Gabriele Suder

Doing Business
in Europe

2ND EDITION

⊘SAGE

Los Angeles | London | New Delhi
Singapore | Washington DC

First edition published 2007
Reprinted 2007, 2008, 2009 and 2010

This second edition published 2011

SAGE Publications Ltd
1 Oliver's Yard
55 City Road
London EC1Y 1SP

SAGE Publications Inc.
2455 Teller Road
Thousand Oaks, California 91320

SAGE Publications India Pvt Ltd
B 1/1 1 Mohan Cooperative Industrial Area
Mathura Road
New Delhi 110 044

SAGE Publications Asia-Pacific Pte Ltd
3 Church Street
#10-04 Samsung Hub
Singapore 049483

Library of Congress Control Number: 2011929701

British Library Cataloguing in Publication data

A catalogue record for this book is available from the British Library

ISBN 978-0-85702-084-0
ISBN 978-0-85702-085-7 (pbk)

Typeset by C&M Digitals (P) Ltd, Chennai, India
Printed in Great Britain by MPG Books Group, Bodmin, Cornwall
Printed on paper from sustainable resources

Gabriele Suder

Doing Business
in Europe 2ND EDITION

SAGE has been part of the global academic community since 1965, supporting high quality research and learning that transforms society and our understanding of individuals, groups, and cultures. SAGE is the independent, innovative, natural home for authors, editors and societies who share our commitment and passion for the social sciences.

Find out more at: **www.sagepublications.com**

Summary of Contents

Contents

This project has been funded with support from the European Commission. This publication reflects the views only of the author, and the Commission cannot be held responsible for any use which may be made of the information contained therein.

With the support of the European Commission's Lifelong Learning: Erasmus – Jean Monnet.

To David, Chantal, Caroline, Ingrid and Rudolf,
and my grandfather Anton

About the Author

Gabriele Suder is currently Professor of European and International Business and Jean Monnet Chair at SKEMA Business School France-USA-China.

Professor Suder holds a German BA, a British MPhil and PhD. She has significant corporate and academic work experience across Europe and worldwide. She teaches and advises on 'Doing Business in Europe', EU market entry and Single Market opportunities for business. She is also visiting fellow at leading business schools, including CEMS and also works for ESCP Europe, Aalto University, the Australian National University and other universities. Among her innovative pedagogical initiatives, she launched the world's first-ever application of Microsoft's integrated intra-organization social network technology, Office 365 with Sharepoint, on three continents in collaboration with Microsoft. Gabriele Suder is the author of numerous books, case studies, media and research articles, and of the YouTube/Dailymotion video series *Doing Business in Europe*.

www.gabrielesuder.com

Acknowledgements

The author would, in particular, like to thank the following people, firms and organizations for their valuable help, suggestions and submission of materials.

First of all my family, in particular David, Chantal and Caroline, and my parents for their love, patience and support, and the role they have played in the intellectual and emotional foundations that made yet another book possible.

Second, my colleagues, friends and contributors, who made important suggestions, provided information and, for some, submitted essential case study material, amongst them, Jean-Philippe Courtois, Vojtech Jirku, Mario Rebello, Jan Muehlfeit, Nicole Fontaine and Claire Holveck, Vincent Lacolare and Nicolas Rougy, Christophe Aulnette, Delphine Foucaud, Ricardo Monteiro, Jacqueline Fendt, William Lightfoot, Gerard Valin, Mohamed Khalil, Ricardo Monteiro, Gijs van IJsel Smits, Laetitia Darnis, Nicolas Rougy, Per A. Havnes, Delphine Foucaud, Martin Seppälä, Matthias Poguntke, Carla Koen, Sak Onkvisit and John Shaw, Hannah Chaplin, Francisco Tur Hartmann, Guillaume Deront, Andreas Klossek, Bernd M. Linke, Irina Jormanainen, Andrei Panibratov, Albert Schram and Ionara da Costa, Joanna Scott-Kennel and Peter Zamborsky.

Third, AIRBUS, BASME Macedonia, Microsoft, Altran, Dari Couspate, Daniel Lefevre, Euro RSCG, Marimekko, Gijs van IJsel Smits, Michael Lucas, Trygve Sten Gustavsen, P.A. Havnes, Philippe Bucaro, Beti Delovska and Vlatko Danilov, David Gillingham, as well as the European Union, World Trade Organization (WTO), World Economic Forum, The World Bank, DBO International B.V., EastWest Institute, Altran, BASME CT, Philips International and Groupe Consultatif Actuariel Europeen, Carrefour, EuroInfoCenter, Agderforskning AS, AHI Roofing and, from academia, my colleagues at SKEMA Business School, Aalto University, the University of Bath and Aberystwyth, ESCP Europe, ANU, GGS and many more, and my anonymous reviewers. Special thanks to Catherine Crochot and Christine Lagadere at SKEMA Business School, Sophia Antipolis campus.

Also, thanks to my research assistants, in particular Hazel Ho, Doris Kukuljan and Todd Wierenga, and my proofreaders, in particular Gillian Rosner, as well as all contributors, my students, and last but not least, the excellent and very supportive team at SAGE Publications, especially Ruth Stitt, for their professionalism and their willingness to provide advice and friendship, and, of course, the readers of the first edition of *Doing Business in Europe* (2007).

I am grateful to the following for permission to reproduce copyright material: Professor Michael Czinkota, Wilf Greenwood, Jacqueline Fendt, William Lightfoot, Gerard Valin, Mohamed Khalil, Ricardo Monteiro, Gijs van IJsel Smits, Dirk Feldhausen, Laetitia Darnis, Nicolas Rougy, Per A. Havnes, Delphine Foucaud, Martin Seppälä, Matthias Poguntke, Carla Koen, Sak Onkvisit and John Shaw, Tanja

Toetzer, Hannah Chaplin, Francisco Tur Hartmann, Guillaume Deront, Andreas Klossek, Bernd M. Linke, Irina Jormanainen, Andrei Panibratov, Albert Schram and Ionara da Costa, Joanna Scott-Kennel, Peter Zamborsky, Vojtech Jirku, Satoshi Inomata, Steven McGuire and Johan Lindeque, companies including Excedea, Carrefour, Haier, Schunk, Marimekko, Microsoft, EuroRSCG, Altran, Airbus, Ariane, Unilever, ECCH European Case Clearing House, to IMF, EUROPA, Eurostat, Eur-Lex, UNCTAD, WTO, EFTA, TEPSA, WE Forum, TUC, INTERPOL, OECD, World Bank, Auswärtiges Amt Berlin, Australian Bureau of Statistics (ABS), and many other individuals and organizations who are named wherever possible in this book.

I acknowledge use of the flag of the EU (http://europa.eu/abc/symbols/emblem/index_en.htm), the geopolitical and river map of the EU after its enlargement to 25 Member States in 2004 and of the candidate countries except for Croatia (http://ec.europa.eu/avservices/photo/photo_thematic_en.cfm?id=&mark=PRO, CART; http://ec.europa.eu/justice_home/doc_centre/asylum/statistics/doc_asylum_statistics_en.htm), extract from European Coal and Steel Treaty (http://europa.eu/scadplus/treaties/ecsc_en.htm and http://eur-lex.europa.eu/en/treaties/ treaties_founding.htm), the Directorates-General and Services (http://ec.europa. eu/dgs_en.htm), Six European Legislative Tools – The three objectives of the structural funds (http://europa.eu.int/scadplus/leg/en/lvb/I60014.htm), A Council, Parliament and Economic and Social Committee conclusion about Single European Market needs (http://ec. europa.eu./internal_market/strategy/docs/comstrat_en.pdf), The first Report on Competition Policy 1972, Evolution of the exchange rate between the US dollar and the euro from January 1999 to July 2005 (http://www.ecb.eu/pub/pub/stats/html/index.en.html) and the table 'Share of EU exports per cent ...' (http://ec.europa.eu/comm/external_relations/asia/rel/ eco.htm) and all other Europa, Eurostat, Eurparl and Eur-Lex data. For these, permissions are granted and all acknowledgement is given to the European Communities and to the source © European Communities. Figure 2.2, Source: map of Europe with 25 members, © European Communities 2007 (http://europa.eu/abc/maps/index_en.htm). All acknowledgement of European Union sources: http://ec.europa.eu © European Union 1995–2011 and © European Union, http://eur-lex.europa.eu/, 1998–2010. Disclaimer: 'Only European Union legislation printed in the paper edition of the *Official Journal of the European Union* is deemed authentic'.

The European Communities consider legislative and quasi-legislative documents published in the *Official Journal of the European Union* and related COM and SEC series as well as charters and treaties and European Court of Justice (ECJ) case law to be in the public domain. Prior written permission is thus not required for their reproduction, and they may be reproduced freely without restriction, including for the purpose of further non-commercial dissemination to final users, subject to the condition that appropriate acknowledgement is given to the European Communities and to the source, and provided that the additional guidelines set out below are respected. For, whenever a document is reproduced verbatim from a source other than the printed version of the *Official Journal of the European Union*, we attract your attention to the following disclaimer that 'Only

European Community legislation printed in the paper edition of the *Official Journal of the European Union* is deemed authentic'.

This is noting that the EU, moreover, does not consider a 'further commercial dissemination' the inclusion, as reference material for consultation purposes, of small amounts of relevant legislative texts in articles/theses/studies/reports/books issued by third-party authors or publishers, whatever the means, and disseminated subject to payment.

WTO Publications for all WTO quoted statistics and tables, as well as 'The EU at WTO negotiations: The United States call for countervailing measures concerning certain products from Europe (Recourse to Article 21.5 of the DSU by the European Communities)' and 'GPA – A case of diversity in multinational negotiations re: government procurement' material.

Thank you for the advice and agreement of companies and organizations mentioned in this book.

While every effort was made to trace the owners of copyright material, in a few cases this may have proven impossible and I would like to offer my apologies in any cases where I might unwittingly have infringed rights. I would appreciate any information that would enable me to trace the owners of such copyright so that I can acknowledge their contribution.

The testimonials, case studies, all material, examples and illustrations, case study teaching notes and other support material are intended to be used as a basis for classwork and discussion rather than to illustrate effective or ineffective handling of business operations or management issues.

Thanks to all my family, friends and supporters.

Companion Website

Be sure to visit the companion website at **http://www.sagepub.co.uk/suder2e** to find a range of teaching and learning materials for both lecturers and students, including the following:

For lecturers:

- **Instructor's manual:** Contains class activities and model answers for review questions.
- **PowerPoint slides:** PowerPoint slides for each chapter for use in class are also provided. These slides can be edited by instructors to suit teaching styles and needs.
- **Multiple Choice Questions:** A testbank of downloadable multiple choice questions are available for lecturers to test students, or make available to students online.
- **Additional case studies:** These additional case studies include discussion questions.

For students:

- **Full-text journal articles:** Full access to selected SAGE journal articles related to each chapter, providing students with a deeper understanding of the topics in each chapter.
- **A country-by-country study:** Important facts and figures about every country in the EU are provided.
- **Video case studies:** Online videos including interviews provide stimulating insight into aspects of European business.
- **Chapter summaries:** These summaries sum up the key points from each chapter, aiding revision.
- **Useful weblinks:** Direct links to relevant websites for each chapter.

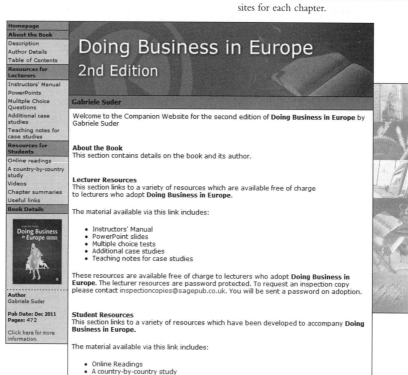

1

Introduction: The New European Business Environment

1.1 The structure of this book

Dear Reader,

Congratulations for choosing the second edition of *Doing Business in Europe*. This new edition is the fruit of its predecessor's international success. It has not only been used throughout Europe, but has also become the reference text in this field in leading universities and training institutions throughout the Americas, in Australia, Asia and many other places in the world.

Great attention has been given to this book and its support material, including the Doing Business in Europe podcast series. This new edition is supported by the European Union's Lifelong Learning – Jean Monnet Programme. The many crucial changes taking place in Europe over the recent years are the reason we decided to publish this new edition. In order to remain consistent with the first edition, the full texts of the original have not been completely altered but the chapters have been better adapted to the new Europe with case studies and examples updated and sometimes replaced.

The book is thus still divided into four parts. Part I sets the foundations that define the Europe of today: a continent with a highly mature and integrated market. Chapter 2, which follows this Introduction, presents an overview of the main European historic landmarks. It discusses the evolution of the numerous treaties and how the European business environment has developed in relation to these. The chapter is complemented by a review of the impact of certain treaties on business, and it briefly presents the tools necessary for the successful implementation of European integration. Chapter 3 then examines past, present and future waves of enlargement and looks ahead to the next steps for a European Union that may accept more new members. The analyses are placed within the framework of integration theories: these help us understand the diversity of motivations that Member States may have towards further market integration, i.e. their willingness to work together in various fields. When European integration makes progress, it appears to foster trade creation but this progress may also cause trade diversion: what does this mean for business interests? What are the opportunities and challenges that come with integration? Chapter 4 studies the framework within which European rules and policies are negotiated, streamlined, debated and decided: it explains the institutions and main actors, and their impact on business in Europe.

Part II is made up of two chapters. Chapter 5 provides a clear understanding of the causes and effects of globalization and the related issues for European and international firms in achieving competitive advantage in increasingly integrated markets. This chapter proposes two complementary perspectives for analysis. Internally, the Single Market opens up opportunities that come with the most highly integrated economic grouping in the world: a business environment that has evolved into a complex but ever-increasing network of opportunities for business activity. Externally, the EU is a major actor in the international geopolitical environment, playing a particular role in globalization. What is this role and what are its implications for international business? What impact does this internationalization have on European firms of different sizes and sectors? Chapter 6 demonstrates how management and knowledge are becoming central to the strategic focus of European firms. In all Member States, we can identify distinct management styles, cultures and structures, which result in various management issues.

Part III focuses on essential 'business activity functions in the European environment'. European economies share a certain number of common policies and harmonized rules. This integration of policies attempts to maximize the benefit that economies and corporations gain from trade and financial integration (it also serves to minimize the effects of crisis) because members share the risks and spillover effects of macroeconomic fluctuations, and experience production and consumption co-movements. Chapter 7 then shows how economic harmonization raises fundamental issues for business and business creation in Europe, and examines the particular characteristics of European economics, finance and fund-raising. Chapter 8 develops the marketing perspective that helps businesses operate with the necessary methodology to approach and manage marketing in the vast European marketplace. European diversity makes the marketing of a product or a service at the European level both challenging and worthwhile. But hidden or subtle differences in pricing, consumer attitudes, specific buying processes, cash flow management, the structure of distribution and communication, legal differences and the practice of arbitration, etc. also add to the complexity of European marketing. The European arena offers opportunities for economies of scale, but requires a sound knowledge of European lifestyles and consumption patterns, buying process and the typology and segmentation of the European markets with appropriate marketing strategies and techniques.

Another essential business function in today's Europe is that of public affairs management and lobbying. An increasing number of public and private organizations are represented at the European institutional level: for this reason, Chapter 9 explores lobbying networks, and analyses the arena, players and competition in the decision-making game. It illustrates the most recognized methods that help companies make their voice heard in Brussels, Strasbourg and Luxembourg. This is where the European business environment and rules are shaped and, thus, where competitiveness either thrives or fails. International competitiveness is the key issue covered in Chapter 10. The chapter examines European trade relations with the main trading partners, and places issues of international competitiveness within a concluding discussion of globalization and Europeanization. It situates *Doing Business in Europe* in the international context.

The last part of the book contains case studies related to the concepts developed in the previous chapters. The case studies illustrate the realities of companies that compete in the European marketplace as it has developed, as it exists today and as it will evolve tomorrow. Their cases demonstrate the crucial need for European and non-European companies engaged in 'doing business in Europe', to participate in pan-European and international activities. As in the first edition, the overall objective of these texts is: (a) to provide you with the fundamentals of theory and concepts; and (b) to link these clearly to the business environment. Each sequence is followed by an evaluation of its impact on business. Short case studies illustrate the way in which corporations experience the realities of the European business environment. The questions following each case study ask you to apply your freshly acquired knowledge and to define the solutions that could be applied to that very case. Testimonials reflect the intimate thinking of business people as regards the issues raised within each chapter. Finally, the web guide leads you to websites on which you can find valuable information about the chapter topics; these are there to help you with your assignments. Do try to answer the review questions after each chapter to make sure that you have indeed acquired the knowledge and are ready to go ahead with the next chapter; this is important because each successive chapter builds on those before. Also, the book concludes with case studies that illustrate a variety of business challenges and asks the relevant questions that are crucial for 'doing business in Europe'. To reduce reading time, if necessary, you may want to ignore the text boxes and testimonials; this may happen under the pre-condition that you are already well experienced in the field of management and do not look for applied examples from elsewhere.

Don't forget that a wide range of resources can be found on the companion web pages for this book (see http://www.sagepub.co.uk/suder2e).

1.2 Centrepiece: the idea of creating a 'unified Europe'

The idea of creating a 'unified Europe' to maintain peace and to create a common European culture has resurfaced repeatedly throughout European history, although the ideal of a united Europe has its origins in classical philosophical thinking. In the fourteenth century, for example, Pierre Dubois[1] proposed a European confederation that was to be governed by a European council, while in the nineteenth century Victor Hugo[2] envisaged a political, federal Europe, uniting nations and unifying people. In a speech to the French National Assembly on 1 March 1871, he said:

Plus de frontières! Le Rhin à tous! Soyons la même République, soyons les États-Unis d'Europe, soyons la fédération continentale, soyons la liberté européenne, soyons la paix universelle! (No more borders! The Rhine for all! Let's be the same Republic, the United States of Europe, let's be the federation of the continent, let's be European freedom, let's be Universal peace!)

Through industrialization and the evolution of trade across frontiers over centuries, nations came to expand their knowledge of different economic systems and trade mechanisms. The end of the feudal system, the mercantilist era from *c*.1600 to *c*.1800 and colonialism shaped societies and their economic and social functioning. The term 'mercantilism' originates from the Latin word *mercari*, meaning 'to run a trade', and from *merx*, meaning 'commodity'. It sets the scene for economic and political interest in internationalization. Ideologically, mercantilism underpinned cross-border trade for long enough to leave its mark, driving exports rather than imports, in so far as a country needed a positive balance of trade to gain more precious metals (gold and silver), and determining that governments introduced tariffs to prevent other countries from gaining an economic advantage. The political economist Adam Smith, who is generally considered the father of economics, popularized the term in *The Wealth of Nations* (1776), where he analyzed the exchange mechanisms that drive economies – and, indeed, every economic system embraces some form of exchange.

The appeal of harmonious trade for economic growth and welfare developed increasingly from the mid-eighteenth century onwards: more than the dream of peace and stability across peoples and nations, the idea of welfare through profitable economic relations was easier to share among all peoples. Adam Smith's book set the foundations for a classical trade theory that evolved strongly in Europe, and that was complemented in later years by the mainly Anglo-Saxon school of international business research, which analysed corporations' cross-border transactions and investments. It is important at this stage to recognize that the convergence of Europe stems from economic and philosophical history, and that during the twentieth century this convergence led to pressure on states that had seen their power and sovereignty erode to the benefit of regionalism and globalization. International trade relations thus became key to the fulfilment of the European idea and ideal.

In Europe, economic and political integration have been driven by one predominant objective: 'Keeping peace among nations'. Interaction between people and their economies has indeed maintained peace for longer than in any other region of the world. Certain European countries have joined together to create a unique organization for this purpose: the European Union (EU). An organization of states that is neither a confederation, nor an organization of the types generally known in international relations, but rather the most advanced form of economic integration in the world that is flirting closely with the temptations of political union. The EU Member States have created a Single Market that marries competitiveness with certain social ideals (welfare, human rights, equality and many others). The European marketplace is both the driver and the stimulus of Europe, as it has shaped and is being shaped by the European ideal. It represents the largest economy in the world, the largest trading partner and the largest donor of development assistance.

This market offers opportunities to those corporations that recognize the pros and cons of convergence, and that make the most out of the diversity of cultures, languages, business practices and management styles. At the same time, the challenge for the institutions of Europe is to maintain European development while staying in touch with its citizens, and to balance a productive economy with social welfare.

The objective of this book is to prepare future managers to face up to both the challenges and the opportunities for doing business in Europe – a Europe enlarged and deepened through continuous integration. Whether you will be working in a local, a European or an international company, you will be confronted with the issues dealt with in this book. Every company operating in or dealing with Europe is exposed to the challenges of globalization and Europeanization.

In this introductory chapter, we take a brief look at attitudes among citizens and at some European foundations and symbols. We shall then introduce some of the terms and concepts that have a bearing on discussions later in the book. The glossary at the end of this book makes reference to further definitions.

1.3 Europe: for European citizens and abroad

The European idea and its ideal are centred on the citizen and her/his welfare. These are driven by economics and politics, in symbiosis with European competitiveness and the role of Europe in the world.

> ### Box 1.1: The European Union
>
> The EU, originally (prior to 1993) known as the European Economic Community (EEC), is a highly advanced form of economic integration. It is a market grouping of more than 27 countries that promotes the economic wealth of its members, not only through free trade but also through many other coordinated activities such as a common competition policy, internal and external trade policy, research and development policy, industrial and social policy and so on. The creation of a central European bank and the adoption of a common currency, the euro, significantly contribute to its singular nature in the world. The EU operates as one economic unit in negotiations about international trade.

Because of this concern with citizen welfare, the EU regularly studies the attitudes of its citizens. It is noteworthy that more than 9 out of 10 EU citizens feel that it is extremely or very important to help others and to value people for who they are, while more than 8 out of 10 believe that it is important to be involved in creating a better society. These societal values are strong in each Member State.

At the same time, EU citizens seem to appreciate specific identity traits and traditionalism. Nearly 7 out of 10 want to live in a world where people live by traditional values. We are a long way from any standardization or homogeneity of the peoples of Europe; for business, this is where the challenges of values and diversity come into play.

....
:
:   **Box 1.2: EU Member States: who are they?**
:
:   In 2007, the EU comprised the following 27 Member States: Austria, Belgium,
:   Bulgaria, Cyprus, Czech Republic, Denmark, Estonia, Germany, Greece, Finland,
:   France, Hungary, Ireland, Italy, Latvia, Lithuania, Luxembourg, Malta, Poland,
:   Portugal, Romania, Slovakia, Slovenia, Spain, Sweden, The Netherlands and the
:   United Kingdom (UK).
:
....

Is there a European identity among citizens? EU statistics, as well as student surveys
conducted by the author at several business schools, illustrate that the majority of EU
citizens feel to some extent 'European'. This is particularly the case for those who travel
or work across frontiers, however at the same time they preserve a strong feeling of
adherence to particular roots and culture. Eurostat (the Statistical Office of the
European Communities) notes that this feeling of adherence differs greatly among
countries: people in Luxembourg are most likely to feel 'European' only. This is a much
higher rate than in any of the other countries and can be explained by the high proportion of citizens from other EU countries that reside in Luxembourg. Nonetheless,
there are seven other countries where people who feel to some extent European are
in the majority: Italy, Spain, France, Belgium, The Netherlands, Austria and Germany.
In the other EU countries, the majority of people identify exclusively with their own
nationality, although in Portugal, Ireland and the newer Member States, this majority
is small. National identity is very strongly felt in the UK, Sweden, Finland, Greece and,
to a slightly lesser extent, Denmark. Europeans' strong adherence to values related to
democracy is an essential part of the identity that drives integration.

When asked which areas the EU should prioritize in the next five years, employment and stability are regular 'firsts', closely followed by research and development
in new technologies. Young people especially appreciate the freedom and ease with
which one can travel (mainly visa-free) from one European country to another. Very
few young people feel that the EU represents negative elements, such as too much
bureaucracy or the loss of cultural diversity, or that the goals of the EU are unrealistic. Rather, young generations adhere to the benefits of cohesion and multiculturalism
in Europe.

We can legitimately conclude that Europe has made unprecedented progress
towards its ideal of peace, political and economic stability and welfare, and this
despite economic and currency crises in the last decade.

1.4 Foundations and symbols

1.4.1 The mystery of 'Europe'

Europe is not only a continent that is turning itself into one vast common market
for companies. It has a rich history and shared culture, much of which is anchored

in Greek and Latin roots. In Greek mythology, Europa was the daughter of the king of Tyre in Phoenicia. Zeus, attracted by her, transformed himself into a white bull, seduced her, and ran away with her on his back to the sea. He took her to the island of Crete and, after revealing his true identity, made her the island's first queen. The semantic root of the name 'Europa' is to be found in the word 'ereb' (dark) – the European continent as seen from Phoenicia was located towards the west where the sun sets. The kidnapping of Europa is a frequently represented motif in ancient Greek and Roman arts. The continent of Europe is now called Europa in all Germanic and Slavic languages that use the Latin and Greek alphabet.

1.4.2 The European flag

The European flag is the symbol of the EU and of Europe's unity and identity in a wider sense. In ancient Greece, the number 12 stood for harmony. Traditionally, this number symbolizes perfection, completeness and unity; thus the circle of 12 golden stars represents the ideal harmony between the peoples of Europe. Also, the Egyptian goddess Isis, representing fertility and compassion, was often represented standing on a crescent moon, with 12 stars surrounding her head. The number of stars does not depend on the number of Member States. The flag has therefore remained unchanged since the beginning of 1986, regardless of EU enlargements. The European flag is the only emblem of the European Commission. Other EU institutions and bodies complement it with an emblem of their own.

1.4.3 The European anthem

The Hymn of Joy from the Ninth Symphony composed in 1823 by Ludwig van Beethoven was adopted by the heads of Member States and governments in 1985 as the official European anthem.

Without words, in the universal language of music, it expresses the European ideals of freedom, peace and solidarity. The anthem does not replace the national anthems of the Member States but symbolically celebrates the shared values encompassed in the EU's motto: 'United in diversity'. The anthem can be heard at: http://europa.eu/abc/symbols/anthem/index_en.htm.

1.4.4 Europe Day

On 9 May 1950, Robert Schuman presented his proposal for the creation of an organized Europe, essential for a prosperous post-war European future and peace between nations. The Schuman declaration is considered to be one of the great landmarks of European integration, and its significance for business will be discussed in Chapter 2. Today, 9 May is 'Europe Day', a symbol, along with the single currency (the euro), the flag and the anthem, that supports the shared identity of the EU. It is a day of activities and festivities across Europe, celebrating political and economic stability and integration. More information on Europe Day can be found online at http://europa.eu/abc/symbols/9-may/decl_en.htm/abc/.

1.4.5 The euro

The EU and its unity are also symbolized by the introduction, in 2002, of a single currency, the euro, which replaced the currency of participating Member States. This was the result of a long process that began in 1969 and was spread over several stages. The preliminary stage, between 1969 and 1993, saw the development of the European Monetary System (EMS); the transitional stage, between 1999 and 2001, saw the official launch of the euro on 1 January 1999; and the final stage, in 2002, saw the introduction of coins and bills for circulation. The euro will be discussed in detail in Chapter 7.

1.5 Some basic terms and concepts

Before you start to read the forthcoming chapters, it is necessary to define some terms and concepts that will be used throughout the text.

1.5.1 Globalization

In the context of this book, globalization refers to a compression of time and space which increases the frequency and duration of linkages between any given actors in the international environment. This implies a complex structure of integrated activities, mainly economic, but also those driven by political, environmental and geopolitical considerations. The compression of time translates into a high sequence of interaction between any of the given actors; for example, it impacts on the rapidity of orders over the Internet or of how long it takes to have a product delivered. The compression of space results in a geographical proximity with countries (and thus markets) that, some decades ago, appeared very far away from each other. The major advances made in transport and in information and communication technology are at the origin of many of the characteristics of globalization. These sectors play an important role in the competitiveness of sectors and markets.

1.5.2 Europeanization

Europeanization is a term used in two senses. The first implies the European integration of economies and the development of common policies of EU Member States. Here, Europeanization is considered as an advanced case of globalization. Thus, the impact of Europeanization in this context can be measured via the importance of EU internal and external trade compared to non-EU countries and market groupings such as NAFTA (North American Free Trade Agreement). An example is the Organization for Economic Cooperation and Development (OECD) which regularly publishes relevant data.

The second meaning of Europeanizaton is used in connection with business corporations. It deals with advanced forms of organization that reflect: (a) the diversity of markets and cultures; and (b) the diversity within companies as well as in the scope of their operations. One example of a Europeanized firm is Eurocopter, the leader in military helicopters and part of the EADS (European Aeronautic, Defence and Space) group. The company was established in 1986 by French and German aerospace leaders, and is now a truly European company in terms of shareholder nationality, partners, employees and management. It has taken what it has learned from trading in the European market and developed this into international competitiveness.

1.5.3 Multinational and transnational firms

International business operations are transactions across borders that may be pursued via different forms of corporate structure and types of transaction, depending on the relation of risks and returns that are expected from investments in those transactions. These may encompass exports and imports, licensing, franchising or subcontracting, outsourcing and offshoring strategies, direct foreign investment into joint ventures or greenfield investment. The basic definition implies that cross-border activity is different from domestic trade. Therefore, an organization with substantial foreign investment may take the shape of a multinational enterprise (MNE), that is, a corporation that has its headquarters in one country but also operates in others. An MNE is typically engaged in the active management of its offshore assets. Another commonly used form of organization is the transnational company (TNC); this defines a firm that coordinates and controls operations across borders through an organizational design that allows for local responsiveness. These firms are typically well adapted through a structure and strategy that responds relatively easily to the changing external business environment, and evaluates the particular advantages of a location at any given time.

1.5.4 The company typology

Large organizations interest us in terms of their ability to profit from Europeanization and to adapt organizational structures and business functions to cross-border networks of decision-making, coordination, control, knowledge management and quasi-institutionalization. However, small and medium-sized enterprises (SMEs) play a particular role in the European business environment: 99 per cent of companies in Europe (i.e. 23 million firms) are SMEs. The European Commission defines SMEs as 'enterprises which employ fewer than 250 persons and which have an annual turnover not exceeding 50 million euro, and/or an annual balance sheet total not exceeding 43 million euro' (Article 2 of the Annex of Recommendation 2003/361/EC; see also the definitions in Table 1.1). We will frequently refer to the role of SMEs and to the importance of flexibility, innovativeness and trade diversion to SME management.

It is also important here to distinguish between private and public sector companies. A private company cannot offer its shares to the public and restricts the right to transfer them. On the other hand, a public company is owned by the public. There are two uses of this term. It may indicate a company that is owned by stockholders who are members of the general public and is traded publicly. Ownership is open to anyone who has the money and inclination to buy shares in the company; the government often owns a minority of shares. A public company may also be fully or mainly owned by a local, regional or national government. Employees may take stock options. For instance, in Belgium between 70,000 and 75,000 employees have received stock options since 1999 and almost all of the 20 largest Belgian corporations (BEL20) operate stock option plans. In Germany, they were introduced in 1997 and by 2006 over two-thirds of companies included in the German stock index (DAX) were running employee stock option programmes. In France, stock options were introduced in 1970 and, presently, approximately 50 per cent of all quoted companies and 95 per cent of companies use stock option plans.

The main European directives on employee participation introduced pan-European structures for a range of business and employment issues in multinational companies over a certain size operating in the EU. Directive 2002/14/EC sets a framework for informing and consulting employees and/or their representatives for all undertakings with at least 50 employees (or establishments with at least 20 employees) that are required to provide employee representatives with information and/or consultation on a range of business, employment and work organization issues. Directives 2001/86/EC and 2003/72/EC expand employee involvement in the European Company and in the European Cooperative Society – the new optional form of Europe-wide company set up under the European Company Statute. The directives add information and consultation structures, procedures and board-level participation (cf. R. Davletguildeev, Trade

Table 1.1 *Staff headcount and financial ceilings determining enterprise categories*

Enterprise category	Headcount	Turnover	Balance sheet total
Medium-sized	< 250	≤ €50 million	≤ €43 million
Small	< 50	≤ €10 million	≤ €10 million
Micro	< 10	≤ €2 million	≤ €2 million

Source: Commission Recommendation 2003/361/EC, Annex 1, Article 2, Official Journal L124, 20 May 2003, p. 39

Unions Advisory Committee to the OECD Third Eurasian Roundtable on Corporate Governance, 29–30 October 2003, Bishkek).

The competitiveness of business depends on innovation, efficient knowledge management and entrepreneurship. In Europe, the impact of multilateral decision-making and policies on competitiveness is recognized by European and third-country businesses working across frontiers. The results can be measured by the attractiveness of the European market for foreign industrial location and investment, and is a subject of vivid debate in political and business circles. The main advantages are based on the European cost base, taxation levels, the availability of skilled, trained labour, effective linkages between research/ academia and the corporate sector business, and the internationalization opportunities of European products and services. But the European business environment is also subject to the struggle between national interests and the efficiency of economic sectors vis-à-vis each other and the world. The EU is thus a microcosm of opportunities and challenges preparing you for global business.

 REVIEW QUESTIONS

1 **What** knowledge is key to success for a company doing business in Europe? Imagine that you want to set up your own company – why would this be different in Europe (as compared to another part of the world of your choice)?
2 **Explain** the ideal of Europe. Do you think that an ideal like that of the EU is still valid today?
3 **What** role does European integration play in business? Would business in Europe support the EU falling apart, and turning back into national states only?
4 Vice versa, **what** role does business play in European integration?
5 **Why** does Europe need symbols?

 INTERNET RESOURCES

General information on the European Union: The EU in brief:
http://europa.eu/abc/index_en.htm

Europe's information society:
http://ec.europa.eu/information_society/index_en.htm

EU news from *European Voice*:
http://www.europeanvoice.com/

(Continued)

(Continued)

The EU – panorama, treaties and more:
http://europa.eu/abc/panorama/howorganized/index_en.htm

Gateway to the EU – activities, institutions, documents, services and more:
http://europa.eu/documentation/official-docs/index_en.htm

Public opinion about European enlargement – European citizens:
http://www.europarl.europa.eu/enlargement/briefings/41a3_en.htm

SMEs in the EU:
http://www.sme-union.org/

Some EU history:
http://www.answers.com/topic/history-of-the-european-union

Gabriele Suder's *Doing Business in Europe* video series (on the SAGE companion website at http://www.sagepub.co.uk/suder2e and YouTube)

Notes

1 Dubois was a royal advocate of the bailliage in Coutances. He was not only an important figure in France's war against Pope Boniface VIII but was also the creative force behind a project to restore Jerusalem to the French king, Philip IV.
2 Hugo was a renowned poet, novelist and dramatist, but also a senator under the Third Republic.

Bibliography

Smith, A. (1776) *Inquiry into the Nature and Causes of the Wealth of Nations* (E. Cannan, ed.). London: Methuen and Co.

PART I

THE EUROPEAN BUSINESS GAME: THE IMPACT OF SIX DECADES

2

Landmarks of European Integration, or How History and Politics Shape the Business Environment

What you will learn about in this chapter:

- The historical evolution of global issues and the European market.
- The main European treaties and their direct impact on business: business Europeanization is underpinned by historic market integration.
- The business opportunities and challenges that result.
- What Europe is really about: objectives that alter the market?

 ## 2.0 Introduction

Doing business in Europe requires an understanding of a set of historical realities, amongst them the European market, its actors, its diversity and its harmonization. The many conditions that constitute this business environment are unique and corporations need to know them well. Understanding this environment requires a look back at the historical development of European integration, in a global setting.

2.1 The past as a basis for the present and the future

The formulation of a plan for cooperation among European states originated after the period between 1870 and 1945, when Germany and France fought each other three times. The last military conflict in the EU-15 area (the area including the 15 western European countries) was World War II, which left more than 50 million people dead and most European economies devastated.

In this context, the only hope for lasting peace and prosperity in Europe was to strive for a new unity on economic and, if possible, political, social and cultural levels. The aim was not to engage in further punishment and revenge against countries that were in chaos and confusion.

A number of leaders, in particular Konrad Adenauer (the first Chancellor of the new Federal Republic of Germany, or West Germany) and Charles de Gaulle (the first post-war President of France), indeed opted rather to set up a process that has been ongoing ever since. This was to provide a diverse but mature market basis for domestic and foreign business in Europe, for European business abroad, and a role for the EU and its corporations internationally.

Box 2.1: The PanEuropa movement

In 1923, Count Coudenhove-Kalergi founded a PanEuropa movement with the aim of uniting the European states. Political and economic tensions (in Germany in particular) – caused not only by upheavals between political parties and politically motivated groups, but also by internal and global economic crises – hindered these aspirations for unification. Indeed, the resentment harboured among European nations after World War I proved to be insurmountable.

Since World War II, efforts to foster reconciliation and partnerships have evolved into widespread economic and political cooperation – and enhanced economic competition. Specifically, the post-1945 period was marked by two phenomena. One was the desire to combat nationalism, which led in parallel to further decolonization; the other was the wish to deal with the new power situation/balance of power in Europe – which was dominated by United States (US)–Soviet relations during the following cold war. The resulting bipolarity in Europe shaped its business environment into diverging economic, political and sociocultural systems. These were divided within Germany and symbolized by the Berlin Wall, which separated East and West, from 1961 to 1989.

However, in the larger international business environment, pre-war and wartime experiences led to the creation of several multilateral organizations that were to have a strong impact on international business. They had a significant influence on the laws and regulations driving the development of European integration too. The United Nations (UN) is just one example.

The emerging landscape of multilateral organizations stimulated the creation of new international arrangements. These led the way to the globalization that was to follow and that has continued ever since. The Bretton Woods Conference in 1944 bore the first fruits of this evolution. At this conference, the representatives of 44 countries were led by the United Kingdom (UK) and the USA into agreement on the establishment of fixed exchange rates, and the establishment of two new bodies. The first of these was the International Monetary Fund (IMF) as a means to deal with balance of payments problems. The IMF was to become the first international monetary authority endowed to some extent with the power of national authorities. It was later to become of great importance in the EU enlargement towards the east of the continent and during the 2008–2010 financial crisis. The second body launched through Bretton Woods was the International Bank for Reconstruction and Development (the World Bank). This was set up as a means to facilitate international trade. Today, EU Member States represent the World Bank's majority shareholders, sharing the leading position of worldwide donors of development aid, in a commonly coordinated strategy with the World Bank for developing and transition countries.

In the same period, the General Agreement on Tariffs and Trade (GATT) was launched as the 1947 predecessor of the World Trade Organization (WTO, established in 1994). Its goals encompassed the reduction of customs, tariffs and trade barriers with the underlying perception that a rise in living standards, the provision of supplies and the exploitation of resources on the world market was dependent on unhindered competition. Since 1995, the EU has been a member of WTO as an entity, while the individual European states are also part of the WTO in their own right. Representation of the EU as a whole – that is, the majority of European states – is in the hands of the European Commission, its executive branch (see Chapter 4). One year later, in 1948, the General Assembly of the UN ratified the Universal Declaration of Human Rights in order to complement the rules governing increasing cross-border relations. The European Union Delegation to the UN, under the authority of the High Representative for Foreign Affairs and Security Policy, supports the priorities of effective multilateralism, the preservation and reinforcement of economic and social progress and fundamental rights and values.

Within these multilateral collaborations, led mainly by the UK and the USA, an unprecedented degree of cooperation between France and West Germany took shape. This gave birth to a 'European integration' that today is wider (geographically) and deeper (in terms of policies and strategic implications) than was ever imagined in those times. As M. Faure, a signatory of one of the earliest treaties (the Treaty of Rome) notes: 'In our vision then, Europe could encompass Spain and Portugal, once they got rid of their dictators. In our opinion, they were part of Western Europe ... We were not even thinking of the communist states ... In 1957, the British question was not posed anymore: it had withdrawn ... ' (*European Voice*, 22 March 2007, p. 3).

The European Recovery Programme, better known as the Marshall Plan, gave rise to the stimuli necessary for this development. It was the basis of a launch of economic cooperation and a customs union, firstly on a small scale and growing to its full size over more than half a century.

After years of cyclical euro-optimism and euro-pessimism, and after decades of adapting to the interests of the different European states, a unique organization has taken shape, which today comprises (on different levels of integration) the quasi-entity of Europe as one market. This is a group of countries that deals as one united force in international negotiations, such as at the WTO.

The Single Market, though still incomplete, is one of the main achievements of European transregional collaboration. This evolution has been driven by the 'Franco-West German engine', that is, the power and influence exercised by these two countries, and their experience of the founding members in dealing with each other during the post-war period. What was initially a successful peacekeeping measure, developed into the largest alliance of countries ever to work together in an economic and (partly) monetary union, complemented by social, cultural, environmental, security and other harmonizing initiatives.

Recognized as the most relevant integrational phenomenon of semi-globalization, the region is a strikingly mature, challenging market that companies cannot neglect. The following chapters will provide you with key insights into this market as a whole and in all its diversity. Internet support for this book will provide you with additional, detailed data about each one of the Member States, their business environments, ease of doing business and the relevant statistics for evaluating specific European locations. The interviews freely and publicly available through Gabriele Suder's *Doing Business in Europe* video series, online, will add further understanding about how small, medium-sized and large firms, both domestic and foreign, handle the many challenges and opportunities that have arisen from European integration.

The various degrees of international integration are illustrated by Figure 2.1, which provides food for thought about the historical (and possible future) development of European integration. It correlates degrees of market integration with the harmonization of policies, the intensity of the resulting correlation defining the level of integration achieved. Indeed, the EU has experienced all the degrees of integration shown by the arrow in Figure 2.1 and has now reached a level where efforts are being made for yet deeper integration. This is clearly a historic and unique development for a business environment. A united Europe, launched with the other founding members of the European Coal and Steel Community (ECSC) (Belgium, The Netherlands, Luxembourg [the Benelux countries] and Italy), has spread its ideas and ideals over a wide area. In the regions of European enlargement, the last war dates from the dissolution of Yugoslavia in the 1990s; in the wider region, events such as the Chechen conflict demonstrate the instability that persists outside of its spheres.

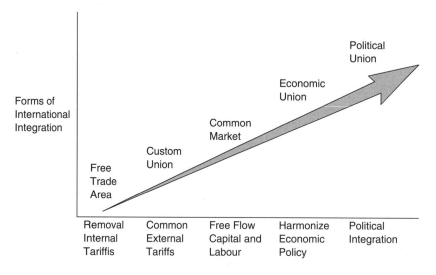

Figure 2.1   *Degrees of international integration*
Source: Suder, 1994

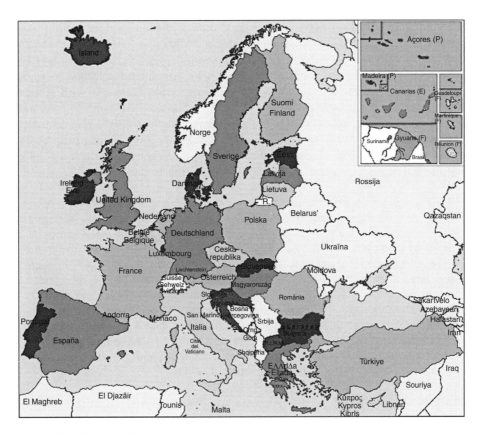

Figure 2.2   *A map of Europe*

Source: http://ec.europa.eu © European Union, 1995–2011

Figure 2.2 shows the European geographical layout with a map of Europe including 27 members (also called Europe 27), that is, its 2007 configuration.

2.2 The Schuman declaration

In 1943, Jean Monnet, a member of the National Liberation Committee of the Free French government (Comité Français de Libération National – CFLN), declared to the committee:

> *There will be no peace in Europe if the states are reconstituted on the basis of national sovereignty ... The countries of Europe are too small to guarantee their peoples the necessary prosperity and social development. The European states must constitute themselves into a federation.*

With this, he highlighted the reason for past conflict, and also how economic integration would effectively increase the resources available to each member county, thus facilitating 'prosperity and social development'.

Jean Monnet, who was in charge of French industrial modernization, is today regarded as one of the main architects of European unity. Together with Robert Schuman, French Foreign Minister, he developed a detailed plan for a united European market of coal and steel production. Schuman proposed the plan on 9 May 1950, for the creation of an organized Europe, stating that it was indispensable to the maintenance of peaceful relations. Schuman (1950) underlined both the motives for, and the planned organization of, European cooperation in the declaration:

> *World peace cannot be safeguarded without the making of creative efforts proportionate to the dangers which threaten it. The contribution, which an organized and living Europe can bring to civilization, is indispensable to the maintenance of peaceful relations ... A united Europe was not achieved and we had war ... Europe will not be made all at once, or according to a single plan. It will be built through concrete achievements, which first create a de facto solidarity. The coming together of the nations of Europe requires the elimination of the age-old opposition of France and Germany. Any action taken must in the first place concern these two countries ... By pooling basic production and by instituting a new High Authority, whose decisions will bind France, Germany and other member countries, this proposal will lead to the realization of the first concrete foundation of a European federation indispensable to the preservation of peace.*

The UK was invited at this stage to participate, but the government thought that such an undertaking would undermine national sovereignty, and so refused.

2.3 Understanding integration: a review of the main treaties

The founding treaties are the result of negotiations between the Member States pursuing two main objectives: to benefit from an efficient and effective European integration, and to promote and defend their own interests. You will now learn about the treaties that were the result of these negotiations. We will only look at those treaties that are considered fundamental and that provide European business with its specific contemporary macroeconomic conditions.

The 1950s and 1960s were rather prosperous in terms of setting the foundations for a united Europe. In the mid 1950s, the founder members of the European Coal and Steel Community (ECSC) agreed to explore further economic and atomic cooperation, and in 1957 they joined with the European Atomic Energy Community (Euratom) to establish the European Economic Communities, also referred to as the Common Market, and later as the European Community (EC). In 1963, the Elysée Treaty became a key component in the eventual creation of the EU because it set the scene for enhanced Franco-German cooperation, and, although only bilateral, it is considered as a milestone agreement between two former enemies that everyone in Europe wished to contain. This treaty had an important positive impact on how the security of Europe was perceived. 'It is good for our children', Chancellor Adenauer and President de Gaulle agreed, and set the basis for cooperation in areas as diverse as education and training, culture, research and technology, foreign affairs, defence and security, and the Europeanization of business.

Nevertheless, from the 1970s to the mid 1980s, several events caused a slowing down of the progress that was being made towards European unity. These events included the hardening of East–West attitudes during the cold war, the increasing North–South divide, the oil crises and, in particular, the geopolitical turmoil in the Middle East.

This period became known as the years of 'Euro-pessimism' or 'Euro-scepticism'. However, the EC grew in size, due to considerable enlargement into the north and south.

From the mid 1980s, treaty reforms seemed crucial to the evolution of European integration. Negotiations intensified and led to the 1986 Single European Act (SEA), the 1992 Maastricht Treaty, the 1997 Amsterdam Treaty, the 2001 Nice Treaty and, later, the Lisbon Treaty of December 2009. These ongoing evolutions have tremendous consequences for the European market and for the opportunities for, and challenges of, doing business in Europe. Table 2.1 shows the main treaties established since 1951.

2.3.1 The Treaty of Paris

2.3.1.1 The first founding treaty

The Treaty of Paris established the ECSC and was signed by six founder members in Paris on 18 April 1951 – that is, France, Italy, Germany and the Benelux countries (Belgium, The Netherlands and Luxembourg). The Treaty was conceived on the basis of the Schuman Plan and set the basis for the four main European institutions: the Council of Ministers, a Common Assembly (later the European Parliament), the Court of Justice and a High Authority. The objectives of the ECSC were to:

- abolish and prohibit internal tariff barriers;
- put an end to state subsidies and special charges;
- outlaw restrictive practices;
- fix prices under certain circumstances;
- harmonize external commercial policy, for example by setting customs duties;
- impose levies on coal and steel production for budgetary purposes.

Jean Monnet was the first president of the ECSC. The economic success of the ECSC provided enough stimuli to launch further initiatives for economic integration. This led to the establishment of the fundamental treaties governing the EEC

Table 2.1 *The main European treaties established since 1951*

Date signed	Treaty	Place of signature	Date entering force	Impact on business
18 April 1951	European Coal and Steel Community	Paris	23 July 1952	A strong impact on business in the coal and steel industries.
25 March 1957	European Economic Community	Rome	1 January 1958	Creation of a free trade area evolving into a customs union that removed internal tariffs on goods and harmonized external tariffs. Establishment of the prohibition of monopolies Launch of the Common Agricultural Policy (CAP).
25 March 1957	European Atomic Energy Community	Rome	1 January 1958	Organization of Member States European atomic activities.
17/18 February 1986	Single European Act	Luxembourg and The Hague	1 July 1987	Elimination of physical and technical frontiers. Liberalization of financial and services markets. Harmonization of national laws on safety and pollution. Increased industrial environmental cooperation.
7 February 1992	Treaty on European Union	Maastricht	1 November 1993	The EU becomes one streamlined market thanks to the single currency, the euro. Significant change for the competitiveness of European manufacturing, primary and tertiary sectors. Disappearance of transaction costs between the members of the euro-zone.

(Continued)

Table 2.1 (Continued)

Date signed	Treaty	Place of signature	Date entering force	Impact on business
2 October 1997	Treaty of Amsterdam	Amsterdam	1 July 1999	Enhancement of the multilateral promotion of employment, placing national controls into a wider European employment strategy. Consumer protection becomes a priority. The protection of the environment introduced important challenges to the production sector. Support for the farm sectors and rural and regional economies, helps to narrow economic and wealth gaps, especially in candidate countries.
26 February 2001	Treaty of Nice	Nice	1 February 2003	Preparation of the path for an enlarged and smooth-functioning European business environment Increase in the efficiency and credibility of the EU's foreign policy for foreign and local investors.
29 October 2004	Constitution	Rome	(Abandoned/partly reworked into Lisbon Treaty)	Attempts to streamline legislation, to set strong priorities and to increase transparency, democracy and solidarity.
13 December 2007	Lisbon Treaty	Lisbon	1 December 2009	Aims to cope with the challenges of EU enlargement and the efficiency of institutionalized decision making. The Lisbon treaty has the goal of simplifying the decision-making process and making the institutions more democratic. Rebalancing business-oriented decision powers between smaller and bigger Member States. Company benefits stem from the increasing transparency.

and its marketplace. The ECSC ceased to exist in 2002 – the Treaty provided for a limited duration of only 50 years. The EU then assumed its responsibilities and assets.

2.3.1.2 The impact of the Treaty on business

The Treaty had a strong impact on business in the coal and steel sectors, and opened the way for further cooperation in the way that the founder members conducted business. Coal and steel were the most important elements in the economic and military power of nations during the post-war reconstruction: steel was the major element in post-war economic reconstruction, and was needed for railways, buildings, ships, vehicles and machinery; coal was the primary energy resource. This treaty was therefore of a commercial nature, establishing a regulated market-sharing arrangement under supranational control. It was designed to:

- balance the six states' particular vested interests in coal and steel;
- facilitate the achievement of national objectives in these two sectors.

In practice, this cooperation increased trade significantly in coal and steel (an increase of 129 per cent in the first five years). Further, this was to:

- unify the market-concentrated supply: this enabled the industry to streamline, leaving only the most efficient producers.

However, the Treaty rapidly became insufficient from an economic point of view. Economically, more durable products challenged the coal and steel markets over time. Indeed, the decline of coal resulted in one of the first challenges for European state aid policies. A debate inflamed decision makers, about the sense of an enduring tradition of granting large amounts of state aid for the purpose of delaying structural adjustments, subsequent to market developments.

   Why is it important to consider this treaty, long past today? This is because, in principle, ECSC market integration was planned and perceived as 'being about the physical movement of goods' alone; in practice, it proved to go far beyond this. The impact on business strategy was significant, and the basis laid is just as important and beneficial for firms today. Let us consider the case of Italian steel price fluctuations during this period as an instructive example: over the first five years of the ECSC's existence, Italy – alone among all the Member States – managed to negotiate a gradual reduction of steel tariffs within the group. Tariffs were finally abolished in February 1958. From January 1957 already, steel prices in Italy began to fall because producers and distributors anticipated the lower prices that firms based elsewhere in the ECSC would be able to offer on the Italian market, i.e. rising competition. At the same time, steel firms in the other ECSC Member States were able to offer low prices in Italy, without lowering their entire price schedule, by aligning with French prices, which were low following currency devaluations in 1957 and 1958. Thus, steel-market integration not only changed business reach and strategic decisions. It also confronted Member State governments with the challenges of microeconomic consequences of macroeconomic policy decisions, relevant well into our times.

2.3.2 The Treaties of Rome

2.3.2.1 The failure of the European Defence Community

The desire for further economic integration coincided with the confirmation of a cold war and a US–Soviet arms race (the 'Sputnik Effect'). Both superpowers exercised pressure upon Europe, in particular Germany. There were also demands from the American government for Western Europe to assume a greater share of its own defence burden. German rearmament was something that many in Europe would have preferred to avoid; however, if it could not be avoided, they would try to control it. It became clear that the question of Germany was a key factor for both superpowers, and hence was going to shape the future of European cooperation and its economic model.

In October 1950, less than six months after Schuman's proposal, French Premier René Pleven drafted the establishment of a European Defence Community (EDC). The Pleven Plan would have put German rearmament under European political control, with German troops serving under the authority of a European defence minister, who in turn would be responsible to the ECSC Assembly. Ultimately, the French Assembly rejected Pleven's proposal. This led to a rapprochement between West Germany and the USA with the Dulles–Adenauer friendship that underlined the subscription of West Germany to the western economic system. In 1955, Germany joined the North Atlantic Treaty Organization (NATO) established in 1949, which assured any member of a common defence in the case of outside aggression. The failure of the plan for a European defence structure illustrated the geopolitical and historical challenges to overall European collaboration plans. It stressed the importance of finding a different common ground if the objectives of Monnet were to be pursued, as desired by international politics and business alike.

2.3.2.2 The main objectives of the EEC Treaty

The success of the ECSC stimulated efforts for further economic integration, the outcome of which was the Treaty of Rome. This treaty symbolized the victory of Jean Monnet's gradualist approach to building a European union. In June 1955, the foreign ministers of the six Member States launched talks in Messina (Italy): it was decided that the time was ripe for the ECSC to move towards a common European market for all products.

On a rainy 25 March 1957 in Rome, the same six countries that had founded the ECSC signed up to the bright future of a continent still scarred by the past war, with two treaties: one created the EEC, while the other, Euratom, was a sector-specific treaty of limited application, promoting and regulating the nuclear industry. Under what was effectively one treaty, the Treaty of Rome, these two new entities (along with the ECSC) merged to form one organization, the EEC. Both treaties entered into force on 1 January 1958, after their ratification by the members' national parliaments.

The Member States committed themselves to removing trade barriers and forming a 'common market' with appropriate institutions governing the communities and a policy framework that would allow a turning of the commitment into practice.

The introduction of a Common Customs Tariff was one of its main objectives. All tariffs and other barriers to trade among the Member States were to be eliminated, while external tariffs became common to all six members and were complemented by establishing the following:

- a common commercial policy;
- an agricultural policy;
- the free movement of people, goods, services and capital;
- equal treatment for all workers with respect to wages, conditions and entitlements to welfare benefits;
- a European Social Fund and a European Investment Bank.

To achieve this, the focus had to be on market liberalization (i.e. its unification), normalization of competition (i.e. the control of monopolies, state aids, subsidies) and economic development.

2.3.2.3 The impact of the EEC Treaty on business

The monumental EEC document of more than 200 articles created a free trade area evolving rapidly into a customs union. It removed internal tariffs on goods and that harmonized external tariffs, thus having a significant impact on import logistics. For a company importing a given product, customs tariffs would no longer differ: choosing a port at which to import a product now became dependent on logistical evaluations rather than on pecuniary ones related to customs. In other words, as the customs tariff became equal across the EEC, only geographical or other logistical considerations defined at which location a good entered the market. Internally, competition and competitiveness were enhanced even further. Nevertheless, the free movement of citizens, capital and services remained limited at this stage.

The Treaty of Rome also launched the Common Agricultural Policy (CAP). As the first expression of 'common' policies, it launched sole EEC decision-making, replacing fragmented national conditions, in certain sectors. Today, three quarters of European business is subject to a rules issue of common policies, including competition and trade policies.

Essentially, the CAP enacted a free market of agricultural products inside the EEC, and formulated policies guaranteeing sufficient revenues to European farmers. The aim of the CAP was to prevent the starvation experienced by the people of continental Europe during and after World War II. Since its inception, the agricultural policy has become subject to a wide range of diverse, complex issues, from how to treat former colonial possessions to a conflict between the desire of the Benelux countries for low tariffs on food imports and that of France, Germany and Italy to use high tariffs to protect their agricultural sectors.

Box 2.2 gives an insight into the development of the CAP up to the beginning of the twenty-first century, and the challenges that it faces under rather different macroeconomic conditions from those of the mid to late 1950s.

Box 2.2: The Common Agricultural Policy – a victim of its own success

The CAP was established with two main objectives: (1) to ensure that the people of Europe would never again experience starvation; and (2) to install a self-sufficiency and independence of the agricultural sector. The system was based on market-sharing, collaboration and common funding policies. It was so successful that it soon resulted in the overproduction of certain agricultural goods, leading to so-called butter 'mountains' and cereal 'heaps' due to the system of market price support payments. The question of what to do with this overproduction quickly arose; immediate but unsustainable and questionable solutions included dumping crops on the markets of Third World countries. In Europe, prices became inflated through distorted export subsidies, with high-volume, low-priced produce replacing quality goods. Attempts to reform the CAP have, on a number of occasions, resulted in quarrels between its members. Countries such as the UK have negotiated budget rebates due to the argument of not being a large agricultural country, much to the annoyance of countries like France and Poland that are high net contributors and receivers of that budget respectively. A heated debate about the distribution and significance of the agricultural budget reflects the many challenges for European leaders in the quest to protect the economic, social and political interests of their respective countries in the overall interest within (or versus?) Europe. This perfectly illustrates the advantages and challenges of cooperation.

The Treaty of Rome also prohibited monopolies, launched some transport policies, granted certain commercial privileges to the colonial territories of the Member States, and set up an investment fund to transfer capital from the more developed to the less developed regions of the EEC.

2.3.2.4 The relevance of the European Free Trade Area (EFTA) and EU relations

Despite its post–war role as an ally, the UK – still strongly attached to its Commonwealth – did not join the Community until 1973, having maintained an independent (though cooperating) role in Europe throughout the 1950s and 1960s.

Instead, the country had joined the European Free Trade Area (EFTA), which was established in Stockholm in July 1959. Members of EFTA entertained bilateral free trade agreements with the EEC, and, later, with the creation of the European Economic Area (EEA) in 1994, adopted about two-thirds of the EEC's body of law. Its members enjoy privileged relations with the EU. Through the EEA, EFTA members have the possibility of taking in the Internal Market of the EU. This only excludes participation in the Common Agriculture and Fisheries Policies, Customs Union, Common Trade Policy, Common Foreign and Security Policy, and the European Monetary Union (EMU). Justice and Home Affairs are also excluded but EFTA countries are part of the Schengen area (see Figure 2.3 for EFTA member states).

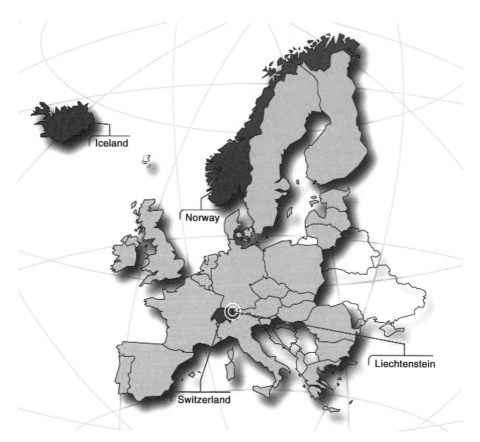

Figure 2.3   *EFTA Member States*

Table 2.2 lists Member States by their year of accession to the EEC/EU, while
Table 2.3 dates the accession of Member States to EFTA. While you study both, note
the shifts from one grouping to the other. You will find, for example, that Denmark
and the UK were among the founder members of EFTA in 1960. They then left in
1973 in order to join the Community. In 1986, Portugal did the same, as did Austria,
Sweden and Finland in 1995. Iceland applied to join the EU in the aftermath of its
financial crisis, in July 2009. By this time, it had become a springboard for those
countries that had EU membership aspirations. The European marketplace was now
vast and well regulated, with different degrees of integration in the region. Note also
that the year 1960 was symbolic for further international multilateral efforts, including
the creation of the Organisation for Economic Co-operation and Development
(OECD) as a forum for economic analysis, debate and solution.

   In 1967, the six founder members of the EEC decided to change its name to
the European Community (EC), a title that corresponded more with the vast
Community aims and objectives.

Table 2.2   *EEC/EU membership by year of accession*

Year	Countries
1952 ('founding members')	Belgium, France, Germany (West Germany only, East Germany in 1990), Italy, Luxembourg, Netherlands
1973	Denmark, Ireland, UK
1981	Greece
1986	Spain, Portugal
1995	Austria, Finland, Sweden
2004	Cyprus, Czech Republic, Estonia, Hungary, Latvia, Lithuania, Malta, Poland, Slovakia, Slovenia
2007	Bulgaria, Romania
2011	Candidate countries: Croatia, Macedonia (received candidate country status in 2005), Turkey, Iceland
	Potential candidates: Bosnia and Herzegovina, Serbia, Kosovo, Montenegro, Albania

Table 2.3   *Internal market EFTA and EEA membership by year of accession*

Year	Countries
1960	Austria, Denmark, Norway, Portugal, Sweden, Switzerland and the UK (the founding members of EFTA)
1961	Finland becomes an associate member (full member in 1986)
1970	Iceland becomes a member
1979	Spain signs the free trade agreement
1991	Liechtenstein becomes a member of EFTA free trade agreement signed with Turkey
1992	Free trade agreements signed with the former Czechoslovakia, Israel, Poland and Romania
1993	Free trade agreement signed with Bulgaria and Hungary. Protocol on the succession of the Czech Republic and Slovakia to EFTA Czechoslovakia agreement signed
1995	Free trade agreements signed with Estonia, Latvia, Lithuania and Slovenia
1997	Free trade agreement signed with Morocco
1999	Free trade agreements with the Palestine Liberation Organization and with Morocco enter into force
2000	Free trade agreements signed with Macedonia and Mexico
2001	Free trade agreements signed with Croatia and Jordan
2002	Free trade agreement signed with Singapore
2003	Free trade agreement signed with Chile
2004	Free trade agreement signed with Lebanon and Tunisia
2005	Free trade agreement signed with the Republic of Korea
2006	Free trade agreement with the Southern African Customs Union
2007	Free trade agreement signed with Egypt
2008	Free trade agreement signed with Canada and Colombia
2009	Free trade agreement signed with Serbia, Albania and Gulf Cooperation countries
2010	Free trade agreement signed with India and Peru

Interestingly, as Eurostat shows, trade in industrial products among the EEC's Member States rose and doubled within the first four years of ratification of the two treaties signed in Rome. The average growth among the economies of the six founder members in the 1960s reached between 5 and 6 per cent. In addition, members with initially weaker economies, in particular France and Italy, increased their trade by far more than the other Member States. This naturally reinforced the founders' belief in the virtues of economic and political integration. Also, barriers to trade were removed more rapidly than had been provided for in the Treaty of Rome.

2.3.3 Main developments from the 1970s onwards

The 1970s saw major developments occur inside and outside the EC. On 1 January 1973, it increased its membership from six to nine countries when Denmark, Ireland and the UK became Member States. During this period, the Community reinforced earlier agreements with neighbouring countries to enhance free trade. The European Parliament used its newly acquired budgetary powers to finance the EC's external market initiatives. In 1975, the EC negotiated the Lomé Treaty which established economic cooperation with, initially, 46 African, Caribbean and Pacific countries (former colonies). In the same year, Norway decided against joining the EC and remained an EFTA country.

A major step towards further integration was taken in 1979 when the European Parliament held its first direct elections. For the first time, a political party system started to exist within and across part of the European continent. Approximately 61 per cent of those eligible voted in these first cross-national elections – not numerically a huge turnout, but symbolically a successful one. The following year saw the introduction of a common unit of currency, the ECU (European Currency Unit), brought in to harmonize exchange rates between the Member States in the long run.

However, by the end of the decade, a sense of Euro-pessimism haunted the Member States with two areas dominating the debate. First, there was dissatisfaction with the many hurdles still to overcome on the path to economic integration. Second, there was a resurgence of doubt about whether national sovereignty should be traded off for the benefits of a harmonious Europe. Also, five years of the most combative negotiations on the side of the British free-market prime minister, Margaret Thatcher, with the socialist leadership of the EC of the time, had resulted in a UK budget rebate that will last until at least 2014. By the early 1980s, inflation was high and growth minimal in most European economies, with desperate devaluations of the French franc, and the need for austerity packages that finally took Europe back out of crisis.

By the mid 1980s, a more optimistic outlook had taken hold of the EC economies once again. Greece had joined in 1981, followed by Spain and Portugal in 1986. The process of integration had received new important political impetus, in particular from Jacques Delors, a French socialist who had been elected President of the European Commission. In 1985, Delors published a startling White Paper that pointed out that the expanding Community potentially could become a single market serving

300 million consumers. However, it also showed very clearly that particular obstacles were thwarting this tremendous potential: queues at border crossings; technical barriers to trade; and closed markets for public contracts. Delors argued that the cost of doing nothing about these inefficiencies – the 'cost of non-Europe' – would be around EUR200 billion, but that they could be overcome by the introduction of 282 specific measures. The pressing challenge of European competitiveness vis-à-vis the USA and Japan became a significant driving force for a revitalized Euro-optimism.

The year of 1985 was also the well-known and appreciated Schengen agreement. The reference made by travellers in Europe to Schengen countries points to that year's agreement of some of the EU Member States to establish common rules and procedures for visa applications for short stays, asylum requests and border controls. When travelling through Schengen countries, in which the collaboration of police services and judicial authorities is enhanced, you normally need not show your passport at borders but can travel as in one single country. Today, just about every EU and EFTA member (for EFTA details, see below) has joined 'Schengen' in one way or another, although regular border controls remain in place for the UK and Ireland. Also, Bulgaria, Cyprus and Romania are not full members.

On the global stage, the optimism of the 1960s had, by 1970, been replaced by the awareness that peace in the world was still a long way from reality. In Europe, the decade had seen a bipolarity of political perspectives develop. On the one hand, the concept of wider and deeper integration through a strengthening of supranational institutions seemed to find its sense in the success of the post-war developments. On the other hand, a Europe of fatherlands, advocated by Charles de Gaulle, resisted any handover of sovereignty to supranational institutions. Indeed, this ideology led to the NATO crisis of 1965. De Gaulle's attempts to take a leading position in Western Europe – between the two blocs – resulted in tensions with the USA. Internally in Western Europe, the end of the 1960s saw student demonstrations, in particular against the war in Vietnam and for freedom; while those countries of Eastern Europe that came under the Soviet sphere of influence imposed ever-tighter restrictions on their populations. Terrorism also became a terrible threat worldwide.

Individual countries within their own borders also experienced major upheavals. For the UK, Northern Ireland became an area of tension and violence, and relations with the USA focused increasingly on economic ties, while the Commonwealth gradually dissolved. In 1974 Turkey invaded Cyprus, which had won independence from the UK in 1960. Turkish troops took control of the northern part of the island where Turkish Cypriots had set up a separate community in 1964 after ceasing to participate in power sharing with the Greek Cypriot community and then refusing to acknowledge a Greek Cypriot government that considered itself to be the government of all Cyprus. After the invasion, the Turkish Cypriots established their own government and state, both of which have only ever been recognized by Turkey. In Spain the following year, an era came to an end with the death of Franco, an era that was marked by internal tension, the omnipotence of its head of state and the growth of the separatist terrorist group ETA (Euzkadi ta Azkatasuna, 'Basque Homeland and

Liberty'). In the same year, Sweden further expanded its prominent social system and reduced the powers of its monarch.

The Soviet economic system continued to concentrate on developing its heavy industry at the expense of adequately feeding its people. Dissenting voices and calls for reform began to become vivid in many of the Eastern and Central European states (such as from Lech Walesa in Poland); in those countries that the USSR had systematically undermined and 'sovietized' from 1945 onwards. There were also signs of a definite thaw in East–West relations, when frictions with China led the USSR to sign a non-proliferation treaty with the USA and the UK.

The 1980s saw the USSR itself undergo change when, between 1982 and 1985, four leaders followed one another rapidly in a symbolic move towards change. The last of these leaders, Mikhail Gorbachev, set in motion a series of liberal reforms that paved the way for the eventual collapse of the Soviet system in Eastern Europe. The fall of the Berlin Wall in 1989 symbolized this collapse and was quickly followed by the toppling of the Ceausescu regime in Romania. At the same time, in Bulgaria an attempt by President Schiwkow to make a 'great leap forward' failed and a new constitution proclaimed the country a socialist democracy. Yugoslavia, a country that had been liberated by a partisan army led by Josip Tito at the end of World War II, enjoyed relative liberty from Soviet influence: Yugoslavia had broken from the USSR (under Stalin) in 1948 and become a federal people's republic. At the time of Tito's death in 1980, the country was collectively led. However, in 1988, Slobodan Milošević became head of state, introducing the systematic discrimination (and, later, elimination) of ethnic and religious minorities that led to the Balkan wars in the early 1990s.

The 1970s and 1980s were also characterized by three important oil crises that put serious strain on the economies of developed countries.

2.3.4 The Single European Act (SEA)

2.3.4.1 The key points of the Act

With the collapse of the Soviet system, the preoccupations of the cold war vanished, and a multipolar world map could be envisaged. Geopolitics were shifting, and regional groupings such as the EU or AFTA (Association of South-East Asian Nations) became increasingly important structural components of the world scene.

In the EU, the White Paper on Completing the Internal Market, finalized under the British Commissioner Lord Cockfield, was presented by the Delors Commission:

Europe stands at the crossroads. We either go ahead – with resolution and determination – or we drop back into mediocrity. We can now either resolve to complete the integration of the economies of Europe; or, through a lack of political will to face the immense problems involved, we can simply allow Europe to develop into no more than a free trade area. (European Commission, Completing the internal market, White Paper for the European Council, Milan, 28–29 June 1985)

It gave birth to the 1986 Single European Act (SEA) that progressively enforced an internal market by 31 December 1992.

Box 2.3: Jacques Delors' definition of the Single European Act's main objectives

'The Single Act means, in a few words, the commitment of implementing simultaneously the great market without frontiers, more economic and social cohesion, a European research and technology policy, the strengthening of the European Monetary System, the beginning of a European social area and significant actions in the environment.'

The SEA covers a broad spectrum of Community law, and contains the first major revision of the EEC Treaty of Rome. It set out a timetable for completing the Single Market by 1993 for goods, capital and services, and citizens within the Community. Whether corporations, professions or trade unions, all actors in economic life incorporated the necessary amendments in their operations without delay. As a result, citizens felt the effects of the measures rapidly: a wider range of goods and services became available; and there were less restrictions on travelling in Europe. Most significantly for internal EC administration, the SEA extended the scope of qualified majority voting (QMV) at the Council of Ministers (also known as the Council of the European Union) and increased the Commission's powers: a decision is adopted if it receives a given number of votes, expressing the favourable vote of the majority of the members of the institution. More explanation about this will be given in Chapter 4, which analyses institutional decision-making for the European business environment.

2.3.4.2 The impact of the SEA on business

As soon as corporations recognized that European integration was the only way forward in an increasingly competitive world market, a Europeanization without precedence followed. For example, the SEA provided the basis for the Directive adopted in November 1997 facilitating lawyers' practice of their profession throughout the EU. The elimination of technical frontiers resulted in the removal of nationally regulated barriers on products and services through general agreement or mutual recognition. Steps were taken to make national laws on safety and pollution consistent across Europe. More generally, EU countries agreed to recognize the equivalence of each other's laws and certification systems. A European company law was established for certain legal entities, and the Member States began to bring their national laws on intellectual and industrial property rights (trade marks and patents) into line with one another.

This created an improved environment for industrial cooperation, which was further enhanced with the elimination of tax frontiers. Agreeing or approximating VAT rates and excise duty overcame the obstacles created by differences in indirect taxes. The SEA also opened the way for even stronger social and cultural cooperation.

2.3.5 The Treaty on the European Union (TEU) – Maastricht

2.3.5.1 The key points of the Treaty

The Treaty on European Union (TEU) signed in Maastricht (The Netherlands) on 7 February 1992 was a turning point in the integration process and changed the official denomination of the EEC to the EU. The Treaty, introduced once the objectives of the SEA had been achieved, is more generally known as the Maastricht Treaty. It was enforced on 1 January 1994. The Treaty assigned the EU with a broad range of objectives, well beyond the politico-economic scope and based on a set of guiding principles, including subsidiarity (the principle that decisions should always be taken as closely as possible to the people and that constant checks should be made to see if Community action is justified, if action is feasible at the national, regional or local level) and a respect for democracy and human rights, governed by an institutional structure presided over by the European Council, that is, the Council of the Heads of State or Government of the Member States of European Union.

Europe was to grow closer and, at the same time, to set the basis for its citizens to live in a monetary, political and social Europe that was to extend the benefits of a free economic area to a more personally appreciable level.

Three pillars of European affairs embodied distinct sets of policy issues in terms of objective and function, legislative basis and modus operandi of the appropriate decision-making process. The first pillar is the EC, that is, the achievement, management and improvement of the Single Market, which includes provisions for customs union and the Single Market, EU competition law, economic and monetary union, trans-European networks, consumer protection and more. This development coincided with important international advancements with regional free trade zones playing an increasing part in economies worldwide. Among others, NAFTA became the world's largest free trade zone – in terms of surface area – in 1991. Mercosur (Mercado Común del Sur in Spanish: Southern [American] Common Market) increased its scale of operations in South America. In 1994, negotiations began throughout the American continent, excluding Cuba and French Guyana, for the establishment of a Free Trade Area of the Americas (FTAA). In Asia, ASEAN (Association of South East Asian Nations) evolved further and the Asia-Pacific Economic Cooperation Conference (APEC) proposed progressive trade liberalization measures to its members – the most populated market group worldwide (see also Chapter 10).

The Maastricht Treaty also recognized the internal and external challenges that a deeper and larger union would be exposed to, with its second pillar. To propose and develop a common currency for EU members was a singular development. Pillar Two added a Common Foreign and Security Policy (CFSP) to the spheres of European integration. The role of the EU, as a whole, in international affairs evolved and needed to be correlated to the Member States' objectives and international challenges. This pillar also comprises foreign policy, a European rapid reaction force, peacekeeping, a European security and defence policy, and more.

The 1990s was a decade characterized by arms reduction efforts. The USA and Russia signed START II (Strategic Arms Reduction Talks) in 1993, and in 1995 the Geneva conference reviewing the 1968 non-proliferation agreement decided to maintain regular contact, in particular because new countries were developing nuclear weapons (such as India, Israel and Pakistan). In the same year, New Zealand protested vehemently against French nuclear trials on the Mururoa Atolls. In 1997, an important United Nations (UN) agreement prohibiting chemical weapons was enforced and signed by 165 members.

The decade was also marked by geopolitical crises and war: the USA under George H.W. Bush engaged in the Gulf War; and what was then considered the periphery of the EU suffered the Balkan wars – to mention just two areas of conflict. This conflict in the former Yugoslavia demonstrated the difficulties that the EU faced in making decisions and reacting to situations quickly. Sweden's president, Olof Palme, was assassinated in 1986: this was an event that profoundly shocked a population known for peace and neutrality. Finland became increasingly exposed to political pressure from Russia.

Former Yugoslavian countries started breaking up from 1992 onwards, leading to the later success of that development when Slovenia became the first former Yugoslavian country to enter the EU (2004) and the euro-zone (2007), and the first former communist country in general to hold the presidency of the EU in 2008.

But let's continue to scrutinize this time period. Elsewhere, more challenges arose for the international community: Russia attempted to reinforce its identity and territory in one of its southern republics, Chechnya; and the Chinese leadership, in the aftermath of the Tiananmen Square events (and despite more economic freedom), brutally put down the internal criticism made about the Communist Party.

The Intifada in Palestine and a rising pan-Arabic nationalism challenged the multilateral peace mechanisms that were so important to European leaders, as well as to Bill Clinton, who had been elected President of the USA in 1992 and again in 1996.

In the Vatican City State, the first non-Italian Pope since 1523, Polish Pope Jean Paul II, increased his international peace missions and attempted in vain to create relationships with Russia and China. While South Africa became a democratic republic abolishing apartheid and freeing Nelson Mandela, the continent experienced ethnic violence and genocide (for example, in Uganda): most of the conflicts originated from former colonial policies and conferred a certain responsibility on the developed world. At the UN, discussions arose as to whether its peacekeeping force should also be peace installing.

The third pillar included Police and Judicial Cooperation in Criminal Matters (PJCC), asylum policy, the Schengen Treaty, immigration policy, trafficking and weapons smuggling, terrorism, trafficking in human beings, organized crime, bribery and fraud. This was particularly significant in the context of Italy because it allowed the Italian authorities to take greater measures to reduce the role of the Mafia in internal politics and the economy. Also, in the context of police and immigration forces across Europe, this pillar provided a response to rising Europe-wide illegal immigration and organized crime. It was a compromise between federalists, confederalists and Eurosceptics, and – in its nature of a compromise – insufficient, and well in need of further development.

2.3.5.2 The impact of the TEU on business

With the TEU, the EU has reached the highest level of international integration, illustrated in Figure 2.1. The EU had become one market, with additional competencies that were to:

- refine economic cooperation;
- enforce political and social convergence;
- include the conduct of monetary coordination and joint monetary actions.

The business impact of the Maastricht Treaty is hence tremendous. It has the virtue of having streamlined the European markets in accordance with the challenges of its time. Also, the Treaty is at the origin of significant improvements in the competitiveness of European manufacturing, in both the primary and the tertiary sectors. It creates further investment and operational opportunities in Europe and ensures cheaper supplies, goods and services. Some reasons for this are cost-efficiencies in European business, stemming from:

- transaction costs disappearing between the members of the euro-zone, not only in terms of currency losses, but also as regards border patrols, customs procedures and red tape;
- reduced uncertainties among those states as to the relative price of currencies. Before the new currency, actors deciding to defer payment in a contract ran the risk of the rise or fall of money value. This facilitates the selling of securities, the raising of funds and capital, and the recruitment of diverse labour;
- credibility and power of a single currency as the demand for the euro will be more important for reserves. European companies potentially save money by having access to lower interest rates;
- increased price and cost transparency on the European markets: an easy comparison of prices facilitates a real competitiveness among companies of EU Member States and encourages efficiencies and economies of scale effects. The competitiveness also has, of course, an impact on companies that are privatized, and/or on those that are not competitive on a European scale, and hence is accompanied by a concentration, consolidation, and outsourcing and offshoring effect. (This will be examined in Chapter 5.)

The Treaty also facilitates the expansion of operations cross-border, giving access to a great many consumers with 'globalized' tastes and values, and that are open to a vast multitude of goods and services, as studied later in Chapter 8. For companies, a pan-European strategy based on trans-regionalism, as introduced by the TEU, streamlines operations in Europe, raises efficiency and improves productivity and the international value chain. Strategic partnerships allow for detailed market knowledge.

2.3.6 The Treaty of Amsterdam

2.3.6.1 The key points of the Treaty

On 2 October 1997, the Treaty of Amsterdam was signed by 15 European states to complement the Maastricht Treaty. The geographical enlargements of the EU in

1973, 1981, 1986 and 1995 had both (a) widened the European integrated market, and (b) challenged the depth of European integration to such an extent that the EU had already started to look even further, in the direction of Eastern and Central Europe. The initial institutional framework, despite some modifications within earlier treaties, needed to be in line with the new Europe.

Thus, this treaty complemented earlier ones and focused on the notion of flexibility, of renewal and adaptation of the preceding texts, and on increasing transparency towards the citizen upon Jacques Delors' view. For this, a number of initiatives had been taken. Citizens were granted the right to access documents of the Council of Ministers. The Schengen agreement and convention among the Benelux countries, and Germany, France, Portugal and Spain, was also incorporated into the treaty and transferred cross-border formalities from internal to external borders. Among other minor amendments for institutions, it is important to remember that the powers of the directly elected European Parliament (EP) were reinforced in Amsterdam, so as to better control the EU internally. As a result, the EP had the power to accept or refuse any proposed candidate for the role of Commission President and his/her college of Commissioners. The treaty created an enhanced cooperation procedure ('flexible cooperation'). For political relations among Member States, arenas of cooperation on levels below that of the 15 were installed, allowing for cooperation meetings involving, for instance, only the UK, Germany and France on certain issues, and within well-defined limits. Most importantly, objectives were formalized that focused on sustainable development, human health protection and consumer protection, and which made firm commitments for cooperation on visas, asylum and immigration. With this treaty, the establishment of a new post of head of the CFSP was to strengthen a policy that was yet to converge at EU level.

2.3.6.2 The impact of the Treaty on business

The Amsterdam Treaty was widely considered as weak. Nevertheless, the Treaty had some impact on business, and this in a variety of areas. It enhanced the multilateral promotion of employment, with a surveillance mechanism monitoring the coherence of policies for a more flexible, effective labour market in Europe. With consumer protection a priority, the provisions of the Treaty changed the regulatory framework for agribusiness and related sectors and organisms. The quest for sustainable development, responsible business and the protection of the environment introduced important challenges to the production sector's target of profit maximization. It also installed leadership aspirations into corporations technologically advanced in:

- waste management;
- industrial compliance;
- personnel resources education;
- activities centred on acquiring a migration methodology to environmentally acceptable technologies, quality management and adapted corporate growth strategy.

The Treaty has played its role in promoting an efficient economy of scale that facilitates movements, amongst which are the flows of trade and investment. At the same time, consumer and labour movement has become even easier in the Schengen countries. It has also contributed to making the consumer ever more European, resulting in (a) citizens aware of the drives and challenges of economic welfare, and (b) consumers with increasingly homogenized product needs and expectations (price, quality, reliability and fair trade principles).

In July 1997, the 'Agenda 2000', following the Amsterdam Treaty closely, complemented the latter by strengthening Community policies, and provided tools needed for further enlargement. Indeed, there was urgency: negotiations were already under way, preparing for a vast evolution of EU membership towards Central and Eastern Europe (CEE). At the same time, some of the richest countries, like Germany, started to be vocal about a perceived imbalance between their contribution to the Community (around 28.2 per cent of the total) and what they received via the European Structural Fund and the common agricultural policy (CAP). Poorer countries refused to sanction a rebalance of contributions. The European Structural Fund and the Cohesion Fund focused on helping regions and countries economically inferior to the EU average. (See Chapter 7 for more information on these funds.)

Agenda 2000 included a much needed revision of the European model for leaner and greener agriculture that would balance expectations for consumer health and a clean and pretty countryside with competitive farming, ecological tourism, a high quality of life and stable spending. What had changed over the past two decades was the awareness that future generations would need a heritage of peace, wealth and also health.

The Treaty also set provisions so that the EU would analyse the effects of enlargement on regional policies of the former communist countries of Central and Eastern Europe, and be prepared to learn for a historical widening of the European market and business environment.

2.3.7 The Treaty of Nice

2.3.7.1 The key points of the Treaty

Another significant step towards the historic enlargement into Eastern and Central Europe (10 countries in 2004 and 2 additional members in 2007) was the Treaty of Nice, signed on 26 February 2001.

Its objective was to increase the role of the Community. The Treaty was also concluded to redefine the size and composition of the Commission by re-weighting the voting system of the Council of Ministers and extending qualified majority voting (QMV).

Two changes were made to the Amsterdam arrangements:

- The first concerned flexible mechanisms to enhance cooperation and to make it potentially more workable: the minimum number of Member States required for flexible cooperation was to incorporate eight members.
- The second concerned the first and third pillars, whereby the Treaty added the possibility of an appeal to the European Council that acts by QMV (for more on this, see Chapter 4).

The key measures prepared for the enlargement of the Union from 15 to 25 and then to 27 Members States and further. This enlargement added 75 million citizens to the 380 million already residing in EU member countries.

Enhanced cooperation was another key objective, with formal authorization given by the Council after receiving the opinion of the Commission. It was decided that with flexible cooperation, no Member State could be excluded, though issues are excluded that deal with military applications or defence matters.

The Treaty also set provisions for the European Court of Justice to operate more efficiently, reduce the backlog of cases and reduce the length of time required to process new cases. Indeed, a new distribution of responsibilities gave increasing powers to the Court of First Instance.

The procedures for managing crises adopted by the Western European Union (WEU) – a body that provided for collective self-defence and economic, social and cultural collaboration among its signatories of 1948 (Belgium, France, Luxembourg, The Netherlands and the UK) – were incorporated into the EU. The aims encompass assistance to each other in resisting any policy of aggression, and the promotion of unity and the encouragement of the progressive integration of Europe.

In addition, the Nice Treaty increased the EU's capacity to fight international crime further. The European Judicial Cooperation Unit ('Eurojust'), formalized in the TEU, was assigned to coordinate action in criminal matters in the Member States, and the European Defence Agency was made an official intergovernmental body in order to coordinate 24 of the European countries' military capabilities, harmonize military requirements, coordinate research and development (R&D), and converge natural procurement procedures (for the first time, part of the internal market programme). The Treaty also designated a new committee, the PSC (Political and Security Committee).

2.3.7.2 The impact of the Treaty on business

The foremost benefit of the Treaty is that it prepared the way for a bigger and better functioning European business environment with accompanying benefits, advantages and challenges in terms of competitiveness, both inside the EU and towards non-member countries. The European common security strategy has increased the EU's foreign policy efficiency and credibility for foreign and local investors, and strengthened the relationships and dialogue among the main trading partners. This deepening and widening market has also helped to reinforce peaceful relationships with its neighbours.

2.3.8 A constitution for Europe? The Treaty of Lisbon

The Union is founded on the values of respect for human dignity, freedom, democracy, equality, the rule of law and the respect for human rights, including the rights of persons belonging to minorities. These values are common to the Member States in a society in which pluralism, non-discrimination, tolerance, justice, solidarity and equality between women and men prevail. (European Communities, 2005: Articles 1–2)

2.3.8.1 The aim of the Lisbon Treaty

The Treaty of Lisbon came into force in December 2009, in the aftermath of a European Constitution project that was abandoned after its rejection by some member states and their populations.

The Constitution's primary objectives encompassed the streamlining of the EU's legal and institutional framework that had singnificantly grown in size and complexity over the decades, and focused on simplification, democracy, transparency, effectiveness and legitimacy for the EU.

Political science teaches us that a constitution is written when a break with tradition forces a government to define how a country is ruled, as was the case, for instance, after the French Revolution, at the end of World War II for Germany (with the introduction of the 'Basic Law' in West Germany), and when independence was obtained by formerly oppressed countries.

Countries, such as the UK, which have not undergone such schisms, are less likely to have a written constitution, and tend to follow a model of governance where tradition, custom and common law prevail. Nevertheless, the leading European thinkers, politicians, business leaders and citizens felt that − with Europe having experienced major upheavals in the past − there was a need for deeper, wider and more challenging integration.

The European Constitution would have been a text subject to the rules of international law and, thus, a treaty. It aimed to answer questions about the distribution of power and objectives, and its functioning.

Its adopted simplified version (not a constitution, but a treaty) of December 2007 provided for a long-term president of the European Council to the EU, and confirmed a foreign policy high representative in charge of diplomacy, aid budget and external relations staff. It stressed the legally binding character of the EU's charter on fundamental rights. Through the Treaty of Lisbon, the EU has become one legal entity with the ability to enter into contract (for example, in the case of an international convention). The treaty also merged the three pillars (remember Maastricht, see above), introduced more democratic voting rules, and provided for increased democratization of overall functioning, for example in terms of citizen's initiatives. Given the diversity of legal traditions and contexts in Europe, some Member States enjoy a special derogation from clauses such as that of fundamental rights (including the UK, Poland, Croatia's adhesion and the Czech Republic). Particular 'bridging' and 'flexibility' clauses were added to the Treaty to make sure that the diversity of interests can be respected but does not hinder decisions for the benefit of European integration.

2.3.8.2 The impact of the Lisbon Treaty on business

The Lisbon Treaty provides for greater transparency of decision-making. It allows for greater subsidiary powers for civil society and thus opens up possibilities for interest articulation and corporate political activity, in which the different actors of the European market and its legislators can better interact. This increases the applicability of policies: it is important that in the vast European market, a diversity of stakeholders have a chance to play a role. Gaining access to EU documents and procedures generally helps stakeholders to obtain information more easily. This is key for companies that need to define their strategy and positions in real time, consistent with rules that will have an impact on operations, markets, opportunities or threats.

In addition, the extension of qualified majority voting (QMV) facilitates the adoption of EU-wide rules and legislation.

The aim of creating a high level of competitiveness through innovation and information systems potentially implies fast and effective decision-making, with European legislation reinforcing business opportunities and vice versa. The Lisbon Treaty's explicit aim was to create a business-friendly environment, leading to both wealth creation (and therefore employment) and a more secure business environment and better functioning Single Market.

With the EU, already the biggest donor of financial aid to the world's trouble spots, reinforcing its peacekeeping and peacemaking operations, a European legislation adapted to the needs and concerns of globalization allows it to play a role in international organizations, in negotiations and in running its many projects which help in practical terms to make human rights and democracy succeed. European integration is hence fostering a secure and liberal business environment across borders, inside and outside the EU.

2.4 European objectives

A chronological review of the main treaties governing European integration has illustrated the sequential evolution of business opportunities and challenges.

Doing business in Europe implies 'doing business within an integrated marketplace', that to its greatest extent is called a Single Market, due to the development of harmonization, deregulation and subsidiarity. But this is also a marketplace characterized by diversity. Business needs to respect that all stakeholders in this community strive for beneficial shared objectives in an area creating freedom, law and justice, and preserving social and human rights and solidarity. European history is at the root of a people striving for a peaceful, prosperous, sustainable independent society, and this, through economic, political, financial, social and cultural harmonization, in domains where compromise can be found and collaborations can be enhanced.

Is the typical European business leader or manager preoccupied by such values and history in everyday business life? The answer is: certainly not. However, he or she moves in a business environment that is, in one way or another, very different from other locations in the world. For non-European corporations, it is essential knowledge that local acceptance of products, services and brands also comes from the intelligent contribution of the firm and its branches to society.

The transregional dimension of Europe opens up many opportunities. In the vast majority, European rules and initiatives constitute a compromise with a purpose of beneficial collaboration, often (but not always) in economic terms.

On a social level, Europe works for a reduction of social exclusion. The share of people with low educational attainment, or living in jobless households, or affected by long-term unemployment has decreased over the past decade, providing a benefit for the business environment. However, the most recent enlargements of the EU have caused unequal regional improvements with more early school-leavers and a need for more lifelong learning.

The EU also plays a role in asylum and immigration policy, guaranteeing the right to seek asylum. The immigration policies of Member States are still relatively disparate. With the freedom of movement of, and limited checks on, people, immigration is difficult to control. Countries such as the UK and Spain have a rather lax stance on immigration, and regularly legalize illegal immigrants. Often, countries with high unemployment rates are increasingly opposed to this practice.

At the same time, the Member States are coordinating their policies for refugees and trying to tackle the problem at source by combating poverty and preventing conflicts in the countries from which people might want to flee. Germany, for example, is known for its particularly humane asylum policy. This divergence among selected Member States' decisions on asylum applications still exists today. Nonetheless, 2009 rules have stipulated the decision-making time, allowing a maximum of six months.

'Asylum shopping', that is, moving across borders in Europe to find the most likely place for successful application, is illegal in Europe. About 70 per cent of asylum applications are rejected.

Europe is ultimately about fewer borders. The advantage of a frontier-free area is the freedom of circulation that is not only simply pleasant when travelling. It also enhances collaborations in an innumerable range of areas. The overall objectives may well be challenged by the fact that freedom and harmonization remain the compromise (more or less well negotiated) of the many countries. The divergences of labour costs, of service and of innovation potential, and the remaining burdensome procedures in some European countries are examples of barriers to full European integration. The Internet-based support site for this book provides you with a country-by-country guide to those conditions.

The true interest in doing business across Europe is in the unique level of integration and harmonization that characterizes this business environment. The speed of market integration and the focus of transnationality are ultimately defined by its members. EFTA integration, the EU's frontier-free Single Market and the single currency, the euro, are symbolic features. They have given a significant boost to trade and business opportunities in Europe.

An agreed strategy of particular interest is the so-called Lisbon Strategy (or Lisbon Agenda), aiming for growth and more and better jobs. In 2009, the EU and its members decided to expand this strategic framework to encourage European cooperation in education and training, under the name of ET (Education & Training) 2020, for Europe 2020. It stipulates that tomorrow's jobs will be created through research, training and education, a spirit of entrepreneurship and innovation, adaptability to new working methods and equal opportunities. This means that Europe is investing (and funding investments) in these fields, with the ambition of supporting contributions that experts, organizations and other stakeholders pursue across borders (Chapter 7 will provide more details about EU funding for corporations).

More than competitiveness, the Gothenburg agenda of 2001 (now called the EU's Sustainable Development Strategy, part of territorial cooperation) supports the Lisbon Agenda for a Europe that is clean, clever and competitive.

About one third of the entire EU budget is taken up by regional funds that promote growth and jobs in less well-off regions, under sustainable development principles. The EU, in particular, favours the advances made by the information society and its sector. The EU is also actively helping European research to achieve scientific excellence. The support and decision of the EU to opt for the technical standards of the global system for mobile communications (GSM) has resulted, for instance, in Europe leading the world in the development and manufacture of mobile telephone systems.

Over time, the European business environment has taken an increasingly transnational character, well consistent with the evolution of the continent's historic integration and it objectives. Today, intra-EU trade constitutes the majority of companies' trade in Europe, but may be endangered by the increasingly nationalistic focus of Member States in times of crisis. The transnational dependence of European interests, however, is clearly evidenced by the tables illustrated below, in particular for the euro-zone.

Table 2.4   *Euro area trade by geographical zone (billion EUR)*

Exports	2002	2003	2004	2005	2006	2007
Total extra-EA-15	1,076.5	1,052.0	1,146.2	1,235.1	1,379.2	1,498.4
Other European countries	529.5	531.9	585.4	628.2	716.0	793.8
Africa	59.4	59.3	64.6	73.3	77.2	86.9
North America	206.7	187.7	195.2	207.9	223.7	218.1
Central and South America	43.4	37.7	40.7	46.9	54.3	61.6
Asia	203.3	201.4	226.3	244.4	271.6	295.5
Oceania	15.8	16.4	18.2	19.3	18.9	20.9
Non-specified	18.4	17.5	15.9	15.2	17.3	21.6
Imports	**2002**	**2003**	**2004**	**2005**	**2006**	**2007**
Total extra-EA -15	938.8	988.3	1,080.7	1,225.7	1,393.8	1,482.7
Other European countries	459.7	467.6	507.3	563.1	644.3	682.0
Africa	67.9	68.9	73.4	96.0	110.1	113.8
North America	140.1	124.6	128.9	136.4	142.4	147.9
Central and South America	39.4	39.6	45.7	53.7	66.0	74.8
Asia	257.4	268.1	310.6	363.0	415.9	447.7
Oceania	7.8	7.9	8.5	9.6	11.0	11.8
Non-specified	11.4	11.6	6.3	3.9	4.1	4.7

Source: compiled from http://epp.eurostat.ec.europa.eu/cache/ITY_OFFPUB/KS-GI-10-002/EN/KS-GI-10-002-EN. PDF, pp. 33–35. Eurostat Pocketbook: External and intra-European Union trade (2009 edition), Data 2002–07 http://epp.eurostat.ec.europa.eu/cache/ITY_OFFPUB/KS-CV-08-001/EN/KS-CV-08-001-EN.PDF, p. 36, © European Union, 1995–2011

Table 2.5 *Exports to other EU members as a percentage of each country's total exports, 2005*

Country	Percentage of total exports
Austria	69.3
Belgium	76.4
Cyprus	71.7
Czech Republic	84.2
Denmark	70.5
Estonia	77.9
Finland	56.0
France	62.6
Germany	63.4
Greece	52.9
Hungary	76.3
Ireland	63.4
Italy	58.6
Latvia	76.4
Lithuania	65.3
Luxembourg	89.4
Malta	51.6
Netherlands	79.2
Poland	77.2
Portugal	79.8
Slovakia	85.4
Slovenia	66.4
Spain	71.8
Sweden	58.4
United Kingdom	56.9

Source: http://europa.eu/abc/keyfigures/tradeandeconomy/
tradingpower/index_en.htm#chart31 and http://europa.eu/geninfo/
legal_notices_en.htm (table for 2005) © European Union, 1995–2011

2.5 Résumé and conclusion

This chapter explained what the European Union is, what it represents and how it grew into what it is today. It reviewed the long-term process of integration that leads from the initial ECSC Treaty up to the Lisbon Treaty and further. The economic cooperation within Europe includes a complex set of stakeholders that lay the foundation of this business environment at a regional and international level. The fundamental Treaties of Paris and Rome defined the institutional structure and policy objectives of the European Communities in the areas of coal and steel (ECSC), atomic energy (EAEC) and economic integration (EEC). The SEA of 1986 created the conditions for the customs union to evolve into a single market, extended the scope of QMV and refined earlier legislation. The Maastricht Treaty of 1992 changed the denomination of this unique organization to the 'European Union' (EU), expanded former treaties and introduced the co-decision procedure and flexible cooperation mechanisms for the Member States. In 1999, the Amsterdam Treaty then set out to prepare the Union for enlargement, and deepened the free movement of people, goods, services and capital.

This increasingly integrated organization was streamlined by the Treaty of Lisbon in December 2009, setting the priorities that define the path of an economic, political, social and cultural union, with its challenges and opportunities. As a conclusion, each treaty has made the European business environment more efficient and more accessible as an entity.

The European Union constitutes the main geographical area and most mature market in Europe. The EU is the most integrated form of economic integration worldwide. Its values might hold no exclusivity, but they have taken the continent the furthest, anywhere, in terms of collaboration and cooperation amongst a defined set of member states. This has resulted in reduced costs, increased efficiencies and a stimulation of a Europeanization for performance over time. By any comparison, Europe represents a low-uncertainty playing field for its firms and organizations. Businesspeople are found to perceive a clear improvement of the business environment in the enlargement countries (EBRC, 2007): exporting firms are about 16 per cent more productive than others. Costs of trade procedures now range from just 2 to 15 per cent of the value of traded goods, and the harmonization of rules has been shown to halve the costs of bureaucratic trade procedures. Indeed, the EU estimates that savings of up to €300 billion a year are achieved for industry operating in Europe, thanks to integrational effects.

Currently, most non-EU firms investing in the EU come from the USA, Switzerland and Turkey, and more and more from Asia and South America. The number of emerging country multinationals (EM-MNEs) investing in Europe continues to grow steadily, often through acquisitions that reduce any liability that may stem from foreignness. Many emerging countries are choosing to invest overseas due to gradual liberalization from their home markets. Threats of domestic dominance within the emerging countries are causing businesses to hone their skills and seek growth abroad to compensate for lost market share in their home country. For example, Hisense, a multibillion-dollar electronics group turned their attention to the overseas market and now owns the best-selling brand of flat-screen TVs in France. Similarly, Mexican company, Cemex, is the world's biggest supplier of ready-mixed concrete. Originally building its business in its neighbouring South American countries (Colombia, Panama, Venezuela), the company began to expand to South East Asia (the Philippines and Thailand) and is now even established in Europe.

Mini case study: Ariane Systems

Ariane Systems is a French firm that offers self check-in/check-out software and products for the international hotelling and hospitality community. Its products are electronic kiosks that act as 24-hour receptionists. The firm was founded in 1998. Since then, it has become Europe's leading provider in the sector with its products being utilized by 24 of the top 50 hotel chains in Europe.

Ariane currently operates in 12 countries. It has subsidiaries in France, Germany, Spain, the UK and also the USA. In addition, it has offices in Denmark, Dubai and a Marine Division in France. The firm uses distributors in Benelux and South Africa

Mini Case

and is just starting to operate in Italy, Poland and Singapore through distributors. The firm began internationalizing in 2004 when it entered Germany. This was followed by the UK and Spain in 2006. Later that same year, Ariane entered the Nordic countries. In 2010, it entered the USA and the Middle East.

The proximity of France to Germany, the UK, Spain and the Benelux countries has aided Ariane in entering these markets. Not only are they short distances to travel, but the culture of these countries is familiar, making it easier to understand local practices and to serve the market. European integration, in particular the development of the Single Market, and the single currency, has helped this process further by removing exchange rate risk in the case of euro-zone countries, and by lowering tariff and regulatory barriers to market entry. Thus, Europeanization has been key in enabling Ariane to develop its overseas capabilities in neighbouring markets. From this European base, it has been able to go global and expand into three other continents: North America, Africa and Asia.

The extent to which Europeanization aided the firm in internationalizing is illustrated by the revenues of the firm. In 2010, at the point at which Ariane started to expand beyond Europe and after only six years of serving European markets, nearly half the revenues of the firm were from outside of its national home market (45 per cent).

When Ariane was considering its strategy for expanding within Europe, it saw a strong potential in having a base in the UK. This was not only because the firm believed that the UK offered a large market, but also because the UK held potential as a springboard into non-EU markets. Ariane entered the UK in 2006, installing six trial kiosks, in three cities, in several well-known budget and business hotels, with the aim of educating and initiating the UK hotelier market to its product. This enabled the firm to raise its profile and enabled users to become familiar with its innovative new service. In doing so, it built its presence in the market backed up by customer support. The latter is an important element of their offer, for which the company seeks a local base in each market through which to provide such services. Locally based support is thought to help to build trust with customers, giving them a sense that the firm will readily be able to offer support when needed. As it developed its operations in 2007, Ariane continued this strategy, implementing further installations on both a trial and permanent basis.

Ariane's next strategic plan was to expand to the Middle East, South Africa and Australia. Carine LeBrun, Managing Director, stated: 'It's very easy to initiate and build relationships in the UK and extend that to other key markets. We're certain we can expand quicker, develop greater awareness and build better business relationships from the UK than from France. Decision makers are more likely to travel to conferences and networking opportunities here.' One such conference, Hostec (Europe's largest technology event), was held in Birmingham and enabled the firm to showcase its kiosks to international audiences. The firm has also benefited from networking and development opportunities through UK Trade & Investment and the UK government's international business development organization, which regularly provide advice and information.

Source: Hannah Chaplin, Economics and Evaluation Team, UK Trade & Investment, London

Mini case study questions

1 As a French firm, Ariane uses the UK as a home base. What are the strengths and threats of Ariane's strategy of expanding within Europe before going global?
2 Why might Ariane have focused on 'old EU Member States' before globalizing? For business, what is Europe about?

 REVIEW QUESTIONS

1 **Explain** the difference between a free trade area and a common market. Why would countries wish to see economic integration deepen, and why would business want this to happen?
2 **Why** has the EU not yet managed to ratify a constitution?
3 **To what extent** does the EU represent Europe as a marketplace?
4 **Does** Europeanization mean that companies have to cover all European markets? If not, what does it mean?
5 **To what extent** has European economic development changed throughout the past decades? Why?

ASSIGNMENTS

- **Imagine** that you are the CEO of a US corporation entering the European market in the year 2012. You know the historic characteristics of the European business environment. How can you use this knowledge to raise acceptance for your investment and your products across Europe?
- **Using Figure 2.1, compare** the threats and opportunities that an Australian exporter faces when dealing with NAFTA, ASEAN and the EU.
- **Case study assignment**: Read and prepare the 'Airbus' case study in Part IV, and discuss the impact of Europe on the company's operations.
- **Internet exercise:** Compare the administrative cost and time requirements for setting up a start-up in three Member States of the EU that joined at different times. How do you explain the divergence of the results?

Further reading

European Commission/Eurostat (2006) EU integration seen through statistics. Key facts of 18 policy areas. Luxembourg.

Knight. G. and Kim, D. (2009) International business competence and the contemporary firm. *Journal of International Business Studies*, vol. 40, pp. 255–73.

Meyer, K. (2001) Institutions, transaction costs, and entry mode choice in Eastern Europe. *Journal of International Business Studies*, vol. 32, pp. 357–67.

Rosamond, B. (2005) The uniting of Europe and the foundation of EU studies: revisiting the neofunctionalism of Ernst B. Haas. *Journal of European Public Policy*, vol. 12, no. 2, pp. 237–54.

Seno-Alday, S. (2010) International business thought: a 50-year footprint. *Journal of International Management*, vol. 16, pp. 16–31.

Trillas, F. (2010) Electricity and telecoms reforms in the EU: insights from the economics of federalism. *Utilities Policy*, vol. 18, no. 2, June, pp. 66–76.

 INTERNET RESOURCES

Education and Training (ET) 2020:
http://europa.eu/legislation_summaries/education_training_youth/general_framework/ef0016_en.htm

European Commission web page (Economic and Financial Affairs) about the euro crisis:
http://ec.europa.eu/economy_finance/index_en.htm

Eurostat – statistics from and about the European Union:
http://epp.eurostat.ec.europa.eu/portal/page/portal/about_eurostat/corporate/introduction/harmonization

Foundation for European remembrance, research and reflection:
http://www.jean-monnet.ch

Foundation supporting European cooperation:
http://www.robert-schuman.org

Franco-German partnership:
http://www.germany-info.org

Gabriele Suder's *Doing Business in Europe* video series (on the SAGE companion website at http://www.sagepub.co.uk/suder2e and YouTube)

History of the European integration:
www.answers.com/topic/history-of-the-european-union

The Schengen area and cooperation:
http://europa.eu/legislation_summaries/justice_freedom_security/

Treaties and Law:
http://europa.eu/abc/treaties/index_en.htm

Bibliography

Almond, G.A., Bingham Powell Jr, G., Strom, K., Dalton, R. and Russel, J. (2000) *Comparative Politics Today: A World View*, 7th edn. New York: Addison Wesley Longman. pp. 148–51.

Behringer, W. (1999) *Europa – Ein historisches Lesebuch*. Munich: Beck'sche Reihe, BsR.

Cantwell, J., Dunning, J. and Lundan, S. (2010) An evolutionary approach to understanding international business activity: the co-evolution of MNEs and the institutional environment. *Journal of International Business Studies*, vol. 41, no. 4, pp. 567–86.

Commission of the European Communities (CEC) (2005) http://europa.eu.int/comm/public_opinion/cf/index_en.cfm

Dinan, D. (2006) *Origins and Evolution of the European Union*, New European Union Series. Oxford: Oxford University Press.

Ebbers, H. and Zhang, J. (2010) Chinese investments in the EU. *Eastern Journal of European Studies*, vol. 1, no. 2, December, pp. 187–206.

European Communities (1951) *Treaty Establishing the European Coal and Steel Community* (ECSC Treaty, or Treaty of Paris). Available at: http://europa.eu.int/abc/obj/treaties/en/entoc29.htm

European Communities (1957a) *Treaty Establishing the European Economic Community* (EEC Treaty, or the Treaty of Rome). Available at: http://europa.eu.int/abc/obj/treaties/en/ entoc05.htm

European Communities (1957b) *Treaty Establishing the European Atomic Energy Community* (Euratom Treaty). Available at: http://europa.eu.int/abc/obj/treaties/en/entoc38.htm

European Communities (1967) *Treaty Establishing a Single Council and a Single Commission of the European Communities* (Merger Treaty of 1965). Available at: http://europa.eu.int/abc/obj/treaties/

European Communities (1987) *Single European Act*. Available at: http://europa.eu.int/eur-lex/en/ treaties/selected/livre509.html

European Communities (1992) *Treaty on European Union* (Maastricht Treaty) [1992] OJ C191/1. Available at: http://europa.eu.int/eur-lex/en/treaties/dat/EU_treaty.html

European Communities (1997a) *Treaty of Amsterdam* [1997] OJ C340/1. Available at: http://europa.eu. int/eur-lex/lex/en/treaties/treaties_other.htm, with [1997] OJ C340/145.

European Communities (1997b) *Treaty Establishing the European Community* [1997] OJ C340/173–308.

European Communities (2000) *The Lisbon European Council – An Agenda of Economic and Social Renewal for Europe. Contribution of the European Commission to the Special European Council in Lisbon*, 23–24 March, DOC/00/7, 28 February.

European Communities (2004) *Treaty Establishing a Constitution for Europe*. Available at: http://europe. eu.int/constitution/index_en.htm

European Communties (2005) *Constitutional Treaty for Europe* (European Constitution). Luxembourg: Eur-Lex 2004/C 310/01.

European Communities/Eurostat (2006) EU integration seen through statistics. *Panorama of the European Union*. Luxembourg: Office for Official Publications of the European Communities

McGuire, S.M., Lindeque, J.P. and Suder, G. (2012) Learning and lobbying: emerging market firms and corporate political activity in Europe. *European Journal of International Management*, vol. 6, no. 2.

Murray, P. (2010) Comparative regional integration in the EU and East Asia: moving beyond integration snobbery. *International Politics*, vol. 47, no. 3–4, pp. 308–23.

Northedge, F.S. (1976) *The International Political System*. London: Faber and Faber.

Schuman, R. (1950) *Declaration of 9 May 1950*. Available at: www.robert-schuman. org/anniversaire_9_mai2006/anglais.htm

Senior Nello, S. (2005) *The European Union: Economics, Politics and History*. Maidenhead: McGraw-Hill Education.

Suder, G. (1994) *Anti-Dumping Measures and the Politics of EU–Japan Trade Relations in the European Consumer Electronics Sector: The VCR Case*. Bath: University of Bath School of Management.

Suder, G. (2007) *Doing Business in Europe*, 1st edn. London: Sage Publications.

United Nations Conference on Trade and Development (UNCTAD) (2008) *World Investment Report: Transnational Corporations and the Infrastructure Challenge*. Available at: www.unctad.org/en/docs/wir2008_en.pdf

Other sources

Various issues of *European Voice, The Economist, Business Week, Le Figaro, Le Monde, Deutsche Welle, Frankfurter Allgemeine Zeitung* and others.

3

Enlargement and the Theories of Integration

What you will learn about in this chapter:

- The meaning of EU enlargements for the European market.
- Business opportunities that are unfolding: the examples of Romania, Turkey and Iceland.
- Challenges for future enlargements.
- The relations, trade and investment flow between current and future Member States.

3.0 Introduction

Doing Business in Europe implies doing business with competitors from all over the Single Market, because of the very nature of this business environment. That means, business partners and competitors originate from many different countries encompassing many diverse market conditions, regulatory frameworks and cultures. These have, however, been linked together by European harmonization, deregulation and freedom of movement and now form a large open market of opportunities and challenges.

The open and democratic structure that we discussed in Chapter 2 predestines Europe's integrated market for further evolution. In addition, Europe believes that integration and collaboration between nations is the best way to enhance peace and welfare. The treaties reviewed in the last chapter established the EU and its common policies, achieving a depth of integration for these nations and their economies. In addition to this 'deepening', the market regularly undergoes 'broadening' through geographical enlargement.

More and more nations are joining the European Union, or declaring their desire to do so. Of course, the many economic, political and sociopolitical conflicts and challenges – from the mid-twentieth century onwards – have given birth to historic ambitions for freedom, democracy and prosperity among European nations. These ambitions have translated into the formal accession of most European states to the EU, EFTA and the EEA, so much so that these associations now regulate practically all of the European market.

The most extensive enlargement of Europe's market blocs took place in 2004 when, for the first time, former Soviet bloc countries were integrated into the European Union. Never before had so many countries applied at the same time for membership of a market grouping. Nor had so many economies with such a substantial wealth and performance gap with current members joined the EU. Never had an enlargement opened up business opportunities on such a scale for both accession countries and established Member States. This fifth EU enlargement took on a truly strategic dimension extended through the accession of Romania and Bulgaria in 2007, Croatia in 2011 and further European states that are joining the market group, from the Balkans and Iceland.

This can be seen as an illustration of the deep roots of the European ideal. Those roots lie in values and beliefs refined over many decades, including human dignity, freedom, democracy, equality, the rule of law, the respect of human rights, peace and the well-being of peoples. These values are not unique to Europe; however, they are at the root of more regional collaboration than anywhere else in the world.

The initial concept of European integration was developed by the six founding members of the EU (Figure 3.1) :

- Germany
- France
- Italy
- Belgium
- Luxembourg
- The Netherlands

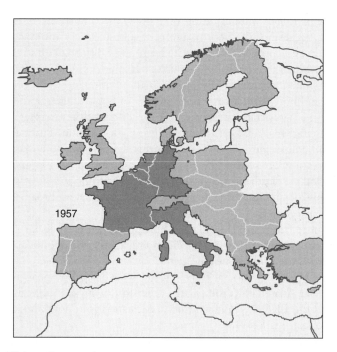

Figure 3.1   *EU founding members*

Source: Auswärtiges Amt (2010)

What started out with the aim of economic cooperation really evolved into long-term political stability. This concept of a peaceful union was based on solidarity and economic development. It was enhanced by the end of the cold war (1989), by the wars in the Balkan region (1990s), the challenges of global terrorism in 2009 and identitarian conflicts of the neighbouring European countries, which have been persistent over recent years. Ideally, the aim of European integration is to progressively and continuously *deepen* and *broaden* business opportunities. This is stimulated by the challenges of competitiveness vis-à-vis:

- the USA and Asia, working with Europe as the 'triad', the three major investment and trade blocs in the world economy; challenged by
- the BRICS, the emerging economies, Brazil, Russia, India, China and South Africa.

Even on a global scale, regionalism is still one of the predominant features of contemporary economics. It is a response to the pressure on states and business to remain competitive. Free trade agreements are spreading across the world more and more rapidly. The World Trade Organization (WTO) reports that in 2008, the greatest number of free trade agreements ever in a year were registered (35), with a total of 422 altogether (Waldkirch and Tikin-Koru, 2010, p. 4) and 371 in force in 2009 (WTO, 2010). Tables 3.1 and 3.2 illustrate the spread of free trade agreements and customs unions worldwide. Accession features and similarities are highlighted for European customs unions.

At the same time, enlargement of the EU has, at times, been perceived as a barrier to deeper and simpler integration of its current members.

Box 3.1: Deeper and broader/wider integration

In Europe, enlargement has sparked off lively debate. The fundamental question is whether the EU should integrate more *deeply*, that is, share more common policies, enhance the authority of the organization and cope with integration – along with the related costs and benefits (for example, economies of scale; the development of the competitive context). Or should the EU increase *wider* integration, that is, enlarge further not only geographically (possibly beyond the geographic borders of Europe) but also in the number of Member States? Are both options feasible for all stakeholders, and are they desirable?

In the past, the deepening and widening of European integration successfully created a market in which people, goods, services and capital moved more freely across the continent than ever before. Supporters of enlargement argue that the business environment has evolved simultaneously on the basis of peace, prosperity and stability. However, critics argue that the many challenges of 'unity in diversity' (the EU motto) are too complex and costly to handle. Some say that national interests will most likely get in the way of any significant progress for integration. In addition, if

Table 3.1 *The Non-European Customs Union*

Agreement Name	Andean Community (CAN)	Central American Common Market (CACM)	East African Community (EAC)	Economic and Monetary Community of Central Africa (CEMAC)	Economic Community of West African States (ECOWAS)	Gulf Cooperation Council (GCC)	Eurasian Economic Community (EAEC)	West African Economic and Monetary Union (WAEMU)
Coverage	Goods	Goods	Goods	Goods	Goods	Goods	Goods	Goods
Status	In force	In force	In force	In force	In force	In force	In force	In force
Date of signature	12 May 1987	13 Dec 1960	30 Nov 1999	16 Mar 1994	24 July 1993	31 Dec 2001	29 Mar 1996	10 Jan 1994
Date of entry into force	25 May 1988	4 June 1961	7 July 2000	24 June 1999	24 July 1993	1 Jan 2003	8 Oct 1997	1 Jan 2000
Current signatories	Bolivarian Republic of Venezuela; Bolivia; Colombia; Ecuador; Peru	Costa Rica; El Salvador; Guatemala; Honduras; Nicaragua	Kenya; Tanzania; Uganda	Cameroon; Central African Republic; Chad; Congo; Equatorial Guinea; Gabon	Benin; Burkina Faso; Cape Verde; Ivory Coast; Gambia; Ghana; Guinea; Guinea Bissau; Liberia; Mali; Niger; Nigeria; Senegal; Sierra Leone; Togo	Bahrain; Kuwait; Oman; Qatar; Saudi Arabia; United Arab Emirates	Belarus; Kazakhstan; Kyrgyz Republic; Russian Federation; Tajikistan	Benin; Burkina Faso; Ivory Coast; Guinea Bissau; Mali; Niger; Senegal; Togo
Original signatories	Bolivarian Republic of Venezuela; Bolivia; Colombia; Ecuador; Peru	El Salvador; Guatemala; Honduras; Nicaragua	Kenya; Tanzania; Uganda	Cameroon; Central African Republic; Chad; Congo; Equatorial Guinea; Gabon	Benin; Burkina Faso; Cape Verde; Ivory Coast; Gambia; Ghana; Guinea; Guinea Bissau; Liberia; Mali; Niger; Nigeria; Senegal; Sierra Leone; Togo	Bahrain; Kuwait; Oman; Qatar; Saudi Arabia; United Arab Emirates	Belarus; Kazakhstan; Kyrgyz Republic; Russian Federation; Tajikistan	Benin; Burkina Faso; Ivory Coast; Mali; Niger; Senegal; Togo
RTA composition	Plurilateral	Plurilateral	Plurilateral	Plurilateral	Plurilateral	Plurilateral	Plurilateral	Plurilateral
Region	South America	Central America	Africa	Africa	Africa	Middle East	Commonwealth of Independent States	Africa
All parties WTO members?	Yes	Yes	Yes	No	No	Yes	No	Yes

Source: Compiled information from Pace (2009), WTO, 'Regional Trade Agreements' and 'Regional Trade Agreements Information System' (RTA-IS), 2011

Table 3.2 *The European Customs Union*

Agreement name	EC (9) Enlargement	EC (10) Enlargement	EC (12) Enlargement	EC (15) Enlargement	EC-Andorra	EC-Turkey
Coverage	Goods	Goods	Goods	Goods and services	Goods	Goods
Status	In force	In force	In force	In force	In force	In force
Date of signature	22 Jan 1972	28 May 1979	12 Jun 1985	24 Jun 1994	28 Jun 1991	6 Mar 1995
Date of entry into force	1 Jan 1973	1 Jan 1981	1 Jan 1986	1 Jan 1995	1 Jul 1991	1 Jan 1996
Accession	Yes	Yes	Yes	Yes		
Original signatories	Belgium; Denmark; France; Germany; Italy; Luxembourg; Netherlands; United Kingdom	Belgium; Denmark; France; Germany; Greece; Ireland; Italy; Luxembourg; Netherlands; United Kingdom	Belgium; Denmark; France; Germany; Greece; Ireland; Italy; Luxembourg; Netherlands; Portugal; Spain; United Kingdom	Austria; Belgium; Denmark; Finland; France; Germany; Greece; Ireland; Italy; Luxembourg; Netherlands; Portugal; Spain; Sweden; United Kingdom	Andorra; Belgium; Denmark; France; Germany; Greece; Ireland; Italy; Luxembourg; Netherlands; Portugal; Spain; United Kingdom	Austria; Belgium; Denmark; Finland; France; Germany; Greece; Ireland; Italy; Luxembourg; Netherlands; Portugal; Spain; Sweden; United Kingdom; Turkey
Current signatories	Belgium; Denmark; France; Germany; Italy; Luxembourg; Netherlands; United Kingdom	Belgium; Denmark; France; Germany; Greece; Ireland; Italy; Luxembourg; Netherlands; United Kingdom	Belgium; Denmark; France; Germany; Greece; Ireland; Italy; Luxembourg; Netherlands; Portugal; Spain; United Kingdom	Austria; Belgium; Denmark; Finland; France; Germany; Greece; Ireland; Italy; Luxembourg; Netherlands; Portugal; Spain; Sweden; United Kingdom	Andorra; Austria; Belgium; Bulgaria; Cyprus; Czech Republic; Denmark; Estonia; Finland; France; Germany; Greece; Hungary; Ireland; Italy; Latvia; Lithuania; Luxembourg; Malta; Netherlands; Poland; Portugal; Romania; Slovak Republic; Slovenia; Spain; Sweden; United Kingdom	Austria; Belgium; Bulgaria; Cyprus; Czech Republic; Denmark; Estonia; Finland; France; Germany; Greece; Hungary; Ireland; Italy; Latvia; Lithuania; Luxembourg; Malta; Netherlands; Poland; Portugal; Romania; Slovak Republic; Slovenia; Spain; Sweden; United Kingdom; Turkey
RTA composition	Plurilateral	Plurilateral	Plurilateral	Plurilateral	Bilateral: one party is an RTA	Bilateral: one party is an RTA
Region	Europe	Europe	Europe	Europe	Europe	Europe
All parties WTO members?	Yes	Yes	Yes	Yes	No	Yes

Source: Compiled information from WTO, 'Regional Trade Agreements' and 'Regional Trade Agreements Information System' (RTA-IS), 2011

expansion implies trade creation (that is, business opportunities), it also results in trade diversion, from streamlined competitive industry, and from replacing a given preference for an outside trade partnership with an internal one. Eurochambers, the European Association of Chambers of Commerce and Industry, calculated that the net cost of EU regulations altogether for each EU consumer over the past 11 years is €2083 for goods and services (2009).

Each wave of enlargement has reinforced competitiveness, trade and investment flows (see Table 3.3 and Figure 3.2), shared know-how, innovation, technological advancement, standards and norms on a European level. Enlargement has also resulted in harmonized regulations, economies of scale and scope for firms, and tax revenue gains for governments.

Nonetheless, in less competitive sectors, it has also resulted in rising unemployment. This is why governments need to rethink their social policy, and reshuffle important factor conditions (labour and capital). Less disputed is the fact that European integration improves the weight of Europe's voice in multilateral trade negotiations, on condition that all members agree upon one stance. Also, it is undisputed that EU membership boosts growth and that the growth rate of the Central and Eastern European countries became most significant following integration.

Table 3.3   *A matrix of inward foreign direct investment (FDI) performance and its map, 2005–2008*

	High FDI Performance	Low FDI Performance
High FDI Potential	**Front-runners** Azerbaijan, Bahamas, Bahrain, Belgium, Brunel Darussalam, Bulgaria, Chile, Croatia, Cyprus, Czech Republic, Dominican Republic, Estonia, Hong Kong (China), Hungary, Iceland, Israel, Jordan, Kazakhstan, Latvia, Lithuania, Luxembourg, Malaysia, Malta, Mongolia, Netherlands, New Zealand, Oman, Panama, Poland, Romania, Saudi Arabia, Singapore, Slovakia, Sweden, Thailand, Trinidad and Tobago, Tunisia, Ukraine, United Arab Emirates and United Kingdom	**Below Potential** Algeria, Argentina, Australia, Austria, Belarus, Brazil, Canada, China, Denmark, Finland, France, Germany, Greece, Ireland, Islamic Republic of Iran, Italy, Japan, Kuwait, Libyan Arab Jamahiriya, Mexico, Norway, Portugal, Qatar, Republic of Korea, Russian Federation, Slovenia, Spain, Switzerland, Taiwan Province of China, United States and the Bolivarian Republic of Venezuela
Low FDI Potential	**Above Potential** Albania, Armenia, Botswana, Colombia, Congo, Costa Rica, Egypt, Ethiopia, Gambia, Georgia, Guinea, Guyana, Honduras, Jamaica, Kyrgyzstan, Lebanon, Namibia, Nicaragua, Nigeria, Peru, Republic of Moldova, Sierra Leone, Sudan, Tajikistan, the former Yugoslav Republic of Macedonia, Togo, Uganda, United Republic of Tanzania, Uruguay, Viet Nam and Zambia	**Under-performers** Angola, Bangladesh, Benin, Bolivia, Burkina Faso, Cameroon, Ivory Coast, Democratic Republic of Congo, Ecuador, El Salvador, Gabon, Ghana, Guatemala, Haiti, India, Indonesia, Kenya, Madagascar, Malawi, Mali, Morocco, Mozambique, Myanmar, Nepal, Niger, Pakistan, Papua New Guinea, Paraguay, Philippines, Rwanda, Senegal, South Africa, Sri Lanka, Suriname, Syrian Arab Republic, Turkey, Uzbekistan, Yemen, Zimbabwe

Source: Pace (2009), http://www.tepsa.be/Enlarging%20the%20European%20Union.pdf, p. 66

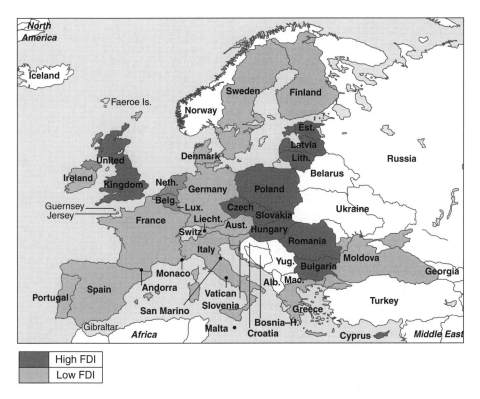

Figure 3.2   *FDI performance in Europe*

Why then does Europe experience different levels of Member State integration? Some Member States are part of the euro-zone, some are not; some are part of the Schengen agreement facilitating cross-border travel, some are not. What is it that drives Member States to have different ideologies about what they want from Europe, what they don't want and what European integration should ultimately look like? To understand the bigger picture, we can find explanations in certain predominant integration theories.

3.1 Integration theories

Chapter 2 introduced you to the different stages of European integration, which resulted in its historic evolution. This evolution is based on a range of integration theories and 'schools of thought' that have been developed since the late 1940s. These beliefs shape Europe even today, and guide the speed and extent to which economies and business have been able to Europeanize (See Table 3.4). The following section introduces and explains these theories.

Table 3.4   *Examples of the effects of accession on New Member States*

Country	Date of accession	Political dimension	Economic dimension
Poland	1 May 2004	Established special relations between the EU and the Ukraine Contributed to the development of the new type of common EU relationship with Russia	Between 1 May and August 2007, Poland experienced an economic growth level reaching 6.5% Declining unemployment rates combined with increased household demand brought about the consumption growth of 6% per annum 2003 Unemployment: 20% Size of GDP: EUR328.93 billion Inflow of FDI: EUR3.50 billion 2007 Unemployment: 11.4% Size of GDP: EUR446.81 billion Inflow of FDI: EUR16.34 billion Approximately 1.2million jobs have been created due to foreign investments
Slovenia	1 May 2004	Achieved goal of state recognition, friendly neighbourly relations and NATO membership	The introduction of the Euro was seen as favourable for the business sector, offering more options for easier international investment and cooperation An opening of markets resulted in the development of a wider financial market and easier access to capital, stimulating import–export activities of large companies and SMEs 2003 Unemployment: 6.7% Size of GDP: EUR29.33 billion Inflow of FDI: EUR216.67 million 2007 Unemployment: 4.8% Size of GDP: EUR38.53 billion Inflow of FDI: EUR1,064.31 million
Bulgaria	1 January 2007	The EU was seen as an alternative to the national government that proved incapable of governing in a transparent and lawful manner	Generally a positive trend of steady economic growth 2003 Unemployment: 13.7% Size of GDP: EUR71.69 billion FDI: EUR1.85 billion 2007 Unemployment: 6.9% Size of GDP: EUR28.87 billion FDI: EUR6.52 billion

Source: Compiled sources. Pace (2009), www.tepsa.be/Enlarging%20the%20European%20Union.pdf, www.oecd.org, www.nsi.bg and others

3.1.1 Functionalism

Functionalism originates from a theory that suggests that states cooperate in specific areas only. Those who support this theory postulate that this cooperation should only take place at a minimal institutional level; it should not aim for deeper political integration. At this level of integration, each state attempts to retain a high level of sovereignty. Functionalism is mainly associated with liberal economies whereby there is little regulatory intervention by the policy-making authority and the economy is considered to be ruled by the 'invisible hand' of its own dynamics. Issues harmonized at European level are therefore mainly defined by technical necessity, answering practical needs, scientific knowledge, expertise and technology. The main subscribers to this theory, in recent European history, are the UK and Scandinavia. The theory evolves in accordance with ideologies that do not subscribe to fundamental legislative texts or constitutions but are based on common law. Authority is rather vested in a supra-territorial concept where specific issues are solved on a regional or global level, depending on circumstances.

3.1.2 Neo-functionalism

As with functionalism, neo-functionalist theory is based on the belief that harmonization and cooperation appear when functional or political needs spill over frontiers and into economic issues. Nevertheless, neo-functionalism recognizes integration as being inevitable. Sociopolitical cooperation is essential in the integration of countries and their economies, such as in Eastern Europe. An important role is played by supranational institutions that become legitimate and gain sovereignty from Member States in the areas which challenge cross-frontiers and lead to sequential cooperation throughout related policy areas. This leads to an integration of power normally reserved for states. A well-known neo-functionalist was Jean Monnet, one of the main founders of European integration.

3.1.3 Federalism

The theory of federalism provides the basis for the main treaties governing European integration, and is guided by the belief that a constitutional framework should govern relations between Member States. In federalism, much subscribed to by Germany for example, a formalized framework dictates the roles of government and institutions that coexist with national and local authorities along a set of shared and independent power lines. Consequently, the theory finds its expression in initiatives including a common currency, common foreign and security policy, or a single constitution. The Treaty of the European Union and then the Lisbon Treaty reflect peak points for federalism.

3.1.4 Further integration theories

Two other integration theories add to our understanding of the way in which European integration has unfolded so far. The collective bargaining orientation of interstate relations is complemented by the need for the pronounced independence of Member States, a limited supranational authority and the preservation of sovereignty via substructures of the system, except in areas that are dependent on cross-border solutions. The common agricultural policy (CAP) is a product of this school of thought. Intergovernmentalism reinforces the belief that bargaining is key to European integration and hence gives a predominant role to the Council of Ministers and the European Council. Supporters of inter-governmentalism reject neo-functionalist objectives. The role of the Commission and the European Parliament (detailed in Chapter 4) are then weakened to give way to the predominance of national control.

3.1.5 The meaning of integration theories

This helps you to understand why different integration theories exist. The different governments believe in them and, in consequence, aim for different scales and scopes of economic policy and integration. Hence, these theories are the very basis for the interests and beliefs of Member States, their peoples and democratically elected governments as to how European integration should both advance and be shaped.

Each Member State is subject to its own nuanced system, political culture and heritage, and particular beliefs and priorities. This political culture and political and economic heritage shape the orientations of citizens, government and corporations in a manner that finds its expression in three main ways:

1 Systems and their legitimacy.
2 Processes in accordance with public expectations.
3 Outputs and outcomes that may or may not satisfy those they affect (see Chapter 2 for a definition of outputs and outcomes). These levels are dynamic and in constant evolution over time, and in response to what are mainly economic, political and sociopolitical challenges.

By way of illustration, a comparison of national pride in Finland, Estonia and the UK indicates lower levels in Finland, medium levels in Estonia and relatively high levels in the UK. National identities and the consequent attachment to national sentiments can shape the way in which sovereignty is shared with supranational groupings and how important sovereignty is perceived to be. These sentiments define how far the population desires a solid fundamental text that anchors the rules of law and the processes attributed to the system. The rejection of the European Constitution and the difficult adoption of the Lisbon Treaty in 2009 served as an example.

Europe has become a mixed system in terms of the structural separation of authority. It combines parliamentary and presidential structural features, with various grades of governance and variations in how this is performed (see Table 3.5).

Economic membership integration and inward-directed foreign direct investment (FDI) performance are positively correlated. As you can see in Table 3.5, besides the EU factor, other FDI-friendly policies were also positively impacted, specifically in

Table 3.5   *The diversity of governance indicators*

2006	Voice and Accountability		Political Stability		Government Effectiveness		Regulatory Quality		Rule of Law		Control of Corruption	
Country	Percentile Rank (0–100)	Governance Score (-2.5 to +2.5)	Percentile Rank (0–100)	Governance Score (-2.5 to +2.5)	Percentile Rank (0–100)	Governance Score (-2.5 to +2.5)	Percentile Rank (0–100)	Governance Score (-2.5 to +2.5)	Percentile Rank (0–100)	Governance Score (-2.5 to +2.5)	Percentile Rank (0–100)	Governance Score (-2.5 to +2.5)
New EU Member States – 2004/2007 enlargements												
Bulgaria	65.4	+0.56	57.2	+0.29	60.2	+0.14	66.3	+0.54	50.0	-0.17	57.3	-0.05
Czech Republic	77.4	+0.96	70.2	+0.75	80.1	+1.01	79.5	+0.96	73.3	+0.73	66.0	+0.36
Estonia	78.8	+1.01	71.2	+0.78	85.3	+1.17	92.2	+1.42	80.5	+0.91	80.1	+0.87
Hungary	87.0	+1.14	66.8	+0.73	72.5	+0.71	85.9	+1.10	73.8	+0.73	69.9	+0.51
Latvia	72.6	+0.83	73.6	+0.81	73.5	+0.73	82.4	+1.06	63.8	+0.52	68.4	+0.38
Lithuania	76.0	+0.93	78.4	+0.89	77.3	+0.82	81.5	+1.02	61.9	+0.45	59.7	+0.11
Poland	76.0	+0.95	54.3	+0.22	69.2	+0.49	69.3	+0.64	59.0	+0.25	60.2	+0.14
Romania	61.5	+0.43	50.0	+0.12	53.6	-0.05	62.0	+0.37	50.5	-0.16	53.4	-0.18
Slovakia	78.4	+0.99	76.4	+0.85	78.2	+0.91	83.4	+1.08	61.4	+0.43	65.5	+0.35
Slovenia	84.6	+1.10	82.7	+1.05	84.4	+1.11	72.7	+0.78	75.2	+0.79	81.1	+0.92
Cyprus	86.1	+1.14	60.6	+0.44	60.6	+0.44	86.8	+1.24	81.9	+0.93	79.1	+0.83
Malta	89.9	+1.24	92.3	+1.21	92.3	+1.21	86.3	+1.22	91.4	+1.47	84.5	+1.19

Source: Pace (2009), http://www.tepsa.be/EnlargingtheEuropeanUnion.pdf, p. 74

the achievement of excellent governance standards. The Worldwide Governance Indicators are measured across several broad dimensions as indicated:

Governance is perceived as those traditions and institutions that confer authority within a state and its territory. 'Governments are selected, monitored and replaced; it is the capacity in which the government can effectively formulate and implement sound policies, and the respect between citizens and the state for the institutions that govern economic and social interactions among them.'

Source: http://info.worldbank.org/governance/wgi/index.asp

Voice and Regulatory Quality (RQ) and Accountability (VA)	• capturing perceptions of the ability of the government to formulate and implement sound policies and regulations that permit and promote private sectors developement.
Rule cf Law (RL)	• capturing perceptions of the extent to which agents have confidence in and abide by the rules of society, and in particular the quality of contract enforcement, property rights, the police, and the courts, as well as the likelihood of crime and violence.
Voice and Accountability (VA)	• capturing perceptions of the extent to which a country's citizens are able to participate in selecting their government, as well as freedom of expression, freedom of association, and a free media.
Political Stability and Absence of Violence/Terrorism (PV)	• capturing perceptions of the likelihood that the government will be destabilized or overthrown by unconstitutional or violent means, including politically-motivated violence and terrorism.
Government Effectiveness (GE)	• capturing perceptions of the quality of public services, the quality of the civil service and the degree of its independence from political pressures, the quality of policy formulation and implementation,and the credibility of the government's to such policies.

Source: http://info.worldbank.org/governance/wgi/faq.htm#2

The many political cultures that characterize European countries do not converge but they do share many common values across Europe (see Chapters 1 and 2). The integration theories help us categorize those cultures and help us understand the ups and downs of European harmonization, in particular its patchwork nature. For companies, this means that the Single Market is not that 'single' and harmonized after all, and firms often call for easier market integration.

The diversity of integrational 'schools of thought' is the basis of discussion for all issues that the EU deals with. In essence, these different schools of thought determine different paths to the same destiny. For example, thanks to company pressure, the EU adopted the European Company Status for firms operating on a European-wide basis. Normally, those companies set up networks of subsidiary companies under different national laws, but since 2004, they can also use the form of a European Company (a 'Societas Europaea' (SE)), governed by a single set of Community rules.

Business interests are an integral part of the European diversity of opinion and are influenced by political and economic culture, nationally and on the European level. Only those companies that are competitive and Europeanized ask for deeper and wider integration. Overall, the proliferation of any regional economic grouping is dependent on the common interpretation of its destiny.

3.2 Waves of European integration: the past, present and future

3.2.1 Past adhesions to the EC/EU

In 1957, six countries signed the Treaty of Rome to create the EEC. The main objective of these founding members was to create a customs union. However, trade cooperation also led to the launch of a number of common policies, in particular the common agricultural policy (CAP). The European Community (EC, later named the EU) was formed in 1967. It was enlarged for the first time in 1973 with the accession of Denmark, Ireland and the UK. This led to the creation of the European Regional Development Fund (ERDF) and a regional policy that was adapted to the UK's agricultural budget.

The second enlargement saw Greece join in 1981. In the third enlargement in 1986, Spain and Portugal become full members. This expansion added poorer and more agriculturally oriented states to the group and led to the creation of the Structural and Cohesion Fund, which became increasingly dependent on richer members' support. In 1987, after 23 years as an associate member, Turkey decided to become a candidate for accession. The Member States refused its application.

The fall of the Berlin Wall and collapse of the Soviet system gave an impulse to new enlargements. In 1990, German reunification added 17 million citizens with no official EU ceremony. Five years later, Austria, Finland and Sweden joined the EU, while a referendum in Norway resulted in a rejection. Increasing use of common policy making and common social policy concerns, and the creation of the CFSP fuelled this 1995 enlargement. This growth to 15 Member States meant that the time

had come to think of streamlining the institutions and their decision-making procedures. The challenges for coherent harmonization of the marketplace to the satisfaction of all now became even greater.

Almost a decade after the transition from planned to market-based economies, and
from totalitarianism to democracy in Central and Eastern Europe (CEE), the EU
underwent its biggest ever expansion. In 2004, 10 new Member States joined and thus
solidified the political and economic stability of the region. The accession of Bulgaria,
Romania, Croatia and other East European states has since followed. Iceland's application was welcomed rapidly in the aftermath of the 2008 financial crisis.

The enlargements are based on the requirement that the candidate states:

- fully accept and apply the *acquis communautaire*, that is, the full body of laws and regulations governing the EU; and
- respect different transition periods.

The obligation includes the general principles of the EU. The *acquis* is negotiated in
31 chapters and accompanied by pre-accession assistance from the original members
of the EU. The chapters include the free movement of goods, services, capital and
people; competition; and the application of rights and rules. Such negotiations take,
on average, from two (Malta, Latvia) to four (Bulgaria, Romania) years. A specific
case was the accession of the 10 Countries of the Central and Eastern Europe
(CCEE), which were formerly part of the Council for Mutual Economic Assistance
(COMECON) (which united communist and socialist countries in the cold war
period). Transition periods were defined:

- for the free movement of goods, people and capital;
- in terms of less than five years for pharmaceutical products;
- in the period up to 2011 for the free movement of goods;
- in the period up to 2012 for agriculture and the full integration of the CAP; and,
  finally
- in the period up to 2015 for the application of environmental rules.

These transition periods are now judged costly and are not applied to any other
accession. All restrictions will end by 2014, and even before, in reality, only Austria
and Germany willkept labour restrictions in place for countries that joined the EU
in 2004 and 2007, that also ended in 2009.

Box 3.2: An example of transition impacts on companies

Expanding his concrete floor polishing activity to Germany was not that easy for
this businessman from Poland in 2010. His main conclusion: 'The bureaucracy
was a nightmare'! In particular, he felt it almost insurmountable to obtain

(Continued)

(Continued)

permission for his employees to work in Germany, and he was looking forward to the end of the coming year when the restrictions would be abandoned. Estimates mention over 1 million people migrating from Poland to Germany, which beats the number of migrants to the UK and Ireland in 2004. Business people in the receiving countries were worried about the qualifications of migrants but were also delighted to welcome the downward pressure that their arrival exercised on wages. ('EU faces threat to migration principle', *Financial Times*, 29 September 2010, p. 2).

3.2.2 Small and medium-sized firms in the enlargement challenge

For corporations, the main impact of enlargement lies in the opening up of the market and in the utility of minor market imperfections. In Europe, common rules are there to harmonize access to countries and market opportunities. Opportunities are diverse. For example, the Czech Republic offers opportunities in automobile equipment, agri-business and fishery; Poland in the environmental sector; Estonia in hotel and restaurant equipment; Cyprus in food and perfume. Questions that need answering internally focus not only on the choice of internationalization strategies, but also on which forms and intensity of competition the firm will encounter from local, European and international competitors in these markets. In particular, 'Euro Info Centres' are there to help understand threats and opportunities, find partners and provide information about prevalent legislation, and in particular to help SMEs cope with the challenges they face.

On average, 1.8 million new enterprises are set up every year in Europe, which represents about 9.7 per cent of all firms. But again, each year about 1.5 million enterprises cease to exist, that is, 8.3 per cent overall leave the market. Start-up activity is particularly important in the newest Member States of the EU. The EU's annual reports observe that (interestingly for an increasingly service-oriented economy) manufacturing SMEs survive better and for longer than service SMEs (see http://ec.europa.eu/enterprise/policies/sme/).

The main external challenges for SMEs in a widening market are:

- to resist market internationalization and globalization impacts (economies of scale, strong competition and pressure on margins, access to distribution networks, etc.);
- to adapt to the tendency of large companies towards offshore production and services; and
- to access financial markets, ensure long-term/reliable financing and cash management.

Internal challenges are:

- critical size and financial resources;
- the transformation of development and diversification opportunities;

- the development and implementation of innovation strategies;
- recruiting or accessing specific competencies; and
- benchmark ambitions, performance, results.

The fastest-growing young SMEs in Europe are those of Estonia, Hungary and Bulgaria. This dynamic SME development (Tables 3.6 and 3.7) is crucial for Europe (as illustrated in the tables below, with the SMEs highlighted). It accounts for high employment and economic growth. euro-zone SMEs account for 99.8 per cent of all firms in the area, and provide for 60 per cent of turnover and 70 per cent of employment. Despite this importance, funding for SMEs is sometimes difficult to access, although we see in the list above that funding is one of the most critical challenges for SMEs. EuropaBio, the European Association for Bio-Industries, is one of many associations that lobby for better access to funding for its members: they speak for over 1800 small and medium-sized enterprises in the sector (agricultural and health-related firms), which receive less than half of the funds available to their counterparts in the USA (see http://www.europabio.org).

Given this situation, the European Central Bank has surveyed SME access to finance since 2009, as an observatory. Also, the EU is paying increasing attention to these challenges and there are new options for accessing European funds. (We will come back to this issue in more detail in Chapter 7.)

Table 3.6 *Employment indicators of non-financial business economy, by size class –*
EU-27 estimates

		Micro	Small	Medium-sized	SME	Large	Total
Levels							
Number of enterprises	x 1000	19,058	1,424	26	20,709	43	20,752
Number of persons employed	x 1000	39,630	27,652	22,665	89,947	43,414	133,362
Persons employed by enterprise	Occupied person/ enterprise	2	19	100	4	1,006	6
Personnel costs	EURbillion	578	772	713	2,063	1,651	3,714
Labour cost per employee	EUR1,000	27	29	32	29	38	33
Percent distribution							
Number of enterprises	total = 100%	92	7	1	100	0	100
Number of persons employed	total = 100%	30	21	17	67	33	100
Personnel costs	total = 100%	16	21	19	56	44	100

Table 3.7 *Number of persons employed, by size class and sector of industry, in the non-financial business economy – EU-27, 2008 estimates*

		Micro	Small	Medium-sized	SME	Large	Total
Non-financial business economy by NACE section	x 1000 total = 100%	39,630 30	27,652	22,665	89,947	43,414	133,362
Mining and quarrying	total = 100%	6	13	13	31	69	100
Manufacturing	total = 100%	14	20	25	59	41	100
Electricity, gas and water supply	total = 100%	3	5	14	22	78	100
Construction	total = 100%	42	30	16	88	12	100
Wholesale and retail trade; repair of motor vehicles, motorcycles and personal and household goods	total = 100%	40	21	13	74	26	100
Hotels and restaurants	total = 100%	45	27	11	83	17	100
Transport, storage and communication	total = 100%	19	15	13	47	53	100
Real estate, renting and business activities	total = 100%	34	17	16	67	33	100

Source: http://ec.europa.eu/enterprise/policies/sme/facts-figures-analysis/performance-review/pdf/dgentr_annual_report2010_100511.pdf © European Union, 1995–2011

Many of those SMEs are Europeanized in that they use the opportunities provided by economic integration of the Single Market. This phenomenon includes the tendency for European-wide 'subcontracting'. The fragmentation of value chains increases inter-linkages across regions, countries and firms. Subcontracting can be expected, logically, to increase through the integration of neighbouring economies. An EU report on this matter declares that:

> subcontracting occurs when one enterprise (the contractor or principal that wants to put a final product on the market), contracts with another enterprise (the subcontractor or supplier), for a given production cycle, one or more aspects of production design, processing or manufacture, or construction or maintenance work, according to the contractor's technical or commercial specifications. (EU, 2009, http://ec.europa.eu/enterprise/policies/sme/files/craft/sme_perf_review/doc_08/eu-smes-subcontracting-final-report_en.pdf, p. 17)

It is reported that about 17 per cent of EU SMEs are subcontractors, and that more of these are located in new rather than older member states.

What is not specified by these figures (Figures 3.3 and 3.4), however, is that more than half of the subcontractors are also contractors. Interestingly, more than twice as many contractors run their subcontracting activity within the EU and EFTA rather than outside those areas. Their contribution to manufacturing production is particularly high in Portugal and particularly low in The Netherlands (EUROCHAMBRES, 2009, p. 209).

Consequently, we can conclude that SMEs are often Europeanized at their creation and can oftentimes be categorized as 'born–Europeans' (a European version of the well-known 'born-global' concept).

3.2.3 Learning from recent and future adhesions

At the 2002 Copenhagen summit, European leaders anticipated further enlargement of the EU, as Bulgaria and Romania, at the frontiers of geographical Europe, suffered extensive oppression from local totalitarian communist dictatorships during the twentieth century. It was therefore important to consolidate political and economic stability in these EU areas. The Western Balkans and Ukraine are close partners, following the example of Macedonia (Former Yugoslav Republic of Macedonia, or FYROM) and Croatia, Serbia, Albania, Kosovo and Montenegro, as well as Iceland, and have received increasing attention from foreign investors because of their status.

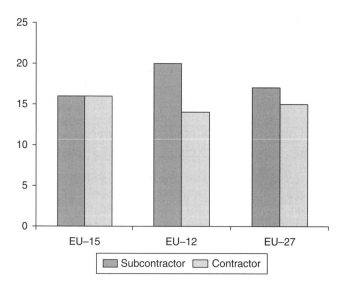

Figure 3.3 *Percentage of SMEs engaged as subcontractors and contractors, EU-12 and EU-15, 2009*

Source: EIM/GDCC Survey, http://ec.europa.eu/enterprise/policies/sme/files/craft/sme_perf_review/doc_08/eu-smes-subcontracting-final-report_en.pdf, Oct 2009 pg. 23/29, © European Union, 1995–2011

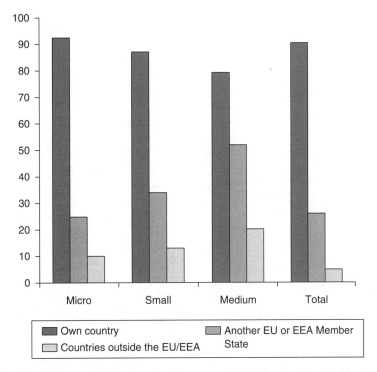

Figure 3.4 *Distribution of SME subcontractors according to the geographical location of client enterprises (contractors), by subcontractor enterprise size and involvement in product/service and process innovations by SME subcontractors, 2009*

Source: EIM/GDCC Survey, http://ec.europa.eu/enterprise/policies/sme/files/craft/sme_perf_review/doc_08/eu-smes-subcontracting-final-report_en.pdf Oct 2009, p. 29 © European Union, 1995–2011

Turkey remains a candidate for accession. In addition, several Mediterranean partners have expressed their interest in closer ties. The following sections provide you with three examples of accession to illustrate the prospects for business opportunities in further EU enlargement. We will now look at some specific contexts of European business – those of Romania, Turkey and Iceland (Figure 3.5). You will find that this textbook's web-support site provides a list of all member and accession countries with the relevant information for business (entry, activity and exit) in those countries.

3.2.4 Romania

3.2.4.1 Historical overview

Romania became a state in 1859. Prior to World War I, it was the principal power in the Balkans; after the war, the Treaty of 1919 doubled its population

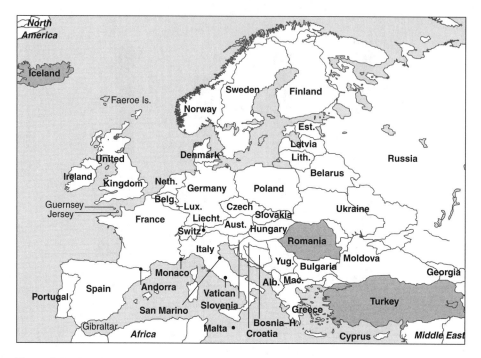

Figure 3.5   *The European Union, with a focus on Romania, Turkey and Iceland*

and territory. During World War II, under Ion Antonescu, Romania sided with
Germany. It was Sovietized after the war. The dictatorship of Nicolae Ceausescu
from 1965 to 1989 left Romania with a complex and difficult political and
economic heritage.

After Ceausescu, the country faced serious difficulties with its economy, administrative and legal system. In addition, minority issues and shifting borders across
Central and Eastern Europe (CEE) required a reconfirmation of state frontiers
through bilateral treaties.

3.2.4.2 EU–Romanian relations

Romania was the first of all the CCEE to engage in official relations with the
European communities. In 1974, an agreement included Romania in the
Community's 'Generalized System of Preferences' (preferential access to the EU
market through reduced tariffs) and an 'Agreement on Industrial Products' was
enforced in 1980.

Romania's diplomatic relations with the EU date from 1990; a Trade and
Cooperation Agreement was signed in 1991. The Europe Agreement entered
into force in February 1995. Trade provisions entered into force in 1993 under
an 'Interim Agreement'. Romania submitted its application for EU membership

Table 3.8   *Basic data for Romania*

General information	2003	2009
Population	21.7 million	22.2 million
Capital	Bucharest	Bucharest
Neighbours	Bulgaria, Federal Republic of Yugoslavia, Hungary, Ukraine, Moldova	Bulgaria, Hungary, Moldova, Serbia, Ukraine
Area	237,500 sq km	237,500 sq km
Ethnic groups	Romanian (89.4%), Hungarian (6.6%), Roma (2.4%), Ukrainian (0.3%), German (0.3%), other (1%)	Romanian (89.5%), Hungarian (6.6%), Roma (2.5%), Ukrainian (0.3%), German (0.3%), Russian (0.2%), Turkish (0.2%), Other (0.4%)
Official language	Romanian	Romanian
Religion	Orthodox (86.8%), Roman Catholic including Greek rite (6%), Protestant (6%), other (1.2%)	Orthodox (86.8%), Roman Catholic (5%), Reformed Protestant, Baptist and Pentecostal (5%), Greek Catholic (Uniate) (1–3%), Muslim (0.2%), Jewish (less than 0.1%)
Life expectancy (at birth)	71.2 years (males: 67.6 years; females: 74.9 years)	71.63 years (males: 68.14 years; females: 75.34 years)
Total GDP	€48.4 billion (2004 est.)	€186.36 billion
GDP per capita	€5,600	€8,300
Currency	1 leu = 100 bani (pl.: lei)	1 euro = 4.2706 New Romanian leu (30 November 2009)
Structure of production		
Agriculture	13.1%	12.4%
Industry	33.7%	35%
Services	53.2%	52.6%
Economic situation		
GDP growth rate	8.1%	7.1% (2008 est.) –6.9%
Inflation rate	9.6%	5%
Labour force	9.66 million	9.33 million
Unemployment rate	6.3%	7.6% (2009 est.)
Budget balance (% of GDP)	–1.49%	Revenue: €36.93 billion; expenditure: €44.72 billion
Current account balance	€-2.62 billion	€-6.20 billion (2009 est.)
Account deficit (rate of GDP)	Revenue: €15.8 billion; expenditure: €16.58 billion	Revenue: €36.72 billion; expenditure: €45.26 billion
Public debt (% of GDP)	23.6%	20%

Source: Compiled data

Table 3.9 *The political situation in Romania*

	Political Situation
Constitution	Adopted in 1991 and revised in October 2003
Head of state	The President
Parliament	The Parliament comprises the Chamber of Deputies (lower house) and the Senate (upper house). The two bodies hold equal powers. Members of Parliament are elected through a proportional system at the national level. Elections are held every four years simultaneously for both houses. The Chamber of Deputies and the Senate have 345 and 140 seats, respectively.

Source: Compiled data

on 22 June 1995. In July 1997, the Commission published an 'Opinion on Romania's Application for Membership of the European Union'. The following year, a 'Regular Report on Romania's Progress towards Accession' was produced. In its second *Regular Report* on Romania, published in 1999, the Commission recommended starting accession negotiations with Romania, conditional on:

- the improvement of the situation of children in institutional care; and
- the drafting of a medium-term economic strategy.

Romania's accession negotiations began on 15 February 2000, and EU membership was obtained in January 2007. From 2000 onwards, its adaptation to the EU was already being supported by pre-accession aid supplied through the Programme of Community aid to the countries of Central and Eastern Europe (PHARE), with funding for institution building and investment. The support of EU accession covered:

- accession preparation funds of €1.5 billion per annum;
- the Instrument for Structural Policies for Pre-Accession ('ISPA') (the pre-accession instrument that provided investments in transport and environmental infrastructure); and
- Special Accession Programme for Agriculture and Rural Development ('SAPARD') (the financial instrument supporting agriculture and rural development), which together provided funding to a level of approximately €700 million per year.

These instruments were phased out after the 2007 enlargement, and replaced by the Commission's Directorate-General for Enlargement with:

- IPA (instrument for Pre-Accession Assistance) 2007–2013;
- National Implementation initiatives;
- CARDS (Community Assistance for Reconstruction, Development and Stabilization) which also funded Turkey, Croatia, Macedonia and others.

We conclude that enlargement countries benefit from significant financial and partnership advantages on their path to full economic integration. With the aim of meeting EU standards on justice and the rule of law, some countries such as Bulgaria and Romania continue to work on special condition progress in the context of corruption, organized crime and judicial reform. In what must be considered to be a 'first' in half a century, Bulgaria was stripped of €220 million EU funds in November 2008 for failing to comply to stipulated standards. In 2009, the dismissal of 500 customs officers and a crackdown on corruption in the energy sector marked an attempt to retrieve most of the 8 per cent of gross domestic product (GDP) lost in annual receipts in the EU's poorest economy at the time.

Amongst EU members, Romania was hit hardest by the 2008–10 global economic crisis, with a large current account deficit and the inability to attract new credit from foreign lenders. Romania was one of those countries that applied for an EU multi-billion emergency fund (available only for non-euro-zone economies and drawn from loans raised on financial markets (via Euro-bonds) rather than the general EU budget), in a context in which most other EU members were struggling with their own public finances.

3.2.5 The Western Balkans

3.2.5.1 The position and history of Turkey

The Western Balkans, the region that separated the Ottoman Empire from the West, were under Turkish control from the end of the fourteenth century. During the eighteenth century, Christianity became established as the major religion in the area. This remained an area stricken by war and conflict well into the twentieth century: Russia against Turkey in 1877–8, Greece against Turkey in 1897, the Balkans from 1912 to 1913, and both world wars. Moreover, ethnic conflicts and the war of 1999 shook both the region and Europe. The region has since been stabilized through the involvement of NATO, the USA and the EU. Consequently, it is now of great geopolitical importance and retains important international military contingents. Political and economic stability is complex and challenging in such a context.

The six Balkan countries (Albania, Bosnia and Herzegovina, Croatia, the Former Yugoslav Republic of Macedonia, Serbia and Montenegro) are part of the EU stabilization and association agreements that established CARDS (see above) in 1999. This was developed for the period 2000–6 with an allocation of €4.65 billion, and prolonged through new initiatives and the 'European Neighbourhood Partnership Instrument' (ENPI). The primary objective of these agreements was to develop relationships with (and within) the region, and to promote democracy, civil society, education, institutions and cooperation regarding justice and internal affairs, as well as political dialogue.

This was complemented by a 'Stability Agreement for South-Eastern Europe' adopted in Cologne in 1999 to ensure the above and focus on economic prosperity.

This agreement encompassed the EU member states, the European Commission, the countries of South-Eastern Europe (Albania, Macedonia, Bosnia-Herzegovina, Bulgaria, Croatia, Hungary, Moldavia Serbia-Montenegro, Romania, Slovenia and Turkey), other partners (USA, Canada, Norway, Japan, Russia, Switzerland) and international organizations. The agreement was replaced by the Regional Cooperation Council (RCC) in 2008. Work towards stability and prosperity is now increasingly regionally owned, with less influence from European and international organizations.

The early 2000s saw significant advances towards democracy in the region, mainly driven by the will of the people. As an example of this, in 2000 the opposition leader in Croatia, Stipe Mesic, was elected president, taking the place of Franjo Tudjman in a drive towards western-style democracy. Democratic forces in Serbia ousted Slobodan Milosevic through the ballot box, and he was eventually arrested and transferred to the International Court of Justice. In Kosovo, Ibrahim Rugova won the election, and Bosnia and Herzegovina mainly stabilized through the international community on the basis of the 1995 'Dayton Peace Agreement' overseen by a Peace Implementation Council. In 2008, the Council set out conditions to end this protectorate. The Serbian controlled 'Republika Srpska' and the Federation of Bosnia and Herzegovina dominated by Bosniaks (Bosnian Muslims) and Croats now come under the auspices of the EU.

The political dialogue between the Balkans and the EU is constructive and Turkey has continuously confirmed its desire to join the EU. Since 2005, when membership talks officially began, a variety of issues (Cyprus, human rights, freedom of expression and the rights of the Kurdish minority) has hindered the full accession of Turkey.

3.2.5.2 EU-Turkish relations

At the World Economic Forum's annual meeting held in Davos in 2005, Turkish Prime Minister Recep Tayyip Erdogan stated that:

> *The EU is no longer a union of steel and coal ... It is not a Christian club. It is a totality of political values.*

EU–Turkish relations are based mainly on a customs union that was established in 1995; indeed, from 1995 to 1999 trade between the two partners increased significantly on the basis of this agreement. Over a 15-year period, Turkey became the seventh biggest export destination for the EU (up from ninth in 1990) and the thirteenth largest exporter to the EU (up from seventeenth in 1990). The Customs Union covers all industrial goods and processed agricultural products but excludes agriculture in general, services and public procurement. Nevertheless, Turkey has been the longest-lasting candidate for full EU membership.

Table 3.10   *Turkey: basic data and economic situation, 2009*

General Information	2004	2009
Population	67,803,927	76. 8 million
Population distribution	64.9% urban population; 35.1% rural population	69% urban population; 31% rural population (2010)
Capital	Ankara	Ankara
Neighbours	Armenia, Azerbaijan, Bulgaria, Georgia, Greece, Iran, Iraq, Syria	Armenia, Azerbaijan, Bulgaria, Georgia, Greece, Iraq, Iran, Syria
Area	779,452 sq km	779,452 sq km
Ethnic groups	Turkish (80%), Kurdish (20%)	Turkish (70–75%), Kurdish (18%), other minorities (7–12%) (2008 est.)
Official language	Turkish	Turkish
Religion	Muslim (99.8% – mostly Sunni), other (0.2% – Christian and Jewish)	Muslim (99.8% – mostly Sunni), other (0.2% – mostly Christians and Jews)
Life expectancy	Male: 66; female: 71 (1995)	71.96 (males: 70.12 years; females: 73.89 years) (2010)
Total GDP	€369.92 billion (2004 est.)	€635.92 billion
GDP per capita	€5,400	€8,100
Currency	1 euro = 1.619 Turkish lira (October 2002 est.)	1 euro = 2.2980 Turkish lira (30 November 2009)
Structure of production		
Agriculture	11.7%	9.3%
Industry	29.8%	25.6%
Services	58.5%	65.1%
Economic situation		
GDP growth rate	8.2%	−6%
Inflation rate	9.3%	6.5%
Labour force	25.3 million	25.3 million; about 1.2 million Turks work abroad
Unemployment rate	9.3% (plus underemployment of 4%)	14.5%
Budget balance	Revenue: $78.53 billion; expenditure: $110.9 billion	Revenue: €105.66 billion; expenditure: €131.33 billion
Current account balance	−€2.64 billion	€−10.15 billion
Account deficit (rate of GDP)	5.1%	5.7% of GDP (2007)
Public debt (% of GDP)	74.3%	46.3%

Table 3.11   *The political situation in Turkey*

	Political Situation
Official name	Republic of Turkey – Türkiye Cumhuriyeti
Constitution	7 November 1982, amended in 1995, 1999 and 2001
Electoral system	18 years of age, universal suffrage, separate parliamentary and local elections (both every 5 years), 10% threshold
Head of state	President
Internal administrative organization	The central administration, headed by the Prime Minister and ministers, is represented in the territory by 81 governors in the 81 provinces. There are sub-governors at district level; the governor is assisted by a directly elected provincial council, and district councils. Several ministries have offices at both provincial and district level. (There are 7 geographical regions in Turkey, essentially for statistical purposes.) An autonomous local administration exists at the municipal level (16 large metropolitan municipalities (MM) – subdivided into sectors – and 3,200 other smaller towns) which elect a mayor and a municipal council. Istanbul MM has a population of 8.5 million, Ankara over 3 million, and Izmir over 2 million. In 50,000 villages, a Council of Elders and a village headman are directly elected by the village assembly.

Box 3.3: Long-term issues for Turkey

Despite the positive developments in trade, Turkey–EU relations are governed by several conflicting long-term issues that need to be resolved.

With more than 65.9 million inhabitants in 1999, Turkey's population had more than doubled since 1960 (see Tables 3.10 and 3.11 for comparative data). With a birth rate of 3.1 per 1,000, the population will be 100 million by 2015. Therefore, one European out of five is of Turkish nationality. Consequently, Turkey as a full member will automatically account for the maximum number of deputies in the European Parliament. Germany is the destination for most Turkish migration, with (including those acquiring German nationality by birth or naturalization) the Turkish community in Germany totalling 2.4 million in a population of 82 million. Turkey, together with Germany, would therefore significantly alter the decision-making structure and balance of power in the EU.

Member States also need to agree on whether the EU is a predominantly Christian grouping.

Other questions have been raised about Turkey's candidacy: How far can the EU make concessions in terms of human rights and equality issues? Can Turkey adapt to the European *acquis* (see 3.2.1)? The question of the Armenian genocide is one issue, which has been resolved. Indeed, the recognition of its Armenian community has been a key to Turkey's change of direction, from its military past and towards democracy. Turkey also needs to re-evaluate its position on the status of Cyprus, divided into two with Greek and Turkish communities since 1983 when the Turkish part declared its separation. A solution to this situation was set as a specific condition

(Continued)

(Continued)

under which the EU agreed to open negotiations for Turkey's accession on 3 October 2005. Reunification talks have intensified, in particular since 2008, in the context of political reshuffles in both governments and thanks to UN supervision.

Besides these questions, the integration of Turkey potentially provides for a large and powerful European Union with ever-increasing geopolitical significance and a unique relationship with Asia. Only 10 per cent of Turkish territory is situated inside geographical Europe (oriental Thrace and European Turkey); the other 90 per cent comprises Anatoly and Asian Turkey, both located on the Asian continent. Among international partners, the USA has traditionally been in favour of Turkish accession to the EU. Within the EU, the Italian government counts amongst its strongest supporters, in opposition to Germany and France.

This accession potentially illustrates – powerfully – that Islam does not necessarily lead to fundamentalism but can be well-matched to and even integrated peacefully into western principles. This adhesion then has a significant effect on the way in which western powers view the Israeli–Palestinian and Iraqi conflicts, and stabilize the region and the business relations within it.

Turkey has received half of the budget allocated to the Instrument for Pre-accession Assistance (INP), that is, a total budget of €11 billion from 2007 to 2013.

Turkey is one of the 12 members of the Euro-Mediterranean partnership, together with Algeria, Egypt, Israel, Jordan, Lebanon, Libya, Morocco, the Palestinian Authority, Syria and Tunisia. This partnership strives for a common area of peace, stability and shared prosperity in the region. It came into existence when, in 2004, the launch of the European Neighbourhood Policy (ENP) of the European Union increased dialogue amongst non-member states of the EU. As a consequence, in 2008, what was known as the 'Barcelona Process' took a new dimension: the creation of a 'Union for the Mediterranean'. The resulting 'Euro-Mediterranean Free Trade Area' aims for the liberalization of trade between the EU and southern Mediterranean countries and also for dialogue amongst southern Mediterranean countries themselves. It is an expansion of the EU's early experiences of political stability achieved through economic collaboration.

Today, amongst other structures, the regions maintain the so-called 'Agadir Agreement' (Tunisia, Morocco, Jordan and Egypt), launched in 2007, which allows for the accession of other Arab Mediterranean countries. Also, Israel and Jordan signed a bilateral free trade agreement. Turkey has signed bilateral agreements with Egypt, Israel, Morocco, the Palestinian Territories, Syria and Tunisia.

3.2.6 Iceland

3.2.6.1 Overview

Iceland formally applied for membership in July 2009, in the context of the economic and financial crisis that left this formerly thriving economy in poor shape. In

2008, the three major Icelandic banks (Glitnir, Landsbanki and Kaupthing) were all put under the control of the Icelandic Financial Supervisory Authorities. The banks' collapse, due to their incapacity to finance their short-term debt, had an impact both inside and outside the country. Across borders, this hit, in particular, a large number of British and Dutch citizens who lost savings deposited in Iceland. The membership application thus supported Iceland's momentum of recovery.

3.2.6.2 EU–Iceland relations

Since its application in 2009, the accession of Iceland has been seen as a smooth process. Iceland had already been a member of EFTA since 1970, and of EEA since 1994. This included a bilateral free trade agreement with the European communities (see Chapter 2) and an extension of the internal market, including all other free movement of goods, capital, services and people (goods here excludes agriculture and fishery).

Ever since 1996, Iceland has been associated with the Schengen area for the free movement of people that includes 25 European countries (only the UK and Ireland opted out). Norway (with Iceland, part of the Nordic Passport Union, along with EU members Denmark, Sweden and Finland) and Switzerland, both EFTA countries, are also part of the area. All members of this area share a common policy on the temporary entry of persons, the harmonization of external border controls, cross-border police and judicial cooperation. Also, Liechtenstein, the smallest German-speaking country and the one with the highest GDP, has been associated with the Schengen area since 2008, meaning that travel without a passport and residence without a work permit is possible there.

Interestingly, Iceland, Liechtenstein and Norway are some of the countries that, in the aftermath of the 2008 crisis, also established increasing trade relations with Canada in the form of free trade agreements in 2010. They are part of the trend confirming the data (above) illustrating increasing creations of trade groupings.

In the context of its EU membership application, it was recognized that Iceland already met the Copenhagen criteria necessary to obtain such membership. Indeed, Iceland is the oldest parliamentary democracy in the world. It is also a founding member of NATO.

Negotiations were opened in June 2010 and were expected to be fast. However, the EU has paid special attention to the weaknesses of the financial service sector in particular, and aimed at guarantees for long-term recovery. Also, policy issues are sensitive when it comes to fishery, accounting for 70 per cent of Iceland's exports (www.economywatChaptercom/economic-statistics/Iceland/Trade_Statistics/) and 10 per cent of its GDP. A report by the authorities of Liechtenstein states that: 'Iceland's annual catch would suffice to cover Liechtenstein's current fish consumption for about 4,750 years' (www.liechtenstein.li/island_e.pdf).

The EU regularly challenges the fishery policy pursued by Iceland as counterproductive towards the conservation needs of resources in the North East Atlantic. Whale hunting, exercised traditionally by Iceland, is another issue that many Europeans want to see resolved.

Table 3.12   *Iceland: basic data and economic situation, 2009*

General information

Population	306,694 (2009 est.) 313,000 (2008) 317,630 (2010)
Population distribution	63% capital and 37% in remainder of country (2010)
Capital	Reykjavik
Neighbours	No immediate surrounding neighbours (Greenland, Sweden, Norway, UK, Ireland are closest)
Area	103,000 km²
Ethnic groups	Homogenous mixture of descendants of the original Nordic and Celtic settlers
Official language	Icelandic
Religion	State Lutheran Church (84%). However, Iceland has complete religious freedom, and about 20 other religious congregations are present
Life expectancy	Males: 79.6 years; females: 83.0 years (2008 est.)
Total GDP	€8.73 billion (2009)
GDP per capita	€27,365 (2009 est.)
Currency	1 euro = 154.479 Iceland Kronur (Sept 2010)

Structure of production

Agriculture	3%
Fishing	3%
Industry	20%
Services	70%

Economic situation

GDP growth rate	GDP growth rate: (2007) 3.8%; (2008) 1.3%; (2009) –6.5%.
Inflation rate	Inflation rate: (2008) 18.1%; (2009) 7.5%
Labour force	185,700 (83.3%) (2010 est.)
Unemployment rate	8.7% (2010 est.)
Budget balance	0.8% of GDP (2006)
Current account balance	€–0.75 billion (2009 est.)
Account deficit (rate of GDP)	149 billion ISK (9.9% of GDP) (2009 est.)
Public debt (% of GDP)	95.1% (2009 est.)

Political situation

Official name	Republic of Iceland
Constitution	Became an independent republic on 17 June 1944
Electoral system	18 years of age, universal suffrage, members of the parliament are elected on the basis of parties' proportional representation in six constituencies, parliament is composed of 63 members, elected every four years unless it is dissolved sooner
Head of state	President (since 1996): Olafur Ragnar Grímsson

(Continued)

Table 3.12   *(Continued)*

Internal administrative organization	The president is elected to a 4-year term and has very limited powers. When Iceland became a republic in 1944, the post of president was created to fill the void left by the Danish king. Although the president is elected and has limited veto powers (s/he can force a public referendum on a proposed law by refusing to sign it), the expectation is that the president should play the same limited role as a monarch in a traditional parliamentary system.
	The prime minister and cabinet exercise most executive functions. The parliament is composed of 63 members, elected every four years unless it is dissolved sooner. Suffrage for parliamentary and presidential elections is universal for those 18 and older, and members of the parliament are elected on the basis of parties' proportional representation in six constituencies. The judiciary consists of the Supreme Court, district courts and various special courts. The constitution protects the judiciary from infringement by the other two branches.

Given the size of its population, Iceland is then the EU's least populous country, with a voting weight and number of MEPs comparable to that of Malta, and adding one official language to the 23 languages already recognized within the EU 27.

3.3 Enlarging business opportunities

Common regulations for free movement of goods, services, capital and people enlarge business opportunities and help facilitate exchanges. They create new opportunities and prolong life cycles. But it is clear that any new operation in new locations also encompasses new risks and uncertainties, new obligations and costs. The annual burden of EU business legislation (that is in general similar across old EU economies) is more costly to accession countries due to the adoption gap that needs to be filled rapidly upon membership. EUROCHAMBRES estimates the overall cost of compliance to business legislation at 12.3 per cent of the EU's GDP (€1.6 trillion). This cost is well below that of frontier-based regional markets. However, the benefits stemming from EU-wide regulation and harmonization are difficult to measure. Most Member States monitor impacts through Impact Assessments; for example, through the Portuguese SIMPLEX programme or the 'Regulatory Management Unit' in Belgium. The Commission claims that overall savings of €30 billion annually are achieved (see EUROCHAMBRES, 2009, p. 14) when it comes to costs for business to comply with legislation.

EU enlargement results in short-term costs that encompass mainly support costs. For the 2004 enlargement, support payments began in the 1990s with about €12.6 billion from the EU, the USA, the World Bank, the IMF and the United Nations Development Programme (UNDP) financing the adaptation efforts made by Central European and Baltic countries. In 2002, €22.5 million was provided through the Open Society Institute: this was then reduced to €7 million in 2004. By then, most entrants had already become net donors to the UNDP; only Latvia and Lithuania owed payments to the IMF. All the states included in the EU and its waves of enlargement subscribe to respect all the general principles of the EU. By extension, this is also true for companies working within the Union.

Business and trade creation opportunities are diverse. In the example of the most recent enlargement of 10 new Member States from Eastern and Central Europe, each country realizes its own specific potential, illustrated in Table 3.13.

The successive waves of enlargement promise to boost the commercial ties with new members. The costs are compensated for by the increase in regional stability and in business opportunities. The growing wealthy internal market offers huge potential benefits that balance the saturation of certain sectors in the EU. Because new markets are accessible under equal conditions of legislation and market access across the EU, the expansion of operations, life cycles and marketing strategies are facilitated. The use of market imperfections allows for cost and resource advantages. Both help economies in new and old members to mature and adapt to the new challenges.

It is estimated that:

- the EU 15 countries gained €15 billion in real income;
- the gain for the 2004 accession countries amounted to €23 billion (Baldwin et al., 1997; Baldwin and Wyplosz, 2004).

Also, within the two years following the 2004 accession wave, more than 800,000 CEE citizens moved to the UK and Ireland, moving knowledge back and forth

Table 3.13 *Selected opportunities in enlargement markets*

Selected Countries	National Focus Sector(s)	Investment Opportunity Sectors
Czech Republic	Freshwater aquaculture, agriculture (wheat, potatoes, sugar beets, hops, fruit, pigs, poultry)	Car equipment, agro food, fisheries, machinery, glass, green technology
Latvia	Biotechnology chemicals and pharmaceuticals, electronics and electrical manufacturing and engineering	Perfumes and cosmetics, renewable energy, forestry and woodworking, textiles and clothing
Cyprus	Banking and financial services, energy, shipping, professional services, R&D	Food and perfumes, ICT, medical services
Romania	Agriculture, aquaculture production, IT & telecommunications, car industry, services (retail, financial, business activities)	Bio-diesel production, alternative energy
Iceland	Fishery, renewable natural resources: fishing, hydro and geothermal power, pastureland	Biotechnology, industrial production
Macedonia	Clothing/textiles/leather, tourism, chemicals, construction, automotive components, ICT, food and tobacco	Pharmaceuticals, agribusiness and food processing industry, energy, mineral resources

across borders (see Table 3.14, referring to the 8 CEE new Member States that joined the EU in 2004).

Though *acceding* to the EU means *abiding* by all rules, even those that are costly, some rules are easier to implement than others. For internal market directives, for example, the worst implementers of regulations have typically been Portugal, the Czech Republic, Greece, Luxembourg and Italy. Amongst efficient implementers of EU rules are Lithuania, Hungary and Slovenia, then Denmark and Finland and also Malta, Spain, the Slovak Republic, Sweden and the UK. The lists of good and bad implementers of business policy-related rules vary from one policy to another. Corporations can benefit from such differences, avoiding costly investments in one market if stepping up operations to another. In agriculture, this has been the case for the use of genetically modified crop plantations.

The implementation gaps can be explained because industry standards, state aid and environmental protection rules, reshape economies extensively. The workforce needs to be educated to be competitive, the infrastructure polished, and access to big markets granted. Low taxation rates, such as in Estonia (where some firms pay 0 per cent corporate tax), as well as low labour costs, put older Member States under strain,

Table 3.14 *Residents in EU-15 countries originating from New Member States (NMS-8) countries*

In 1000 persons	2000	2002	2003	2004	2005	2006
Austria	60.4	44.6	41	53.7	80.5	78.9
Belgium	9.3	12.2	9.5	15.6	25.6	59.9
Denmark	8.7	10	10.2	10.5	11.3	13.3
Finland	12.9	14.8	15.8	16.5	18.3	17.8
France	37.8	44.9	35.1	34	46.8	29.6
Germany	416.5	453.1	466.4	480.7	438.8	481.7
Greece	13.8	14.9	16.4	15.2	20.6	20.1
Ireland	6.4	8.6	49.1	54.1	58.5	58.5
Italy	34.4	41.5	42.2	55.6	67.8	79.8
Luxembourg	1.1	1.2	1.1	1.1	0.7	0.7
Netherlands	9.4	11.2	12.2	13.1	17.9	23.2
Portugal	0.4	0.7	0.6	0.7	0.8	0.3
Spain	10.6	30	41.5	46.7	61.8	74.3
Sweden	23	22.9	21.4	21.1	23.3	26.9
United Kingdom	52.7	62	78.6	81.4	180.8	328.6
EU-15	697.3	772.3	841.1	909.0	1,053.40	1,293.50

Source: National Population Statistics, Eurostat (cited from Brückner, 2007; Breitenfeller et al., 2008 © European Union, 1995–2011)

Key

Experienced at least 500% growth in 2000–2006

Experienced a decrease in migration in 2000–2006

Migration has stayed approximately the same in 2000–2006

because in the first years of membership, new Member States' relatively sluggish regulation and significant growth attract high levels of inward investment.

3.4 Competitiveness in the enlarged market: leveraging benefits

How should competitive strategies best target the enlarged market? What are the opportunities for a given company? Should export strategies be generalized or differentiated? What type of presence in the market is best for my company? Should I go for subcontracting or prefer other options? With regard to the threats of doing business in the enlarged Europe, what type of competition will I encounter? What prices can I target? What product or service is best adapted to the customer in this market? What qualifications and human resources legislation will count?

3.4.1 Cross-border advantages

These questions require answers before cross-border decisions are made. Economic theory has shown that internationalization is good for corporate competitiveness. The costs of trade procedures typically eat up between 2 and 15 per cent of the value of traded goods worldwide. Harmonization of rules in the EU halves the cost of bureaucratic trade procedures.

Box 3.4: An example for the use of the EU's Tariffs and Customs Data Base (TARIC)

TARIC Information Goods Code 0905 – Country Mauritius – MU (0373)

Section II Vegetable products

Chapter 9 COFFEE, TEA, MATÉ AND SPICES

0905 – Vanilla

Mauritius	Spain
TARIC Information	TARIC Information
Goods code 0905 – Country Mauritius MU (0373)	Goods code 0905 – Country Spain (excluding XC XL) ES (0011)
Description [show]	Description [show]
No restriction	No restriction
Measures	Measures

(Continued)

(Continued)

ERGA OMNES (TOUT)

Import

Third country duty: 6.00 per cent R2204/99

Source: http://ec.europa.eu/taxation_customs/dds2/taric/measures.jsp ?Lang= en&SimDate=20101116&Area=ES&Taric=0905

The EU estimates savings of up to €300 billion a year for industry operating in Europe. We understand that low operational and environmental risks foster cross-border business activity in that area. At the same time, both internationalization and Europeanization have been detrimental to firms that have not been capable of responding to integration.

While gains and losses are intrinsic to any business operation, choosing the right cross-border location represents an efficient solution to obtain competitive advantages that will make a difference by:

- optimizing or reducing costs;
- providing opportunities for growth;
- developing new strategic strengths.

Typically, the prerequisites of internationalization are based on the certainty that foreign countries offer advantages. These encompass ownership-specific advantages, internalization, to a certain degree, and location-specific advantages.

A firm must also assess the operational risks and threats of this move.

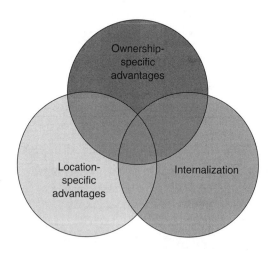

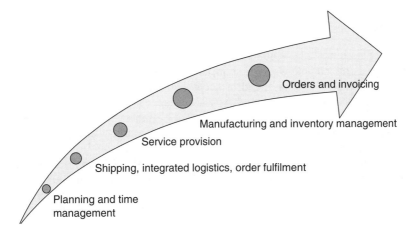

Orders and invoicing

Manufacturing and inventory management

Service provision

Shipping, integrated logistics, order fulfilment

Planning and time management

3.4.2 Adapting the value chain

In its international value chain, this includes the assessment of conditions related to the factors in Figure 3C.

These elements involve all aspects of management, from human resources management to marketing and sales strategies. Before the internationalization process is undertaken or expanded, a crucial decision for a company is the choice of location. In the case of delocalization, the new location is also crucial to both home and receptor markets. A firm's decision is based on the balance that can be established between risks and returns, costs and benefits: local externalities and research and development spillovers are enhanced; and cost of knowledge transfer and/or transport costs are reduced. As an example of the geographical dimensions in Europe, consider that the distance between Paris and Prague is the same as that between Paris and Barcelona (1031 km), and that any entrepreneur will have as much travel (or less) from Helsinki to Talinn, Estonia, as from Helsinki to Mikkeli further north in Finland, to run his or her business within this harmonized business environment.

Transaction cost advantages make relocating more attractive, as do the gains from cost benefits and from entering foreign markets and resources. Often, investors do not await a country's official accession to invest there.

Box 3.5: Moving ahead of accession

The Central Chamber of Commerce of Finland, for example, assesses the performance of European economies for its member organizations and corporations, along specially developed indicators. These indicators comprise growth and stability

(Continued)

(Continued)

components as well as investment, labour, production and infrastructure criteria. Scores on a 280-company survey show that 80 per cent of firms invested in the Polish and Baltic countries ahead of accession, due to expectations of positive progress of those criteria. Firms indicate that they mainly entered these markets firstly through their own exports, and subsequently established subsidiaries, formed partnerships with local firms and increased subcontracting, with a preference for Estonia as a first point of entry. That country was in the top four for growth and stability with a relatively small national export. On a scale of 4 (worst) to 10 (best), firms awarded Estonia with the top score of 7.15 in 2001 and 7.56 in 2005. Its main challenges were named as low price levels and low levels of purchasing power. Business impatiently awaited full free labour movement and the common currency that were introduced in 2011 onwards. Estonia is now ranked number 17 out of 183 economies as a high income category (based on the ability to start a business, get credit, protect investors and trade across borders). The business community values its similarity in culture and language, with a 12-point jump in receiving credit, with indicators such as:

- the strength of their legal rights (the degree to which collateral and bankruptcy laws protect the rights of borrowers and lenders and thus facilitate lending), scoring 7 out of a possible 10 points (vs 6.6 for Eastern Europe and Central Asia);
- the depth of their credit information index (measuring rules and practices affecting the coverage, scope and accessibility of credit information available through either a public credit registry or a private credit bureau), scoring 5 out of a possible 6 points (vs 4 for Eastern Europe and Central Asia).

Finland remains Estonia's largest trade partner after the great leap in 2005, with exported goods from Estonia to Finland increasing by 50 per cent. The Finnish-Estonian Trade Association (SEKY) helps bilateral operations; and the Finnish-Estonian Chamber of Commerce (FECC) mediates business contacts, as well as provides its members with information about the Estonian economy.

Source: www.doingbusiness.org/data/exploreeconomies/estonia#getting-credit; www.vm.ee/?q=en/node/69; www.keskuskauppakamari.fi/site_eng/About-Us/Chambers-of-Commerce

Any corporation that engages in business across the enlarged Europe must have appropriate organizational capabilities. It must be able to leverage its strengths internally, in sufficient supply, to counterbalance external market mechanisms.

3.4.3 Organizational structures for knowledge transfer

Corporations possess geographic organizations that are shaped into international divisions (for example, Haribo), geographically linked via a matrix structure combining functions and business units to regions (for example, Microsoft EMEA), and have different degrees of transnationality (Bartlett and Ghoshal, 1992). The particular advantage of the transnational corporation lies in the efficient and effective transfer of knowledge about global and local conditions. This includes tacit knowledge (that is, experience, accumulated tacit knowledge, networking motivations) and explicit knowledge (for example, geographical proximity, logistic ease and risk diversification motivations) about location decisions. Management decides which knowledge and competencies, yielding ownership and internalization advantages, are transferred to external parties at a particular location, and which knowledge needs to remain internal.

The success of going cross-border depends on strategic competencies and ownership-specific advantages that counterbalance a knowledge gap in a particular location and its markets. This is the liability of foreignness, part of the cost of going abroad.

In Europe, this level of unfamiliarity with new (enlargement) markets is relatively low and access to information is easy.

Box 3.6: Foreign investment after enlargement – not everything is rosy

Greece joined the EU in 1981. Despite expectations of strong inflows in foreign direct investments (FDI), in 2003 the country had still only received 0.2 per cent of the total investment flow to Member States, as the OECD found. UNCTAD, the United Nations Conference on Trade and Development, found that the total investment stock for 2003 only amounted to 9.8 per cent of GDP, compared with 32.8 per cent of GDP in the other Member States. This was one year before the biggest enlargement of the EU took place and started to distract its focus from the south towards the east. Enlargement countries tend to catch up within a decade of accession. But the reasons suggested for the Greece phenomenon, which is rather exceptional, were its isolated location: it had no direct border with other EU members, until Bulgaria joined in 2007 to bridge the geographic gap.

Even today, the domestic market of Greece with its 11 million consumers is relatively small. One would expect its industry to take full advantage of the Single Market. However, the contrary occurred: 'EU accession had a negative effect on the country's export performance, instead of improving it. One of the reasons for this effect is that the export subsidies, during the time period that they were available, just improved the exporters' revenues and were not used for creating new comparative advantages for the Greek products' (Koukouritakis, 2006).

Foreign Direct Investment (FDI) is somewhat hindered by tax rates (in particular, compared to those of Member States such as Estonia). Bureaucracies process applications, licences and permits slowly. Time for export red-tape is above the average of OECD countries (20 days), and delays are even worse for imports (25 days). The *Financial Times* reported in 2005 that it still took about two years to complete the paperwork required before foreign investment. As a result, most investment is made indirectly through acquisitions.

(Continued)

(Continued)

Also, in 2005, the World Competitiveness Report (Schwab, 2005) ranked Greece 50; in 2009, 71; and in 2010, 83; (Schwab, 2010). It is ranked below El Salvador and before Trinidad and Tobago, and is last on the list of EU countries. All other EU countries are listed between rank 2 for Sweden, and 71 for Bulgaria. For market efficiency, it is ranked 94, and for the macroeconomic environment, 123 of 139 countries.

Year	Rank
2005	50
2006	42
2009	71
2010	83

Because structural funds flow into the newest enlargement countries, the Greek government had to rethink its domestic business environment from 2004 onward; even though it continued to be a net gainer from the EU budget, Greece pocketed a net gain of €3.4 billion in 2008. To put this in perspective, Germany alone contributed €8.8 billion ($11.9 billion) more to this EU budget than it received.

As an example of improvement in Greece, corporate tax was reduced to 25 per cent from 2007 onwards. Public–Private Partnership (PPP) ventures are encouraged and start-up legislation has been facilitated, and now requires 20 permits and 30 days for paperwork; the government website that facilitates such registrations continues to be accessible only in the Greek language.

Nonetheless, Greece has great potential: it excels in high-quality infrastructure with distinct know-how of local and regional markets. The neighbouring Balkan economies are growing fast, moving closer to the Single Market, and Greece has turned into a springboard for firms from older Member States to enlarge operations. Its most attractive sectors for inflowing investment today include tourism, the life sciences, sustainable energy, information and communication technology (ICT) and nutrition.

Source: Compiled from EuroInfoCenter; FT; UNCTAD; IMD; WE Forum; OECD; 2005–2010; Invest in Greece 2010; and Suder (2010).

The progress of FDI performance in new EU Member States (cf. Table 3.3) is a significant phenomenon, and cross-border strategy has to be adapted to each context.

The first movers into the CEE markets were firms from Germany and Austria, followed by the USA. Proximity, educational levels and the expected growth of the GNP, due to consumption of equipment (TV, cars, etc.), led the corporate sector to move rapidly into these markets. Its dynamics also proved attractive to US investors, third in terms of FDI inflow into the region.

Investors received support from the EU in the shape of structural funds that amounted to €40 billion for 2004 to 2006 with respect to the 2004–7 wave of integration, and will receive similar funds for investments in new candidate economies. These funds are attributed to regional development projects in particular, encouraging firms to create structures now that will open markets for the future.

Typically, it can be observed that within a decade of joining the EU, increasing regional integration results in the close proximity of European demand structures. The gap between labour costs, public aid structures, and harmonization of all norms and standards helps to reduce the differences between older and younger accession countries, which typically balance out over 10 years. Indeed, the younger members of the EU show dynamic economies that leave some older members envious.

3.5 Pricing and enlargement

An interesting case of enlargement effects is that of the French car manufacturer Renault: Renault's Romanian-built, low-priced Logan car was conceived around 1998 with versions at €5000 for the CEE market. It also turned out to be a success across the whole of Europe when it hit the market in older Member States in 2004. Despite a higher price and models starting at about €7000, it remained at the top of sales. In 2008, the Logan accounted for 35 per cent of Renault sales. Since then, sales have been increasing by 85 per cent of low-cost sales per annum.

Pricing policies generate the specific pricing objectives of a corporation. Common strategies include price skimming, penetration pricing, life-cycle pricing, above/at/below competitors and customer value in order to develop list or base prices for publication. These prices are calculated via cost-based, competitive-based or demand-based methods of calculation. They need to adhere to an EU set of rules of fair competition, in accordance with anti-dumping regulations, for example. Discounts are used in order to provide reductions from list prices for different consumers, depending on the situation, location and consumer behaviour, in the shape of variations in quantity, season, credit and special sales. They also provide allowances to the distribution channel to perform services. These services may be advertising, stocking or trade-in. Again, although several types of adjustment are feasible (and these always depend on the industry and the nature of the products), generally speaking, rebates and discounts must not be discriminatory.

European competition laws prohibit dissimilar conditions for equivalent transactions. Adjustments are also made for geographical and cultural considerations. Lower income levels in some foreign markets may require firms to set lower prices to achieve sales, and fierce competition may call for a low price level.

Despite lower costs, a product may be more expensive in the foreign market because of transport and other add-ons, but intra-EU and intra-EEA tariff costs are irrelevant.

A firm may reconsider that the cost of exporting is strategically less decisive if management considers that research, development and other costs are already covered by domestic sales. Consequently, the firm will be more likely to cross borders than in other circumstances. This is important because one main advantage of international operations is the leverage of charging country-specific prices that reflect differences in a willingness to pay, normally related to affluence (Rossini and Zanghieri, 2008).

A company's pricing in one country can help create separate channels in another country and affect their pricing. This means that pricing decisions in different countries cannot be made in isolation. A corporation needs to consider the consequences of the resulting prices in separate channels, and to link these prices to form a coherent pricing policy in accordance with its strategy. Pricing policy that attempts to differentiate prices based on buyers' willingness and ability to pay in order to extract consumer surplus and maximize profit potentials in different countries, often leads to a price difference for the same product. In many cases, the price difference is large enough for an enterprise to purchase the products in country A (the lower-priced country), ship and distribute them into country B (the higher-priced country), and still make a profit. This is when the price difference between two countries exceeds a certain threshold; parallel imports may emerge and create a channel of unauthorized product flows. This has been observed between the markets of older EU Member States and those of accession countries in the very early stages. Parallel imports are often costly to the manufacturer since they cannibalize the sales of the manufacturer's authorized channel in country B and deteriorate the relationship with distributors. When companies are forced to compete against their own trademarked items, profits decrease prohibiting domestic distributors from continued promotion of the product. The net change may be positive or negative. Overall, the effects of parallel imports on the manufacturer's global supply chain are:

- a shift in the middle market segment's sales volume from the higher-priced country to the lower-priced country;
- the creation of a new market segment at the lower end in the higher-priced country;
- an increase in the total sales volume in the global marketplace and a potential increase or decrease in the total profit, depending on the profitability of various market segments;
- a modification of the company image based on product usage information, service, warranty and safety protection.

Economic growth usually leads to increased demand which raises price levels. It was predicted that price differences in Europe would merge in the long-term (Terpstra and Sarathy, 1991; Yang et al., 1998). We know today that this is not necessarily true.

3.6 Résumé and conclusion

In this chapter, you have studied the enlargement effects of free trade agreements, in particular that of the European Union for its market. The successive waves of enlargement offer business opportunities for European and international firms operating in the Single Market. The successful integration of countries boosts the growth of formerly weak economies and provides the essentials necessary for corporations and Member States to combine competitiveness with welfare.

The European market has grown into a microcosm of the global business environment, marrying unique integration with singular diversity. Trade creation is, as expected, accompanied by trade diversion. The applications of further potential members, as well as the special relations that the enlarged EU possesses with non-EU countries, benefit both intra- and extra-EU trade for both European and non-EU corporations.

Regarding wider consecutive integration, the key question continues to be: Where do the borders of the EU begin and end? For many partisans of economic integration, the EU cannot be built politically if there is no delimitation of its borders. Borders are limits that demark sovereignty, define community identity and determine harmonious or hostile relations with neighbours. Historically, the question of borders is a sensitive one in Europe. Borders have been at the origin of threat and conflict, expansion and exclusion. The enlargements of European integration have ended schisms of the past but have not truly answered this debate. The opportunity for geographical enlargement outside Europe has arisen: Where will the borders be drawn? Does the EU need to consolidate, homogenize economies and obtain deeper integration before it can create a truly powerful and competitive Europe?

Mini case study: On the path to accession – the BASME C&T story in Macedonia

When Beti Delovska and Vlatko Danilov decided to leave their steady jobs, one at the National Entrepreneurship Promotion Agency and the other at one of the largest Macedonian commercial banks, to set up a private business, BASME C&T (Balkan Small and Medium Enterprise Consulting & Training), many of their friends and colleagues found the move very risky. BASME C&T has since become one of the most successful consulting companies in Macedonia.

Although Macedonia had already spent almost 12 years in transition, private business was still perceived as a career reserved for vocational college graduates and the unemployed. The prevailing mindset of most intellectuals considered steady jobs a much more secure and promising alternative.

In 2003, BASME C&T was born. It took almost the entire savings of the two partners. Suddenly, Beti and Vlatko found themselves in a situation of rapid change.

The original enthusiasm and virtues of 'being one's own boss' quickly dissipated. 'As partners in the team of the first Macedonian entrepreneurship agency, we had hundreds of seminars behind us. We helped many start-ups in their most difficult years. We were teaching them that starting a private business is a very serious, rewarding adventure; that it takes a lot of dedication, knowledge, personal stamina and managerial virtues, and that very often, family life suffers. While we were good with the theory, in real life we found ourselves making the same mistakes as everyone else. Things were changing all the time. You try to plan your moves, but soon find yourself in the role of a medical surgeon in a military hospital who doesn't know whether the next patient be will be suffering from a head injury, a bullet in his chest, or be in need of serum against a deadly snakebite. You get on with the job, with the agenda, but something much more important and critical calls your immediate attention. You need to be alert and vigilant all the time, and able to switch topics "in the blink of an eye"', says Vlatko. This is, they say, a 'go-go' phase, when business is more chaotic than smooth and organized.

Today, things are different. BASME is a well-established consulting company, known by many European counterparts, which implements various EU-funded projects in the region. Members of the team are in charge of planning the activities and personal workload months in advance and there is a network of capable associate consultants. However, it was not easy to reach this stage; the challenges were tremendous. Indeed, the founders' private lives were jeopardized since they were always busy with the company and had insufficient time for private obligations.

BASME's small team mastered the virtues of implementing various development projects. One helpful development in this was that Macedonia became closer to the EU and the profile of the projects changed from start-up issues to business assistance in the pursuit of EU funds and in expanding markets into the EU in this pre-accession era.

'We have no time to rest,' said Vlatko already in 2006. 'Recently, we have started a project with Invent from Germany, on setting up an export promotion agency for small and medium enterprises, and we are looking for partners to make joint applications on projects which will use various accession funds that we expect to be opened up for Macedonian companies when the country starts its formal accession process. We have to be prepared for that stage, and we have already started acquiring the necessary knowledge.'

When BASME planned to go international, the company started to respond to requests for proposals and expressions of interest for projects in the region. Beti obtained a project in Montenegro and was very successful. BASME has also signed a contract with the UNDP Offices in Tirana, Albania. In particular, BASME has always opted for assignments in partnership with established consulting companies from an EU country. This strategy allowed the BASME team to jump years of learning. With fast access to the practices and know-how of the leading consulting houses, 'we learned that the percentage of the share you have in a venture is irrelevant. What really matters is how big the pie is. Plus, the possibility to learn from our partners is priceless. We offer this winning strategy to our clients too. It worked for us in the consulting business; it will work for any other service and industry, even for government units', say Beti and Vlatko. By 2010, the company had accelerated its growth. The client base has diversified, including bigger clients such as governments, ministries and international consortia. BASME's main market is limited for its home base, boosting diversification in terms of geographies, services and partners. Vlatko concludes: 'we have invested much of our time to improve our capacities, to teach new staff, become familiar with EU fundings; we understand

Mini Case

that if we sell advice we have to be one step ahead before the others'. In Macedonia, he says, consulting remains a rare profession (BASME C&T, 2010).

Source: BAMSE C&T, (Macedonia 2011/Authors: B. Delovska, V. Danilov and G. Suder)

Mini case study questions

1　Macedonia is a candidate country to full EU membership. What benefit can organizations derive from this status?
2　Is BASME C&T a typical European company?

？ REVIEW QUESTIONS

1　**Which** integration theories drive integration the most?
2　**Which** integration theory would be supported by a large US corporation operating in the European market? Why?
3　**Should** long-time Member States contribute to EU structural funds that help enlargement countries financially, and that may then help to lure jobs and industries away to countries with cheap labour and low tax rates? If so, why?
4　**Discuss** the future of Europe. Would business benefit more from deeper or from wider integration?
5　It was reported by major analysts that the 10 enlargement countries of 2004 are losing out to India on wage costs and skilled labour advantages, and to China for R&D investment location. **Why** then are the Baltic countries still booming?

ASSIGNMENTS

- **Imagine** that you are the CEO of a Turkish corporation producing Turkish delight. To what extent does the customs union with the EU enhance your international business opportunities? What would full membership to the EU mean for your company?
- **Compare** the threats and opportunities of further enlargement across the European geographic delimitations.
- **Case study assignment**: Read and prepare the case study 'Investment consulting in Eastern Europe with Excedea' in Part IV, and discuss the impact of Europe on the company's operations.
- **Internet exercise**: How do corporations make their international location decisions? Prepare an analysis on the basis of statistics for Europe and find a short case example.

 Further reading

Adam, A. and Moutos, T. (2008) The trade effects of the EU–Turkey Customs Union. *World Economy,* vol. 31, no. 5, May, pp. 685–700.

Brenke, K., Yuksel, M. and Zimmermann, K. (2009) EU enlargement under continued mobility restrictions: consequences for the German labor market. *CEPR Discussion Paper* no. 7274. London: Centre for Economic Policy Research.

Dobson, J.R. (2009) Labour mobility and migration within the EU following the 2004 Central and East European enlargement. *Employee Relations*, vol. 31, no. 2, pp. 121–38.

Hix, S. and Noury, A. (2009) After enlargement: voting patterns in the sixth European Parliament. *Legislative Studies Quarterly*, vol. 34, no. 2, May, pp. 159–74.

Lefilleur, J. and Maurel, M. (2010) Inter- and intra-industry linkages as a determinant of FDI in Central and Eastern Europe. *Economic Systems*, vol. 34, no. 3, September, pp. 309–30.

Mikecz, R. (2006) Cross-cultural communication: the challenges faced by Finnish organizations in Estonia. *Economic Interferences*, no. 20, June, pp. 69–77.

Onaran, O. and Stockhammer, E. (2008) The effect of FDI and foreign trade on wages in the Central and Eastern European countries in the post-transition era: a sectoral analysis for the manufacturing industry. *Structural Change and Economic Dynamics*, vol. 19, no. 1, March, *Special Issue: Relocation of Production to Central and Eastern Europe – Who Gains and Who Loses?* pp. 66–80.

Stefanova, B.M. (2006) The political economy of outsourcing in the European Union and the East-European enlargement. *Business and Politics*, vol. 8, no. 2, article 3.

 INTERNET RESOURCES

A comprehensive report on SME activity across Europe:
http://ec.europa.eu/enterprise/policies/sme/files/craft/sme_perf_review/doc_08/eu-smes-subcontracting-final-report_en.pdf

Council of the European Union:
http://europa.eu/institutions/inst/council/index_en.htm

Enlargement towards Central European countries:
http://www.dree.org/elargissement/def2.htm

Enlargement website of the European Commission:
http://ec.europa.eu/enlargement/

EU relations with Iceland:
http://www.eeas.europa.eu/iceland/index_en.htm

European Neighbourhood Partnership:
http://www.enpi-info.eu/indexmed.php

Foundation supporting European cooperation:
http://www.robert-schuman.org

(Continued)

(Continued)

Government of Romania (constitution, programmes, objectives): http://www.gov.ro/main/index/l/2/

Worldwide Governance Index (also used as source): http://info.worldbank.org/governance/wgi/faq.htm#2

Gabriele Suder's *Doing Business in Europe* video series (on the SAGE companion website at http:// www.sagepub.co.uk/suder2e and YouTube)

Bibliography

Baldwin, R. and Wyplosz, C. (2004) *The Economics of European Integration*. Maidenhead: McGraw-Hill.

Baldwin, R.E., Francois, J.F and Porter, R. (1997) The cost and benefits of eastern enlargement: the impact on the EU and central Europe. *Economic Policy*, vol. 24, pp. 125–70.

Bartlett, C. and Ghoshal, S. (1992) What is a global manager? *Harvard Business Review*, September–October, pp. 124–32.

Breitenfellner, A., Crespo Cuaresma, J., Mooslechner, P. and Ritzberger-Grunwald, D. (2007) *The Impact of EU Enlargement in 2004 and 2007 on FDI and Migration Flows Gravity Analysis of Factor Mobility*, Monetary Police and the Economy, Q2/08/OECD. Available at: http:// www.imf.org/external/pubs/ft/wp/2008/wp08264.pdf

Breitenfellner, A., Cuaresma, J.C., Mooslechner, P. and Ritzberger-Grünwald, D. (2008) The impact of EU enlargement in 2004 and 2007 on FDI and migration flows: gravity analysis of factor mobility. *Monetary Policy and the Economy* (Austrian Central Bank), no. 2, pp. 101–20.

Bruckner, H. (2007) *Labor Mobility after the European Union's Eastern Enlargement: Who Wins, Who Loses?* A Report to the German Marshall Fund of the United States. IAB Nuremberg and IZA Bonn.

Czinkota, M., Ronkainen, I. and Moffet, M. (2005) *International Business*, 7th edn. Mason, OH: South-Western Thomson.

Dinan, D. (2006) *Origins and Evolution of the European Union*, New European Union Series. Oxford: Oxford University Press.

EIM (2009) EU SMEs and subcontracting (EIM Business & Policy Research, Ikei Research and Consultancy, in cooperation with local partners of ENSR). Available at: http://ec.europa.eu/enterprise/policies/sme/files/craft/sme_perf_review/doc_08/eu-smes-subcontracting-final-report_en.pdf

EUROCHAMBRES (2009) *Counting the Cost of EU Regulation to Business*. Available at: http://www.eurochambres.eu/content/default.asp?PageID=1&DocID=1834

European Communities (2002–5) *Eurostat Metadata in SDDS format*. Available at: http://europa.eu.int/ estatref/info/sdds/en/gov/gengovt02_sm.htm

Herder (ed.) (1989) *Der farbige Ploetz*, 12th edn. Freiburg: Herder Verlag.

Iyer, V. (1992) *Managing and Motivating Your Agents and Distributors*. London: Financial Times/Pitman.

Komet (ed.) (2003) *Der grosse Ploetz*, 32nd edn. Cologne: Komet Verlag.

Koukouritakis, M. (2006) EU accession effects on export performance: the case of Greece. *South-Eastern Europe Journal of Economics*, vol. 2, pp. 147–66.

Mercado, S., Welford, R. and Prescott, K. (2001) *European Business*, 4th edn. Harlow: FT Prentice Hall.

Pace, R. (2009) 'The effects of EU enlargement on Malta' in G. Avery, A. Faber and A. Schmidt (2009) *Enlarging the European Union, Effects on the New Member states and the EU*. Brussels: Trans European Policy Studies Association, pp. 45–54.

Rossini, G. and Zanghieri, P. (2008) What drives price differentials of consumables in Europe? Size? Affluence? Or both? *Open Economies Review*, vol. 19, no. 1, pp. 121–34.

Sarathy, R. (1991) *International Marketing*, 5th edn. New York: Dryden Press.

Schwab, K. (ed.) (2005) *World Competitiveness Report*. Davos: World Economic Forum.

Schwab, K. (ed.) (2010) *World Competitiveness Report*. Davos: World Economic Forum.

Senior Nello, S. (2005) *The European Union: Economics, Politics and History*. Maidenhead: McGraw-Hill Education.

Suder, G. (ed.) (2006) *Corporate Strategies under International Terrorism and Adversity*. Cheltenham: Edward Elgar.

Suder, G. (2010) Europe must focus on value creation: the Greek crisis was a distraction from Europe's project to create value through integration, harmonization, and diversity. Let's get back to the future. *Business Week*, 15 April.

Terpstra, V. and Sarathy, R. (1991) Pricing in international marketing, in *International Marketing*, 5th edn. Fort Worth, TX: Dryden Press.

Waldkirch, A. and Tikin-Koru, A. (2010) North American integration and Canadian foreign direct investment. *B.E. Journal of Economic Analysis and Policy*, vol. 10, no. 1, article 74.

World Trade Organisation (WTO) (2011) Regional Trade Agreements, Geneva. http://www.wto.org/english/tratop_e/region_e.htm

Yang, B., Reza, H. and Kent, B. (1998) Pricing in separable channels: the case of parallel imports. *Journal of Product and Brand Management*, vol. 7, no. 5, pp. 279–94.

Other sources

Primary sources from EuroInfoCentre, Nice, and various articles and data from the *Financial Times*, UNCTAD, IMD Lausanne European business school and OECD, as acknowledged.

4

Institutional Players: How the Rules and Agendas of the European Business Environment are Set

What you will learn about in this chapter:

- Which main EU institutions does business need to be familiar with, and why?
- How is EU decision-making which shapes most of the market rules handled?
- What are the EU's main tools for implementation of its projects and initiatives? Does business benefit from them?

4.0 Introduction

The institutions of the EU were set up on the basis of the Treaty of Rome. As discussed in the chapter before, at this stage the EC comprised six Member States. An ambitious project such as a single European market needed an organizational structure large enough to run multi-actor projects, initiatives and programmes, and to carry out negotiations. The Treaty of Rome gave the European institutions wide discretion for further integration and closer union among Member States: the aim was to deal with present needs and to prepare for the future.

Economics and business have been important drivers for European integration from its earliest stages onwards. This is why the original design of the institutions focused on establishing a common market and on a convergence of Member States' policies. The aim was to harmonize economic activities: to encourage business across borders to create (and maintain) economic and political stability. This would hopefully result in a peaceful and prosperous community of formerly hostile countries, making sure they could work together in the long run. The progressive improvement of living standards was to serve as a tool for the continuous evolution of common activities. 'The more collaboration, the less animosity,' was the underlying logic. Like this, businesses would – at the same time – increasingly share resources, streamline and become more competitive through a larger home market.

The institutions have changed over time, of course: since their inception, their size and weight in the power balance of EU decision-making have evolved. The Lisbon Treaty of December 2009 noted these changes and worked on making them more suited to a more recent, contemporary EU, aiming at greater transparency. These aims were pursued in response, among other things, to major demands from the private and public sector. Business in Europe was interested in a solution to the two main challenges facing the EU at the time:

- the great geographical enlargement experienced by the European Union; and
- the progressive deeper integration resulting from increasing harmonization and deregulation across the Single Market.

Both these challenges required that the EU's organizational structure adapt to deal with their expected continuation over time. This way, the EU should open further opportunities for economic, political and social benefits in the long-term. The Lisbon Treaty made the EU a *legal entity*, i.e. an entity that could sign international conventions, become a member of an organization and sign contracts on behalf of all members. It structured the EU as a multi-stakeholder model with its decision-making process suited to today's regionalization, modifying earlier treaties like Rome and Maastricht and giving legitimacy to this vast organization and its members as a whole.

During all stages of EU decision-making, the institutions of the EU play an essential role in forming both legislative and executive policy. Companies that operate in Europe are subject to EU and Member State legislation. Such companies had long asked for processes of institutional decision-making to be more transparent. Understanding the institutions' role and nature is therefore essential for understanding the European business environment.

4.1 The institutions

4.1.1 The European Commission

The European Commission, or Commission of the European Communities (CEC),[1] was first established on the basis of the EC Treaty's Articles 155 to 163, which regulate the CEC's relations with the Council of Ministers (Council) as well as with the European Parliament (EP).

Article 4 of the EC Treaty prescribed the function and operation of the four principal EC bodies: the CEC, the EP, the Council, and the European Court of Justice (ECJ), empowered to carry out the tasks assigned to the EC. The CEC's powers (Box 4.1) are mainly of an executive nature, but are also political, legislative and administrative in cooperation with the powers entrusted to the Council and the EP.

The CEC possesses *exclusive* powers to initiate legislation and the setting up of proposals, with a resulting diversity of the workload. The CEC is often complemented by and embedded in expertise from the outside: national civil servants via committees or other knowledgeable parties, such as Eurogroups (pressure, interest or lobbying groups), are consulted to make sure that the CEC has sufficient knowledge of stakeholders and issues before a rule or legislation is initiated. Participation from outside the institutional setting is considered pluralist: the CEC recognizes the diversity of stakeholders and interests, and is dependent on the input of data from public and private sources. This creates elements of corporatism in the decision-making process, that is, institutions mediate between businesses, trade and employee interests, governmental and non-governmental voices, with the objective of enhancing collaboration, regional economic independence and welfare. We will return to these issues in Chapter 9.

Box 4.1: The Commission's main objective

The main objective of the Commission is to *ensure the proper functioning and development of the Common Market*. The Commission mainly:

1 Proposes legislation to Parliament and the Council.
2 Manages and implements EU policies and the budget.
3 Enforces European law, together with the European Court of Justice.
4 Represents the European Union internationally.

4.1.1.1 Composition

The CEC's president and his or her vice-presidents manage its composition. The Treaty of Amsterdam had taken steps to strengthen the role and position of the President of the European Commission in terms of powers of organization and cohesion. Indeed, the President holds powers defining the broad policy lines that the CEC has to follow, and determines the allocation (and possible reorganization) of portfolios.

The governments of the EU Member States designate the person they intend to appoint as *president* by common agreement. Since the Treaty of Nice (1 February 2003), the Council meeting that unites the Heads of State and Government (the European Council) designates the president by a qualified majority. The EP is then asked to approve the appointment, typically for five years. This term of office is renewable, as we can see in the case of José Manuel Barroso (2004–9 and 2009–14) from Portugal. Mr Barroso, with his education in law, European studies and political science, is particularly known in business circles for his vision of the EU as a main actor in crisis settlement and for his view of the progress necessary for a sustainable environmental and social agenda. As an extension of the same logic beyond EU borders, the CEC president has been a driving force in the EU–MERCOSUR negotiations restarted in May 2010, for the world's largest free trade agreement (FTA), of 700 million consumers.

The High Representative for the Union in Foreign Affairs and Security Policy is today also Vice-President of the CEC: this mode of operation was introduced by the Lisbon Treaty to enhance the coherence and visibility of external action. Baroness Catherine Ashton from the UK was the very first High Representative. She had previously also been Trade Commissioner so she was well known to business interests in Europe, in particular in the fields of ACP relations (African, Caribbean and Pacific countries), the FTA with South Korea, and the WTO Doha negotiations. She had also played a role in dispute settlements with EU international trade partners. Another example of her role has been in the extension of EU monitoring of stability and normalization for Georgia (in collaboration with the United Nations (UN) and the Organization for Security and Cooperation in Europe (OSCE). This is the sort of political action where the EU helps create and maintain peaceful prosperity, opening doors to new potential markets for business in Europe.

The CEC is organized around *commissioners* in charge of a policy area, and nominated by national governments with each running a part of the CEC, that is, one of the directors general (DGs). These officers take up their duties six months after European Parliamentary elections. The commission president makes the final decision about the policy area, and thus the DG that a commissioner will take care of. There are, for example, DGs of Internal Market and Services, and for Economic and Monetary Affairs.

The president can reshuffle the attribution of DGs when necessary and can ask a commissioner to resign. Until the Nice Treaty, each Member State was entitled to have at least one, but no more than two, commissioners. In practice, France, Germany, Italy and the UK were the countries that normally nominated two commissioners due to the size of their populations. Since Nice, however, each Member State can only propose one commissioner. The Lisbon Treaty confirmed the 'one member one commissioner' rule. An additional reduction of commissioner numbers to two-thirds by 2014 – as proposed by the draft European Constitution – was put on hold because Ireland and other smaller members were worried about their potential loss of influence in the CEC. For this, it was stipulated that commissioners be chosen by a rotation system based on equal rights of all Member States.

The European Council endorses the list of commissioners prepared by national governments and approved by the president. Once the president and the Commission members have been approved by Parliament, they are appointed to the Council by qualified majority vote.

The commissioners are appointed for a renewable term. This term of office may be terminated early by death or resignation. The commissioners are required to be independent of any national government or other agency in the performance of their duties, and the CEC is politically independent. Nonetheless, it is worth mentioning that many commissioners served as ministers in their national governments before nomination to the CEC.

The body of commissioners is often referred to as the *College*. Within the College, each commissioner is assigned responsibility for a particular policy area. The EP may force the whole college to resign by passing a censure motion by qualified majority vote.

The commissioners are assisted by a cabinet or departmental staff headed by a director general. Each director general reports to a particular commissioner. In each case, the nationality of the director general is different from that of the commissioner. The staff members of each commissioner are appointed at his or her discretion and personal choice. When the commissioner's term of office ends, the staff members also leave their positions in Brussels, Belgium. The directors general vary in size and are differentiated by the policy area transferred to them (see Box 4.2).

Box 4.2: The Commission's policy areas

- Agriculture and rural development
- Competition
- Economic and financial affairs
- Education and culture
- Employment, social affairs and equal opportunities
- Enterprise and industry
- Fisheries and maritime affairs
- Environment
- Health and consumer protection
- Information society and media
- Internal market and services
- Joint research centre
- Justice, freedom and security
- Regional policy
- Research
- Taxation and customs union
- Transport and energy

The CEC also hosts external relations, including:

- Development
- Enlargement
- European aid
- External relations
- ECHO – the humanitarian aid office
- Trade

Its general services comprise:

- European anti-fraud office
- Eurostat
- Press and communication
- Publications office
- Secretary general

There are also nine directorates for internal services.

Source: © European Commission, 2010, Departments and Services, http://ec. europa.eu/about/ds_en.htm

4.1.1.2 Role

The CEC constitutes a collective body which commits its members and Member States to shared responsibility for actions and policies that often cut across sectors, concerning, for example, anti-competitive practices as well as consumer, environmental and R&D issues. The CEC's major responsibilities are the initiation, formulation and coordination of Community policy. If you read this chapter in the summer or are involved in the cosmetics and pharmaceutical sector, you might want to know that the European Commission is considering changing labelling on sunscreen products, requiring not 'sun block' or 'total protection' references but a new UVA seal. If you are affiliated to the Information and Communications Technology or automotive sectors, you are likely to respond to the Commission's (Internet-accessible) public consultation about the deployment of in-vehicle emergency calls.

The cabinets, in particular, can be considered important players in the decision-making process. Within these cabinets, private senior officials reporting to each 'Chef de Cabinet' specialize in a given subject and play a central role in developing regulations and decisions. The CEC implements, manages and controls, checks the proper application of EU law, plans and implements common policies, executes the budget and manages Community programmes.

Altogether, the CEC functions through the articulation of European interests. These interests are based on a maximum consensus of diverging approaches, attitudes and impacts which are brought before the CEC. It acts as an observer of what is enacted by the treaties and takes violators to the European Court of Justice (ECJ). It also suggests policies and is in charge of drafting EU policy proposals. The 2010 Monti report on the Single Market refers to the CEC's specific role in the progress of economic integration. Agricultural and trade policies may also, in certain cases, be implemented by the CEC on a day-to-day basis.

You will often come across EU stakeholders speaking of *comitology*: they refer to the provision that the CEC can be assisted by committees and ascertain continuous dialogue with national administrations (and, thus, actions close to their needs) who assist the CEC, in particular regarding measures that implement legislation adopted by the EP and the Council of Ministers, and can ask for amendments or block drafts. The national government can, within the eight weeks available for review of legislative proposals, stop the co-decision process, and may or may not be outvoted by the institutions. If national governments are dissatisfied with the subsidiarity of a legislative text, this can then be taken to court. For business, this is a way to ensure that rules are not contrary to local and national needs and objectives.

As the EU negotiator, the Commission officially conducts relations with international organizations as well as with non-EU countries. Box 4.3 provides you with an illustration of these activities, and the weight of one strong European voice for business.

Box 4.3: The European Union at World Trade Organization negotiations: the Commission with one voice for Europe's access to raw materials

Many EU companies depend on raw materials (bauxite, coke, fluorspar, silicon carbide and zinc) as inputs for further processing in the steel, aluminium and chemical industries. Those resources are part of global trade flows, and access is dependent on the liberalization of international trade. In the years leading up to 2009, China applied an increasing number of export restrictions – quotas and export duties – on such key raw materials. As a result, competition was distorted, global prices rose and downstream industries in China enjoyed access to cheaper materials than their non-Chinese competitors. In this context, the EU, Mexico and the USA asked for a dispute settlement panel at the World Trade Organization (WTO). Indeed, China also started putting export duties on those raw materials open to global trade on 373 tariff lines at the 8-digit level, worth an estimated €4.5 billion in 2008 for EU imports. The EU thought that this was contrary to the general and specific agreements signed by China's accession to the WTO that are, as always, based on reciprocity.

The export duties amounted to: the 10 to 15 per cent on bauxite (depending on the product); 40 per cent on coke; 15 per cent on fluorspar; 10 per cent on magnesium; 15 to 20 per cent on manganese (depending on product); 15 per cent on silicon metal; and 5 to 30 per cent on zinc (depending on the product, see Table 4.1).

Table 4.1 *Export duties (election results, July 2009)*

Element	Export duty (%)
Bauxite	10–15% (depending on the product)
Coke	40%
Fluorspar	15%
Magnesium	10%
Manganese	15–20% (depending on the product)
Silicon metal	15%
Zinc	5–30% (depending on the product)

Source: http://ec.europa.eu © European Union, 1995–2011

In addition, China imposed additional requirements and procedures for the export of these materials. The criteria were different for foreign-invested enterprises in comparison to domestic firms. Exporters were to pay fees and a minimum export

(Continued)

(Continued)

price system was established. All export contracts and export prices were subject to the examination and approval of the Chinese authorities through its ministries as well as chambers of commerce.

In the EU, the restrictions on raw materials and price increases were estimated to affect about 4 per cent of EU industrial activity and around 500,000 jobs. The main sectors indirectly affected included automotive, construction and fire retardants. The European Commission, representing all members of the European Union, its industries and corporations, handled this matter which was settled in 2010.

Source: European Union, 2010, http://trade.ec.europa.eu/doclib/press/index.cfm?id=483, EU Memorandum: Dispute settlement, Brussels, 4 November 2009, and WTO 2010, http://docsonline.wto.org/GEN_highLightParent.asp?qu=%28%40meta%5FSymbol+WT%FCDS395%FC%2A%29&doc=D%3A%t2FDDFDOCUMENTS%2FT%2FWT%2FDS%2F395%2D7%2EDOC%2EHTM&curdoc=9&popTitle=WT%2FDS395%2F7

Some myths and rumours surround the activities of the CEC and its role, and you can find explanations of these on the Commission's website. For example, the CEC is *not* in charge of harmonizing women's clothes sizes, nor banning Britain's construction workers from taking off their shirts in summer, nor is there legislation banning curved cucumbers, nor can the typical EU official retire at age 50 with a massive pension. However, coming back to cucumbers, the CEC did set grading rules that B2B buyers had asked for, and that help those buyers in one country to have a precise estimate of the quality and quantity of produce, without travelling to the seller in another Member State to scrutinize the boxes. These rules were adopted to help facilitate trade and reduce costs and are 'identical to pre-existing standards set down both by the UN/OECD and the UK' (http://ec.europa.eu/dgs/communication/take_part/myths/fact_033_en.htm).

4.1.2 The European Parliament

Within the Lisbon Treaty, the role of the European Parliament (see Box 4.4) encompasses *powers for legislation, budget and political decision-making*. This is particularly important for a democratic Europe, in which EU citizens directly elect this institution. Through its powers of co-decision, it is on an equal footing with the Council of Ministers, which represents the national governments. It represents, together with increasing 'subsidiarity' (closeness to the basis), the legitimacy of European decision-making.

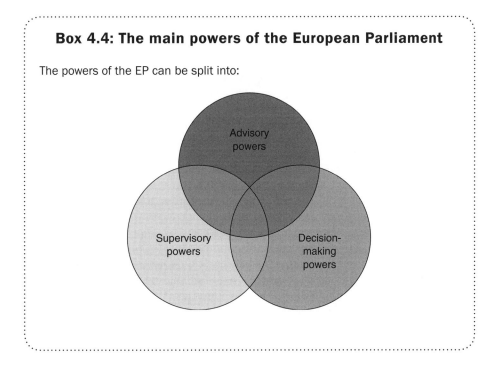

Box 4.4: The main powers of the European Parliament

The powers of the EP can be split into:

4.1.2.1 Composition

The EP is the only directly elected institution of the EU. It consists of Member States' representatives who hold annual sessions as well as extracurricular sessions in case of requests either by a majority of its members or by the Council of Ministers or the CEC.

The EP's president is elected from among the MEPs, that is, among a maximum of 751 MEPs, following the Lisbon Treaty. Any given Member States can have a maximum of 96 and a minimum of 6 MEPs.

The EP president has a mandate of two-and-a-half years and is helped by 14 vice-presidents. The president and the President of the Council (whom we learn about later in this chapter) both sign all legislative acts adopted under co-decision, the most common EU decision-making process. These include decisions regarding agriculture, energy policy, immigration, and EU funds. Examples of what is voted on range from the rights of bus passengers to new bio-waste agreements, and from the rules that apply for Internet governance to the arrangements necessary for efficient and safe imports of aquaculture products into the EU. If you are a great user of mobile phones and text messaging when abroad, you might want to thank the MEPs for having voted that roaming charges across Europe be restricted to a maximum limit from 2010; however, if you are running mobile phone operations, this legislation might have worried you!

In Parliament, MEPs do not sit in national blocks, but in political groups. These groups represent the political ideology (as closely as possible) of the different national parties to which the MEPs belong (see Figure 4.1). The groups comprise, among others:

- a European People's Party (Christian Democrats) and European Democrats group;
- a socialist group;
- an Alliance of Liberals and Democrats for Europe group;
- a Confederal group of the European United Left-Nordic Green Left;
- an Independence/Democracy Group; and
- a Union for Europe of the Nations group.

MEPs can be contacted directly by all citizens and business interests. The EU website provides a listing by name or political group, and allows you to find your MEP by region and constituency. It also helps you find out which sectors and fields each MEP works in and what his or her function is. This is of major interest to stakeholders: the main bulk of decision-making is prepared in the 20 parliamentary committees, subcommittees and special working groups in which MEPs hold specific positions. The EP meets for its main plenary sessions in Strasbourg but its main business is conducted in Brussels.

The EP comprises delegates of Member States who act as 'representatives of the peoples of the States brought together in the Community' (European Communities, 1957a: Article 137). Since June 1979, EP members are not designated by Member States' Parliaments but are elected to the EP by direct universal suffrage. MEPs are elected for a five-year period. In keeping with the logic of European integration, EU citizens whose country of residence is not that of their nationality have the right to vote or to stand as a candidate in elections to the EP.

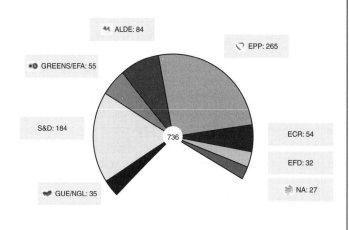

GUE/NGL:
Confederal Group of the European United Left and Nordic Green Left

S and D:
Group of the Progressive Alliance of Socialists and Democrats in the European Parliament

GREENS/EFA:
Group of the Greens/European Free Alliance

ALDE:
Group of the Alliance of Liberals and Democrats for Europe

EPP:
Group of the European People's Party (Christian Democrats)

ECR:
European Conservatives and Reformists Group

EFD:
Europe of Freedom and Democracy Group

NA:
Non-attached

Figure 4.1   *EP sitting order (election results, July 2009)*

Source: http://ec.europa.eu © European Union, 1995–2011

Administrative staff recruited by the European Communities Personnel Selection Office (EPSO) seconds MEPs. The EPSO organizes open competitions to select highly qualified administrative staff for positions in the institutions of the EU: not only in the EP but also in the Council, the CEC, the ECJ, the Court of Auditors, the European Economic and Social Committee (EESC), the Committee of the Regions (CoR) and the European Ombudsman.

4.1.2.2 Role

Due to its composition, the EP has not always worked as a parliament in the sense that national parliaments do. Because the entire Parliament and its committees consist of political and national representatives, political party majority does not determine the EP's organization or its operations. Historically, the EP has been more a consultative body of the EC with only limited powers. It could suggest amendments of CEC or Council proposals, delay legislation, and, importantly, dismiss the entire CEC. The Council consults the EP on proposals received from the CEC when legislation is not handled by co-decision. This is the case when the Council is the only final decision maker (such as in the field of taxation or for accession of new members).

In general, we note that a minimum of parliamentary formal *opinion* is required on most proposals before the Council can adopt them. On the basis of the SEA, most Single Market proposals as well as those concerning social policy, economic and social cohesion and research were made subject to the cooperation procedure. In this case, the EP gives a first opinion on a CEC proposal. The Council decides on this proposal in principle, and the Parliament then gives a second opinion. As noted above, the Lisbon Treaty of December 2009 transferred much more power to the EP and it has now become one of the two instruments necessary for rules covering the EU, including justice and home affairs.

To summarize the EP's role in the decision-making process, we note three levels of implication:

In *Consultation,* the EP approves the Commission's proposal, rejects it, or asks for amendments that will be made by the CEC or the Council of Ministers

In *Assent,* the EP has to provide its assent by absolute majority to proposed legislation before the Council can adopt this (alone). The EP cannot amend the texts: it accepts or rejects them

In *Co-decision,* the EP has equal and shared powers with the Council of Ministers: the legislation is adopted jointly

For example, the European Parliament rejected a European Commission pro-posal to exempt self-employed truck drivers from EU working-time rules because of health and safety concerns. These rules stipulate that an average working time of 48 hours a week for a truck driver can rise to 60 hours a week under the condition only that it does not exceed an average of 48 hours a week over a four-month period. The rules also stipulate at least three nine-hour breaks a week, two 11-hour breaks and one 24-hour break between driving shifts. An opt-out from this rule for self-employed truck drivers was rejected by the MEPs voting 383 to 263, with 23 absten-tions. Votes for the proposal came from the centre-right European People's Party (EPP) and the Alliance of Liberals and Democrats (ALDE); the votes that gained the majority were led by Members of the centre-left Socialist and Democrats (S&D) group and the Greens-European Free Alliance group who led objections in a process that was run as co-decision but failed before reaching the Council of Ministers.

It is again of particular interest to business in Europe that the treaties stipulate the following: a citizen, resident or registered office in the EU has the right to address a petition to the EP, either individually or in association with other citizens, persons or organizations. This is possible if the issue of the petition concerns EU activity affecting the petitioner directly. For such a case, there is an independent ombudsman: this ombudsman has the official authority to manage complaints from any citizen, resident or registered office in the EU that may concern maladministration in the activities of the European institutions or bodies. You should note that this excludes the activities of the ECJ and the Court of First Instance, which have a judicial role.

As noted above, the role of the EP includes the power to approve the designation of the commissioners and to dismiss the CEC as a whole via a motion of censure (with a two-thirds majority). It used these powers in 1999 when the Santer Commission was forced to resign en bloc. In 2004 and in 2009, the EP imposed the change of certain commissioner designates for the then forthcoming five-year CEC.

Indeed, the EP scrutinizes the work of the CEC: the supervision of the CEC's administrative function includes questions, both oral and written, put to the other EU institutions, and the right to be heard by the Council. Also, the EP sets up com-mittees for inquiry into Community policy and its application. The EP also has the right to bring issues before the ECJ.

The budgetary powers of the EP include control not only over its own budget but also over that of the Community as a whole, thus once again sharing powers with the Council, over which it now has the final word. The EP president's signature gives approval to the annual budget whose implementation is also controlled by the EP.

4.1.3 The Council of Ministers or Council of the European Union

The Council of Ministers or Council of the European Union (herein called the Council) (Box 4.5) *represents national interests* on a European level, and has long been of foremost importance in European decision-making. This institution was set up by Article 145 of the Treaty of Rome and modified by the Lisbon Treaty of December 2009.

Box 4.5: Main objectives of the Council

The main objectives of the Council are to:

1 Ensure the coordination of the general economic policy of the Member States.
2 Use its power to make decisions and approve European laws.

In most cases, the Council makes decisions about proposals from the CEC, deciding jointly with the EP under the 'co-decision procedure'. Following the Lisbon Treaty, the Council meets in public and has improved the democratic basis of its voting rules (which we shall study a little later in this chapter).

4.1.3.1 Composition

The Council is typically composed of one representative from each Member State. The representatives meet either in ministerial meetings or working groups of officials whose composition depends on the matters to be discussed. There are General Council meetings as well as those of the Council of Ministers that deal with major issues of policy in foreign affairs, finance, labour, industry, research, internal market, budget, environment and social affairs, with the Foreign Affairs Council coordinating the activities of the specialized Councils. So-called specialized Council meetings hence refer to meetings to decide on one particular area of policy.

The members of the Council are appointed by their national governments. They are ministers from Member States who normally meet in Brussels and, less frequently, in Luxembourg. Permanent representatives and experts also take part in these meetings. There is also always one representative of the CEC who attends the meetings as a non-voting participant. Decisions are prepared by the Committee of Permanent Representatives of the Member States (Coreper), assisted by working parties of national government officials.

4.1.3.2 Role

The Council is a truly *intergovernmental* tool in which Member States negotiate according to national and transnational priorities. Meetings are chaired by the Member State holding the presidency. The Presidency of the Council of the European Union rotates every six months in alphabetical order of the Member States' names as they appear in their mother tongues (see Table 4.2).

The state holding the presidency, together with the preceding one and the state that will follow, constitute the so-called Troika. The Troika used to have a particular function representing the EU in external relations within the CFSP, assisted by the CEC and the Secretary General of the Council who acted as High Representative. This position has now become that of the High Representative for Foreign Affairs and Security Policy, a position created in December 2009 that is close to being a Minister for Foreign Affairs.

One difficulty with the rotation system remains: when a particular country's presidency coincides with that country's national elections or other important national

Table 4.2   *Council of the European Union presidency by country, 2011–2020*

Hungary	January–June	2011
Poland	July–December	2011
Denmark	January–June	2012
Cyprus	July–December	2012
Ireland	January–June	2013
Lithuania	July–December	2013
Greece	January–June	2014
Italy	July–December	2014
Latvia	January–June	2015
Luxembourg	July–December	2015
Netherlands	January–June	2016
Slovakia	July–December	2016
Malta	January–June	2017
United Kingdom	July–December	2017
Estonia	January–June	2018
Bulgaria	July–December	2018
Austria	January–June	2019
Romania	July–December	2019
Finland	January–June	2020

Source: © European Union, http://eur-lex.europa.eu/, 1998–2010

issues, the result may be either an inefficient presidency or a postponement of issues on the EU agenda that may not lie in that country's direct interest. This can be an inconvenience for companies awaiting the EU-wide application of rules. Integration can thus be promoted or delayed by a particular country's Presidency of the Council.

The Council is assisted by Coreper (see above) as well as by the General Secretariat, which has its own legal service to cover EU activities. Coreper serves the Council as the 'ambassador' of the EU Member States and mainly prepares for Council meetings. Both the Council and Coreper are assisted by civil servants, council officials, technical advisers, the CEC, the Council working groups, the EP and the ESC, which provide opinion on any drafts before they are officially passed on to the Council.

As the main decision-making body, the Council takes decisions by simple majority voting, QMV or unanimously. QMV now applies in most cases, in areas such as agriculture, the Single Market, environment, transport, employment and health. At all meetings, translation into the official languages of the EU is assured, and all official documents are also translated into these languages. This also applies to the other institutions. The Lisbon Treaty reinforced the joint decision-making powers of the Council and the EP, in that most decisions need approval from both institutions to ensure that they are as democratic and legitimate as possible when implemented across the Member States.

As stipulated in the Lisbon Treaty for 2014,[2] the Council is required to make its decisions on the basis of a double majority of Member States and people, which means that a decision is only taken if 55 per cent of the Member States representing at least 65 per cent of the Union's population supports it. At the same time, the qualified majority voting in the Council is extended to new policy areas. A blocking minority is obtained when at least four Member States object to a proposal.

4.1.4 The European Council

The European Council is the EU institution that, as its main objective, defines the general political guidelines of the EU. With the Lisbon Treaty, it was decided that the European Council elects a president by qualified majority, for a mandate of two and a half years that can be renewed once. This full-time President of the European Union does not hold any national mandate.

4.1.4.1 Composition

The European Council is made up of the Heads of State or Government of the EU, its president and the President of the Commission. Since December 2009, it has held a quarterly *European Summit*, chaired by its president, the first being Herman Van Rompuy, formerly a Belgian politician.

4.1.4.2 Role

Set up in 1974, the European Council was legally recognized by the SEA in 1986. The Treaty on European Union (TEU) provided it with official status in 1992. The Council makes decisions that are the major impetus in defining the general political guidelines. These help to set priorities and political direction and to resolve issues.

Each Summit is opened by a presentation from the EP president. The European Council reports to the EP after each meeting and issues an annual report.

In this context, let us recall that since the Lisbon Treaty, a High Representative for Foreign Affairs and Security Policy has been nominated as the Council's representative for the CFSP (Common Foreign and Security Policy), the President of the Foreign Affairs Council and a Vice-President of the Commission. Baroness Ashton is the first to hold this five-year position; she manages the EU's foreign policy and common defence policy and represents the EU on the international stage in this policy field. The European External Action Service has been created to help fulfil this function, also exercizing authority over about 130 EU delegations in third countries and international organizations.

The High Representative is appointed by the European Council with the agreement of the President of the CEC and the EP's consent.

4.1.5 The European Court of Justice

The supremacy of EC law over Member States' national law provides the ECJ with a powerful role (Box 4.6), set out by Articles 164 to 189. Its practices are based on rules of procedure that are adopted by the Court by unanimous approval (Treaty of Rome, Article 188). The ECJ is also called 'the General Court'.

Box 4.6: Main objective of the European Court of Justice

The main objective of the ECJ is to ensure that the interpretation and application of EU legislation is observed, and that the freedoms and rights guaranteed by the Treaty of Lisbon and set out in the Charter of Fundamental Rights of the European Union are respected. It also interprets EU law for national courts and in specific cases on request, and settles disagreements at EU level. It thereby also guarantees the subsidiarity principle.

4.1.5.1 Composition

Judges appointed to the ECJ are drawn from EU Member States, and are chosen by common agreement of the Member States' governments in the Council. The number of judges corresponds to that of the number of Member States at a given time. They are assisted by advocates general, and are appointed for six years. The President of the ECJ is elected among these judges for a renewable term of three years.

Cases are generally brought to the ECJ by the CEC or transferred to it by national courts. The cases are examined in three stages: the first stage, in writing, initiates the procedure by submitting a complaint with the Registrar. The President of the Court then appoints a juge-rapporteur who is one of the Court's judges. The juge-rapporteur has the task of reporting on this particular matter, for the consideration of the court. Subsequently, the First Advocate General assigns one of the judges to the case.

4.1.5.2 Role

The general ECJ procedure consists of an exchange of submissions, that is, the claiming and defending statements of the parties concerned. These cases may concern breaches of European rules or conducting policy-making procedures or implementing policy. For example, cases in the area of EU anti-dumping policy concern the interpretation of rules, such as on the determination of 'the like product or the calculation of constructed values' (SEC(92)716 final: 18), and can be initiated by any interested party, such as consumer associations or enterprises. If necessary, a preparatory inquiry has to be approved by the ECJ; this presents the juge-rapporteur's report orally and is followed by the judges' questioning of agents and counsel. After hearing the parties' arguments, the judgment of the ECJ is drafted by the juge-rapporteur and delivered in open court when approved by unanimous vote. It is binding from that date onwards. The main procedures of the Court are divided into written (direct actions and appeals, or references for preliminary rulings) and oral proceedings (Hearings, Opinion of the Advocate General, Deliberations of the Court, Judgment).

The ECJ is assisted by the Court of First Instance, which was set up in 1989. The role of the Court of First Instance is to examine the direct actions brought by individuals and the Member States at an initial level to make sure that only appropriate actions are brought before the ECJ. Its composition is similar to that of the ECJ, though it does not have permanent advocates general. All cases heard first by the Court of First Instance may be subject to a right of appeal to the ECJ on points of law only. Since 2003, the Treaty of Nice has provided for 'judicial panels' to be created in certain specific areas and, in 2004, the Council adopted a decision establishing the European Union Civil Service Tribunal due to the increasing number of cases. Today, citizens and corporations may bring claims to the courts even if not personally affected. Subjects of direct actions include matters regarding agriculture, state aid, competition, commercial policy, regional policy, social policy, institutional law, trade mark law, transport and staff regulations.

Another court of the EU is the Court of Auditors. This court is independent and, since the 1970s, has been responsible for auditing the collection and spending of EC/EU funds, analysing and recording as well as making sure those funds are subject to legal and regular execution, and ensuring their economic management. The composition of the European Court of Auditors is similar to that of the ECJ. This court also assesses the regulatory framework and control approach that the CEC has developed to simplify customs procedures for imports.

These intra-EU procedures are an essential tool for European integration and its customs policy. They help move goods across borders more quickly, and are subject to fewer controls. The Court of Auditors has found that these procedures are widely used, with more than two-thirds of all EU customs declarations for imports being carried out using simplified procedures. The Special Report recommends that Member States need to enhance controls so that traders comply with the obligations deriving from the common trade policy. The application of an EU-wide automated risk analysis has only become mandatory since the end of 2010, and ensures that only reliable traders can operate simplified procedures (European Court of Auditors press release, Luxembourg, 7 June 2010, ECA/10/11 Special Report: 'Are simplified customs procedures for imports effectively controlled?').

4.2 The EU decision-making process

The decision-making process in the EU is both multi-institutional and multilateral. It has great implications for business in Europe, considering that most of the European business environment is subject to EU legislation.

The continuous enlargement of the European market underlines the increasing (nation-state) bargaining character of decision-making at the same time as the alteration of relative powers by the SEA and the Maastricht and Lisbon Treaties.

Decision-making at the European level relates to specific policy sectors in which the EU holds competencies that were transferred by its Member States. Because these rules and opinions have an impact on the whole of Europe, a large number of actors compete for influence. Power at the decision-making level may shape the outcome of the process.

Every proposal for a new law or rule is based on a treaty article, referred to as the 'legal basis' of the proposal. These proposals mainly concern harmonization, deregulation and subsidiary-focused solutions to cross-border issues. As noted above, three decision-making processes may be used: 'consultation', 'assent' and 'co-decision'. These are presented below in simplified form.

| All decision-making process is normally initiated by: • a request from the Council on behalf of a Member State; or • by the CEC itself or on behalf of third parties; or • by the EP within a general debate | Following this request for action, a first proposal is drafted by the relevant directorate general in the CEC. This proposal is then send to one or more study groups consisting of CEC officials as well as national civil servants and experts. After discussion of the draft proposal, the final draft is produced and must be formally approved by the CEC Commissioners | The proposal is then sent out for 'consultation', 'assent' or 'co-decision' |

Under the *consultation* procedure, the Council consults the EP as well as the EESC and the CoR. The EP may approve the proposal, reject it or ask for amendments. If the EP makes amendments, the CEC considers the suggested changes, but is not obliged to accept them. If the EP does accept any suggestions, then it sends an amended proposal to the Council. The Council Secretariat typically transfers the proposal to the Permanent Representatives of the Member States. The governments then put forward their official opinion. Meanwhile, advisory opinions are sought at the EESC, which links civil society organizations to the EU. This is a committee whose functions are very similar to those of the EP. The Council examines the amended proposal and either adopts or amends it unanimously; after approval it then enacts the proposal as a directive, a regulation or a decision. On less important issues, a decision is adopted without debate if Coreper agrees to it unanimously. Otherwise, more important issues are discussed in detail during Council meetings.

In the *assent* procedure, the Council has to obtain the EP's assent before decisions are taken. This applies to decisions of foremost importance to the EU. The EP cannot amend a proposal, but will either accept or reject it. Acceptance requires an absolute majority of the vote. At all other stages, the procedure is equivalent to that of 'consultation'.

The *co-decision* procedure applies to most EU law-making. Here, the EP not only gives its opinion but shares legislative power with the Council on equal terms. If they cannot agree, then a conciliation committee, made up of equal numbers of Council and Parliament representatives, is asked to reach an agreement. Following that agreement, the text is sent back to the EP and the Council for final adoption as law (see Figure 4.2).

Since the Lisbon Treaty of December 2009, most decisions are taken by co-decision. This means that decisions about the European marketplace are made in an increasingly democratic and transparent manner, so business and other

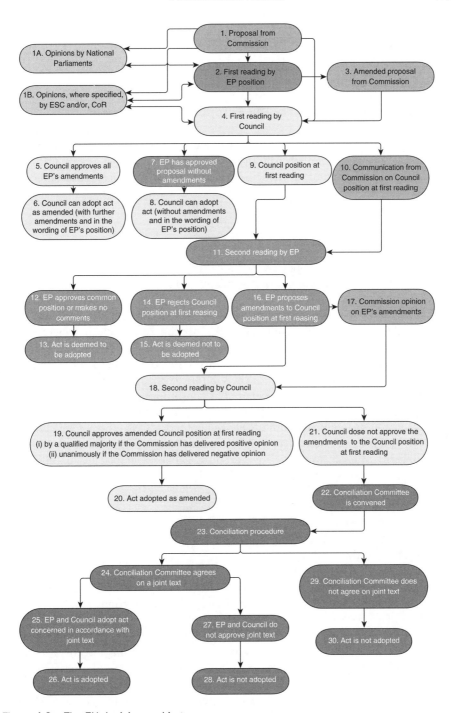

Figure 4.2   *The EU decision-making process*

multi-stakeholder interests can be well presented and considered during the process. (We will come back to this in the following chapters, and analyse the pluralist nature of this interaction in more detail in Chapter 9.)

4.3 Implementing rules for the European market: tools

How does the EU implement its objectives and outputs, and reach the appropriate outcomes? Several instruments help the institutions and Member States in this quest. We will now study two of the principal tools to this end: legislative instruments and the EU budget.

4.3.1 Legislative implementation tools

The EU institutions are supported by a number of agencies in the decision-making process and its implementation and control functions.

Among these agencies is the European Economic and Social Committee (EESC), which expresses the opinions of organized civil society on economic and social issues. EESC membership consists of a cross-section of European society and its economic actors.

The Committee of the Regions (CoR) expresses the opinions of regional and local authorities and is responsible for the subsidiarity that we have mentioned as one of the EU's main concerns. It is a rather young institution, its first session being held in March 1993. CoR officials comprise regional presidents, mayors and chairpersons of city or county councils who are elected into the CoR for a four-year term. Consulting this Committee is compulsory in the EU decision-making process when this concerns issues related to trans-European networks, public health, education, youth, culture, and economic and social cohesion.

The European Central Bank (ECB) is responsible for monetary policy and managing the euro, while the European Investment Bank (EIB) helps achieve EU objectives by financing investment projects. In this context, the European Ombudsman deals with citizens' complaints about maladministration by any EU institution or body.

The ECB stands behind the diverse powers of the EU, based on Community law that can be distinguished as constitutional legislation (primary law), conventions between Member States, and Community agreements (secondary law). We have already studied primary sources, in particular treaties, above.

Secondary sources create rules on the basis of primary sources: these rules may be obligatory or not. 'Binding' legal instruments include regulations, directives and decisions. 'Non-binding' instruments are resolutions and opinions and a series of other legislative tools, such as the institutions' internal regulations and action programmes.

A particular note should be made here: Community law has priority over Member States' national law, and its judicial legislation is enacted by the ECJ through case law.

This does not mean that national governments have no say; because, as you learned in this chapter, they are the key actors in the formulation of primary law (that is, the main treaties) and within all EU decision-making processes.

However, even if EU laws have priority, they are implemented in national frameworks according to different degrees of obligation. Let's observe what this means in the following section.

Table 4.3 gives a brief summary of the main legislative tools, their nature and the institutions engaged in issuing them.

Do note that the different institutions also issue communications, case law, judgments and orders. Some apply in a more direct and immediate manner to a region, Member State or business, whereas some are indirect: it is very useful for business to know the difference between a rule and its real applications. This helps to evaluate which legislation is relevant for a given business sector, a corporation or a business operation.

4.3.1.1 Binding legislation
The following are considered as binding legislation.

Regulation: regulations are 'binding in their entirety' and addressed to everyone. They are used as an instrument guaranteeing uniformity within the EU, and are directly applicable in all Member States as law. They are adopted by the Council in co-decision with the EP, or by the Commission alone. A regulation creates law that takes immediate effect in all the Member States just like national legislation, without any further action by national authorities. Some regulations, such as an anti-dumping duty on the applicants' exports of retail electronic weighing-scales, also apply retrospectively to imports of these products registered in accordance with Commission Regulation (EC) 1408/2004 (Council Regulation [EC] 692/2005 of 28 April 2005). Another example of a regulation, amongst many others, is Commission Regulation (EU) 330/2010 of 20 April 2010 'on the application of Article 101(3) of the Treaty on the Functioning of the European Union to categories of vertical agreements and concerted practices' (L103 of 23 April 2010). Such

Table 4.3 *Six legislative tools of the European Union*

Legislative Tools	Nature	Institution
Law	Legislative Acts	Proposal from the Commission, adoption by the Parliament and the Council of Ministers
Framework law Regulation	Non-legislative Acts	Commission or Council of Ministers (delegated regulations or execution acts)
Decision Recommendation Opinion	Point of view	Commission, Council of Ministers, European Central Bank

Source: http://ec.europa.eu © European Union, 1995–2011

vertical agreements can increase efficiencies. They can also result in market sharing that is controlled by the EU for fair competition.

Directive: addressed to the Member States, a directive is adopted by the Council and the EP or through the Commission alone, to align national legislation. While the Member States are bound to the directive in terms of outcomes, they have entire discretion about the form and method of adoption. In cases where a directive is not transposed into national legislation or only incompletely or with a long delay, citizens can invoke the directive in question directly before the national courts. 'Council Directive 2009/47/EC of 5 May 2009 amending Directive 2006/112/EC as regards reduced rates of value added tax' (VAT) is an example of a directive with a significant impact on business (L/116). Entering into force in June of the same year, it promises the optional use of reduced VAT rates for particular labour-intensive services, including restaurant services, window cleaning and hairdressing, amongst others. Such services are by nature local and therefore a reduced VAT option does not affect competition across Europe. However, some directives are not aligned in time by national governments. In the VAT case, most Member States failed to respect the December deadline for implementation of the directive, mainly because of a diversity of national formalities and procedures that had to be dealt with before implementation.

Decision: a decision is a legislative tool that is adopted either by the Council, or in co-decision with the Commission. It provides Community institutions with a binding ruling, in its entirety, on a particular issue. It can ask a Member State or a specified citizen to take or refrain from taking a particular action, or confer rights or impose obligations on a Member State or a clearly specified citizen. The following are some examples of Decisions that illustrate the variety of fields concerned.

The Commission Decision of 18 February 2004 established a model health certificate for non-commercial movements of dogs, cats and ferrets from third countries (European Communities, 2004b), which is a text with EEA relevance.

The Regulation on the marketing of products, applicable since 1 January 2010, was backed up by provisions of a Decision (Decision 768/2008/EC of the European Parliament and of the Council of 9 July 2008 on a common framework for the marketing of products, repealing Council Decision 93/465/EEC), useable immediately but operational only once fed into existing Directives when revised.

This legislative package reinforced (amongst other things):

- EU-wide market surveillance of harmful products;
- notification rules for accreditation and quality control valid across the EU;
- clarification of the CE mark and measures against any abuse of this collective trade mark;
- the harmonization of EU trade for products not subject to EU harmonization, including bread and pasta, furniture, bicycles, precious metals and more, which constitute altogether more than 15 per cent of intra-EU trade in goods (http://ec.europa.eu/enterprise/policies/single-market-goods/regulatory-policies-common-rules-for-products/new-legislative-framework/).

Yet another Council Decision, in July 2010 (the Council decision of 26 July 2010 concerning restrictive measures against Iran and repealing Common Position 2007/140/CFSP), influenced the rules applying to companies with business interests, this time outside the EU. In establishing restrictive measures against Iran, this Decision had consequences for international trade, prohibiting any imports or exports of material, software or training that might in one way or another be associated with the nuclear weapons sector. These restrictions were disapproved of by China and favoured by the USA and Israel.

These are only a few of many examples. We can therefore legitimately conclude that European binding rules have a fundamental impact on European business, its rules, its agendas and its overall environment.

Now let us turn to non-binding legislation and the reason why it is also useful to know about this.

4.3.1.2 Non-binding legislation

The following tools fall under the category of 'non-binding' legislation.

Recommendation: a recommendation allows institutions to make their views known. The institutions suggest a line of action but do not impose any legal obligation for action on those to whom it is addressed (i.e. the Member States, other institutions or in certain cases the citizens of the Union). An example is Commission Recommendation 2004H0345 of 21 October 2003, which deals with measures for road safety. The Commission reminds Member States to be more effective regarding speed control, road infrastructure, drink-driving control and seat belts in the context of keeping death off the roads (European Communities, 2004a). The action programme helped reduce the average number of deaths on the road 'per one million inhabitants from 113 in 2001 to 69 in 2009 for all current 27 Member States' (EU, MEMO/10/343, Brussels, 20 July 2010, Road Safety Programme 2011–2020: detailed measures, p. 4), and was reinforced with a Road Safety Programme 2011–2020 which focused, in addition, on smart technology and motorcyclists.

Opinion: an opinion is an instrument that allows EU institutions to make a statement in a non-binding fashion, in other words without imposing any legal obligation on those to whom it is addressed. The aim is to set out an institution's point of view on a specific question. Council Opinion 10839/10-UEM of 8 June 2010 was a published opinion on an updated stability programme for Cyprus, when its economy shrank for the first time in more than 30 years at the turn of this decade. The opinion recommended measures based on EU experience-sharing.

Joint action: a joint action is a legal instrument in which Member States have to achieve commonly defined objectives unless major difficulties arise. Joint action in police and judicial cooperation in criminal matters is based on decision, framework decision and joint action (police and judicial cooperation in criminal matters). Since the Treaty of Amsterdam, decisions and framework decisions have replaced joint actions in the field of police and judicial cooperation in criminal matters. There are also joint actions in areas such as health. In this sector, human, financial, knowledge and material resources are coordinated amongst the Member States.

Framework decision: such a decision binds Member States, in terms of the result to be achieved; however, the different national authorities are left to choose the methods by which the result will be achieved (in this, the framework decision is similar to the directive in the Community context). Decisions are used in the field of police and judicial cooperation in criminal matters for any purpose other than the approximation of the laws and regulations of the Member State, which is the preservation of framework decisions. The harmonized European definition of corruption and undue advantage and the fight against these in the private sector are based on such a framework (Council Framework Decision 2003/568/JHA of 22 July 2003), which covers both profit and non-profit activities. Indeed, the EU Observer reported in 2010: 'Fewer than 1 in 10 respondents in Bulgaria, the Czech Republic, Hungary, Lithuania and Ukraine considered government anti-corruption efforts to be successful' (Pop, 2009).

4.3.2 Other important sources of information

We have observed that even so-called non-binding legislation significantly determines what is happening on the European level and within the Member States. We shall mention in the following just a few other important documents that business interests in Europe regularly consult.

Commission communication: the vast majority of communications from the Commission (COM documents) are proposals for decisions that are passed on to the EP and the CEC for decision. The other most important COM documents are listed below. For example, in its communication COM(2004)636 on 6 October 2004, the Commission explains how to move to the deployment and operational phases of the European satellite radio-navigation programme (European Communities, 2004d). A 2008 Communication (Communication from the Commission to the European Parliament, the Council, the European Economic and Social Committee and the Committee of the Regions on the protection of consumers, in particular minors, in respect of the use of video games, 22 April 2008 – COM(2008)207 final) dealt with the assessment of content and age ranking of video game products, including on the Internet and on cell phones. Based on an EU-wide survey about the market and consumer behaviour, this work provided the basis for Pan European Game Information (PEGI) (http://www.pegi.info/en), the single European voluntary, self-regulatory system organized by the software industry.

Green Paper: this is written to stimulate discussion and to launch consultations at European level about a particular subject. The consultations that result from a Green Paper can then lead to the publication of a White Paper, which proposes a set of concrete measures for Community action. For example, the 2010 Green Paper on Pensions (EU, MEMO/10/302, Brussels, 7 July 2010) will hopefully set the scene for your generation to obtain pensions when you retire – despite the demographic challenges that have started to shrink the workforce in 2012 in Europe. Another Green Paper, on 'Unlocking the potential of cultural and creative industries' (COM(2010)183, 30 April 2010), launched a discussion of how to help creative SMEs, in particular in analysing the challenges they face in the European market.

White Paper: this contains a set of proposals for action by the Community in a particular field. They sometimes follow from Green Papers. If the Council favourably receives a White Paper, then it can lead to an EU action programme in the field concerned. For example, the White Paper on 'European transport policy for 2010: time to decide' (COM(2001)370 final, White Paper, Brussels, 12 September 2001) lists 60 measures for a European transport policy. These measures deal with business-related issues such as the saturation of air space, easier passage through the Pyrenees, integrated ticketing and standardized containers across Europe for cargo.

Report from the Court of Auditors: this is the annual report of the Court of Auditors, presenting its comments on the handling of the Community's finances. The report is forwarded to the Community institutions and published in the *Official Journal*. The report highlights points where improvement would be possible or desirable. The institutions then reply to the Court of Auditors' observations. These reports are thus interesting sources of information for business.

Case law: all the decisions handed down by bodies exercising judicial powers constitute case law. The ECJ and the Court of First Instance are the judicial institutions of the EU. It is the task of the Court to ensure that Community law is respected in the interpretation and implementation of the founding treaties. The Court is assisted in its work by advocates general, who draw up opinions as mentioned above. This case law provides business with interesting guidelines when it comes to dealing with conflicts between corporations or the public and private sectors in Europe.

Judgments: the ECJ and the Court of First Instance hand down judgments that are decisions that conclude a litigation procedure. There is no appeal against judgments of the ECJ. An appeal against a judgment of the Court of First Instance can be brought before the ECJ. These instances are important in case of recourse against European legislation.

ECJ Opinions: the EP, the Council, the Commission or a Member State can seek the opinion of the ECJ on whether an agreement between the Community and non-member countries or international organizations is compatible with the provisions of the EC Treaty. An agreement on which the Court has given a negative opinion can enter into force only under the conditions laid down in Article 48 of the Treaty on European Union (TEU) (procedure for amending the treaties). This provides an opportunity for European business in case of international frictions.

Orders: the ECJ and the Court of First Instance issue orders in a variety of instances, as laid down in the Rules of Procedure, which fall broadly into three groups: instances during the investigation of a case (for example, acts ordering the preservation of evidence, or separating, joining or suspending cases); instances where the Court takes a decision without considering the substance of the case (for example, in the event that the case be manifestly inadmissible outside the Court's jurisdiction); and instances where the Court takes a decision on the substance of the case. The orders are in fact simplified judgments that are used when the case is identical to others on which a judgment has already been handed down. Orders can, in principle, be amended or revoked.

You will have recognized from these examples that it is important to understand the legal and institutional business environment in Europe. Given the diversity of national legal and institutional traditions, corporations have taken much interest in knowing about and supporting European harmonization and deregulation plans, simply because they increasingly help standardize strategy across this vast mature market.

These legal traditions stem from the historical melange of Roman law, which itself was influenced by the Greeks, later consolidated with characteristics that can be found in the contemporary codified civil law of most parts of continental Europe. These laws were convenient for cross-border commerce because they were written down and concise but they were too slow to apply to local customs; much later, through the influence of Norman and Islamic law, parts of northern Europe started to use what is today known as common law with its case-based basis on precedents, as used in the UK for example, but this was too extensive to be a convenient tool for use over long distances. The medieval *lex mercatoria* that helped merchants base their business on self-stipulated shared texts, set the foundations for international commercial law and cross-border codification, with the convergence of civil and common law that can be observed, for example, in Internet-based trade and related usages and customs.

Institutional objectives are deeply embedded into such traditions. They reflect the past learning and future objectives of a democratic society, and hence add to the diversity of European rules and agendas for business.

The implementation of these European rules and agendas is operational within Member States and has significant financial implications. This is where the EU budget becomes important. Where do funds come from, and on what are they spent?

4.3.3 Budgetary tools

European income comes mainly from value added tax (VAT), averaging typically about 40 per cent of the budget. About the same percentage can be attributed to national contributions. This GNP-based resource is obtained by applying a rate fixed each year under the budget procedure to a base representing the sum of the GNPs at market price. The contribution is calculated by reference to the difference between expenditure and the yield of the other own resources. Own resources ideally furnish most of the EU budget. These include customs duties that are levied on imports at frontiers outside the Union. Agricultural levies are charged on trade in agricultural products with non-member countries and vary according to price levels on world and European markets. (Besides agricultural levies, there are also levies on the production and storage of sugar and isoglucose. The latter levies are internal to the EU only.)

Historically, VAT own resources were introduced by a 1970 Decision because the traditional own resources were not sufficient to finance the Community budget.

Currently, each member has to pass on the equivalent of a 1.4 per cent VAT rate to the EU budget. Other 'specific resources' are yielded through taxes and contributions paid by staff, income from interest, guarantees and diverse other charges.

For reference, the EU had a budget of €109 billion for 2004, and a budget of €141.5 billion for 2010 (see Table 4.4 and Figure 4.3). You can easily find the current year's budget information on the European Union website (http:// ec.europa.eu/budget/budget_detail/current_year_en.htm). On average, the EU budget represents 1 per cent of the economic wealth generated by the countries of the EU each year, and costs each taxpayer about €240 per year; 6 per cent of EU expenditure goes to the running of the EU institutions and its translation services for its 23 official languages.

With the Lisbon Treaty, the EU opted to continue multi-annual financial frameworks for its budget. This framework needs approval from the EP s mentioned earlier in this chapter. The EP and the Council commonly determine all expenditure, with a balance between the two institutions.

Once the budget has been allocated to policy areas for a given year, the Commission implements it according to EU rules. Mainly, these rules are laid down by the DG budget that monitors the budgetary procedure internally and is responsible for the annual accounts. The Court of Auditors controls its external legal and continuous implementation. Also, on the Council's recommendation, the EP may grant a discharge in respect of the management of Community funds. Each directorate general and service is in charge of the efficient use of its corresponding budget. This use of the budget includes sector and regional spending.

Its four structural funds are there to help specific regions, sectors or activities in the Member States, sharing a budget of more than €345 billion, i.e. 35.7 per cent of the total EU budget on the principal of subsidiarity:

- the European Regional Development Fund (ERDF);
- the European Social Fund (ESF);
- the Guidance section of the European Agricultural Guidance and Guarantee Fund (EAGGF);
- the Financial Instrument for Fisheries Guidance (FIFG).

We distinguish between the ERDF, the ESF, the Guidance section of the EAGGF and the FIFG. All of them operate under a common set of rules which issue EU grants, classified into three objectives: support for regions lagging behind in

Table 4.4   *The EU budget, 2007–2010*

2007 – €126 billion
2008 – €131 billion
2009 – €136.5 billion
2010 – €141.5 billion

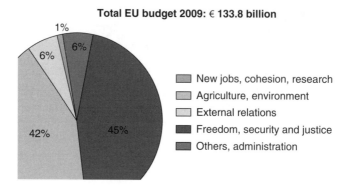

Total EU budget 2009: € 133.8 billion

- New jobs, cohesion, research
- Agriculture, environment
- External relations
- Freedom, security and justice
- Others, administration

Figure 4.3   *How the EU's money is spent*

Source: http://ec.europa.eu © European Union, 1995–2011

development; support for regions in structural crisis; and regions needing support for education, training and jobs. Table 4.5 illustrates the importance given to each objective.

The future of the European Cohesion policy is part of Report 2020, presenting an analysis that is part of the overall Europe 2020 strategy. This analysis covers European vulnerabilities and challenges throughout that decade by region, where the separation of social and cohesion policies has become a challenge for opinion leaders. Interestingly, up to 2006, more than 40 per cent of the EU budget was dedicated to *agricultural markets*, causing regular debate between Member States, with markets being agriculturally, industrially or service oriented. Another approximately 35 per cent were typically spent on the *structural funds* mentioned above. Less then 10 per cent were used for overseas aid, administration, R&D and miscellaneous (in declining order). At the turn of the decade, the biggest share of funds moved to growth and employment measures, rising by 3.3 per cent from 2009 to 2010 due to the economic crisis. Direct aid and market-related expenditure ate up

Table 4.5   *The three objectives of European structural funds*

Structural Funds	Convergence Objective (Formerly 'Objective 1'): 81.54% of Funds	Regional Competitiveness and Employment Objective (Formerly '2'): 15.95%	European Territorial Cooperation Objective (Formerly '3'): 2.52 %
Why?	Regions lagging behind in development	Regions in structural crisis	Regions needing support for common solutions for development
EU funds available (in €bn)	135.9 in 2000–2006 283.3 in 2007–2013	22.5 in 2000–2006 55 in 2007–2013	24.05 in 2000–2006 8.7 in 2007–2013
Which funds?	ERDF, ESF, Cohesion Fund	ERDF, ESF	ERDF

Source: European Communities, 2004 and EU, 2010: 'The three objectives of the structural funds', http://ec.europa. eu © European Union, 1995–2011

31 per cent to stimulate trade and economic growth. The Common Agricultural Policy (CAP) is a system of European Union agricultural subsidies implemented to protect agriculture throughout the EU by controlling prices and levels of production. It represents a large part of the European budget (40 per cent), costing about €55 billion per year. Agricultural funds now focus on milk, water management, animal welfare and organic farming. For example, following a fall in milk prices, in 2009, the EU agreed to give €17.9 million to the EU dairy industry in 2010–13 after protests from EU farmers.

Both the budget and the legislative tools of the Union ensure the smooth functioning of the EU as a whole. They are the result of a complex formula made up of Member State negotiation, the willingness of members to give up or retain sovereignty and power, and structural complexity that needs to suit many varying wishes and needs.

Business in Europe is well advised to keep abreast of the who's who of European institutions. These institutions are the *past, present and future* of 'doing business in Europe' because, together with the Member States, they are essential actors in the regulation of the European business environment at both national and cross-border levels.

4.4 Résumé and conclusion

This chapter has shed light on the different institutions that govern the European decision-making process, and the democratic process that is helping – slowly but surely – to change the European business environment from different national markets to a harmonized, deregulated and subsidiarity-focused Single Market.

The CEC is the driving force and executive body of the structure; the EP is the only directly elected body, elected by the peoples of the Member States, and the main legislator together with the Council of Ministers. The Council of the European Union represents the governments of the Member States, with the president of the European Union as head of the organization. Another important entity is the ECJ which guarantees compliance with the law. The Economic and Social Committee has a major role to play in the representation of opinions of organized civil society on economic and social issues.

Other institutions, agencies and bodies complete the structure that operates in three alternative decision-making modes, depending on the policy area and issue to be decided. The co-decision procedure is the main route to pan-European decision-making that will regulate the business environment for both European and non-European firms in the Single Market and international affairs.

The EU budget is essential for the accomplishment of European objectives in this vast and mature market. It is made up of VAT, agricultural levies, customs duties and own resources, and benefits the business environment through sectoral and regional spending and funds. The budget itself is an illustration of the convergence of legal and institutional traditions in the European political economy.

Mini case study: Blending wines?

On 27 April 2009, the blending of red and white wine was planned to be authorized through an EC regulation project for making rosé. This idea was unthinkable for most French winemakers: the Comité Interprofessionnel des Vins de Provence (Interprofessional Committee for Provence-region Wines) instantly asked the French authorities to put significant pressure on EU stakeholders, and make sure that this project was withdrawn. This regulation project, the mix of red and white wines – that is nonetheless authorized by the OIV (the International Organization of Vine and Wine) – would become *in extenso* (and thus be recognized as) a common oenological practice in the EU!

Part of European efforts to increase the competitiveness of its wine sector was to accomplish a move from the image of 'old wines' to a modern process that would enable EU wine makers to benefit from the same cost-saving techniques as those used by their competition in third countries.

Amongst other European wine markets, it became apparent that the UK market, for example, had long been dominated already by wines from the USA and other non-EU producers. Those producers claim that traditional rosé has too short a shelf life. But using stocks of red and white wines (the latter being the main ingredient for the blend) facilitates the production of rosé on demand. In this context, it was no surprise when one European Commission spokesman was reported as saying: 'Wines made in this way are already sold on our market, but only those produced outside the EU ... That makes no sense to us. Why should we allow others to do it and ban our own producers from doing so?' (*The Wine Spectator*, 2009). For the European Member States, the rosé issue turned into a question of adapting the production of rosé table wines to the international market and, possibly, a question of survival of a distinguished (but expensive) sector.

Traditionally, rosé wine has been made in the following way, ensuring high quality and a distinct taste: crushing red grapes, letting the juice extract colour and flavour from the skins and draining off the juice before fermentation.

The New World Wine Maker lobby, comprising of the new wine-making countries (South Africa, Australia, the Americas), was in favour of the mixing, because they would be able to sell those wines in the EU too, and the lobby was of course hoping that the legislation would make it easier for the process of mixing wines to be accepted within the EU.

Opposition to the mixing was represented in particular by CEVI, the European Confederation of Independent Winegrowers, but French, Austrian and other MEPs also played a role. One Austrian MEP from the EEP-EP political party group pointed out the competitive advantage of quality for Austrian wine growers. One Italian MEP cited the successful petition drawn up in her region in defence of rosé wines that had also been signed by the general public in Holland, France, Spain, Belgium, Luxembourg, Slovenia, Poland, Lithuania and Ukraine. Some MEPs made reference to others' various divergent positions on the matter at the time of European election campaigning.

So let's listen in to a sample of the questions raised in this context and asked in the EP debate, on behalf of three groups:

In the context of the discussion of the regulations implementing the CMO in wine, the Commission intends to rescind the provisions in force until 31 July 2009 concerning oenological practices so as to lift the ban on blending white wines with red wines without a protected designation of origin (PDI) or protected geographical indication (PGI) to produce rosé wine.

In recent decades, wine-growers in many regions in Member States have made considerable efforts, accompanied by substantial investment, to develop high-quality rosé wines which are recognised as such as wines in their own right and which meet a growing demand.

These efforts have helped to achieve balance in local and regional economies and in land use. Operators in the industry in the regions concerned have expressed their strong concern, inter alia to Parliament through the Viticulture-Tradition-Quality Intergroup, about the serious economic, ecological and employment impact of a decision which will make it possible to produce cheap rosé wine. This measure is liable, in particular, to cause confusion between traditional rosé wines and blended wines and to give rise to unfair competition which, even in the short-term, could destroy traditional production of rosé wines.

In view of these concerns and the possible disastrous impact of a hasty decision, will the Commission:

1   Postpone the contested decision, which is scheduled for the end of April?
2   Undertake a broadly-based consultation exercise with the industry on the basis of a thorough study of the possible economic, social and environmental impact of lifting the ban on blending?
3   Propose options which will make European wines more competitive on the European market and in third countries, while safeguarding traditional rosé wines against unfair competition?

Source: EP debate, 5 May 2009

And indeed, on 8 June of the same year, the commissioner for agriculture and rural development announced that the project had been abandoned: 'It's become clear that a majority in our wine sector believe that ending the ban on blending could undermine the image of traditional rosé. I am always prepared to listen to good arguments and that's why I am making this change,' said the commissioner (EU/UK Press Release, 2009). The exemption from the ban for French rosé champagne and the derogation allowing Spanish table wine to be blended and marketed since 2004, will persist.

The consumption of rosé table wines is currently increasing throughout the world: it accounts for nearly 30 per cent of wine consumption. EU wine consumers collectively drink about three-quarters of the world's rosé wine. While France still leads this category, it is followed by the USA where wine consumption is on a continuous rise; a 10 per cent rise for rosé in the past decade was noted on the online foodnavigator-usa.com/; Spain, Italy, Germany, the UK and the emerging countries follow it closely.

Mini Case

Mini Case

Reuters reports that 'France is the world's top rosé wine producer with about 29 per cent of global output ... Italy and Spain are the world's second and third largest rosé producers, with annual production of 4.45 and 3.85 million hectolitres apiece. Rosé accounts for roughly 10 per cent of each country's overall wine output; both countries are net exporters ... The USA produces around the same volume as Spain. For consumption, some 21 million hectolitres of rosé wine are drunk around the world each year – or 9 per cent of overall wine consumption. Nearly 30 per cent of this is made in France.'

In New Zealand, the planted area for wine grapes has increased by 240 per cent, in Australia by 169 per cent and in China by 164 per cent, in recent years. A major Australian wine producer was quoted as saying: 'They're [the EU] shooting themselves in the foot yet again by making laws that disadvantage their wine producers ... It astonishes me that they are still legislating themselves into a corner in the 21st century' (http://www.abc.net).

The EU, with an annual budget of approximately €125 million, now focuses on promoting the specific quality of European wine in the newly emerging developing countries market. The European Commission has also proposed a reform of wine labels across the Single Market which is under scrutiny at the WTO. As Reuters notes, around 22 million hectolitres of rosé wine are made each year worldwide, equivalent to 8 per cent of overall wine production. Of this production, about three-quarters originate from EU countries; about 90 per cent of rosé wine comes from the macerating of grapes rather than blending or mixing. Under these circumstances, the strong adverse reaction to the planned regulation is hardly surprising, is it? By the way, even rosé should be drunk in moderation!

Source: http://www.winespectator.com/webfeature/show/id/A-Rose-by-Any-Other-Method_4663. On Reuters via http://www.flex-news-food.com/pages/24152/France/Wine/profile-europes-rosewine-sector-production.html, 8 June 2009, 'Europe's farm chief has bowed to weeks of pressure from EU winemakers and withdrawn a plan that would have allowed rosé wine to be made by blending red and white types'; Daily News Alerts: http://www.abc.net.au/worldtoday/content/2008/s2596932.htm; http://www.foodnavigator-usa.com/Financial-Industry/US-to-lead-global-wine-consumption; http://ec.europa.eu/unitedkingdom/press/press_releases/2009/pr0948_en.htm; http://www.europarl.europa.eu/sides/getDoc.do?pubRef=-//EP//TEXT+OQ+O-20090067+0+DOC+XML+V0//EN; for the debate on 5 May 2009, see http://www.europarl.europa.eu/sides/getDoc.do?pubRef=-//ep//text+cre+20090505+item-013+doc+xml+v0//en

Mini case questions

1 What interests did the 'traditional' and 'new world' rosé producers have in the project for a new rosé Regulation of the EU?
2 Why would an EU Regulation significantly change the market in the EU and internationally?

REVIEW QUESTIONS

1 **Draw** a graph or diagram that visualizes the EU decision-making process clearly. Consider what impediments to the smooth and expedient operation of EU decision-making might exist.
2 **What** is the sense of subsidiarity? Why does Europe focus on subsidiarity whilst harmonizing and deregulating its market?
3 **Why** do the EP and the Council of Ministers decide together on the EU budget?
4 **How** do you keep your business informed about European decisions?
5 **What** are the underlying legal traditions that shape Europe's decision-making across the Single Market?

ASSIGNMENTS

- Find the most recent examples of the different types of legislation analysed in this chapter. **Imagine** the consequences for a given business sector.
- **Compare** Regulations, Directives and Decisions: in which cases does Europe use the different types of binding legislation?
- **Case study assignment:** Read and prepare the case study 'The Expansion into Europe of Multi-Latinas: a new breed of competitors' in Part IV, and discuss the impact of Europe on the company's operations.
- **Internet exercise:** Some legislation is not implemented at all, not completely implemented or implemented late in the Member States. Analyse the latest statistics and try to find explanations for this phenomenon.

 Further reading

Farhang Niroomand, F. and Edward Nissan, E. (2007) Socio-economic gaps within the EU: a comparison. *International Advances in Economic Research*, vol. 13, no. 3, pp. 365–78.

Hix, S. and Marsh, M. (2007) Punishment or protest? Understanding European Parliament elections. *Journal of Politics*, vol. 69, no. 2, May, pp. 495–510.

König, T. (2008) Analysing the process of EU legislative decision-making: to make a long story short. *European Union Politics*, vol. 9, no. 1, pp. 145–65.

Poguntke, T., Aylott, N., Ladrech, R. and Luther, K.R. (2007) The Europeanization of national party organizations: a conceptual analysis. *European Journal of Political Research*, vol. 46, no. 6, October, pp. 747–71.

INTERNET RESOURCES

Budget and financial information:
http://ec.europa.eu/budget/index_en.cfm

Decision-making:
http://europa.eu/institutions/decision-making/index_en.htm

ECJ and legal institutions:
http://curia.europa.eu/

The EU institutions:
http://europa.eu/institutions/index_en.htm

The Lisbon Treaty and fact sheets:
http://europa.eu/lisbon_treaty/full_text/index_en.htm
http://www.robert-schuman.eu/doc/divers/lisbonne/en/10fiches.pdf

Portal to EU law:
http://ec.europa.eu/budget/index_en.cfm

Regional policy, structural and cohesion fund:
http://ec.europa.eu/regional_policy/index_en.htm

Gabriele Suder's *Doing Business in Europe* video series (on the SAGE companion website at http://www.sagepub.co.uk/suder2e and YouTube)

Notes

1 For convenience, we will continue to abbreviate the Commission as CEC in this book.
2 Until 2014, the Council must use qualified majority voting, meeting the conditions of a majority of Member States approving (in some cases a two-thirds majority) and a minimum of 255 votes in favour of a proposal out of a total of 345 votes. In the transition period between November 2014 and March 2017, Member States can ask for the former weighted voting system to be applied, instead of the new double majority system.

Bibliography

Deards, E. and Hargreaves, S. (2004) *European Union Law Textbook*. Oxford: Oxford University Press.
Dinan, D. (2006) *Origins and Evolution of the European Union*, New European Union Series. Oxford: Oxford University Press.

European Communities (1951) *Treaty Establishing the European Coal and Steel Community* (ECSC Treaty, or the Treaty of Paris). Available at: http://europa.eu.int/abc/obj/treaties/en/entoc29.htm

European Communities (1957a) *Treaty Establishing the European Economic Community* (EEC Treaty, or Treaty of Rome). Available at: http://europa.eu.int/abc/obj/treaties/en/entoc05.htm

European Communities (1957b) *Treaty Establishing the European Atomic Energy Community* (Euratom Treaty). Available at: http://europa.eu.int/abc/obj/treaties/en/entoc38.htm

European Communities (1967) *Treaty Establishing a Single Council and a Single Commission of the European Communities* (Merger Treaty of 1965). Available at: http://europa.eu.int/abc/obj/treaties/

European Communities (1987) *Single European Act*. Available at: http://europa.eu.int/eur-lex/en/treaties/ selected/livre509.html

European Communities (1992) *Treaty on European Union* (Maastricht Treaty) [1992] OJ C191/1. Available at: http://europa.eu.int/eur-lex/en/treaties/dat/EU_treaty.html

European Communities (1997a) *The Treaty of Amsterdam* [1997] OJ C340/1. Available at: http://europa.eu. int/eur-lex/lex/en/treaties/treaties_other.htm, with [1997] OJ C340/145.

European Communities (1997b) *Treaty Establishing the European Community* [1997] OJ C340/173–308.

European Communities (2001) Treaty of Nice Amending the Treaty on European Union (Treaties Establishing the European Communities and Certain Related Acts). *Official Journal* C 80, 10 March.

European Communities (2004a) Commission Recommendation, 2004H0345, Communication from the Commission concerning the Commission recommendation of 21 October 2003 on enforcement in the field of road safety (OJ C93, 17 April 2004).

European Communities (2004b) Commission Decision of 18 February 2004 establishing a model health certificate for non-commercial movements from third countries of dogs, cats and ferrets (notified under document number C(2004)432-2004/203/EC).

European Communities (2004c) Council Regulation (EC) 1590/2004, Community programme on the conservation, characterisation, collection and utilisation of genetic resources in agriculture and repealing Regulation (EC) 1467/74. *Official Journal of the European Union*, 30 September.

European Communities (2004d) COM(2004)636 on 6 October 2004, *Deployment and operational phases of the European satellite radio-navigation programme in many detailed issues*. Available at: http://europa.eu.int/eur-lex/pri/en/dpi/cnc/doc/2004/com2004_0636en01.doc

European Communities (2004e) Judgment of the Court (Second Chamber) of 7 October 2004, *Sintesi SpA versus Autorità per la Vigilanza sui Lavori Pubblici, in reference to a preliminary ruling of the Tribunale amministrativo regionale per la Lombardia in*

Italy, the Directive 93/37/EEC on Public works contracts and awards of contracts (Case C-247/02). Available at: http://europa.eu.int/eur-lex/

European Communities (2004f) White Paper on the review of Regulation 4056/86, applying the EC competition rules to maritime transport, 13 October.

European Communities (2004g) Commission to the council and to the European Parliament on the Commission Decisions of 20 October 2004 concerning national allocation plans for the allocation of greenhouse gas emission allowances of Belgium, Estonia, Finland, France, Latvia, Luxembourg, Portugal, and the Slovak Republic in accordance with Directive 2003/87/EC.

European Communities (2004h) *Treaty Establishing a Constitution for Europe.* Available at: http://europe.eu. int/constitution/index_en.htm

European Communities (2005) Commission Regulation (EC) 1408/2004 (Council Regulation [EC] 692/2005 of 28 April 2005).

Frank, M. (2009) *A Rose by Any Other Method.* Available at: http://www.winespectator. com/webfeatures/show/id/A-Rose-by-Any-Other-Method_4663. Accessed 17 March 2011.

Pop, V. (2009) Europeans see corruption in private sector as economic crisis hits. *Valentina Pop*, 3 June. Available at: http://www.Euobserver.com.

Suder, G. (1994) *Anti-Dumping Measures and the Politics of EU–Japan Trade Relations in the European Consumer Electronics Sector: The VCR Case*. Bath: University of Bath School of Management.

Van Schendelen, R. (2002) *Machiavelli in Brussels: The Art of Lobbying the EU*. Amsterdam: Amsterdam University Press.

PART II

BUSINESS EUROPEANIZATION

5

The Europeanization of a Business Environment

What you will learn about in this chapter:

- The evolution of the European market observed through the lens of theory.
- European sector dynamics and related EU issues.
- Competition, competitiveness and competivity: what does it mean for Europe?
- The main common business-related policies and their impact on business.

5.0 Introduction

This chapter sheds light on the European business environment as a whole. For the most part, this business environment is made up of a multitude of countries. They share many of the rules and policies across the EU, EFTA, the EEA and regional clusters. Most of geographical Europe is covered by the EU and its partners. Internally, the creation of a single market allows for ever-widening and deepening networks of infrastructures and opportunities for corporate activity. However, this network also represents challenges. Can firms consider an entire market grouping as their home market? This chapter reviews some of the most important international trade theory related to this issue. It examines, in particular, the elements and contexts that are common to this vast business environment, and focuses on the policies that managers in Europe need to be familiar with.

The European business environment has been subject to rapid transformation ever since the mid 1990s when the Single Market became a reality. The introduction of a common currency in 1999, the extension of the Single European Act rules (SEA, see Chapter 2) to new areas such as e-commerce, and the ongoing trend towards supranational business taxation regulations are developments that have largely contributed to the construction of an increasingly harmonized business environment.

Developments towards a single market led to the diversification of firm structures. More and more *multinationals* have become European transnational companies that compete worldwide, from a sound, vast home market. *SMEs* increasingly operate on a European scale (as micro-multinationals) and are locally, nationally and internationally exposed to large-scale competition.

European integration has boosted the pace of economic developments throughout Europe and its neighbouring countries. Similarly to globalization, Europeanization compresses time and space. To understand this better, consider the following example: during the cold war era, it was difficult, if not virtually impossible, to export goods, services or capital from Western Europe (which was already integrating), to certain Eastern and Central European countries (which were politically, logistically and culturally oppressed under the Soviet system). Following developments during the 1990s and the EU enlargements, Member States have become ever closer, both politically and culturally. Logistically, improved infrastructures as well as virtual and real means of transport seem to have reduced distances and the time taken to cover them. Market harmonization rules apply to all actors within the Single Market, resulting in a permanent race for competitiveness while respecting the social values pursued by most European peoples.

A cartography of the European business environment and its networks would ideally also represent relative economic power, distribution of income, capital, labour, entrepreneurship, knowledge and corporate risk. Most of these are difficult

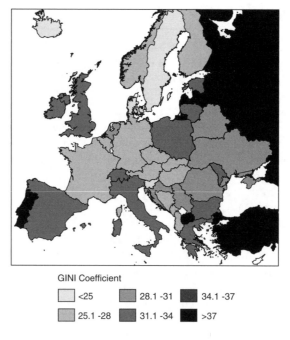

GINI Coefficient

<25	
25.1 -28	
28.1 -31	
31.1 -34	
34.1 -37	
>37	

Figure 5.1   *GINI index for Europe*

Source: http://dev.null.org/blog/item/200904210031_ginieuroa

to represent, given that the cartographer is situated in a particular time and location – both of which, as stated above, evolve ever more quickly.

One example for such cartography is that of income inequality: the GINI coefficient (see Figure 5.1) is one of the most commonly used measures of inequality. The coefficient varies between 0 (reflecting complete equality) and 1 (reflecting complete inequality), i.e. one person has all the income while all others have none. As shown above, the general pattern appears to be an equitable core comprised of Scandinavia, Germany, France and Central Europe. There appears to be greater inequality approaching the Anglophone, Mediterranean and Slavic countries. Turkey has the highest GINI core at –43.6.

5.1 The main impacts of Europeanization

The opening up of business opportunities is accompanied by rising competition within markets. Some of today's European markets were entirely inaccessible (or difficult to access) in the past. Examples are the deep-seated past animosity that historically opposed Germany and France (see Chapter 2), or inaccessibility due to oppression by another country such as in Eastern Europe (see Chapter 3).

In addition to ever-more market access, corporations benefit from inherently lower costs of doing business in an integrated market. These effects are mainly based on economic and political integration automatisms. The resulting business environment helps save costs, thanks to:

- the integration of major, mainly economic, decision-making at EU level;
- the widening and strengthening of the Single Market;
- an evolving form of federalism through monetary unification;
- common policies;
- an intensification of competition;
- liberalization and deregulation;
- the free movement of labour, goods, services and capital;
- the removal of barriers to entry and to trade, for production and investment;
- harmonized norms, standards and legal frameworks;
- simplified tax regimes.

Consequently, it is possible to obtain significant cost economies in the Single Market if the mix of factor costs and skills is optimal. The resulting *trade creation* is the main positive outcome of freer and more integrated trade; it also delivers lower prices for consumers within the EU. Nevertheless, the impact of integration with regard to *trade diversion and reinforced competition* is negative. The basis of these Europeanization principles lies in the internationalization of firms; international trade theory deals with this issue.

5.2 The ideological background

The ideology behind the Europeanization of the business environment in Member States is based on globalization and free market concepts that were prevalent in the 1990s. The internationalization of capital markets, technological advances, products and people's way of life accelerated globalization across the world, and marked the evolution of trade groupings.

5.2.1 The main international trade and business theories

Among the leading classical economic and international trade theories (see Figure 5.2), we find that those of Adam Smith and David Ricardo, as well as those of Heckscher-Ohlin, explain the importance of business operations that reach across frontiers. *Mercantilism*, a theory developed at the very beginning of international business and colonial commerce, states that a country shall best run a balance-of-trade surplus, in a zero-sum game towards other countries. The theory calls rather for government intervention in the interests of each trading nation.

In *The Wealth of Nations* (1776), Adam Smith looked deeper into the reasons why trade exists between countries. To summarize, he put forward the theory that any given country has an *absolute advantage* in the efficient production of goods; other goods should therefore be imported. David Ricardo then expanded this theory to that of *comparative advantage*, explaining that within this framework imports may also include goods that could be produced, though less efficiently, in the domestic market. In this manner, free trade without restrictions on the basis of comparative advantage is to turn trade into a positive-sum game that obtains higher-world production levels.

The theories of Smith and Ricardo were reinforced by the Heckscher-Ohlin model that analyses international trade patterns based on *factor endowment*. This model indicates that those goods that are imported or exported are defined on the basis of local resource levels. The factors studied in this theory are labour and capital. In short, a country that is relatively labour-abundant should specialize in the production and export of that product which is relatively labour-intensive; the same would apply for capital. Hence, this demonstrates why certain countries specialize in certain goods and not others, as a reinforcement of the theory of comparative advantage. However, the theory in itself does not explain the phenomenon completely. For example, some countries have minimum wage laws that result in high prices for relatively abundant labour. The *Leontief paradox* using this framework demonstrated that countries like the USA in the post-war period actually exported relatively more labour-intensive goods and imported capital-intensive goods. A more and more nuanced approach to cross-border trade is therefore necessary. Linder, amongst others, has engaged in research into these nuances; his resulting *Overlapping Product Ranges Theory* holds that trade in manufactured goods is dictated not only by cost concerns, but by a similarity in

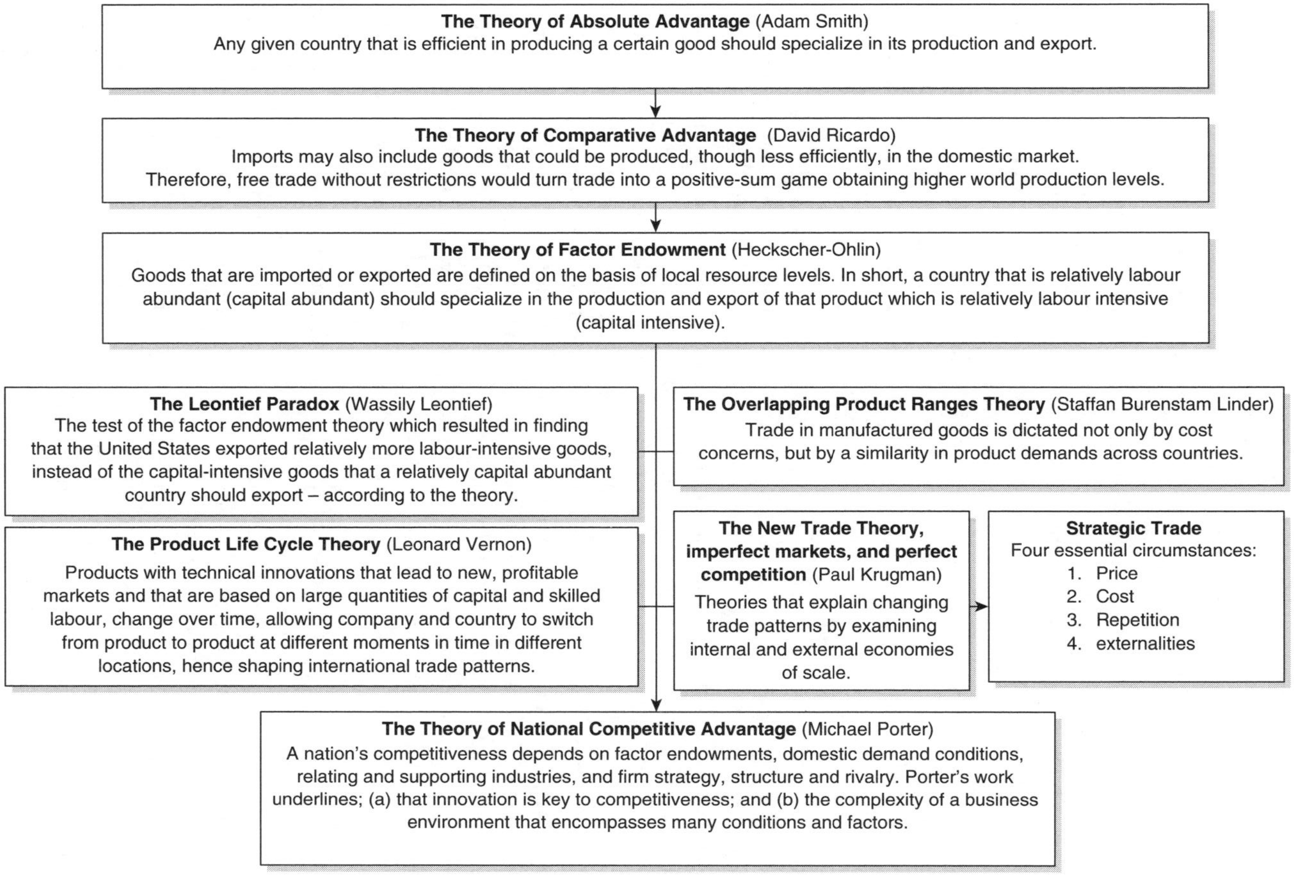
The Theory of Absolute Advantage (Adam Smith)
Any given country that is efficient in producing a certain good should specialize in its production and export.
The Theory of Comparative Advantage (David Ricardo)
Imports may also include goods that could be produced, though less efficiently, in the domestic market. Therefore, free trade without restrictions would turn trade into a positive-sum game obtaining higher world production levels.
The Theory of Factor Endowment (Heckscher-Ohlin)
Goods that are imported or exported are defined on the basis of local resource levels. In short, a country that is relatively labour abundant (capital abundant) should specialize in the production and export of that product which is relatively labour intensive (capital intensive).
The Leontief Paradox (Wassily Leontief)
The test of the factor endowment theory which resulted in finding that the United States exported relatively more labour-intensive goods, instead of the capital-intensive goods that a relatively capital abundant country should export – according to the theory.
The Overlapping Product Ranges Theory (Staffan Burenstam Linder)
Trade in manufactured goods is dictated not only by cost concerns, but by a similarity in product demands across countries.
The Product Life Cycle Theory (Leonard Vernon)
Products with technical innovations that lead to new, profitable markets and that are based on large quantities of capital and skilled labour, change over time, allowing company and country to switch from product to product at different moments in time in different locations, hence shaping international trade patterns.
The New Trade Theory, imperfect markets, and perfect competition (Paul Krugman)
Theories that explain changing trade patterns by examining internal and external economies of scale.
Strategic Trade
Four essential circumstances:
1. Price
2. Cost
3. Repetition
4. externalities
The Theory of National Competitive Advantage (Michael Porter)
A nation's competitiveness depends on factor endowments, domestic demand conditions, relating and supporting industries, and firm strategy, structure and rivalry. Porter's work underlines; (a) that innovation is key to competitiveness; and (b) the complexity of a business environment that encompasses many conditions and factors.

Figure 5.2 *The evolution of Trade Theory*

product demands across countries. This theory therefore centres around preferences of consumer demand. Today, we speak of market segments.

In addition, an essential question about the timing of import and export needs
to be answered: When is it the right time to engage in trade across borders?
Raymond Vernon's *Product Life Cycle* theory was a first valiant attempt to respond
to this question. The theory suggests that products with technical innovations that
lead to new, profitable markets and that are based on large quantities of capital and
skilled labour, go through different phases. These begin with introduction,
through maturity to standardization, allowing company and country to switch
from product to product at different moments in time in different locations, hence
shaping international trade patterns. The complexity of today's operations and
productions, and the importance of the service economy limit the importance of
this approach in the current understanding of international trade and business. It
is worth noting that the theory mainly still holds for technologically based mass
production merchandise.

In the 1970s, the *New Trade Theory* was developed. This held that when a
country produces specialized products, economies of scale and low production
costs can be achieved by exporting across borders. This results in relatively
cheaper goods as well as more consumer choice. Paul Krugman and Anthony
Venables (Krugman and Venables, 1995), among other leading thinkers, contributed to the modern understanding of cross-border trade through an examination of internal and external economies of scale that are developed from
microeconomics and market structure analysis and that result from *imperfections*
of the larger market. He notes, for example, the beneficial role that government
can play, and expands the study of the political economy. The theory is based on
the understanding that firms' output is differentiated and that market conditions
and outputs are heterogeneous (in real or imaginary ways). This stands in opposition to *perfect competition* in which these are interpreted as homogeneous, that
is, very similar or equal. The works of Hymer and others explore these imperfections in detail.

The resulting *strategic trade* extracts four essential circumstances in which strategic
trade may apply: price, cost, repetition and externalities. Nevertheless, this thinking
is challenged by the trends that may incline governments to turn to protectionism
and incline companies to seek this protection for themselves, even though this may
result in retaliation from trade partners.

In the EU, the free movement of goods, services, labour and capital and market
integration have been established to allow for cost economies by centralizing production in locations with particular factor wealth and specialization of particular
resources, whether these be raw materials, supplies, human or capital resources,
knowledge or cultural factors. The New Trade Theory also explores the predominance of first movers and oligopolies (industries comprising a limited number of
large firms, for example European Aerospace or the petroleum industry), and of
government intervention by means of subsidies.

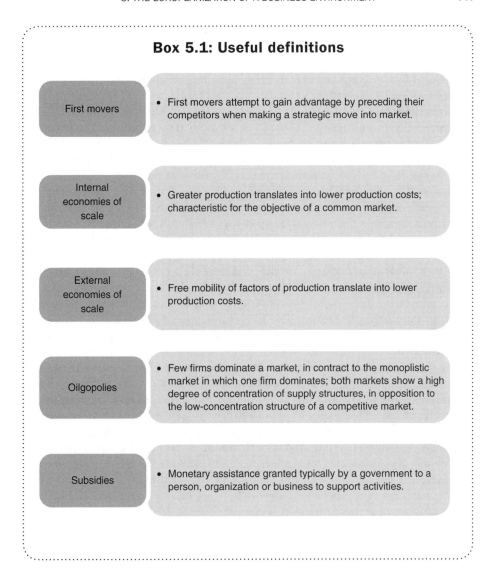

Box 5.1: Useful definitions

First movers
- First movers attempt to gain advantage by preceding their competitors when making a strategic move into market.

Internal economies of scale
- Greater production translates into lower production costs; characteristic for the objective of a common market.

External economies of scale
- Free mobility of factors of production translate into lower production costs.

Oilgopolies
- Few firms dominate a market, in contract to the monoplistic market in which one firm dominates; both markets show a high degree of concentration of supply structures, in opposition to the low-concentration structure of a competitive market.

Subsidies
- Monetary assistance granted typically by a government to a person, organization or business to support activities.

F.T. Knickerbocker (1973) suggested that the imitative behaviour found in oligopolies can also be observed in the investments of equity funds abroad and in general in FDI. This is often referred to as herd behaviour. In an extension of the theory, it becomes clear that international firms compete in a complex environment like a network of intertwined linkages. They compete at different locations and times and in different industries and markets. In Europe, the increasing competition in Europeanization efforts has led to MNE strategies that favour market share increase through the use of mergers, acquisitions and alliances, or operations through FDI, rather than simple import and export activities. Knickerbocker's theory can hence also help understand the streamlining of, for example, the European mobile telecom industry and other sectors that compete across the Single Market. Let us mention here that, in Europe, joint ventures are rarely used as a means of market entry because of the low level of uncertainty.

Michael Porter's (1990) theory of *national competitive advantage* is very helpful to understand the main attributes of trade of a nation that encompass the so-called 'diamond' of factor endowments: domestic demand conditions, relating and supporting industries and firm strategy, structure and rivalry. Porter's work underlines: (a) that innovation is key to competitiveness; and (b) the complexity of a business environment that encompasses many conditions and factors. Porter adds that competitive clusters form in fields that constitute cutting-edge, highly successful markets. These locate in a concentrated manner to gain the advantages of stimulating network effects in both the corporate and the public environment, and in particular in knowledge transfer. You will find examples of relevant clusters in Europe in the R&D science park of Sophia-Antipolis or the Canceropole in Toulouse in France, the technology park in Brno in the Czech Republic, the Cambridge Avlar Cluster which focuses on biotech and venture capital in the UK, the Austrian bioenergy cluster or InternetBay in Sweden. The European Cluster Alliance and the European Cluster Observatory are part of the EU's support mechanisms for innovation-related business activity.

The writings that constitute international trade theory have helped substantially, not only in understanding the phenomenon but also in structuring corporate and governmental thinking about the opportunities and threats of trade across borders. In Europe, mainstream thought has gradually driven deep and broad market integration. The *Theory of International Investment* reinforces the above concepts, in that companies are considered to be making a significant investment and hence contribution to the host economy when they produce in another country. This move is dependent on the mobility of capital at the international level. If the firm invests directly across borders, production, organization, resources management and knowledge management become increasingly complex. The firm will seek advantages from this diversification of opportunities in resources, factors, knowledge, security and markets. It will strive to profit from access opportunities that may otherwise be difficult (for example, because of import restrictions), from factor mobility and from management imperfections such as managerial or marketing techniques or financial resources. In addition to this, the theory holds that companies will be able to internalize, that is, keep in their possession non-transferable sources of advantage such as trade secrets or other specific expertise.

Successful trade and investment in Europe is dependent on adaptable approaches of how to weigh options and exploit opportunities. The European business environment demands *careful market segmentation and sound internationalization strategy*. It benefits to an important degree from the advantages that trade theories stipulate, and also defines the resulting challenges, depending on sector, production stage and location. Various studies shed light on the effects of market integration using the arguments of trade theory. These studies confirm that business in Europe remains complex despite the elimination of duties and the progressive harmonization of technical and safety standards, administrative barriers and local fragmentations.

Major studies into market integration effects in Europe demonstrate that firm size and market size are interrelated in that *industries tend to consolidate and get bigger when markets enlarge and competition grows*. It was found that corporations are exposed to an adjustment phase, because integration leads to profit losses through shifting factor advantages, conditions and price decreases. These losses may be short term because, increasingly, less competitive firms fall while prices rise, mergers and alliances flourish and consolidation takes place. The faster industry adapts, the less loss it has to bear. *The more familiar non-European corporations are with these business realities when targeting Europe, the better they adapt.*

For example, the consolidation of the IT industry in Eastern Europe between 2008 and 2010 had significant implications for Russian business interests in the CEE markets engaging in acquisition activity across the region and further eastwards. EU firms have become careful in their IT outsourcing, making sure that despite consolidations, these outsourcings continue to yield savings from less overheated (and thus less over-demanding) labour markets.

What do we learn from these theories? For both European and non-European firms, doing business in Europe engages management in strategic decisions, primarily those of location and market entry. As we learned in earlier chapters, the fact that most of Europe is part of free trade agreements, a customs union and the EU's Single Market, location and market entry decisions can focus on a wide range of options and will be based on market imperfections. (Internet support for this textbook provides a guide to the Member States and their business environments one by one.)

These decisions are underpinned by international trade theory. Location decisions clearly reflect the discussed concepts of international trade theory when it comes to the specific evaluation of corporate and market specialization, resources, factor endowments and economies of scale objectives. Corporate strategies in terms of first movers may be influenced by those considerations too. Also, government policy is greatly influenced by economic theory. In the defragmentation of the European market and the consolidation of competition for scale economies and profit sustainability, governmental policy may be seduced by state aid and subsidy solutions to counterbalance the social costs of lay-offs and inefficiency. Trade barriers that are based on some of the theories mentioned above, act as impediments to corporations' ability to internationalize; other examples of resulting protectionist policies can be intervention through infant industry protection, local content requirements, voluntary export restraints or anti-dumping duties. This is where common European policies have a role to play in restricting anti-competitive practices.

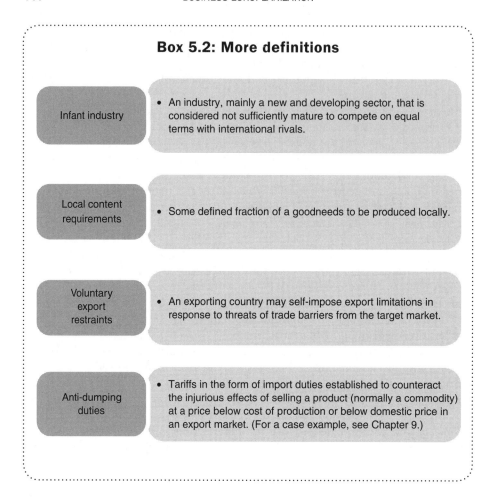

Box 5.2: More definitions

Infant industry
- An industry, mainly a new and developing sector, that is considered not sufficiently mature to compete on equal terms with international rivals.

Local content requirements
- Some defined fraction of a goodneeds to be produced locally.

Voluntary export restraints
- An exporting country may self-impose export limitations in response to threats of trade barriers from the target market.

Anti-dumping duties
- Tariffs in the form of import duties established to counteract the injurious effects of selling a product (normally a commodity) at a price below cost of production or below domestic price in an export market. (For a case example, see Chapter 9.)

Fair trade principles are the objective of common policies such as the common commercial policy towards non-EU states, for the sake of economic cohesion. Curative measures are applied punctually, and are ad hoc interventions depending on functionality and need. While, politically, some European states have yet to structure sound governance adapted to Europeanization, corporations have taken the lead in this challenge. Corporate Germany leads the world in export figures (overtaken only by China) and Italy owes a rise in employment figures to its Biagi law, which loosens labour regulations; in France, the CAC-40 indexed companies broke records in profit generation and Bulgaria shows record growth rates.

As shown in Table 5.1 and Figure 5.3, both Italy (an EU, Schengen and euro-zone member) and the United Kingdom (an EU member) demonstrate a steady increase in total employment up until 2009, although Italy's yearly employment increase shows greater strength. The global economic crisis hit the UK economy and its labour market hard, resulting in a higher unemployment rate than in many other EU countries.

Table 5.1   A comparison of the evolution of employment in Italy and the UK

| Year | Italy | | United Kingdom | |
	Total Employment	% Change	Total Employment	% Change
2000	21,225,000		27,166,000	
2001	21,634,000	1.93%	27,408,000	0.92%
2002	21,922,000	1.33%	27,557,000	0.54%
2003	22,134,000	0.97%	27,820,000	0.95%
2004	22,404,000	1.22%	28,008,000	0.68%
2005	22,562,000	0.71%	28,665,400	2.35%
2006	22,988,000	1.89%	28,926,300	0.91%
2007	23,222,000	1.02%	29,094,900	0.58%
2008	23,405,000	0.79%	29,443,600	1.20%
2009	23,025,000	−1.62%	28,832,200	−2.07%

Source: http://stats.oecd.org/Index.aspx?DatasetCode=ALFS_SUMTAB

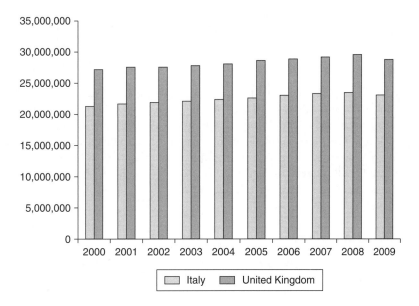

Figure 5.3   *Employment: is Europeanization good for the job market?*

In 2009, China officially overtook Germany and became the world's leading exporter. Germany had held the title of global export leader since 2003 when it surpassed the USA. China's exports recovered more rapidly than most countries' exports in 2010, partially due to the low value of China's currency (renminbi), which keeps Chinese goods relatively inexpensive in foreign markets. Amongst European economies, the German economy remains the most dynamic in this sense (see Figure 5.4).

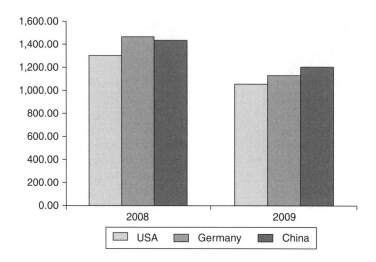

Figure 5.4 *World export leaders (USA, Germany, China) (billion euros)*

Source: Compiled sources (www.destatis.de/jetspeed/portal/cms/Sites/destatis/Internet/EN/Content/Statistics/
Internationales/InternationalStatistics/Topic/Tables/BasicData__Export,templateId=renderPrint.psml#AnkerAsia,
OECD)

Figures 5.5 to 5.8 illustrate that Bulgaria can be considered to be a rapidly advancing nation in Europe, as demonstrated by the graphs shown above. Its geographical location in the far east of the European Union offers great employment opportunities. Bulgaria is utilizing considerable infrastructure and general expertise available within the EU to enhance its own economic development at all levels. However, as was the case for all other countries, Bulgaria too experienced a hit during the economic crisis, resulting in a decrease in all sectors.

5.2.2 Business realities

Corporate Europe (that is, business entities and industries in Europe) has the opportunity to move to international markets from a home base of the one single market. Economic cohesion creates an inherent and incremental advantage that lies in Europeanization. In this context, international trade theory takes on its full sense.

We need to study this theory just one step further for yet more insight into European complexities: the so-called market imperfection theories (internalization theories) stipulate that corporations favour FDI above export or licensing strategies because of market impediments. The Europeanization of business is driven by internalization: within the market, these impediments may be trade or tariff barriers or cultural or administrative hurdles. They result in costs or benefits or advantages and disadvantages that vary from one market to the other.

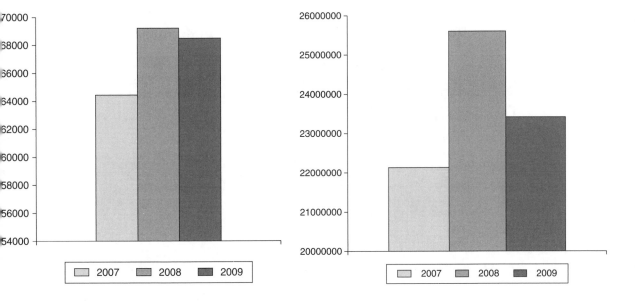

Figure 5.5   *GDP production (in million levls)*   Figure 5.6   *GDP by income*

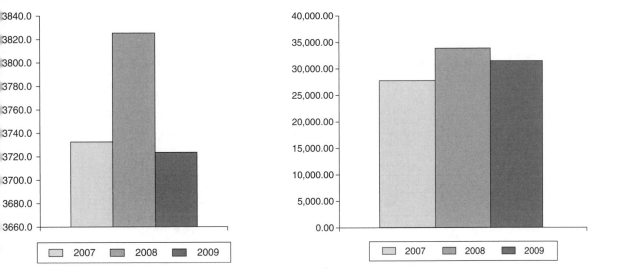

Figures 5.7   *Employment (in thousands)*   Figure 5.8   *Annual gross income*

Box 5.3: Foreign direct investment directions

Horizontal	• Equity funds invested across borders in the same branch of activity. Typically this is motivated by cost and market-access considerations.
Vertical	• Equity funds invested across borders with product stages in different locations, providing inputs (backward) or outputs (forward) for the domestic production process. Typically this is motivated by the fragmentation of production and relative factor costs.

Because of this, horizontal FDI (FDI in the same industry of a given company) is of particular interest when market imperfections, transaction costs, location advantages and/or life-cycle serve to decrease the efficiency of less risky modes of international business such as exporting or licensing. Attracted by market similarities and relatively low risk factors among Member States, companies in Europe use the entire range of internationalization strategies, including horizontal and vertical FDI (that is, providing input or output for a firm's operations), that may take different forms according to the degree of investments to be made and risk involved.

Box 5.4: Strategic choices for Europeanization

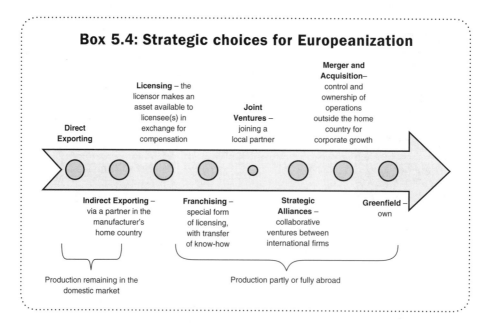

One substantial advantage for firms in terms of subsequent internationalization outside Europe is that their experience curve is at its peak. This is because cross-border trade has become a continuous business reality in Europe. *The Europeanized firm is hence an instrument that allows countries and organizations to locate production, services, capital, knowledge and distribution effectively.* It enters into a resource transfer that benefits both 'emitter' and 'receptor' of goods, services and capital (see Figure 5.9). However, the Europeanized company might be less experienced than others in the entry modes used in high-uncertainty markets, including joint venturing.

The theoretical and ideological underpinning that we discussed above has succeeded, accelerating Europeanization. For example, the UK is one of the Member States most open to FDI, but it also intervenes when it comes to national interests. Most European countries are rather pragmatic when it comes to the costs and benefits of free trade. The import of skills, capital, technology and know-how, as well as employment, is appreciated and can drive the wealth of an economy, for example that of Ireland. Some Member States actively attract FDI through policies such as tax breaks and grants. Investment incentives may also encompass reduced land prices, infrastructure advantages or personnel training support.

However, it is important to note that there are dangers in Europeanization. Profits from investments may leave the host country and regions. Supplies may come from abroad and basic or traditional knowledge can be lost (see the mini case study in this chapter); operations may turn into assembly only. Factor mobility does not benefit each country in the integrated market. Therefore, bargaining for greater benefits

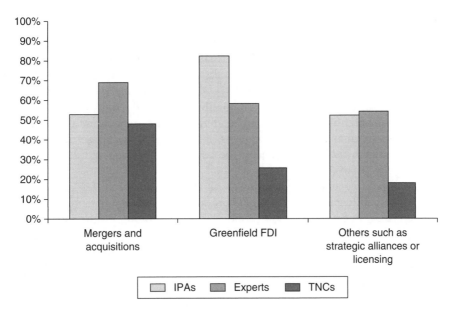

Figure 5.9 *Expected modes of global investment 2005–6 (per cent of responses)*
Source: UNCTAD, 2005

(rather than costs) leads general European policies to encourage FDI, and for country of origin rules to preserve a certain amount of local identity.

Box 5.5: Country of origin rules

Country of origin rules refer to the criteria needed to determine the national source of a product. These rules are of particular importance because they determine duties and restrictions that depend upon the source of imports. Governments vary in terms of criteria: some governments apply the criterion of change of tariff classification, others apply ad valorem percentage criteria, and still others use the criterion of manufacturing or processing operation. For example, the EU rules of origin for cotton clothing stipulate that the manufacturing process must 'manufacture from yarn', implying that imported cotton fabric cannot be used and that the yarn must be sourced locally. US rules of origin are more restrictive: a change of tariff heading defines the determination of imported cotton fabric, imported yarn and imported cotton thread. The rule requires that the production of cotton thread, spinning this into yarn, weaving the yarn into fabric, and the cutting and making up of fabric into clothing must all be undertaken locally. In 2011, the CEC launched new rules of origin, more favourable then ever for developing countries and a new procedure for demonstrating proof of origin: the responsibility of operators will be enhanced and, from 2017, the certification of origin system for third country authorities will focus on statements of origin issued directly by exporters (registered via an electronic system).

According to the above theories, adequate competition from inside and outside allows markets to function efficiently, in that more competitors will drive prices down, thereby increasing consumer welfare and choice. Once again, following theory, competitors will *invest more in R&D, personnel training, knowledge and equipment transfer*, to win the race for competitiveness, productivity and innovation (remember Chapter 3). In this scenario, complementary product and service industries flourish simultaneously. Nevertheless, this does not tackle all the challenges: increasingly, much thought is given to the issues of offshoring and outsourcing in Europe (see Box 5.6).

The European general public tends to look at these issues with fear of unemployment and loss of identity. When specific products, close to a population's heart, are produced elsewhere, protests of some kind are not uncommon. For example, in 2011, Prada announced their intention to produce a 'Made in' series, collaborating with different artisans to produce their designs utilizing the traditional craftsmanship, materials and manufacturing techniques of specific regions. Products would include items such as kilts from Scotland and alpaca knitware from Peru. Consumers were troubled that the move would dilute the quality of the brand and voiced their negative opinions online.

Box 5.6: Offshoring, out- and insourcing

Offshoring: undertaking FDI to serve the domestic market, that is, relocating a service, like a hotline or any other service that can be carried out remotely from a foreign location. Control of the company remains with the company owner although the activity is carried out in another country. Local employment legislation covering salary or advantages applies. European offshoring focuses mainly on Eastern or Far East countries as well as the Maghreb countries. For example, France Telecom's 'hotlines' are located in Morocco.

Outsourcing: external acquisition and purchase of services or products that were previously produced in-house. That is, subcontracting part of the service or the business to an external company. In some industries, outsourcing is either a company strategy or a necessity because the company does not have the required resource internally. In the pharmaceutical industry, those companies are referred to as contract research organizations (CROs), and they undertake all or part of the R&D process.

Insourcing: where operations or activities within a business are channelled to a specific internal entity that specializes in that operation, often in another country than the headquarters. This is used in production to reduce the cost of taxes, labour, transportation, etc. and in R&D to preserve knowledge.

Offshoring and outsourcing bring several advantages. According to liberal economic theory, when offshore production serves the domestic market, it frees up resources so that a country can focus on sectors of activity that generate comparative advantage. Prices from offshore production are relatively lower than those from domestic production. Companies remain competitive vis-à-vis their international competition which also uses offshoring. Based on this theory, the negative effects on employment are outweighed by the long-term benefits to both companies and consumers (see also the discussion on subcontracting for SMEs in Chapter 3).

This is indeed a weak argument for the employee who loses his job because of offshoring or outsourcing. For the corporation and the economy as a whole, the phenomenon is underpinned by theory. Issues of location are therefore ever closer to the consumer and the labour market. Such issues map out the pattern of Europeanization.

5.3 Choosing a location

Choosing a location implies that a firm opts to seek direct or indirect gains. The theories established by Vernon (1979), Dunning (1989) and many others help to understand what drives a firm to become international or transnational, with different degrees of host economy integration and linkages across borders (definitions of the terms 'international' and 'transnational' in international business were provided in Chapter 1).

5.3.1 Determining your cross-border location

Locations and modes of internationalization are defined by corporate management (see, for an example, the Schunk case study in the latter part of this textbook). This takes place on the basis of the particular advantages that the firm gains from operations that reach beyond the national market. These are outlined in Dunning's (1989) leading work on internationalization on a global scale, which he called the eclectic paradigm consisting of the so-called OLI advantages (Box 5.7). *The main benefits of going European in terms of market scale and operations depend on the degree to which a firm remains owner of its resources and the internalization that it may benefit from.*

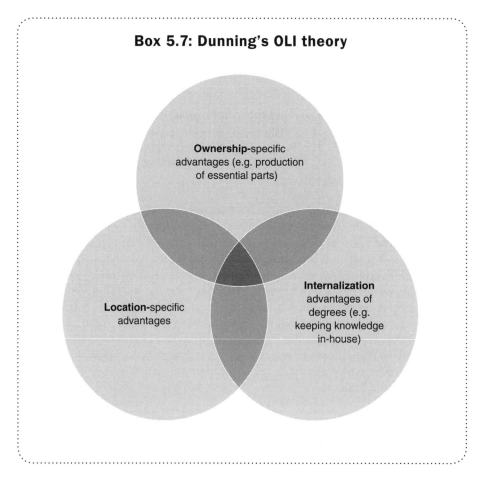

Box 5.7: Dunning's OLI theory

Ownership-specific advantages (e.g. production of essential parts)

Location-specific advantages

Internalization advantages of degrees (e.g. keeping knowledge in-house)

These advantages differ on local, regional, national and global scales, depending on company criteria (nature, organization, sector of activity). Choosing a European, cross-frontier location is therefore a crucial decision and – in some cases – an important first experience for a company in its internationalization process.

Location decisions are related to either offensive or defensive strategies (Howell, 2001; see also Bouchet, 2005: 445). *Offensive internationalization* means that a firm will move faster than its competitors and anticipate market developments on the basis of strong marketing and finances. This is the case, for example, for firms that invest in candidate countries before their definitive accession to the EU. On the contrary, *defensive internationalization* is conducted to preserve market share and competitive advantage in response to other players in the same or in a supplementary market. This strategy is different in terms of its timing because it is conducted at a later stage than offensive internationalization. It may require supplementary efforts to succeed in a complex environment that is already dominated by competitors: differentiation and knowledge of the terrain are essential requirements; one option is to reinforce local product or service adaptation, for example in McDonald's decision to sell salads in its French fast-food restaurants. The chain is the market leader in France despite fierce competition from national and international players in that market (Quick, Kentucky Fried Chicken, etc.).

Cross-border development may be a first move for the firm, or it may be part of an established strategy, and add to or change a location of earlier internationalization stages. Decisions are made on the basis of existing alternatives, and are often based on previous experience or an arising opportunity. In particular in European SMEs, first cross-border locations are determined more by 'knowing people' or 'following another firm's example' than by rigorous market research, given that uncertainties are reduced thanks to certain market harmonization effects of economic integration.

While gains and losses are intrinsic to any business operation, choosing the right international location is the best solution to obtain competitive advantage. The main advantages gained from successful internationalization are:

- optimization or reduction of costs; and/or
- creation of new opportunities for growth; and/or
- development of new strategic strengths.

For this, the firm screens its environment. In the EU, this environment can offer important advantages along the international value chain, that is, the path that links primary and support activities for providing goods and services. This value chain covers all stages that lead from procurement up to order fulfilment (see Chapter 3). No matter whether the location decision is primarily based on market research or opportunism, the value chain is key to the appreciation of a business environment and influences all aspects of management, reaching from human resources management to marketing and sales orientations.

In operational terms, corporate executives generally use four main criteria for location decisions:

1 Operational.
2 Financial.
3 Local.
4 Risk.

The *operational* criterion deals with all aspects relating to operational activities, that is, the quality of transport, logistic and telecommunications infrastructure; the level of local labour skills and education, and their availability; and the proximity of a target market (competition). The quality of operational resources is seen as more important than the potential of target markets. The *financial* criterion directly concerns the finances of the company and its management of revenue. In particular, it concerns not only potential gains in productivity, tax burdens and the cost of labour, but also public aid, the proximity of financial markets, the flexibility of labour law, special treatment of foreign investments, the availability of grants and subsidies, access to financial investors and the integration of a particular monetary zone. This criterion mainly ranks second in international location decisions but remains essential, knowing that labour costs and social charges and the level of tax burden are omnipresent. The location, or *local*, criterion concerns the operating environment of the company of a given country or region and the extent to which they offer the necessary means to develop the firm: this includes the availability of sites, the cost of land and regulations, specific skills developed in the region, the availability of specific expertise, local language, values and culture, the proximity of centres of innovation and research, as well as quality of life. In addition to these criteria, the *bandwagon or herd effect* explored by Knickerbocker (1973) is illustrated by Europeanization. Competitors follow firms into emerging markets; this move is accompanied by an investment en bloc into a specific region. Chapter 3 on enlargement considered investments made by media corporations in the Eastern European Member States; this is only one example of massive en bloc investments in Europe.

The consideration of relocation or location change is often necessary when a firm needs to adapt to local externalities, research and development spill-overs, the costs of knowledge transfer and/or transport (Krugman and Venables, 1995). This scenario applies if the costs of operating in a market are greater than the returns. But a firm may also adapt its cost/return ratio by shifting to a different mode of operation with differently adapted levels of internalization.

As an example, let us examine the situation in European textiles. Italy is at the forefront of European textiles, followed closely by Portugal and Spain. In recent years, European markets have been inundated with textile products from India, which boasts 40 per cent of the world market, and China, with some categories of textile increasing by 1500 per cent a year. This huge shift of activity to Far East countries is due to several factors:

- increasing costs in Europe;
- international competition;
- resource advantages;
- very low labour costs;
- counterfeit products from some locations;
- specific illegal imports.

The escalating rise in costs in Europe has threatened some industries with disappearance, for example the above-mentioned textile industry, but also the aircraft industry or the defence sector. These owe their survival to Europe-wide consolidation, the use of highly sophisticated machinery and equipment for quality and innovation, and an adjustment in recruitment of workers and managers to those adaptable and skilled to work well in a variety of cultures and teams (we will discuss these competencies in Chapter 6). If the current generation of workers is neither very flexible nor polyvalent, then the labour associations and trade unions which represent these workers will find it increasingly difficult to retain work in Europe.

One of the most prestigious labels in the textile and clothing industry is 'Made in Italy'. It is the leading sector in the Italian economy and primarily consists of small and medium-sized companies. In fact, 95 per cent of the companies have an annual turnover of less than €2 million. The Italian fashion industry employs nearly a million people, including about 200,000 self-employed workers.

However, in this sector in Europe, more than 250,000 workers have been laid off in recent years. One additional reason for this phenomenon is that of competencies, or rather the lack of them: semi-skilled and unskilled workers have a low demand profile in many European countries. Also, while well-educated employees benefit from Europe-wide recognition of their qualifications and can become geographically mobile, unskilled labour is less fortunate. In Italy, the various employers' associations welcome the introduction of extensive and more efficient training schemes for workers. Employers, as well as the trade unions, agree that to remain competitive in the international market, labour costs must be rationalized, productivity fostered and quality further upgraded.

Although it may seem that workers in high-wage countries cannot compete with those in fast-developing, emerging market countries, steps can be taken to help industries survive. In textiles, many firms do so by focusing on luxury brands (such as Prada and Giorgio Armani in Italy), innovative products (for example, Marimekko in Finland – see case study in Part IV) and related products and services. Advances in technology for textile development are increasing exponentially through 'intelligent materials', including micro, thermo-regulator, anti-stress and perfumed fibres, bio-protective fibres, etc. Amongst innovative services, we can mention Swarovski, the luxurious Austrian crystal company, which has created an initiative called 'Create your style', enabling customers to create unique and personally inspired jewellery. This *savoir faire* is a key success factor that Europe has in its favour. In addition to this positioning, Europe also presents innovative technologies and processes for the apparel sector such as:

- 3-D body scanning and automated body measurement;
- on-screen visualization of clothes and virtual try-ons;
- 'wearable technology' and multi-functional clothing;
- industrial made-to-measure and mass customization;
- multimedia applications for fashion retailers;
- online retailing and other e-commerce solutions for the sector.

In this way, European industry remains competitive, Europeanization helps to converge competencies and standards, and low-cost clothing serves a different market.

5.3.2 Yielding benefits from market-serving, resource-seeking Europeanization

Vernon (1979) and Dunning (1993) argued that firms can leverage resources through FDI, namely with a resources-based perspective. Birkinshaw and Hood (1998) added that the strategy of transnational companies (TNCs) is as much market-serving as it is resource-seeking. TNCs reach scale economies of knowledge using knowledge management (KM) tools on a horizontal transfer of information, talent, skills and innovation across borders. These approaches thus spread across global or regional levels, and Europeanized companies often constitute TNCs to yield benefit from market integration strategy.

The mode of entry that a firm chooses reflects the answer to a multitude of variables that are priorities for the European firm, and are relatively easy to screen in the European marketplace. Firms will pay attention to specific variables that determine their cross-border options:

- local advantages: currency, resources, market-related needs, cultures and knowledge management;
- transaction costs;
- infrastructure;
- decomposition possibilities of activities;
- company taxation;
- company law and legal issues;
- regional policies;
- sociocultural forces;
- product life cycles;
- network effects;
- government policies;
- organizational resources;
- knowledge transfer options;
- risk-diversification possibilities;
- cross-border factor mobility;
- herd or first-mover behaviour.[1]

The complete and careful screening of these variables means gathering information on a European, national and local level. At the European level, CEC databases are particularly useful and available online. In addition, Eurostat is a very complete research tool; it provides, among other data, information about all the main trade areas in Europe and their trends. At the national level, most useful are DTIs (Departments of Trade and Industry) and similar institutions, as well as trade organizations and business information services such as national and CEC representatives. Company registration offices and local legal offices may also be helpful. The environmental screening process allows the firm to evaluate the potential costs and benefits of locations. Also, operational risk can be limited if managed within a framework of diversification of sourcing and suppliers and flexibility in entry and exit strategies, on the basis of a firm-specific set of location modes. The European market allows firms to apply these diversification modes.

International trade is dominated by a high degree of cross-investment between the highly developed economies. Inward FDI into developing countries is rising because firms are aware of the importance of this knowledge for their international mapping. Emerging market MNEs (EM-MNEs) started to invest in developed markets, such as in the EU for market access and knowledge sourcing, and in underdeveloped countries, such as in Africa and South America, for resource reasons. Most non-EU firms investing in the EU are from the USA. The EU and USA are each other's main trading partners. Trade flows across the Atlantic amount to around €1.7 billion every day. Switzerland is the fourth largest trading partner in the EU. In 2008, trade figures show €80 billion in imports and €97.6 billion in exports. Further important trading areas include Turkey and, more and more, Asia and South America. The European Union and Australia share a strong economic relationship, with the EU having been Australia's largest single economic partner for more than 25 years. The EU is Australia's largest partner both in two-way trade in goods and two-way trade in services. On a balance of payment basis, which takes into account trade in goods and services, foreign investment income and transfer payments, economic activity between the EU and Australia is estimated to have exceeded $A126 billion in 2008, representing 18 per cent of all Australian overseas transactions. This figure, compared with Australia's other major economic partners (ASEAN economies 14 per cent, USA 13 per cent, Japan 12 per cent, and China 11 per cent) demonstrates that the EU remains Australia's largest economic partner by a significant margin (see Chapter 10).

European TNCs favour investment in historically close markets or in markets that are governed in special partnership with the EU; we note from the above that this is also the case vice-versa: *market groupings reduce political risk incrementally as integration improves, and the periphery of special relationships expands this stability.* The reduction of risk encompasses that of economic risk, financial and transfer risk, exchange risk, cultural environment risk, legal and contractual risk, regional contamination risk (spill-over effect), and the systemic risk associated with any global crisis.

5.4 Income discrepancies and labour movements in Europe

As noted earlier in this chapter, factor mobility does not benefit each country or region in a market grouping equally. The benefit can be measured by examining the distribution of wealth and profit, and it is generally evaluated on the basis of values and the worth of assets. These assets may be stocks and shares, that is, marketable wealth, or assets like property and land resources that are difficult to assess unless sold. Non-marketable wealth may include rights and wealth support by origin and heritage that include the values of networking, creativity and innovation. For instance, in

Germany small firms producing innovative machinery and equipment are interlinked (for an example, see the Schunk case study in Part IV).

The distribution of marketable wealth is less even than the distribution of income. Market groupings are often characterized by inequalities in the distribution of income between regions of the same country. The EU is no exception to this.

Within its Member States, parts of Poland, Portugal, Greece, southern Italy and Spain, eastern Germany, eastern Finland and the west of Ireland traditionally show the lowest income figures. In the UK, there is a north–south divide in the distribution of incomes, in Germany this is reflected in an east–west divide, and in France, the highest incomes can be found in the Île-de-France area including Paris and its surroundings, and the lowest incomes in Guadeloupe, Guyana, La Réunion and Martinique.

If one relies on market mechanisms, then the rationale indicates that labour flows to high-income regions (workers migrate), while capital flows to low-income regions due to profit rates. In this case, is policy intervention the key to combating regional income inequalities? Any reflection about international geo-economic history indicates that inequalities also occur in planned economies under strong governmental intervention. While the reply to this question has hitherto been negative, regions differ regarding high and low resources; the household composition differs in urban and rural regions and educational attainment and skills are not the same. Statistical analyses have shown a positive correlation between settlement density and working population: the working population was significantly higher in urban areas than in rural regions. For people of working age, urban areas tend to be more attractive than rural areas; this holds particularly true for the well-educated (see Table 5.2 below). Immigration and minority issues can play a significant role in regional income disparity.

Table 5.2   *Correlation between density of urban fabric (CLC 11) and proportion of population by level of education in Austria and Slovenia*

Austria	University	College	Vocational academy	Upper secondary vocational school	Upper secondary general school	Apprentice-ship	Basic education
clc11	0.612**	0.390**	0.154**	0.252**	0.609**	−0.288**	−0.311**

Slovenia	Higher post-graduate	Higher undergraduate educational attainment	Short-term tertiary educational attainment	Upper secondary educational attainment (technical, professional and general)	Basic educational attainment	Incomplete basic educational attainment	No education
clc11	0.563**	0.467**	0.467**	0.469**	−0.264**	−0.581**	−0.162*

*p<0.05
**p<0.01

Source: Totzer, 2008, http:// www.vlm.be/SiteCollectionDocuments/Rurality%20near%20the%20city/rnc_proceeding_totzer_06.08.08.pdf

5.4.1 Labour

In practice, labour is in fact relatively immobile because if labour migrates, it takes its purchasing power with it so the region's income is reduced. Local commerce also obtains less income; shopkeepers, estate agents, solicitors, etc. reduce their spending and all this results in a further reduction of regional income. Moreover, in reality, labour is *not* a homogeneous factor, for example a skilled carpenter is not a perfect substitute for a pharmacist or an accountant. In addition, there is no substitute for labour if the population is not sufficiently skilled. Following this, an area with relatively unskilled labour is less attractive for business and FDI. The reverse is true for highly skilled labour.

Interestingly, highly educated Scandinavia shows the least variability between income levels in Europe and has for years been at the head of the World Economic Forum's Competitive Ranking. Table 5.3 below shows the GCI Index for the top 10 countries, including three Scandinavian countries: Sweden, Finland and Denmark.

Highly skilled labour increases the human resource capital of a country, and normally benefits the balance of payments through investment into the host economy. Low-skilled labour exercises a less important impact on the balance of payments because revenues are often sent back to families in the home country. Nevertheless, labour still contributes significantly to the economic health of the host country. This means filling in demographic gaps, counterbalancing labour shortages in specific areas, and offering education and training to a diversity of potentials. Labour may move in and out of Europe, or freely within Europe. The Schengen agreement explained in Chapter 3 encourages labour movement through low-administration common rules and procedures for internal and external border controls for citizens of participating countries. The Schengen agreement was also signed by some EFTA countries (Iceland and Norway in 1996, and

Table 5.3   *Global Competitiveness Index 2010–2011 rankings and 2009–2010 comparisons*

Country/Economy	GCI 2010–2011		GCI 2010–2011 Rank	GCI 2009–2010 Rank
	Rank	Score		
Switzerland	1	5.63	1	1
Sweden	2	5.56	2	4
Singapore	3	5.48	3	3
United States	4	5.43	4	2
Germany	5	5.39	5	7
Japan	6	5.37	6	8
Finland	7	5.37	7	6
Netherlands	8	5.33	8	10
Denmark	9	5.32	9	5
Canada	10	5.40	10	9

Source: http://www.weforum.org/documents/GCR10/Full%20rankings.pdf

Switzerland in 2005). The agreement also facilitates the transit of goods through increased customs cooperation.

In terms of labour and employment policies, the overall European focus on a services-oriented economy since the mid 1990s has resulted in services employment accounting for more than double that of industry, and even more than that of agriculture. In a breakdown by gender, more men work in agriculture and industry, while more women are employed in services. Europe encompasses several socioeconomic models: the mainstream models are Nordic, Latin, French, Italian, new Eastern European and German. In each model of capitalism, the labour market is different. The UK with its limited government intervention, decentralized pay bargaining and flexible working arrangements appears to be the most flexible of the EU economies. Ireland and The Netherlands are also examples of comparatively flexible labour markets.

Member States maintain their exclusive competence in confronting unemployment and encouraging job creation. However, EU governments treat employment policies as a matter of common concern. As a result, joint employment guidelines are published annually and each Member State submits a National Action Plan (NAP) for employment. For example, Malta's National Action Plan against Poverty and Social Exclusion is working towards eradicating poverty and achieving an inclusive society. The targeted vulnerable/at-risk-of-poverty groups involve a wide range of categories (children, youths, families; victims of domestic violence, addiction, mental health problems; irregular immigrants, etc.) (see http://www.epasi.eu/$-project-study.cfm?PID=247).

The European labour market is not as 'single' and harmonized as might be imagined; several employment models operate in disharmony within the EU. The four main models are cited below:

- The Mediterranean model (Italy, Spain, Greece): this model is often criticized for inefficiencies both in creating employment and in combating poverty.
- The Continental model (France, Germany, Luxembourg): this model has the reputation of being good at combating poverty but bad at creating jobs.
- The Anglo-Saxon model (Ireland, the UK and Portugal): this model is relatively efficient at creating employment but bad at preventing poverty.
- The Nordic model (Denmark, Finland and Sweden, plus The Netherlands and Austria): this model is successful at both creating jobs and preventing poverty.

Table 5.4 provides an overview of the main characteristics of these models.

There is a great variety of employment conditions, unemployment and retirement benefits and working hours across the EU. The European Commission's monthly labour market monitor is one source of data for labour market conditions. Each wave of regional enlargement: (1) expands the market for firms; (2) adds to the diversity of the labour market in the integrated Europe; and (3) alters expectations for the future of sectors that are increasingly service and financials-oriented (see Figure 5.10), despite the effects of the 2008 financial crisis. This adds additional challenges to corporate Europeanization.

Table 5.4   *Four employment models operating in disharmony within the EU*

Model	Countries operated in	Characteristics
Mediterranean model	Italy, Spain, Greece	Social spending concentrated on old-age pensions and a focus on employment protection and early retirement schemes
Continental model	France, Germany, Luxembourg	Insurance-based, non-employment benefits and old-age pensions and a high degree of employment protection
Anglo-Saxon model	Ireland, UK, Portugal	Many low-paid jobs, payments linked to regular employment, activating measures and a low degree of job security
Nordic model	Denmark, Finland, Sweden, Austria, Netherlands	High spending on social security and high taxes, little job protection but high employment security

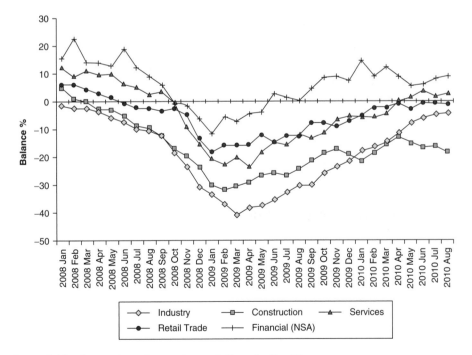

Figure 5.10   *Sectoral employment expectations for the EU*

Source: http://ec.europa.eu © European Union, 1995–2011

5.4.2 *Capital*

In contrast to labour, capital is very mobile, not only between regions but also between countries. Therefore, the market mechanism works as capital flows (but it flows globally). The global financial crisis in 2008 had a severe impact on domestic output, reflecting the pre-crisis dependence of many countries on international bank and bond-lending to finance domestic expenditure. The debt crises in some of the high-income European countries (i.e. Greece, Italy, Portugal) and their diminished growth prospects have created uncertainty for developing Europe. The combination of extremely deep falls in 2009 and a modest recovery is characterized by high unemployment. Registered unemployment has risen by 3 million and exceeded 10 per cent of the labour force in several countries, including Latvia, Turkey, Estonia, Lithuania, Slovakia and Hungary. The most vulnerable countries in the overall region include Albania and Azerbaijan, for which Greece, Italy, Portugal and Spain represent more than 20 per cent of their total exports.

Governmental and supranational agencies like the EU intervene mainly through financial assistance programmes and regional funds, research and training initiatives. These aim at making Europe more attractive for internal and external economies of scale on the basis of factor mobility, reinforced flexibility of labour and capital factors, and the highest educational standards recognized EU-wide. The move of the EU towards a knowledge-based economy reinforces these efforts.

The European Monetary Union (EMU) brought about the creation of the European Central Bank (ECB). The Maastricht Treaty detailed the role of the Euro system in defining and implementing monetary policy in the euro-zone, conducting foreign exchange operations, holding and managing official reserves, promoting the smooth operation of payment systems, and issuing banknotes and coins. A tendency towards monetary integration following the principles of federalism guides the primary objective of the ECB to maintain price stability (Maastricht Treaty). Overall, the EU has successfully centralized its monetary policy and harmonized interest rates. (This topic will be analysed further in Chapter 7.)

5.5 The competitiveness of European manufacturing and service industries

The EU 2020 strategy, replacing the so-called Lisbon strategy in 2009, was launched as the CEC's new economic, environmental and social framework strategy. The main focus of the EU 2020 strategy is to combat the effects of economic and financial crisis.

The strategy, set up to boost competitiveness, follows a concept that can be defined in several ways: one definition may refer to competitiveness as being industrial, technological or enterprise-related (Box 5.8). In all three cases, the term is used to cover several principal factors: price- or non-price (such as high quality, superior design and technical innovation); lower cost; and profitability.

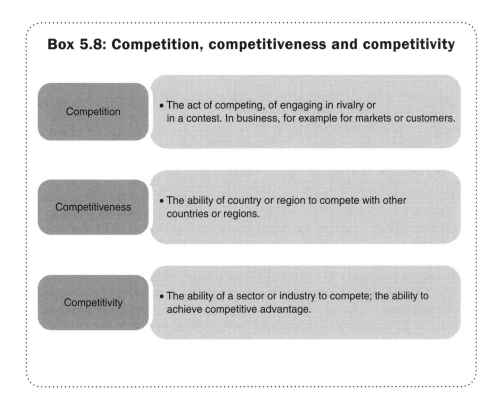

Box 5.8: Competition, competitiveness and competitivity

Competition
- The act of competing, of engaging in rivalry or in a contest. In business, for example for markets or customers.

Competitiveness
- The ability of country or region to compete with other countries or regions.

Competitivity
- The ability of a sector or industry to compete; the ability to achieve competitive advantage.

There is a wide range of *indicators of competitiveness* that may give different results depending on which measures are adopted for assessment. We can distinguish quantitative and qualitative indicators (Buckley and Casson, 1988):

- *Quantitative* indicators include export market share, market share, export measures, per centage of world manufacturing/GNP and percentage of domestic manufacturers in total output, balance of trade, comparative advantage, cost competitiveness, technology and profitability.
- *Qualitative* indicators are ownership advantage, marketing aptitude, commitment to international business and globalization, relations with intermediaries, proximity to market, cultural advantages, cross-licensing and acquisition of technology.

Buckley and Casson (1988) conclude that competitive advantage stems primarily from the ability to reach targets at the least possible cost, defined as efficiency, and second to choose the right goals, defined as effectiveness. The achievement of these goals is related to the historical situation, existing competitors and the existence of a well-defined counter-factual competitiveness. In terms of international competitiveness, these factors will, together with cost and price developments, either improve or deteriorate the performance of a country or firm.

Box 5.9: Long-term strategies for sustainable competitiveness

- long-term contracts or exclusive distribution agreements;
- an increase in product differentiation;
- technological innovation through R&D;
- concentration by means of merger or takeover;
- globalization by means of investment and acquisition policies;
- the establishment or elimination of certain barriers to entry.

The result of market behaviour and a particular market structure is mirrored in the company's market *performance*. It can be measured by a firm's profit margins, sustained growth, the degree of capacity utilization, and product quality. Also, incomes are interpreted as identifications of the degree of competitiveness and the market performance of a company. The aim is to increase incomes as rapidly as the competitors and to make the necessary investments to remain competitive in the long-term. Income is a good indicator of company competitiveness. However, net income in a pure competitive environment is the last thing to increase in a company. In fact, any profit that a company makes and does not reinvest would weaken its current position relative to the competition. Academics argue that the lower the level of nominal wages, the lower the external value of the currency and the faster an increase in productivity appears; consequently, the greater the international competitiveness of the country's industry.

Following this theory, there are three main options to increase competitiveness:

- low-wage strategy: nominal wages are decreased while productivity and exchange rate remain at their normal level; it will result in higher volume sales without a loss in profit margins and will therefore create an effect equivalent to a direct fall in production costs. However, this strategy would have an adverse effect on the international division of labour and is therefore problematic in terms of international competitiveness;
- devaluation strategy: devaluation of a country's home currency enables its industry to sell products in foreign markets at lower prices than at home. This facilitates the success of domestic sales, because the prices of foreign products in terms of the devalued currency are higher than those of domestic manufacturers;
- innovation strategy: stimulation of innovation increases productivity in a country where growing incomes stimulate import demand.

These options aim to improve trade conditions and to benefit the economy as a whole. Designing a particular strategy like this must evolve from the growth of demand, the relevant production costs which depend on location, distribution marketing and transaction costs, and the situation of the industry in general. In Europe, these factors are subject to the forces of the Single Market.

5.6 Competition, competitive sectors and business-related common policies

Strategy and company policies are not entirely under management control. The dynamic evolution of the European economy means that demand and cost conditions continuously change. It is important for corporations to monitor the 'uncontrollable' variables of competitiveness, such as the strategies of competitors, and to impose even marginal adjustments that may be necessary for sustainable competitiveness. This might mean that costs can be cut quickly or resources attributed differently. The enterprise can then keep in close touch with demand conditions, thus keeping ahead of competitors.

The preceding discussion could lead to the conclusion that competitivity could be defined simply as the result of commercializing a product or service at the right time in the right place under the right conditions. It is quantifiable through the sustained performance improvement of industry. However, competitivity ultimately depends on economic choices, financial and market, operational and technological, as well as on human resources and organizational issues. On a global scale, European corporations are among the leaders in the chemicals, pharmaceuticals, electrical engineering, IT, telecoms, food and beverages, metals, motor vehicles, banking, insurance and financial services sectors. Yet, European companies are deeply rooted in their home markets (although transnational companies like Nestlé, Unilever, Philips Electronics, Glaxo-Wellcome and Electrolux are exceptions to that rule). In telecoms and its applications, Europe is highly competitive vis-à-vis its trading partners. The same applies to the fields of nanotechnology and biotechnology. The EU is China's biggest trading partner, and benefits from important FDI opportunities there.

Structural weaknesses that leave the market with high production, capital and labour costs, rigid labour legislation, and heavy social laws that undermine employment flexibility: all of theses factors nevertheless hamper EU competitiveness. Moreover, R&D spending is relatively low in terms of European GDP compared to that in the USA and Japan. Business is therefore calling upon the EU and its members, as a common European institution, to facilitate and stimulate economic activity by:

- eliminating bureaucracy;
- increasing the efficiency of procurement processes;
- raising the participation of various societal groups in decision-making processes;
- encouraging education as a key factor to foster information access and content production;
- improving the dissemination of best practice, ultimately leading to better services for citizens and businesses.

Common policies, with supremacy over or to complement national policies, were set up by European treaties to monitor intervention where outcomes may distort Europe-wide benefits. This has been the case in agriculture, transport, social policy and also regional policy since 1987. Foreign and security policy are governed with increasing harmonization. This chapter will now analyse those competition and commercial rules that constitute common policies.

5.6.1 Common policies: competitive market structures and related costs

Competition policy has been part of European integration efforts since the Treaty of Paris and the Treaties of Rome. Its aim is to preserve and stimulate efficiencies and effectiveness in the European market.

The CEC is the main institution in charge of anti-trust policy, merger policy and state aid controls. The objectives of competition policy are to:

- promote competitive market structures;
- discourage anti-competitive behaviour;
- guarantee fair competitive trade in the Single Market;
- benefit consumers and citizens of the EU.

The Common Competition Policy complements national measures that are and were taken by Member States under the principle of the supremacy of EU law in case of conflict. It prohibits any agreement as anti-competitive and 'incompatible with the common market' that affects intra-EU trade with an objective to prevent, distort or restrict competition. Collusion is therefore generally prohibited, with a few exceptions of cooperation between corporations where this does not harm consumer welfare. It also prohibits the abuse of dominance, whether by an individual firm or jointly. Mergers and acquisitions are subject to prior clearance under the merger control.

Of major importance also are state aid rules against distortion of competition across Europe, with few exceptions. In anti-trust policy, national competencies share much of the EU application of rules. In mergers, the role of Commission investigations was extended beyond that of market dominance towards a focus on the general effect of mergers. The rather limited numbers of staff at the CEC's competition directorate means that there is a relatively fragmented control mechanism. The case of the *Commission* v. *Microsoft* illustrates the difficulties in pursuing this policy, starting in 2003 and running over many years.

These commercial policy areas are underpinned by an industrial policy that is not a 'common' policy per se. Since the end of the1980s, Europe has seen a sharp increase in mergers, acquisitions, joint ventures and other cooperative agreements between firms, identified as cluster building or concentration (Cawson et al.,

1990). Also, there was a significant rise in FDI within the Single Market as part of the Europeanization of business, underlining the movement towards international economic integration. With this development, European industrial policy shifted the traditional national focus of sponsoring 'sunset' champions with sectorial aid, to an economically more sensitive approach of supporting 'sunrise' innovation with horizontal aid (El-Agraa, 2004). In conclusion, the inherent objective of industrial policy is to increase competitiveness in tandem with the requirements of the market.

Altogether, the prime objective of the European competition policy is to eliminate distortions and enhance the proper functioning of market mechanisms. The main challenge is to avoid 'protectionist' behaviour that would lead to low levels of knowledge and information flows and hinder innovation. Such behaviour would also increase the difficulty of picking champions, and result in retaliation by trade partners. Counter to this incentive, R&D-supportive initiatives are justified by external factors such as the social returns associated with economic returns. Innovation has become key to European competitiveness. Its promotion typically takes the shape of financial assistance, public contracts, tax incentives, one-off trade barriers in case of unfair competition, and export assistance. Ideally, measures of industrial policy should not intervene actively and directly, with the exception of occasional actions. Rather, measures that stimulate the diffusion of knowledge, innovation and entrepreneurship are to be encouraged.

5.6.2 The Common Commercial Policy

Given that the EU industrial policy is fragmented and sector-specific, the Common Commercial Policy (CCP) is there to help domestic and foreign corporations to benefit from a single market. The CCP is part of the EU external trade policy and is the first single coherent, common European policy. It allows for a common tariff and a common commercial policy towards non-EU countries, with basic common rules in three commercial fields:

- trade with state-trading countries;
- import quotas; and
- anti-dumping measures.

The CCP allows for the common conclusion of tariff and trade agreements, the negotiation of changes in tariffs and the achievement of uniformity in measures of liberalization. European export policy and EU-wide trade protection measures, for example anti-dumping and anti-subsidy measures, are occasionally imposed when this is in the Community's interest (consumer and industry). Box 5.10 summarizes the *trade instruments* that are at the disposal of the EU to make this happen. (Later, in Chapter 10, *trade agreements* will be discussed further.)

Box 5.10: Trade policy instruments and types of intervention

- Balance-of-payment measures, including export rebates (restitutions) refunding the difference calculated by the Commission between EU and world market price, applied foremost in agricultural policy, and restrictions on hire purchase.
- Productivity, price and income policies.
- Common customs, taxation and tariff instruments, including import quotas, transit duties, preferential duties and anti-dumping duties.
- Import monitoring associated with Voluntary Export Restraints (VERs), local content requirements and rules of origin.
- Legislation to control not only companies, mergers and restrictive practices within the Single Market, but also to monitor illicit action in third countries where EU firms encounter obstacles to market access, through the 1995 trade barriers regulation, leading to negotiation and/or recourse to the WTO if necessary.
- Control of scientific research and structural aspects of technology.

Overall, European industry excels in the automotive sector and its components, in engineering and electrical skills, in aerospace and in the mobile phone industry. LVMH, Armani, Gucci and Dior are leaders in the luxury fashion industry, while Carrefour, H&M, Zara and Metro are highly efficient retailers worldwide (Doz et al., 2001). The Europeanization of the business environment has had a largely positive impact on competitiveness and has enhanced the focus of the market towards specific and functional specializations that enhance effectiveness and efficiency. Financial integration in the shape of a common currency in the euro–zone stimulates this effect.

5.6.3 Business-related policies: implications

The EU is responsible for a large number of common policies. Among them, you can find the common agricultural policy (CAP), the Common Foreign and Security Policy (CFSP), fisheries, environment and energy, regional, certain social and employment policies, as well as transport, trade and aid policies.

On a *micro and meso level*, common policies are not only advantageous but also challenging. We can observe the potential costs of EU Directives with the example of labour. Those common rules harmonized many important areas, making compulsory employment conditions in and across borders in Europe more transparent, in regard to job contracts, working time (see Table 5.5), young workers, pregnancy, parental leave and part-time work.

Table 5.5 *Full-time employee average hours worked per week, 2010*

	Weekly working hours
United Kingdom	42.2
Germany	40.6
France	39.4

Source: Trades Union Congress at http://www.tuc.org.uk

Employers in Europe bear the costs of:

- social security;
- high protection standards (such as higher rates per hour);
- individual cases for exemption rights (such as absence for a medical check-up);
- improved health and safety protection;
- additional administrative burdens (bookkeeping, scheduling, additional writing requirements).

On *a macro level*, trade policy links the public and private sector to the WTO and deals with global trade issues, sectorial and horizontal issues, and bilateral agreements with one common approach. At the WTO, the Member States are represented by the EU. The advantage is that the EU together has more negotiation power; the challenge is that specific issues may well get diluted in the overall objective setting that encompasses all Member States' views. These multilateral negotiations have an important impact on business activity worldwide (see Chapter 10). In global trade, the EU supports developing countries in as much as it helps them integrate into the trading system. The objective is to help these economies mature so as to benefit from liberal trade. The Generalized System of Preference (GSP) runs a *system of non-reciprocal tariff advantages* with the EU for these economies. Similarly, the Commission is engaged in sustainable development initiatives and researches the impact of trade negotiations on developing countries, on social welfare, the environment and civil society. The EU concludes bilateral agreements and devises specific trading policies with non-EU countries and regional groupings. These *bilateral agreements are legally binding* for the partners, as custom unions, free trade associations, cooperation or partnerships. At the same time, European trade policy deals with the horizontal and vertical sectoral issues. *Horizontal issues* may be those of trade and competitiveness, intellectual property (IP), market access policy, trade and competition, trade facilitation, government procurement – as in the example cited above – and export credits are also part of these. As an example, *export credits* that are typically government supported may create unfair competition: they are used when a foreign buyer of exported goods or services defers payment. Export credits are hence subject to OECD agreements and the EC Directive on harmonization of export credit insurance for transactions with medium- and long-term cover. They are therefore under supervision from the EU for all Member States.

An essential part of European trade policy is dispute settlements, trade barrier regulation, anti-dumping, anti-subsidy and safeguarding policies, and a range of fair trade defence and monitoring tools. These mechanisms complete the sectoral policies that structure a common market for agriculture, fisheries, services and merchandise on a *vertical level*. For example, the EU is the world's largest producer of chemicals and cosmetics (CEC, 2010, figures). Those firms that export need to overcome a number of obstacles such as complex standards and technical regulations, intellectual property laws, registration and certification procedures, while those chemicals companies that enter the EU market need to be familiar with European regulations such as REACH, the European regulatory framework for the registration, evaluation and authorization of chemicals for early identification of the properties of chemical substances. The EU, through its trade policy, attempts to facilitate trade in the sector and engages in agreements such as those elaborated under the WTO Chemical Harmonization Tariff Agreement (CHTA). It hence has an important role to play in the competitiveness of the sector.

Another important example for the implications of common policies on business is the European Research and Technology Development (RTD) policy. European centres of excellence are scattered across the continent and need adequate networking. The Commission's directorate general for research aims to establish a common market for research, the European Research Area. This supports and coordinates research activities and the convergence of research and innovation policies at national and EU levels. Some main areas of support are mobility and training, women in science, and a Community patent policy, and there is also support for SMEs. (More information can be found online at: http://ec.europa. eu/enterprise/enterprise_policy/cip/index_en.htm.)

5.7 Résumé and conclusion

The Europeanization of the business environment is based on the effects of globalization as well as geo-historical and geo-economic evolutions. International trade theory makes a strong case for the internationalization of firms that can obtain important advantages from going abroad. Also, the theories sustain the argument that integration is beneficial for the competitiveness of a nation or, in the case of Europe, a market grouping. The European business environment has been subject to major harmonization, liberalization and deregulation efforts that are illustrated by the common policies that govern important policy areas. Nevertheless, income distribution is not equal, and the EU promises huge potential if harmonization efforts continue.

The dynamic though streamlined corporate sectors in the Single market prove that Europeanization increases business efficiency and effectiveness. Most governments sustained their 'national champion' expansion with non-tariff trade and investment barriers directed against foreign competitors and strong borders protecting national markets. But these policies failed and caused low growth, unemployment and inflation after the first oil crisis in 1973. The European Commission then decided to work on an integration programme to eradicate the main trade and investment burdens. The Single Market programme had a positive effect. The manufacturing industry was the main target of EU initiatives; this focus shifted towards the service industry around 2000. Consequently, 'national champions' and championing governments had to adapt to focus on becoming European leaders. Firms whose activities were highly dispersed from the outset benefited more than others from the Single Market by rationalizing and concentrating their operations on the EU market. As a result, competition within the EU has largely enhanced general international competition and competitiveness worldwide (De Voldere et al., 2001).

Competitiveness is a key issue in the EU. This chapter has reviewed the main rationale and business-related instruments that drive the common response to challenges of market mechanisms. In Europe, there is a tendency to apply occasional direct intervention in cases of market distortions. In all other cases, the EU role is to monitor and stimulate competition and fair trade. This includes, for example, fair access to non-EU markets.

Mini case study: AHI Roofing from the Pacific Rim to Europe

AHI Roofing, a New Zealand firm, is a world leader in the production of steel roof tiles. In 2007, it had manufacturing facilities in New Zealand, Malaysia and California and contemplated its strategy for Europe. New Zealand has been increasingly trying to link its future to the fast-growing Pacific Rim area, where AHI's manufacturing facilities were located. However, the company also recorded strong and rising sales in Europe, particularly in the emerging East European nations. AHI had to decide whether it should establish a production operation in Europe, and, if so, how and in which country.

The company invented the world's first steel roof tile in 1957 and now sells its products in over 80 countries. A subsidiary of Fletcher Building, one of New Zealand's largest corporations, AHI's key regional sales offices are located in New Zealand, Malaysia, Australia, Japan, China, the United Arab Emirates, Slovenia, Poland and France. Exports to Europe began in the 1970s, with licensed manufacture in Belgium in 1979 and Denmark in 1981. These operations were later terminated and sales offices were established in Central Europe (1991), Turkey (1999), Slovenia (2000), Poland (2001) and France (2004). In 2007, the company's distribution warehouse for Europe was in the UK and the marketing office for Europe was in Slovenia (see Table 5.6 for the location of AHI's key European sales offices and their country coverage).

Table 5.6   *AHI Roofing in Europe*

Sales office location	Countries covered by the office
Toulon, France	Andorra, France, Spain, Portugal, Belgium, Netherlands, Libya, Morocco, Tunisia, Algeria
Holsworthy, UK	UK, Bulgaria, Estonia, Lithuania, Latvia, Romania, Russia, Turkey, Azerbaijan, Kazakhstan, Turkmenistan, Uzbekistan
Ljubljana, Slovenia	Albania, Austria, Bosnia, Cyprus, Greece, Croatia, Italy, Kosovo, Montenegro, Macedonia, Slovenia, Serbia, Hungary, Czech Republic
Warsaw, Poland	Belarus, Poland, Slovakia, Ukraine

The decision about a new manufacturing facility in Europe had to be seen in the context of growth opportunities elsewhere. The USA operations, where a plant in California was established in 1989, had exceptional sales in 2005, driven by hailstorm damage in southern states. However, sales in 2006 were somewhat disappointing and there were already signs of a cooling construction market in the USA in 2007. Exports to Asia have been strong from the 1980s on, with a licensed manufacturing plant in Malaysia established in 1985 and upgraded after a purchase from the licensee in 2005. In 2006, manufacturing plants in New Zealand and Malaysia achieved record production and sales volumes rose annually by 13 per cent overall that year. Earnings in 2006 rose 23 per cent but the margins on exports from the New Zealand plant were negatively affected by a strong New Zealand dollar.

Sales in Europe were also growing rapidly after 2000, to the point that AHI was often not able to meet the peaks in demand. A new European production facility would allow AHI to provide better service to European customers, decrease transport costs, increase penetration in these relatively high-margin markets and allow for expansion to meet longer-term growth expectations. AHI's products were in high demand, particularly in the fast-growing East European nations, which were seen by the company as lucrative and the centre of AHI's market in Europe. There was a considerable building boom in these parts of Europe, and the new EU members were attractive bases for manufacturing foreign direct investment due to their central location in Europe and relatively low wages and high skills of workers.

Author: Dr Peter Zámborský, lecturer in management and international business, University of Auckland Business School, Auckland, New Zealand.

Source: Compiled data

Mini case study questions

1 Should AHI build a manufacturing plant in Europe? If yes, should it be a wholly owned Greenfield plant, a licensed operation or some other form of entry? Why?
2 In which country should AHI locate its manufacturing facility for Europe? Which factors does it have to consider in this decision?

 REVIEW QUESTIONS

1 **Explain** in which cases offshoring is economically sensible.
2 **Explain** the importance of internalization advantages for a Europeanizing firm.
3 **Based** on international trade theory, to what extent can a firm be an instrument of effective production and distribution on a European scale?
4 **Where** can you find trade diversion effects in Europeanization?
5 **Can** market mechanisms combat regional income inequalities?

ASSIGNMENTS

- **Imagine** that you are the manager of a company in the luxury fashion industry. You decide to have your main production transferred to Asia. Why is this subject sensitive? Find a recent example.
- **Compare** income distribution disparities in your home country with that of any (other) EU Member State's. Discuss your findings.
- **Case study assignment:** Read and prepare the case study 'The European market for Schunk: an audit of Europeanization' in Part IV, and discuss the impact of Europe on the company's operations.
- **Internet exercise:** On the Internet, find the main competitiveness charts. Which organizations publish them and what criteria are they based on? Compare the top rankings for the 20-year period 1985–2005 and interpret your findings.

Further reading

Coeurdacier, N., De Santis, R.A. and Aviat, A. (2009) Cross-border mergers and acquisitions and European integration. *Economic Policy*, vol. 24, no. 57, January, pp. 55–106.

Dahan, N.M. and W.J. Frech (2008) A review of European business integration: does European business exist? *International Journal of Business Research*, vol. 8, no. 5, pp. 15–27.

Knight, G.A. and Daekwan, K. (2009) International business competence and the contemporary firm. *Journal of International Business Studies*, vol. 40, February/March, pp. 255–73.

Marin, D. (2010) The Opening Up of Eastern Europe at 20-Jobs, Skills, and 'Reverse Maquiladoras' in Austria and Germany. *Münchener Wirtschaftswissenschaftliche Beiträge (VWL) 2010–14*. Available at: http://epub.ub.uni-muenchen.de/11435/

Sagic, L. and Schwartz, S.H. (2007) Cultural values in organizations: insights from Europe. *European Journal of Management*, vol. 1, no. 3, pp. 175–90.

INTERNET RESOURCES

Competitiveness and Innovation Framework (CIP) Helpdesk for Intellectual Property Questions:
http://www.ipr-helpdesk.org/home.html

European Business Forum website:
http://www.europeanbusinessforum.com/home/ebfhome.asp

EuropeInnova European Cluster Observatory:
http://www.clusterobservatory.eu/index.html

(Continued)

(Continued)

Internal Market Scoreboard:
http://ec.europa.eu/internal_market/score/index_en.htm#score

United Nations Conference on Trade and Development:
http://www.unctad.org

World Bank website (information on countries):
http://www.worldbank.org

Gabriele Suder's *Doing Business in Europe* video series (on the SAGE companion website at http://www.sagepub.co.uk/suder2e and YouTube)

Note

1. Some parts of this section are based on published material in Suder (2006).

Bibliography

Baldwin, R. and Wyplosz, C. (2004) *The Economics of European Integration*. Maidenhead: McGraw-Hill.

Birkinshaw, J. and Hood, N. (1998) Multinational subsidiary evolution: capabilities and charter change in foreign-owned subsidiary companies. *Academy of Management Review*, vol. 23, pp. 773–95.

Bouchet, M.H. (2005) *La Globalisation*. Upper Saddle River, NJ: Pearson Education.

Buckley, P. (2004) Cartography and international business. *International Business Review*, vol. 13, pp. 239–55.

Buckley, P.J. and Casson, M.C. (1976) *The Future of the Multinational Enterprise*. New York: Holmes and Meier.

Buckley, P. and Casson, M. (1988) A theory of cooperation in business, in F.J. Contractor and P. Lorange (eds), *Cooperative Strategies in International Business*. Lanham, MD: Lexington Books.

Campbell, J. and Hopenhayn, H. (2002) Market size matters. *NBER Working Paper* 9113. Cambridge, MA: National Bureau of Economic Research (NBER).

Cawson, A., Morgan, K., Webber, D., Holmes, P. and Stevens, A. (1990) *Hostile Brothers: Competition and Closure in the European Electronics Industry*. Oxford: Clarendon Press.

Commission of the European Communities (CEC) (1996) *The 1996 Single Market Review: Background Information for the Report to the Council and the European Parliament*. Commission Staff Working Paper, Brussels. Available at: http://europa.eu.int/en/update/impact/index.htm

Commission of the European Communities (CEC) (1999) The Competitiveness of European Enterprises in the Face of Globalisation – how it can be encouraged, Brussels, 20 January.

Commission of the European Communities (CEC) (2004) *Internal Market Scoreboard*. Brussels: European Communities.

Commission of the European Communities (CEC) (2006) *Europe in Figures*. Eurostat yearbook 2006–07, Catalogue no.: KS-CD-06-001-EN-CA, Brussels, February 2007.

Commission of the European Communities (2010) *European Commission Trade – Industrial Goods, Chemicals*. Available at: http://ec.europa.eu/trade/creating-opportunities/economic-sectors/industrial-goods/chemicals/

Czinkota, M., Ronkainen, R. and Moffett, M. (2005) *International Business*, 7th edn. Mason, OH: South-Western Thomson.

De Jong, E. (1988) The contribution of the ECU to exchange-rate stability: a reply (with H. Jager). *Banca Nazionale del Lavoro Quarterly Review*, vol. 166, pp. 331–5.

De Voldere, I., Sleuwaegen, L., Veugelers, R. and Van Pelt, A. (2001) *The Leading Firms in Europe from National Champions to European Leaders*. Management School Working Paper Series 2004/12, Vlerick Leuven, Gent.

Dicken, P. (2003) *Global Shift: Reshaping the Global Economic Map in the 21st Century*, 4th edn. London: Sage.

Doz, Y., Santos, J. and Williamson, P. (2001) *From Global to Metanational*. Boston, MA: Harvard Business School Press.

Dunnett, A. (1998) *Understanding the Market*, 3rd edn. Harlow: Longman.

Dunning, J. (1977) Trade location of economic activity: a search for an eclectic approach, in B. Ohlin, P. Hesselborn and P. Wijkman (eds), *The International Allocation of Economic Activity*. New York: Holmes and Meier. pp. 395–418.

Dunning, J. (1989) The study of international business. *Journal of International Business Studies*, vol. 20, pp. 411–36.

Dunning, J. (1993) *Multinational Enterprises and the Global Economy*. New York: Addison-Wesley.

El-Agraa, A. (2004) *The European Union: Economics and Policies*, 7th edn. Harlow: FT Prentice Hall.

European Communities (1999) The Strategy for Europe's Internal Market; Communication from the Commission to the European Parliament and the Council 1. COM(1999)464 final 2. B5-0204/1999. Available at: http://europa.eu.int/comm/internal_market/en/update/strategy/strat2en.pdf

European Communities (2000) The Lisbon European Council – an agenda of economic and social renewal for Europe. Contribution of the European Commission to the special European Council in Lisbon, 23–24 March 2000, DOC/00/7, 28 February.

General Agreement on Trade in Services (GATS) (2005) Working Party on GATS Rules, Report of the Meeting of 21 September 2005, Note by the Secretariat.

Gramlich, E. and Wood, P. (2000) Fiscal federalism and European integration: implications for fiscal and monetary policies. *Board of Governors of the Federal Reserve System International Finance Discussion Paper*, no. 694, Washington, DC, December.

Howell, L. (2001) *The Handbook of Country and Political Risk Analysis*. East Syracuse, NY: The PRS Group.

Inderbrand Corporation (2006) The 100 best global brands. *Business Week*, 9–16 August, pp. 58–61.

Johnson, G. and Sholes, K. (2002) *Exploring Corporate Strategy*, 6th edn. Harlow: FT Prentice Hall.

Kirzner, I. (1973) *Competition and Entrepreneurship*. Chicago, IL: University of Chicago Press.

Knickerbocker, F. (1973) *Oligopolistic Reaction and Multinational Enterprise*. Boston, MA: Division of Research, Graduate School of Business Administration, Harvard University.

Kogut, B. and Zander, U. (1993) Knowledge of the firm and the evolutionary theory of the multinational corporation. *Journal of International Business Studies*, vol. 24, no. 4, pp. 625–45.

Krugman, P. and Venables, A. (1995) The Seamless World: A Spatial Model of International Specialization, (August 1995). *National Bureau of Economic Research (NBER) Working Paper Series*, vol. w5220.

Lamfalussy, A. (1997) Address of the President of the European Monetary Institute, to the Euromoney Conference in New York, 30 April.

Nello, S. (2005) *The European Union: Economics, Policies and History*. Maidenhead: McGraw-Hill.

Porter, M.E. (1990) *The Competitive Advantage of Nations*. New York: Free Press.

Rugman, A. and Collinson, S. (2006) *International Business*, 4th edn. Harlow: Pearson Education.

Sagic, L. and Schwartz, S.H. (2007) Cultural values in organizations: insights from Europe. *European Journal of Management*, vol. 1, no. 3, pp. 175–90.

Smith, A. (1904) *Inquiry into the Nature and Causes of the Wealth of Nations*, 5th edn (E. Cannan, ed.). London: Methuen and Co. (First published 1776.)

Suder, G. (1994) *Anti-Dumping Measures and the Politics of EU–Japan Trade Relations in the European Consumer Electronics Sector: The VCR Case*. Bath: University of Bath School of Management.

Suder, G. (2006) *Corporate Strategies Under International Terrorism and Adversity*. Cheltenham: Edward Elgar.

Tötzer, T. (2008) Relationships between periurban-rural regions: the first findings from the EU-Project Plurel, Rurality near the City. Available at: http://www.vlm.be/SiteCollectionDocuments/Rurality%20near%20the%20city/rnc_proceeding_totzer_06.08.08.pdf

Vernon, R. (1966) International investment and international trade in the product cycle. *Quarterly Journal of Economics*, vol. 80, pp. 190–207.

Vernon, R. (1979) The Product Cycle Hypothesis in an international environment. *Oxford Bulletin of Economics and Statistics*, vol. 41, no. 4, pp. 255–67.

Volvo Company (2004) Company News Feed (formerly Regulatory News Service), March.

United Nations Conference on Trade Development (UNCTAD) (2005) [1992/1996] Expected modes of global investments 2005–2006: prospect assessment, in J.M. Letiche (ed.), *International Economic Policies and their Theoretical Foundations*. Toronto: Academic Press. pp. 415–35. Available at: http://www.unctad.org/fdiprospects

6

The Europeanization of Business Management

What you will learn about in this chapter:

- Cultures and identities in Europe, and the Europeanization of business management.
- Does a European strategy make sense?
- The convergence issue: intellectual property (IP) rights for Europe, or What the people expect.
- Subsidiary management and knowledge transfer issues.

6.0 Introduction

Does management 'Europeanize' too? This chapter will inquire into this question through a quest of management styles and cultures.

In all EU Member States, distinct management styles, cultures and structures, and resulting management and human resources (HR) issues can be identified. This chapter will therefore deal with a synthesis of these distinctions and their complementarities for Europeanized business through the examination of key themes. Also, you will learn about some of the main issues that managers have to adapt to in a large marketplace, such as intellectual property (IP) rights. Finally, the organizational structures that managers use to adapt, and the particularity of diversity and knowledge management in Europe will be considered.

6.1 Does business management 'Europeanize'?

In this chapter, we will find out whether a European management exists, on the basis of European competence, culture, identity and leadership qualities. Does a unique European way make sense in business management? Let us first take a cross-cultural management, leadership and strategy perspective. The following chapters will then shed light on financial, marketing, regulatory and international challenges to European business performance.

A World Bank study into certain business operations (presented in Tables 6.1 and 6.2) ranks a set of countries as the best and worst business performers in the world. Interestingly, few of them are EU Member States: EU members are rather situated in the 'middle' of such criteria. Is this caused by Europeanization? Does Europeanization focus on values other than 'business performance'?

It is interesting to note that Luxembourg is the most efficient country worldwide in enforcing contracts' 'procedures, time and cost to resolve a commercial dispute'.

Within the EU 15 countries, it is easiest to obtain a credit in the UK. Tax procedures are most efficient in Ireland in comparison to all the OECD countries, followed by Denmark (3), Luxembourg (4) and the UK (5).

Luxembourg is number one for efficiency in enforcing contracts' 'procedures, time and cost to resolve a commercial dispute', followed by France (5) and Germany (6). Three Nordic EU countries hold the first three positions in trading across borders:

Table 6.1   *A ranking of best and worst business performance of the 183 included worldwide countries (selected business operation areas)*

Ease of ...	Best performer (1st)	Worst performer (183)
Doing business	Singapore	Central African Republic
Starting a business	New Zealand	Guinea-Bissau
Dealing with construction permits	Hong Kong, China	Eritrea
Employing workers	United States	Bolivia
Registering property	Saudi Arabia	Maldives
Getting credit	Malaysia	Palau
Protecting investors	New Zealand	Afghanistan
Paying taxes	Maldives	Belarus
Trading across borders	Singapore	Afghanistan
Enforcing contracts	Luxembourg	Timor-Leste
Closing a business	Japan	Burundi

Source: International Bank for Reconstruction and Development/World Bank: Economy Rankings, 2010

Table 6.2   *A ranking of best and worst performances of 27 OECD countries in various business operation areas*

Ease of ...	Best performer (1st)	Worst performer (27th)
Doing business	New Zealand	Greece
Starting a business	New Zealand	Spain
Dealing with construction permits	New Zealand	Portugal
Employing workers	United States	Portugal
Registering property	New Zealand	Belgium
Getting credit	United Kingdom	Luxembourg
Protecting investors	New Zealand	Switzerland
Paying taxes	Ireland	Italy
Trading across borders	Finland	Slovakia
Enforcing contracts	Luxembourg	Italy
Closing a business	Japan	Czech Republic

Source: International Bank for Reconstruction and Development/World Bank: Economy Rankings, 2010

Finland (1), Denmark (2) and Sweden (3). It would be the most difficult to close a business once established in the Czech Republic (last position 27), Hungary (26) and the Slovak Republic (22) compared to the other studied OECD countries.

We note again that European business is subject to a great diversity of formal and informal conditions. This is mainly due to cultures and identities that Member States preserve voluntarily. These cultures nonetheless overlap to some extent. This is the driving force for coherence or quasi-convergence of European business management: the phenomenon is interesting to European managers and to non-European managers alike as a matter of comprehension of business attitudes. Indeed, Jean Monnet, a founding father of European integration, was quoted to have said that if he could start again, he would start with cultural integration, as a driving force of all other harmonization in Europe. While it is questionable whether a complete cultural integration (and complete harmonization) is desirable, it is certain that communities and organizations benefit vastly from cultural understanding.

6.2 Intercultural management in Europe

Despite its conception of unity, Europe constitutes a microcosm of *diversity* that experiences convergence around certain common interests. In the increasingly global and multicultural world of European business, managers hence need to understand how people act and react in international, national, regional and even locally based organizations. Even more importantly, any company seeking to do business outside the comfortable base of its own culture is dependent on a sound comprehension of *mindsets*. This comprehension, or expertise, facilitates relations with customers and clients, suppliers, intermediates, distributors or agents, and also with those public officials whose backgrounds and cultural expectations may be quite different from one's own. Moreover, the *culture of an organization* is not expressed in a singular and unique trait, but by its diverse and ever-changing management process.

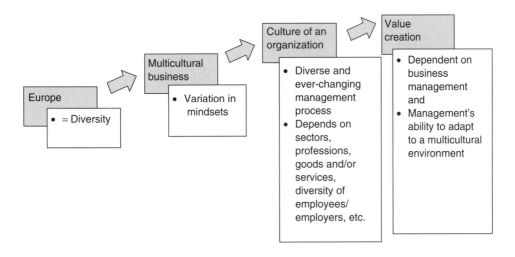

The culture of a company depends on sector(s), professions, goods and/or services, diversity of employees' and employers' backgrounds, its origin and the markets that the company operates in. Value creation in Europe depends on business management that is capable of adapting to an environment that is intrinsically and inevitably multicultural.

Increasingly, the same is true of organizations which function in a purely 'national' context, because diversity is the norm in Europe. Corporate Europe is reflected not only in a broad, multicultural customer base, fast communication between people and organizations, and strong corporate power, but also in environmental pressure and turbulence stemming from different points of view and perspectives. These pressures must find their answer in efficient diversity management.

Europeans share an increasing set of common traits. For example, in general, people worry increasingly about the impact of such issues as environmental hazards, natural disasters, poverty in the world, global warming and rising sea levels, the Kondratieff cycle, epidemic diseases, civil destabilization, global conflict and terrorism. Many of these preoccupations which reach beyond borders are based on historical experiences, and Europeans strive for peace through multilateral coordination. They try, typically, to understand the impact of risks, uncertainties and conflicts on a large scale so as to deal with them together and, hopefully, better. The desire for steady growth, open boundaries and a cosmopolitan community are based on this.

At the same time, Europeans have a historic-cultural tendency to fear nationalism, war and military conflict, but also any crisis of the welfare system through demographic changes, an increase in unemployment, and inequalities. The notion of Europe therefore encompasses a strong psychic dimension, of shared fears and of confidence in a better management of those challenges together, rather than separately.

6.3 A management definition of culture

For business management, the focus on culture necessitates the study of:

- systems of shared ideas;
- the value of diversity;
- conceptual designs supporting learned behaviours;
- beliefs, values and norms;
- patterns of symbols and artifacts;
- the sum total of all of these in relation to the specific corporate culture of one's firm.

Efficient European business management is prepared to cope with various languages (verbal and non-verbal). The first challenge in this context is always to find a solution in a multi-language environment, and to make sure that a common language is found for communication and negotiation.

Sound language skills help significantly in information gathering and evaluation. Language provides access to local societies, ensures that company communication is efficient, communicates in the right way and reduces the risk of cross-cultural misunderstanding – and thus of corporate disaster.

Box 6.1: (Mis-)interpretations of the same term, written/ expressed in English

'Yes': 'I understand/I agree/I hear you/I listen/I confirm' ...

'We need to communicate about this': formally/informally/restricted sharing/ sharing with all concerned ...

'Eventually': 'In the event of/automatically/maybe' ...

'Collaboration': may refer to a wide range of degrees of implication, responsibilities, deontology ...

'You should do this': may mean 'must' or 'should' ...

A general recommendation is to speak and write at least three languages which give essential access to communications in Europe – that is, English, German and French or Spanish. Interestingly, the three first mentioned languages are also relay languages at the EU institutions' language centres, that is, they are the languages that permit translation between two other languages.

Apart from spoken language, the interpretation of contexts that influence business operations also includes non-verbal signals: this includes mainly an interpretation of time, space, body and facial expressions, social patterns and behaviours, and agreements. The analysis of any announced communication therefore includes various criteria that influence the reaction of the receiving party. The criteria are:

- pronunciation;
- speech rate;
- message content;
- code competence and code-switching competence.

Humour, in the context of business management, can be more important in some cultures than in others. Some companies or nationalities may even be a victim of such humour, as illustrated in Box 6.2.

Box 6.2: Cross-cultural complexity: jokes

Humour is an excellent tool which helps us to understand cultures. In addition, laughter breaks down possible cross-cultural frontiers. Humour might be considered inappropriate or offensive, depending on the way that it is presented. Here are some examples from Spain:

Porqué los gallegos cuando se ponen crema en la cara, cierran los ojos ? Porque la crema dice <<Nivea>>. = Why do Spanish people close their eyes when applying facial cream? Because it may be the facial cream marked 'Nivea' (Don't look).

Porqué cuando los Gallegos se lavan los dientes, se cuelgan? Porque en la pasta dice <<Colgate>>. = Why would Spanish people hang themselves when they brush their teeth? Because the toothpaste is called 'Colgate' (Hang yourself).

One ambiguous example follows here:

A given culture: how international corporations work, explained with the help of cows

A French corporation: You have two cows. You go on strike because you want three cows.

A German corporation: You have two cows. You re-engineer them so they live for 100 years, eat once a month and milk themselves.

(Continued)

(Continued)

An Italian corporation: You have two cows, but you don't know where they are. So you break for lunch.

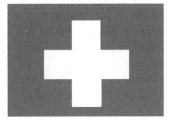

A Swiss corporation: You have 5000 cows, none of which belong to you. You charge others for storing them.

Source: http://culturalmoments.blogspot.com/2007/12/european-stereotypes. html

The (real or assumed) perception or understanding of underlying cultural values of communications, literature, media publications and humour, is evident to the receiver of such a message on the condition that he/she is well acquainted with it or an insider and part of it. Taken from a different cultural stance, it may well be baffling and misinterpreted.

6.3.1 The relevance of identity

When unfamiliar with a particular culture, you may consider it strange, threatening or exotic. Its habits may be acquired with difficulty. This is sometimes so when one thinks of other religions, customs and other variables, on which cultural traits depend and which characterize one's adherence and identity. They include:

- religion;
- values and attitudes;
- manners and customs;
- material elements;
- aesthetics;
- education;
- social institutions.

From the list above, one example is education. We receive our education from parents, institutions, social networking, media and publications that we choose to look at, our travel and our surroundings as a whole. They are the primary factors that shape our *mindset* and our way of thinking and behaving in a particular situation. For example, the use of first names in business relations is common in the UK and Ireland, while last names and the use of titles is recommended in Austria and Germany. German employees may find it normal and convenient to eat lunch at their desk; French employees will find it important to take that time to leave the office and take more time for lunch (often from 12 to 2 p.m.); Scandinavians will take their lunch rapidly and early (as of 11 a.m.); and in Spain, lunchtime is traditionally long and late (around 3 p.m.). In France, colleagues often use kisses on the cheeks to greet each other, unknown of in Poland and relating to the different appreciation of space and intimacy. This is also relevant in the evaluation of office space and distribution, in regard to privileges or tendencies one may observe. For example, in some places, the key executive will have the nicest and most spacious office while, in other places, she or he may share an open office space with others.

Second, the notion of time and space vary and are culture-, sector- and situation-dependent. In the north of Europe, meetings will start on the hour, while further to the south, participants will find it normal to arrive later. Manners related to time are learned from the social environment, from institutions and from educational contexts at any given time in life.

Attitudes, including those related to time, can then shift when one changes any of these three contexts over a longer period. This goes further than *punctuality*. In negotiations in southern Europe, for instance, the first meeting may be just a 'get to know you' session and it can well take several meetings to get to business. In northern Europe, they are straight to business in the first meeting. Hall and Hall (1990, p. 15) also analysed time in terms of *monochronic* and *polychronic commitments*. *Monochronicity* translates into dealing with one issue at a time, along deadlines, with a high focus on the job, short-term relationships, low contexts and a need for information inputs to enable this promptness. *Polychronicity* is characterized by dealing with several issues at a time, with flexible time frames and roles, a focus on high contexts (attention to the unspoken) and a dedication to long-term relations and information sharing. Amadeus Group, the European leader in transaction processing for travel and tourism, is one example of a European company that has decided to opt for flexible working and meeting hours in order to respect various international customs. Hofstede also uses the dimension of time and long- or short-term orientation (see below).

The challenge for companies that work across borders and cultures is to reduce the gap that employees perceive between new cultures and their own, and to help them deal with this. The aim is to shorten the period of time that it takes employees to understand different ways of doing, of working and of knowledge; in this way, productivity and team efficiency can be maintained or increased, rather than (even if only temporarily) lost because of 'culture shocks'.

Third, systems of shared ideas in one culture are, more often than not, not the same in another. They may appear complex, interpersonal, process-oriented or not, relational or contradictory.

6.3.2 Synergy and diversity: the impact of communication

Many of these tensions are antithetical to our taught ways of doing things and to apprehending reality, especially in a 'scientific' context. So how can one survive in this 'jungle' of cultures? Is there *the* right way to communicate and to negotiate in a multicultural environment such as that in Europe? What will one need to expect as a European expatriate? How does one best prepare to deal with partners or subsidiaries across Europe? Carey (1989) developed communication models that explain the 'symbolic process whereby reality is produced, maintained, repaired and transformed'. Herein, communication is based on the following.

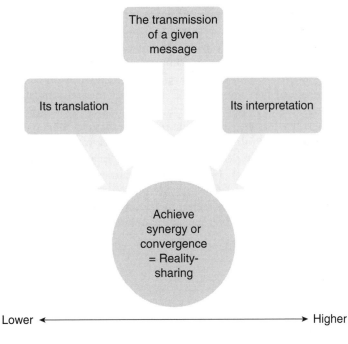

These three stages take place, ideally, within a desire for reality-sharing, because the emitter/sender needs to ensure that the message is well understood. The message is only well understood when intentions, behaviours and interpretations surrounding the message are jointly believed to be viable, that is, when a certain level of *synergy* or *convergence* can be achieved between the communicator, on the one hand, with one cultural background, and the receptor on the other, with possibly another background. For example, in recent times, sustainable development has become a focus for managers in very different countries, and messages about the business impact in this matter are convergent. With this, knowledge is transmitted more easily from one actor to another, and can be translated into different cultures, or even into common shared legislation, and the protection of ideas and concepts.

Synergy between the emitter and the receiver can, in most cases, only be partial: it is situation-dependent. Take the example of a team that needs to boost innovation in the communication of a product. For the team leader, the term 'innovation' might refer to e-related advertising. For some team members, it might rather mean communicating through academic, NGO or similar stakeholder channels. For yet others, it might mean cross-border communication, or the addition of service-related features to existing communication tools, or opt-in membership groups, or a change in the speed of communication in existing channels. The interrelation of cultural comprehension and of situations hence adds complexity to communication, and requires explicit communication.

6.3.3 The value of diversity

The value of diversity (upon condition of understanding) is beneficial for organizations because it leads to an exchange of knowledge, expertise and experience stemming from different contexts – for example, a speaker with a banking background from London expects an audience with a banking background in Frankfurt to have 'appropriate' synergy originating from competence and from appropriate norms for language use. However, the speaker is deceived if perspectives on banking issues do not diverge because of the 'brainstorming' effect that these divergences have. If the speaker does not make any effort to seek the values of synergy and diversity, this will normally be perceived as negative, even more so than incompetence (Giles and Noels, 2002; see also their other numerous publications in the field).

Haven't the different eating cultures of Europeans helped McDonald's *improve its customer services and product lines*? Haven't country cultures that are supportive of innovation, R&D and technologies (such as Sweden, the UK and The Netherlands) changed the EU-wide (sometimes sceptical) acknowledgement of the *economic potential* of GM (genetically modified) crops for farmers, the food industry and European economic development?

6.3.4 Negotiations

For companies, culture also has a direct impact on *negotiations*. Negotiation may well be easier with similar counterparts abroad (not sharing the same common national

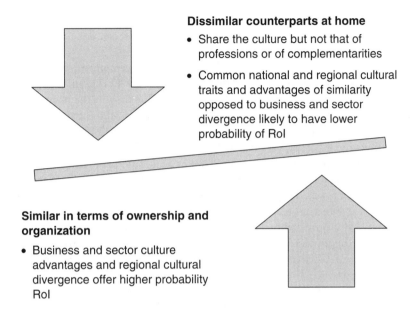

Dissimilar counterparts at home

- Share the culture but not that of professions or of complementarities

- Common national and regional cultural traits and advantages of similarity opposed to business and sector divergence likely to have lower probability of RoI

Similar in terms of ownership and organization

- Business and sector culture advantages and regional cultural divergence offer higher probability RoI

or regional culture) than with dissimilar counterparts at home (sharing that culture but not sharing that of professions or of complementarities): when doing business across borders, it would be easiest to start with firms that are similar in terms of ownership and organization (Sparrow et al., 2004), because of comparable business and sector cultures. In this case, *business and sector culture advantages opposed to national and regional cultural divergence* grant a higher probability of return on investment in the negotiation and operation phases than *common national and regional cultural traits and advantages of similarity opposed to business and sector divergence*. For example, it may be easier for an Italian textile producer to handle negotiations with a Polish or Russian counterpart in the same or complementary sector, than to negotiate with a Spanish banker about the funding of the operation.

6.3.5 The impact of business management Europeanization on human resources management

Human resources management is directly affected by European diversity, European integration and the Europeanization of business management. The relative ease of constituting European teams and partnerships is a benefit for all stakeholders, i.e. organizations, labour and institutions. National institutional contexts are rather predominant in this field, and EU initiatives complement or – in the long run – will substitute certain sets of national legislation (through, for example, the part- and fixed time directives of 1999 for equal employment protection). The EU Regulation 1408/71 of 1971 set the scene and facilitated mobility within Europe by offering the possibility for employees to remain in their previous social security scheme when abroad in Europe, given the diversity of social security systems. This applies for limited periods (1 + 1 years), with an extension of up to 5 years, but, again, due to the differences in systems, is technically complex to implement.

Also, the field of information and consultation of employee representatives is regulated at European level. A 1994 European Directive introduced European Works Councils (Council Directive 94/45/EC of 22 September 1994). The broad-scale use of contingent employment practices (that is, 'the ability to adapt without undue pain or cost to the requirements of the market' (Tregariskis and Brewster, 2006, p. 112)) through different types of employment contract is facilitated, in some Member States more than in others, by social security, trade union support and employment protection (Koene et al., 2004).

The EU thus aims to encourage companies in specific areas to facilitate mobility in order to avoid classical lay-offs as far as possible, and to provide subsidies for mobility and training. The European Social Fund (ESF) launched actions to fight against some potential discrimination: the Quinqua Competencies Project is an example of this. It analyses the impact of the ageing of salaried employees on cross-border companies; the Franco-German–Spanish helicopter company Eurocopter was acting as one pilot company for this project. The challenge in this context is to adapt and explain retirement policies according to the evolution of legislation, the social rules and conventions; manage the transfer of competencies between generations; enhance and manage the ends of careers along adapted remuneration and recognition criteria; and define organization and working hours (that is, flexi time, part time, full time). Part of this involves the adaptation of work stations and their environment to the challenges of European human resources (HR) policies in response to demographic and economic necessities (ageing workforce, equality, etc.).

Of course, diversity and HR management across borders and cultures is by nature a complex matter, on a technical and human basis. Comparative research into management styles and norms reveals the main features of different models, of which the table below is a relevant example.

Table 6.3 *A tentative comparison of two selected HR models in Europe*

The Anglo-Saxon model	The so-called Rhineland model
Short-term benefits (contracts; recruitment based on technical or experience match; high wage disparencies; profit-sharing or reward upon individual merit and position)	Long-term orientations (contacts; recruitment policies based on complete reviews of files, interviews, references, aptitude testing; performance-related reward for group)
A highly flexible and fluid labour market (few in-house promotions, hire and fire)	Low degrees of flexibility of labour markets (dismissal complex)
Generalist management training (business-school type)	Specialist management education (engineering, sciences, law, etc.) and in-house training
Low degree of vocational training	Close industrial relations (important union and bargaining structures)
High degree of specialization of staff	Low staff specialization (in-house mobility)

Source: Koen, 2005: 198–243

Effective and efficient business is optimal in the case of information convergence, starting from the very basis of well-adapted recruitment and staffing policies. Every level of the corporate value chain (most commonly studied alongside Porter, 1987, as explained in Chapter 5) is affected by cultures, ideally by the search for useful synergies. This allows business to preserve the benefits of diversity. In HR, different backgrounds allow for a range of perspectives that are useful with staff members who travel, work and/or live across borders but, also, technological development benefits from a diversity of education, conceptual thinking, preferences in design, and an understanding of consumer needs and desires. In procurement, cultural diversity helps by giving a wider perspective to what is happening in the field and where opportunities lie; in logistics and in operations, value is added when execution excels through transnational knowledge, which is a key to marketing, sales and service efficiencies and effectiveness across Europe (Schueffel and Istria, 2006).

6.4 Crucial cross-cultural and convergence management methodology

Management across borders necessitates an expertise of cross-cultural management methodology that can be acquired through training or experience.

On the one hand, the advantage of *training* is that trainees show a fast learning curve in regard to reference points that are useful when facing particular situations. On the other hand, nothing can replace real *experience*, because training always *stereotypes* to some extent. Also, monocultural staff may experience subconscious barriers to the penetration of other cultures and, therefore, if selected for an international assignment because of rare professional competence in the firm, need particular attention. The selection of adapted staff is hence key to cross-border efficiency, as detailed in Box 6.3.

Box 6.3: The value added when joining the two methodologies of training and experience

- The level and frequency of cross-cultural clashes are reduced.
- The adaptation phase to foreign cultures is shortened.
- The efficiency of managers in a foreign environment is immediate.

This efficiency is strongly influenced by what can be called the 'life cycle of adaptation' that the international manager (or manager of an international team) is living. Danckwortt (1959) is one of the precursors of this life cycle, and separated the cultural adaptation process into the four main periods of observation, interpretation, consolidation and leaving.

The key to multicultural management is the creation of trust and confidence between cultures. Though European cultures are relatively similar, each of them has a particular way of achieving this feeling of *security* that:

- drives common achievements on a business operations level;
- motivates people;
- enhances efficient communication.

While each business case is different, specific models, concepts and 'dimensions' help calculate potential options to exploit and traps to avoid. Hofstede's five fundamental cultural dimensions (see Box 6.4), researched across a sample of 55 countries, offer this kind of help, and was fundamentally complemented by the works of Hall (above), Trompenaars, the GLOBE study and others. An early acquisition of expertise about a host country's cultural dimension, set in relation to its own culture, reduces the country-of-origin/liability of foreignness effects of cross-cultural management.

Box 6.4: Hofstede's five cultural dimensions

- Power distance (PDI)
- Individualism–collectivism (IDV)
- Masculinity–femininity (MAS)
- Uncertainty avoidance (UAI)
- Time orientation (LTO)

6.4.1 The large or small power-distance culture (PDI)

Power distance highlights the way in which less powerful members of a society accept that power is distributed unequally. In large power-distance cultures, such as Belgium, France, Poland and Portugal, everybody has his or her place in a hierarchy. In the UK, Germany, The Netherlands and Scandinavia, this idea of hierarchy is less important and more transparent. These countries are said to be in cultures of small power distance. Hierarchies are rather flat in these societies, and the focus on collaboration of different power levels is higher. Management decisions, negotiations, HR policies and business–government relations are influenced by the power-distance culture.

6.4.2 The individualist or collectivist culture (IDV)

In individualist cultures, people emphasize their own concerns, even those of their own family, and want to differentiate themselves from others. In collectivist cultures, people belong to in-groups, which support them in exchange for loyalty, and are preoccupied with a common goal rather than an individual one. In collectivist cultures, the need for harmony may translate into higher degrees of conformity and acceptance of challenges. Northern Europeans are typically considered to tend towards individualism and southern Europeans towards collectivism. The goals of your staff, management and corporate culture are mainly influenced by this; for example, your reward policy may need to vary from one geographically based business unit to another. Also, we can argue that a public sector entity is by nature one that is driven by collectivist goals, though that does not imply that all individuals herein are driven by collectivism in their career management. This leads us to the awareness that culture is not only linked to nationality but also to industries, sectors, professions and other factors.

6.4.3 The masculine or feminine culture (MAS)

In masculine cultures, the dominant values are achievement and success. The dominant values in feminine cultures include care for others and quality of life; a focus on performance and achievement is less important while key for pride in masculine cultures. In addition, status is not interpreted equally in the two approaches. In Europe, a tendency towards masculinity can be found in the cultures of the UK and Italy. Examples of feminine cultures are The Netherlands and the Scandinavian countries. Depending on the origin of your company, the origin of its executives or that of the majority of its employees, the Europeanized enterprise will tend to satisfy more one or the other culture. For example, employees may push for involvement in social and humanitarian initiatives that stimulate the corporate culture through ethical standards and stakeholder satisfaction. Conversely, a company may focus its corporate governance on shareholder satisfaction and translate this into an essentially Milton Friedman-type of profit focus. Friedman, the recipient of the 1976 Nobel Memorial Prize for economic science, forwarded in *Capitalism and Freedom* (1962) that corporate social responsibility (CSR) is a 'fundamentally subversive doctrine' in a free society, and that in such a society, 'there is one and only one social responsibility of business – to use its resources and engage in activities designed to increase its profits so long as it stays within the rules of the game, which is to say, engages in open and free competition without deception or fraud'. We can then assume that its CSR initiatives are driven by marketing and communication objectives rather than deep long-term moral and resource-related investments. This does not necessarily connect to the individualism or collectivism measures.

6.4.4 High or low uncertainty avoidance (UAI)

Uncertainty avoidance is the extent to which people feel threatened by uncertainty and ambiguity, and hence try to avoid these scenarios. In cultures of strong uncertainty avoidance, rules and formality provide for a feeling of structure and security. In weak uncertainty avoidance cultures, people tend to be more innovative and entrepreneurial, in other words more risk taking. Some countries of southern and Eastern Europe score highly on uncertainty avoidance, England and Scandinavia lower.

The dimension of LTO (time orientation) has been discussed above, and plays a role in the manner in which corporations and managers develop strategies and negotiate contracts. Indeed, Hofstede's dimensions (Box 6.4), though accused of a certain rigidity and somewhat criticized, allow for insights into the way in which both HR management and business negotiations need to be ruled by cross-cultural knowledge. Such dimensions categorize cultures, in showing, for example, that:

- power distance needs to be taken into account more so in Poland than in Sweden;
- people might be more individualistic in/from The Netherlands than in/from Germany;
- we can count on a much stronger masculinity tendency for Germans than Swedes;
- the same holds for uncertainty avoidance; and
- the long-term orientation of Dutch employees can be expected to be more pronounced than that of their Swedish counterparts.

Aviat and Coeurdacier (2007, p. 28) and others demonstrate, on the basis of a gravity equation model, that countries with common borders trade more with each other than with others. The Uppsala School of internationalization teaches us that there is a tendency for companies to first internationalize into countries that are culturally related. Because market integration stimulates trade, this trend is sustained in Europe: 'Trade between people who know each other is less costly and as a consequence people who belong to the same social networks trade more' (Aviat and Coeurdacier, 2007, p. 28).

European cultures have increased peoples' shared economic, societal and even political links. There is a feeling of belonging to a shared cultural space that underlies social, economic and political cohesion, as much as there remains national patriotism, together creating a prosperous breeding ground for a transnationality of business.

The feelings that define cohesion, that is, the identity of the European people, is based on the identification of what is shared ('us') and what is different ('the other'). Only this in- and out-group identification (subconsciously often more than consciously) enables the construction of a true European identity (Box 6.5). On the one hand, the successful construction of European relations over old fractures is in itself a shared 'us' – a characteristic that (situated in time rather than in space) separates contemporary Europeans from 'the other', that is, past wars and conflict. Demorgon (2005), particularly, stresses this basis of a European culture in that antagonisms can, by use of adaptive mechanisms that benefit from the overlaps that always exist, turn from hostility to the emotive and cognitive conditions for intercultural comprehension. On the other hand, economic crisis and competition boost the definition of the 'other' in terms of space (markets), GDP, corporate revenue and similar characteristics.

Box 6.5: A 'European tribe'?

Feeling excluded from the 'European tribe', Caryl Philips stated that ' ... a large part of finding out who I was, and what I was doing here, would inevitably mean having to understand Europeans ... They all seemed to share a common and mutually inclusive, but culturally exclusive culture.'

Source: Phillips, a British national of African–Carribean descent (1987)

Management needs to be responsive, proactive, flexible and knowledge-based in order to make it through the European *complexity* of cultures. The required qualifications for managers that work across borders are clearly different to those that are recruited for local assignments only. Also, for those working in local firms but relating to non-local customers, distributors, suppliers and partners need to be enabled to deal efficiently with various cultures. Which meetings with those partners are followed up on? Will the partners work for the implementation of decisions taken in meetings, regardless of how they feel about them personally, such as in Germany, or need they be personally convinced of its rightness, as is often the case in The Netherlands, or can they raise objections freely that might hinder implementation, as one finds in Spain? Will you reward your teams for the efficient implementation of decisions, and rather award the group or the individuals? The key to appropriate behaviour, is, as a rule of thumb, to observe the values of the society and the norms within the group you are dealing with, and to develop:

- empathy, appreciating difference and diversity in a non-judgemental manner;
- interpersonal skills and the ability to cope with misunderstandings;
- team efficiency capabilities and constructive behaviours;
- tolerance for uncertainty and ambiguity.

6.5 Intellectual property: a case for European convergence

A recent study of culture, work dependence and local embeddedness demonstrated that, on the basis of sound research data from the public relations sector, employees from high power distance, high uncertainty avoidance and high-context cultures are likely to favour *standardization*. In marketing, factors resulting in standardization preferences have also been studied (Laroche et al., 2001; Newburry and Yakova, 2006). In these studies, standardization is recognized to have an effect on coherence-raising, cost-saving, improved planning and control, and greater ease in exploiting ideas (Buzzel, 1968). This leads directly to a reflection on the utility of IP protection as a case of convergence and standardization across Europe. You will note that Europeanization of IP is very much dependent on international synergies and regulations, and on the will of the people. In Europe, in particular, the preservation of identity and ownership rights is valued as essential.

IP refers to creations of the mind: inventions, literary and artistic works, and symbols, names, images and designs used in commerce. IP is important to preserve, and it is costly when lost for an enterprise. We will see in this section that IP is well protected in Europe, but less so in its neighbouring countries. The International Criminal Police Organization (INTERPOL) Database on International Property (DIIP) Crime is an autonomous iBase database that contains information regarding organized IP crimes. The database was created to perform criminal analysis to monitor links between transnational and organized cross-industry sector IP criminal activity, and to facilitate criminal investigations. It is particularly useful because it facilitates law enforcement interventions in transnational organized IP crime, and helps to improve the flow of communication between stakeholders, strengthening the efficacy of international law enforcement. Figure 6.1 (below) shows which member countries the INTERPOL Intellectual Property Rights Programme works with (in black). It is evident that all of Europe is covered, though many of the neighbouring countries are not.

The enforcement of intellectual property rights in Europe has been threatened over the last decade due to extremely skilled counterfeiters operating on a global scale. These counterfeiters are known to make expert use of technology and trade to produce every imaginable fake item. This includes luxury goods, fashion and film products, cosmetics, hygiene products, medicine, toys and various types of technical and electronic equipment. These sectors are at the heart of European culture, identity and competitiveness for their quality. The EU has therefore implemented a number of legal instruments such as the Enforcement Directive, and seeks to improve the administration cooperation

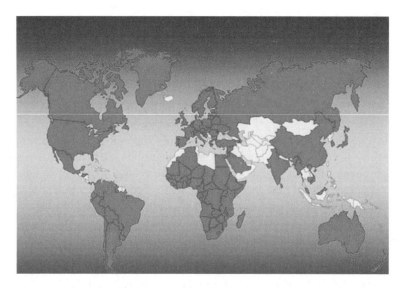

Figure 6.1   *INTERPOL member countries working with the INTERPOL Intellectual Property Rights Programme, September 2010*

Source: © INTERPOL, http://www.interpol.int/Public/FinancialCrime/IntellectualProperty/DIIP/Default.asp, 2011. In black: members

between authorities at all levels to fight piracy and counterfeiting. One result is the 2008 European Observatory on Counterfeiting and Piracy – a Resolution on a comprehensive EU anti-counterfeiting and anti-piracy plan.

Altogether, areas that IP covers include:

1 Copyrights, including original literary and artistic works, music, television broadcasting, software, databases, advertising creations and multimedia: automatically applicable (no need for formal application or registration).
2 Industrial property, including patents, utility models, designs, trade marks, plant variety rights, topography of integrated circuits and geographical indications: registered in each individual EU country.
3 Commercial strategies, trade secrets, know-how, confidentiality agreements or rapid production.

6.5.1 Patents

By definition, a *patent* is an exclusive right granted for an *invention*, that is, a product or process that provides a new way of doing something, or offers a new technical solution to a problem. The process of turning an invention into an innovation is *culturally biased*: an interpretive process is a prerequisite in its diffusion, and ideas have to be put into an abstract form for 'export' and protection as a *property*.

The first step in securing a *patent* is the filing of a patent application. The application contains the title, an indication of the technical field, the background and a description of the invention in enough detail so that an individual with an average understanding of the field could use or reproduce the invention. An invention must fulfil certain specific conditions, in that it must be of practical use, show novelty and add on existing knowledge. Also, in Europe you must be 'first to file'. If these conditions are satisfied, the patent is then granted by a national patent office or by a regional office that does the work for a number of countries, such as the European Patent Office (EPO, http://www.european-patent-office.org). The EPO, located in The Hague, offers patent protection in 36 European countries. Cooperation and European patents can be obtained from national IP agencies (such as the French 'Institut National de la Propriété Industrielle', http://www.inpi.fr; the Slovakian 'Slovak Industrial Property Office', http://www.epo.org/about-us/european-patent-network/ssp/sk-po.html; or the Latvian 'Latvijas Republikas Kulturas Ministrija', http://www.km.gov.lv/lv/).

In 2009, the EU reached a political agreement to set up a single EU patent. However, in practice, a common patent was blocked by some Member States, including Italy, and innovators continue to acquire national patents for protection, suffering administrative and financial burdens, including for translation.

The patent examination will take between three and five years. Once you are awarded the patent, protection for an invention to the owner of the patent is granted for a limited period of time that generally covers 20 years. The patent protection in the USA also ends 20 years from the date of the first application, however the patent examination can be a lengthy process depending on the number of patents received in a year and the kind of patent to be reviewed (i.e. biotechnology and software design patent applications tend to take longer). The process can last from two to six years. China's patent term length is also 20 years, however the length of time it takes to get a patent varies depending on the type of patent received. There are three types of patents in China: the Patent for Invention (similar to the Utility patent in the USA), the Patent for Utility Model (similar to the Utility Model patents in Europe) and the Patent for Design. China has been working to decrease the amount of time it takes to have a patent issued and, similar to the USA, the length depends on the number of applications received, as well as the technology involved. Presently, invention patents typically take two to four years after entry into substantive examination and utility model patents take 4 to 15 months (no examination is required). This patent protection excludes the invention's commercial make, use, distribution or sale without the patent owner's consent. As the patent owner, you may give permission to, or license, other parties to use the invention on mutually agreed terms. You may also decide to sell the right to the invention to someone else, who will then become the new owner of the patent.

Box 6.6: Patent costs

In Europe, covering all of the market with a patent costs an overall EUR70,000 using regional and national agencies, compared with EUR20,000 in the USA and less in Asia. Savings of more than EUR150 million for companies potentially stem from a full harmonization.

Source: 'EU takes big step towards common patent system', *EU Observer*, 2009, http://www.euobserver.com/9/29099

Infringement and validity issues of patent rights are judged in national court. This may happen if, for example, after communication about an invention, the right to claim it as a patent may have been lost or the innovation may not be unique. European countries are working on an EU patent court system to set up a single European appeals court for patent infringement disputes.

Patents are a crucial part of business protection: they provide incentives to individuals because they offer recognition for creativity and material reward for marketable inventions. These incentives encourage innovation. Patented inventions can be found in everything from electric lighting (patents held by Edison and Swan) and plastic (patents held by Baekeland), to ballpoint pens (patents held by Biro) and microprocessors (patents held by Intel, for example). All patent owners are obliged, in return for patent protection, to publicly disclose information on their invention in order to enrich the total body of technical knowledge in the world. Such a seemingly unlimited pool of public knowledge promotes further creativity and innovation in others.

For a reach beyond European frontiers, the World Intellectual Property Organization (WIPO)-administered Patent Cooperation Treaty (PCT) allows for the filing of a single international patent application with the same effect as national applications that would be filed in the designated countries (Box 6.7). Variation in the cost of a patent application is due to the application being composed of three categories of costs: (a) the official fees (this varies both by country and in the way in which the application is filed, i.e. paper vs. electronically); (b) the costs made by the patent attorney; and (c) extras/reductions, e.g. some cases will incur additional charges if the application exceeds 30 pages in length or one could receive reductions of 90 per cent if the patent is filed from a Third World country. The time required for a patent to be granted depends on the country's registration procedure. In countries where no examination is required, the patent can generally be registered within a few months. However, countries with thorough examination processes can take at least one year. With one application, you may request protection in as many signatory states as necessary. Consequently, your invention cannot be commercially made, used, distributed or sold without the patent owner's agreement. A court can ensure the patent owner's rights in case of infringement, or also declare a patent invalid due to rightful recourse by a third party. By comparison, in the USA, you will be subject to the 'first to invent' (instead of the 'first to file') principle, in which the patent is attributed to the name of an inventor (individual or group); in this market, it is easier to risk communication about an invention because the law allows for a one-year period after first communication to request and obtain the patent (http://www.uspto.com).

Box 6.7: Main treaties governing patent law in Europe and internationally

The Paris Convention, signed by 164 states, grants: (1) a one-year priority, from your national deposit onwards, for international filing; and (2) that communication about the innovation does not inhibit your patent rights.

The Patent Cooperation Treaty (Treaty of Washington, 19 June 1970) provides the possibility of depositing the same patent in 121 countries, simultaneously.

The Munich Convention on European patents (5 October 1973) helps to obtain the European patent, which has the same characteristics as the national patent, covering 36 countries.

6.5.2 Trade marks, industrial designs and other IP

A *trade mark*, a distinctive sign, serves to identify goods or services as those produced or provided by a certain person or enterprise only. The first objective of trade marks is to make sure that consumers identify and purchase a product or service with a specific image, reputation, nature and/or quality through words, letters and numerals, or other signs. Simultaneously, the owner of the trade mark enjoys exclusive use of its rights, or can authorize others to use these rights in return for payment. Therefore, trade marks foster recognition and financial profit. They are related to a specific company culture.

Renewed simply via the payment of additional fees, trade marks can be held for as long as judged necessary. Again, protection is enforced by the courts against counterfeiters who could potentially use similar marks to market inferior or different products or services.

The registration of a trade mark requires an application to an appropriate national or regional trade mark office. A reproduction of the sign filed for registration, including any colours, forms or three-dimensional features are needed, along with a list of goods or services to which the sign would apply. The applicant must demonstrate that the sign is sufficiently distinctive, so that consumers identify it as a particular product or service clearly separate from other existing trade marks. Most countries in the world register and protect trade marks, with offices that maintain a Register of Trade Marks, which contains all application information on registrations and renewals. WIPO again allows for the international registration of marks, on the basis of the Madrid Agreement Concerning the International Registration of Marks and the Madrid Protocol, and covers over 60 countries.

Industrial designs help protect a very large array of industrial and handicraft products, including, for instance, electrical appliances and textile designs. The design must be recognizable from an aesthetic point of view, but the protection does not cover its technical features; the first objective here is the marketability of the product. Protection against unauthorized copying or imitation of the design by third parties is meant to encourage creativity, and also to preserve and boost traditional arts and crafts. A new industrial design must be registered in order to be protected under industrial design law, but this is generally inexpensive. The registration certificate issued grants a term of protection of mostly five years, but can often be extended to 15 years. Generally, industrial design protection is limited to the country in which protection is granted. Under The Hague Agreement Concerning the International Deposit of Industrial Designs, another WIPO-administered treaty procedure for international registration is possible.

Geographical source indications are signs used on goods that have a specific geographical origin relating the product or service characteristics to those created in that place of origin. A place name, for example, may be that of perfume from Paris, English tea or Belgian chocolate. The efficiency of such signs in terms of market share or financial profits depends on national law and consumer perception. In the EU, geographical source indications are required by law and protected under European regulation. An appellation of origin is a particular case for products that have a certifiable exclusivity quality, or one that is substantially due to geographically dependent climates, resources or handicrafts. In contrast to a trade mark, geographical source indications may be used by all producers who make their products in the very place designated by a geographical indication, and whose products share typical qualities.

The laws against unfair competition, consumer protection laws, laws for the protection of certification marks or special laws for the protection of geographical indications or appellations of origin give the basis for this protection. From national to regional to international agreements, the WIPO again provides protection, this time mainly based on negotiations at the

Paris Convention for the Protection of Industrial Property of 1883, and the Lisbon Agreement for the Protection of Appellations of Origin and International Registration. Also, the Agreement on Trade-Related Aspects of Intellectual Property Rights (TRIPS) covers the matter, this time within the framework of the WTO. In some countries where protection extends over a lengthy period of time, consumers transpose geographical terms (for example, Dijon mustard, a style of mustard originally from the French town of Dijon) to a type of product, even if not produced at that location. The same may happen to trade marks of specific companies, such as Scotch and Tesafilm for adhesive tape.

A different case of protection is that of *copyright*, in which rights protect creators' literary and artistic works. For business management, this concerns in particular communication and advertising, or companies in specific related sectors, such as Internet-based firms. Copyright applies to works such as novels, reference works, newspapers, computer programs, databases, films, musical compositions, artistic works such as paintings and photographs, and also architecture, advertisements, maps and technical drawings. These rights protect the original creators of works and their heirs who hold exclusive rights in their use – prohibiting or granting to a third party reproduction, public performance, recording, broadcasting, translation or adaptation within a time limit (under WIPO legislation, this is 50 years after the creator's death). No official filing is necessary for copyright because the work's pure existence is protected at once.

IP protection in Europe, if not filed under WIPO, does not cover the USA, China or any other third-party markets. In manufacture, in services or in capital markets, successful companies protect innovations that may relate to sales (for example, outsourcing with or without technology transfer), through the Contract Research Organization (CRO) and the Contract Manufacturing Organization (CMO). For any company that works across borders, national protection does not suffice because it most often engages in the transfer of know-how, programmes, license-in or license-out for specific periods, or the transfer of patents if the innovation is to be sold or joint ventured.

IP laws preserve the values and ethical basis of business management in different societies with regard to creativity, knowledge and innovation, which are the underlying elements for a sound corporate culture. The satisfaction of stake- and shareholders depends on these values. A harmonization of European and international norms is essential for this type of return on investment: the convergence of principles and behaviours helps people (and business management altogether) to Europeanize and internationalize efficiently, based on European culture, diversity and identity.

6.6 Corporate culture and subsidiary management

The most common cross-border structures in Europe are functional structures, international divisional structures and product structures. Functional structures are usually used in the early stages of a company going European, since no international specialists are in place and only a few products are positioned in a limited number of cross-border market segments. When growing, the international divisional structure serves the company when it opts for standardized production or servicing in response to European consumer needs. In this structure, one particular division of the firm deals with all international business activities. Product structures are usually used in corporations that have acquired significant international experience. In this structure, each product or service division is in charge of its own R&D, production, marketing and sales departments. Many food, beverage, car and pharmaceutical companies, in particular, use a geographical structure in addition to the functional one, well adapted to a relatively homogeneous range of products that require a fast and efficient distribution channel. In this structure, each country department has its own production, marketing and financial services. Close to this is the matrix structure, organized on a two-dimension basis that emphasizes product and geographical areas, often all of Europe or as an EMEA region (Europe–Middle East–Africa). This structure is widely adopted in MNEs that have large ranges of products to sell in a geographically widespread market. Each subsidiary management depends on the firm's particular knowledge of the market, and the level and share of cross-border activity of the company. Stopford and Wells (1972) demonstrated that foreign product diversity and sales, as a proportion of total sales, encourage the turn to a matrix structure with geographically extended product divisions or area structures.

Hence, corporations change structure as they grow (Daniels et al., 1984, among others), and respond in this manner to the competing forces of local responsiveness and global integration (Bartlett and Ghoshal, 1988; Prahalad and Doz, 1987; Rosenzweig and Singh, 1991, among others). Some indications were found by Brock et al. (2007) that those firms which use the highest integrative structures globally are less effective then those with relatively lower integration structures, arguing that going straight to standardized global structures hurts effectiveness; regional structures based on diversity values may hence be considered more efficient than (a) firms structured with low degrees of integration, that is, favouring locality or (b) highly globalized firms. The structures described above increase the involvement of business management at different degrees of cross-border activity if well adapted to localities only. We can argue that the more business management engages in Europeanization, the faster it climbs up structures that we can call the 'subsidiary management ladder'.

Indeed, a study published by the European Commission in the mid 2000s and realized by EOS Gallup Europe, based on the response of 200 companies, shows that the strengthening of organizational and human capital represents key assets in establishing competitive advantage. This suggests that managing diversity is a real business asset, which delivers long-term benefits. Thanks to a multicultural Europe and an economic vitality of the European marketplace, European companies are well positioned to turn diversity into a source of growth and motivation for their employees – and to structure their subsidiary management efficiently. Companies know how to deal with local standards, adopt responsiveness and innovate accordingly. This may be very costly for

SMEs in particular, but is a main key to survival. For MNEs, the advantages of a Europeanized business environment are easier to exploit, marrying responsiveness to innovative efforts. For instance, ST Microelectronics is continuously ranked number four in the world semiconductor industry because it continues to adopt a 'system on a chip' strategy by accessing and combining European knowledge. Within the European companies that gained worldwide market share, we note a successful management of corporate development by stimulating innovation and by sharing cross-European knowledge of different environments, sociopolitical institutions and cultures. European companies attain a learning curve of diversity that provides business with a diversity of knowledge applicable in the US and Asian markets. It was found that the rapid growth of American companies in the EU is also due to this strategic orientation: Starbucks, for example, pays great attention to European behaviour, tastes and coffee cultures. This means that the described effects apply for European firms as much as they do for companies from non-EU countries which operate intensively and efficiently in the European market.

Early and rapidly internationalized structures can be found in *Born Globals*, that is, firms that are international by 'birth', such as global start-ups or instantly globalizing high-technology firms, online services and IT (information technology) security solutions. These corporations, often of SME size, rely heavily on their network structure and the diversity of the value added of each component of this structure: advantages in the use of resources, procurement, distribution and cross-border sales characterize this form of diversification and corporate risk reduction. At the same time, *Born Globals* need to be run with a global vision and a network relying on the 'know your customer, your supplier and your distributor' principles more than traditionally internationalizing firms. In Europe, start-ups are increasingly *Born Europeans*, given entrepreneurs' increasing awareness of the value creation that is possible through harmonized networks of transportation and communications, of market expertise through the proximity of European markets, and cross-cultural competencies.

Subsidiaries sometimes compete amongst each other and with local firms. The challenge is to use the best available structure so as to link knowledge retained in these subsidiaries to that relevant for efficient cross-border management (Brock et al., 1999). The relatively low level of risk in Europe, coupled with the resulting relatively high trust levels that issue from European integration on various levels reinforce a unique feature of internationalization: European firms tend to move up the subsidiary ladder of structures in Europe faster and more voluntarily than when it comes to the internationalization of non-EU countries.

The differences across Europe in culture and behaviour, in management styles, in factor efficiency and in price competitiveness are responsible for cost and price differentials that do not quickly vanish despite a high degree of market harmonization efforts. They will, rather, lead to the rationalization and streamlining of an organization. Efforts to reduce costs include diversity management and the search for cost-beneficial overlap that are necessarily good for international competitiveness, and bad for those firms that do not succeed in coping.

The structure of the organization helps or hinders the manager, and so does his or her ability to lead the organization efficiently.

6.7 The role of European leadership

The necessary charisma and qualities of leadership and management constitute a set of features that vary between one culture and another. Recent studies (Fendt, 2005, a.o.; see also the CEO case study in Part IV) demonstrate that some overlap can be found which helps us characterize successful *European leadership*.

A convincing leadership is a key competitive resource in cross-border structures and markets, and therefore essential in European business. Because three-quarters of all international business assignments are connected with the transfer of knowledge (Weir, 2004), and because intercultural communication is an elementary skill area in these transactions, the leadership of a corporation can be characterized ideally by a profile that knows how to:

- involve and listen to people (motivate and stimulate effective interaction);
- work multiculturally (in terms of countries, cultures, sectors and professions);
- recognize value diversity (flexible, intuitive and based on a broad vision);
- converge and protect value (of human resources, negotiations and IP skills).

(Adapted from Calori and De Woot, 1994, p. 237; and Paulson et al., 2002, p. 410–11)

European business management is relationship-based, and engages economic determinism in inescapable cultural convergence, with its leads and lags.

While the role of managers consists essentially in rationality, control and problem solving, the role of a leader reaches much further. Leadership in Europe is the art of recognizing the meaning of decisions and actions to a set of highly diversified people that are to share a common goal, in an integrated business environment. Its tool is the recognition of *what is shared* and *what national and international teams can share* with people, individually and collectively.

Leadership is the power exerted 'in altering moods, evoking images and expectations, and in establishing specific desires and objectives, it determines the direction a business takes' (Zaleznik, 1992, p. 128).

The locus and transfer of knowledge management in the European Single Market is best distributed through the use of writings (texts, books, emails), training, (best) practices, and in particular through individuals that have expertise and that can be observed, asked and listened to – the latter being identified as a crucial element for efficient management and leadership. Suitable knowledge for a diversified European market is scientific, positivistic or causal; it may be quantitative, linear, context-free or public. Alternatively, it may be lay, narrative, exemplary, qualitative, recursive, and is surely context-bound and idiosyncratic. Its transfer, and hence its convergence at company level across borders, is largely dependent on trust – a sentiment that can be fostered by efficient leadership.

Box 6.8: What are the skills that a global manager should have? A European opinion

For me, a global manager knows how to coach a diverse array of people. This is a person who has good relations with people and is characterized by loyalty, people assets, and so on – a person who is willing to take chances, and work them through within a long-term approach. It is a listener who is careful to approach a decision. (Jean-Philippe Courtois, CEO Microsoft International, formerly CEO Microsoft EMEA)

Source: Suder, 2005

6.8 Trust and diversity

A 'diverse workforce ... will increase organizational effectiveness. It will lift morale, bring greater access to new segments of the marketplace, and enhance productivity' (Thomas and Ely, 1996). This statement comes from an article entitled 'Making differences matter', diversity being the main research topic of Thomas and Ely in the *Harvard Business Review*, which reviews the topic (or similar ones) regularly: thinking of diversity management in a holistic manner is based on a feeling of trust that may foster or hinder knowledge transfer across cultures, along the paradigms (Thomas and Ely, 1996) of:

1 Discrimination and fairness: in HR management.
2 Access and legitimacy: in marketing and internationalization.
3 Learning and effectiveness: in knowledge management.

In academic literature, trust is typically classified as *etic*, that is, general or universal, or as *emic*, that is, culture-specific: these two notions help understand trust in cross-cultural business. They help understand which conditions, strategies and structures of a firm generate symmetries or asymmetries of trust. For example, what types of relation (communication tools, knowledge transfer tools ...) generate trust between subsidiaries, and, by consequence, may be acceptable to all or limited only to a few individuals or units? In an alliance, what are the best available patterns of ownership and distribution of resources?

Lane and Bachmann (1998), in an analysis of the foundations of trust along cultures, found that they differ significantly in terms of the meaning and significance of trust and the manner in which it can be obtained. These conditions depend, in particular, on social and institutional characteristics of cultures. For example, in Germany, technical expertise is one main precondition in the acknowledgement of managerial power, and in trust in managerial capabilities. However, personal relationships are predominant in trust-creation in Latin cultures. Stereotypes, though useful reference points for cross-cultural relations, may reduce trust-creation between partners in

foreign countries (Arino et al., 2001; Zaheer and Zaheer, 2006). Consequently, motivations and expectations are preconditioned by trust patterns and influence cross-
border partnerships and operations in terms of investment volumes and investment
modes, institutionalization of relations, internalization and knowledge transfer,
monitoring and controlling (Zaheer and Zaheer, 2006).

Any culture-, gender- or colour-blindness is detrimental to the values that originate
in diversity. If the knowledge of any of a company's cultures (at headquarters and
subsidiaries or at agents) is not fully taken into account, knowledge is not at its best.

The Europeanization of the business environment of more than 27 countries provides a unique chance for corporations. In terms of business management, strategy
and knowledge management conditions, a firm has the opportunity to benefit from
shared cultural, social, economic and business conditions that converge at a fast pace.
In terms of the constant striving for competitive advantage, the Europeanization of
this business environment underlies corporations' ability 'to integrate, build and
reconfigure internal and external competencies to address rapidly changing environments' (Teece et al., 1997). Its diversity makes organizations capable of identifying
the most valid and promising conditions.

6.9 Résumé and conclusion

This chapter positioned Europeanization issues in the area of business management.
It offered the chance to learn about the cultural differences and similarities in
European management; and to reflect on the question of whether a European strategy makes sense, and whether that concerns the HR management or any other stages
of the value chain that are influenced by diversity. We learned that diversity could be
of great competitive advantage to corporations in many different fields. But also a
certain convergence of interests, values and priorities in business helps it to remain
on top of the competition. The use of synergies and convergence facilitates the efficient application of resources and the protection of ideas and inventions. International
property rights were the main example when studying convergence, but we also
looked at equality issues, given their significance for economic growth and diversity
value creation. The same phenomena of diversity and synergy were found in subsidiary management, across the value chain of business in Europe, and underline the
utility of knowledge transfer.

Cultures, structures, roles and behaviour are ongoing but ever-changing challenges
for the European firm, from the inside and the outside; they are essential to the evolution of a European self-concept and identity with its particular contexts, situations,
personalities and leaders, literatures and emotions.

The knowledge and expertise of multiculturalism is a key competitive resource in
global markets that is acquired day after day in the European business management.
The following chapters shed light on those particular stages of the value chain and
competitive edging that are crucially influenced by European diversity and convergence phenomena.

Mini case study: Cargo business – cultural perspectives

For several years, I acted as a senior manager in a Finnish logistics company, which specialized in door-to-door delivery of various types of cargo from around the world to Russian clients. Finland is one of the most important transit routes to Russia as it has a good infrastructure and favourable customs procedures and regulations. Thus, products that are manufactured in Asia, the Americas and Europe are often delivered to Russia through Finland.

The nature of this business implies that employees of the company have to interact on a day-to-day basis with business partners and customs authorities from many countries. The major challenge in my job was to achieve understanding and smooth communication between partners in the logistic chain of each delivery, which was a particularly difficult task due to the geographic and cultural differences. There were three main groups of actors that our employees had to interact with: Russian clients, forwarding agents and customs authorities. Each of these groups had their own ways of working, requirements and interests. Our main task was to coordinate their activities in order to deliver cargo in the required time and at minimum cost. Indeed, the specific feature of transport logistics – as a type of business operations – is that delivery of cargo involves many actors and stages: the coordination and understanding of what is going on at each of the stages is essential for achieving the desired outcome. The Russian clients always put the receipt of their cargo at the top of their priorities, regardless of the time of day or day of the week; whereas our Finnish employees treated the job as just one of the various tasks to accomplish within their working hours. Hence, when the Russians required us to do extra work to follow their tight schedules, the Finnish employees simply refused to stay longer. This was certainly due to the high value they placed on their personal lives. The job is not valued above their own personal time and family activities, and hence Finnish employees would not spend any Friday evening waiting for a delivery, though this was often demanded by our Russian clients. On the contrary, as Russian business is very competitive and firms and employees are under continuous pressure to perform, Russian employees are expected, without question, to do extra hours where required to keep their jobs intact and businesses successful. Also, Finnish customs authorities are very rigid in their work procedures and follow rules and timetables without exception, even when the situation is 'urgent'. For example, I realized that Finnish working hours span from 8.00 to 16.00, while Russians work from 10.00 to 20.00 (often 22.00). As a Russian manager in Finland, I specifically had to motivate the Finnish employees to satisfy our customers' expectations and to take more proactive attitudes towards their work.

At the same time, it was essential to explain to the Russian customers that in Finland things are not done at any time and that people live according to their own priorities. However, over time, the ways and means of overcoming these differences were found through close interaction and discussions, allowing for an expression of opinions and attitudes. A new flexibility ensured the success of our company and

Mini Case

Russian clients often referred to our expertise as being 'understanding' and 'efficient', as compared to many other Finnish companies. It is worth noting that the company's rapid development and provision of financial rewards were very persuasive for the employees in proving the necessity of implementing a 'tailored' approach to their work. After all, we have created a highly positive spirit of mutual understanding and cooperation. Management involvement decreased over time because employees were eager to support the 'organizational culture' and pass it on to new workers.

Source/Author: Irina Jormanainen, Aalto School of Economics, Finland

Mini-case study questions

1   How did cultural differences affect the development of the cargo business?
2   What skills are required to overcome difficulties associated with cultural differences?

REVIEW QUESTIONS

1   **Explain** the difference between business cultures and national cultures.
2   **Why** does the EU strive to complement national rules affecting human resources management?
3   **To what extent** does the European social agenda influence business management?
4   **Does** Europeanization phase out and equalize cultures, norms and behaviour?
5   **To what extent** does the valuation of diversity sustain or even increase the competitive edge of European corporations?

ASSIGNMENTS

- **Imagine** that you are the operations manager of an English company. You are being relocated to Austria. How will you go about obtaining the trust and confidence of your staff in a location that is new to you?
- **Compare** the threats and opportunities that innovative companies face: Are international property rights really useful?
- **Case study assignment**: Read and prepare the 'European Chief Executives in the Merger Maze' case study in Part IV, and discuss the impact of European mergers on management styles.
- **Internet exercise**: Compare the social security systems of three EU states of your choice. Discuss your findings and their significance to a firm with staff working across these three countries.

Further reading

Brewster, C. (2007) A European perspective on HRM. *European Journal of International Management*, vol. 1, no. 3, pp. 239–59.

Fischer, R. and Mansell, A. (2009) Commitment across cultures: a meta-analytical approach. *Journal of International Business Studies*, vol. 40, no. 4, pp. 1339–58.

Pudelko, M. and Harzing, A.-W. (2007) How European is management in Europe? An analysis of past, present and future management practices in Europe. *European Journal of International Management*, vol. 1, no. 3, pp. 206–24.

Sagiv, L. and Schwartz, S.H. (2007) Cultural values in organizations: insights for Europe. *European Journal of International Management*, vol. 1, no. 3, pp. 176–90.

 INTERNET RESOURCES

Corporate social responsibility network for sustainable development in Europe, with information about business leaders and campaigns:
http://www.csreurope.org

Council of Europe site with information about European identity, human rights, social cohesion, education, culture and heritage, youth and sport, of 46 nations:
http://www.coe.int

The EU's official site with links to employment, social policy and other fields:
http://ec.europa.eu/social/main.jsp?catId=750&langId=en

European Patent Office:
http://www.european-patent-office.org

Examples of national European IP offices (UK and Hungary):
http://www.patent.gov.uk; www.hpo.hu

Functions and history of US patents and trade marks:
http://www.usgovinfo.about.com

Organization for Security and Cooperation in Europe's 55-country activities in Western Europe, including women, children, security and preventive diplomacy:
http://www.osce.org/

Site of the European Business summit, network of business leaders and policy makers:
http://www.ebsummit.org

(Continued)

(Continued)

Site of the European intellectual property authority and watchdog:
http://www.uspto.gov

United Nations Economic Commission for Europe site, illustrating the values
important to the European economic sector and linking to the population activities unit working on gender, ageing and generation issues:
http://www.unece.org

World Intellectual Property Organization:
http://www.wipo.int//portal/index.html.en

Gabriele Suder's *Doing Business in Europe* video series (on the SAGE companion
website at http://www.sagepub.co.uk/suder2e and YouTube)

Bibliography

Arino, A., Torre, S.D.L. and Ring, P.S. (2001) Relational quality: managing trust in
corporate alliances. *California Management Review*, vol. 44, p. 1.

Aviat, A. and Coeurdacier, N. (2007) The geography of trade in goods and asset holdings. *Journal of International Economics*, vol. 71, March, pp. 22–51.

Bartlett, C. and Ghoshal, S. (1988) Organizing for worldwide effectiveness: the transnational solution. *California Management Review*, vol. 31, no. 1, pp. 54–74.

Beeth, G. (1997) Multicultural managers wanted. *Management Review*, American
Management Association, May, pp. 17–21.

Brewster, C. and Hegewisch, A. (eds) (1994) *Policy and Practice in European Human
Resources Management*. London: Routledge.

Brock, D., Powell, M. and Hinings, C.R. (1999) *Restructuring the Professional
Organization: Accounting, Health Care and Law*. London: Routledge.

Brock, D., Siscovick, I., Thomas, D. and Burg, J. (2007) Global integration and local
responsiveness in multinational subsidiaries: some strategy, structure and effectiveness contingencies, *Asia Pacific Journal of Human Resources*, vol. 45, no. 3,
December, pp. 353–73.

Buzzel, R. (1968) Can you standardize multinational marketing? *Harvard Business
Review*, vol. 46, November–December, pp. 102–13.

Calori, R. and De Woot, P. (eds) (1994) *A European Model of Management: Beyond
Diversity*. London: Prentice Hall.

Carey, J. (1989) *A Cultural Approach to Communication*. New York: Routledge.

Chandler, A. (1966) *Strategy and Structure*, Anchor Books edn. New York:
Doubleday.

Claus, E. (2003) Similarities and differences in human resources management in the
European Union. *Thunderbird International Business Review*, vol. 45, no. 6,
November–December, pp. 729–56.

Commission of the European Communities (1999) *Employment and Social Affairs*. Luxembourg: Office for Official Publications of the European Communities; Council Directive 94/45/EC of 22 September 1994.

Danckwortt (1959) *Internationaler Jugendaustausch*. Bad Neuenahr: Juventus.

Daniels, J., Pitts, R. and Trotter, M. (1984) Strategy and structure of US multinationals: an explanatory study. *Academy of Management Journal*, vol. 27, no. 2, pp. 223–307.

Demorgon, J. (2005) *Critique de l'interculturel*. Paris: Economica.

Egan, M.L. and Bendick, M. (2003) Workforce diversity initiatives of US multinational corporations in Europe. *Thunderbird International Business Review*, vol. 45, no. 6, November–December, pp. 701–27.

European Commission and EOS Gallup (2003) Flash Eurobarometer 151b 'Globalization' (realized by EOS Gallup Europe upon the request of the European Commission (Directorate General 'Press and Communication'): survey organized and managed by Directorate General 'Press and Communication' (opinion polls, press reviews, Europe direct). Available at: http://ec.europa.eu/ public_opinion/ archives/flash_arch_fr.htm

Fendt, J. (2005) *The CEO in Post-Merger Situations: An Emerging Theory on the Management of Multiple Realities*. Delft: Eburon Academic Publishers.

Festing, M., Kabst, R. and Weber, W. (2003) Personal, in W. Breuer and M. Gürtler (eds), *Internationales Management*. Wiesbaden: Gabler. pp. 163–204.

Frankel, J. and Rose, A. (2002) An estimate of the effect of common currencies on trade and income. *Quarterly Journal of Economics*, vol. 117, no. 2, May, pp. 437–66.

Friedman, M. (1962) *Capitalism and Freedom*. Chicago, IL: University of Chicago Press.

Gallois, C. and Callan, V. (1997) *Communication and Culture: A Guidebook for Practice*. London: John Wiley & Sons.

Gannon, M. (2001a) *Cultural Metaphors: Readings, Research Translations, and Commentary*. Thousand Oaks, CA: Sage.

Gannon, M. (2001b) *Working Across Cultures: Applications and Exercises*. Thousand Oaks, CA: Sage.

Giles, H., and Noels, K.A. (2002) Communication accommodation in intercultural encounters, in J.N. Martin, T.K. Nakayama and L.A. Flores (eds), *Readings in Cultural Contexts: Experiences and Contexts*, 2nd edn. Boston, MA: McGraw-Hill. pp. 117–26.

Grant, J. (2006) Golden Arches bridge local tastes regional strategy. *Financial Times*, London edn. Business Life, 9 February, p. 9.

Hall, E. and Hall, M. (1990) *Understanding Cultural Differences*. Yarmouth: Intercultural Press.

Hampden-Turner, C. and Trompenaars, A. (1994) *The Seven Cultures of Capitalism: Value Systems for Creating Wealth in the United States, Japan, Germany, France, Britain, Sweden, and The Netherlands*. London: Piatkus.

Hampden-Turner, C. and Trompenaars, F. (2002) *Building Cross-Cultural Competence*. London: John Wiley & Sons.

Hickson, D. (ed.) (1993) *Management in Western Europe: Society, Culture and Organization in Twelve Nations*. Berlin: De Gruyter.

Hofstede, G. (1980) *Cultures's Consequences*. Thousand Oaks, CA: Sage.

Hofstede, G. (1991) *Cultures and Organizations: Software of the Mind*. New York: McGraw–Hill.

Hofstede, G., Hofstede, G.J. and Minkov, M. (2010) *Cultures and Organizations: Software of the Mind*, 3rd edn. Maidenhead: McGraw-Hill.

Holden, N. (2002) *Cross-Cultural Management: A Knowledge Management Perspective*. London: FT Prentice Hall.

Karra, N. and Phillips, N. (2004) Entrepreneurship goes global. *Ivey Business Journal*, November–December, pp. 1–6.

Koen, C. (2005) *Comparative International Management*. Maidenhead: McGraw–Hill.

Koene, B., Paauwe, J. and Groenewegen, J. (2004) Understanding the development of temporary agency work in Europe. *Human Resources Management Journal*, vol. 14, no. 3, pp. 53–73.

Lane, C. and Bachmann, R. (eds) (1998) *Trust Within and Between Organizations*. Oxford: Oxford University Press.

Laroche, M., Kirpalani, V., Pons, F. and Zhou, L. (2001) A model of advertising standardization in multinational corporations. *Journal of International Business Studies*, vol. 32, pp. 249–66.

Ledent, B. (2002) *Caryl Philips*, Contemporary World Writers Series. Manchester: Manchester University Press.

Maalouf, A. (1998) *Les Identités Meurtrières*. Paris: Éditions Bertrand Grasset. (Published in English as *On Identity*. London: Harvill Press, 2000).

Morosini, P. (1998) *Managing Cultural Differences: Effective Strategy and Execution Across Cultures in Global Corporate Alliances*. Oxford: Pergamon Press.

Newburry, W. and Yakova, N. (2006) Standardization preferences: a function of national culture, work interdependence and local embeddedness. *Journal of International Business Studies*, vol. 37, pp. 44–60.

Paulson, S., Steagall, J., Leonard, T. and Woods, L. (2002) Management trends in the EU: three case studies. *European Business Review*, vol. 14, no. 6, pp. 409–15.

Phillips, C. (1987) *The European Tribe*. New York: Farrar, Straus and Giroux.

Pitts, R. (1980) Towards a contingency theory of multi-business organizational design. *Academy of Management Review*, vol. 5, no. 2, p. 203–10.

Porter, M. (1987) The state of strategic thinking. *The Economist*, no. 23, May.

Prahalad, C. and Doz, Y. (1987) *The Multinational Mission: Balancing Local Demands and Global Vision*. New York: Free Press.

Redding, G. (ed.) (1995) *International Cultural Differences*. Aldershot: Dartmouth.

Rogers, E. (1995) *Diffusion of Innovations*, 4th edn. New York: Free Press Division of Simon & Schuster.

Rosenzweig, P. and Singh, J. (1991) Organizational environments and the multinational enterprise. *Academy of Management Review*, vol. 16, no. 2, pp. 340–61.

Schueffel, P. and Istria, C. (2006) Winning through diversity. *European Business Forum*, vol. 21, Winter 2005–6, pp. 41–4.

Sparrow, P., Brewster, C. and Harris, H. (2004) *Globalizing Human Resource Management*. London: Routledge.

Stopford, J. and Wells, L. (1972) *Managing the Multinational Enterprise*. New York: Basic Books.

Strang, D. and Soule, S. (1998) Diffusion in organizations and social movements: from hybrid corn to poison pills. *Annuel Revue Sociologique*, vol. 24, p. 265–90.

Suder, G. (2005) The CEO interview: Jean-Philippe Courtois, CEO Microsoft EMEA. *Thunderbird International Business Review*, vol. 47, no. 2, March–April, pp. 153–61.

Suder, G. and Lefevre, J. (2006) The diffusion of corporate governance paradigms: the role of sustainable development in the shareholder and stakeholder model. Paper presented at the Research Colloquium on Sustainable Development as a Tool of Competitiveness in the Multinational Enterprise, Georgia Tech, Atlanta, October.

Tayeb, M. (2000) *International Business*. London: Prentice-Hall/Pearson Education.

Teece, D., Pisano, G. and Shuen, A. (1997) Dynamic capabilities and strategic management. *Strategic Management Journal*, vol. 18, no. 7, pp. 509–33.

Thomas, D. and Ely, R. (1996) Making differences matter: a new paradigm for managing diversity. *Harvard Business Review*, September–October, pp. 70–90.

Tregariskis, O. and Brewster, C. (2006) Converging or diverging? A comparative analysis of trends in contingent employment practice in Europe over a decade. *Journal of International Business Studies*, vol. 37, pp. 111–26.

Warner, M. (2000) *Management in Emerging Countries*. London: Thomson Learning.

Warner, M. and Joynt, P. (2002) *Managing Across Cultures*. London: Thomson Learning.

Weir, D. (2004) Teaching material. Sophia Antipolis: Ceram.

Zaheer, S. and Zaheer, A. (2006) Trust across borders. *Journal of International Business*, Commentary, vol. 37, no. 1, January, pp. 21–9.

Zaleznik, A. (1992) Managers and leaders: are they different? *Harvard Business Review*, March–April, pp. 126–44.

PART III

BUSINESS ACTIVITY FUNCTIONS IN THE EUROPEAN ENVIRONMENT

7

European Economics, Finance and Funding

What you will learn in this chapter:

- How Europe attempts to master macroeconomic fluctuations.
- The impact of a single currency for business.
- How to obtain capital funding.
- Selected analyses of other efforts towards harmonization and convergence.
- The consolidation of European financial markets.

7.0 Introduction

Now, you will obtain an insight into macroeconomic fluctuations which the EU attempts to regulate through harmonization and the single currency that the majority of EU members have adopted. Moving from the macro to the micro level, we then shed light on the opportunities for firms to raise funds in Europe. Finally, you will learn about crucial convergence efforts that go hand in hand with the region's broader characteristics (ageing, retirement, taxation, accounting and stock market consolidation efforts).

European economics are characterized by the harmonization of rules that attempt to maximize the benefit gained from trade and financial integration through:

- risk sharing (the main traditional argument for cross-border asset trade);
- spillover of macroeconomic fluctuations; and
- product and consumption co-movements.

One of the main steps towards common measures was the introduction of the single currency in 1999, which provided the euro-zone members with a unique chance for economic cohesion. Also, it stimulated financial flows in an unprecedented manner, and linked the monetary fates of Member States to each other:

- for better in the case of saving costs and facilitating commercial transactions;
- and for worse, for example when members are unable to cover their debt and thus hamper economic wealth across the area.

Geographical proximity is a strong stimulation factor for cross-border equity flows (Portes and Rey, 2005). Increasing flows can be observed, even if informational asymmetries might increase transaction costs and vice versa. This finding was further confirmed (Aviat and Coeurdacier, 2007, p. 27) using evidence from data on bilateral tax treaties and institutional proximity variables, linking trade in goods (based on geographical determinants and transportation costs) to bilateral financial claims. In this study, the notions of *proximity and distance are geographical but also institutional*: proximity was found to affect asset holdings across borders, because trade in goods has a significant impact on asset portfolios, and stimulates their engagement.

This confirms that, as we saw in Chapter 6, institutional and cultural proximity has a positive effect on cross-border bilateral asset holdings. It appears therefore that financial Europeanization and globalization 'has gone much further on the financial side than on the real side' (Aviat and Coeurdacier, 2007, p. 27).

Table 7.1 shows 'advanced EU economies' current account positions, which reflect a variety of interesting features and serve as a basis for discussion.

Table 7.1 *Advanced EU economies' current account positions as a percentage of GDP at times of financial crisis*

Country	Current account position (% of GDP) observation		Currency
	2009	2010	
Germany	2.9	3.6	Euro (€)
France	−1.2	−1.4	Euro (€)
Italy	−2.5	−2.3	Euro (€)
Spain	−6.0	−4.7	Euro (€)
Netherlands	7.0	6.8	Euro (€)
Belgium	−1.0	−0.9	Euro (€)
Greece	−10.0	−9.0	Euro (€)
Austria	2.1	2.0	Euro (€)
Portugal	−9.9	−9.7	Euro (€)
Finland	0.5	2.0	Euro (€)
Ireland	−1.7	0.6	Euro (€)
Slovak Republic	−8.0	−7.8	Euro (€)
Slovenia	−3.0	−4.7	Euro (€)
Luxembourg	7.6	7.0	Euro (€)
Cyprus	−10.0	−9.8	Euro (€)
Malta	−6.1	−6.1	Euro (€)
United Kingdom	−2.0	−1.9	British pound (GBP)
Sweden	6.4	5.4	Swedish krona (SEK)
Czech Republic	−2.1	−2.2	Czech koruna (CZK)
Denmark	1.1	1.5	Danish krone (DKK)

Source: IMF *World Economic Outlook*, October 2009, p. 75

Table 7.2   *Emerging Europe*

Country	Real GDP observation		Current account balance (% of GDP)	
	2009	2010	2009	2010
Turkey	−6.5	3.7	−1.9	−3.7
Estonia	−14.0	−2.6	1.9	2.0
Latvia	−18.0	−4.0	4.5	6.4
Lithuania	−18.5	−4.0	1.0	0.5
Hungary	−6.7	−0.9	−2.9	−3.3
Poland	1.0	2.2	−2.2	−3.1
Bulgaria	−6.5	−2.5	−11.4	−8.3
Croatia	−5.2	0.4	−6.1	−5.4
Romania	−8.5	0.5	−5.5	−5.6

Source: IMF *World Economic Outlook*, October 2009, p. 78

Within this data, out of the 20 EU countries that the IMF defines as economically advanced, only four do not have the euro as currency. At the time of the 2009/10 financial crisis, 'data from Europe suggest that the pace of decline is moderating. In the second quarter of 2009, euro area GDP contracted less than previously expected, with France and Germany posting positive growth and the United Kingdom registering a more moderate decline' (http://www.imf.org/external/pubs/ft/weo/2009/02/pdf/text.pdf).

In Table 7.2, we can observe that seven out of 27 EU countries (and two candidates at that time) were still classified as emerging countries by the IMF in 2009. The IMF's definition of emerging Europe states that 'Emerging Europe is especially vulnerable to further contractions in cross-border funding, and large cross-border exposures by Austria, Belgium, and a number of other advanced economies remain a risk to banks in these countries' (http://www.imf.org/external/pubs/ft/weo/2009/02/pdf/text.pdf, p. 96/226).

7.1 Macroeconomic fluctuations

7.1.1 The euro

The euro was introduced on 1 January 2002 as the new currency of 12 of the (then) 15 EU Member States: Austria, Belgium, Finland, France, Germany, Greece, Italy, Ireland, Luxembourg, The Netherlands, Spain and Portugal. Since then, another five EU countries (which joined in 2004) have also adopted the euro as their currency: Slovenia in 2007, Cyprus in 2008, Malta in 2008, Slovakia in 2009, Estonia in 2011, and more were about to join.

This was the culmination of the EU's plan for Economic and Monetary Union (EMU). The precursor and foundation of the euro, the ECU, was the official currency of the EC but was never – under this denomination – in citizen's wallets. Its value was defined in terms of a 'basket' full of all Member States' currencies. This basket was composed of fixed proportions of Community currencies.

The ECU had no independent value on its own, but was calculated from the value of those 12 currencies, each reflecting its economic and financial strength and the relative economic importance of each Member State within the Community. The value of the ECU was revised every five years or on request if the external value of a currency had changed by 25 per cent, in accordance with a Council Resolution.

Since the original ECU was based on a mixture of currencies, the value of the ECU against any particular EU currency did not alter much over time. The Maastricht Treaty did not allow for any new currency in Europe, even if the EU was enlarged. This explains why, for example, the Austrian, Finnish and Swedish currencies could not be included in the basket calculations.

The ECU was used for non-cash transactions, such as cheque or bank transfers, for deposits on savings accounts, the purchase of bonds or other forms of investment. It was used mainly for loan issues on the international capital market by the Community institutions. Also, the EC budget was drawn up in ECUs and accounts were in ECUs; financial aid and Community loans were expressed in ECUs. The Commission used the ECU for billing and as an instrument of payment (El Kahal, 1998). Given its importance, it is necessary to briefly review its foundation.

7.1.1.1 A brief history of the euro

On 2 December 1969, The Hague Summit of Heads of State and Government decided to make EMU a main goal of the Community. The EU's history of monetary integration effectively began with the organization of a series of formal financial instruments designed to limit exchange rate volatility in the EEC markets of the 1970s. The Summit ended with a signature to create the EMU: European leaders saw the Bretton Woods system as deteriorating in the late 1960s and considered that it was probably time to weigh up the benefits of exchange rate coordination and the possibility of establishing a truly European monetary union. The main aim of this was to *limit exchange rate volatility*.

The Economic and Finance Committee (ECONFIN) now established the Werner Committee, which proposed the management of a three-stage currency arrangement: this was launched to facilitate the establishment of a full EMU within the following 10 years. In August 1971, the Bretton Woods system effectively collapsed when the US president, Richard Nixon, unexpectedly announced that the USA would discontinue the convertibility of the US dollar to gold. Given the shock that this caused on the financial markets, it was decided to put the EMU on hold. On 24 April 1972, the six founding Member States set up a 'snake in the tunnel' mechanism that floated the European currencies within set limits (the tunnel) against the US dollar. The oil crises, however, put the system under harsh pressure and it was soon abandoned.

In 1978, the EC decided to relaunch the process of monetary integration. At the Brussels European Summit, a European Monetary System (EMS) was created that entered into force in 1979. Its main goal was to *initiate monetary integration* and, through the introduction of a currency basket (with the ECU), a monetary *stabilization* mechanism, the Exchange Rate Mechanism (ERM) and a mechanism to *finance monetary interventions*, the European Monetary Fund (FECOM).

On 28 February 1986, the SEA was signed to modify the Treaty of Rome. It included significant reinforcement of the free movement of capital across Europe. With those and further advances in the field, on 7 February 1992, the Treaty of Maastricht was ready to pave the way for European monetary integration: installing a union and stipulating the following conditions that would later allow Member States to join the euro-zone, as listed here.

Euro-zone conditions:

- A country's inflation rate: no more than 1.5 per cent higher than the average of the rate in the three countries with the lowest inflation rate.
- A country's budget deficit: no more than 3 per cent of GDP and its national debt no more than 60 per cent of GDP.
- A country's long-term interest rate: no more than 2 per cent of the average of the rate in the three countries with the lowest interest rates.
- A country's currency: not devalued against any other Member States' for at least two years prior to monetary union.

At the beginning of the 1990s, public debt had reached its highest level ever in several European countries and could not be reduced during the resulting recession. With this experience in mind, EU Member States agreed to diminish the ratio of deficits and debt to GDP for the benefit of introducing a single currency, with a pact that was to reduce dramatically if not eliminate the phenomenon in the future.

At the December 1996 Dublin Summit, euro-zone members thus established a *Stability and Growth Pact*, which set rules for euro-zone members. The pact, confirmed at the Amsterdam Summit in 1997, determined that *government debt and deficit levels should be mastered over the long-term at/or below the EMU ratios (60 per cent and 3 per cent of GDP, respectively)*. The pact was also to protect against individual Member States' forcing interest rates to increase for all other members.

At the same time, the Stability and Growth Pact was made for a *stable economic environment*, despite national difficulties in implementing and maintaining its obligations. During times of economic growth in the markets, the pact was to restrict members' budgetary policy to avoid inefficient expenditure and increasing deficit. However, in times of recession, some flexibility in budgetary policy would be needed to enable financing of social help and restructuring, as was shown by the 2009/10 financial and Greek crises.

From 1 January 1999 onwards, the euro-zone experienced a transition period with the introduction of the euro, which was essential for accounting purposes. Restating all existing financial contracts (bond issues, etc.) in the euro was a huge and complicated process. With this development, companies succeeded in significantly reducing the intra-European exchange risk. On 1 January 2002, the euro became the official currency of the EU under the control of the ECB, and a reality for all financial interaction at every level in the euro-zone. Beyond the euro-zone, the euro has grown to be the second most traded currency in the world, after the US dollar.

Today, the main issue to be tackled apart from debt-related challenges, is the full integration of intra-euro-zone non-cash retail payments. In this field of payments, in contrast to large-value payments, the customer still needs to obtain euro-area-covering, comprehensive services, procedures and instruments. But let us first look at the overall business impact of the only common currency in Europe.

7.1.1.2 The benefits and consequences of the euro

- Lower transaction costs

The euro represents a natural progression towards complete economic union. Companies do not have to deal with foreign exchange risk costs. Therefore,

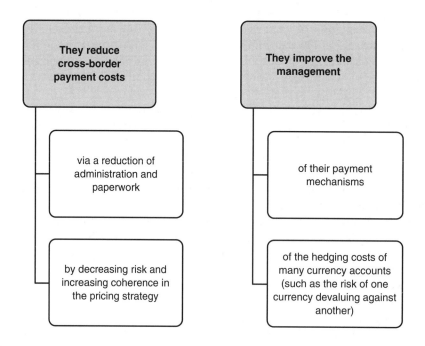

There is also greater liquidity in financial instruments. Since the introduction of the euro, countries that participate in EMU have saved an estimated $30 billion per year in the reduction of such costs ('The euro', *The European*, 2004, p. 154).

A decrease in currency risk decreases a country's risk premium, which then makes the single European market much more attractive to foreign investors.

- Macroeconomic stability and growth

The primary goal of EMU, and the subsequent introduction of the euro, served two objectives:

- on the one hand, to ensure inflationary and employment stability; and
- on the other hand, to enable EU members to remain competitive in a globalized market.

In terms of economic stability and further economic prosperity, the euro-zone saw tremendous economic growth between 1998 and 2001, characterized by increasing levels of FDI; the worldwide economic slowdown then led to a subsequent decrease in FDI influxes into the EU. It is noteworthy that the lesser developed countries enjoy an increase in FDI from the stronger EU economies, while the stronger EU economies are the main FDI recipients of and donors to non-EU states. However, the 2010 Greek crisis (that then hit other markets in the euro area) proved that not all challenges were covered: 'Confronted with debt and public deficits incompatible with euro zone policy, Greece spooked its European Union neighbours (and world markets), even though many of those EU members are only doing slightly better' (*Business Week* online, 17 April 2010). The traditional thinking about debt-to-GDP ratios was compromised, and the ability to finance high debt levels became the EU's main focus of euro-zone crisis management. In this context, the European Parliament voted to insist that financial supervisory bodies have genuine powers over national affiliates to ensure there is no repeat of the financial crisis. A note of interest: frustrations about EU budget policy became apparent during this crisis, too, as 'Germany alone contributed €8.8 billion ($11.9 billion) more than it received from the EU budget in 2008; Greece at the same time pocketed a net gain of €3.4 billion ($4.6 billion).'

In this context, the measure of per capita GDP demonstrates the positive effect of economic value creation in the euro-zone. In the 10 years after it joined the EU, Austria's per capita GDP grew 23.4 per cent, while Portugal's jumped 90.5 per cent and Spain's 149 per cent. This value creation is also perceived by European business leaders: the current business confidence index was once more on the rise only shortly after the peak of the fiscal crisis at the beginning of 2010, although it had been in free fall during the global crisis of 2008.

Table 7.3   *Price comparison in the EU at the launch of the euro: examples within the European market for consumers and corporations*

City	1 litre of milk	Music CD	Fast food hamburger meal
Madrid	€0.60	€20.95	€5.80
Berlin	€0.75	€16.99	€5.15
Paris	€1.20	€17.99	€5.85

Source: Collected and compiled from http://www.expatistan.com/price/milk/madrid and www.finfacts.ie/costofliving.htm

- Efficient capital markets

The euro and the single European market facilitate financiers', borrowers' and consumers' access to capital markets. Even though the emerging markets in India and Asia are very competitive, the emerging economies in Eastern Europe provide investors with the low-cost benefits associated with a developing economy that has the stability of a single European currency.

The euro allows for price and purchase transparency for goods and services (see Table 7.3). The European market has become more dynamic, especially when combined with Internet accessibility.

Capital, from both domestic and foreign investors, is accessible on a European scale. With a European market as one's domestic hunting ground, obtaining capital is simpler but also, if capital markets concentrate, prices rise. For corporations, the European market is behind the strong competition across all levels of the value chain, with free information flows which confront prices and intra-EU transfers of goods, services and capital.

- Transparency, discipline and competition

One major benefit of a single currency and market is a homogenous monetary policy that expects full financial transparency from each Member State. Some challenges have appeared since the introduction of the euro. Greece's budgetary deficits, the legitimacy of budgetary statistics and the need for Member States to remain well within the obligations of the pact are examples (see, for example, http://www.EUobserver.com). As a result of the pact, the euro-zone Member States' finances need to be transparent; this should result, in principle, in a coherent budgetary discipline. On this basis, the advantages of the single currency encompass *stable cross-border trade* and the *ease of movement of people, goods, services and capital.*

The disadvantages include increased cross-border competition, squeezed margins and a more complex management of European economies: the ECB must set common interest rates that are suited to rural as well as urban regions, and adapted to more or less advanced economies. Note that thanks to the euro and the Stability and Growth Pact, the EU has significantly improved the inflation record of the EU economies.

- The single European policy and the loss of autonomy by individual states

The loss of autonomy incurred by adhering to the single currency means that countries are not able to use monetary policy as a fix. For example, lowering interest rates when Ireland was booming could have caused the Irish economy to overheat as the added liquidity could spill over into worse investments and lead to inflation. An example to the contrary would be to have increased interest rates when southern Italy was in near recession. This would not have stimulated growth and consumption, but would have lead to deeper recession than if a looser economic policy had been followed. It can be assumed that the larger countries such as Germany and France have more of a say in the direction that the policy takes. This is advantageous or not, depending on one's standpoint.

It is debatable whether regional or country monetary policy is a 'good thing' or not. Indeed, in the highly integrated European markets, fiscal policy is potentially more effective than monetary policy. So, forgoing this advantage might not be such a tremendous loss after all. However, the Stability and Growth Pact also limits the extent to which fiscal policy can be used to stimulate an economy. The aim of this policy is to strengthen the conditions for price stability.

All Member States that are part of the euro-zone had to give up some cherished symbols of identity and nationhood when adopting the common coins and notes. The Greek drachma, for example, originated in the times of Alexander the Great, while the Deutschmark was a sign of post-World War II recovery and economic strength throughout a region beyond Germany, into Eastern and Central Europe. These references to the past were given up to be replaced by the euro, with a symbol from each nation portrayed on one side of its coins, which circulate throughout Europe.

- Different business cycles

Within Europe, monetary and fiscal policy freedom has been restricted. The implications of this are tremendous when one looks at differing business cycles: the difference in business cycles in Europe calls for a range of policies that individual countries are not able to set; however, in the case of differing cycles, economic shocks can be smoothed out by absorbing them throughout the euro-zone. However, it needs to be noted that if business cycles are synchronized, then big economic shocks will tend to extend to other countries through spill-over effects, thus worsening the situation in times of downturn. This is why an optimum currency area (OCA) was defined by Mundel (1961), one of its founding fathers, as a currency area for which *the costs of relinquishing the exchange rate as an internal instrument of adjustment (that is, within the area) are outweighed by the benefits of adopting a single currency or a fixed exchange rate regime.*

This implies that factor mobility, in particular in labour, throughout Europe is sufficiently large and highly dynamic. Unfortunately, there are many barriers to the various forms of mobility. European countries vary in culture, the main difference being that of language. It is unthinkable for a German factory worker to leave his or her country to go to France or Italy in search of a new job. It is true that more service-based and international jobs, such as consulting, require and enable factor mobility, thanks to a common business language. But the assumption of human mobility in Europe is still unreasonable. This means that the increased factor mobility must be found elsewhere.

One could argue that wages influence mobility. If prices rise with no corresponding increase in wages, mobility is influenced. Instead of companies moving to countries with cheaper labour, the harmonization of prices through Europe is the mobile factor: increasing prices with no wage increase is equal to a discrete reduction in salary. For example, workers in Germany recently agreed to lower wages in order to remain competitive ... Is this the first sign of an adjustment to larger international trends by the German workforce?

Box 7.1: A student's perspective on how Europe stimulates mobility even at the educational stage

A very positive point: the mobility of students, Erasmus program for example. I read that 'According to the European Union, student and teacher mobility is an important factor for growth and employment.' The third indicator relies on data from the Erasmus programme, in which the number of participants is progressing regularly (+9.4 per cent in 2003/04 and +7.4 per cent the previous year). Every year, this programme involves approximately 0.8 per cent of the European students (or, approximately 35 per cent of the intra-European flows of students). The EU aims to reach a level of 2 per cent per year, so as to include 10 per cent of the total EU students if considered as a '5-year class'. (http://www.euractiv .com/en/education/student-mobility-positive-factor-eu/article-140514)

From my personal experience I have heard only the best about the Erasmus student exchange programs ... Students really love it. And I believe that after an experience like that, they are more open to go for an internship or for a permanent employment in another EU country. (Doris Kukuljan, Croatian and Slovenian national, MSc student in International Business (SKEMA Business School); trainee in marketing and portfolio department [for the NECSE region – northern, eastern, central and southern Europe], Amadeus IT Holding SA)

One can see that since the 2004 '10-member' enlargement in particular, labour has exploited mobility opportunities, with a record immigration of Polish citizens into the British economy after the accession of Poland, and that of seasonal Polish workers into Germany. Companies thus benefit from cheaper labour and greater negotiation power in their national labour market.

Italy provides an example of one of many scenarios for the impact of labour mobility through European integration. Immigrants from the new Member States of 2004 (NMS-10), of 2007 (NMS-2) and of the six candidates (CAND-6) represent an essential resource for the Italian labour market, and have provided a significant input for national employment growth, especially in the years around their accession/candidacy.

A study by Makovec (2007) found that immigrants from these countries are a complement rather than a substitute for Italian labour; this is related to the high national demand for unskilled manual and non-manual workers and for personal and domestic care staff. In 1997, the presence of immigrants from Romania, formerly at 5 per cent of migrants from European countries, began to increase exponentially,

Table 7.4 *Labour market indicators by nationality (Census 2001)*

	Men		Women		Men and Women	
	Employment rate	Unemployment rate	Employment rate	Unemployment rate	Employment rate	Unemployment rate
Italy	54.3	9.5	31.8	14.7	42.6	11.6
NMS-10	71.1	8.2	43.7	20.5	50.0	16.9
Poland	72.4	9.1	45.6	20.9	52.1	17.3
NMS-8	71.4	8.2	44.1	20.5	50.3	16.9
NMS-2						
Bulgaria	73.9	10.2	48.1	19.6	58.0	15.2
Romania	84.2	6.7	49.8	19.7	65.5	12.6
CAND-6	77.7	8.3	31.3	26.8	57.6	13.5
Albania	77.8	8.7	29.2	30.8	57.2	14.6
Bosnia & Herzegovina	78.5	6.3	40.9	18.4	61.4	10.3
Croatia	77.9	5.2	45.2	14.0	60.2	9.0
Macedonia	85.2	5.2	20.7	31.1	61.7	9.4
Serbia & Montenegro	72.5	10.8	33.7	23.9	54.6	15.0
Turkey	74.2	7.7	25.2	23.6	53.4	11.4

Source: http://ec.europa.eu © European Union, 1995–2011

rising to the second most important immigrant group to Italy from the European countries (after Albanians). The main drivers of migration from the CEE countries into Italy were women.

Evidence since 2009 indicates, however, that migration balances out across Europe insofar as, for example, net immigration flows from the NMS are in decline, in particular from high-income NMS. This also shows the convergence of wages and labour market conditions over time, that local populations remaining in the home country are less likely to emigrate, and that the brain drain reverses after several years.

- Taxation

The mobility phenomenon is amplified by persistent tax differentials in Europe. Of course, companies are not going to constantly move from place to place to benefit from lower taxes. But the decision to locate and/or headquarter in a particular European country is influenced by these differences. Ireland, for example, has long run a 12.5 per cent tax rate for corporations. In 2010, other European company taxes still vary from a low of 9 per cent in Montenegro to a high of 35 per cent in Hungary (see Table 7.5).

Since 2001, the EU has worked on a common tax base that used a 2003 public consultation on the use of International Accounting Standards as a starting point. The *Common Consolidated Corporate Tax Base* (CCCTB) was set up as 'a single set of rules that companies operating within the EU could use to calculate their taxable profits. In other words, a company or qualifying group of companies would have to comply with just one EU system for computing its taxable income, rather than different rules in each Member State in which they operate' (CEC, 2011), as proposed by the Commission in March 2011: 'In addition, under the CCCTB, groups using the CCCTB would be able to file a single consolidated tax return for the whole of their activity in the EU. The consolidated taxable profits of the group would be shared out to the individual companies by a simple formula so that each Member State can then tax the profits of the companies in its State at the tax rate that they – each Member State – chooses (just like today).'

The Taxation and Customs Union Directorate General aims to define a common consolidated tax base for companies operating in the EU, its basic tax principles, the structural elements necessary and technical mechanisms that allow for 'sharing' a consolidated tax base between Member States. The EU states that cross-border activity still leads to high company tax and VAT compliance costs for companies in Europe, with relatively higher costs for SMEs than for large companies; it is thus proposing a home state taxation for SMEs: in this case, an SME is also allowed to use its home base's tax system for its foreign European subsidiaries for calculating taxable profits.

Overall, the highest implicit tax rates in Europe are typically found on labour in Italy, on consumption in Denmark and on capital in the UK.

For those of us who work cross-border, bilateral double taxation treaties tackle the tax problems that individuals and business may well experience in Europe: such

Table 7.5 *Eurostat – top statutory income tax rates (%)*

	Tax on personal income				Tax on corporate income			
	2000	2009	2010	Difference 2000–2010	2000	2009	2010	Difference 2000–2010
EU27*	**44.7**	**37.1**	**37.5**	**−7.2**	**31.9**	**23.5**	**23.2**	**−8.7**
Belgium	60.6	53.7	53.7	−7.0	40.2	34.0	34.0	−6.2
Bulgaria	40.0	10.0	10.0	−30.0	32.5	10.0	10.0	−22.5
Czech Republic	32.0	15.0	15.0	−17.0	31.0	20.0	19.0	−12.0
Denmark	59.7	59.0	51.5	−8.2	32.0	25.0	25.0	−7.0
Germany	53.8	47.5	47.5	−6.3	51.6	29.8	29.8	−21.8
Estonia	26.0	21.0	21.0	−5.0	26.0	21.0	21.0	−5.0
Ireland	44.0	41.0	41.0	−3.0	24.0	12.5	12.5	−11.5
Greece	45.0	40.0	45.0	0.0	40.0	25.0	24.0	−16.0
Spain	48.0	43.0	43.0	−5.0	35.0	30.0	30.0	−5.0
France	59.0	45.8	45.8	−13.2	37.8	34.4	34.4	−3.4
Italy	45.9	45.2	45.2	−0.7	41.3	31.4	31.4	−9.9
Cyprus	40.0	30.0	30.0	−10.0	29.0	10.0	10.0	−19.0
Latvia	25.0	23.0	26.0	1.0	25.0	15.0	15.0	−10.0
Lithuania	33.0	15.0	15.0	−18.0	24.0	20.0	15.0	−9.0
Luxembourg	47.2	39.0	39.0	−8.2	37.5	28.6	28.6	−8.9
Hungary	44.0	40.0	40.6	−3.4	19.6	21.3	20.6	1.0
Malta	35.0	35.0	35.0	0.0	35.0	35.0	35.0	0.0
Netherlands	60.0	52.0	52.0	−8.0	35.0	25.5	25.5	−9.5
Austria	50.0	50.0	50.0	0.0	34.0	25.0	25.0	−9.0
Poland	40.0	32.0	32.0	−8.0	30.0	19.0	19.0	−11.0
Portugal	40.0	42.0	42.0	2.0	35.2	26.5	26.5	−8.7
Romania	40.0	16.0	16.0	−24.0	25.0	16.0	16.0	−9.0
Slovenia	50.0	41.0	41.0	−9.0	25.0	21.0	20.0	−5.0
Slovakia	42.0	19.0	19.0	−23.0	29.0	19.0	19.0	−10.0
Finland	54.0	49.1	48.6	−5.4	29.0	26.0	26.0	−3.0
Sweden	51.5	56.4	56.4	4.9	28.0	26.3	26.3	−1.7
United Kingdom	40.0	40.0	50.0	10.0	30.0	28.0	28.0	−2.0
Norway	47.5	40.0	40.0	−7.5	28.0	28.0	28.0	0.0
Iceland	n/a	n/a	46.1	n/a	30.0	15.0	18.0	−12.0

* Arithmetic average
n/a Data not available

Source: Eurostat/TAXUD © European Union, 1995–2011

conventions are entertained by EU Member States with each other and with non-EU states. They are subject to scrutiny by the ECJ (European Court of Justice, see Chapter 4) for equal treatment of EU residents and for triangular situations (applying double-taxation conventions to cases with more than two countries).

Furthermore, it is planned to harmonize VAT, the consumption tax assessed on the added-value of deliveries, throughout the Union. It is paid by the buyer but transferred by the seller. In the EU, merchandise sold for export or services sold to customers abroad are 'normally not subject to VAT', with VAT for services payable where the service is supplied. Imports into the EU are taxed so that they are sold on 'equal terms on the European market' (EU, 2010). Because of the characteristics of the Single Internal Market, VAT is not collected at intra-EU borders, and the VAT Information Exchange System (VIES) VAT number validation on the DG's website helps check any other organizations' VAT number validity in case of intra-Community supply. In the long run, the EU is working on a common VAT system with the tax charged by the seller of goods, i.e. an origin-based VAT system. For the time being, taxable transactions are taxed at the rates and under the conditions set by the EU country where they take place. The standard rate of VAT is set as a percentage of the taxable amount, which, until 31 December 2015, may not be less than 15 per cent.

Let us conclude this taxation sub-chapter with a mention of environmental taxes in Europe. They can be divided into four broad categories: energy (which includes CO_2 taxes), transport, pollution and resource taxes. Transport fuel taxes are predominately used in the NMS amongst the total, for some constituting 40 per cent of environmental tax revenue. This level can also be found in Ireland, Malta, Greece and Norway, while Sweden, for example, collects more on electricity and natural gas. In Denmark, companies may be eligible for tax refunds if they have concluded an energy saving agreement

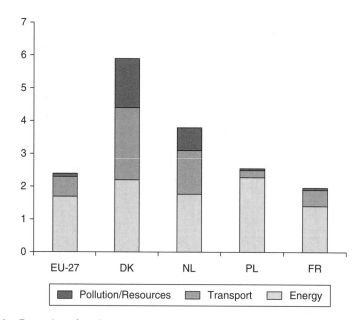

Figure 7.1 *Examples of environmental tax revenues by some Member States and type of tax (2007, in % of GDP, weighted averages)*

Source: http://epp.eurostat.ec.europa.eu/cache/ITY_OFFPUB/KS-DU-09-001/EN/KS-DU-09-001-EN.PDF, p. 118, © European Union, 1995–2011

with the Danish government. In the EU 27 (2008), environmental taxes accounted for 2.4 per cent of GDP, ranging from 1.6 per cent GDP in Spain to 5.7 per cent in Denmark. The Member States with the highest environmental taxes in GDP were Denmark (5.7 per cent), The Netherlands (3.9 per cent), Bulgaria and Malta (both 3.5 per cent), and the lowest were Spain (1.6 per cent), Lithuania (1.7 per cent), Romania (1.8 per cent) and Latvia (1.9 per cent). These taxes made up 72 per cent of total environmental taxes in the EU 27, while transport taxes made up 23 per cent and taxes on pollution and resources made up 5.5 per cent. Examples are given in Figure 7.1.

- Changeover costs: prices, money, machinery

There were and are many costs associated with the transition into a single currency. Wherever a Member State changes over to the common currency, these costs include collecting and destroying the former currency, printing the new money, changing accounting systems to deal with the euro, etc.

Many of the 'menu costs' have increased. According to the British Retail Consortium, transition costs in the UK for the retail industry alone were £3.5 billion in the context of the 2002 transition, and this was so even though the UK did not participate in the currency. This would amount to approximately 3 per cent of turnover for small businesses (including training personnel, and changing machinery and price tags).

Another significant challenge is simply one of *people*. Many argue that changing from one currency to another can be confusing, especially if people continue to count in the 'old' currency as well.

The 2002 transition to a single currency led to *specific costs for businesses* within Europe as well as abroad. Menu costs increased. All the big retailers and most companies implemented a dual pricing system during the transition and this can still be seen today in most euro-zone countries. The European Commission recommends to new euro-zone members that retailers give up the dual pricing system for a single pricing system so that citizens will get used to the euro as soon as possible.

The cost of changing IT systems and accounting procedures is not negligible: estimates show that the cost associated with IT changeover can reach between 0.25 per cent and 1.25 per cent of turnover. During the transition process, accounting in two currencies makes it even more difficult to cope. For EU members not part of the single currency, such as Denmark, coping with the situation is different: participating in the euro would most likely:

lead to slightly lower interest rates, a small increase in foreign trade and lower transaction costs. In normal, calm periods, interest rates will only be marginally lower than under the current fixed-exchange rate regime. Over a longer horizon, adopting the euro will have a certain positive overall effect on growth in Denmark … Denmark's Nationalbank's rough estimate is that, in the long term, euro area membership would permanently boost GDP by between 0.5 and 1 per cent … All along, we have been aware that the advantages of euro area membership would be accentuated in periods of financial turmoil. The lessons from the financial crisis have more than confirmed this. (Bernstein, 2010)

However, as the Governor of the Danish National Bank estimates, when a state is a member of the euro-zone, it is not 'and should not' be sure of any easy access to foreign borrowing, because only sound economic policy can guarantee that. 'But when you are a small open economy and a storm of this magnitude sweeps through the markets – you would rather not have your own currency to worry about.'

The British pound was lower in value than ever before around the time of crisis, and had also experienced certain difficulties. At the same time, the euro proved to be stable and strong in coping with the crisis to monitor prices.

- SEPA: The Single Euro Payments Area

The Single Euro Payment Area (SEPA) is an ambitious part of the Single Market initiatives that aims to abolish any differences that might possibly remain in the euro area between national and cross-border retail payments. This includes the use of debit cards, making cross-border bank transfers, direct debit, avoiding hidden charges, and using one bank account across the euro-zone. Significant savings result from euro payments across the EU as they are as easy, efficient and secure as domestic payments: 'a market potential of up to €123 billion in benefits (cumulative over 6 years, namely 2007 to 2012) with a significant upside for all demand side stakeholders while allowing banks to retain current margins' (ECB MEMO 08-52). For example, the possibility of cross-euro-zone common SEPA mechanisms for e-invoicing services, were estimated as a potential net benefit to the market of 238 billion euros over the same period. Box 7.2 provides the testimonial of an ECB representative working on the SEPA mechanisms.

Box 7.2: Testimonial from the ECB

SEPA for businesses

The Single Euro Payments Area (SEPA) project is a natural step following on from the introduction of the single currency in the area of cashless payments. With SEPA, all cashless payments in euros will be treated as European, i.e. there will be no differentiation between national and cross-border payments. This will be achieved by using a single set of payment instruments, i.e. SEPA credit transfers and SEPA direct debits, which are as simple, safe and efficient as those used in the national context today. SEPA thus provides the payment platform, which will facilitate the realization of a fully fledged internal market.

For SEPA to function effectively, the EU must have harmonized legislation on payments. To this end, the Payment Services Directive (PSD) came into force on 1 November 2009. Among other aspects, the PSD ensures that the full amount of a transaction is transmitted and that the payer and payee each bear only the cost of their own bank's charges. Faster execution of payments, which is also guaranteed by the PSD, will enhance firms' cash flow and liquidity. In the past, it could take as

(Continued)

(Continued)

long as five days or more for a payment to reach the beneficiary's account. This was true even for some national payments let alone those across borders. With SEPA credit transfers, as of November 2009, all payments in Europe are credited to the beneficiary's account in a maximum of two days and, from 2012, in just one day, in accordance with the PSD. In addition, no value dates are lost, as the payment will be credited to the beneficiary's account as soon as his/her bank receives it.

But SEPA has far more advantages than just a more user-friendly and harmonized regulatory framework. SEPA will pave the way for a European payments market in which any bank in the SEPA area is able to provide SEPA payments to any customer. In this respect, SEPA will be a key driver for more competition among payment service providers, leading to lower costs, enhanced services and more innovation. The same applies for card payments: card payment terminals will also conform to a European standard, meaning that merchants will benefit from competition between terminal manufacturers and between acquirers. Merchants will no longer be limited to choosing an acquirer based in the same country. Moreover, companies and merchants present in several EU countries will be able to centralize their payments in one country and will thus no longer have to adapt to different standards and rules.

SEPA is not only about traditional retail payment instruments. It is also about innovation. A European e-payment scheme, i.e. for making online payments, is being prepared as part of the SEPA framework and – once realized – will offer further benefits. In addition, small and medium-sized enterprises (SMEs) are increasingly using the Internet as a channel for doing business. Growing numbers of consumers, especially young people, prefer to use the Internet and e-commerce to make online web purchases and do not always have a credit card to hand. In countries such as Germany, The Netherlands and Austria, safe and efficient e-payment schemes are already available, but are not connected, and in many countries they are still lacking. A common European e-payment scheme will allow any merchant or SME present on the Internet to receive payments from consumers securely and efficiently.

These benefits will be available to all companies conducting cross-border business or operating locally.

Making use of the opportunities that SEPA offers simply requires the use of international account and bank identifiers, namely IBAN and BIC, rather than national identifiers. Countries such as Italy, Latvia, Luxembourg, Poland, Romania and Slovenia have already successfully switched to using these account identifiers without a problem. Banking software may need to be updated, but this can be accomplished in the course of the normal investment cycle of a firm.

SEPA has been designed to benefit end customers, consumers and companies, including SMEs. Several years have passed since the Single Market and the euro banknotes and coins were introduced, and Europe now needs a single market for cashless retail payments as well. SEPA will deliver this.

Source: Francisco Tur Hartmann, Adviser, Directorate General, Payments and Market Infrastructure, Market Integration Division, European Central Bank, 12 August 2010

7.1.2 The European Central Bank (ECB)

The ECB, mentioned above in particular in the discussion of the euro currency and SEPA, was set up in June 1998 under the Maastricht Treaty.

From its location in Frankfurt, Germany, the ECB began operations in January 1999. It introduces and manages the currency, conducts foreign exchange operations and ensures the smooth operation of payment systems. It is important that the ECB focuses on price stability and keeps up pressure on members to retain inflation lower than 2 per cent, which is measured by the Monetary Union Index of Consumer Prices (MUICP) for the area within the euro-zone. In July 2009, euro area annual inflation was found to be at 1.9 per cent; in the same month one year later, it was estimated at 1.7 per cent.

In order to achieve its aim, the ECB may cut or raise interest rates. The ECB is responsible for holding and managing the official foreign reserves of the euro area countries (portfolio management). The bank has exclusive rights to authorize the issue of banknotes within the euro-zone, and collects the necessary statistical information, either from national authorities or directly from economic agents.

At the same time, its main responsibility is to frame and implement the euro-zone economic and monetary policy. Therefore, the bank works closely with the European System of Central Banks (ESCB) which groups the central banks of all EU Member States. The institution is governed by a board of directors, headed by a president and a board of governors. Within this structure, only governors from national banks that belong to the euro-zone are involved and are responsible for the decision process. The EU institutions and the European Member State governments must respect the independency principle of the ECB.

On the one hand, critics argue that the ECB sets interest rates with a view to controlling inflation, but does not necessarily take into account objectives such as employment and sound exchange rate stability. The complexity of its tasks seems particularly challenging, and the analysis of the collected data relies on the accuracy of its sources. On the other hand, the ECB works in relation to (and taking account of) other main international financial institutions, and adapts accordingly.

7.1.3 The European Investment Bank (EIB) and other sources of capital

The EIB was set up by the Treaty of Rome and is the main financing institution of the EU. Its main task is long-term lending for capital investment projects which promote European integration and cohesion on social and economic levels. Like a development bank, it raises its resources on the financial and capital markets, mainly through bond issues or other specialized capital market operations. Its Eurobonds are listed mainly on Euronext, Luxembourg and the London Stock Exchange, and price quotations can be found most easily on the Reuters and Bloomberg systems. These debt contracts engage the borrower in paying interest at a given rate and the principal amount of the bond on defined dates.

The EU's sovereign Member States own the AAA-ranked bank, and its board of directors is mainly constituted of one member representing each EU Member State and the European Commission. It has a subscribed capital of around €223 billion (by comparison, €165 billion in 2006). Statutory lending goes up to 250 per cent of this capital.

In accordance with the EU institution's political and economic objectives, the EBI focuses on raising very significant volumes of funds that are used for the financing of capital projects on highly favourable terms: this mainly targets projects inside the EU and also components of development aid and cooperation projects in non-EU countries. EIB loans that were launched in 2010 supported small and medium-sized projects in Slovenia for €25 million to Banka Celje d.d. and €25 million to Gorenjska banka d.d., to 'co-finance projects promoted by SMEs and priority investments of public authorities in particular energy and environment infrastructure' (EIB, 2010).

The objectives that need to be satisfied for EIB loans have to serve any of the following: the EU's economic development, competitiveness, human capital, ICT networks, R&D and innovation, transport, telecommunications and trans-European networks (TENs), the environment, SME development and/or critical infrastructures in the EU. Projects of non-EU countries are dealt with in two categories that are accession countries and other non-EU countries: in accession country projects, the focus remains on the transfer of EU expertise and legislation, and the development of infrastructural and other economic activities.

For projects from other non-EU countries, initiatives such as the 2012 Euro-Mediterranean Partnership of a Customs Union, link the EU to non-EU Mediterranean countries with the same perspective, to African, Caribbean and Pacific (ACP) countries, to Asia and Latin America in terms of mutual interests, and to the Balkans regarding the Stability and Growth Pact for the reconstruction of infrastructures and regional development (EIB, 2010, Annex). The bank is, for example, involved in the financing of the EuroMena fund in Beirut, Lebanon, in the infrastructure development project in Medina, and in the modernization of Budapest's healthcare system.

In Turkey, the bank supports economic development to facilitate the country's moves towards integration into the EU, at about €2.5 billion per annum, with 57 per cent of this lending going to SMEs.

The projects are submitted officially or informally via potential promoters (such as companies), commercial banks, public authorities, or international or national development finance institutions (cf. 'The Project Cycle', EIB, 2010); those that are eligible to benefit from the EIB's financing facilities will have been scrutinized in terms of economic, technical, environmental and financial viability in accordance with EU objectives. They are accepted upon a sound evaluation of risks and benefits. Since 2001, the projects have been publicly listed at an advanced stage on the bank's website.

The bank's *loans* are credit lines made available for the funding of small and medium-sized projects (ventures of SMEs or infrastructure schemes) through intermediary banks; these are projects that are not big enough for direct EIB funding. Non-reciprocal *aid and assistance* is granted to EU development and initiatives such as operations under the Lomé Convention and the Cotonou Agreement with

79 countries from Africa, the Caribbean and the Pacific (ACP). Altogether, EIB is the world's largest borrower on the capital markets, with the issue of large, liquid benchmarks in the main currencies (the euro, British pound and US dollar), and specific securities in a range of currencies.

7.1.4 Venture capital and private equity

Venture capital (VC) and business angels are an important alternative financial source in the EU. Venture capitalists appeared tentatively in the EU around 1997, the year in which the EIB started to engage in this activity in collaboration with the banking and financial sector. By the year 2000, VC had begun to show a strong presence in Europe, and its evolution coincided with that of the Internet as a major force to consider in business and innovative activity, nationally and even more easily across borders. Today, VC investments flourish and are a main basis for innovation in Europe, with a particular focus on being in the Czech Republic, Poland, Romania, Hungary and Bulgaria.

The European adoption of private equity as a means of business funding started in the UK. It made its way rapidly into the other European economies. Amounts invested in this manner are at historic levels in Europe. In Germany, where traditionally only banks had funded companies, the share of investments into start-ups by private entities is today most significant, amounting to approximately 20 per cent of investment capital.

The European Investment Fund (EIF) is one of Europe's main VC instruments for stimulating innovation in SMEs and entrepreneurship. Its funds are dedicated mainly to the early stages of development of technology-oriented ventures. The fund relies on capital from the group which includes the EIB and the EIF. Within its mandate, the EIF also manages the resources of the EIB. In addition, capital from the CEC is allocated through the ETF Start-up Facility and Seep Capital Action for investment in new funds. These two actions are part of the Multiannual Programme for Enterprise and Entrepreneurship, and cover the EU Member States, candidate and potential candidate countries and the members of the European Free Trade Association (Iceland, Liechtenstein, Norway and Switzerland; see Chapters 2 and 3).

The EIF is a tripartite shareholding consisting of the EIB (its main shareholder), the CEC and the EU, as well as the public and private banks and financial institutions that receive returns. Among these public and private institutions are Bank Austria Creditanstalt AG, Encouragement Bank AD of Bulgaria, Vaekstfonden of Denmark, BGL Investment Partners SA of Luxembourg and NIBC of The Netherlands. It is managed by a chief executive, a board of directors and an audit board, holds an annual general meeting and is monitored by a range of authorities.

Direct investments in SMEs are excluded from the EIF scope of action. Rather, working under market conditions, the Fund supplies SME financial guarantees to facilitate access to debt finance, and acts through intermediaries for its VC.

Many small Internet entrepreneurs, however, prefer to operate without VC because they prefer to remain independent from VC returns, and sell off activity before growing becomes costly. Because they have lower fixed costs for servers, storage and software, self-funded micro enterprises can deal with costs for much longer than larger companies, and they exploit ICT evolutions. Web design and programming are often outsourced for cost efficiency. However, semiconductor and mobile technologies do rely on higher, mainly external, funds.

7.1.5 Business angels

Business angel investment is the most significant source of external equity finance for young companies. About 75 per cent of this money is invested in businesses at an *early stage of development*. Providing straightforward deals and staying with the investment for longer than more traditional sources of capital investment, business angels also provide knowledge, expertise and business contacts because they only invest in projects or firms that they feel an affinity for.

Although some deals are put together by groups of investors, the majority of business angels are individuals with widely different preferences and styles who make infrequent investments, maybe every three or four years, and are rarely actually searching for investment opportunities. Typically, they are top executives of companies, high-level managers or wealthy people who feel a passion for their work or a particular business sector. They tend to be between 35 and 65 years old. With the passion and the capital that business angels provide, they generally want to be involved in the companies they support, which makes the relationship between the investors and the companies rather close. Indeed, investment takes place in the shape of direct capital, and not as a loan. Indeed, this is a 'patient' investment, where capital stays in the company for at least three years. A benefit for the business angel is thus generated from selling shares at the moment of early maturity of the business. In most EU countries, sums invested are usually between around €25,000 and €250,000.

The main interest for this type of investment will be found in the first stages of a company's development, during the development of a prototype or during a diversification of activities such as internationalization. By taking the risk to invest early, business angels hope to reap benefits from the company's success.

Business angels invest in all sectors. However, they rarely invest in social projects or in order to acquire recognition from the community. Rather, their 'business passion' is inflamed by their belief in the competitive advantage of the product or service commercialized by the company and its potential for growth. Where traditional funds are less accessible or expensive, business angels can step in and often operate at smaller levels than venture capitalists. However, while business angels are less demanding than other sources of equity finance, such as the public sector or venture capitalists, they will always make sure that the business plan is convincing, the risk suits the potential return and the information supplied is accurate. Confidence and interpersonal affinity are key here: the more the angels know about the entrepreneur seeking investment, the more likely they are to invest.

7.1.5.1 Searching for an angel?

Business angels are looking for investments capable of achieving a return of 20 per cent or more. To avoid wasting time in chasing investors, it is important to make sure that this condition can be satisfied. Also, this type of investor typically invests locally, nationally or on a well-defined level such as that of the EU. The most likely place to find an angel is within the region around your main business premises. In terms of numbers, for example, there are around 1500 active business angels in Scotland, but the number of potential investors is likely to be much larger (see http://www.businessangels.com). However, they are less easy to recognize than venture capitalists or other sources of funding.

The search for such investment mainly concentrates on contacting successful leading individuals within a similar sector or industry, because business angels provide not only capital but also advice, and thus look for investments in areas where they have a lot of expertise. Given the informality of this approach, the first meeting is particularly important because business angels invest along the lines of their feelings and affinities and hence tend to place an emphasis on the human relations with the entrepreneur and management team. Networking and listing contacts who are or have been in the same business sector or industry is essential, as is mixing with them (through making direct contact or at business events); this helps to spread the word about your activities and your search for investors. In general, business angels who are contacted but not active in your sector will be happy to refer you to someone more suitable.

The CEC supports the European Association of Business Angels (EBAN) financially. Its members and indirect members in the 28 member states of EBAN alone review some 40,000 business plans each year. EBAN also represents the interests of early stage investors (regulatory, fiscal, etc.) at European institutions. (This is an activity that we will review in Chapter 9 on lobbying.)

7.1.6 More sources of capital for established corporations

European Union funding is not only a source of capital but also a proof of the valence and financial health of one's business project and its consistency with EU objectives and evolution. It is thus worthwhile also applying for funding from specific EU programmes. These programmes, which are not exclusively destined for companies, are very precise, detailed and regularly monitored.

Generally, organizations that are already established are eligible for such programmes. Only this type of company satisfies the conditions stipulated for those funds. Some indirect mechanisms can also help start-ups to obtain support, because they are at the heart of the EU's Europe 2020 agenda for innovation and competitiveness. They can, in addition, benefit from funded actions such as conferences at universities and business schools.

'Gate2Growth' offers individual financial advice for high-tech projects and is a partner for actions of the EU. Also, Business and Innovation Centres (BICs) help business creation (http://www.ebn.be, for example), and regions co-finance certain initiatives (see EuroInfoCenters and your local Chamber of Commerce and

Industry). Some regions are supported by European regional policy and businesses are well advised to refer to the information provided in INTERREG; here you will find the main objectives of this funding and learn that these funds are allocated as an integral part of local aid complemented by regional funds.

The EU does not provide any direct funds for export, employment or specific corporate development. Rather, support is indirect in the form of:

- investment aid (structural, non-reimbursable funds);
- co-financing (non-reimbursable);
- loan or bank guarantee (by EIB and EIF);
- participation (VC through intermediaries);
- non-financial aid (technical tools such as Ecolabel, or information);
- payment of service or purchase (calls for tender in case of programmes with non-EU countries).

In addition to legislative tools (mainly directives and rules) that open up possibilities for funding, the EU defines technical programmes that specify objectives, requirements and budget lines. In this context, the EU's Framework Programmes (FP7 for the time period to 2013, FP8 for the five following years) are the EU's main instrument for funding research and development. Framework Programmes are proposed by the European Commission and adopted by the Council and the Parliament following a co-decision procedure. The Programmes were first implemented in 1984 and generally cover a period of five years, with the last year of one Programme and the first year of the next overlapping. FP6 was running up to the end of 2006, when it was replaced by FP7, which runs for seven years to ensure consistency and economic convergence. It has been fully operational since 1 January 2007 and expires in 2013 when FP8 will be defined and launched.

FP7 is designed to build on the achievements of its predecessor towards the creation of the European Research Area, and carry it further towards the development of the knowledge economy and society in Europe. With over €70,000 million for the period 2007–13, FP7 focuses on cooperation, convergence, knowledge sharing, international research (with the establishment of the European Research Council) and a simplification of operations internally. This field refers to gaining leadership in key scientific and technology areas by supporting cooperation between universities, industry, research centres and public authorities across the EU and with the rest of the world. Transnational cooperation is the main instrument for carrying out research. This programme is organized into nine sub-programmes with nine different thematic research areas in which Community support can be obtained (the so-called thematic priority areas). FP6 thematic priorities continue to be supported in FP7. Only one new priority, 'space and security', has been added to the previous set of themes. Joint, cross-thematic approaches to research subjects of common interest are also encouraged. Thematic programmes include eContent, to make digital content more accessible, usable and exploitable, through best practice, cooperation and awareness, SaferInternet Plus (to combat illegal e-content) and also IDABC (Interoperable Delivery of European eGovernment Services to Public Administration,

Business and Citizens), TENs (trans-European networks), and LIFE (natural habitat improvement), among others. CIP (Competitiveness and Innovation Framework), with €4.21 billion to 2013, is a new programme in FP7.

The EU's CORDIS (the Community Research and Development Information Service for Science, Research and Development) website proposes a 'Practical Guide to EU Funding Opportunities for Research and Innovation' that helps evaluate the eligibility of organizations for funding (http://cordis.europa.eu/). When filing for EU funding, it is of primary importance to satisfy not only the expectations and objectives of the EU, but also the specific file components and information criteria (Box 7.3). For any directorate general's (DG) grant programme, an information unit of the relevant DG is indicated and will advise.

Obtaining a European fund, chair or project has several advantages that are not only *financial (co-funding)*. They also lie in improved access, stemming to networks of:

- recognized and distinguished experts; and
- potential partners in one's field, and strengthened opportunities to share knowledge; and
- best practice on a European and international level; and finally to
- help institutional actors to disseminate (and maybe obtain) expertise.

In the starting phase of a project proposal for funding at the EU, it is essential to organize the distribution of tasks and finance among partners and to arrange intellectual property rights among them. Which organizations are involved, who is the legal representative, who is the project leader, and who is the contact person for your project? Also, the organization's usual sources of finance are important, as the EU usually only co-finances projects. A steering committee for intermediate and final reports needs to ensure liaison with the EU at all relevant stages and during auditing.

Project outcomes must be well defined in the shape of business plans, databases and web-supported dissemination of findings, reports, conferences and publications. They must be well in line with the objectives of European integration, cohesion and its future.

Box 7.3: The crucial parts for a submission of proposals to an EU call for tender consist of specific application items

- Application form (including acknowledgement; the receipt proves registration of your file at the EU).
- Budget form (total budget estimation with all sources of funding, quantitative measures and expected revenues). Any application needs to state precisely the objectives, the duration of activities and the project methodology. What is the rationale, problems identified, match with programme and EU objectives? Is your project innovative? How will its results make a difference that benefits all partners and the Community?

(Continued)

(Continued)

- Checklist.
- Compulsory appendices.
- Possible appendices: MEPs' (of the right working groups) or local representatives' letters of support or other; details on aspects, information on subcontractors and on methods of calculation.

Calls for Tender are top-down calls in which the EU predefines needs that companies may respond to and execute if selected. Sometimes these calls are restricted to certain organizations or to actors having already submitted to calls for interest. In *Calls for Proposals*, a bottom-up strategy, the EU asks for the creative promotion of its objectives through projects defined by the applicant according to guidelines.

Your partners, depending on the call that you answer, may be required to cover a specific number and/or location of EU Member States, but in most cases can or must also include EFTA, candidate or other countries.

In terms of budget, an application is sound when it shows a *balance of expenditure and revenue*, in euros, in respect of financial conditions set out clearly in the call for proposals published by the EU in its *Official Journal* (C and S) and on its website (http://ted.europa.eu, the EU's dedicated public procurement site). This includes realistic *costs*/prices that can be found through benchmarking, analytical accountancy and record calculation methods for possible later audits. In these measures, one should take into account that organizations privilege low translation costs, travel costs (rather using ICT, see EU objectives), staff costs and subcontracting costs. For example, the cost of equipment (firsthand, secondhand or rented), are stated at the depreciation rate – usually 10 years for electronic equipment – and only for the period of time calculated for the project, supplies, consumable goods, services and (limited) subcontracting. This includes costs linked to dissemination (printing, photocopying, communication, etc.). For staff costs, ISCO international standards can be applied but are not compulsory because of the variation of wages across EU countries. You may use the rates of specific markets, but may want to explain them. Staff costs (excluding incentives; day rate x no. of days) exclude secretarial tasks that are part of usual job tasks, but can be included for placements, or if the precise job tasks are exclusively dedicated to the project to a percentage, for example 10 per cent. For travel, private car use is calculated as first-class train fare, while the air fare is always benchmarked on economy rates. Once the project is running, all reservation details and boarding cards are proof of evaluation and audit by the EU. For subsistence allowance, the calculation is made for two meals, accommodation, local travel and other necessities on travel (per diem rates or real costs). *Other eligible direct costs* on your budget may include particular financial services (a financial guarantee, if necessary; costs for a specific bank account), and those stated on the call for proposal. Indirect, overhead costs can be stated but must be limited to 7 per cent of eligible direct costs. Any expenses that concern, for example, interest paid, exchange losses, unestimated costs, provisions or representation costs, or VAT (except for organizations that pay VAT and cannot recover it) are excluded.[1]

The only *revenues* that are eligible are those generated by your project, financial contributions by the applicant and partners, grants and certain other contributions. *Contributions-in-kind* are non-eligible costs, that is, part of the total budget but not of the funding budget. They are revenues on the total budget, not on the funding budget.

In addition to the qualitative and quantitative soundness of the application, there are other details, which enhance the probability of being in line with the institution's ways of working. For the papers themselves, staples are not recommended, signatures should be in blue (not black) ink, and plastic covers (in open folders) make it easier for papers to be extracted and make the life of your evaluators easier. A good acronym for the title of your project helps in its understanding and dissemination, and English is often the main language when filling in the forms because the majority of evaluators read it. Early and continuous contact with the Commission is useful; it helps to ensure that your project is in line with those of the EU in the programme.

While consultants and advisors can help you fill in your application, make sure that the main actors of the project are an integral part of the formulation of the contents to ensure consistency. All funding by the EU is subject to specific reports. The granting of the funds is subject to a highly competitive evaluation procedure. The funds may attribute very important support to projects. Information can be obtained on the above-named CORDIS website and also from Heads of Unit of the European Commission. Chapters 3 and 9 are also useful for information on funding, opportunities for enlargement and the importance and techniques of public affairs management.

7.2 European harmonization efforts

While not exhaustive, due to the ever-changing EU financial and economic regulatory framework, some developments in specific European harmonization efforts differ from other international business environments. We have already discussed VAT harmonization above. Indeed, European Member States still control most parts of sales taxes, excise duties, and income and corporate taxes, but increasing efforts are made to obtain at least partial harmonization, such as with that of VAT. For this, the unanimous approval of all Member States is required. Hence, a full common European tax regime remains unlikely.

However, certain rules and legislation stimulate tax convergence, such as those on state aid. From the corporate side, firms are not necessarily hoping for fiscal harmonization in Europe, because its divergence helps business benefit from the tax regime that may be the most suitable for its activity or organization. Also, elected politicians tend to avoid potentially unattractive tax reforms.

7.2.1 International accounting standards (IAS)

Within the evolution of IAS, most of Europe has harmonized rules governing financial statements in order to guarantee the protection of investors. The main objectives are:

- a better integration of financial markets and activities; and
- easier cross-border and international securities trading.

> One of the strongest conclusions of the G20 was the shared commitment to reform together and to ensure convergence of accounting standards at an international level. To this end, we need to find the right balance between a faithful representation of a company's financial situation and wider financial stability. (http://www .iasplus.com/europe/1002barnierecofin.pdf, M. Barnier, Comissioner for Internal Market and Services, 16 February 2010 presentation, 'Acting Without Delay to Clean Up Financial Markets' to Ecofin Council [the council of economic and finance ministers of EU Member States])

IAS in Europe are adopted to improve the element of trust between companies working together in the international value chain, in which the *Know your customer* principle is key to risk reductions. The IAS are now International Accounting or Financial Reporting Standard (IFRS), along with the similarly structured Generally Accepted Accounting Principles (US-GAAP) that are accepted throughout the world, and adopted in the EU, to improve the credibility of European corporations towards the non-EU countries and vice versa.

EU Member States were free to adopt the standards until their final implementation in the middle of 2007. IAS standards have been adopted and used in the EEA overall, that is, including the EU and EFTA countries. Within these countries, listed companies (including banks and insurance companies) prepare consolidated accounts in accordance with ISA that facilitate the marketability of securities, cross-border mergers and acquisitions, and the raising of finance. The mini case study for this chapter examines IAS and their impact further. It appears less and less acceptable and feasible that investors could not compare like with like, and obtain information, say interim information, about costs of goods, when costs of raw materials, packaging or transport, for example, are volatile. Harmonization serves to provide transparency for investors, analysts, bankers and other actors in the field.

7.2.2 Stock exchange consolidation

The introduction of the single European currency, the euro, has enhanced transparency and eased profit-making opportunities on the European stock exchanges. The consolidation of these stock exchanges constitutes an essential basis for the harmonization of capital market conditions for corporate benefit. In this type of convergence, costs are reduced and cross-border trading is facilitated. Exchange places make economies of scale both in operations and in trading (Steil, 2001). As a result, market liquidity increases, market fragmentation is reduced, and investment and perfor-mance ratios of capital assets in Europe increase (McAndrews and Stefanadis, 2002). With the euro being the currency in most parts of Europe, intra-European currency exposure has fallen, meaning that risks associated with an unexpected change in exchange rates have disappeared, or (for non-euro members) diminished. This results in easier and more attractive cross-border investment.

The simultaneous removal of certain regulatory restrictions on intra-European capital flows enhances this phenomenon. Investors hold more assets from countries whose returns are positively correlated with their own stock market (Aviat and Coeurdacier, 2007). Also, equity has risen in importance in the past decade.

The degree to which capital moves freely through the EU is critical to its Member States' balance of payments. Sound integration of the appropriate economic and political measures can dramatically reduce capital flight – a sudden outflow of capital from the economy that indicates the onset of crises – which was significant before the Asian crisis in the late 1990s, and in Argentina and Turkey in 2000/1, for exam-ple. This was not observed in the same manner in the 2009 European euro crisis.

Typically, stock exchanges in Europe are national institutions that trade on a national or restricted cross-European level. However, developments can be noted in this area, such as in an increasing number of stock exchanges that operate on a wider European level. A full-scale consolidation of European stock exchanges will be a long process since regulatory, legal and economic barriers and national interests may ham-per the process on a large scale and for a long time to come. The consolidation and takeover speculations by Deutsche Börse of the London Stock Exchange was one example of this: on 3 May 2000, Deutsche Börse, the sixth largest stock exchange in the world at the time, announced that it was interested in merging with the London Stock Exchange, which is number three worldwide with US$5169 of shares traded at the time. This would have created the second largest exchange after New York, thereby consolidating the European stock exchange market to a degree as yet unknown. Werner Seiffert, then chief executive of Deutsche Börse, offered 530p a share, or £1.3 billion, for the London Stock Exchange; the bid was rejected. Nevertheless, Deutsche Börse submitted another bid at the same price in January 2005; this was also rejected.

The rejections reflected not only the fact that the London Stock Exchange con-sidered itself to be undervalued, but also the difficulty in playing one's hand at man-agement control. It also appeared that the main shareholders of Deutsche Börse (TCI and Atticus) tended more towards continuous dividends rather than investment in another stock market, and emphasized this interest through a shareholder petition that was reported to have ultimately removed Seiffert from his position. Deutsche Börse, however, did reserve the right to return as a bidder if Euronext made an offer.

Euronext then also showed interest in the London Stock Exchange and was seen as being more knowledgeable about the management of multinational exchange, for example with the London Future Exchange (Liffe). However, Euronext made no formal offer at the time.

The London Stock Exchange (LSE) has continued to be a target of takeover speculations and investors from the European continent and non-EU countries, such as the Macquerie Bank, an Australian bank that has little experience in financial exchanges, preferring to invest in roads, airports and property. The European competition authorities investigated the potential consequences of a monopoly status of the European stock exchange. This interest in the stock exchange led to a significant rise of stocks and the FTSE 100 was able to double its gains in 2004.

Three years later and after further moves in Europe, Deutsche Börse dropped out of merger negotiations with Euronext, making way for another form of consolidation for greater economies of scale and a move into new trading products: Euronext merged with NYSE group in April 2007. Since 2008, Deutsche Börse – the German exchange and Europe's largest venue by market capitalization – expressed its interest in a merger of the two entities to create the world's largest exchange. In 2009, the Luxembourg Stock Exchange moved its securities to the NYSE Euronext UTP platform, and consolidation continues in Europe. Euronext operates primary exchanges in France, The Netherlands, Belgium and Portugal, and since 2010 also in the UK, where more than half of daily trading on Euronext comes from international investors based in the UK with the euro-zone. Its connection to the euro-zone is therefore an advantage versus LSE. Its biggest international listings market remains that of Paris, where the majority consists of Chinese companies.

The London Stock Exchange Group operates mainly the UK and Italian primary markets, has a joint venture with Tokyo Stock Exchange, and is reaching out to France and other international marketplaces. Its major shareholders in 2010 were from Dubai and Qatar.

Chi-X Europe is the largest venue for trading in the most liquid European equities markets. Operating in a low-margin, high-competition market, Ch-X Europe, Bats Europe and Turquoise are the main actors in a market in which Nasdaq OMX Europe decided to close to business in 2010 for lack of market share evolution (FT, 2010).

The European financial world is mainly influenced by the activities of the European Commission, European Parliament, EcoFin Council, the European Securities Committee, and the Committee of European Securities Regulators. The European Association of Central Counterparty Clearing Houses (EACH) and European Central Securities Depositries Association (ECSDA) work closely with the Federation of European Securities Exchanges (FESE). FESE represents 46 exchanges in equities, bonds, derivatives and commodities in 30 countries, including European emerging markets, and is part of their interest representation towards the EU institutions. Altogether, the financial market infrastructures in Europe are, even by the CEC, interpreted as rather unspectacular: 'Infrastructure has often been compared to the plumbing in the building of the EU financial market: vital, but unglamorous and forgotten until something goes wrong' (http://ec.europa.eu/internal_market/financial-markets/index_en.htm).

7.3 Résumé and conclusion

This chapter has reviewed the most important features of the convergence and divergence of European finance, emphasizing those features that have a significant impact on the economy and corporate activity. Following the argument that investments and movements of financial assets are more frequent and intense when conditions of economic and political proximity grant stability, we have been able to observe two main phenomena. On the one hand, national interests, governmental income, electoral considerations and social policy have a significant impact on willingness to negotiate the consolidation of financial markets and harmonized market conditions. On the other hand, public and private initiatives and interests across Europe drive the Europeanization of compatibilities that increase balance of payments (BOP) stability; this enhances the liquidity of financial markets in Europe. Also, a European approach in monetary, fiscal and financial policy altogether provides some degree of stability during economic and financial crises, on condition that it preserves the flexibility necessary in times of recession.

In the following chapter, we will look at the way in which the single currency, harmonization, and convergence and diversity influence the purchase and sales of products and services in Europe. Consequently, the next chapter focuses on marketing.

Mini case study: Auditing in Europe today

Where does auditing come from? As a reaction to the collapse of the New York Stock Exchange in 1929 and the following world economic crisis, the 1934 Securities and Exchange Act required all publicly traded companies to disclose certain financial information. This financial information has to be viewed by an auditor as an independent and qualified party. The general focus is to assure the shareholders and other stakeholders that the reported financial statements represent a true and fair reflection of the company's financial status.

Since that time, companies in most countries have been obliged to have their financial statements audited by certified auditors. Clients and the public are dependent on the reliability of the auditor. Therefore, the legislator, as well as the auditing profession itself, has written out professional duties and general standards of auditing over the years. The auditing standards underlie a continuous development. In the past, auditing procedures were only based on verifying separate balance sheet items and the audit process was often motivated by taxation. Today, auditors have to use the risk-oriented audit approach. They have to evaluate companies' business models and their individual economic environment, as well as their specific processes and workflows.

Some of the spectacular accounting affairs like ENRON, WorldCom or Parmalat have shown in the past that a good accounting policy is an indispensable precondition for cross-border capital markets.

How about a harmonization of accounting and auditing then? Global companies are competitors in the global capital markets. To get access to these markets, companies need comparable financial statements, so that investors have access to comparable financial information about all participants. This is one of the most important issues and the main reason for the necessary harmonization of accounting and auditing worldwide and especially in the EU. The main assumption for the harmonization of the economic audit service is the creation of consistent accounting principles and the adaption of supervisory authority in the EU.

The harmonization of accounting principles in the EU is one of the basic elements of the harmonization of European corporate law and, for that, the formation and embodiment of a European domestic market of financial services. A bare unification of accounting principles is not the main ambition and – because of the differences in 'accounting traditions' – not realizable. Growing pressure on the part of capital markets led to a ratification of accounting guidelines that resulted in a noticeable convergence of various traditions. Instead of developing its own accounting principles, existing standards (IAS) were imported. These former IAS are now called IFRS, as well as the similarly structured US-GAAP (Generally Accepted Accounting Principles), which are accepted throughout the world. While US-GAAP are used mainly in the USA for SEC-listed companies, IAS/IFRS are common in the EU.

The IAS/IFRS have been permanently modified since their creation. They are becoming more and more relevant. Importantly, the IFRS also contain most of the core statements of US-GAAP and these two accounting standards converge towards each other constantly. Along with this, the IASB (International Accounting Standards Board – IFRS) and the FASB (Financial Accounting Standards Board – US-GAAP) agreed a Memorandum of Understanding that described concerted action in improving accounting standards and a substantial convergence between IFRS and US-GAAP in 2006. A further Memorandum of Understanding exists between the IASB and the Accounting Standards Board of Japan (ASBJ), in order to achieve substantial convergence between IFRS and Japanese-GAAP.

Due to these agreements, in 2007, SEC removed the requirement for non-US companies to reconcile their financial statements with US-GAAP if they use IFRS instead.

At present, the IFRS are the most important accounting principles in the world and more than 100 countries require or permit their use.

The simple absorption of the IFRS, however, would cause multiple problems regarding accounting and taxation, and also in terms of guidelines of assessment, publicity requirements and facilities for SMEs. For this reason, the use of local GAAPs (e.g. German HGB rules) in several states of the EU is stipulated too.

Given its cross-border dimension, the European Commission is the relevant authority for ratifying the IFRS as guidelines for its Member States. In addition to the guidelines for assessment and disclosure, the EU guidelines include the responsibilities of independency and the professional principles of the auditor. In cases of external quality control (peer review), the guidelines guarantee supervision of the auditor and enhanced cooperation of the different supervisors in the EU.

The different national professions of auditors each founded international organizations to accomplish exchange of information, transparency, conception and

Mini Case

Mini Case

implementation of standards. The International Federation of Accountants (IFAC) aims at a worldwide harmonization of accountancy professions. Also, the above-mentioned International Accounting Standards Board (IASB) was founded to develop accounting standards for public benefit and to enhance their acceptance as well as their compliance. The IASB is committed to improving and harmonizing cross-border accounting principles, and is therefore an essential component of their convergence.

On a European level, the Fédération of Experts Comptables Européens (FEE) represents the interests of accountants. It comprises of 43 professional associations from 32 countries, including all Member States of the European economic area. Altogether, the federation has 500,000 members, approximately 95 per cent of whom come from EU countries. In the course of the progressive adjustment of the accounting standards and their implementation in Europe, other committees were founded: the purposes of the Contact Committee, the European Financial Reporting Advisory Group and the Accounting Regulatory Committee consist primarily in their consultation and advice to the European Commission regarding the extension of and changes to the guidelines and standards. The long-term objective of the European Commission is hence to efficiently and effectively establish uniform professional auditing and standards of accounting and auditing across its Member States.

Source: Dirk Feldhausen, auditor and tax advisor, BDO Deutsche Warentreuhand AG, Germany

Mini case study questions

1 Why does the EU aim for the adoption of uniform accounting standards by all of its Member States?
2 What role can accountants play in these efforts towards harmonization?

 REVIEW QUESTIONS

1 **Explain** why the euro currency is important for business, and how the single currency helps master macroeconomic fluctuations.
2 **Why** (and in which case) may it be crucial to approach business angels?
3 **To what extent** does the present euro-zone advantage (or disadvantage) its member economies and their companies?
4 **How** does SEPA work?
5 **What** funding can you expect to gather in the EU for a new innovative project, and under which conditions?

ASSIGNMENTS

- **Imagine** that you are a new financial auditor in Europe. How will you go about obtaining the relevant information on EU standards?
- **Compare** the advantages and disadvantages that companies may encounter due to corporate tax divergence in European Member States.
- **Case study assignment**: Read and prepare the case study 'Marimekko' in Part IV, and discuss the impact of the European currency on corporate financial management.
- **Internet exercise:** Compare the price of fixed phone services in three EU Member States of your choice. Discuss your findings, and the impact of the euro for business opportunities across the European market in this context.

Further reading

Axel, B.S., Ludwig, A. and Winter, J. (2006) Ageing, pension reform and capital flows: a multi-country simulation model. *Economica*, London School of Economics and Political Science, vol. 73, no. 292, November, pp. 625–58.

Bancel, F. and Mittoo, U.R. (2004) Cross-country determinants of capital structure choice: a survey of European firms. *Financial Management*, vol. 33, no. 4, pp. 103–132, Winter.

Larrson, A., Gaco, N. and Sikström, H. (2011) Monetary Integration and Business Cycle Synchronisation: Evidence from the Nordic Countries. Available at: people.su.se/~annla/pub/RBC110322.pdf

Schipper, K. (2005) The introduction of international accounting standards in Europe: implications for international convergence. *European Accounting Review*, vol. 14, no. 1, pp. 1–125.

 INTERNET RESOURCES

ECB website:
http://www.ecb.int/home/html/index.en.html

EIB website:
http://eib.eu.int/

EIF and VC information:
http://www.eif.org/venture

Euro-area economic and financial data:
http://www.ecb.int/stats/keyind/html/sdds.en.html

(Continued)

(Continued)

European budget:
http://europa.eu/pol/financ/index_en.htm

European Economic Area:
http://www.efta.int/eea.aspx

Financial service information of the EU:
http://ec.europa.eu/internal_market/finances/index_en.htm

Fiscal policy in European countries:
http://www.europarl.europa.eu/factsheets/3_4_9_en.htm

Free circulation of capital in the EU:
http://ec.europa.eu/internal_market/capital/index_en.htm

European funding sources (CORDIS):
http://cordis.europa.eu/eu-funding-guide/finding-sources_en.html

IAS standards:
http://ec.europa.eu/internal_market/accounting/ias/index_en.htm

Interactive map of the euro area:
http://www.ecb.int/euro/intro/html/map.en.html

Stability and Growth Pact and economic policy coordination of the EU:
http://europa.eu/legislation_summaries/economic_and_monetary_affairs/stability_and_growth_pact/index_en.htm

Taxation in the EU:
http://ec.europa.eu/taxation_customs/

VC in Europe:
http://www.europeanvc.com

Gabriele Suder's *Doing Business in Europe* video series (on the SAGE Companion Website at http://www.sagepub.co.uk/suder2e and YouTube)

Note

1   Text based on: Information & Enterprise, 1992 in Suder, 1994; WelcomEurope 2005; ETI, 2006; interviews at CEC; own project experience).

Bibliography

Aviat, A. and Coeurdacier, N. (2007) The geography of trade in goods and asset holdings. *Journal of International Economics*, vol. 71, March, pp. 22–51.

Baldwin, R. and Wyplosz, C. (2004) *The Economics of European Integration*. London: McGraw-Hill Education.

Barysch, K. (2005) East versus West? The European economic and social model after enlargement, Essay, Centre for Economic Reform. Available at: http://www.cer.org.uk

Bernstein, N. (2010) The Danish krone during the crisis, Speech by Nils Bernstein, Governor of the National Bank of Denmark, at the Copenhagen Business School, Copenhagen, 22 March. Available at: http://www.bis.org/review/r100325c.pdf

Brenneman, D. (2004) The role of regional integration in the development of security markets: A case study of the EU accession process in Hungary and the Czech Republic (Manuscript available at http://www.law.harvard.edu/programs/pifs/pdfs/david_brenneman.pdf).

Commission of the European Communities (CEC) (2011) Market access database (Trade). Available at: http://madb.europa.eu/mkaccdb2/indexPubli.htm

Deppler, M. and Decressin, J. (2004) How to help european fiscal policy: a commentary, by Deputy Division Chief, EU Policies Division, European Department, International Monetary Fund, *Financial Times*, 15 February.

El Kahal, S. (1998) *Business in Europe*. Maidenhead: McGraw-Hill International.

European Central Bank (ECB) (2002) *Evolution of the exchange rate between US$ and the euro from January 1999 to July 2005*. Frankfurt: ECB.

European Central Bank (2008) Single Euro Payments Area (SEPA): Commission publishes major cost-benefit study (IP/08/98). MEMO/08/52, Brussels, 28 January.

European Central Bank–Eurosystem/Schmiedel, H. (2007) The economic impact of the single euro payments area, *Occasional Paper Series*, No. 71, August.

European Commission Taxation and Customs Union (2010) *How VAT Works*. Available at: http://ec.europa.eu/taxation_customs/taxation/vat/how_vat_works/index_en.htm

European Communities (2000) International exchange of VAT information within the EU, Donato Raponi, DG Taxud, Head of the Unit. Available at: http://www.itdweb.org/VATConference/Documents

European Communities (2001) The reform of taxation in EU Member States, Final Report for the European Parliament, *Report for the European Parliament*, Tender No. IV/2000/05/04, Final Version, 9 May, CEPII, Paris.

European Communities (2005) Framework for fiscal policies, *European Parliament Fact Sheets*. Available at: http://www.europarl.eu.int/facts/5_5_0_en.htm

European Documentation Series (1987) *The ECU*, 2nd edn. European Documentation 5/87, Luxembourg European Investment Bank (2001) The Project Life Cycle at the European Investment Bank, 12 July. Available at: http://www.eib.org

European Investment Bank (EIB) (2010) EIB increases its support to SME projects in Slovenia. No. 2010-048-EN, Luxembourg, 25 March. Available at: http://www.eib.org/projects/press/2010/2010-048-eib-increases-its-support-to-sme-projects-in-slovenia.htm

European Union (EU) (2010) What is VAT? http://ec.europa.eu/taxation_customs/taxation/vat/how_vat_works/index_en.html

EUROSTAT/DG TAXUD, STAT/10/95 of 28 June 2010, Taxation trends in the European Union: EU 27 tax ratio fell to 39.3 per cent of GDP in 2008, *Eurostat News Release.*

Financial Times (FT)/Stafford, Ph. (2010) BATS and Chi-X eye new landscape, http://www.ft.com/cms/s/0/c1fc6ac6-0ec0-11e0-9ec3-00144feabdc0,s01=1. html#axzzlOxpdapJK

Government of Australia (2005) *Export EU: A Guide to the European Union for Australian Business.* Available at: http://www.dfat.gov.au/publications/eu_exports/exporteu_2005.pdf

Government of the United Kingdom of Great Britain (1997) *Fiscal Policy.* Available at: http://image.guardian.co.uk/sys-files/Guardian/documents/2003/06/09/policyframeworks2.pdf

International Monetary Fund (IMF) (2009) *World Economic Outlook,* October 2009, p. 75.

Inforeg (2004) *Guide des Financements européennes pour les enterprises: Tout savoir sur les mechanismes des aides européennes.* Paris: Gualino Editors, EJA, CCI Paris, Euro Info Center.

Jeffs, L. (2010) Nasdaq OMX to close European trading platform, *Financial Times,* 28 April. Available at: http://www.efinancialnews.com/story/2010-05-28/nasdaq-omx-shuts-neuro

Lord Currie of Marylebone, D. (1998) *Will the Euro Work? The Ins and Outs of EMU.* London: Economist Intelligence Unit.

Lord Currie of Marylebone D. (1999) EMU: Threats and opportunities for companies and national economies, in M. Baimbridge, B. Burkitt and P. Whyman (eds), *A Single Currency for Europe.* Basingstoke: Palgrave Macmillan.

McAndrews, J. and Stefanadis, C. (2002) The consolidation of the European Stock Exchange. *Current Issues in Economics and Finance,* vol. 8 no. 6, June, Federal Reserve Bank of New York. Available at: http://www.newyorkfed.org/research/current_issues/ci8-6/ci8-6.html

Makovec, M. (2007) Labour mobility within the EU in the context of enlargement and the functioning of the transitional arrangements. Country Study: Italy, European Integration Consortium IAB, CMR, fRDB, GEP, WIFO, wiiw-VC/2007/0293, Deliverable 8 Fondazione Rodolfo Debenedetti (fRDB). Available at: http://publications.wiiw.ac.at/?action=search&id=searchfulltext&fkeyword=labour+mobility&step=2&foptsearch=exact&ff[]=Mattia+Makovec

Mercado, S., Welford, R. and Prescott, K. (2001) *European Business.* Upper Saddle River, NJ: Prentice Hall.

Mundel, R. (1961) A theory of optimum currency area. *American Economic Review,* vol. 51, pp. 657–65.

Pagano, M. (1998) The changing microstructure of European equity markets, *CSEF Working Papers* No. 4. Salerno: Centre for Studies in Economics and Finance (CSEF), University of Salerno.

Portes, R. and Rey, H. (2005) The determinants of cross-border equity flows. *Journal of International Economics,* vol. 65, no. 2, March, pp. 269–96.

Stark, J. (2010) Economic recovery and exit strategies, Speech by Jürgen Stark, Member of the Executive Board of the ECB. Delivered at a debate on 'The post-crisis strategy for growth and jobs' and 'Modernisation of the global financial architecture' between the Committee on Economic and Monetary Affairs of the European Parliament and national parliaments, Brussels, 16 March. Available at: http://www.ecb.int/press/key/date/2010/html/sp100316.en.html

Steil, B. (2001) Borderless trading and developing securities markets. Paper presented at the World Bank, International Monetary Fund, and Brookings Institution Third Annual Financial Markets and Development Conference, Washington DC, April 4–6.

Suder, G. (1994) *Anti-Dumping Measures and the Politics of EU–Japan Trade Relations in the European Consumer Electronics Sector: The VCR Case*. Bath: University of Bath School of Management.

Suder, G. (2010) Europe Must Focus on Value Creation: Viewpoint, *Business Week* online, 15 April. Available at: http://www.businessweek.com/globalbiz/content/apr2010/gb20100415_271686.htm

WelcomEurope (2005) *Eurofounding – Complete Guide*, 7th edn. Paris: WelcomEurope.

Wildavsky, A. and Zapico-Goni, E. (eds) (1993) *The Role of Budgeting Procedures for Improving the Fiscal Performance of the Member States of the EC: National Budgeting for Economic and Monetary Union*. Boston, MA and London: EIPA/Martinus Nijhoff.

Other sources

AFX News, Daily Telegraph, Deutsche Welle, The Economist, The European, Financial Times, Herald Tribune, Time, Wall Street Journal, http://www.bseindia.com, www.businessangels.com, http://www.EUobserver.com, and many others.

EUROPA (2009) European labour market. Available at: http://www.eurofound.europa.eu/areas/industrialrelations/dictionary/definitions/europeanlabourmarket.htm

EUROPA (2010) Benefits of the euro. Available at: http://ec.europa.eu/economy_finance/publications/publication_summary7313_en.htm

8

Marketing in Europe

What you will learn about in this chapter:

- European marketing diversity and points of convergence.
- The dos and don'ts in European marketing.
- The future of the European marketing mix.
- Opportunities and challenges for the marketer in Europe.

8.0 Introduction

The introduction of the single currency and the relative harmonization of financial management tools illustrate an increasingly competitive EU market. Easier price comparison transparencies have an increasing impact on pricing strategies and marketing investment. The need to excel through innovation and creativity to differentiate your product is a determinant force of marketers in Europe. It is reflected in communication and brand-building strategies.

Indeed, harmonization and diversity in Europe establish marketing paradigms that are based on a *Europe-wide* strategy and on the opportunities of standardization versus niche positions. Similarly to international marketing, these strategies depend on the definition of the product, the market and the timing.

But European marketing theory has been recognized as different from typical 'international marketing' theory. Marketers are positioning their product or service in a highly integrated market and face high Europe-wide levels of competition. All developments in the political economy and in the frame of business transactions and relationships in the market have a direct consequence on the work of marketers. This concerns marketing departments, advertising agencies and market-research companies on a level that encompasses all EEA countries (see Chapter 2), whether the firms or products concerned be of European origin or not. European marketing translates into far-ranging, long-term marketing strategies in which diversity management and strategic partner relationships are key. Also, the high rates of adoption of new communication technologies in Europe force the marketing manager to reinvent or readapt strategies in accordance with Europe-wide solutions. For example, the Internet and third-generation telephoning have significantly altered the tools available to marketers for advertising and promotion as well as for managing transactions.

The main question of how European marketing approaches consumers is: Does ongoing European integration allow the company in general, and the marketer in particular, to approach the market as one single entity, that is using a standardized approach, or not? On the one hand, there is a greater number of consumers than in the USA; in certain regions, they have comparable purchasing power and are situated in one single market almost comparable to that of the American market. On the other hand, Europe is more diverse in terms of culture, distinct local and regional roots and attachments. Can we talk of a convergence of the European consumer? Can Europe-wide business act as an agent of change to 'standardize' the European consumer, hence facilitating the work of European marketers?

The business reality shows that, for example, Europeans show similar behaviour towards low-cost airlines, but differ considerably when it comes to purchasing in-flight meals on these carriers. German and Dutch clients tend to bring along their own food but, if served, expect sufficient quantity and quality. French and Spanish clients don't mind purchasing their meal in-flight.

This chapter reviews the main concepts that characterize European marketing and its realities. It provides you with the distinctive knowledge and tools for marketing in Europe.

The breakdown of barriers, increasing harmonization of educational standards, continuous evolution of financial-product ownership beyond national borders and the emergence of pan-European media enhances the feeling among consumers and marketers that Europe is one entity. Nevertheless, we will see in this chapter that the more the market converges, the more the consumer likes to be considered as unique and locally rooted.

The view of Europe as a homogeneous market is erroneous and this view can only be considered appropriate for a few strongly branded products and services. This approach is interesting in terms of economies of scale, but for most markets, market heterogeneity reigns in Europe. In a context of cultural, linguistic and remaining regulatory differences between European countries, it is a mistake to think of Europe in terms of standardization. Rather, it is important to know how to adapt your marketing approaches and strategies to customers in their own contexts. Economies of scale can apply to some of these, but by no means to all.

A European or non-European firm that effectively benefits from the Single Market typically pursues Europe-wide strategies, rather than local or regional-based marketing, for several reasons similar to those seen in Europeanization. These centre on issues of potential convergence or divergence of demand and potential efficiencies on the supply side, such as:

- advantages from wider business volume on an incremental basis;
- expansion of life-cycles when the domestic market has reached a certain level of maturity;
- with fixed costs being committed, achievement of economies of scale;
- high sales figures that obtain high additional volume;
- first-mover advantages or advantages in following competitors, or following clients, for example in financial services or specific components supply;

(Continued)

(Continued)

- defence or anticipation of potentially growing European and international competition towards the local, regional or European market;
- streamlining of marketing services in terms of return of investment, risk diversification, accountability for efficiency, speed and quality in creativity.

From earlier chapters, we have acquired a sound knowledge of the European market. For example, a single market has the advantage that import duties of non-EU members are payable only at one given point of entry into the EU, and not again upon transportation of the product within the EU. Nevertheless, we also learned that the harmonization of the European market does not eliminate the diversity of micro-indicators that analyse the potential acceptance of the product or service. For instance, highly varying factors in different Member States influence the rate of, say, coffee consumption, or tourism, or the number of farms or 5G telephones. This is essential knowledge, but not sufficient for doing business in Europe. We will now need to study how market research is conducted in Europe. Understanding consumer behaviour is every firm's principal preoccupation.

8.1 Understanding consumer behaviour

The basis of successful marketing is the screening and assessment of opportunities: the screening process typically reviews specific selection data that include size and growth of the market, political and social conditions, competition, and market similarities. Since 9/11 and the ensuing build-up of awareness of a new global risk of international terrorism, marketers increasingly also look at potential shifts in consumer behaviour due to threatened or experienced violence. Risk diversification has been given more thought in investment and in marketing. A stable business environment such as that of the EU is hence of vital importance as a basis for international operations because, for the marketer, it represents a microcosm of reactions and reactivity.

Macro-level data help select general market potential that is then considered relative to the specific product or service. This market-level screening helps to obtain answers to the most important market condition inquiries (see Box 8.1).

Box 8.1: Market conditions

- Existence and evaluation of similar existing products/services or substitutes for it.
- Likelihood of cultural adaptation.
- Market size.
- Taxes and duties.
- Stages of development.

The availability of data in the EU underpins the advantages that can be obtained from a single market strategy in marketing, but also allows you to learn about the cultural, linguistic, geographical and social differences that exist.

As a market grouping, the EU is the most advanced entity in the world, and *proxy variables* in the research of market potential, that is, studying a similar or related product or service for indication purposes, becomes a particularly powerful tool. Methodologically, marketing studies traditionally use four types of research tool:

- qualitative marketing research;
- quantitative marketing research;
- observational tools;
- experimental tools.

We add also the much more recent addition of Six Sigma analysis.

The research tools necessary for our purposes can be found in the traditional market research toolbox of international marketing (see Figure 8.1); there are, however, differences in the availability of data and their source and the diversity of findings for any Europe-wide approach.

Qualitative marketing research is generally used for exploratory purposes to analyse the perception of a small number of respondents to your product or service. The

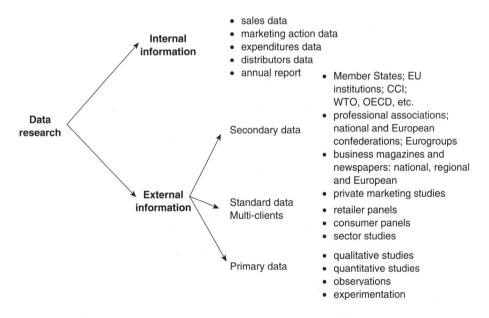

Figure 8.1 *Information research for European marketers*

study is not made to be generalized to the whole population and is typically already based on sound knowledge of the target customer. Qualitative marketing research is not calculated for statistical significance; rather, it tells us about the needs, desires and purchasing availabilities of a given focus group, using in-depth interviews and projective techniques. This tool may help you study the common or divergent elements between consumers of, say, the same level of education and professional background but from different cultures and will help, for example, to position e-learning tools or e-government initiatives for a specific clientele.

Quantitative marketing research allows you to draw conclusions regarding a specific hypothesis. This tool typically requires the use of random sampling techniques and involves a large number of respondents from many different backgrounds answering surveys and questionnaires. This is a common marketing research tool for consumer products such as dairy products, but is increasingly being used for commodities such as gas and electricity.

Observational tools demand the direct involvement of the researcher to observe social phenomena in everyday routines. These observations may well occur on a cross-sectional basis, with a number of observations made at one moment in time. Another approach is longitudinal, that is, a smaller number of observations are confirmed over several time periods. Examples include product-use analysis and computer cookie traces.

Experiments may then follow, complement or stand alone in market research. Experimental tools create a quasi-artificial environment that excludes non-controllable forces as much as possible. At least one of these variables is then manipulated in the environment, for example in test markets. This is of major significance for service marketing in which the consumer not only receives information but also interacts with it, and is hence involved in the consumption process rather than only with the outcome (Hollensen, 2004, p. 73). None of these tools guarantees the success of a marketing operation; normally you will use more than one of the above tools based on secondary research that is only refined by this primary data at a second stage. It is best to obtain the secondary data at the national, regional and European level, adding up complementary sources that convert a puzzle into a comprehensive picture. Figure 8.1 illustrates the main sources available for this external information, which needs matching with the internal information so as to be able to evaluate whether the pieces of the puzzle actually fit together – whether your product or service indeed fits with the target market and whether you should envisage a Europe-wide or segmented market strategy.

The best market research is a long-term exercise in which a consumer database is continuously updating the corporate understanding of consumers, their purchasing behaviour and the risk factors that may lead to changes in this behaviour.

The market study helps define a commercial strategy based on highlighting the firm's strengths and weaknesses compared to those of the competitors. Only with this information does the firm choose its commercial actions. Internally, the validation of appropriate marketing strategies can be based on techniques such as the Six Sigma quality-control concepts made famous by Jack Welch at GE, and which have great potential in terms of process discipline and performance value in marketing: Quelch and Harris (2005, p. 33–5) discuss the successful experiments of senior management using Six Sigma in these areas. The experiments focused on enhancing marketing criteria generally known to quality management as:

- Applicability
- Visability
- Manageability
- Replicability
- Receptivity
- Profitability
- The criteria of sigma techniques such as value mapping

These techniques can lead to best practices that may be replicated in European and, later, in international markets. Therefore, these techniques are particularly suited to vast and complex markets where market research and practice may cause high costs and encounter diverse levels of performance due to the diverse market requirements. Evaluations based on the marketing study, return on investment and quality criterion of your specific product or service will define the marketing approach best applicable in the European environment, either as a market grouping, or considering specific Member States or regions. Figure 8.2 illustrates the process followed for market segmentation. Market segmentation into single Member States or into regions of the EU can only be pursued on the basis of the micro and macro conditions that define your task as a marketer. You need to assess your product or service and its targeted business environment.

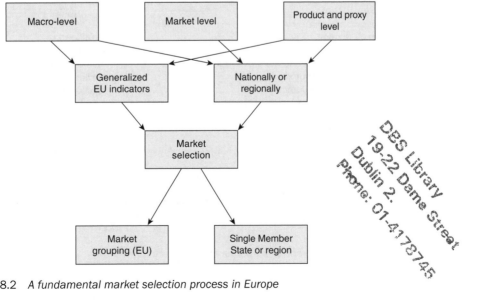

Figure 8.2 *A fundamental market selection process in Europe*

8.2 Assessing the product or service and the targeted environment

The traditional approach to international marketing focuses on the definition of the most suitable marketing mix, based on the work of Kotler (1988). This marketing mix includes the right product, at the right price, known through the right promotion, and available at the right place (the 4Ps).

The *best product scenario* is that in which the quality, features, options, style, brand name, packaging, sizes, services, warranties and returns are ideally adapted and adaptable to the price, promotion and place conditions. The *best price scenario* balances the list price, discounts, allowances, and payment, period and credit terms with the product, its promotion and the outlets where it will be available. The *best promotion scenario* deals with the adaptation of advertising, personal sales, promotion and publicity to the product, price and selling location. Finally, the *best place scenario* defines the channels, geographical coverage, locations, inventory and transport conditions for the product, at its price, and in accordance with its promotion (cf. Kotler and Armstrong, 1991, p. 41). The 4Ps provide us with a wonderful tool that deals primarily with the micro level of marketing decisions; therefore, the marketer in a complex marketplace needs to recognize that the 4Ps bathe within a diversity of perceptions – and deal with this accordingly. Figure 8.3 provides the main criteria that are needed to gear towards a strategy in the search for Six Sigma.

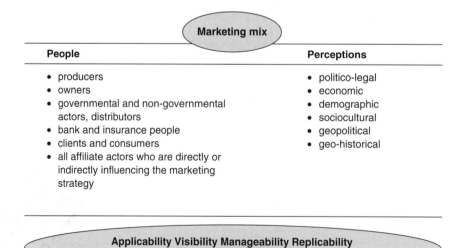

Marketing mix

People	Perceptions
• producers	• politico-legal
• owners	• economic
• governmental and non-governmental actors, distributors	• demographic
• bank and insurance people	• sociocultural
• clients and consumers	• geopolitical
• all affiliate actors who are directly or indirectly influencing the marketing strategy	• geo-historical

Applicability Visibility Manageability Replicability Receptivity Profitability

Figure 8.3   *People and perceptions for a marketing mix*

8.2.1 Segmentation in Europe: targeting similarities

Segmentation aims at identifying distinct groups of consumers whose purchasing behaviour differs significantly from others. It works by subdividing a market into distinct subsets of customers that behave in the same way or have similar needs. Several segmentations can be used and combined by marketers. Usually, marketers identify niches (or sub-segments of segments), which are more narrowly defined groups seeking a mix of benefits. There are unlimited bases of segmentation: from geographical to psychosocial and behavioural. The ultimate segmentation is one based upon the benefits sought by a particular set of customers for the product or service in question.

Nevertheless, not all segmentations are useful. A segment has to be at least measurable and differentiable – there are distinct marketing-mix elements and programmes distinct from one segment to another – and reachable.

The conditions outlined above lead the marketer to search for similarities in the perception of the product or service that is to be positioned. On a purely socio-cultural basis, a separation of Europe into the following similar but not identical segments or perception lines, is a good way to start. Table 8.1 illustrates possible distinctions.

A similar table needs to be drawn up for economic, demographic, sociocultural, geopolitical and geo-historical conditions, but the main politico-legal and economic cross-border conditions in Europe are highly integrated. A comparison on the basis of these analyses creates the mapping of opportunities on the grounds of segmentation, in response to the diversities of the European market and the advantages stemming from the Single Market. However, because of differences in purchasing power, national and personal income levels, attitudes to savings, and lifestyles across Europe, the standard socioeconomic group segmentation often applied in national markets may not provide a sufficiently refined definition. To date, only a few products have become relatively homogeneous.

Table 8.1 *A general European segmentation table, adaptable as needed*

EU member	Perception lines
Spain and Portugal, southern Germany, northern Italy, south-eastern France	West Mediterranean
South Italy, Greece, Malta, Turkey	Eastern Mediterranean European
UK and Ireland	Anglo-Saxon
Central and northern France, south Belgium, central Germany, Luxembourg and Austria	Centre
Northern Germany, Netherlands, northern Belgium, Iceland, Norway, Finland and Denmark	Northern
Eastern and Central European countries	Eastern, Central or Baltic

Source: Compiled and adapted from VanderMerwe and L'Huillier, 1989; Harris and McDonald, 2004 and others

These include household cleaning products, soft drinks and cigarettes, as well as computers, computer applications and Internet services. All of these were formerly dominated by American or British brands at the beginning of European Single Market opportunities, and have been marketed with a Europe-wide standardization strategy.

Clearly, only a sound assessment of the business environment can allow a company to best price, promote and locate a product or service in a market as complex as Europe. We will now study more of the specific characteristics of this European market.

8.2.2 Political and legal conditions

Although political and legal conditions within European countries are only partially harmonized, they allow the marketer to include various crucial criteria in evaluating the marketing mix. For example, essential to defining the price, promotion and potential of a product or service are the existence, non-existence or level of trade barriers, taxation rates and restrictions on foreign ownership or assembly operations, rules of origin, distribution of profits on capital movements, protection of intellectual property, labour laws and other aspects of business law.

The degree to which European countries adopt EU legislation and opt for integration defines the degree of harmonization of politico-legal factor advantages. A homogeneous political and legal framework does not exclude significant differences in taxation rates within the EU.

Administrative differences between European countries can hence be a hurdle for both trade and marketer: in agricultural goods, European law on food traceability can hamper marketers. However, in advertising, the EU sets standardized regulations to harmonize communications legislation, making it easier and cheaper to carry out Europe-wide advertising campaigns. European legislation also stipulates conditions that apply to packaging, for example in language requirements.

A non-exhaustive list provided in Box 8.2 summarizes the main politico-legal challenges that may hinder corporate marketing across borders. Stimuli are also available through governmental policy; for instance, the EU eases conditions for technological and digital business across the Single Market to enhance knowledge transfer, innovation and competitiveness. Some of the disadvantages of politico-legal intervention are relatively unimportant for business within Europe; others may serve as non-tariff barriers at particular moments in time. For example, the EU may well use customs and entry procedures as non-tariff barriers to entrance. In 1986, France insisted that all EU imports of video recorders came through one particular small customs point in Poitiers causing delays and logjam (Suder, 1994). In an example involving quotas, the Japanese car industry faced particular restrictions in Europe a few years ago; in consumer electronics and semi-conductors, the use of anti-dumping policy is a means of one-off intervention.

Box 8.2: Politico-legal challenges

The impact of political-legal frameworks:	Customs and entry procedure:	Product requirements:
• Administrative risks • Administrative guidance • Subsidies • Government procurement and state trading	• Product classification • Product valuation • Documentation • License to permit • Inspection • Health and safety regulations	• Product standards • Packing, labelling and marking • Product testing • Product specifications

Quotas: export and import:	Financial control:	Other policies and requirements:
• Absolute • Tariff • Voluntary	• Exchange control • Multiple exchange rates • Prior import deposits • Credit restrictions • Profit remittance restrictions	• Market reserve policy • Performance requirements

Source: Adapted from Onkvisit and Shaw, 1988

In terms of Place from the 4Ps, specific locations give access to particular conditions in price, product and promotion or image. While London has an important image in financial services, it is costly in terms of location; the Baltic countries allow cost savings in production and have the highest IT skills, but links with the rest of the region need to be improved. Visa laws in Sweden are relatively harsh compared to those in Greece, and may define your location of HR. Also in Sweden, advertising is strictly regulated, particularly at times when children watch TV. On the other hand, the politico–social stability and quality of life may be advantageous depending on the product or service to be marketed. The Czech Republic is the German airline Lufthansa's data-processing operations hub because of a stable politico-legal environment, while Zara, the Spanish fashion store, produces most of its materials in Europe and opened its first non-Iberian store in Paris. Li & Fung, an important Hong Kong-based trading company, operates in Europe from two Eastern European Member States.

8.2.3 Economic conditions, national income and quality of life

For successful marketing, it is best to have stable economic conditions. Economic instability results in risks associated with inflation rates, balance of payments, exchange rate stability, government budgets and growth. Within the euro-zone in particular, these indicators are likely to present similar macroeconomic trends. However, the more members there are, the more imbalances are likely to exist. Fostering the strong competitiveness of the Single Market through EU-wide initiatives can counterbalance these imbalances. The countries that implement these initiatives most fully are likely to be those that perform best economically in the long run, and are most suitable for constituting a whole market segment. A measure for this is the annual report of Eurostat that rates Member States' adoption of EU legislation. This information is easily accessible on the Europa website.

Economic conditions have a strong impact on consumer behaviour. During recessions, consumers prefer to save money; in times of economic risk and crisis, they invest differently. In periods of growth, consumers have a tendency to spend more and borrow more. National income usually explains some of the EU-wide differences in consumption, but in a more homogeneous economic, legal and technical environment such as the European market, how does consumption differ? In Europe, variations in income can explain a lack of convergence between the euro-zone countries and others. Where we find similar economic and politico-legal conditions, some product and service consumption tends to converge at first, and is then followed by divergence. For example, new technology converges at a macro-level, but differs at the micro level. National income gaps typically exist between new entrant countries and between new and old member states, and even more so with Bulgaria and Romania and candidate countries including Albania, Bosnia-Herzegovina, Croatia, Macedonia, Serbia and Montenegro, and Turkey.

In addition, personal income (discussed in Chapter 5) and quality of life will influence the marketing mix. The 15 'older' European members have been more intensively exposed to the marketing mix and its influences than newer European Member States. This means that the product or service may need to be more innovative and promoted differently in older Member States. Consumers may be less sensitive to price issues, and have reached a higher level of consumption saturation. Marketers need to think in terms of questions similar to: Why buy another car if you already own two? What would motivate your client to purchase another or different mobile phone if everyone in the household and workplace already owns one or more? For new members or applicants, which fashions will lead consumers to purchase your goods or services? Is there a desire to resemble other Europeans, and do consumers wish to obtain the same quality of life, or even a higher one?

8.2.4 Demographic conditions

Demographic variations and disposable incomes per head can also have a significant impact on the assessment of the EU market and its opportunities. We can estimate the levels of demand, size and development of the market, its regions or single Member States via information about demographic movements. Also, price movements in these markets, the level of development of financial, physical and supporting HR infrastructures are influenced by demography. Analysing similar or supplementary products or services is a way of assessing marketing conditions very precisely. While the size of the population in a given market is important, its specific characteristics with regard to the product or service are more crucial. The identification of the right clientele and a reliable population with similar behaviour and attitudes can be found in country reports and sector analysis provided by EU and international institutions such as the OECD, or market studies. The sources obtainable from governmental and non-governmental agencies are most useful for SMEs, which might not have their own departments for this exercise, whereas larger enterprises typically keep themselves informed about the market through their own researchers and consultants.

Market segmentation takes demography into account because it aggregates prospective buyers, sharing common needs or desires and responding in similar ways to marketing actions in groups. Segmentation seeks communities rather than individuals, although the promotion will also have to correspond to the desire of Europeans, particularly in northern Europe, to be individual and unique.

Segments must be measurable in purchasing power and size. This means that marketers must be able to promote and serve the segment effectively. The segment must be sufficiently large for sound profit potential, and must also match the corporation's marketing capabilities. Age defines some segments, for example the teenager segment (12–19 years) and the senior citizen segment (from age 70 onwards). In the ageing populations of Europe, these two segments are most interesting because the first has a growing (relative) purchasing power and decision impact in the buying process, while the latter is increasing in size. Both segments also exhibit very similar needs or behaviour across borders, and are part of the most important subcultures in Europe. However, purchasing power does vary between these segments. Both require the corporate sector to provide specific products and services in terms of comfort and lifestyle. Since 1999, the EU population has fewer children but its citizens are living longer than two generations ago. Eurostat figures show that between 1997 and 2007, only Ireland experienced a baby boom.

A demographic segmentation by gender may be useful, given that women's equal rights are protected by EU legislation and women's equality in society and the workplace is more prominent the further the given society is towards the north of the EU. The participation of women in economic, social, political and civic spheres, as well as equal treatment on pay, desegregation, family and working life provides households with additional purchasing power and evolving preferences on an individual and family level.

Marketing needs to recognize that European society faces important demographic challenges that may have positive or negative impacts on its activities. These changes open up opportunities for products and services that are adapted to needs: European societies need to find solutions for pensions, healthcare and welfare through such measures as raising the retirement age, increasing taxes or cutting benefits. Europe's demographic problem of a large elderly population is a challenge to pension funds and other financial organizations in this sector. At EU level, a pension forum exists to improve collaboration between the Member States, align their different points of view, solve issues and propose solutions to pension management in consultation with the private sector. The forum also aims to agree a general strategy on the pension programme that will satisfy the member countries.

Indeed, the absence of a common regulatory framework for pension rights still leaves barriers to the free movement of workers, which is difficult for social policies and labour needs. At the same time, immigration from other continents brings in a temporary and permanent workforce between the two sides of the international division of labour. On one side, guest workers often arrive under substandard conditions as a result of a shift in labour resources away from underdeveloped countries. Refugees and asylum seekers avoid persecution by coming into the most liberal countries of the EU; for example, in the UK, where the administrative requirements for the job market are less strict than in other EU countries. On the other side, highly educated migrants from non-EU countries come to Europe as part of a so-called brain drain in order to earn higher western salaries and to experience more liberal attitudes. This phenomenon attracts a niche customer base whose first generation is quite different from the traditional 'European' clientele, with cultural and societal behaviour and preferences that should interest the marketer. The second generation is normally a segment desiring fast integration into society while being soundly rooted in the parent's identity. Again, this is a segment for the marketer that is comparable to that of the segments in future candidate countries.

Europe needs cheap labour in order to keep its industry and competitive edge vis-à-vis low-cost competition from all over the world (this will be studied further in Chapter 10). In France, immigrants providing this come mainly from the Maghreb (North African Mediterranean countries), in the UK from India and Pakistan, in Germany from the Ukraine and Eastern Europe, and formerly from Turkey, in Poland from Russia, in Italy from Albania and other countries from this region; with people coming in legally or illegally.

8.2.5 The social agenda and sustainability

The sustainability of marketing in Europe is dependent on issues resulting directly from the conditions developed in the analysis above. This sustainability is profoundly influenced by the EU's vital interest in economic growth and welfare. The current challenges are defined by an analysis of the unemployment deficit, through the European Commission, forwarding crucial factor disadvantages stemming from:

- a services gap: employment in the services sector is much smaller in the EU than in the USA;
- a gender gap: only half of European women are part of the workforce compared to two-thirds in the USA;
- an age gap: the rate of unemployment in the 55–65 age group is high;
- a skills gap: skill requirements in the EU are not matched by supply, particularly in the IT sector;
- long-term structural unemployment: about half of those out of work have been so for over a year (EU, 2005).

As a solution to these issues, demographic evolution and education are key to the EU socio-economic agenda. Social issues accompany demographic developments and particular challenges to (or from) minorities. An illustration of this was the rioting in French, Greek and other European suburbs. With the support of European institutions, various organizations exist to combat discrimination against minorities and promote equal rights and opportunities. Institutions include AGE (European Older People's Platform), ILGA Europe (International Lesbian and Gay Association – Europe), ENAR (European Network against Racism) and the EDF (European Disability Forum) (more information can be accessed online at http://europa.eu.int/comm/development). Engaging in these anti-discriminatory or humanitarian initiatives, as well as in conflict prevention, raises the image and brand reputation of firms. In Europe – again more in the north than in the south – corporate social responsibility is a clear necessity and at the same times a value-added to marketing efforts. The main parties that interact in corporate social responsibility are the business, workers, investors and consumers (Monks, 2004). All stakeholders are concerned with ethical labour standards, which should conform to those set by European institutions for working conditions, child labour, forced labour and pension systems. Also in this context, sustainable development is at the top of the agenda.

There is yet another new social phenomenon that the attentive marketer can detect in Europe and in all rich economies; this is caused by commercial and industrial changes due to technology. Developments in this field have caused an individualization and intensification of work resulting in increasing stress and work accidents. The concept of 'wellness' has become important in marketing in Germany, and has great marketing potential.

A firm cannot pretend to be something or believe in an action; it has to show that that very thing is part of the corporate reality. The transparency required by Europeanization and globalization ensures that image can only be created from real actions, if companies are to avoid a boomerang effect leading to corporate disaster in terms of marketing.

Efficient marketing takes account of these different phenomena and adapts to them in the quest for message sustainability. Some of the phenomena that we have studied are similar among EU Member States and may invite an EU-wide marketing approach. Others are more diverse from one country or region to another and may require further segmentation. The sociocultural conditions of the European environment will provide further insights.

8.2.6 Sociocultural conditions

Understanding cultures is crucial for marketing across borders because cultures define norms and values, behaviours and perceptions, as well as consumer preferences. A successful marketer thus has to be able not only to be aware of different cultures but, even more, to adapt to them. Chapter 6 explained that the concept of culture includes national or regional, professional, industrial and functional, and company cultures (Schneider and Barsoux, 2003). All of these shape how the firm markets and how the consumer acts and reacts.

The temptation to over-generalize stereotypes is strong for marketers since culture conveys basic values, consumer perceptions, wants and individual behaviour in every society. Although consumer needs and perceptions may vary from one region to another within the same country, consumers from different bordering countries may share common values, attitudes and behaviour. A response to the unique needs of consumers in more than one market mostly requires a customized process, in order to satisfy fully consumers' local needs or characteristics. On the other hand, standardizing a product or service reduces expenditure, and allows for economies of scale. How can one know how clients will act and react in a given cultural context?

Some basic cultural information about European countries is most useful for understanding the European market. While direct exposure to different cultures is the very best way of learning about them, this is only possible for a few countries given the fact that it is unrealistic to go and live in every single targeted market across Europe. Thus, we need tools that help us to recognize marketing opportunities and/ or threats based on certain cultural traits. Understanding cultures (see Box 8.4) and being adaptable to different contexts is key to marketing in Europe.

Box 8.3: The marketer's sociocultural understanding focus

- Different ways of thinking and behaving.
- Different tastes and preferences (aesthetics, religions, personal choices).
- Different lifestyles (brand images, signs and values, family).
- Different priorities (individualist versus collectivist; dedication to work, family, leisure; attitude to change).

By identifying difficulties in intercultural relations, the marketer can relativize 'different' or 'disadvantageous' elements by comparing these to similar situations already encountered. An example is the acceptability of foreign languages in the media: in Germany, for instance, English words are regularly adapted to the German context, and this is considered normal, modern and a sign of openness to others (an interesting illustration is that, in Germany, the mobile phone is called a 'Handy', which leaves Anglophone visitors stunned). In France, any English wording in a product or service promotion needs translating and is restricted in number (the French Académie Française controls the proper preservation of the national language); in Sweden and Finland, most TV programmes are shown in the original language, often in English, and the consumer is used to that. This is the reason why case studies are excellent tools for this exercise. They can illustrate failures and successes in translation, for example that of Carrefour (which translates into 'happy family' in China). When self-acquired, firsthand information is missing or incomplete, you can avoid making mistakes by getting information from commercial sections of embassies and consulates, or academic and consultancy services in the targeted cultures.

Marketing a good or service can be based on a better understanding of the customer achieved through comparison and analysis. Consequently, the product and price can be adapted and a sound basis for communication can be set up through promotion. The study of consumer behaviour in relation to culture provides determinant information to firms and organizations. In what Kotler named core cultural values (1988, p. 160), certain beliefs and values persist over a long time and the firm needs to adapt to these. In Europe, people believe in freedom, particularly freedom of expression, in equality of people and chances, in the benefit of democracy, in social networks, to mention just a few common beliefs. In what Kotler (1988) calls secondary beliefs and values (which may change at a much faster pace), Europeans generally accept that marriage or partnerships may be hetero- or homosexual, that monoparental families are relatively frequent nowadays, and that social security networks and pension policies need to be adapted to demographic necessities so as to maintain an appropriate quality of life for all.

Most of these values are clearly rooted in religious ideas or social history. In Europe, Christianity has been the most common religion for centuries. Mainly, you will expect to encounter Catholics, Protestants and Orthodox Christians, a result of the religious division of the eleventh century. In 1904, German sociologist Max Weber made a famous connection between Protestant ethics and 'the spirit of capitalism' that had many repercussions in the Anglo-Saxon world – and for the economists influenced by this school of thought – because it was in opposition to Catholic doctrine that salvation arrives in life after death, and is not connected to wealth. The Islamic religion is becoming increasingly represented in Europe due to immigration, and this phenomenon plays yet another role in European consumer behaviour.

This perception of religions may lead to stereotypes that are too rigid to be true. Nevertheless, any classification or segmentation is subject to a certain tendency to stereotype and this is not necessarily bad if used as a reference point. If this reference point becomes a point of comparison for realities, it will have served a useful purpose.

Stereotypes may be enhanced through differences in interpersonal communication, either more expressive (in the south) or rather reserved (towards the north), or with a variable expressive culture (Eastern Europe). Verbal communication has to do with words and their meanings. Para-verbal language refers to how loudly (or quietly) we speak those words, the meaning of silence and the significance of conversational overlap. With non-verbal communication (also called body language), we communicate without using any words at all. For example, in Estonia, women do not shake men's hands in business when greeting each other. In France, you may be greeted by being embraced and kissed on the cheeks (with two, three or four kisses, depending on the regional culture), and this may also happen in Spain; in Germany and Austria, greeting someone means shaking their hand. Body language can also be different from one culture to another as is the perception of personal space and intimacy – again, while there is much diversity, certain similarities can be found. In northern Europe, priority is given to work, and behaviour reflects this in the life-style there; in the Latin and Mediterranean cultures, people say that 'there is life after work', and give a relatively high priority to personal relationships. There, commu-nication is more dynamic and warm-hearted. A business meeting may well start with a discussion about one's children and the presentation and discussion of your marketing report may extensively include the personal perceptions of colleagues at the meeting. Again, similarities may be found in several countries or regions. The next testimony illustrates the necessity for adaptation with the example of Euro RSCG's activities in southern Europe.

Box 8.4: Testimony of Ricardo Monteiro, CEO Euro RSCG Group Portugal and CEO Euro RSCG Latin America, and Executive Committee Euro RSCG Worldwide, March 2006

I've been an executive for Euro RSCG Worldwide for the past seven years. I previ-ously worked for BBDO, an American advertising firm, and for Unilever, the con-sumer goods giant. In my career, I've worked in Portugal, Spain, France and completed my university studies at the Université Catholique de Louvain, in Belgium. I'm currently CEO for Euro RSCG Portugal and CEO for Euro RSCG Latin America, where we employ about 2000 people in 18 countries. We do advertising and provide marketing services across the world for the likes of Peugeot, Citroen, Volvo, Danone, L'Oréal, Reckitt-Benckiser, Airbus, and many others, making us the fifth largest communications conglomerate in the world.

What particular value does southern Europe add to Euro RSCG's activities? Southern Europe is becoming less and less southern Europe in the sense that cul-tural and social values are, albeit slowly, converging across the European region and, I would even dare say, into some Latin American (LatAm) countries, such as Argentina or Chile, and even large groups in North America and Canada. The Latin characteristics that used to stand out are becoming part of everyone's values and only a few things subsist as being peculiar to southern Europe. Among those, I would underline family traits (young people staying at home with parents until they get married, even though they might hold jobs and have a career), eating habits (two full meals a day, long lunch and dinner hours) and a certain *joie de vivre* that still stands out, particularly when compared with northern countries. These are sufficient for a certain number of industries to behave differently in south-ern Europe. Banks direct their mortgages to new university graduates rather than towards the general population, as in more northern countries. Restaurant adver-tising is in its infancy, but taking off from where McDonald's or Pizza Hut have been an advertising feature in, say, the UK for the best part of the last 20 years, and product categories such as rum or vodka either make it in Spain and Italy or they're bound to fail in Europe. Keep in mind also that Spain, Italy, Portugal and

(Continued)

(Continued)

Greece stand out among the world's favourite tourist destinations. This propels all of these countries to the top of marketing know-how in that category and brings with it a cultural mingling that transforms the atmosphere here into a vibrant location, a true crossroads of peoples and cultures that all create an atmosphere of hospitality and understanding that might justify why, anywhere in the world these days, you'll find Spanish companies on the prowl (they dominate the scene in Latin America) and vast diasporas of Italians, Greeks and Portuguese that have strong positions in restaurants and small 'mom and pop' businesses that proliferate in the landscape. Being a southern European gives one the advantage of centuries' old cultures that have learned to listen, not to impose, to adapt, not to dictate. Don't forget, southern Europeans colonized the world and were first to learn that rule by force will only get you ousted faster.

Do we see any particular difference between advertising and communication (its tools, techniques, strategies, targets, etc.) in Europe and that conducted in Latin America? There are things, such as language and folklore, which are shared with Latin America, mainly by Spain and Portugal. And they're important. And, most of the African legacy in, for instance, Brazil, can also be found in Angola or on the streets of Lisbon. The Catholic inheritance in the whole of the Latin American region harks back to Spanish missionaries and it has, in many ways, shaped the mentality there. So, the ethics behind advertising messages, the total ignorance of certain important aspects of society today, such as homosexuality, divorce or the rule of the powerful, are still treated or, should I say, ignored by not only advertising but also mainstream media. Therefore, a certain conservatism prevails in the language and only beauty sells – no 'real imagery' or 'real people'. Not the gruesome reality of day-to-day life in the *favela* but rather the projective way of the lifestyle anyone would love to have. I think that in southern Europe – a possible line of division with Latin America – we're now getting closer to a certain, 'westernized' reality where social tensions of a basic nature – inequality, rich versus poor, socialism as a solution, fighting corruption – are no longer important. Our (European) speech has moved towards 'employment stability' and 'social Europe' whereas in LatAm they're still going for those very basic values. All of this reflects in advertising and communications.

What works better here, what works better there? In southern Europe, we're looking at indulgence, appeal to luxury and gadgetry, far away places, second cars, second homes. In LatAm, we're moving up from basics to the first car, the first mobile telephone, the first house, a better detergent, a fuller ice-cream.

Is European diversity (of people, perceptions, cultures and its business environment) an advantage or disadvantage for Euro RSCG's business? It can be an advantage if you come from an open culture, such as those in southern Europe or Scandinavia. It can be a terrible hindrance if one comes from France or the UK, where ignorance of other cultures and motivations is prevalent and people tend to concentrate on their national problems and do not see or accept experiences from other countries as valid for their own. Indeed, I always find it more difficult

(Continued)

(Continued)

to explain to a Frenchman what Brazil is like – his or her standard reply usually starts with 'In France, we ... ' – than, for instance, to a Swede who will ask questions and try to find out as much as possible about the country before he or she ventures into advice. But generalizations are always misleading. There's a growing number of people, mainly young people, who have gone through Erasmus and other European programmes that are coming out as truly diverse and open in their approach and, no matter where they were born, come across as a first generation of 'Europeans', as we like to think of them: open-minded and diverse, with cultural texture and density.

On the contrary, language barriers are more difficult for marketers in Europe who find that for communication campaigns customization is crucial. The other alternative is to find 'universally applicable' methods of communicating a message, for example by using a minimum of text but tackling issues that appeal to people across Europe, that is, shared core values (used for beauty and hygiene products, for instance, but also for high-tech products or cars).

Language problems can give the wrong impression and images about a product, a service or a company, and can easily be avoided through the help of competent translators of the desired mother-tongue. European legislation requires that content description on packaging be in all languages of the targeted markets.

In addition to the above, symbols and colours have an impact on promotion and media planning. In this framework, the well-informed advertisement marketer in Europe studies preferences for cinema, commercial or satellite TV. For instance, in Germany, 30 per cent of homes view satellite TV. The Internet, newspapers, posters and billboards are supports that work to different degrees; their applicability depends, for instance, on the tendency of people to live outdoors and to travel, in which case billboards and neon signs are attractive tools. Their use in the EU is, however, constrained. Radio and ICT provide important alternatives, mainly at rush hour: Scandinavians sometimes finish work at 4 p.m., the French at 5.30 p.m. Drive times vary from urban to rural regions, and radio and rush hours vary too.

Overall, promotion in print is still the biggest single share for advertisement in Europe, while Internet advertising has a small but growing percentage (Gillingham, 2005). On an EU scale, it can be observed that media spending is much higher in Germany, the UK and France than it is in Italy.

8.2.7 Geopolitical and geo-historical conditions

In Europe, geopolitical and geo-historical conditions influence the manner in which you can position a product in different markets. As mentioned above, some language barriers stem from sociocultural variations but these are often also based on other conditions. In West Germany between 1945 and 1990, for example, the US government engaged in geopolitical interests in opposition to the interests of those living on the other side of the Iron Curtain. The Marshall Plan and US forces therefore had a particularly strong influence on economic developments and lifestyles after World War II. As a consequence, English remains an easily accepted language for promotion, and trends from an English-speaking environment are often readily adopted. In another example, in some of the accession countries, the socialist past is a rather negative reference point; for subgroups, however, this past reminds them of perceived advantages no longer provided by their newly capitalism-focused economies (full employment, free child care, etc.).

Perceptions of products or services are influenced by these conditions. In our era, the threat of global terrorism is vastly perceived and not limited to particular places or regions. The events of 11 September 2001 had a worldwide impact on marketing too. First, the Madrid and London bombings demonstrated that Europe is at risk as well as the USA and tourist locations such as Bali. Second, the attacks affirmed that some European countries serve as transit places for 'sleepers' (extremists covered by neutral identities, well integrated into society and who may be dispatched for attacks). Third, terrorist groups recruit certain young Europeans or second-generation Europeans into their ranks and employ them for their local knowledge and for geopolitical reasons of their own. The challenges stemming from these phenomena force marketers into yet another sensibility about people and perceptions. For example, after the London bombings, the bicycle industry was able to position its product by maintaining that it was safer to travel by bike than by other forms of transport. (By the way, in other locations, this industry also reacts to people's preoccupations with the environment and with well-being and health into old age.) After each attack, consumers around the world perceived the threat of terrorism as being based on striking with an element of surprise against innocent bystanders and attracting as much media impact as possible. For the security sector also, important market opportunities appeared. In the retail industry, a tendency to store more basic food products is measurable. In clothing, fashion stores such as Zara turned to darker clothes (expressing grief) in Europe after the attacks. In terms of brand marketing, it was recently demonstrated that, on a worldwide level, US brands have generally lost market share while European brands using a multiple brand strategy have improved their place in the market because they are less exposed to the psychological association of being the 'prime target' (Suder et al., 2007; Suder and Suder, 2011).

Finally, a particular market can be promising in terms of image due to governments' geopolitical interests. For example, the marketing of science parks in Turkey boosts the potential for developing marketing opportunities in the Middle East; these opportunities are supported by EU funds that encourage collaboration with or within accession countries.

8.3 The Ps and AIDA: a marketing mix for Europe

Just as for the complexities in international marketing, European marketing strategy depends on the number of segments that the company has decided to target. There can be either a standardized marketing strategy with a standardized marketing mix applied to all targeted groups, or a concentrated market dividing a marketing mix to reach a single segment of the global market, or differentiated global marketing with different marketing mixes for each target group. The crucial factor in deciding whether to standardize marketing strategy is the similarity of the benefits sought by segments in different geographic markets.

When a marketer has defined a specific target, the marketing solution for the consumer must be developed through:

- a product or service that is well designed and adapted;
- its placement;
- a well-defined price; and
- being sold with the right choice for its promotion and communication.

Before the development of this strategy, marketers have to be sure of the targeting process. The best means can be classified into three main categories as presented in Box 8.6: the Pull strategy, the Push strategy and the Contact strategy.

Box 8.5: Marketing strategies

- The Pull strategy creates customer demand through all promotional efforts and 'pulled' demand through distribution channels, that is, leading the consumer to the product, for instance via advertising.
- The Push strategy pushes the product through the distribution channel into the retailer.
- The Contact strategy establishes direct contact with the consumer through canvassing and follow-up. (Kotler, 1988)

Which strategy is the most suitable and why depends entirely on the product or service and its target market. Do the size and growth potential of the targeted market allow for a long-term standardization strategy? If not, high competition might need to be avoided, unless you satisfy an unsatisfied consumer better than the competition. Within your European strategy, is the targeted market compatible with the company's goals?

Non-European companies wishing to establish a European operation may need to adapt their marketing strategy depending on the company's status, as illustrated in Table 8.2.

Table 8.2 *Company responses to European markets*

Company status	Challenges	Response
Established multinational	Exploit opportunities from improved productivity	Pan-European strategy or regional/country segmentation
Established multinational markets	Meet challenge of competitors Cater to customers/intermediaries doing same	
Firm with one European subsidiary	Competition Loss of niche	Expansion Strategic alliances Rationalization Divestment
Exporter to Europe	Competition Access	European branch Selective acquisition Strategic alliance
Moderate interest in Europe	Competition at home Lost opportunity	Any entry

Source: Material drawn from Magee, 1989, and adapted from Czinkota et al., 2003, p. 262

Another strategic question is whether a company has the minimum resources (competencies/human resources/financial resources, etc.) to do well. Pricing will be dependent on this.

8.3.1 The marketing mix in Europe

Decisions on pricing are crucial because of the effect on returns on investment, revenues and hence profits. At the same time, the price of a good or service will shape the perception and willingness of people to engage in a first or repeat purchase, in terms of quality, image and positioning vis-à-vis the competition of similar or complementary value. The purchasing power of the market segment needs to be taken into account. By worldwide comparison, price differences in Europe are relatively small, although there are some exceptions as follows:

- goods or services taxed by governments, for example petrol;
- goods or services which have obtained a particular brand recognition in a particular country and which are more expensive there than elsewhere, such as cars; and
- goods or services positioned in a more or less deregulated market, such as telephone services.

However, if the brand image is strong in Europe, then relatively homogeneous pricing can be expected for products (such as Nutella, a well-known hazelnut chocolate spread) and for services (such as in the online purchasing of flowers or books). This is also the case for retail groups that have obtained strong Europe-wide or international buying power, for sales to big European customers, and for cases of parallel imports and grey markets.

Pricing in the form of EU-wide standardization is based on the company setting a price as the product leaves production, with adaptations in terms of foreign exchange rates in non-euro-zone countries, and in terms of variances in the regulatory field; this is facilitated through the Single Market and the euro-zone effects because adjustments are not necessary. Standardization neglects the diversity of the market but, due to its low risk, allows for high-level sales and a clear price reputation.

Price differentiation is defined, rather, at a regional or local level and is based on the distinction of cultural differences and consumer perception in different markets. This strategy allows for adaptation to market conditions, local competition, terms and conditions and price awareness, but it may also invite grey market or parallel import activities across borders. This is the case, among other examples, for tobacco products, which are subject to different levels of national taxes.

Price differences within the euro-zone tend to decrease with time, which is interesting in terms of sourcing. Prices converge primarily in sectors where the market is broad and logistics are less important, such as industrial supplies and mobile and price transparent products and services sold over the Internet. However, attitudes to Internet security, personal spending and savings, and choice of preferred means of payment differ between regions. In France, where credit card payments predominate, the relationship of consumer behaviour and spare change is less developed than in Germany, where most payments are made in cash.

We have seen that exchange rate risks only apply to pricing in those European countries that are not members of the euro-zone. Nonetheless, differences in VAT have yet to be completely eliminated by the EU (see Chapter 7). This is important in transfer pricing, that is, prices set for intra-firm movement of goods and services establish the value of these for taxation purposes when travelling from one country to another. Typically, the ideal solution when setting these prices is to define them on the basis of the tax rates in the countries of manufacture and distribution (Hollensen, 2004, p. 509). The difficulty of setting the right price, at cost, at arm's length or at cost plus, can be expected to diminish if the EU completes its harmonization of tax regimes. Altogether, the key issue in making price decisions is the question of what price the customer is prepared to pay. If this differs significantly from market to market (for whatever reason), then standardized prices make no sense.

Promotion is crucial to the marketing mix in the cases of standardization and segmentation developed above. Advertising is key to perception and this in turn is key to competitive positioning and pricing.

Consequently, in the context of prestige brands, pricing translates into high pricing for products or services. Examples are Audi TT cars, perfume and golf clubs. Positioning and pricing reflect the value and position of the service or good in the market. However, low price low value strategies in Europe include particular products where consumers are prepared to accept low value, for example generic brands. The UK's Marks & Spencer and Sweden's Ikea (the largest single furniture retailer in the world) use medium-priced, good-value strategies. Lastly, in penetration pricing strategies, we find European mobile phones. A quite different strategy which has had much success is pre-booking: variable pricing where prices increase or decrease as a direct function of demand, for example in online bookings for low-cost airlines, pioneered in Europe by easyJet and Ryanair.

Altogether, prices reflect what is happening in the market, in terms of quality and value, competition and placement. Benchmark brands influence their competitors' pricing, for example Perrier and San Pellegrino in bottled waters. But do not forget that segmentation, discussed earlier, always comes before setting prices, placement and promotion. However, even if the core product remains the same, its marketing may differ depending on the market and the culture. The same product, such as water, may be sold differently because it may be more or less treated, more or less available, more or less considered valuable and used according to different needs (drinking, cleaning, watering gardens, filling up pools, farming, etc.), and hence at different prices.

In terms of placement, the marketer in Europe quickly recognizes that channel structures and the degree of retailer *power* is not the same in all EU countries. Some national distribution systems are closed networks of producers, transport companies, wholesalers and retailers, but more and more of them are challenged by European competition. The 2011 takeover of TDG (via holding company Laxey Logistics Ltd) by the French group Norbert Dentressangle, is an illustration of pressures for consolidation in Europe in many sectors, approved by the Commission (CEC). Also, the *means* of distribution are influenced by the transport and logistics systems and of consumer goods by wholesaling and retailing systems. These systems yet differ for legal reasons, especially in transport laws, environmental rules on emissions and congestion, planning laws that restrict where production, distribution and retailing operations take place, and technical factors (Harris and McDonald, 2004). For example, in France, hypermarkets were invented because the French did not allow supermarkets in cities.

As mentioned above, good promotion depends on the most researched perceptions and demand. Their taxonomy influences the behaviour of consumers, who in Europe are typically exposed to between 2000 and 3000 messages per day through advertisements, most of which go unrecognized, while others raise awareness.

Legal conditions influence promotion policies because laws on advertising and promotion activities vary across European countries. But cultural differences often require different types of promotion too. Language differences hinder much of Europe-wide word of mouth, and may hinder large-scale reputation building and effective promotion. Technical factors often require differences in the demographic and geographical coverage of newspapers, and television and ownership of telephones and Internet connections also influence the possibility of adopting the same promotion package.

Harris and McDonald (2004) propose the following combination of products and promotion packages in this single but diversified European market:

- the same product and the same means of promotion: has the least costs and permits economies of scale and scope;
- the adapted product and the same means of promotion;
- the same product and different means of promotion;
- the adapted product and different means of promotion: has the highest costs and limits economies of scale and scope.

The AIDA-toolbox (Weilbacher, 1984) summarizes the main stages in communication and marketing, and consists of:

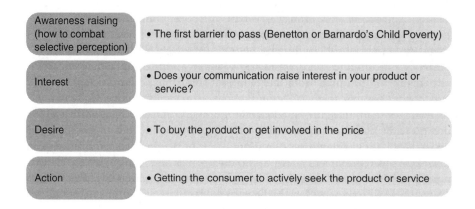

In all promotion activity, the main questions are the following: Who is your target market? What is its demography and culture? Does it contain conservative or modern groups, religions, etc.? Could it be that your advertisement offends people? Are the people you may offend your customers? Consumer freedom depends on particular standpoints, cultures and backgrounds. If controversial ads are used, these need to be studied in terms of positive or negative impact on sales. Advertising, personal selling, sales promotion and PR arise as part of AIDA – perhaps the most affected by culture; even if the product is the same, the way you promote it will often be different.

Is the promotion about brand or product? How saturated are the target customers by your or your competitors' campaigns? Are you as the marketer solely generating revenues or are you also pursuing other goals (for example, stakeholder satisfaction through social or environmental concerns)? Do you want to raise awareness or get people to buy your product immediately? In Box 8.7, you will find a non-exhaustive checklist of 'must-dos' in advertising.

Box 8.6: The 'must-dos' in controlling your advertising: a checklist

- Who is the target customer of the advertisement?
- What benefit does the advertisement best emphasize?
- What is the message?
- How effective is the advertisement at reaching the target and at communicating the message?
- Can you think of a better way to communicate with the target audience?
- What are the perceptions shown in test marketing with a sample group?

The advertisement's message has to be driven by information rather than the artistic aspirations of an advertising agency; these aspirations can nevertheless be useful if used positively to attract awareness through creative and innovative approaches. The marketer's message to the agency must be explicit. With perfume, for example, men mainly make purchases for their partners; the promotion, therefore, must mainly target men.

The integrated European market gives people a great choice of consumption in terms of quality and quantity, and illustrates its great freedom of expression (Gillingham, 2005).

8.3.2 The future of European marketing

In the diversity of Europe, we can expect marketing to develop into segments that grow in size due to increased harmonization in the environment – without necessarily becoming one single segment for all goods and services. Interestingly, the US market appears to be developing in the opposite direction, from generally standardized marketing towards diversity marketing; this phenomenon is due to ethnodemographic and economic developments in recently immigrated communities. However, we can expect that, in the USA, marketing will not reach the same level of heterogeneity as it does in Europe. Consequently, a convergence of marketing approaches will take place in the long-term that – together with the increasing integration of European and North American markets – holds significant promises for the marketer. Again, Europe is a microcosm that allows for the development of strategies applicable in the international environment. Its composition of markets of various degrees of maturity opens up a set of important opportunities.

8.4 Résumé and conclusion

A European market study is the collection of information on a market that is particularly diversified but that also benefits from market group similarities for efficient marketing. These advantages are based on EU integration as well as on conditions that shape Europeans' perceptions. As a selection of these perceptions, we have studied politico-legal, economic, demographic and sociocultural conditions. These conditions help the marketer to identify opportunities and challenges according to a product or service's needs, to demand and to the environment. Knowing these conditions means adapting the 4Ps of the marketing mix efficiently:

- Know the characteristics and needs of customers in order to satisfy them as well as possible.
- Modify a new product according to consumers' needs.
- Design a new product.
- Test a new product.
- Know the threats and opportunities of a market.
- Analyse sales and forecast the demand.
- Evaluate the firm's reputation and brand image.

Situational analysis of the European environment, customers, other actors such as distributors and suppliers, competition, opportunities and threats can be based on a multitude of freely accessible data. The main challenges for market studies may be language barriers for in-depth studies in some of the newer Member States.

In accordance with the firm's internal objectives, strengths and weaknesses, a segmentation of target markets may be undertaken or a standardized European-wide marketing strategy adopted. The latter option is certainly the most cost-efficient, but only applies to relatively few products and services. Among them, we have found those characterized by strong cross-border brand images, and Internet services that allow for high mobility and flexibility. Also, when logistics are unimportant and European harmonization is required, an EU-wide strategy makes sense.

In conclusion, the leakage effects of traditional marketing approaches in a European context make national approaches less effective, but still useful because of important diversities in the perceptions of European peoples. Any corporation is well advised to market its goods or services in Europe because trade flows, investment and sourcing in the EU reduce the specific advantages that a firm would achieve from outsourcing or foreign supply. Marketing can hence underpin a sound European strategy wherever possible in terms of adapted product or service. Because all efficient marketers utilize the possibilities that the Single Market provides (on a regional or an EU-wide basis), only those firms that still only act locally lose out on these opportunities.

The true key to success lies in adapting a marketing strategy to either an EU-wide or a country or regional segmentation, in which the marketing mix of the good or service accords with people's perceptions. The factor advantages in European marketing are anchored in the best possible compromise between cost savings, quality management and local knowledge. Product or service features, the right price, an efficient promotion and the place best adapted are dependent on the heterogeneity of successful marketing.

Mini case study: The Xbox Kinect in Europe – the key part of a Guinness World Record

Kinect, the motion-sensing system of Microsoft's Xbox, arrived on the European market in 2010, revolutionizing computer gaming: the Xbox console detects players' body movements for control input, replacing the traditional remote systems through (simply put) an invisible infra-red beam reflection captured by sensors and a 3D camera. The cornerstone track mechanism, based on machine learning, was devised at Microsoft Research Cambridge in the UK.

The Xbox Kinect had been launched in the USA on 4 November 2010. It was then launched throughout Europe, the Middle East and Africa on 10 November 2010, in line with Microsoft's regional structure. Within that one week, the company had made it possible to deliver a sufficient supply of Kinects to 60,000 stores in 38 countries.

Earlier that year, in June 2010, Microsoft had showcased Kinect as a 'first' in Europe at the Cannes Lions International Advertising Festival. The launch took place at the famous 'Promenade de la Croisette' on the French Riviera, to show innovation in regard to, amongst other things, consumer space and experience management.

> We are committed to investing in Europe and the crucial role it plays in Xbox's global success.

Microsoft VP of Interactive Entertainment Business EMEA, Chris Lewis, announced this in August 2010 at GamesCom in Germany, which is the biggest show in this sector in the region. At the same time, Microsoft announced expected sales of over 2 million Kinects across the region by the end of 2010, which would account for 40 per cent of global sales forecasts for the EMEA region.

Today, it is estimated that, in just 11 days of sales time in the USA and in less than 7 days in Europe, Microsoft sold its first 1.3 units. By the beginning of March 2011, Microsoft had sold more than 10 million units. Guinness World Records 2011 announced that:

> We confirm that no other consumer electronics device sold faster within a 60-day time span, an incredible achievement considering the strength of the sector. (G. Davies, Editor, http://www.techflash.com/seattle/2011)

The recommended pricing for Europe was decided as EUR149, selling for £129.99 in the UK. In fact, in Germany, a customer can purchase the 'Kinect Sensor with Kinect Adventures (Xbox 360)' for EUR99.99 since a 'Preiskrieg' (price war) started there when one of the biggest retailers, Saturn, reduced its prices for an anniversary promotion, and was followed by its main competitors, Amazon and Media Market. It is now also on offer at the reduced price on Amazon's UK site: 'RRP: £132.76; now: £99.98' and at similar prices for competing retailers in the UK. At the time of this study, the Kinect remains at the initial recommended price of EUR149.99 in Spain and in The Netherlands, and sells at EUR167 in Romania.

In the games industry, Microsoft continues to challenge directly Nintendo's Wii and Sony's PlayStation, the latter suffering from 2011 legal issues in Europe due to important privacy leaks. In April 2011, EU authorities announced that they were looking into the PlayStation gaming network regarding how much data the company stores and why.

Microsoft itself is regularly under investigation in the EU. However, the company is at the same time one of Europe's important partners for public–private partnerships supporting, amongst other initiatives, the Europe 2020 strategy (see Chapter 2).

The Nintendo Wii had played a significant role in the industry when it redefined gaming because it removed the need for a handset, and made gaming more accessible to a broader audience.

Microsoft had moved into this market with the first-generation Xbox to compete with Sony's Playstation 2 (PS2) and Nintendo's Game Cube. The seventh generation

Mini Case

of gaming consoles integrated new developments, with Internet access and online services of varying kinds. These gave extra potential for allowing access to content, prolonging gaming time, generating additional income and building relationships with users. These consoles also make extensive use of avatars to represent the players in a game, different consoles allowing differing degrees of personalization. Microsoft's acquisition of Skype and its technology in May 2011 enable even more personalized interaction among users.

For the Kinect, Microsoft identified five main segments in the video gaming market. The core targets are 'social' and 'independent' gamers, who constitute 35 per cent and 28 per cent of the customer base respectively.

The *Social Core* is made up of advanced Internet users, at ease with technology and using the Internet for video streaming, online gaming, music downloads and more. This demographic is predominantly male (thought this is lessening), aged 14 to 18, and connected to the Internet from morning to night. For these individuals, video games are an integral part of life and an important source of social recognition from peers. They subscribe to Xbox Live and take great pleasure in comparing scores with friends. They use the Xbox to link up with friends and will play with them while chatting. Proud to own an Xbox and often critical of other consoles, they may enjoy playing on a friend's Wii but will find the games lacking in sophistication. These gamers were once tempted by a PS3 but now try to convert friends to the Xbox. The Kinetic adds a social and dynamic side to such gaming and word of mouth is an important element here.

The *Independent Core* is the largest category of gamers for the Xbox. They are older than the Social Core (aged 18 to 35) and are attracted to realistic, long-lasting games. These gamers are attracted to the Xbox because of the games (Forza, Halo, Gears of War, Fable) and the value for money in terms of high definition. They were potentially wary of the impact on the kinds of games that Kinect offers: they do not want the games they cherish to be replaced by lighter forms of entertainment. Some of these players see the handset as an essential part of gaming and all require hi-definition games.

In addition, Microsoft reaches out to two other segments in particular: the Hyper Socials and the Family Timers, who – by the end of 2010 – made up 16 per cent and 6 per cent of the customer base respectively.

The *Hyper Social* segment is largely female, between 15 and 30 years old. They are extraverts and spend large amounts of time on social networks, such as Facebook, Windows Live Messenger and Twitter. They also enjoy challenging their friends to games on social networks. Their priority is to stay connected with their friends, either by being with them, or through the web or a mobile phone. They often have a Wii and love to play games such as dancing, karaoke or sport with their friends.

The *Family Timer* segment involves parents around the age of 40 who live in the suburbs with their family. They do not frequent social networks and use mass-market brands such as Nike and Gap. They spend time watching TV, enjoying social games such as Monopoly and being with their family. They like to take photos and typically enjoy playing on the Wii, particularly Mario Kart, Wii Play or Wii Sport. For them, technology has to be user-friendly.

Adding these two segments to the Xbox's existing core audience would translate into doubling its audience.

Finally, there is also a smaller segment that might also provide potential in the future. These mainly young adult females have no great affinities with video games and the few that they have played are on the Wii. They are ill at ease with a handset, but enjoy games that involve physical activity, providing exercise or allowing weight loss. They typically like pop music and reading fashion magazines.

By February 2011, UBISOFT, the French computer and video game publisher and developer, had conquered 21 per cent of the European market for the games developed for Kinect, proclaiming itself as the number one third-party publisher on Kinect.

Because of the potential of Kinect's technology going well beyond games, its applications hold the promise of a bright future. An associated software development kit (SDK), with its 'starter kit', allows for business, science, health and educational applications through immersive experience.

Source/authors: Gabriele Suder and Peter Spier, SKEMA Business School. Data used: by permission of Microsoft Corp./International.

Mini case study questions

1   Despite the single recommended price announced for the region, why are the prices of the Xbox Kinect different across Europe?
2   Why is Europe a key element in the success of the XBox Kinect? What market characteristics explain the phenomenon?
3   Given the information in the case study, what marketing strategy(-ies) has Microsoft used for Kinect in Europe, and what further elements do you think contribute to this success?

 REVIEW QUESTIONS

1   **How** does culture impact on consumer behaviour in the buying decision processes?
2   **How** do environmental conditions affect the marketing mix for firms acting in European countries?
3   **What** are the pros and cons of a pan–European marketing strategy?
4   **What** are the fundamental steps to take in conducting a market study (in general and in Europe)?
5   **Is** the European consumer comparable to the Latin American consumer?

ASSIGNMENTS

- **Imagine** a product and a service that you wish to market in Europe. Why are the approaches different from those used in other markets?
- **Compare** the promotion of a given product, for example that of a middle-sized car, in Europe and in the USA. What is different in the marketing approach?
- **Case study assignment**: Read and prepare the case study 'Managing change at Unilever' in Part IV.
- **Internet exercise**: Which Internet sources are most useful for market studies of the European market?

Further reading

Albayrak, M. and Gunes, E. (2010) Implementations of geographical indications at brand management of traditional foods in the European Union. *African Journal of Business Management*, vol. 4, no. 6, June, pp. 1059–68.

Douglas, S.P. and Craig, C.S. (2011) Convergence and divergence: developing a semi-global marketing strategy. *Journal of International Marketing*, vol. 19, no. 1, March, pp. 82–101.

Hunter, M.L. and Soberman, D.A. (2010) The 'equalizer': measuring and explaining the impact of online communities on consumer markets. *Corporate Reputation Review*, vol. 13, pp. 225–47.

Kuenzel, S. and Vaux Halliday, S. (2010) The chain of effects from reputation and brand personality congruence to brand loyalty: the role of brand identification. *Journal of Targeting, Measurement and Analysis for Marketing*, vol. 18, pp. 167–76.

Levy, J. (2007) Demographic changes in Europe: opportunity or threat? *Journal of Medical Marketing*, vol. 7, pp. 287–93.

Rossini, G. and Zanghieri, P. (2006) *What Drives Price Differentials of Consumables in Europe? Size? Affluence? Or Both?* Bologna: University of Bologna/Centre d'Etudes Perspectives et d'Informations Internationales (CEPII).

 INTERNET RESOURCES

Case studies of European firms:
http://www.maporama.com/home/fr/societe/case+studies.asp

Consumer behaviour and marketing:
http://www.consumerpsychologist.com

European marketing conference:
http://www.emc.be/activities.cfm

(Continued)

(Continued)

European Marketing Research Centre:
http://www.emrc.be

Gabriele Suder's *Doing Business in Europe* video series (on the SAGE companion
website at http://www.sagepub.co.uk.suder2e and You Tube)

Bibliography

Czinkota, M., Ronkainen, I. and Moffett, M. (2003) *International Business*. Mason,
   OH: South-Western Thomson Learning.
European Communities (2005) *Social Policy Agenda 2005–2010*. DG Employment,
   Social Affairs and Equal Opportunities, Brussels.
Gillingham, D. (2005) *International Marketing Seminar*. Nice: Ceram.
Halliburton, C. and Hünerberg, R. (1993) *European Marketing: Readings and Cases*.
   Wokingham and Cambridge: Addison-Wesley.
Harris, P. and McDonald, F. (2004) *European Business and Marketing: Strategic Issues*.
   London: Sage.
Hill, C. (2005) *International Business Competing in the Global Marketplace*, 5th edn.
   Maidenhead: McGraw-Hill.
Hollensen, S. (2004) *Global Marketing: A Decision-Oriented Approach*, 3rd edn. Harlow:
   FT Prentice Hall.
Kotler, P. (1988) *Marketing Management*, 4th edn. London: Longman.
Kotler, P. and Armstrong, G. (1991) *Principles of Marketing*, 5th international edn.
   London: Prentice Hall.
Magee, J. (1989) 1992 moves Americans must make. *Harvard Business Review*, vol. 67,
   May–June, pp. 78–84.
Mercado, S., Welford, R. and Prescott, K. (2001) *European Business*. Upper Saddle
   River, NJ: Prentice Hall.
Monks, J. (2004) *The European Social Model: Myth or Reality?* May Day Celebration,
   EU Enlargement Speech, European Trade Union Confederation (ETUC) General
   Secretary, Gorizia. 01 May 2004.
Muhlbacher, H., Leihs, H. and Dahringer, L. (2006) *International Marketing: A Global
   Perspective*, 3rd edn. London: Thomson Business Press.
Onkvisit, S. and Shaw, J. (1988) Marketing barriers in international trade. *Business
   Horizons*, vol. 31, no. 3, pp. 64–72.
Pardo, P., Rodríguez, L.S. and Alarcón, E.T. (2005) *Marketing in the European Union*.
   Alicante: Economía Financiera, Contabilidad y Marketing, MEU.
Quelch, J. and Harris, B. (2005) Six sigma comes to marketing. *European Business
   Forum*, vol. 22, Autumn, pp. 33–5.
Schneider, S. and Barsoux, J.-L. (2003) *Managing across Cultures*. London: Pearson
   Education.

Suder, G. (1994) *Anti-Dumping Measures and the Politics of EU–Japan Trade Relations in the European Consumer Electronics Sector: The VCR Case*. Bath: University of Bath School of Management.

Suder, G. and Suder, D. (2011) *Brand Sensitivity Revisited: Learning from Ten Years of Brand Value and Ranking Fluctuations*. Nagoya: Academy of International Business.

Suder, G., Chailan, C. and Suder, D. (2007) Has terrorism an effect on brand value? An empirical study on the 100 biggest world brands. *Ceram Working Paper*, Sophia Antipolis.

The Economist (1989) The myth of the Euro-consumer, 4 November, p. 79.

Tordjman, A. (1994) European retailing: convergences, differences and perspectives. *International Journal of Retail and Distribution Management*, vol. 22, no. 5, pp. 3–19.

VanderMerwe, S. and L'Huillier, M. (1989) Euro-consumers in 1992. *Business Horizons*, January–February, pp. 34–40.

Webb, J.R. (1992) *Understanding and Designing Marketing Research*. London: Dryden Press.

Weilbacher, W. (1984) *Advertising*, 2nd edn. New York: Macmillan.

Other sources

http://www.consumerpsychologist.com/international.htm: Lars Perner
http://www.mckinsey.com/practices/marketing/ourknowledge/pdf/WhitePaper_MarketinginThreeDimensions.pdf

9

Lobbying the Playing Field

What you will learn about in this chapter:

- What is lobbying, and what are the opportunity networks for lobbying?
- Why is European lobbying increasingly important, and what do you lobby for?
- How do you lobby the EU?
- Who lobbies, when, and where do you lobby?
- Further recommendations about contemporary lobbying strategy and action in Europe.

9.0 Introduction

The last chapter examined marketing in Europe and highlighted the importance of diversity management tools when it comes to carrying it out. A rather different kind of 'marketing' – this time not that of a product or service, but that of a company and its sector of activity – will now be considered: that of lobbying the EU. Why is this just as important as traditional management tools?

First of all, both European business and international corporations from non-EU countries have recognized the importance of *institutional opportunity* networks at EU level. These opportunity networks can be defined as 'more or less loosely organized relations among (in our case) business and governmental authorities that are potentially beneficial to the involved parties'.

These networks play an important role in the search for sustainable competitiveness. We now examine these networks, and analyse the mode of operation that prevails in the *relations between firms and institutions*, that sets the rules governing European business. With this knowledge, your chances for playing a role in the dynamics of the European political economy strengthen considerably. Why would your organization simply put up with rules set upon the opinions and objectives of others? Why not, instead, exchange information with the policy makers and be one of those stakeholders that promote a point of view, comparable to a corporate marketing exercise? This seems essential in a business environment that is dynamic, ever changing and highly competitive.

In the diverse and multilayered context of European rule making, lobbying is recognized as a dynamic capability of a corporation.

This chapter therefore studies the most efficient and recognized ways of getting a business voice heard in Brussels, Strasbourg and Luxembourg. This is key to the essential competitive advantages for any firm that wants to do business in Europe.

The focus of the subsequent sections is as follows. First, we will define 'lobbying' and explore European opportunity networks, that is, the network of stakeholders that focus on setting rules in the European marketplace. European lobbying has increased with each wave of European integration, bringing with it increased recognition of the EU as an international player and its legitimacy as a supranational organ. 'Interests are happy to ignore Europe until something from Europe hits their wallets!' argues J.J. Richardson in his important works (Richardson and Mazey 1996, 1999, 2001). The more opportunity structures there are, the more corporations will operate on a European scale, and the more they will engage with power centres at the heart of institutions in Brussels and affiliated locations like Strasbourg and Luxembourg, and in locations of national and regional power.

The underlying culture of lobbying originates in Anglo-Saxon models of interest representation; indeed, to date, more US and UK lobbyists work in Brussels than lobbyists from continental Europe. But organizations from all over the world work in this area, increasing their say. For instance, you will find a person in charge of following up on EU activities in each embassy in Brussels (those of Arab or Asian countries, for example). A number of companies from these countries also employ in-house lobbyists. More than 15,000 lobbyists work in Brussels.

Box 9.1: Veolia in Brussels

Veolia Environment, supplier of water services worldwide, owns an office in the EU neighbourhood/district in Brussels, and is a member of professional associations and specialized lobbying groups (such as EUREAU, the European Union of National Associations of Water Suppliers and Waste Water Services). This is one of a range of corporate lobby groups, which participates in workshops and conferences with European institutions. Because the company manages drinking water, industrial water supplies and waste water services, it talks in particular to the Directorate General for the Environment at the CEC. Veolia's clients are 67 per cent public authorities and 33 per cent are industrial companies. The Veolia Brussels representative chairs BUSINESSEUROPE's Task Force on Services of General Interest, and is highly visible across the European policy-making arena. BUSINESSEUROPE is an association of 40 central industrial and employer federations from 34 countries. Association members aim for growth and competitiveness in Europe and represent small, medium and large companies. For example, it represents companies such as A.C. TECHNOMETAL, a medium-sized firm from Nicosia, Cyprus, producing aluminium products, accessories and frames, through the Cyprus Employer & Industrialists Association and its Cyprus Metal Industries Association. The SME is also part of the Cyprus–Czech Republic Business Association that has an indirect influence in Brussels.

Critics claim that information exchanges are prone to show omissions of relevant data; overall, firms' engagements in the European network are nonetheless judged impressive and are part of a diversity of influences. (Corporate Europe Observatory, 2008; Cyprus–Czech Republic Business Association, 2010; etc.)

To meet the expectations of shareholders and stakeholders in general, corporations increasingly fear missing out in the intelligence-gathering game that is a key aspect of access to resources. The EU legislator is the biggest market creator in Europe, and all corporations in the European market face international competition from other business, which is, of course, also shaped by this regulator. The practice of public affairs management has become an integral part of effective business strategy and has become increasingly professional through special training programmes, qualifications of a federation of experts and a code of conduct.

In the following text, we examine what lobbying means. In this context, we will enlarge upon the reasons why European lobbying is increasingly important. Business in Europe is experiencing strong trends towards risk-avoidance strategies, anticipation and proactivity, which are underpinned by Europeanization: Can you take the risk of losing out on the opportunities that Europeanization and lobbying may bring? Can you take the risk of losing out when the public administration decides upon issues? These factors may make or break your operations and affect your decision making, as well as your customers' choices or investment policies.

Previous chapters have characterized the European business environment as mature, democratic and competitive. It is an integrated system of economies illustrated by distinct management cultures run upon a set of harmonized rules and certain complementarities in their objectives: European integration reaches across economic, social and geopolitical divides, and its governance is highly accessible for communication purposes, when you possess interesting and appropriate knowledge. So why take unnecessary risks? How, then, does a corporation represent its interests in the EU in the most efficient and effective manner?

This chapter is about EU lobbying. This EU activity is different from lobbying attitudes, techniques and practices in London, Madrid or Prague. The Union is multifaceted, with many arenas in which major decisions that shape the business environment are made; this calls for a sound understanding of the decision-making processes introduced in Part II. In this context, we will also analyse the essential *When*, *Who* and *How* questions: you will learn that there is no way to control the trajectory of a policy game consistently. However, there is a stable setting for participation and consultation – that is, where corporations develop best practices in what is professionally called 'lobbying'.

9.1 Lobbying and European opportunity networks

What is 'lobbying'? The term is generally used interchangeably with public affairs management, interest intermediation and corporate political activity. The main function of this activity is to make one's voice heard and known, and thereby to influence a given public administration. The objective of any organization is to ensure that decisions are taken to coincide with its interests. Lobbying is a legal and beneficial activity that allows institutions to receive the various inputs necessary for elaborating adequate and equitable decision-making.

> ### Box 9.2: Defining opportunity networks
>
> A political opportunity structure can be defined as the degree to which people or groups are able to gain access to power and to manipulate the political system. (McAdam, 1996)

In this framework, the main lobbying tool is the exchange of information and expertise and the transfer of in-depth knowledge and competencies, which provide a corporation with the opportunity to benefit from inputs and outputs at the policy level. (For a reminder of the theory underpinning this logic, refer back to Chapter 4.)

Efficiency in the formulation and implementation of public policy is directly associated with the need of economies to stimulate competitiveness and consumer welfare, which are typically at the core of western government intervention. This search for overall efficiency in political, economic and social terms, gives rise to a need for consultation: government bodies and institutions need to maintain a strong link with civil society, business society and political society; they are hence constantly on the lookout for expertise and support. This can be explained by the lack of a certain in-house expertise in institutions that may not be up to date with innovations and trends; an institutionalized dialogue ensures equity and the respect of law and codes of conduct.

EU 'pressure' groups are generally welcomed, once they are shown to provide the administration with high-value information about the 'real' world and its development potential. Groups with high resources easily tackle some structures because they are able to engage in individual and group lobbying on many levels, maximizing contacts. Sometimes, however, less rich, lower-resourced groups are favoured for their unique and down-to-earth expertise. Many officials in their information gathering value this because, as stated above, the most common size of enterprise in Europe is the SME. In general, institutions value representatives in proportion to their uniqueness of expertise and experience, or weight of representation.

The concept of the lobbying 'arena' or 'playing field' illustrates the setting in which this process of influencing takes place and the space in which a lobbying campaign is played out.

For any party or actor in the arena, efficient and timely lobbying within the public–private matrix and proactive anticipation of institutional agenda-setting play an essential role: three keys to long-term competitiveness can be built this way. They are:

- resilience;
- flexibility;
- speed of action (proactivity and reactivity).

Table 9.1   *A conceptual matrix of structured interrogation*

Screening tool (interrogation)	Best-case scenario (targets)	Strategies (means)
WHY	The vision or issue upon which persuasion needs to be instigated	Prioritizing
WHEN	Before the agenda is set Before and during every stage Risk analysis sets the readiness level	Anticipation Multi-timing along life cycle
HOW	Maximize positive input and alliances and forestall opposing lobby	Scenario planning
WHERE	Multiple access points	Venue shopping Alliance
WHAT	Constructive lobbying Dissuasive lobbying	Business firewalls
WHO	Multi-arena, multiplayer	Partnerships

Source: Suder and Greenwood, 2004 (p. 10)

All three key factors are necessary either to:

- (a) gain from the political economy; or to
- (b) prevent, deflect or minimize potential corporate disaster.

This disaster may, to cite some examples, be that of failure to secure support for mergers (as experienced by Ryanair in 2010 when planning to take over Aer Lingus), for subsidies (as in a Nokia case in 2008), for legal cases (for example, the ECJ rule against privileged protection for in-house lawyers of international MNEs), including anti-trust decisions (such as that against Intel, accused of dominance and fined €1.06 billion), or for anti-dumping action (such as in the case of Chinese exporters of fasteners in 2010).

Also, business players and others can express opinions about the economic impact of EU legislation and provide their expertise to the policy maker. This is why lobbying, also termed 'public affairs management', has obtained a special role in European business competitive strategy. Table 9.1 summarizes the main information on successful European lobbying. You may wish to refer to it while you are reading this chapter.

9.1.1 Historical and academic background

9.1.1.1 The what and why of EU lobbying

European lobbying issues have attracted the interest of scholars and researchers from diverse backgrounds, particularly from business and academia. The latter can be divided into two main groups: international business scholars and political science scholars. Both find their origins in the thinking of international law and international relations. They play an essential role in raising awareness among corporations and as consultants to businesses that plan to engage in or improve their lobbying activities.

Since 1640, the word 'lobby' defined 'in the House of Commons, and other houses of legislature, a large entrance hall or apartment open to the public, and chiefly serving for interviews between members and persons not belonging to the house' (OUP, 2005). In the USA in the nineteenth century, the term 'lobbying' developed into the 'influence [of] members of a house of legislature in the exercise of their legislative function by frequenting the lobby. Also to procedure in the passing of a measure ... by means of such influence' (US Congress, 1953). Indeed, Washington was and remains the world's hotspot of lobbying, which has long been regulated by law (Foreign Agents Registration Act 1938; Federal Regulation of Lobbying Act 1946).

In continental Europe, lobbying remained a local, regional and national exercise until its art and techniques were imported from the UK. Its development was shaped by the necessity for business to tackle issues covered by the step-wise progression of European integration, and also by decisions in regard to corporate and industrial activity. The underlying concepts in the study of lobbying are rooted in the expertise of lawmaking, formal institutions, procedures and (originally, foreign) policy and power. The most recent business theorists examine the 'dual roles of both a receiver and a sender of influence efforts' (Van Schendelen, 2010) in the private sector, the public–private sector, and the public sector.

Research on corporate lobbying has increased at a pace exponential to that of lobbying itself, and is – as a result of its origins – strongly influenced by Anglo-Saxon literature. Here, political scientists typically emphasize the role of government, and traditionally exclude this power centre from what is considered as legitimate lobbying at the EU (cf. Laurencell, 1979), that is, private interest groups, pressure groups and NGOs. The lobbyist is then analysed in his role in the shaping of decision-making (Hix, 1999; Rosamund, 2000).

Corporate public affairs management in Europe has a different face to that of the Anglo-Saxon world, traditionally the leaders in this field. As US businesses have to learn, in Brussels social issues are of great interest. The regulator will be interested in a company's working environment and the way its workforce is treated. Also, what is the company's contribution to environmental protection, to sustainability and to citizenship? Is its interest in accordance with that of a body in charge of Member States?

UK and US lobbyists were for a long time predominant in the corridors of institutions, while German and French corporations preferred fostering relations with their national institutions. Deregulation and privatization in an increasingly competitive European business environment have changed this. European and international interests alike ferociously defend their positions on issues ranging from the services directive, the REACH chemicals registration and evaluation directive for manufactured products, to banana tariffs, chocolate labels, vegetable sauces and corporate images (*International Herald Tribune*, 5 April 2005, pp. 1–4).

The theory of 'conceptualizing' prevails in the study of European integration: it questions to what extent Member States are willing to negotiate on sovereignty, state power and federation, as well as consocation (Taylor, 1996) and multilevel governance (Hix, 1999). 'Theorizing' consists mainly of the intellectual frameworks that analyse functionalism, institutionalism, supranationalism and interdependency theory (Rosamund, 2000): what is important in practice is that each one of these approaches sets a different priority for and technique of a given actor (and consequently which time frame the lobbyist uses) that allows for efficient lobbying input and output. (We will come back to this in more detail below in a model of lobbying strategy.)

9.1.2 Who lobbies European decision-makers?

Some pressure groups engaged in their first lobbying activity as European institutions were being created. However, awareness of the importance of lobbying only really started in the 1970s.

Many interest groups arrived as the different landmarks of European integration occurred. Even more started to invest resources in lobbying when it became clear that EU-wide regulations influenced a wide range of business and societal interests, either in particular cases or more generally influencing the business environment. Pressure groups involved in the EU lobbying process are typically classified into eight categories:

- European associations (for example, EACEM and the Greenpeace International European Unit).
- National associations (for example, the Confederation of British Industry).
- Individual firms or groups (for example, Microsoft or the EADS group).
- Lobbying consultancy firms (for example, Hill & Knowlton and government policy consultants).
- Public representatives (for example, regional governments and local authorities).
- Ad hoc coalitions (coming and going for different issues).
- Single issue groups (for example, Software Action Group for Europe).
- Organizations of experts (for example, the European Heart network).

Box 9.3: The role of a European lobbyist, public affairs manager or adviser

- Seek to shape democratic decisions in own clients' best interests.
- Collect and disseminate information.
- Analyse impacts.
- Complement the knowledge of legislators and bureaucrats in the making of laws; present and shape a case in accordance with the political and corporate agenda.

While some of these groups are non-profit-making organizations (professional and non-governmental associations, industry federations), others such as legal advisers, public relations and public affairs firms, and consultants are 'for profit' organizations.

In 1985, 500 European associations were found to have lobbied the EU institutions (Butt-Philip, 1985). In 2000, according to CEC figures, there were over 700 European associations, among 3000 groups of various kinds. Some sources estimate that, by 2005, the number of lobbyists and advisory bodies around the EU institutions will amount to between 15,000 and 20,000 (*European Voice*, 2005–2010; Corporate Europe Observatory, 2008; EP, 2010), making both Washington and Brussels the most densely lobbied locations in the world. Altogether, among special interest groups in Brussels are mainly European and international federations (members belong to more than 5000 national federations), offices representing *Länder* (German provinces), regional and local authorities, individual firms with direct representation, consultants and law firms. It is impossible to know precisely how many groups are accredited given that the accreditation process has been changed.

Although there is no obligation to register, the CEC has over 3000 stakeholders in its Register of Interest Representatives/Lobbyists; the EP has over 4570 accredited lobbyists (see Table 9.2).

Table 9.2 *Register of interest representatives*

(Sub)categories	Number of interest representatives
Professional consultancies/law firms involved in lobbying EU institutions	**221**
Law firms	14
Public affairs consultancies	111
Independent public affairs consultants	42
Other (similar) organizations	54
'In-house' lobbyists and trade associations active in lobbying	**1,685**
Companies	431
Professional associations	949
Trade Unions	90
Other (similar) organizations	215
NGO/Think-tanks	**1,064**
Non-governmental organizations/associations of NGOs	825
Think-tanks	108
Other (similar) organizations	131
Other organizations	**442**
Academic organizations/associations of academic organizations	109
Representatives of religions, churches and communities of conviction	16
Associations of public authorities	58
Other (similar) organizations	259

Source: http://ec.europa.eu © European Union, 1995–2011

Operational lobbyists that act for firms, minority associations, workers' unions or expressive groups, such as Greenpeace or workers' educational associations, will normally be involved in minor (i.e. routine) political issues. However, representative groups like 'Business Europe' (formerly known as UNICE) or propagational ones such as 'The European Movement' get involved in major political decisions and therefore target higher politics debates and higher-level representatives.

'Players' in the lobbying arena are not only lobbyists and pressure groups. In the denomination of actors, we also find professionals and NGOs (also known as issue groups), associations, federations and confederations, corporations, citizens and consumers.

Box 9.4: The citizens' voice

One good example of the direct impact of citizens on European rules is that of petitions. The Lisbon Treaty stipulates that 'not less than one million citizens' (of the 501-million population) need to agree on an issue, in a 'significant number of Member States' and sign a petition for it to invite the CEC to draft a proposal (see Chapter 4 for the legislative process). This is part of the European Citizenship Initiatives, agreed after a vast public consultation between 2009 and 2010. Even before its rules were finalized, more than 20 petitions were submitted to the CEC, for issues ranging from calls against genetically modified crops to improved rights for disabled citizens.

On the other hand, institutions are also players that seek to influence others, and others also influence them. All players engage in 'individualist' action that is more often than not complemented or exercised through 'collectivist' ad hoc or permanent partnerships and cooperation agreements. These collaborations serve to increase power and to control potential competition. With *hostile brotherhoods*, that is, matching up different interests on specific common interests, the firms may be partners in lobbying despite their competition in the marketplace and on other issues. This requires an 'open dialogue' in the private–public arena, a term first used by former President of the Commission Jacques Delors, and which has evolved significantly ever since, into the necessity of timely and agenda-adapted strategy (Suder and Greenwood, 2004).

9.1.2.1 The practitioner's perspective

At each landmark of European integration (cf. Chapter 2), the lobbying networks also evolved. More and different actors have joined, and power relations have altered. For instance, the Treaty of Maastricht modified the arena of EU lobbying through the increased power of the EP, and altered the primacy of the European Commission within the regulatory institutions (Pedler, 2002). EU enlargement, in particular since the 1990s, increased the competition for access to policy makers and the resources available for lobbying.

Many lobbyists set action plans depending on their place in the lobbying arena and their set objectives; this results in a specific role for each actor. It would be difficult to act in many different fields as in any search for strategy, priorities have to be made.

Ideally, a corporation or pressure group plays a role in the decision and/or its implementation by participating in lobbying. We also note that this player has a role in providing feedback to governance, either directly, or via agents such as the Euro Info Centres. In addition, the increasing role of the EU in the global market that we will discuss in Chapter 10, and the interactions of the EU and Member States' public, make lobbying a strategic activity for companies of any size and sector.

Box 9.5: SMEs and lobbying

The CEC's SG Enterprise & Industry notes that: 'For SMEs – often the largest group of enterprises to be affected by new policy – there are clear difficulties in putting their views across to policy-makers. SMEs do not usually have the resources which large firms dedicate to influencing policy-making or lobbying. For this reason, the Commission has appointed an SME Envoy and encourages an effective and wide-ranging consultation of SMEs as one element of its "Think Small First" principle.' This principle is anchored in the Small Business Act of 2008. Business organizations representing SMEs in Brussels are typically small, were established earlier than those of MNES, and horizontal lobbying organizations with indirect compulsory membership are generally large, with about three quarters of members from micro and small enterprises (cf. EIM, 2009). Overall, UEAPME, the European Association of Craft, Small and Medium-Sized Enterprises represents SMEs on a large scale.

Players in the lobbying arena access certain powers, which can lead to *influencing* agendas, but which can also significantly *write* agendas of policy development. For instance, if your corporation is the leader in a technology that stimulated certain objectives set by the EU (say, best available technology in waste management, good for the environment and sustainable development), you may be able to initiate tighter legislation favouring the use of your technology – at the same time widening your market opportunities (Suder, 2007). Successful firm representations position this strategy within a 'move from reaction to pro-action' (Pedler, 2002, p. 134). This is even easier if there is a close association between corporate lobbying strategy and institutions, that is, when your information input is valuable and rare enough to lead to its being 'institutionalized' (the systematic association of particular pressure groups to the policy process for consultation in a certain field) (see Richardson and Mazey, 2001).

9.1.3 The 'how' question

The different strategies used in lobbying can be categorized into three predominant techniques. They can be distinguished by their main objectives of being dissuasive (negative), risk minimalizing (reactive) or constructive (proactive) (see Box 9.6).

Box 9.6: Lobbying techniques

- Negative strategies – opposing Commission proposals directly or through counter-proposals: a dissuasive lobbying technique.
- Reactive strategies – monitoring and answering to meetings and consultations: a risk minimalization technique.
- Proactive strategies – taking initiative, writing agendas and constructively partnering: a constructive lobbying technique.

A standard strategy in public and private lobbying at the European level consists of 'venue shopping' (Baumgartner and Jones, 1991), in which the complexity of the European framework and the diversity of players and interests are at the origin of a normative multi-level, multifaceted exertion of pressure. This strategy is used in all three techniques, at different intensities. The particular complexity of this kind of lobbying is mainly considered as opportunity-rich (see, for example, Rosamund, 2000; Peterson, 2001; Van Schendelen, 2002).

How do professionals qualify the complexity of EU lobbying? It is 'a chance for those who have been able to develop long lasting relationships based on content, trust and win–win situations. Clever lobbyists know how to diversify their contacts and not to allow disproportionate friendship,' says N. Rougy, Policy Officer, Club of Madrid, while 'it is a multi-levelled conciliation process between Commissioners and Cabinets, Members of Parliament, the Directorates General and Services'.

Each official brings his or her own cultural, administrative and national filters to any single issue, enforced by the different interest groups involved in any given debate. 'Multiply this complexity by the many different lobbying groups on each side. Understanding how to navigate through these different schisms will provide valuable intelligence to a lobbyist making important decisions', writes R. Pinto, Government Affairs Coordinator, Law and Corporate Affairs (LCA), at Microsoft Europe, Middle East and Africa.

Lobbyists attempt to reach satisfaction at the different venues and, ideally, do so simultaneously. This requires players to function effectively at the different levels of policy making.

The way that decisions are made can be compared to a project being managed within a corporation, and follows the concepts applying to project management.

Decisions are made that either:

- introduce, modify or abolish legislation;
- rule upon an action or measure to be taken;
- distribute, modify or suspend the distribution of specific resources; and/or
- in any other manner alter the economic or political environment of a firm, industry, sector or economy directly or indirectly.

A decision at its infant stage is called an *issue*. Any given actor in the arena may introduce this issue into public debate. If an issue obtains enough attention to become a social and political problem and if it is recognized at government level, then corporations have a variety of input possibilities that potentially shape the agenda writing (that is, the sequence and timing of the issue's path through the decision-making process) and the output of the decision maker. This variety and number of actors and strategies in issues explains the increasingly competitive nature of EU lobbying.

But there are many ways of lobbying. The institutionalizing of pressure groups or lobbyists inside the decision-making process appears to constitute *best practice*. It establishes vast opportunities, an image close to that of a brand for a product, and a reputation and credibility that is the source of the comparative advantage of any actor enjoying this position. This scenario maximizes opportunities to be heard and, even more, opportunities to be taken into account by the different levels and diverse actors in the policy- and decision-making process. The adoption of strategies is dependent

An *issue* (a decision in the infant stage) may be introduced into public debate by any given actor in the arena

Once the issue obtains enough attention to become a social and/or political problem and is recognized at a governmental level, corporations can have a variety of input possibilities that potentially shape the agenda-writing (that is, the sequence and timing of the issue's path through the decision-making process) and the output of the decision maker

This varirty and number of actors and strategies in issues explains the increasingly competitive nature of EU lobbying on several vital factors that are mainly defined by the resources available to the actor. Does an individual or a group best exercise lobbying? Is this actor based close to the institutions or not, and is the actor well resourced or not?

Actors seek factor advantages and compete against each other for:

Information	Contact	Networks	Influence	Image
Institutionalization	Resources distribution	Access to actors and agendas	Recourse opportunities	Power

These factors are interlinked and depend on each other. They are challenging, intensive in nature and may alter at any given moment through interior or exterior 'disaster', which could include anything, from misbehaviour to corporate fraud. Any of these will directly lead to a loss of factor advantages.

Again, group strategies may be beneficial for the inexperienced actor in the EU arena: in a collective context, risks are diversified and factor advantages – though shared – may be more sustainable. It appears that emerging market MNEs, including firms from European transition countries, start their political activity in Brussels through collective lobbying in partnership with experienced interest groups.

Strategies engaged by the different pressure groups vary in tactics depending on looser (in the USA) or tighter (for instance, in Canada, the UK, Germany and the EU) control of the executive, shaping their preference for bargaining before or behind closed doors. Activity on a national level therefore influences the preference formation of national governments before delivery to the EU (Richardson and Mazey, 1996). In general, it was observed that national governments sometimes disappoint interest groups in favour of other policy goals in last-minute bargaining; the study of spill-over effects of corporate public affairs management and its time-sensitivity mainly explores those international regimes, using the regime theory definition (Hopkins and Puchala, 1983), with its 'principles, norms, rules, and decision-making procedures around which actor expectations converge in a given issue-area'.[1]

A corporation can exploit the multiplicity of access points for an issue efficiently if it engages in writing, influencing and utilizing time frames adapted to the validated strategy of constructive lobbying, risk minimalization or dissuasive lobbying. It is hence important for any player to:

- screen the arena, and identify actors and their interests;
- analyse the potential ad hoc or permanent agreements that exist or may arise in terms of threats and opportunities;
- evaluate strengths and weaknesses, opportunities and threats (SWOT) (in the same way as the SWOT analysis in corporate strategy) and consider correcting them through appropriate action, partnership or timing strategies;
- set an agenda-oriented time frame of action.

Issue-specific techniques of ad hoc partnerships include building *firewalls*, that is, a method of protecting from wider oppositions, and playing off threats in regard to industry- or sector-focused lobbying (Suder and Greenwood, 2004). In this, particular government–industry patterns may influence the degree to which hostile brotherhoods may be efficient and firewalls can be effective (Cawson et al., 1990, p. 286): Mainly, the public–private (or government–industry) relationship serves to develop responses to market challenges. The power of firms in this context depends on the protectionist or liberal orientation of the economy, because this orientation results in a higher or lower impact of input on the output of the government system.

We observe, once more, that corporate performance is directly linked to the political economy in which the corporation is placed. Gilpin (1975) and Spero (1990), among others, argue that the government may, in the context of internationalization, see the corporation as a threat. The internationalizing company has a set of objectives and the government authority may have aims that are similar or that diverge. This needs to be knowledgeable and informed by the private entity to avoid a normative retaliatory approach by the institutions that may attempt to preserve power. This explanation is at the root and the ends of lobbying, and gives insight into the competitive edge that it provides for corporations.

The toolbox of any individual or group engaging in EU lobbying is well stocked (see Figure 9.1).

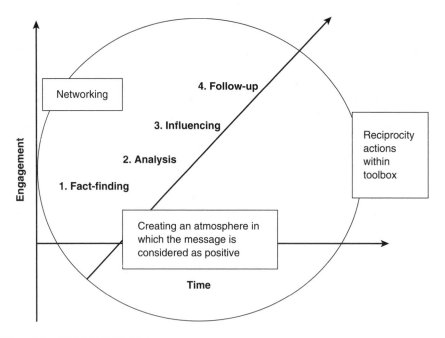

Figure 9.1   *EU lobbying toolbox*

The earlier the lobbyists intervene in the process, the more likely it is that they will be able to influence legislators and other actors, installing trust, credibility and maybe even dependence on others. Monitoring institutions, issue and agenda building are the very basis of efficiency and are enhanced through communication with policy makers: knowledge of issues, of access points to legislators and potential partners, and of the legislative process are incomparable commodities that can be further enhanced by efficient economic intelligence games. The more rare and distinctive is your knowledge about an issue and about its impact on the business or political environment, the greater your chances of being heard and taken into account.

The EU lobbyist (unlike those at national level, for example in Berlin or Warsaw) is more like an adviser, advocating and influencing the arena, who will define the strategy and organize the campaign for clients for his or her own interests.

Interestingly, when a government authority such as the EU sets structural objectives in the intervention it chooses, for example through competition policy, it will be less concerned with the interests of one single specific firm (because the issue will affect many diverse stakeholders). This means that the individual firm will have less power in the policy-making process (Cawson et al., 1990, p. 361–3), and will need to lobby more through groups than individually, or combine the two. Also, the higher the degree of concentration in an industry, the more vigorous are its attempts to exclude foreign competition, particularly through high-resourced, highly concentrated lobbying activity (Suder, 1994; Suder and Greenwood, 2004).

Outside of the EU, European business typically engages in national lobbying. This is also the case for organizations operating in or originating from EFTA Member States who lobby their national governments rather than EFTA as a whole. EFTA-level political activity is certainly limited by the small (though powerful) size of the economic group, and the lobbying activity is comparable to that found in particular European regions such as across the Nordic countries or, outside of the EU, the Euro-Med agreement mechanism. One prominant organ for interest representation at EFTA is its Consultative Committee of the European Free Trade Association which serves as a forum for trade unions and employers' organizations in the EFTA member states. The European Trade Union Confederation (ETUC) and BUSINESSEUROPE are also members of this committee.

EFTA countries represent EFTA interests (as defined by the governing body, the EFTA Council in Geneva) through political lobbying within the EEA (European Economic Area) when matters of concern are being debated inside the European Parliament. EFTAs Parliamentary Committee is a venue for Members of Parliament of the EFTA States to discuss issues twice a year, with EFTA Ministers, who wield a certain influence there too.

The main lobbying activity from this region focuses on EEA conditions. This takes place through the EFTA authority and among Members of Parliament. EFTA also sees national parliaments of the EU and the Nordic Council as a cooperative tool to make its voice heard at the EU. The Nordic Council is the inter-parliamentary cooperation of Nordic countries including those from Denmark, Finland, Iceland, Norway, Sweden and three autonomous territories: the Faroe Islands, Greenland and Åland.

Despite the differences in status of these countries in Europe, Nordic interests remain closely related and 'Nordic business has integrated rapidly through acquisitions and mergers between big corporations in two or more countries. The best example is perhaps the Nordic banking group Nordea, but Arla, Stora Enso, Tieto, TeliaSonera and Sampo Bank (within Den Danske Bank) all arose out of Nordic alliances' (www.norden.org). Particular interests represented here and at European authorities centre around the importance of maintaining world-class infrastructure, education, research and social welfare.

9.2 When is the best time to lobby?

If any interest group or individual, desiring to get a voice heard at governmental level, competes to influence decision-making, then agenda setting defines the competition that takes place at any moment in the decision-making process, its preparatory phase and ending/transposition phase. This *time-sensitivity* is based on the matrix of input and output constraints that the corporation or the institutions are subject to. It is hence useful to screen the environment early and to draw up a matrix of constraints, so as to better structure the message communicated to any of the actors in the arena, and to identify the time slot that appears most efficient to launch this communication and repeat it. The strategy will vary according to the lobbyist and his/her background, the corporation represented, its sector of activity and the issue in question.

Given the rising number of actors and policy issues that are targeted by lobbying, 'the moment of setting the agenda is the key time to influence process' (Pedler, 2002, p. 315): it is crucial to be well known and valued, and to have your timing right in accordance with the political objectives of the policy maker. A comparison can again be drawn with corporate marketing, in which you need to know your environment, your competition and the right time for your actions – getting your marketing mix, or rather, your 'lobbying mix' right.

Any appropriate strategy needs to follow the time frame that surrounds the issue. Van Schendelen (2002) established a life cycle of an issue, which typically may start silently, enter the public arena for a period normally shorter than 10 years, then be settled in some form, and then vanish from agendas, to be replaced by another issue (see also Tombari, 1984). On the basis of this issue life cycle, the time frame surrounding a dossier or issue can be developed in six phases, as illustrated in Figure 9.1 (adapted from Van Schendelen, 2002). The life cycle here is separated into sub-elements that show the development of professional and public attention in more detail.

The life cycle, where applied to a specific dossier, is a powerful tool for defining relevant time slots for individual or collective action. It also helps define the moment at which lobbying may help raise attention, and hence the probability that an issue will be taken into account. This is because the interactions of public and private interests are interlinked in bureaucratic politics. They compete on the basis of the resources, interests and needs of each structure at different venues. This conception includes public awareness of EU lobbying strategy; it includes the need to evaluate the life-cycle programme that defines the key moments for action, for strategies in the:

- long-term (for example, for further integration processes);
- medium-term (for example, for the reform of the Human Rights Council of the UN);
- short-term (for example, for funding projects);
- ongoing positioning process.

9.3 Where is lobbying most effective?

We have seen that EU lobbying is a crucial activity for corporations doing business in Europe, and for those monitoring EU activities. It was pointed out that this activity required action on various levels, applying suitable strategies and using them in particular time slots. Also, going alone is not always a wise option. Choosing a good partner is essential for optimal results. The different levels of EU decision-making require complete knowledge of EU institutions and their interactions. This needs effective lobbying at several levels of policy making: these are the institutional levels that we discussed in Chapter 4.

Box 9.7: Main levels of European lobbying

- the national level(s);
- the Commission (CEC);
- the European Parliament (EP);
- the Council of Ministers; and
- the numerous additional venues at the EU and at national or regional governmental agencies that can be lobbied, including sometimes:
- the European Court of Justice (ECJ) and the Court of First Instance through recourse, or any of these levels identified as most strategic to your interests.

The main venues of EU lobbying are concentrated in Brussels at the EC and the EP for committee meetings and additional sessions; at the EP in Strasbourg for monthly plenary sessions; at the general secretariat in Luxembourg or anywhere in the EU where MEPs are located. Another key venue is the ECJ in Luxembourg, and the Court of First Instance. The Council of Ministers can also be approached in Brussels, except in April, June and October when all meetings take place in Luxembourg. All national governments of Member States, their representatives and regional or local authorities are also key points. Given the number of these venues and the distance between them, a low-resource representation is generally likely to favour indirect lobbying at local and regional level. Medium-resourced groups will cover these venues and be present in Brussels, the venue of most direct channels of interest representations. High-resources groups cover a maximum of entry points for high input levels.

The CEC is the key venue in Brussels. Its organizational structure emphasizes consultation, because its task (as discussed in detail in earlier chapters) is one of the key policy formation roles that has remained largely unchanged by the more recent treaties (Maastricht, Amsterdam and Nice), despite some shifts in power balances. The CEC deals with problems, policies and interests, and all proposals undergo detailed scrutiny and processing. In the assessment and formulation of policy proposals, much technical detail (standards, parameters, procedural rules, etc.) prevails and requires specific expertise. Due to its tasks, the CEC provides a predominantly bureaucratic/technical setting for routine day-to-day policy making. This establishes a good opportunity for a continuous process of building on, refining and extending existing policies and elaborating new policy to respond to the needs of an ever-changing business and societal environment. Ongoing consultation is thus an essential requirement for this institution. Also, consultative bodies like advisory committees, advising on, for instance, safety, hygiene and health protection at work or the Industrial R&D Advisory Committee, surround the CEC. We can speak of a European 'committology' as defined by all the expert committees that work with the institutions to draw up legislation (N. Rougy, Club of Madrid, Brussels).

Further bodies for consultation and identification of key issues and actors are ad hoc groups like the Conference on Environment and Employment (jointly between the CEC and the EP); or the Symposium on aerospace and defence regions and SMEs. These committees, listed on http://www.europa.eu.int/comm/secretariat_general/regcomito, exercise a high level of power through information shaping and knowledge transfer. Lobbyists and pressure groups therefore strive for input opportunities at these levels, with the procedural ambition of their recognition as key policy shareholders within the EU policy process. At its best, they are involved in the institution's agenda setting, that is, in the early process of problem identification and options search on a particular issue.

At the Commission level, neo-functionalist expectations (see Chapter 3 for a reminder of this concept) stipulate a preference for working with and through Euro groups. However, the Commission additionally welcomes direct contributions from companies (McLaughlin et al., 1993: 199) and non-corporate actors. Companies thus opt ideally for multiple lobbying strategies (p. 195; cf. also Richardson and Mazey, 2001; Butt-Philip and Porter, 1993). The resulting interrelations of actors and levels within the various time slots are shaped by coordination and cooperative relations, replacing – for the duration of the issue held in common – competition. These relationships are based on a certain shared sense of interest reinforced by the very nature of European integration and harmonized policy making and policy application. It is also Europe's strongest driving force, pressing for further integration, a more transparent system that is open and accessible in the struggle for higher levels of power.

So, where do you best lobby the EU? The answer depends on the nature of the issue, the actors and the arena as a whole. All regulatory institutions attract interests, particularly business interests. Corporations cannot afford to be left out, whatever the cost. Firms and groups recognize that governments matter because all business activity is subject to particular rules and practices in what constitutes the business environment. Europeanization has intensified this phenomenon in Europe, adding multiple layers to the playing field. All stages of policy and decision-making are targets of lobbying, some more and some less, some more directly and some indirectly. You will best lobby at all stages in the policy-making process and at national and international levels, complementing your actions with those of other organizations and actors that may influence preference formation. This requires a *constant flow* of updated information.

9.4 Resource factors

The CEC has established a set of behavioural norms, rules, procedures (formal and informal) and organizational structures that allow for high involvement in any lobbying, and so has the EP. The register of expert groups is set up by the CEC to provide a transparent overview of advisory bodies. It lists those formal and informal advisory bodies that are established either by CEC decisions or informally by CEC services. The listing helps to find information about groups working in given policy areas, and gives direct links to CEC websites that publish more detail about expert groups on their own websites.

Lobbyists have their own code of conduct, which requires them to identify themselves by name and company and to state the client they represent. The EP also has its own 10-point code of conduct for lobbying.

The level of implication and the strategy of any lobbyist depend strongly on their resources. These resources include financial means, knowledge and economic intelligence, and available networks of actors and sympathizers. The heavy emphasis on consultation at the CEC includes a standard consultation exercise for proposals that are sent out to all relevant groups for comments. Much of this happens via the Internet. When the main key issues are identified through the feedback received, actors gather in conferences and workshops. Any corporation has a stake to take or defend in this consultation, and it is important also that low-resourced SMEs answer to consultations because, otherwise, they are subject to decisions made by 'others', which may be fatal to parts of, or all, operations. Low financial resources do not stop anyone from monitoring and lobbying the EU.

In Brussels, specialized advisory committees (permanent and ad hoc) join forces at the CEC to complement the daily meetings between officials and group representatives; correspondence and telephone conversations make for efficient contacts with the institution on any resource level. At the EP, where most legislative power is shared between the Council and the EP under co-decision, the role of MEPs can be a threat to or an opportunity for business, whether they debate the adoption of rules on the patenting of new generic material, of chemical regulations or of the 'Auto oil programme' to control pollution from motor vehicles. The list of issues that influence the business environment is never-ending. MEPs are thus a decisive target group for lobbyists and are available easily and without complication for their electorate and the different actors of their constituency. A list of MEPs' names and contacts can be obtained from the EU or any national and local authority, and communication is mainly based on e-mails, telephone conferences or direct meetings.

In the numerous EP 'intergroups', informal meetings of MEPs are held to discuss policy issues, such as the Pharmaceutical Intergroup. EP committees also hold public hearings. As a result of these, the EP Committee on External Relations on the Agenda of the WTO Millennium Round, on 22 April 1999, included presentations from Oxfam, Greenpeace, ETUC (European Trade Union Confederation), Committee of Professional Agricultural Organisations (COPA) (Agriculture) and ERT (European Round Table of Industrialists). The EP is hence an interesting option for all types of resource.

The ECJ and the Court of First Instance are, through recourse, part of a standard lobbying strategy when a group fails to get satisfaction at its national venue, at the CEC, EP and the Council of Ministers. This is, however, an option that is costly and time-consuming. Hence, many cases take the form of test cases that are backed by many groups; or else, lobbyists attempt to persuade the CEC to bring the case to court.

The Council of Ministers' task of striking bargains between national governments (through what we earlier named inter-governmentalism) in the decision-making process is either merged into co-decision, in which the EP takes part, or highly intense when it comes to the most important and historic decisions. In any case, all EU policies are approved in agreement with the Council or Coreper. However, the Council is the EU institution that is the least directly accessible for lobbying, and may be at the low end of priorities for groups that have few resources. Lobbying the Council is based on mainly indirect techniques and target national delegations in Brussels, that is, members of the Permanent Representations, or through participation in Council working groups (more than 200 such groups exist), to prepare meetings of Coreper and ministerial councils. This requires a multiple-level and multiple venue approach that requires relatively important resources. Another technique consists of lobbying members of the many Council working groups that pass on technical expertise to the relevant national representatives. For instance, groups composed of national officials working on vehicle pollution will see Renault lobby its French civil servant.

One lobbying strategy towards the Council that does not require many resources is the indirect targeting of national governments. This technique is relatively cheap, close to both EU and domestic affairs, and is an example of the continuing use of traditional channels of information and exchange developed over decades. Under the qualified majority vote, a lobby cannot be sure that its national government will deliver the desired outcome (Richardson and Mazey, 1996), because national governments sometimes disappoint interest groups in favour of other policy goals in last-minute bargaining. The national level is therefore important in the long-term for a multitude of similar issues rather than a guarantee for short-term output. In the same way, lobbyists will set up or attend seminars, conferences, advisory committees, breakfast briefings and gatherings in the institutions and around them.

A key recognition of the value and importance of pressure groups takes shape when actors experience the institutionalizing of their input activity; this translates into the quasi-systematic consultation of the lobbying group by a given EU institution on a given issue (Richardson and Mazey, 1999). An example for institutionalized lobbying at the CEC is the biannual meetings with the Platform of European Social NGOs and with the 'Group of Eight' (that is, the biggest pan-European environmental NGOs) and others.

All those engaged in lobbying for or against particular issues help to construct the strongest possible links with government actors. These contacts may be formal and informal, or both. For instance, on a macro level, UNICE, the European employers' association, enjoys observer status in the Council of Europe, as well as at EFTA, the UN Conference on Trade and Development, the UN Industrial Development Organization, the European Patent Office and other international organizations, and can therefore take part in timely strategic lobbying. At the same time as the influence is exercised upon Europe, the organization may benefit from spillover effects into those markets that are regulated by affiliate institutions. On a micro level, civil servants, ministries and governmental agents, Member States' Permanent Missions in Brussels and governmental experts are also interlinked by what they do; they are affiliated to the consultation and advisory mechanisms within European Member States and institutions, and can be accessed for multiple lobbying purposes, covering various issues and venues.

9.5 The competition is open: lobbying strategy in action

There are many actors whose knowledge of how time is spent and of the competition involved in lobbying, is crucial. Olson (1965) assumes that all pressure groups are equal, and that the health of democracy benefits from the competition between them because the decision maker takes the role of referee, choosing the most useful input and the best policy presented. However, in reality the actors are not equal, neither in their interests nor in their resources, size or level of influence. This does not mean that low-resources lobbying is condemned and that high-resources groups automatically hold the winning hand.

Most significant interests in the EU have formed associations, because all areas of public policy are covered by EU regulations, and because the association of interests maximizes entry points into the arena. But Commission officials hardly rely solely on Euro associations, and because there is no guarantee that your opinion is the most influential one, you need to seek out the most influential person to lobby. Because of the opportunity lobbying provides to influence legislation at its very roots, this person is usually the one who drafts proposals of an issue, and not the person who signs it (who will be lobbied later).

Lobbying depends on the resources available to persons, groups or associations who devote these (that is, mainly human and financial resources) in proportion to their organization's perception of what is required for a winning situation in the EU policy game. This perception, inherent to the organization in the framework of an issue, shapes the level, time and strategy applied to a lobbying effort, and is a direct result of its environmental screening and scenario planning in relation to a perceived level of competition in the arena for the issue in question. The chosen lobbying strategy is hence comparable to a function of the perception of the arena, that of competition in the arena, and the resources that are available to the person or group for its lobbying activity (Box 9.8).

Box 9.8: The equation defining the choice of a lobbying strategy

Lobbying strategy x = function (perception of arena, a; perception of competition, c; resources available, r; time frame available, t), i.e., $x = f (a;c;r;t)$

Also, geopolitical and societal developments shape the most efficient formula for interest representation. Trade unions, for instance, are interest groups that organized efficiently at EU level so they could counteract already organized business groups, and promote interests that are increasingly difficult to pressure for at national level. Internet and multimedia techniques benefit NGOs and e-governments that are more connected and adept than others. These evolutions underpin the emergence of a dense and mature pressure group system. The density of the lobbying arena is proportionate to the opportunities and venue points that are open to influence and input, therefore defining for every arena a different relation between competitors for power. This is the reason for trends towards risk avoidance through the above-mentioned venue shopping, and an increasing spread of resources.

9.6 Lobbying today

More than ever, doing business in Europe is accompanied by lobbying activity. European regulation may have an adverse affect on interests, but new rules may also furnish opportunities that may be exploited to the disadvantage of others. Business in Europe has become aware of the competitive advantage that public affairs management on an EU scale offers. The opportunity network is complex and dense. It distributes costs and benefits between interests unevenly, and it is in the interest of any actor to secure all direct benefits where possible.

Involvement in lobbying today requires detailed expertise that accentuates chances to gain rather than lose out on benefits, similar to that in striving for competitiveness in a given market. Actors representing a company need to construct an information network that provides the firm with a crucial alert system and access to essential information. Lobbyists need to be proactive because the earlier you know and engage in an issue, the more effective you will be; even better, you may initiate the issue. Representatives need to understand how to communicate to institutions and actors, and how to 'sell' their message best, providing administrations with market data, industry information and expertise: marrying the interests of all for a win–win situation for all actors by playing the role of actor, supplier and customer at the same time. Here, alliances and hostile brotherhoods are key to knowing and controlling the competition while enhancing the firm's power.

Lobbying the EU requires long-term investment. While on one hand, it is crucial to get known early, on the other, lobbyists must respect the policy-making process and its institutional actors, and try to understand what is required for the issue at hand. Attention to detail and mediation between actors may be key to the willingness of officials to grant access to information, discussion or permanent representations; they are a valuable resource that needs to be followed up for every issue.

The Internet and the media are efficient tools in the complexity of EU lobbying. Few genuine media outlets specifically support EU lobbying, but there are exceptions such as *European Voice*, edited by *The Economist*. Attempts to influence the news content of newspapers, television and radio guarantee that opinions are communicated.

Writing or advertising in specialized European media for government and lobbying agents focuses on the Three I's:

- Influence domestic preference formation.
- Influence behaviour of governments.
- Influence public perceptions on European issues.

The perceived increase in lobbying activity has given a growing role to tools including press releases, press briefings, press conferences, interviews in the media, and public service communications, with advertisement of training sessions and paid advertisements. Ad hoc groups may favour these methods in addition to grassroots lobbying (activating the relevant contacts in one's personal and professional network), but lobbyists who anticipate attention given to a particular issue that is central to the governmental agenda will also use the media at a specific moment in time.

9.7 Résumé and conclusion

Efficient multi-networked public affairs management helps corporations reduce risk and uncertainty, and is recognition of the strategic importance of Europeanization. Indeed, the role of firms as political actors is today recognized in international business and international political economy studies alike.

The firm is regulated by an increasing number of actors, at state level as well as multilaterally in the competition of the two for power through the expression of redistributive welfare, and hence the benefits from wealth creation through corporate activity. Each wave of European integration has given rise to ever more

EU-level lobbying activity, at the speed at which EU public policy and the power of institutions have expanded. The landmarks of European integration that we reviewed in the early chapters of this book have incrementally fostered lobbying activity: in 1986 with the SEA, in 1992 with the Treaty on European Union (TEU) at Maastricht, in 1997 with the Amsterdam Act, and in particular through the waves of enlargement.

The Europeanized business environment and management have increased corporate awareness of the opportunities that lobbying can bring. Similar to the issues that you studied about cross-cultural management, about marketing and diversity management, and about the important efforts towards financial integration, Europeanization has influenced the way in which business deals with public affairs. Firms need to be aware *which* institutions are the most important to talk to, and *how* institutions matter, and then adapt accordingly. Integration history shifted the power venues and actors that are the most likely to grant an 'output' return on (lobbying) investment.

Corporations need to build a message and transfer this message with the help of other actors in the arena. This happens through, at a minimum, replies to consultations and, at a maximum, EU lobbying that has to be committed to the EU process, procedures and objectives. We note that the EU policy network consists of national and EU institutions and non-governmental actors. Non-EU, international organizations and foreign governments that exercise power also heavily influence it. Hence, lobbying involves interaction at different levels with directly or indirectly concerned state actors, policy professionals and experts, companies and interest groups of different kinds.

Lobbying means that a person or a group of people tries to influence legislators so that an individual or organization's point of view is represented in the government. A lobbyist is a person who is, most of the time, paid to influence legislation and public opinion. Most large corporations hire professional lobbyists to help promote their activities as agents, or open their own representation in Brussels, and their main objective is to maintain a positive regulatory environment for their organization.

The activities of lobbyists, that is, intelligence, can be compared to service functions. Parts of this activity are information gathering, dissuasive, constructive or risk minimization, implementation and participation of policy implementation. Another function is that of feedback to the public administration.

Lobbyists define their strategies along scenario planning and best practices that are defined similar to environmental screening in marketing. The many access points in the European opportunity structure offer all actors the possibility to lobby the arena, whether directly or indirectly, individually or through partnerships and federations, in Brussels or at any other location in Europe, or wherever European actors are represented, and, finally, whether European or from a non-EU country. For all players, the arena is complex, competitive, dynamic and unpredictable, and unavoidable for any risk minimization strategy when doing business in Europe. In this lobbying 'marketplace', there are no guaranteed results … but this is what you need to be looking for.

Mini case study: Regulatory risk or better lookout for consultations

A small local company imports hand pallet trucks exclusively from China. On 18 July 2005, the Council adopted Regulation No. 1174, imposing 'a definitive anti-dumping duty and collecting definitely the provisional duty imposed on imports of hand pallet trucks and their essential parts originating in the People's Republic of China'. The consequence for the company? Its costs increased exponentially due to a new anti-dumping duty that amounts to 46.7 per cent if they want to keep on buying products from the same providers. Other competitors, who have other Chinese suppliers, pay 'only' 7.6 per cent. Why such a difference? Could the company have done something to avoid this situation?

The Commission had opened a one-year investigation of dumping and injury (2003–4). At the time, 'all interested parties' were informed about the EU project for an imposition of an anti-dumping duty on the basis of Council Regulation No. 384/96 of 22 December 1995, on protection against dumped imports from countries not members of the EC. These interested parties were granted a period within which they could give oral and written comments. This company knew about that, but did not take the time to respond, to articulate its interests or opinions on the matter, whereas other competitors did act. That is why some European importers – even very small ones – succeeded in having their suppliers named individually on a shortlist of Chinese companies paying much lower duties than the 46.7 per cent rate.

Source: Delphine Foucauld, Director of EuroInfoCentre, Nice, France

Mini case study questions

1 What are the consequences of this company's lack of awareness of EU procedures?
2 Despite its restricted resources, how could the company have influenced the outcome of this case?

 REVIEW QUESTIONS

1 **Explain** the strategic difference between short-term and long-term lobbying.
2 **Who** are the key institutions to approach for efficient EU lobbying?
3 **What** are the main advantages of collective lobbying?
4 **What** are the advantages of codes of conduct compared to laws regulating lobbying?
5 **Why** do non-EU interests also lobby in Brussels, and for what current issues?

ASSIGNMENTS

- **Imagine** that you are the main lobbyist for a confederation of European textile manufacturers, lobbying for quotas against Chinese textile imports. Which institutions will you mainly lobby, and from which actors can you expect competition?
- **Compare** the resources available to an SME and an MNE of your choice. In your opinion, how do differences of resources potentially influence lobbying strategy?
- **Case study assignment**: Read and prepare the 'Altran' case study in Part IV, and discuss the challenges of setting up a representation in Brussels.
- **Internet exercise**: Search for evidence of whether the Internet is a main tool in European public affairs management. Which sites are, in your opinion, the most relevant? Present your findings and compare them with newspaper support material in this context. What type of readership is the target of those different media (Internet, newspapers, radio and so forth)?

Further reading

Barnard, H. (2010) Overcoming the liability of foreignness without strong firm capabilities: the value of market-based resources. *Journal of International Management*, vol. 16, no. 2, pp. 165–76.

Coen, D. and Richardson, J. (2009) *Lobbying the European Union: Institutions, Actors, and Issues*. Oxford: Oxford Univerity Press.

Johannesson, J. and Palona, I. (2010) The dynamics of strategic capability. *International Business Research*, vol. 3, no 1, pp. 1–10.

McGuire, S., Lindeque, J. and Suder, G. (2011) *Learning and Lobbying: Emerging Market Firms and Corporate Political Activity in Europe*. Basingstoke: Palgrave Macmillan.

Mitchell, N. and Bernhagen, P. (2009) The determinants of direct corporate lobbying in the European Union. *European Union Politics*, vol. 10, no. 2, June, pp. 155–76.

Van Schendelen, R. (2010) *More Machiavelli in Brussels: The Art of Lobbying the EU*. Amsterdam: Amsterdam University Press.

🖱 INTERNET RESOURCES

Access to the CEC and EP Register of Experts and Lobbyists:
http://europa.eu/lobbyists/interest_representative_registers/index_en.html

Advice for persons outside the Union who are thinking of launching business operations:
http://www.eurolegal.org

(Continued)

(Continued)

CEC's Directorate Generals, e.g. for the environment:
http://ec.europa.eu/environment/index_en.htm
Essential information for EU lobbying:
http://europa.eu.int/comm/secretariat_general/sgc/lobbies/docs/

European Citizen Initiative:
http://ec.europa.eu/dgs/secretariat_general/citizens_initiative/index_en.htm

Services, directory, key topics, jobs:
http://www.eubusiness.com; www.euractiv.com

Website of the Groupe Consultatif Actuariel Européen:
http://www.gcactuaries.org

Gabriele Suder's *Doing Business in Europe* video series (on the SAGE companion website at http://www.sagepub.co.uk/suder2e and YouTube)

Plus the websites of all embassies and foreign representations in Brussels, trade missions and chambers of commerce, European and foreign associations of manufacturers, NGOs and other actors.

Note

1 Parts of this text are based on Suder and Greenwood (2004).

Bibliography

Baumgartner, F. and Jones, B. (1991) Agenda dynamics and instability in American politics. *Journal of Politics*, vol. 53, pp. 1044–74.

Bellier, I. (1997) The Commission as an actor: an anthropologist's view, in H. Wallace and A.R. Young (eds), *Participation and Policy-Making in the European Union*. Oxford: Clarendon Press. pp. 91–115.

Broscheid, A. and Coen, D. (2002) *Business Interest Representation and European Commission For a Game Theoretic Investigation*. Cologne: MPI für Gesellschaftsfors chung. Cologne.

Bück, J.Y. (2003) *Le Management des connaissances et des compétences en pratique*, 2nd edn. Paris: Edition d'Organization.

Buckley, P.J. (1992) *Studies in International Business*. Basingstoke: Palgrave Macmillan.

Butt-Philip, A. (1985) *Pressure Groups in the European Community*. London: University Association for Contemporary European Studies.

Butt-Philip, A. and Porter, M. (1993) Eurogroups, European integration and policy networks. Unpublished working paper, University of Bath, Bath.

Cawson, A., Morgan, K., Webber, D., Holmes, P. and Stevens, A. (1990) *Hostile Brothers: Competition and Closure in the European Electronics Industry*. Oxford: Claredon Press.

Coen, D. (1997) Evolution of the large firm as a political actor in the European Union. *Journal of European Public Policy*, vol. 4, no. 1, pp. 91–108.

Coen, D. and Grant, W. (2000) Corporate political strategy and global policy: a case study of the transatlantic business dialogue. *London Business School Regulation Initiative Discussion Chapter*, (November). London: London Business School.

Congress of the United States of America (1953) Lobbying Investigation Unconstitutional: Constitutional Law. Free Speech Lobbying. Congressional Committee Lacks Power to Investigate Indirect Lobbying. Right to Remain Silent before Congressional Committee protected by First Amendment, *Stanford Law Review*, vol. 5, no. 2, February, pp. 344–9.

Corporate Europe Observatory/Pigeon, M. (2008) *Turning on the taps in Brussels – Veolia Environnement's lobbying activities on water at an EU level*, December. CEO, Brussels (see http://archive.corporateeurope.org/docs/turning-on-the-taps.pdf).

Cutler, A., Haufler, V. and Porter Tony (eds) (1999) *Private Authority and International Affairs*. New York: Suny Press.

Cyprus-Czech Republic Business Association (2010) Available at: http://www.cyprusczech.org

Danton de Rouffignac, P. (1991) *Europe's New Business Culture*. London: Pitman.

European Voice (2005–2010) including in particular 'Brussels lobbying', 11 (13) 7 April 2005; 'MEPs look to make it easier to lanch citizens' initiatives', vol. 16, no. 40, 4 November 2010.

EIM (2009) Study on the representativeness of business organizations for SMEs in the European Union, *EIM Business & Policy Research*, Zoetermeer.

Figstein, N. and McNichol, J. (1998) The institutional terrain of the EU, in W. Sandholz and A. Stone Sweet (eds), *European Integration and Supranational Governance*. Oxford: Oxford University Press. pp. 59–91.

Gardner, J. (1991) *Effective Lobbying in the EC*. Boston, MA: Kluwer.

Gilpin, R. (1975) *US Power and the Multinational Corporation: The Political Economy of Foreign Direct Investment*. New York: Basic Books.

Gray, P. (1985) *Free Trade or Protection? A Pragmatic Analysis*. London: Macmillan Press, and New York: St. Martin's Press.

Greenwood, W. (2003) *Objective Setting*. London: Project World, Imark.

Hix, S. (1999) *The Political System of the EU*. London: Macmillan.

Hopkins, R. and Puchala, D. (1983) International regimes: lessons from inductive analysis, in S. Krasner, (ed.), *International Regimes*. Ithaca, NY: Cornell University Press.

International Herald Tribune, Paris edition, various issues.

Keohane, R. (1984) *After Hegemony: Co-operation and Discord in the World Political Economy*. Princeton, NJ: Princeton University Press.

Klemperer, P. (2000) What really matters in auction design. *Journal of Economic Literature*, Nos D44 (Auctions), L41 (Antitrust), L96 (Telecommunications).

Laurencell, S. (1979) *Lobbying and Interest Groups: A Selected Annotated Bibliographie*. Washington, DC: Congressional Research Service.

Lawton, T. (1997) *Technology and the New Diplomacy*. Aldershot: Avebury.

McAdam, D. (1996) Conceptual origins, current problems, future directions, in D. McAdam, J. McCarthy, and M. Zald (eds), *Comparative Perspectives on Social Movements. Political Opportunities, Mobilizing Structures, and Cultural Framings*. Cambridge: Cambridge University Press, pp. 23–40.

McLaughlin, A.M., Jordan, G. and Maloney, W.A. (1993) Corporate lobbying in the European Community. *Journal of Common Market Studies*, vol. 31, no. 2, pp. 192–211.

Mazey, S. (2000) Introduction: Integrating gender – intellectual and 'real world' mainstreaming. *Journal of European Public Policy*, vol. 7, no. 3, pp. 333–45.

Moravscik, A. (1998) *The Choice for Europe: Social Purpose and State Power from Messina to Maastricht*. Ithaca, NY: Cornell University Press.

Nugent, N. (1999) *Government and Politics of the EU*, 4th edn. London: Macmillan.

Olson, M. (1965) *The Logic of Collective Action*. Cambridge, MA: Harvard University Press.

Oxford University Press (OUP) (2005) *The Compact Edition of the Oxford English Dictionary*. Oxford: Oxford University Press.

Palan, R. and Abbot, J. (1998) *State Strategies in the Global Political Economy*. London: Pinter.

Pedler, R. (2002) *European Union Lobbying: Changes in the Arena*. New York: Palgrave.

Peterson, J. (2001) The choice for EU theorists: Establishing a common framework for analysis. *European Journal of Political Research*, vol. 39, no. 3, pp. 289–318.

Pollack, M.A. (1998) The Engines of European Integration: Delegation, Agency and Agenda Setting in the EU. Oxford: Oxford University Press.

Porter, M.E. (1985) *Competitive Advantage: Creating and Sustaining Superior Performance*. New York: Free Press.

Rauch, J. (1994) *Demosclerosis: The Silent Killer of American Government*. New York: Times Books.

Richardson, J.J. (ed.) (1993) *Pressure Groups*. Oxford and New York: Oxford University Press.

Richardson, J.J. (2001) Policy-making in the EU: interests, ideas and garbage cans of primeval soup, in L.Cram, D. Dinan and N. Nugent (eds), *European Union: Power and Policy-Making*. Oxford: Oxford University Press.

Richardson, J.J. and Mazey, S. (1996) 'EU policy-making: a garbage can or an anticipatory and consensual policy style?', in Y. Meny et. al. (ed.), *Adjusting to Europe*. London: Routledge. pp. 41–58.

Richardson, J.J. and Mazey, S. (1999) 'Institutionalising promiscuity: Groups and European integ ration', in W. Sandholz and A. Stone Sweet (eds), *The Institutionalising of European Space*. Oxford: Oxford University Press.

Richardson, J.J. and Mazey, S. (2001) 'Interest groups and EU policy-making: Organizational logic and venue shopping', in L. Cram, D. Dinan and N. Nugent (eds) *European Union: Power and Policy-making*. Oxford: Oxford University Press.

Rosamund, B. (2000) *Theories of European Integration*. London: Macmillan.

Schmitter, P.C. (1996) Imagining the future of the Euro-polity with the help of new concept, in G. Marks, F. Scharpf, P. Schmitter and W. Streek (eds.), *Governance in the EU*. London: Sage. pp. 121–150.

Spero, J. (1990) *The Politics of International Economic Relations*. London: Longman.

Stone Sweet, A. and Sandholtz, W. (1998) Integration supranational governance and the institutionalization of the European polity, in A. Sandholtz and W. Stone Sweet, (eds), *The Institutionalising of European Space*. Oxford: Oxford University Press. pp. 1–26

Stopford, J. and Strange, S. (1991) *Rival States, Rival Firms: Competition for World Market Shares*. Cambridge: Cambridge University Press.

Strange, S. (1982) Cave! Hic Dragones: a critique of regime analysis. *International Organization*, vol. 36, Spring, pp. 479–96.

Suder, G. (1994) *Anti-Dumping Measures and the Politics of EU–Japan Trade Relations in the European Consumer Electronics Sector: The VCR Case*. Bath: University of Bath School of Management.

Suder, G. (2004) *Public policy implications of constraint theorem, Ceram Working Paper*. Sophia Antipolis.

Suder, G. (2007) The municipal solid waste incineration sector in Europe: a study of harmonization and its impact. *International Journal of European Waste Management*, no. 2, pp. 391-405.

Suder, G. and Greenwood, W. (2004) *Time-Sensitive Lobbying: Approaches to Corporate Disaster Impact Reduction*. Washington, DC: International Association of the Management of Technology Annual Conference.

Taylor, P. (1996) *The European Union in the 1990s*. Oxford: Oxford University Press.

Tombari, H. (1984) *Business and Society*. New York: Dryden Press.

Van Schendelen, R. (2002) *Machiavelli in Brussels: The Art of EU Lobbying*. Amsterdam: Amsterdam University Press.

Van Schendelen, R. (2010) *More Machiavelli in Brussels: The Art of Lobbying the EU*. Amsterdam: Amsterdam University Press.

Wallace, H. and Young, A.R. (1997) The kaleidoscope of European policy-making: Shifting patterns of participation and influence, in H. Wallace and A.R. Young, (eds), *Participation and Policy-Making in the European Union*. Oxford: Clarendon Press. pp. 235–255.

Wills, A. and Quittkat, C. (2004) Corporate interests and public affairs: organized business–government relations in EU Member States. *Journal of Public Affairs*, November, vol. 4, no. 4, pp. 384–399.

10

Competing Internationally

What you will learn about in this chapter:

- The EU's relations with its main trading partners, and a comparison of conditions and sectors.
- Trade partners as competitors on the international scene.
- The EU's link to the WTO and other major international organizations.
- Competitiveness and globalization: the European way.

10.0 Introduction

This final chapter, 'Competing Internationally', covers issues that are crucial to international competitiveness and the relations that the EU pursues with its trading partners. This chapter provides a concluding discussion of the role of Europe in advanced globalization. This is guaranteed food for thought and debate for business students and future and current managers in Europe!

Before we come to discuss the issues in this field, you will be asked to remember the basis that defines the very existence of a European Union, and that also defines its international relations. We then discuss the most important trade partners of the EU, which are both partners and competitors on an international scale. In this context, what contribution does Europe make to positive globalization? What role does European business play in this, and how does non-European business enter the playing field? The concluding mini case study illustrates, with some final words, the manner in which non-EU country corporations do business in Europe to make a success of international competition.

Let us start by noting that, in its early stage, the foremost concern of the EU was to gather the nations and peoples of Europe. European states were to work with other countries and with international organizations in order to remove economic, political and cultural animosities; and to develop economic regions and promote worldwide relations governed by peaceful principles. The main objective was (and still is) to spread the European values of freedom, democracy, human rights and peace, based on the dramatic experiences of World War II, and on a resulting strong belief in the benefits of cooperation on a multilateral level. The evolution of European international relations and international trade has gone hand in hand with this belief.

Trade and foreign investments constitute an essential part of international relations, that is, the relations that countries establish between each other. The meaning of the term 'relation' can take diverse forms and expressions: these may concern diplomacy, propaganda, military operations and/or economic activities; all of these can be seen as parts of a state's potential for power. In general, this is to influence other states or actors so that they will demonstrate certain behaviours or so that they will become economically dependent on the state exerting power. International relations consist of interaction between bodies of decision makers of two or more countries with interests in each other. For instance, in trade and investment, we saw that the multinational company is an important player in international relations.

International trade is primarily based on the international voluntary exchange of assets. Because all international transactions play a role in nations' wealth, much effort is devoted to recording and analysing them, and solving trade frictions. Even more energy goes into competing efficiently within the international business environment. The EU actively deals with the particular challenges of terrorism, international crime, drug trafficking and illegal immigration, and also with crucial global issues such as poverty and the preservation of nature and the environment. A potential force for world stability, the EU is characterized by a common belief that economic stability and cooperation are the foundation of peace and security.

The EU is entitled to negotiate bilateral trade agreements with countries or regional groups of countries as one single entity. However, some fragmentation of foreign policy outputs has weakened the impact of EU power on the international scene, where the EU has relations with many non-EU countries and groups:

Switzerland: no other country has as many agreements with the EU as Switzerland. Relations include the liberalization of trade in processed agricultural products and a liberalization of services. Switzerland mainly exports chemicals and medical products, machinery, instruments and watches. The country participates in the Schengen and Dublin agreements on border control and asylum policy (see Chapter 2), and on savings and taxation, and in EUROPOL ECURIE (European Community Urgent Radiological Information Exchange).

Russia, Eastern Europe and Central Asia: relations include partnership and cooperation agreements (concerning trade, cooperation in science, energy, transport and the environment), political dialogue and joint actions to combat crime, drugs and money laundering. For Russia, the EU is of particular interest as its main trade partner and its main inward investor. The EU provides the Balkan region with financial aid and promotes stabilization. Association and accession agreements also exist between the EU and certain Balkan states. Tables and Figures 10.1 and 10.2 show the variation between EU–Balkan trade relations and trade relations with Russia.

USA: the EU has had intensive trade relations with the USA since its very beginning, constituting the largest bilateral trade and investment relationship in the world. This encompasses business dialogues and dialogues between consumers, trade unionists and environmentalists, talks about competition law and recognition of technical standards. The relationship also includes an agreement on scientific and technological cooperation, on extradition, on mutual legal assistance and on satellite navigation systems (Galileo and GPS). The Transatlantic Economic Council oversees and accelerates government-to-government cooperation to advance economic integration between the two partners.

Table 10.1 *The EU's trade balance with Western Balkan countries (millions of euro, %)*

Period	Imports	Variation (%, y-o-y)	Share of total EU imports (%)	Exports	Variation (%, y-o-y)	Share of total EU exports (%)	Balance	Trade
2006	11.573	28.6	0.9	25.204	16.8	2.2	13.631	36.777
2007	13.340	15.3	0.9	29.374	16.5	2.4	16.034	42.712
2008	13.928	4.4	0.9	33.030	12.4	2.5	19.102	46.957
2009	11.183	−19.7	0.9	25.459	−22.9	2.3	14.276	36.642
2010	13.789	23.3	0.9	26.491	4.1	2.0	12.702	40.279
Average annual growth (2006–2010)		4.5			1.3			2.3

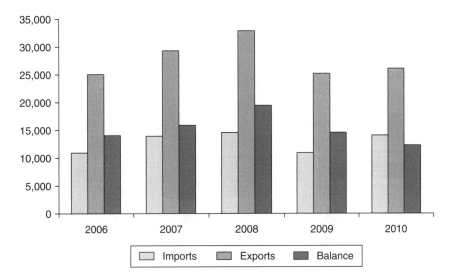

Figure 10.1 *The EU's trade balance with Western Balkan countries (millions of euro, %)*
Source: http://ec.europa.eu © European Union, 1995–2011

Asia: Asia–Europe meetings have increased in number and issues have been raised over the past decade in which high-income industrialized partners engage with dynamic emerging economies and poor countries and societies. The dialogue aims to strengthen mutual trade and investment flows, promote the development of the region's less prosperous countries, address causes of poverty, protect human rights, and spread democracy, good governance and the rule of law in this region, the world's main highly interrelated production hub.

Association of South East Asian Nations (ASEAN): in particular in Asia, the EU and ASEAN members Brunei Darussalam, Cambodia, Indonesia, Lao PDR, Malaysia,

Table 10.2   *The EU's trade with Russia (millions of euro, %)*

Period	Imports	Variation (%, y-o-y)	Share of total EU imports (%)	Exports	Variation (%, y-o-y)	Share of total EU exports (%)	Balance	Trade
2006	140.916	25.2	10.4	72.328	27.6	6.2	−68.589	213.244
2007	144.459	2.5	10.1	89.137	23.2	7.2	−55.322	233.596
2008	177.762	23.1	11.4	105.028	17.8	8.0	−72.733	282.790
2009	117.254	−34.0	9.7	65.614	−37.5	6.0	−51.640	182.868
2010	154.899	32.1	10.4	86.577	31.9	6.4	−68.322	241.476
Average annual growth (2006–2010)		2.4						3.2

Source: http://ec.europa.eu © European Union, 1995–2011

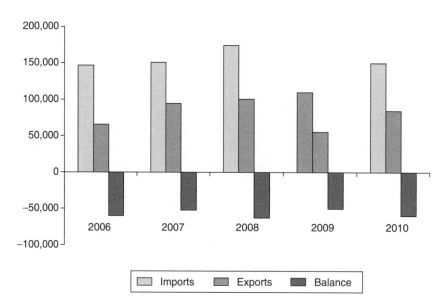

Figure 10.2 *The EU's trade balance with Russia (millions of euro, %)*

Source: http://ec.europa.eu © European Union, 1995–2011

Myanmar (Burma), Philippines, Singapore, Thailand and Vietnam, meet regularly to stimulate discussion of economic integration, political and security issues. The EU is ASEAN's 3rd largest trading partner and ASEAN is the EU's 5th largest trading partner with its 600 million consumers. A first ASEAN-EU business summit, in May 2011 in Jakarta, set the basis for regular meetings between entrepreneurs, private and public investors. Main exports from the EU to ASEAN include chemical products, machinery and transport equipment. FTA negotiations have succeeded with Singapore, where more than 8000 European companies are present.

Japan: over the past few decades, Europe has put significant pressure on Japan to remove non-tariff barriers; an example is the 'Gateway Japan' and 'EXPROM' initiatives, which were established to stimulate EU exports. Japan is particularly important for European supply chains because of its highly sophisticated production technologies and its embeddedness in Asian regionalism. It is the sixth largest import source for European industry (after China, the USA, Russia, Switzerland and Norway). Bilateral dialogues include arrangements in science and technology, competition policy, development assistance, environmental policy, industrial policy, industrial cooperation, macroeconomic and financial affairs, and transport. Policy cooperation is close, for example at WTO. The 2011 earthquake was another sign of the solidarity that federates Europe and Japan.

India: the historic links between the EU, in particular the UK, and India set the basis for a strong partnership which is still hindered by specific tariff – and non-tariff – barriers. The 2011 scheduled free trade agreement will stimulate opportunities for both sides, where export and imports are balanced and FDI continues to be stronger into India. Indian MNEs are increasingly interested in investments in the European market, following the Tata Group and other emerging international players.

Australia: with an emerging free trade agreement, the two partners hold mutual science and technology agreements, mutual recognition of conformity assessment (testing, inspection and certification of products traded between Europe and Australia in the exporting country rather than at destination), wine agreements (protection of intellectual properties in wine terms, prevention of false representation to consumers), agreements on the export of coal and an agreement on the transfer of nuclear material. Their cooperation includes environmental and energy issues. Figures 10.3 and 10.4 demonstrate the importance of EU–Australian trade.

New Zealand: the Joint Declaration on Relations of 1999 set a solid basis for cooperation, and includes science and technology, a sanitary measure agreement, and a mutual recognition agreement of conformity assessment (cf. Australia). The EU continues to import mutton, wool, dairy products, fruits and wine, and a range of other products from New Zealand, although in smaller quantities than the Asia Pacific Rim. The two partners share and consult on many common concerns including climate change and security.

Canada: on the basis of a Framework Agreement on Economic Cooperation, a 1976 commercial and economic agreement established mechanisms for cooperation in trade, industry and science. The Joint Political Declaration on EU–Canada Relations and Joint EU–Canada Action Plan 1996 deals with bilateral and multilateral issues that Canada and the EU have shared for many decades: it is Canada's oldest formal agreement with an industrialized country. There is a large range of agreements in different sectors (such as the Agreement Regarding the Application of Competition Laws or the Agreement on Customs Cooperation and Mutual Assistance to Customs Matters), completed by the 2011 free trade agreement for trade, investment and open procurement of each other's goods and services.

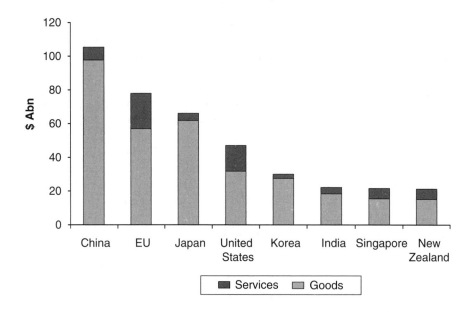

Figure 10.3   *Australia's two-way trade in goods and services by major partners, 2010*

Source: Delegation of the European Union to Australia 2011, based on Australian Bureau of Statistics 2011, International Trade in Goods and Services, Australia, June 2011, cat. no. 5368.0, and International Trade in Services, by Country, by State and by Detailed Services Category, Calendar Year, 2010, cat. no. 5368.055.004.

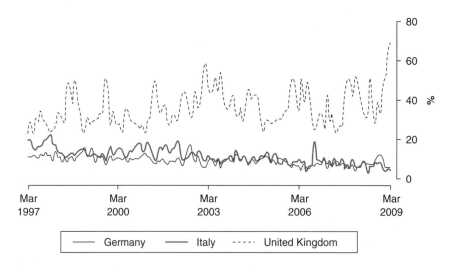

Figure 10.4   *Export shares with selected EU countries, 2009*

Source: International Trade in Goods and Services, Australia, http://www.abs.gov.au/ausstats/abs@.nsf/Products/ BDD4202C398F744DCA2575C400174636

Central and Latin America: relations include the Association Agreement between the EU and Central America (Costa Rica, El Salvador, Guatemala, Honduras, Nicaragua and Panama). The EU supports the Central America Common Market, and has had close links with Latin America since the 1960s; the EU is the leading donor in the region, first foreign investor and second most important trade partner. There is specialized dialogue with MERCOSUR, the Andean community and, specifically, Mexico (free trade area in goods and services) and Chile.

Brazil, part of MERCOSUR (see below), holds a special interest in the EU, which is its biggest trade partner and also its biggest foreign investor. For EU companies, the Brazilian market remains challenging because of remaining trade barriers. Brazil is a member of the G20 group of advanced and developing countries, in which the EU is the 20th and only regional member. Amongst the many sectors of common interest, that of aviation has been a striking example for trade openings, with the 2011 agreement for EU airlines eliminating restrictions on routes, prices, number of flights and destinations: this generated up to €460 million p.a. in consumer benefits for an estimated traffic 'growth of 335,000 additional passengers in the first year' in Brazil alone (European Commission, 2011). The agreement complements those already in place with air transport agreements between the EU and Switzerland, Morocco, the Western Balkan countries, Georgia, Jordan, the USA and Canada.

The Union for the Mediterranean: the Barcelona Process has created EURO-MED, a partnership that was relaunched in 2008, for financial support, peace and the promotion of democracy, within a framework of political, economic and social relations. The 16 southern Mediterranean partners include Albania, Algeria, Bosnia and Herzegovina, Croatia, Egypt, Israel, Jordan, Lebanon, Mauritania, Monaco, Montenegro, Morocco, the Palestinian Authority, Syria, Tunisia and Turkey. Libya has been under observer status since 1999 as part of the European Neighbourhood Policy (ENP). The EU suspended all contractual relations with Libya in the 2011 period during the pro-democracy civil unrest. At the same time, the EU pooled its resources to support the movement, repatriate its citizens (as part of the Civil Protection Mechanism), channel humanitarian aid with the help of ECHO (EU humanitarian aid and civil protection), and deal with migration flows. After a UN Resolution in March 2011, a summit on Libya between the European Union, the Arab League and the African Union launched a European-led intervention in Libya. Euro-Med also includes initiatives around business creation, maritime and land highways and initiatives allying its partners for solar energy investments.

Box 10.1: The Export Helpdesk

As part of the stimulation of trade between the Mediterranean countries and Europe, the EU opened its Export Helpdesk in Arabic in 2011. The helpdesk also functions in English, French, Spanish and Portuguese. It provides essential

(Continued)

(Continued)

information and documents, as an online service furnished by the CEC, to help market access to the EU for developing countries' firms. Amongst useful information about a country's preferential market access conditions, tariff and non-tariff conditions, or rules of origin, non-EU companies also obtain the Customs Import Declaration (SAD): 'All goods imported into the European Union (EU) must be declared to the customs authorities of the respective Member State using the Single Administrative Document (SAD), which is the common import declaration form for all the Member States' (http://exporthelp.europa.eu/). Preferential arrangements include the Generalised System of Preferences (GSP), preferential duty regime for the African, Caribbean and Pacific (ACP) states, autonomous trade preferences (ATPs) and FTAs with their specific rules. Import duty into the EU is calculated on the type of goods, value and country of origin, but once an importer has paid this duty at customs (i.e. it is released for free circulation), no duty is payable anymore in another EU country if circulating normally in the Single Market. VAT also needs to be paid, and is different from the import duty (see Chapter 7). Vice versa, European exporters to non-EU countries can access a similar database and support site called the Market Access Database (http://madb.europa.eu/mkaccdb2/indexPubli.htm) with a guide to formalities, tariffs and a complaint register that feeds into EU monitoring and policy-making mechanisms.

Gulf Cooperation Council: the GCC countries (Saudi Arabia, Kuwait, Bahrain, Qatar, the United Arab Emirates, and the Sultanate of Oman) entertain a Cooperation Agreement with Europe, to facilitate trade relations and to strengthen stability. Working groups focus on industry, energy and environment, university cooperation, business cooperation and the preparation of a free trade agreement. There are bilateral relations with Iran, Iraq and Yemen, including an EU–Iraq Partnership and Cooperation Agreement 2011.

The League of Arab States (the Arab League) is a regional organization of Arab states in north and north-east Africa and the Middle East. Its 22 member states mainly collaborate to increase cooperation and aim for independence and sovereignty.

Africa, Caribbean and Pacific (ACP): the Cotonou Agreement (now succeeded by Caribbean Forum of African, Caribbean and Pacific States (CARIFORUM) links the EU to 77 ACP countries. With its Economic Partnership Agreements (EPAs), the EU supports ACP governments' aim to create a balanced macroeconomic context, expand the private sector, and improve the quality and coverage of social services. The Fourth Lomé Convention frees the ACP countries from customs duties on 94 per cent of their exports to the EU. For example, 'One of Papua New Guinea's exports to the EU, canned tuna, on the other hand will continue to enter the EU duty and quota-free, with significantly more advantageous and simplified Rules of Origin to facilitate sourcing the raw tuna for processing' (European Commission, 2011). Among other initiatives, the EU is a stakeholder in the 'Kimberley Process' to prevent circulation of conflict diamonds in African war zones.

Other African relations: relations with the African Union, established in 1999, have thrived particularly since the pro-democracy movements in 2011. The union was launched to promote peace, solidarity and cooperation, and encompasses 53 member states (except Morocco). The EU opened a delegation at the OAU in 2008 in recognition of its importance.

The EU has established strong links with the UN, the WTO, NATO, the Organization for Security and Cooperation in Europe (OSCE), the Council of Europe and regional organizations on the other continents to defend its interests and to contribute aid to the Third World, in particular through its numerous Economic Partnership Agreements.

10.1 The international business environment: some key facts for European business

Compared to its trading partners, the EU enjoys a relatively open economy with an openness degree of almost 27 per cent (exports + imports/GDP). The trading power of the Member States is embodied by their common role as the world's leading exporters of goods (see Table 10.3), with more than 17 per cent of the world total; the world's leading exporter of services, with about 25 per cent of the world total and the world's leading source of foreign direct investment (FDI) and the second largest home for foreign investment. *The EU's members represent approximately 7 per cent of the world's population and account for more than a fifth of global imports and exports.* It is the world's largest market, with more than 500 million people. Member States enjoy comparatively sound rates of GDP, both as a whole and on a country-to-country basis. In comparison to other trade powers worldwide, Europe benefits from an exceptional business environment that we have studied throughout this book.

This environment is as much an opportunity as it is a challenge to business. On the one hand, the unemployment rate in Europe is higher than in other developed countries. On the other hand, the EU plays a major role in the WTO as one voice. EU tariffs on industrial products are among the lowest in the world and, in fact, most have been dismantled.

Table 10.3   *Worldwide exports of the EU*

Country	Percentage of total EU-15 trade	Percentage of total EU-25 trade
1 USA	21.0%	23.3%
2 Switzerland	6.5%	7.4%
3 China	5.8%	6.5%
4 Japan	5.6%	6.4%
5 Russia	3.9%	5.3%

Source: COMEXT, IMF, European Communities, 2003, http://ec.europa.eu © European Union, 1995–2011

10.2 Europe's trading partners

China has overtaken Germany as the world's largest exporter, accounting for 9.6 per cent of the global total in 2009 (Germany's share was 9 per cent, and that of the USA 8.5 per cent). Six of the 10 leading exporters last year were European countries.

Table 10.3 illustrates the growth of EU exports to five main partners, pre- and post-2004 enlargement. Trade and investment relations with other countries, market groupings and emerging countries represent a huge opportunity for EU firms. This opportunity is generated from international policies that reach out to create and sustain relations worldwide.

10.2.1 Relations with market groupings

Because of its role as a highly integrated, large market, the EU entertains privileged relations not only with major trading partner countries, but also with most other market groupings. For business that operates in such an enlarged market, the opportunities of other market groupings are part of the life cycle. Market grouping representatives from across the globe come to the EU to understand how regional policy works to successfully stimulate less advanced Member States' growth, such as Spain in the 1980s, Ireland in the 1990s, Poland in the 2000s and Croatia in the 2010s.

The main trading partner of the EU is NAFTA, comprising the USA, Canada and Mexico. This free trade area, established in 1994, encompasses 426 million inhabitants, with a total GDP for NAFTA of approximately US$12 trillion worth of goods and services. The main aim of NAFTA is to eliminate impediments to trade of goods and services, facilitate their movement across Member States and boost commerce and internal investments. These objectives also characterize the FTAA project, which is to cover the entire continent except for Cuba and French Guyana. NAFTA's dispute settlements concern investment, anti-dumping and countervailing, among other subjects.

The EU's geographically closest market grouping is EFTA, consisting of Iceland, Liechtenstein, Norway and Switzerland (see Chapter 2). EFTA members have incorporated two-thirds of EU legislation since 1992, following EFTA's partnership (except for Switzerland) with the Union to form the EEA. Subsequent easy accession to the EU is possible for EFTA members. Many of the countries that joined the EU in the 1980s and 1990s were formerly EFTA members.

The Southern American Common Market, MERCOSUR, comprising Argentina, Brazil, Paraguay, Uruguay and Venezuela, was established in 1991. It has about 270 million inhabitants, with a common total GDP of more than US$1.9 trillion. The grouping was formed to encourage integration among members via the free movement of goods and services. Members also apply a common external tariff. The main objective is to ensure the economic and political stability of the region. MERCOSUR influences other regional economic structures and is looking into expansion through a pan-American (FTAA) or a MERCOSUR–EU pact. The most tangible outcomes of the grouping encompass important infrastructural projects such as gas pipelines, bridges and motorways.

APEC, founded in 1989, is the largest market grouping with privileged EU relations. APEC members are Australia, Brunei, Malaysia, Singapore, Thailand, New Zealand, New Guinea, Indonesia, Philippines, Taiwan, Hong Kong, Japan, China, South Korea, Canada, USA, Mexico and Chile: 21 members of over 2.5 billion people, a combined GDP of over US$19 trillion and 47 per cent of world trade (Members Economies, 2006 – available at: http://www.apec.org/content/apec/member_economies.html). However, APEC presents a relatively low degree of unification, although its core mission is to facilitate trade and FDI by removing barriers.

The members of the Association of South-East Asian Nations (ASEAN) are mostly also members of 'Asia – Pacific Economic Cooperation' (APEC), the regional economic forum of the most dynamic part of the world with more than 30 bilateral free trade agreements. APEC trade facilitation initiatives reduced 'transaction costs by a further 5 per cent between 2007 and 2010' (APEC, 2011).

ASEAN is constituted by Indonesia, Malaysia, Philippines, Singapore, Thailand, Brunei Darrussalam, Laos, Vietnam, Myanmar and Cambodia, set up in 1967, with 590 million inhabitants and a total GDP of more than $1.5 trillion. ASEAN was created to accelerate economic growth, social progress and cultural development and is equipped with a dispute settlement. Its free trade area, AFTA, was created in 1993 to stimulate growth through a decrease of government control on national economies, and as a response to the EU's and NAFTA's regional peace and stability initiatives. It has reduced intra-regional tariffs and non-tariff barriers significantly, i.e. through cross-notification mechanisms. Amongst AFTA's FTAs, its trade relations with the EU evolved into the Trans-Regional EU–ASEAN Trade initiative (TREATI) in 2003, and the EU negotiates FTAs with its members, having started such agreements with Singapore. European companies are the largest investor in ASEAN countries, and Europe is ASEAN's top export destination, amounting to 11.2 per cent of ASEAN's total exports (2009).

Asian–European interests started to take serious shape in the 1980s. From Japanese management models, Asian natural resources and corporate cultures, to the evolution and crisis of the Asian Tigers, the region quickly attracted Europe with its potential. Contacts between Europe and ASEAN were established in 1993, resulting in the first ASia–Europe Summit (ASEM) in 1996 in Bangkok. The 19 Asian countries and the EU 27 regularly meet to stimulate economic, political and social relations. At the ASEM meeting in October 2004, both continents approved the enlargement of each other's grouping for equally enlarged talks. Since October 2004, the Asia–Europe meeting, held every two years, has included Japan, China and South Korea, and since 2010, also Australia, New Zealand and Russia.

Inside ASEM, the ASia Europe Foundation (ASEF) promotes cultural and intellectual exchanges between Europe and Asia to reduce the risk of cultural misunderstandings. Intellectual exchange is fostered through seminars and conferences, bringing together experts from different areas supported by ASEF (for example, on issues of security, the environment and cultural dialogue). People, cultural exchange and communication reinforce the system. The annual Asia-Europe Business Forum (AEBF) is a forum of exchanges for the private sector from Asia and Europe.

Relations with African market groupings include those with the East African Community (EAC) and the eastern and southern African countries (ESA). The EAC was, from December 1999 onwards, re-established among Kenya, Uganda and the United Republic of Tanzania, Burundi and Rwanda, with its seat in Arusha, Tanzania. This grouping has run a customs union since 2005. EAC goods enjoy duty- and quota-free access to the EU as well as favourable rules of origin. Mainly coffee, tea and spices originate from the EAC countries, while the leading European players in the region sell machinery there.

Trade liberalization and EU tariff reductions are also practised for and by ESA which mainly excels in textiles and sugar. A recent grouping in African integration is the Southern African Development Community, a free-trade zone since September 2000; it groups together Angola, Botswana, Congo, Lesotho, Malawi, Mauritius, Mozambique, Namibia, Seychelles, South Africa, Tanzania, Zambia and Zimbabwe. Angola, Botswana, Lesotho, Mozambique, Namibia, Swaziland and South Africa mainly entertain relations with the EU (ESA's largest trade partner, in particular in natural resources) via an Economic Partnership Agreement which constitutes the oldest customs union in the world (COMESA – see European Commission, 2011). A 2005 EU strategy for the first time addressed Africa as one entity for support, aid, security and politico-economic relations.

10.2.2 Business relations with selected partners

The European Commission predicted in 2011 that within a very few years, 90 per cent of world growth would be generated outside of Europe. Therefore, the European corporate world is dependent on European external relations and on furnishing an attractive business environment for investments.

10.2.2.1 Relations with the USA

The USA and the European Union are allies in a long relationship and have, for decades, been the two largest economies in the world. They enjoy the world's biggest bilateral trading and investment relationship (Table 10.4 compares geographical data) and share common concerns on political and security issues. In accordance with this relationship, there is a high frequency of meetings, negotiations and debate. Though the goals are usually the same, ideas about how to achieve them often differ.

The President of the United States and the Presidency of the European Union meet twice a year for presidential summits. The US Congress confers with the

Table 10.4   *A short comparison: the EU and the USA*

Country	Population (millions)	Area (1,000 km²)	Population density (inhabitants/km²)
EU	502	5000	100
USA	310	9372	33

European Parliament. Among agreements on political and economic issues, we note the New Transatlantic Agenda (1995) and the Economic Partnership (1998).

It is estimated that trade and investment flow across the Atlantic is at a rate of nearly EUR1.7 billion a day (EU source) to $2.7 billion a day (US source, 2011). The US-owned FDI is greater in the EU than in any other region of the world. The USA receives one-quarter of EU exports and supplies 20 per cent of its imports, and hence serious economic disputes are relatively rare – less than 2 per cent of total transatlantic trade – but make media headlines (such as beef hormones, steel or disagreement about the military invasion of Iraq in March 2003 that caused the decline of certain French, German and other EU market shares in the USA due to a guided change in consumer perceptions). For decades, the EU and the UAS have trodden a fine line between free trade principles and protectionism in trade.

A comparison of partners is useful for any trans–Atlantic business. This comparison may be based, for example, on the Lisbon Strategy's dimensions of EU Member States' competitiveness (see Table 10.5).

Following Table 10.5, the EU as a whole is less competitive than the US economy. In seven out of eight Lisbon dimensions, including social cohesion, the EU as a group is less competitive than the USA. However, the EU outperforms the USA in telecommunications, social protection and sustainable development. In this

Table 10.5   *Lisbon scores comparing the EU, the USA and East Asia, 2010*

Lisbon dimension	EU-27 average	USA	East Asia	EU-27 average relative to the USA	EU-27 average relative to East Asia
Information society	4.73	5.79	5.56	−1.06	−0.83
Innovation and R&D	4.23	6.03	5.24	−1.81	−1.01
Liberalization	4.80	5.05	5.10	−0.25	−0.30
Network industries	5.39	5.73	6.06	−0.34	−0.67
Telecommunications	5.62	5.54	5.89	0.07	−0.27
Utilities and transport	5.16	5.91	5.24	−0.75	−1.07
Financial services	5.05	5.22	5.41	−0.17	−0.36
Enterprise	4.60	5.07	5.17	−0.47	−0.56
Business start–up environment	4.80	5.31	5.14	−0.51	−0.33
Regulatory environment	4.41	4.83	5.20	−0.42	−0.79
Social inclusion	4.51	4.71	4.93	−0.20	−0.42
Returning people to the workforce	4.97	5.39	5.41	−0.42	−0.45
Upgrading skills	4.47	5.09	5.09	−0.62	−0.61
Modernizing social protection	4.10	3.66	4.30	0.44	−0.19
Sustainable development	5.16	4.59	4.74	0.57	0.42
Final Index Score	4.81	5.27	5.28	−0.46	−0.47

Source: The Lisbon Review 2010 © 2010 World Economic Forum, http://www.scribd.com/doc/30852400/The-Lisbon-Review-2010

comparison, one may look at individual countries in the EU and compare them to the USA: some are progressing better. In particular, the Nordic countries have comparatively higher scores than the USA in all areas. The other Member States either outperform the USA in specific areas of the Lisbon criteria (for example, Austria, France, Luxembourg) or perform worse in all areas (for example, Italy, Greece, Portugal; this coincides with the economies that suffered most from the 2009/10 financial crisis). Although the US economy is separated into different independent large states, the economy consists solely of one entity, while the EU consists of many nationalities and economies. The recent accession of new members to the EU hinders its performance in the short-term because the existing infrastructure of these members does not yet support economic growth, especially in the areas of the information society, innovation and R&D, and social inclusion. In the long-term, an increase in prosperity is expected for all.

Based on the world market share of each industry, we can compare sectors (see Tables 10.6 and 10.7). For instance, if the EU is the second leading exporter

Table 10.6   *US competitive industries ($ billion)*

Industry	World export ranking	World market value (WMV)	US export value	Percentage of WMV
Agriculture	1	783	79.57	10.2%
Chemical	2	976	112.86	11.6%
Electronic data processing (EDP) and office equipment	2	421	43.9	10.5%
IC and electronic components	1	331	49.3	14.9%
Automotive	3	847	76.42	9%

Source: WTO, 2005 data

Table 10.7   *EU-25 competitive industries ($ billion)*

Industry	World export ranking	World market value (WMV)	EU-25 export value	Percentage of WMV
Agriculture	2	783	78.41	10%
Iron and steel	1	266	29.20	11%
Chemical	1	976	190.86	19.6%
Electronic data processing (EDP) and office equipment	3	421	31	7.4%
Telecom equipment	2	383	44	11.5%
Automotive	1	847	125.88	14.9%
Clothing	3	258	19.13	7.4%
Textiles	2	195	24.31	12.5%

Source: WTO, 2005 data

after China in telecommunications equipment, we conclude that the telecommunication equipment industry is one of the most competitive sectors in the EU economy.

Judging from the data in Table 10.6, the US economy remains competitive in the integrated circuits (IC) and electronic components industries and in agriculture. American companies like Intel and AMD lead the world in integrated circuits technology. The USA is the leading exporter of agricultural products such as grains, oilseed and livestock (the three products account for $36.31 billion in exports). The main market for its agricultural products is Asia. In the automotive sector, the US industry significantly lost momentum during the 2008/9 financial crisis; it is now exporting less than the EU and Japan. Oil prices also have an effect on the world consumption of automotive products and on innovation needs in the sector.

European car manufacturers such as BMW and Mercedes are performing well as the leading exporters of automotive products in terms of world market share (see Table 10.7). As mentioned above, in telecommunication equipment, the EU is second only to China. Telecommunication companies like Nokia, Ericsson and Siemens lead in technology, while Asia does so in production costs. Enlargement adds to the export volumes of the EU, for example in the clothing industry. (The numbers in Table 10.7 take into consideration only exports of products from the EU 25 to countries outside the EU and not exports between the EU countries.)

Unfortunately, no similar comparison was published with the Asian trade partners. Therefore, the following analysis of Asian–European relations will be based on European and WTO material.

10.2.2.2 The Asia-Pacific region

The Asian and Asia-Pacific region is home to more than half of the world's population, and to most of the world's production. Moreover, it accounts for a significant part of world trade. In spite of the economic and financial problems it faced in the 1990s, the region is one of the most dynamic in the world, accounting for approximately one-third of world value of import–export. European production within the Asian region is part of the highly integrated intra-regional production networks and many European companies are dependent on them.

Asia – as a whole – accounts for 21 per cent of EU external exports, and is the third-largest regional trading partner, after non-EU Europe (31 per cent) and NAFTA (28 per cent). Asia also exports more than NAFTA and the EU. Table 10.5 (above) illustrates that the first seven scores beat the EU, but East Asia is still lagging behind in sustainable development.

Asia accounts for a significant share of EU foreign investment flows, while certain Asian countries are also increasingly important investors in the EU (see below). The outward investment flows from China and Japan between 1985 and 2000 set the scene for the emergence of Asian integration into the world economy (see Figure 10.5).

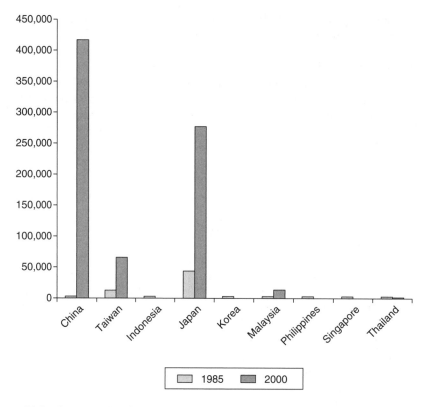

Figure 10.5   *Outward FDI of Asian countries (sample), 1985 and 2000*
Source: Data compiled from Suder et al., 2011; UNCTAD, 2009

Indeed, the 'favoured location for foreign affiliates of the largest EM-MNEs (Emerging Market multinationals) is not another developing country, but the United States and the United Kingdom (UNCTAD, 2008: 30), with European countries notable for their presence in UNCTAD's list' (Box 10.2, McGuire et al., 2011).

Box 10.2: Preferred location of foreign affiliates for the top 100 developing economy MNEs

1 US	5 Hong Kong (China)	
2 **UK**	6 **Netherlands**	
3 China	7 Brazil	
4 **Germany**		

Source: UNCTAD, 2008; McGuire et al., 2011 (p. 346)

Asian countries play an important role within the WTO, and as China and Vietnam's entry into the WTO strengthen this role, so will Russia's. In particular, China, India, the Republic of Korea, Hong Kong and Singapore all experienced high inflows from worldwide sources. Flows to the region remain unevenly distributed and strongly inter-related, with a shift towards China in the early and mid 2000s. Figure 10.6 illustrates this interrelation, showing that the main production network hubs can be found around China and Japan, but include the crucial contribution of various other Asian players.

The sheer number of consumers and markets, which are emerging and are more open than ever, have turned China, Hong Kong and South East Asia into fast-growing business environments that attract a large amount of foreign investment. Major advantages for trade and investment in Asia are factor advantages that lie in

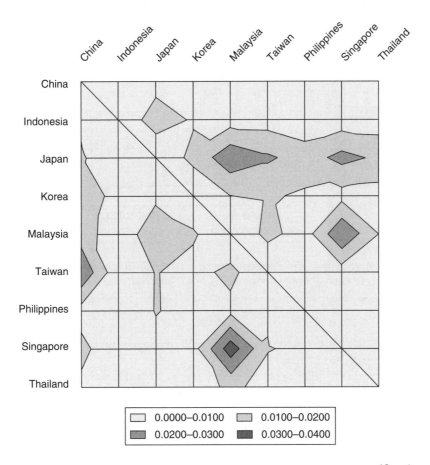

Cross-national linkages: 2000

(Continued)

(Continued)

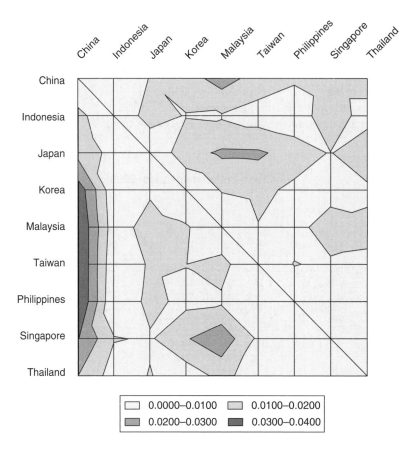

Cross-national linkages: 2000

Figure 10.6   *Spatial economic interdependence in East Asia (production networks in three industries: manufacturing, textiles, machinery), 2000 and 2005*

Source: By permission, S. Inomata; The Asian International Input–Output Table, 2000 and 2005 (preliminary), IDE-JETRO, 2011

the cost of production and/or country-specific advantages such as technology and regional network advantages.

Despite the fact that each country in this region has a different policy for foreign investment, most of them entertain sound relations with the EU and encourage investment in the region through tax reduction and incentives. Each country in the Asia-Pacific region has a different way of doing business: business cultures are very diverse, similar to the situation in Europe, but without the EU's historical, economic and political integration of the marketplace.

Table 10.8   *Business sector performance in the EU and Asia*

Sector	World trade value ($ billion)	EU		ASIA (includes Japan, Taiwan and China)	
		Ranking in world export	Share in world export (%)	Ranking in world export	Share in world export (%)
Agriculture					
Fuel and mining	1281	4	4.62	7	2.46
Manufacturing					
Iron and steel	266	2	10.98	1	22.83
Chemical	976	1	19.60	2	15.40
Pharmaceutical	247	1	27.00	3	5.22
EDP and office equipment	420	3	7.38	1	52.83
Telecom equipment	383	2	11.49	1	48.06
Automobile	847	3	14.90	1	19.70
Textiles	195	2	12.50	1	41.70
Clothing	258	4	7.40	1	35.80
Commercial services					
Transportation	500	1	32.40	2	17.00
Travel services	625	1	34.00	5	7.90
Other	1000	1	42.60	3	13.40

Source: WTO, International Trade Statistics, 2005

Relations with Japan, the most mature though crisis-stricken Asian economy in this area, have always been challenging but important. In the post-World War II period, the EU had little exchange – limited to textile, cutlery and sewing machines – with Japan. However, during the 1980s and early 1990s, while the Japanese economy was booming, European business became fascinated with Japanese management tools (such as Just-in-Time) and Japan's market. But European business faced tariff and non-tariff barriers when approaching the Japanese economy. Through important negotiations and partnership initiatives, the EU significantly improved relations with Japan during the 1990s, and European business has progressively become the major foreign investor there. Since 2001, the EU and Japan are engaged in an action plan that has widely expanded bilateral cooperation on trade and investment to political and cultural issues, reinforced again in the aftermath of the 2011 unprecedented triple crisis in Japan, of earthquake, tsunami and nuclear accident.

Certain Asian countries, notably Japan and South Korea (the latter in an FTA with the EU since February 2011), are also major investors in the EU.

Box 10.3: South Korean free trade

Negotiations for an EU–South Korea free trade agreement were launched in 2007. Initiated by the CEC in 2009, the EP adopted this agreement in February 2011 and the Korean Parliament in April 2011. This FTA is the second largest in the world and the most ambitious for both parties. It eliminates 98.7 per cent of duties in trade value for industrial and agricultural products between 2011 and 2016. The EU states that this 'deal will create new trade in goods and services worth €19.1 billion for the EU; another study calculates that it will more than double the bilateral EU–South Korea trade in the next 20 years compared to a scenario without the FTA' (http://trade.ec.europa.eu/doclib/press/index.cfm?id=680).

However, the European car industry needs to adapt to the more restrictive standards in Korea, such as stricter emission standards; if not complied with, the agreement could even be harmful for the Europeans, since it also makes it easier for South Korean car and truck makers to compete. This FTA completes an earlier Agreement on Co-operation and Mutual Administrative Assistance in Customs Matters of 1997, for shared competition policy, and the EU–Korean Framework Agreement on Trade and Co-operation of 2001, for cooperation in transport, energy, science and technology, industry, environment and culture. The EU machinery exporters estimate savings of €450 million in duties per annum; the chemical sector approximately €150 million. In textiles and clothing, more than €60 million in duties will disappear. Finally, the FTA has a 'mediation mechanism to tackle non-tariff barriers. The procedures envisaged under the dispute settlement chapter foresee arbitration ruling within 120 days, i.e. much faster than in the WTO'[(European Union, 2010). A safeguard clause was also put in place, in case of excessive increase in imports from South Korea to the EU. MEPs and industry groups can activate the clause.

US President Obama pursued a similar agreement between the USA and South Korea in March 2011. The country signed an FTA with Peru in the same year and a three-way FTA between South Korea, China and Japan is in the making.

The relationship with China significantly increased in political, economic affairs and institutional exchanges, particularly during China's run-up to WTO membership in December 2001. The same phenomenon appeared in the 2011 talks about a global monetary systems reform in which China became an important negotiator. While the USA ranks first among its trading partners, the EU is the first source of Chinese foreign investment, ahead of both the USA and Japan.

With regard to North Korea (DPRK), the EU supports the inter-Korean reconciliation process and shares international concerns about the North Korean uranium enrichment programme, which is in breach of its non-proliferation commitments. The EU's policy of dialogue is underpinned by market accessibility opportunities for North Korea.

With India, current relations are based on the 2000 EU–Indian summit meeting and the 2011 FTA negotiations. The EU is India's biggest trading partner and provider of foreign investment. Relations started via trade agreement and now embrace political and business, cultural cooperation and joint research projects. This market excels in technology, engineering competencies and expertise in languages and is an essential part of EU companies' sourcing of services in particular.

Figure 10.7 and 10.8 illustrate the importance of EU firms sourcing internationally, and the sourcing of engineering functions which European companies entertain with China and India. The results (from this sample of country origins) show that older Member States' firms are more likely to source outside of the EU than those from newer countries.

Today, negotiations between the two parties focus on a trade and investment agreement, transport negotiations for maritime transport, and joint work on climate change.

Despite the fact that Asia is a large market, diversities in economic performance are more obvious in the Asia-Pacific region than in the EU and the continent does not show the same depth of integration but rather a great number of bilateral

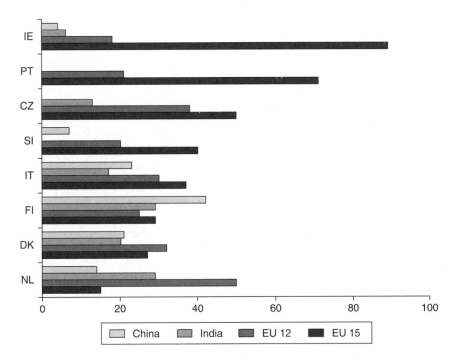

Figure 10.7   *Destinations for sourcing engineering functions; share of enterprises sourcing those functions (%), 2001–2006*

Source: http://epp.eurostat.ec.europa.eu/statistics_explained/index.php?title=File:Destinations_for_sourcing_
engineering_functions;_share_of_enterprises_sourcing_those_functions_%28%25%29,_2001-2006.png&filetimest
amp=20110308162656 © European Union, 1995–2011

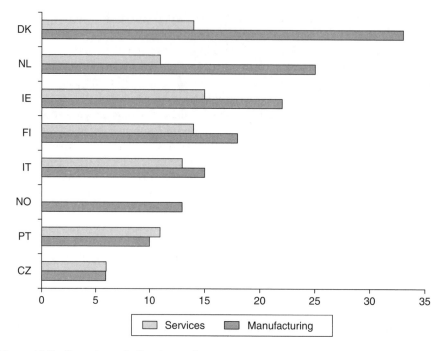

Figure 10.8   *Sourcing to India: share of enterprises having sourced core and/or support functions internationally, by sector (%), 2009*

Source: http://epp.eurostat.ec.europa.eu/statistics_explained/index.php?title=File:Sourcing_to_India_-_Share_of_
enterprises_having_sourced_core_and_or_support_functions_internationally,_by_sector_%28%25%29,_2009.png&fil
etimestamp=20110308153906 © European Union, 1995–2011

agreements. In comparison, the EU therefore enjoys higher degrees of relative homogeneity in its market grouping. The value of the market compared with the average income per capita of EU countries is higher than that in Asian countries. At the same time, the Asian-Pacific region has a considerably high trade/GDP ratio, and in some regions higher growth rates than the EU; it is a region of extremes in that context. There is a significant difference in the level of the trade/GDP ratio among the individual economies within the region.

Import tariffs have been significantly reduced in the Asia-Pacific region over the last decade, largely due to the effects of regional and global trade arrangements. For example, as a result of China's WTO accession, its average tariff dropped by 75 per cent in 2000 in all products (primary and manufactured). On the social side, the EU is more competitive than Asia in education, with a more efficient public health sector and a highly developed infrastructure. But Asia continues to catch up, with important growth potential vis-à-vis the maturity of most European markets and sectors and its demography.

Altogether, whether doing business in the EU or in Asia, you need to have the understanding and tools for adapting to the uniqueness of each region and be experienced in diversity management. Also, you must be able to recognize the firm- and country-specific advantages that allow your business to benefit from similarities in markets or modes of doing business. The Global Competitiveness Report, in formulating the range of factors that go into explaining the evolution of growth in a country, identifies 'three pillars': the quality of the macroeconomic environment, the state of the country's public institutions, and, given the importance of technology and innovation, the level of its technological development. A *Growth Competitive Index* position is the comprehensive outcome. As the study notes, the Nordic European countries have held the leading position for many years in the global growth competitive ranking together with Switzerland, followed by Singapore. Other countries also highly ranked in the chart are, for Asia, Taiwan, Japan, Malaysia and China.

Using world trade value and share of world trade statistics from the WTO, you are now able to analyse trade in the world market that has been grouped into five major sectors: only extra EU export is considered when comparing competitiveness to other regions (see Table 10.9). Equally, only Asian exports to non-Asian markets are measured. Table 10.10 illustrates both economic groups' performance in all business sectors.

According to this table, the most competitive sectors in the EU are the manufacturing of chemical and pharmaceutical products and commercial services. These competitive sectors draw from the EU's strength in technology competitiveness such as entrepreneurship, information and communication technology (ICT), human resources and sustainability. For example, Finland and Germany are very competitive in the quality and standards of labour, innovation and ICT. On the other hand, small countries like Luxembourg, Poland and Hungary exploit their strength in entrepreneurship. Although single EU Member States are not strong enough in all sectors, it is clear that complementarities can drive further growth potentials in commercial services sectors. Through free movement of resources and capital, the EU encourages the business environment to gain competitive strength in the commercial service sector, including financial and business consulting, and R&D centres. The EU is shifting its competitive focus from manufacturing sectors to a knowledge-based economy. However, the EU also needs to maintain its competitiveness in the manufacturing sector to have a balanced market.

Again, as Table 10.8 shows, Asia currently excels in the manufacturing sectors. These can be sub-sectored into eight generic types, as shown in the table. If you consider Asia as one integrated economic group, then it obtains its main share in exports from the many sub-sectors in manufacturing. For example, while Japan makes a big contribution in the automotive sector, China and India count for a major share in Asia's textiles and clothing. Despite the small amount of share, other Asian countries like Thailand and Malaysia also contribute significantly to the development of sectors such as office equipment and telecommunication and multimedia equipment. The Asian-Pacific pool of essential human, natural and technological resources is vast, though unevenly distributed. The lower cost of production, both from labour and material, convey Asian competitiveness in mass production, while Australia and New Zealand follow the economic trends of

Table 10.9 *Share of goods and commercial services in the total trade of selected regions and economies, 2004 ($ billion and percentage, based on balance of payments data)*

	Exports			Imports		
	Value	Share		Value	Share	
	Total	Goods	Commercial services	Total	Goods	Commercial services
World	**11,140**	**80.9**	**19.1**	**11,060**	**81.1**	**18.9**
North America	**1,709**	**77.8**	**22.2**	**2,284**	**85.3**	**14.7**
Canada	378	87.6	12.4	335	83.3	16.7
Mexico	202	93.1	6.9	216	91.1	8.9
United States	1,129	71.8	28.2	1,733	85.0	15.0
South and Central America	**347**	**83.9**	**16.1**	**293**	**80.3**	**19.7**
Argentina	39	87.7	12.3	28	76.7	23.3
Bolivarian Republic of Venezuela	40	97.5	2.5	22	80.2	19.8
Brazil	108	89.4	10.6	79	79.6	20.4
Chile	38	84.5	15.5	29	78.2	21.8
Colombia	19	89.2	10.8	20	80.7	19.3
Europe	**5,032**	**77.6**	**22.4**	**4,864**	**78.9**	**21.1**
Austria	159	69.7	30.3	154	69.4	30.6
Belgium	294	83.2	16.8	284	83.0	17.0
Czech Republic	77	87.4	12.6	77	88.1	11.9
Denmark	111	67.4	32.6	99	66.2	33.8
Finland	70	87.3	12.7	60	80.4	19.6
France	531	79.4	20.6	525	81.7	18.3
Germany	1,044	87.2	12.8	911	78.8	21.2
Ireland	146	67.8	32.2	118	50.3	49.7
Italy	428	80.8	19.2	417	80.7	19.3
Netherlands	374	80.5	19.5	344	79.0	21.0
Norway	109	76.2	23.8	73	67.3	32.7
Poland	95	86.0	14.0	99	87.6	12.4
Spain	269	68.6	31.4	302	82.3	17.7
Sweden	161	76.5	23.5	132	75.0	25.0
Switzerland	175	79.0	21.0	144	85.3	14.7
Turkey	91	73.8	26.2	101	89.8	10.2
United Kingdom	521	67.0	33.0	591	77.0	23.0

Source: WTO, 2005

highly developed economies. The fast development of socio-technology, manufacturing technology and rising awareness of the environment sustains investments and improves product quality.

In the chemical and pharmaceutical sectors, Asia is catching up with large investments in very important equipment and high levels of education and technology.

Table 10.10 *Share of goods and commercial services in the total trade of selected regions and economies, 2005 ($ billion and percentage, based on balance of payments data)*

	Value	Share		Value	Share	
	Total	Goods	Commercial services	Total	Goods	Commercial services
World	12,690	81.0	19.0	12,610	81.4	18.6
Commonwealth of Independent States (CIS)	389	89.2	10.8	281	77.8	22.2
Azerbaijan	8	92.5	7.5	7	62.4	37.6
Belarus	18	88.7	11.3	18	93.3	6.7
Kazakhstan	30	93.3	6.7	25	71.0	29.0
Russian Federation	268	90.9	9.1	164	76.5	23.5
Ukraine	44	79.7	20.3	43	83.9	16.1
Africa	340	83.3	16.7	311	77.7	22.3
Egypt	31	51.9	48.1	33	71.5	28.5
Morocco	18	58.4	41.6	22	85.8	14.2
Nigeria	37	88.7	11.3	19	67.7	32.3
South Africa	65	84.5	15.5	68	83.0	17.0
Tunisia	14	74.3	25.7	14	86.1	13.9
Asia	3,551	85.2	14.8	3,312	82.7	17.3
Australia	134	79.4	20.6	149	80.6	19.4
China	836	91.2	8.8	711	88.3	11.7
Hong Kong[a], China	352	82.3	17.7	330	90.2	9.8
India	153	63.3	36.7	187	72.1	27.9
Indonesia[b]	94	92.0	8.0	87	73.4	26.6
Japan	676	84.0	16.0	607	78.2	21.8
Korea, Republic of	333	86.8	13.2	313	81.6	18.4
Malaysia	161	88.2	11.8	130	83.4	16.6
Philippines	45	90.0	10.0	54	89.2	10.8
Singapore[a]	273	83.5	16.5	236	81.4	18.6
Taipei, Chinese	224	88.6	11.4	212	85.2	14.8
Thailand	130	84.2	15.8	134	79.4	20.6
Viet Nam	35	87.4	12.6	39	86.3	13.7
Memorandum item:						
European Union (25)	4,978	77.5	22.5	4,893	78.8	21.2

Note: Trade in goods is derived from balance of payments statistics and does not correspond to the merchandise trade statistics given elsewhere in this report. It is likely that for most economies trade in commercial services is understated.

a Trade in goods includes significant re-exports or imports for re-exports.
b Secretariat estimates.

Source: www.wto.org/english/res_e/statis_e/its2006_e/its06_overview_e.htm, Table 1.9

While EDP, office equipment and telecommunication equipment constitute the world's largest share, this to date concerns manufacturing competitiveness. But rates of innovation and technological competitiveness are growing.

10.3 The future of European business: 'unity in diversity'

Doing Business in Europe is a dynamic, ever-changing challenge and opportunity, in a market characterized by deep and vast economic integration. The best-adapted company is a networked, born-global, flat organization with a highly diversified workforce. But this is not the only structure to succeed in the European business environment, that Single yet diverse Market.

Europe continues to provide business with opportunities and challenges that stem both from harmonization, (de-)regulation and the schism between the functionalist and federalist objectives of its Member States. The 2009/10 crisis forced European nations to reconsider the mechanisms that they believed would keep the market protected but only did so partially. Instead of isolating themselves through nationalist and self-centred interests, these nations have made the (sometimes costly) decision to continue their engagement in a profoundly democratic, peace-enhancing and collaborative regionalism that is open to the world.

In the context of this book, we considered Europeanization as a particularly advanced case of globalization: the compression of time and space that increases the frequency and duration of linkages between any given actors in the international environment. Is the world flatter? Certainly not – rather, its landscape has become more varied thanks to more cooperation and interconnectivity between states, economies and people. While incomplete, the high sequence of interaction between any given actor is prone to increase knowledge, awareness and progress in political, social and economic issues that reach beyond borders. The consumer knows more and expects more. Companies need to adapt faster and act responsibly across borders. Economies need to support each other as well as their institutions and peoples. European economies strive increasingly for European independence through regional interdependence and support. Business will continue to play an essential role in this endeavour.

Europeanization was always a term with two meanings, where the first applied to whole economies, and the second, to companies. The first meaning is thus the integration of European economies and the development of common policies of EU Member States. Europeanization in this sense is considered as an advanced case of globalization compared with other forms of market grouping and regional economic integration. The term Europeanization used in its second sense in connection with business corporations, describes advanced forms of organizations that reflect: (a) the diversity of markets and cultures; and (b) the diversity within the company as well as in the scope of their operations. As for the whole phenomenon of globalization, some sectors or industries are more concerned than others. This is the case for financial markets, in- and outsourcing and FDI. In Europe, social, ethical and environmental issues are of increasing concern: both people and companies show high levels of awareness about the role that organizations play in these fields.

Doing Business in Europe, experiencing its diversity and similarities and knowing how to best tackle the resulting opportunities: this is the key to international success.

Mini case study: The rise of Russian multinationals – the Lukoil case

According to Platts top 250 Global Energy Company 2009 ranking, Lukoil is the second largest Russian private oil company and the twelfth worldwide; it acts in the area of exploration and production of oil and gas, the production of petroleum products and petrochemicals as well as in the marketing of these. The proven reserves of the Russian giant in 2009 amounted to 14.5 million barrels of crude oil and 29.5 billion cubic feet of natural gas. The company declares its share in global oil reserves as about 1.1, and that of the world oil production as about 2.3 (Lukoil Factbook, 2009). Its main resource base is in the western part of Siberia. Lukoil possesses modern oil refineries, gas-processing and petrochemical plants located in Russia, Eastern and Western Europe, as well as in the neighbouring countries of the CIS (Commonwealth of Independent States). Most of Lukoil's production is sold in international markets, including the countries of the EU and the USA.

The organization officiates as a successful oil and gas supplier on the territory of the former Soviet Union and is strongly involved in projects for oil and gas prospecting in Central America and the Middle East. Lukoil possesses a 'Lukoil' gas-station chain in European countries, and also operates under the brand 'Getty' in the USA, and 'Teboil' in countries of the CIS (Table 10.11). The company owned a total of 6748 gas stations at the end of 2008.

Table 10.11   *Lukoil gas stations in the world*

Country	Number of gas stations
USA	1,524
Turkey	777
Finland	456
Romania	319
Ukraine	285
Bulgaria	209
Serbia	184
Belgium	157
Lithuania	120
Poland	106
Moldova	95
Hungary	74
Belarus	66
Latvia	45
Georgia	44
Czech Republic	43
Estonia	37
Cyprus	31
Azerbaijan	27
Croatia	15
Slovakia	13
Macedonia	8
Montenegro	7

Mini Case

One of the central objectives of Lukoil today is the global expansion of its sphere of influence and that is why the company intends to conquer western market share.

For Lukoil, the crux of the matter has always been in achieving a stronger position in the petrochemical industry and aiming to be among the top three companies in the oil and gas centre. To enter new markets, Lukoil had to implement an appropriate expansion strategy, which requires high capital investments and significant efforts to compete successfully with oil and gas suppliers already present.

Although Lukoil explored international operations in the countries belonging to the CIS, in the Middle East (Saudi Arabia, Egypt and Iraq), western Africa (Ghana and Ivory Coast) and Latin America (Colombia and Venezuela), its activity in Europe was not prominent.

However, Europe is closer to Russia than most of those other destinations; moreover, Europe needs Russian petroleum more than other regions and continents. In the last 10 years, OECD Europe's reliance on Russian crude oil exports has grown from around 12 per cent of total imports to around 30 per cent (2008). More than 1.2 million barrels of oil a day flow from Russia through the Druzhba ('Friendship') pipeline, providing almost a quarter of Germany's needs and 96 per cent of Poland's imports, as well as supplies to other Central and East European countries.

After two years of decline in worldwide oil consumption, the petroleum demand in Europe is expected to grow in the near future. The role of Russian energy for Europe may increase dramatically because of the pessimistic outlook for supply growth in Brazil and Central Asia which constitute the bulk of the non-OPEC oil supply. Moreover, US oil output fell by about 70,000 bpd (barrel of crude oil per day) in 2011 as the moratorium and BP's 2010 crisis delayed deep water projects.

For natural gas, Russia is the second-largest source of energy in western Europe. Demand for natural gas is expected to rise significantly over the next 15–20 years, coincidentally with a steady depletion of reserves in EU countries. Russia currently supplies around 40 per cent of Europe's imported gas, with projections indicating a percentage increase to roughly 60 per cent by 2030. Given dwindling reserves and political and logistical restrictions on other potential natural gas suppliers, Russian energy companies are in an excellent position to capture the lion's share of the European gas market.

These trends and considerations may explain the rising interest of Russian multinationals in European energy markets. In the second half of the years 2000–2010, Lukoil had already decided to invest in active European expansion, getting off to a good start when obtaining a leading market position in Italy, through the establishment of a sales network created and run by its Italian subdivision. In the middle of 2008 after a long series of negotiations, Lukoil also executed an agreement to acquire a 49 per cent stake in a newly established joint venture company, namely ERG SA, operating the ISAB refinery in Sicily.

The refinery was jointly operated as a cost centre with separate responsibilities for crude oil supply and product marketing. This allowed for highly effective strategic flexibility for both Lukoil and its Italian counterpart because the whole transaction process was based on an equal partnership. Through the joint venture with ERG, the

Russian oil giant achieved significant benefits such as an improvement in its earnings (via a better local network) as well as an improved balancing out of the company's strategic portfolio. With this acquisition, the proportion of Lukoil's foreign oil-processing facilities grew, making up about 35 per cent of the company's total.

Bearing in mind the need to expand through diversification, Lukoil's management continued to purchase numerous gas stations on Italian territory. According to forecasts, Lukoil was to acquire approximately 1000 gas stations within a few years after its market entry. Two options were considered, either purchasing already existing and operating gas stations belonging to rivals such as Agip, Shell or Tamoil (all also acting on the Italian market), or attracting smaller domestic gas-station owners, who were fighting for survival, into the franchising system.

Continuing its European strategy into 2009, Lukoil acquired 45 per cent of Total Raffinaderij Nederland (TRN) of The Netherlands: one of the biggest and most modern petroleum refineries in Europe. It was partially acquired for a transaction amounting to €570 million. If in Italy Lukoil started with the acquisition of only five stakes, in The Netherlands the company strove to take the maximum from the very beginning of operations. In this region too, Lukoil already had a network of gas stations. From 2009 onwards, Lukoil was hence able to distribute its own oil products through those filling stations – either its own or those under Lukoil's control.

Source/author: author Andrei Panibratov, Graduate School of Management, St Petersburg State University, Russia

Mini case questions

1   Should Lukoil change its approach to European market entry, since the world financial crisis influenced the oil and gas sector and since those commodities may in addition become increasingly rare in the future? If so, how?
2   What are the chances of Lukoil cooperating with other actors in the European markets? What forms of cooperation would you recommend?

REVIEW QUESTIONS

1   **Explain** the position of the EU in its relations with NAFTA and ASEAN. Compare the objectives of these agreements. What is the strategic role of the EU in relation to them?
2   **Why** does the EU have a particular relationship with ACP countries?
3   **How far** have relations with Asia evolved and why?
4   **Does** Europeanization potentially have a positive impact on globalization?
5   **To what extent** can non-EU international business benefit from doing business in Europe?

ASSIGNMENTS

- **Imagine** that Europeanization and economic integration come to a halt, that nationalism takes over in Europe and breaks up the Euro area and Single Market. Do international trade relations have a role to play in the development of a future European Union? What pressure would the international community exercise?
- **Compare** the working hours in Europe with those in emerging countries. Discuss your findings. Can we expect convergence in the future? What would this imply for international business?
- **Case study assignment:** Read and prepare the case study 'Haier: A Global Chinese Corporation Feels at Home in Germany' in Part IV.
- **Internet exercise:** On www.wto.org, review the most recent negotiations at the WTO. What is the European stance on the most recent topics? Analyse the reasons for these standpoints.

Further reading

Caporale, G.M., Rault, C., Sova, R. and Sova, A. (2009) On the bilateral trade effects of free trade agreements, between the EU-15 and the CEEC-4 countries. *Review of World Economics*, vol. 145, no. 2, pp. 189–206.

Communication from the commission to the European Parliament, the council, the European economic and social committee and the committee of the regions. An integrated Industrial Policy for the Globalisation Era Putting Competitiveness and Sustainability at Front Stage COM(2010)614 SEC(2010)1272.Eur-Lex, Brussels.

European Commission (2010) *European Competitiveness Report 2010*. Accompanying document to the communication from the Commission to the European Parliament, the Council, the European Economic and Social Committee and the Committee of the Regions: An Integrated Industrial Policy for the Globalisation Era Putting Competitiveness and Sustainability at Front Stage [COM (2010) 614} {SEC (2010) 1272}. Eur-Lex, Brussels.

Nicolas, F. (2009) Chinese Direct Investment in Europe: Facts and Fallacies, *International Economics*, June, Chatham House Briefing Paper. London: Royal Institute of International Affairs.

Qureshi, M.S. and Wan, G. (2008) Trade expansion of China and India: threat or opportunity? *World Economy*, vol. 31, no. 10, October, pp. 1327–50.

Ramos, M.P., Bureau, J.-C. and Salvatici, L. (2010) Trade composition effects of the EU tariff structure: beef imports from Mercosur. *European Review of Agricultural Economics*, vol. 37, no.1, pp. 1–26.

INTERNET RESOURCES

Candidate countries' information and status:
http://europa.eu.int/comm/trade/issues/bilateral/regions/candidates/

Delegation of the European Commission in the USA and its website:
http://www.eurunion.org

East–West Institute's site as an example of not-for-profit international networking
for the building of fair, peaceful and prosperous civil societies:
http://www.ewi.info

EU's Europe Aid website:
http://ec.europa.eu/europeaid/where/asia/regional-cooperation/index_en.htm

European aid and support for developing countries:
http://ec.europa.eu/comm./europeaid/index_en.htm

European Industrial Relations Observatory Online:
http://www.eiro.eurofound.eu.int

European Neighborhood Policy:
http://ec.europa.eu/world/enp/index_en.htm

Eurostat's global value chains – international sourcing to China and India:
http://epp.eurostat.ec.europa.eu/statistics_explained/index.php/Global_value_
chains_-_international_sourcing_to_China_and_India

Regionalism: friends or rivals? And more articles, studies and data:
http://www.wto.org

UN information about competition:
http://www.un.org/ecosocdev/geninfo/afrec/vol14no3/afstocks.htm

Gabriele Suder's *Doing Business in Europe* video series (on the SAGE companion
website at http://www.sagepub.co.uk/suder2e and YouTube)

Bibliography

Alden, J. (2002) *U.S. Competition Policy*. Geneva: Freedom Technologies, Inc., ITU
Presentation.

Allegretto, S., Bernstein, J. and Shapiro, I. (2005) *The Lukewarm 2004 Labor Market
Despite some Signs of Improvement, Wages Fell, Job Growth Lagged and Unemployment
Spells Remained Long*. Washington, DC: Economic Policy Institute and Center for
Budget and Policy Priorities.

Blanke, J. and Lopez-Caros, A. (2004) *The Lisbon Review 200': An assessment of Policies and Reforms in Europe.* Cologne/Geneva: World Economic Forum.

Buch, C. (2000) *Financial Market Integration in the US: Lessons from Europe?* Kiel: Kiel Institute for World Economics.

Commission of the European Communities (2005) *EU Report on Millennium Development Goals 2000–2004.* Brussels: Directorate General Development.

Economic Research Service and Foreign Agricultural Service (2005) *Outlook for US Agricultural Trade* 2005, Washington, DC: United States of Department of Agriculture (USDA).

EEC Council Directives 89/429/EEC, *89/369/EEC on the reduction of air pollution from waste-incineration plants,* Directive 2000/76/EEC, Opinion 1998/0289 of 11/10/2000.

EUROFOUND (2000–6), *European foundation for the improvement of living and working conditions 2000–2006,* and *European survey on working time and work-life balance.* Available at: http://www.eiro.eurofound.eu, Dublin.

European Commission (2001) *A Sustainable Europe for a Better World: A European Union Strategy for Sustainable Development,* May, COM(2001)264 final. Luxembourg. European Communities.

European Commission (2002a) *Report on EU Financial Integration,* European Economy Economic Papers No. 171, May. Brussels Economic and Financial Committee (EFC). European Communities.

European Commission (2002b) *Manuscript for Information Brochure,* December. Brussels/Luxembourg. European Communities.

European Commission (2005) *Online Availability of Public Services: How is Europe Progressing?* Luxembourg: Directorate General for Information Society and Media.

European Commission (2011) *Report from the Commission to the European Council Trade and Investment Barriers Report 2011 – Engaging our Strategic Economic Partners on Improved Market Access: Priorities for Action on Breaking Down Barriers to Trade.* Luxembourg. European Communities.

European Communities, *Decision of 21 November 1997 on Code of Conduct Concerning Public Access to Documents of the European Foundation for the Improvement of Living and Working.* Luxembourg. European Communities.

European Union (2010) MEMO/10/423 EU-Korea Free Trade Agreement, Brussels, 17 September. European Communities.

Federal Government of the Federal Republic of Germany (2004) EU sustainable development strategy: position of the Government of the Federal Republic of Germany on the consultation process 2004, Berlin, 1 November.

Gowan, P. and Anderson, P. (eds) (1997) *The Question of Europe.* London: Verso.

IDE-JETRO (1992) Asian International Input-Output Table 1985, *IDE-SDS,* 65.

IDE-JETRO (2006) Asian International Input-Output Table 2000, *IDE-SDS,* 89, 90.

IDE-JETRO (2011) Asian Input-Output Table 2005 (preliminary), *IDE-SDS.*

Keegan, W. and Schlegelmilch, B. (2001) *Global Marketing Management.* London: FT Prentice Hall.

Lukoil Factbook (2009) Available at: http://www.lukoil.com/static_6_5id_2133_.html

McGuire, S. M. Lindeque, J. P. and Suder, G. (2011) Learning and Lobbying: Emerging Market Firms and Corporate Political Activity in Europe. *European Journal of International Management*, vol. 6, no. 2, p. 346

Mercadon S., Welford, R. and Prescott, K. (2001) *European Business*, 4th edn. London: FT Prentice Hall.

OCO Consulting (2005) *Attracting FDI to the US: Challenges in a Global Economy*, September. Chicago, IL: IEDC.

Riedmann, A., Bielenski, H., Szczurowska, T. and Wagner, A. (2006) *Working Time and Worklife Balance in European Companies*. Dublin: EUROFOUND.

Sen, A. (2000a) Competition and demand change in selected Asia Pacific countries. Presentation, Isik University, Isik.

Sen, A. (2000b) How applicable is the European Union experiment for a regional integration form in Asia Pacific. Isik University, Isik.

Smismans, S. (2004) *EU Employment Policy: Decentralization or Centralization Through the Open Method of Coordination?* Florence: Department of Law, European University Institute.

Suder, G. (2007) The municipal solid waste incineration sector in Europe: a study of harmonization and its impact. *International Journal of Environment and Waste Management*, vol. 2, no. 1, pp. 391–405.

Suder, G., Inomata, S., Jormanainen, I. and Meng, B. (2011) International input-output dynamics as a measure of the geography of value distribution across Asia and of market integration in three industries, AJBS Nagoya.

United Nations Conference on Trade and Development (UNCTAD) (2008) World Investment Report: Transnational Corporations and the Infrastructure Challenge. Available at: http://www.unctad.org/en/docs/wir2008_en.pdf

United Nations Conference on Trade and Development (UNCTAD) (2009) World Investment Report: Transnational Corporations, agricultural production and development. New York and Geneva: UNCTAD.

Virmani, A. (2004) *Development of World Economy & Global Governance*, Indian Council for Research on International Economic Relations (ICRIER), virmani.

West, D.M. (2000) *Assessing e-government: The Internet, Democracy, and Delivery by State Federal Governments*. Providence, RI: Brown University.

Williams, J. (2005) *Strategy Driver for International or Global Business* (3 of 5), political factors using the EU as an example, and other topics. Available at: http://www.answers.com/topic/european-union, downloaded November.

World Trade Organization (WTO) (2005) *UNCTAD World FDI Flows in $ Billion* (http://www.unctad.org/ tdistatistics) and *International Trade Statistics* (2006). Geneva: WTO.

PART IV

CORPORATE CASE STUDIES

Airbus: A Catalyst of European Integration

By Professor Gabriele Suder, SKEMA Business School

The first A380 flight announced a European success story that has evolved with the deepening of European integration and the resulting business environment. The European Aerospace and Defence sector is a significant catalyst of an integration that has gained business recognition over time, and that has been business-driven. This case therefore studies the link between the growing role of the European aerospace industry and European integration. 'Defence' was at the very heart of the European settlements after World War II: peacekeeping and security concerns were the main driving force behind post-war economic cooperation[2].

Over time, the EU has set out clear objectives that aim to improve the security and economic prosperity of its members. The Cologne European Council recognized the need for sustained efforts for a competitive and dynamic industrial and technological defence industry in support of Europe's capacity to respond to international crises. At the Lisbon Council, the Heads of State and Government set the strategic goal of becoming the most competitive and dynamic knowledge-based economy in the world within a decade. This message was reinforced at the Barcelona Council, which called for a significant boost in the overall R&D and innovation effort in the Union. More recently still, the Thessaloniki Council decided that the time had come to take concrete steps in the field of defence, of which the aerospace industry is the most integrated part.

Why aerospace? As a high-technology, high skill dual-purpose industry, the European aerospace industry is uniquely placed to contribute significantly to these economic and strategic aims: it is a crucial component in maintaining Europe's industrial and technological capability for:

- transportation
- communication
- observation
- security and
- defence.

Airbus[1] was one of the first firms created as a truly European company. Its main shareholders and stakeholders are four major European nations (Germany, Spain, UK and France). The firm is now one of only two worldwide aircraft manufacturers in the market for large commercial airliners that design, build, sell and provide support for commercial aircraft with a capacity of 100 seats or more. Airbus boasts the most modern and comprehensive airline families in the world and consistently captures about half of all commercial airline orders.

Airbus history

Airbus Industrie, as it was formerly known, began as a consortium of European aviation firms that joined together to compete with American companies such as Boeing and McDonnell Douglas. In the 1960s, European aircraft manufacturers had been competing as much with each other as with the American firms that were already giants in the sector. In the mid 1960s, tentative negotiations commenced that were to give birth to a true European collaboration that, it can be argued, saved a fragmented sector from forecasted decline.

At its very beginning, in September 1967, the British, French and German governments signed a Memorandum of Understanding (MoU) to start the initial development of a 300-seat Airbus A300. This was the second major joint aircraft programme in Europe, preceded only by Concorde, for which no ongoing consortium had been devised.

An earlier announcement had been made in July 1967 but was condemned by the British Aircraft Corporation (BAC). The British government refused to back its proposed competitor, a development of the BAC 1-11, and instead waited to support the Airbus aircraft. In the months following the agreement, both the French and British governments continued to express some doubts about the project. One of the issues was the development and requirement for a new engine that was to be developed by Rolls-Royce, the RB207. In December 1968, the French and British partner companies, Sud Aviation and Hawker Siddeley proposed a revised configuration, the 250-seat Airbus A250. Renamed the A300B, the aircraft would not require new engines, and hence reduced development risks and costs, and the project started to make progress. In 1969, the partnership was shattered by Hawker Siddeley's withdrawal from the project. Given the participation by the British partner up to that point, France and Germany were reluctant to take over its wing design. Finally, the British company agreed to continue as a major subcontractor.

Airbus formed: changing mindsets

Airbus Industrie was set up formally in 1970 following an agreement between Aerospatiale France and Deutsche Aerospace (Germany); they were joined by *CASA* (Construcciones Aeronáuticas SA) of Spain in 1971. Each company would deliver its parts of the plane components as fully equipped, ready-to-fly items. The name *Airbus* was taken from a non-proprietary term used by the airline industry in the 1960s to refer to a commercial aircraft of a certain size and range. The term was linguistically acceptable to both the French and Germans.

In 1972, the A300 took off for its maiden flight. Its first production model, the A300B2, entered service in 1974. Initially, the success of the consortium appeared to be short-lived but, over time and by 1979, 81 aircraft had entered into service and the partners continued their cooperation. The launch of a new aircraft project in 1981 confirmed Airbus as a growing competitor in the aircraft market: the A320 had over 400 orders before its first flight, compared to the 15 pre-orders clocked up by A300 in 1972.

In the meantime, the 1977 merger of Hawker Siddeley with BAC formed British Aerospace (BAe). In 1979, BAe (now BAE SYSTEMS) formally joined the consortium again, taking a 20 per cent stake in it. This left the Germans and French with 38 per cent each, and the Spanish firm with 4 per cent. It was a fairly loose alliance that only significantly changed in 2000 when DASA, Aerospatiale and CASA merged to form EADS. DASA DaimlerChrysler Aerospace AG, which had been founded by Deutsche Aerospace at the end of the 1980s, merged with Aerospatiale-Matra of France and Construcciones Aeronáuticas SA (CASA) of Spain to give birth to the European Aeronautic Defence and Space Company (EADS). Since this merger, the former DASA has operated as EADS Germany. In 2001, BAE and EADS then formed the Airbus Integrated Company. Airbus SAS employs about 57,000 people, mainly in six countries, all located in Europe.

The creation of Airbus SAS coincided with the development of the Airbus A380, as yet the world's largest commercial passenger jet. Airbus was ready for its most ambitious European adventure yet with this economic mega-jumbo.

Forging a common corporate mentality over time

Driven by high R&D costs, aerospace companies started to cooperate much earlier than their counterparts in other sectors. Over several decades, from soon after World War II, firms learned to work together, first to check on each other's activities, for political reasons and finally for reasons of efficiency.

They gradually developed a dense network of joint ventures that served as a basis for a wave of consolidation in the industry at the end of the 1990s. It is noteworthy that, in comparison to this, land system companies and naval shipyards have never reached a similar degree of cooperation in Europe: during the cold war, R&D costs in these sectors were lower and (as far as land armaments are concerned) production runs longer, making purely national programmes and production facilities sustainable. This situation changed with procurement cuts in the early 1990s. The ensuing period, however, has been too short to make up for the delay in production networking over several decades, in particular since almost no intergovernmental programmes had been launched that could have structured industrial cooperation.

The aerospace industry, despite its military origins, realizes more than 70 per cent of its turnover in the civil market. The importance of commercial business is due to a reduction in military orders in Europe, the growth of civil aviation in general and the competitiveness of Airbus in particular.

Airbus is in many ways both the result of and the driving element for cross-border consolidation. First, cooperation within the consortium has led to a considerable *degree of specialization among the partner companies, binding them together* in a core area of activity. Secondly, the transformation of Airbus into an integrated company meant a *wider restructuring of the whole aerospace sector*, including defence activities. Again, this stands in opposition to the land systems or naval shipbuilding sectors where producers are often highly specialized, with little diversification, and are rarely associated with big commercial groups (except in Germany).

A market under pressure

Between 1993 and 1997, a wave of consolidation in the USA led to the creation of aerospace and defence giants with turnovers several times greater than those of the biggest European groups. The only way for Europe's national champions to sustain competition with companies the size of Boeing, Lockheed-Martin and Raytheon was to *pool R&D resources, broaden market access and reform the Airbus system*. The temptation to *move from cooperation to integration* was all the more irresistible because competition with the US was high across both the civil and the defence markets. Since the 1997 MDD-Boeing merger in particular (in which Boeing was hoping to diversify and yield further competitive edge from military interests), European governments actively supported the Europeanization of their aerospace industries.

Historical opportunities and challenges

The early evolutions of European integration gradually introduced freedoms of movement for goods, services, capital and people and the harmonization of most business-related red tape. Today, companies can sell their products anywhere in the Member States and consumers can buy where they want with no penalty; citizens of the Member States can live and work in any other country and their professional qualifications should be recognized there; currencies and capital flow freely between the Member States, and European citizens can use financial services anywhere in the Union. European integration has taken care of professional services such as banking, insurance, architecture and advertising, and these can be offered in any Member State, for use by the citizens of any other Member State.

In particular in 1992, cross-border companies in Europe were given further leeway. A company could organize its structure, or establish subsidiaries or branches, across national borders without any extra costs resulting from different national regulatory requirements on company organization. Specifically, European industry, like that of Aerospace, relies on this point in order to improve distribution of its activities – and increase productivity.

European integration of rules and regulations underlies the relative ease with which Airbus can establish strategic cooperation agreements with firms based in other Member States. In this way, 2002 and 2003 marked two essential events: the adherence of the EU to Eurocontrol, and the signature of a cooperation memorandum between the two parties on 22 December 2003. The cooperation memorandum stimulates five fields of cooperation, all essential to Airbus:

- the settlement of a Single European Sky;
- R&D;
- gathering and data analysis in the fields of air traffic and environment;
- aerial navigation by satellite (like Galileo);
- international cooperation in aerospace fields.

Due to the increasing demand of aerial space capacity, the European Commission also launched a major initiative in the shape of an Advisory Council for Aeronautics Research in Europe (ACARE), launched in 2001, that would guarantee close collaboration between major R&D players in aeronautics.

ACARE defines and updates the Strategic Research Agenda (SRA) that maps out plans for research programmes. The SRA takes account of five principal challenges to competitiveness: quality and economic access, environment, security, safety, and the efficiency of the air transport system in Europe. The agenda thus aims to create innovative tools and initiatives to improve the efficacy of current research, setting up further mechanisms inside the European area of research thanks to additional public and private investment. This agreement is fundamental because it provides a solid basis to strengthen partnerships amongst firms of the aeronautics sector inside Europe that constitute the backbone of Airbus.

These political stimuli have also translated into the possibility, for any company in Europe, to establish stages of its supply chain across European Member State borders, using production factors located or sold in other Member States wherever suitable and economically advantageous. This opportunity has not only generated delocalization, in- and outsourcing, but also contributed to balance out some economic differences between the European states. The firm is able to define and determine a product's specification and how to market it without consideration of national barriers. Thanks to the integrated market, Airbus has the possibility to promote, distribute and sell its products, goods and services to wherever its management finds it desirable or profitable in Europe, without any extra costs other than those due to geography and local preferences, such as costs of broadcasting advertisements in national markets.

Consolidating cooperation

The creation of Airbus and its structure was first organized by Natco, a network of geographically separate specialized sites of manufacturing coordinated by a Central

Entity, that is, one nation named to be responsible for the production of aircraft parts. Airbus Manufacturing manages the production of Airbus aircraft, which takes place at different sites in Europe. Typically, manufacturing is organized as a transnational process, structured around key manufacturing units. Each one is responsible for producing a complete section of the aircraft for delivery to the final assembly lines.

Airbus organizes its structure, operations and manufacturing through Centres of Excellence. These are transnational in several fields and thus represent still greater European corporate integration: Airbus employs around 40,000 people in several European countries. Construction takes place at a number of plants across Europe. Airbus sites are located throughout Europe, while its main factory is situated in Toulouse, France. The two final assembly plants of Airbus are located in Toulouse, France and Hamburg, Germany.

Given distance and diversity, the corporation has worked and is still working to strengthen cooperation, and harmonize the processes, ways of working, procedures, cultural differences and operations for increased productivity. For instance, specially enlarged jets, called 'Beluga', were created to move aircraft parts between the different factories and the assembly plants; the system relies on aircraft capable of carrying entire sections of fuselage of the Airbus aircrafts. This means it is not in use for the A380, which has exceptional width of fuselage and wings; the parts are mainly shipped to Bordeaux, France, and then transported to Toulouse (via a specially enlarged road) for final assembly.

Case Study Figure 1   *Airbus A380 (by permission of Airbus SAS 2010)*

Civilian and military product innovation

Over its existence, Airbus has developed from the role of challenger to that of market leader in both civilian and military sectors, and has profited from unique integration based on EU history and political will.

While the civilian Airbus product line started with the A300, a shorter variant of it – known as the A310 – was also conceived to confirm market presence. Airbus then launched the very successful A320 with its innovative fly-by-wire control system. The A318 and A319 followed as shorter derivatives with some of the latter under construction for the corporate *biz-jet* market (Airbus Corporate jet). A stretched version known as the A321 proved competitive with later models of the Boeing 737.

In January 1999, the Airbus Military SAS was launched to conceive and support development and production of a turboprop powered military transport aircraft (the Airbus Military A400M). The aircraft represents a joint development of seven NATO members, that is, Belgium, France, Germany, Luxembourg, Spain, Turkey and the UK, and is an alternative to the C-130 Hercules. Longer-range products in civil aircraft, the twin-jet A330 and the four-jet A340, have efficient wings enhanced by winglets. The Airbus A340-500 excels with an operating range of 13,921 km (8650 nautical miles) – the second longest *range of any commercial jet* after the Boeing 777-200LR (with a range of 17,446 km, or 9420 nautical miles). Here, integration is further illustrated inside civilian and military planes with the use of fly-by-wire technologies and the common cockpit systems in use throughout the aircraft family.

International challenges

Boeing has continually protested over the support that Airbus receives from the governments of the partner nations. In July 2004, for instance, Airbus was accused of abusing a 1992 non-binding agreement covering launch aid. Airbus has received launch aid from European governments, repayable through strict commercial contracts and (the company contends) fully compliant with the 1992 agreement and WTO rules. The agreement allows up to 33 per cent of the programme cost to be met through government loans, fully repayable within 17 years with interest and royalties. These loans were held at a minimum interest rate equal to the cost of government borrowing plus 0.25 per cent, which would be below market rates available to Airbus without government support. In 2010, the WTO ruled that Boeing's complaint about excessive subsidies to Airbus was justified, with the USA claiming that government subsidies to Airbus included $1.5 billion in R&D subsidies, $1.7 billion in infrastructure subsidies, $2.2 billion in equity infusions, and $15 billion in launch aid (comprising $4 billion for the A380).

Airbus, on the other hand, argues that some of the (directly or indirectly) government-funded military contracts awarded to Boeing (the second largest US defence contractor) are in effect a form of subsidy (see the Boeing KC-767 military contracting scandal). The significant US government support of technology development via

NASA (National Aeronautics and Space Administration) also provides significant support to Boeing, as do the large tax breaks offered to Boeing that are suspected of violating the 1992 agreement and WTO rules. For its recent products, such as the 787, Boeing has also been offered substantial support from local and state governments. Airbus and Boeing are also in dispute regarding the American company's offering of the 787 Dreamliner. EU trade officials are questioning the funds provided by the Japanese government and Japanese companies for the launch of this aircraft. In March 2011, the WTO ended a six-year-old lawsuit judging that some $5.3 billion of US subsidies to Boeing, much of it in export subsidy and tax breaks, was illegal.

The competition is fierce. In 2003, Airbus delivered more jet-powered airliners than Boeing for the first time in its 33-year history. With a market share of 50.7 per cent, Airbus confirmed its (close) leadership again in 2010 for aircraft orders and deliveries, mainly for its 320 (versus the B373 for Boeing). With 510 units delivered in one year, Airbus has excelled, in particular, in emerging markets and the low-fare sector.

After losing supremacy to America in the battle of commercial airliner sales in the 1950s and 1960s, Europe seems to have regained the upper hand. Industry analysts widely attribute this to Airbus's more efficient product line, compared to many of Boeing's older designs; the 737, for example, still uses components designed in the 1980s. The 747 was designed in the late 1960s and the 757 and 767 were conceived in the late 1970s. Boeing claims the Boeing 777 has outsold its Airbus counterparts, which include the entire A340 series, as well as the A330-300. The smaller A330-200 competes with the 767, and dominated that class until the introduction of the 787.

Currently, there are around 4540 Airbus aircraft in service in the A320 range alone. But Airbus products are still outnumbered six to one by in-service Boeings (there are over 8000 Boeings in service, altogether). Airbus entered the modern jet airliner market relatively late (in 1972 compared to 1958 for Boeing) and its sales are mainly civilian (as compared to the numerous Boeing aircraft used by the military in the USA and other countries). However, the company has won a relatively greater share of orders and delivered more aircraft in 2003, 2004 and 2005 than its main competitor, and broke its deliveries record in 2010.

More than just commercial competition, the challenges for Airbus and Boeing are frequently perceived as a political and geopolitical quarrel. In this duopoly, Airbus is an emblem of EU influence on the economic and geopolitical scene and has helped Europe gain politico-economic influence, improve its image as a competitive market and build a true identity.

Key success factors

At Airbus, European values and the integration of market, labour, capital and services represent a tool in the search for efficiencies, such as human resources (HR). The group's corporate culture and philosophy are critical success factors in its own integration which goes hand-in-hand with that of its home region.

Internal corporate communications are heavily based on European values and identity, and, with these, a feeling of Europeanism is created internally. Internally,

Airbus promotes a strong message to staff to get involved in multicultural teams, cooperating and sharing experiences, to move internationally and to recognize and use beneficial differences as complementarities. The resulting feeling of cohesion and appreciation of diversity is actively used in initiatives that aim to motivate people to participate actively in company integration. For instance, personal training sessions are regularly organized for managers and operational staff to enhance people's inter-cultural management skills and career development: how to collaborate efficiently with those many different cultures that make up the corporation.

Airbus' corporate culture is built on innovation, creativity and free-thinking. Our organization reinforces transnational working patterns while preserving the diver-sity of cultures and languages which has proved a key asset in the company's development and growth. (Source: http://www.airbus.com/about/philosophy.asp)

Cultural diversity and European progressive integration constitute a value to the company.

The Airbus Company culture

Proud of our past

Thirty years of European partnership producing a family of aircraft

Making history with new technology

Changing the face of the industry'

'Confidence in a challenging future

One organization working together as a truly integrated team

Taking advantage of and developing our cultural diversity

Taking a leading part on the world stage

Designing and manufacturing the world's largest commercial airliner

(Source: http://www.airbus.com/careers/life/company.asp)

Opportunity creation in Human Resources

The Human Resources Director of the Central Entity explains the extent to which Airbus's HR management is based on EU-created opportunities in the following interview:

Question: What sort of working environment does Airbus offer?

Airbus strongly believes in the multicultural value of its workforce. With 45,000 employees, representing more than 30 nationalities speaking 20 languages, we are creating a business culture of openness, originality, drive and enthusiasm. We do not believe in forcing everyone into a company mould. Our cultural diversity is a major business advantage – enabling us to work closely with a wide range of customers, understanding their needs and speaking their own languages. We offer exciting opportunities for international 'players' who are able to adapt to a multicultural team, enjoy working on a project basis and are willing to learn from others, while contributing their own ideas and experience.

The transfer of knowledge and cross-cultural cooperation are key factors in our success. We promote cross-functional and international mobility and we seek to recruit graduates with an international mindset. International experience is increasingly needed for a successful career within Airbus.

Question: What does cultural diversity mean at Airbus?

Over the past 30 years, we have mastered the art of creating effective teams of individuals with different nationalities, backgrounds and skills. Airbus boasts at least 80 different nationalities and 20 languages amongst its employees.

We do not try to standardise our employees. On the contrary, we encourage individual originality, drive and enthusiasm. Preserving diversity also presents a key business advantage. It enables us to work closely with customers by understanding their needs and speaking their language.

Question: What are the opportunities for working internationally?

Within Airbus, there are a number of opportunities to work internationally – via transnational work teams, exchange programmes and international transfers. Vacancies are advertised internally across the Airbus organization worldwide. Transnational and cross-functional moves are encouraged throughout the company.

(*Source*: Interview release of Airbus.com: http://www.airbus.com/careers, information L. Darnis, February 2005)

The location of Airbus' headquarters in Toulouse is not random: the main aerospace schools (ENAC, Sup Aero, etc.) are located in this attractive south-western city of France which boasts engineers from all over Europe. Airbus Central Entity and Airbus France are also both located in Toulouse.

Cooperation, integration and innovation

Of equal importance to borderless HR management for Airbus is borderless innovativeness. The one may go in hand with the other through a diversity of educational backgrounds, cultures and ways of thinking and doing.

The need for innovation and continuous technological development is crucial for customer satisfaction and company competitiveness. Because competitors and customers are relatively scarce in this market, research and development programmes represent very heavy costs. To respond to this problem, the European Commission decided to get involved with the STAR 21 programme, launched in 2002. STAR 21 deals with five prime objectives:

- Opening markets with a single set of competition rules and relaxation of the 'Buy American Act'.
- Developing a coordinated research policy in order to secure EUR100 billion of R&D finance over 20 years.
- Creating and extending the '*single sky*' with the EU as the decision-making and control authority in all areas of civil aviation.
- Harmonizing operational requirements, equipment and defence budget, and reduction of capability deficits.
- Developing a coherent space policy along with the necessary funding based on the Galileo and GMES (Global Monitoring for Environment and Security) projects.

The harmonization of industrial policy favours innovation and R&D, and clearly helps industry to maintain market share. For example, the A380 competes directly with the B747 (the B version being the longest aircraft ever, test-flown for the first time in March 2011) on long-distance carriers with a far bigger passenger capacity (from 550 to 800 passengers). Due to a high degree of innovation, it is also an economical aircraft. In the middle-distance carriers market, the 7E7 by Boeing, launched in 2008, competes with the A330 and carries between 200 and 250 passengers. With kerosene consumption 20 per cent lower than that of its competitors for a 0.85 Mach speed, kilometre price per passenger is decreased.

Moving towards alternatives, Lufthansa, the German airline, in 2011 started the world's first scheduled daily flights specifically based on the use of biofuel blended jet fuel, adding further challenges to both corporations' race for innovation. TAM, Brazil's largest airline, had run the first Jatropha-based biofuel flight in 2010 and is turning to alternative solutions.

Further challenges also arise from emerging countries such as India that experienced a 43 per cent growth of passenger transport for civil aviation alone between 2008 and 2010. Its Hindustan Aeronautics Limited (HAL) is an emerging player in the defence sector, ranked 34 in the top 100 defence aircraft producers worldwide and benefiting from strong ties into Indian R&D competencies. For private jets, Airbus's private jet company record for 2010, delivering 15 planes worth US$1.5 billion, confirms the role of China as the firm's fastest-growing and most challenging market in terms of innovation and customization.

European and international suppliers

The quality and flexibility of subcontractors and suppliers is crucial because they provide Airbus with all parts of the final product. An aeroplane is made up of thousands of parts or components provided by different firms: systems for engines, electronics (for semi-conductors for instance) and information technology (IT). Around a thousand subcontractors are involved in manufacturing an aircraft.

The corporation has links with suppliers from all over the world. For instance, some parts supplied in 2003/4 came from:

- USA: engines in collaboration with SNECMA, security, navigation system;
- Europe: electronics, development, fuselage, opening door system;
- Asia Pacific: front doors, access doors, wings, body, tools;
- Africa: cables.

For the very large A380, Airbus has reorganized its purchasing policy by widening some of its vetting of tender for new suppliers. It has also tried to minimize the number of suppliers. The firm's aim is to negotiate as best as possible in order to have the most cost-efficient products. This means building up real partnerships and the evolution of European integration and its administrative procedures increasingly facilitate this process. On the supplier side, EU integration offers suppliers three main options for cost and operational efficiency:

- Joining the firm, to reduce costs and benefiting from each other's capabilities.
- Relocating their production into Eastern EU countries, to use lower-cost labour.
- Offering innovative products to the firm, to differentiate themselves from competitors.

In the supply chain process, the integrated system chosen by Airbus aims to reduce costs for both parties. Programmes, operations and functions are thus transversal and transnational, and are reinforced by means of conference calls, video conferencing, regular shuttles, networking and air-bridges from site to site, e-portals and e-room collaboration.

IT tools infrastructure: linking people and knowledge for greater and faster integration

IT plays a key role in corporate integration, particularly in strengthening transnational cooperation and enhancing reactivity and constant and regular communication and exchanges. Airbus has created an integrated internal portal named 'Airbus People' and e-rooms offering all employees a shared, secure collaborative space to exchange data, documents and planning. Airbus People and other portals open to external stakeholders (suppliers, customers, etc.) are now the basis and structure of 'Airbus Collaboration'. These tools provide the drive to harmonize ways of working, processes and procedures, documents, messages and identity.

Altogether, Airbus makes extensive use of portal technology to work with three different groups: the air transport community (airlines and legal authorities), worldwide suppliers (subcontractors and forwarders), and employees and on-site subcontractors.

The company's portals promote cultural integration, enable process optimization and facilitate information systems harmonization and file sharing.

Sup@irWorld Solutions

Sup@irWorld Solutions, one of the main integration projects, provides web-based collaborative tools to enhance working efficiency between Airbus and its suppliers. Its solutions have been running since March 2005. It provides solutions for integration internally and externally by harmonizing all the procurement processes on each international site and entity. With such tools and solutions, Airbus's suppliers obtain one common strategic policy and objective, whichever site they deal with. Internally, this tool and shared solutions enhance inter-site cooperation, offering a single way of working for all the Airbus entities.

Airbus manages this tool as one policy regarding procurement, customer relationships, human resources and other fields – creating a single point of contact, a working place and a source of information for its corporate activities and its stakeholders.

Sup@irWorld covers all exchanges for both flying and non-flying materials, goods and services and acts as the 'backbone' of both the procurement channel for Airbus People and in the Airbus supply chain through its supplier portal. Sup@irWorld consists of four interlinked domains, which address four key channels with suppliers: sourcing, e-procurement for non-flying goods, e-collaboration for flying goods and procurement master data management.

- *Sourcing*   The sourcing domain allows current and potential suppliers to register with Airbus and tells buyers about their products and capabilities. Suppliers and buyers can also exchange information about requirements through a secure connection.
- *BuySide*   This e-procurement domain covers the purchase of general, non-flying goods and services from initial request through to final approval of payment. By simplifying and standardizing procurement processes, BuySide has significantly reduced administrative costs and purchasing lead times. Requisitioners order from electronic catalogues, which are created and updated by suppliers, and which Airbus hosts free of charge. Automation has reduced the time required to process an order from five days to two hours, and cut delivery time from 72 to 24 hours. BuySide automates specific e-procurement terms and conditions, resulting in purchasing that is automatically fully compliant with the contracts set by the European Aeronautic Defence and Space Company, which owns 80 per cent of Airbus.
- *eSupplyChain collaboration*   This domain allows Airbus and suppliers of flying goods to collaborate through the entire supply-chain cycle. They can exchange information in real time about forecasts, purchase orders, physical logistics, and the receipt and storage of goods and invoices. Airbus sends immediate notification of changes in requirements or quantities to its suppliers, so that procurement plans can quickly adapt to production changes. It tracks the shipping of purchased goods after they have left the supplier. The supplier has to commit himself to the procurement plan or

propose some recovery plan. Inventory is reduced and visibility on forecast and the ability to track logistics flows also reduces the risk that shortages and late deliveries pose for manufacturing. Reduced risk also means greater assurance that schedules are met for final delivery of airplanes to customers.

- *Found@tion* By consolidating data from 70 different databases in Airbus across France, Germany, the UK and Spain, this domain gives the company, for the first time, a comprehensive view of its suppliers. The constantly updated database provides cross-referenced information about the nature and quality of the suppliers' products and services, purchasing history, comprehensive reporting, and the status of the approval process for suppliers and their products. These services are the cornerstone of the BuySide and eSupplyChain operations.

Sup@irWorld gives Airbus a common way of dealing with suppliers across the organization. The company acts as a single integrated entity in its procurement and presents a single face to its suppliers.

Airbus: 'A European adventure'

The development of Airbus has required gradual cohesion and cooperation over time in concordance with the evolution of the Single Market. The development of the A380, the world's largest passenger jet, has required significant, if not unique, investments in skills, research and technology. Industrial cooperation in the EU is the basis for the success of new aerospace products within an intensively competitive global market. The former French President, Jacques Chirac, expressed this in March 2005 at the official unveiling of the Airbus A380:

> *The launch of this giant of the airways is the crowning achievement of a fantastic human and industrial adventure. A European adventure of perseverance, innovative spirit and ardent determination ... Today I share the enthusiasm, the emotion and the deserved pride of all the men and women who are part of this immense industrial success story: the engineers, journeymen, assemblers, sales and administrative staff of Airbus and its suppliers. All of you, who have given the best of yourselves to bring this aeroplane into being, I pay you the warmest homage. Whether you work in Germany, the United Kingdom, Spain, France or other countries, notably in Europe, it is your common dream that is taking shape here at AéroConstellation, the A380 assembly site. This is the culmination, I know, of years of effort, imagination, sacrifice and willpower ... First of all, it is the success of a European company: EADS, the parent company of Airbus with BAE Systems, is probably the first truly European company, in its ownership structure, its working methods and the common culture that has developed between the French, Germans, Spanish, British and their partners from other countries of the EU. It is also the success of an innovative Europe. A Europe where every nation contributes what it does best. A Europe that is demonstrating its capacity to master and integrate the most advanced technology. (Source: http://www.ambafrance-au.org/article.php3?id_article=888)*

Questions

1 Why is a globally competitive aerospace industry central to the achievement of Europe's economic and political objectives?
2 How does Airbus manage corporate integration? As Airbus stands for the European Union microcosm with all its cultural differences, challenges, stakes, etc., what are the key success factors and barriers that helped Airbus in this challenge?
3 Transnationality is a main characteristic of Europeanized firms. Identify the key operational assets of Airbus.
4 Why has innovation become crucial for the European agenda? Find examples in the Airbus case.

Notes

1 The author would like to thank Laetitia Darnis, Ceram, SKEMA and Airbus, for their valuable assistance by providing the material for this case study.
2 This case is based on documentary research: internal information and documents, web and press articles. It is exclusively descriptive and analytical. Most material was directly made accessible by Airbus. Its first version was published in 2007.

Investment Consulting in Eastern Europe with Excedea

By Dr Martin Seppälä, CEO and Partner at Excedea; Hanken Swedish School of Economics and Business Administration

I still clearly remember the first time I was in Latvia. The year was 2000. I had been selected for a consulting project at very short notice, and flew to the capital Riga the next day. At the time, I had been a management consultant in Helsinki, Finland, for only a year, and the Latvian assignment was one of the first projects where my role was more central. Our Latvian client was a large former state-owned monopoly, whose management was still very heavily politically connected.

For a young Finnish consultant, everything about Latvia seemed different. Big companies placed guards (in dark green army uniforms) by all entrances, and all the buildings seemed to have an 'old world' feeling to them. As we approached the large oak doors of the company's headquarters, our project manager (who had some experience of doing business in Latvia) gave us some final advice: 'First, these people really value decades of experience, so don't bring up your age or limited time with our company. Second, you should know that in this country men don't shake hands with women.' A few seconds after these words, the large oak doors were opened, and we proceeded to meet the management of the company in a large and gloomy hall-like room. And, indeed, following what I later learned was commonly accepted business behaviour in Latvia at the time, the women in the room did not make any effort to shake our hands. My colleague and I firmly shook the hands of the 60+ Latvian male executives and shyly nodded towards the women in the room (some of whom we later found out were also high-ranking executives).

After that initial trip to Latvia, I ended up returning there about 40 times during the next three years. I began to understand the Latvian mentality and all the challenges and opportunities linked with an economy in rapid transition. Although the people and the culture could have been described as very different from a Nordic or western perspective, I realized that these differences were mostly about people adapting to the economic environment; in private, people had basically the same sources of joy and sorrow as anywhere else in the world. Perhaps the biggest differences I experienced in Latvia compared to the Nordic countries were related to a male-dominated culture and a clear lack of trust in business relations. Later, I realized that these are not only typical characteristics for Latvia, but for Eastern Europe in general.

Trust is something that is especially reserved only for very close relationships, and it often takes a long time to build up to a level which in the Nordic countries would be considered normal in business relations.

After finalizing my last project in Latvia, my career headed more westwards, with work in Sweden, the UK and France. Even though these working environments were much closer to 'home', I couldn't help feeling that something was missing. In Western Europe, people seem to be more satisfied with their standard of living and this, in my view, can result in a sort of lack of inspiration. What I had instead experienced in Latvia was a sort of unbiased energy, which could be felt among the young, local managers (although less so among the politically elected 'old dinosaurs'), and which gave an edge to all business transactions.

Now, over 10 years later, I am the CEO of Excedea, a strategy and investment advisory company specializing in Eastern Europe.[1] The 100+ projects that my team and I have delivered over the last five years have brought me to places like Macedonia, Belarus, Kazakhstan, Azerbaijan and Ukraine (to mention some of the more exotic locations of our projects. Naturally, we have also been active in countries such as Russia, Poland, the Baltics, etc.). The role of an advisor like Excedea is to be a reliable source of information and to mainly advise our Western European clients. In practice, this means analysing markets, creating market entry and operational strategies, doing background checks on both companies and people and also often assisting in acquisitions.

The last five years have had an interesting pattern. It seems that most investors follow the same logic and share the same interests at any given time. In 2005–2006, everyone's focus was on Ukraine. The country had just gone through the 'orange revolution', where western-minded politicians overthrew the existing Russian-minded leaders. As a result, many western companies wanted to enter the market, based on the belief that this would result in a rapid positive development of the economy and society (as we know, history has later shown that the truth is more complicated than that). In 2006–2007, the same investors started to shift their focus towards Bulgaria and Romania, who became EU members at the beginning of 2007. Investments were pouring in, and reliable advisors were needed to make sure the targets were carefully selected and proper caution was used in all strategic moves. Later in 2007 and at the beginning of 2008, the investment hype was extremely strong. Companies went further and further to look for higher returns on investment and many of my team's projects were set in countries such as Azerbaijan, Kazakhstan, Georgia and rural Russia. In 2008–9, however, the global recession started to kick in, and the companies and investors that were clients of Excedea suddenly didn't need any additional risks in far away and seemingly exotic places. Instead, the demand turned to securing profitability of investments already held, and for some industries and firms, we saw a 'return to safe single market' in the related strategies. Also, boosting of sales and restructuring of market-facing efforts were in high demand. With recovery, the pendulum has swung again and the appetite for new risk is back. My team and I are again working with acquisitions and expansions to new markets (including Eastern Europe's true 'final frontier', i.e. Belarus).

All in all, my experience is that Western Europe has some very exciting neighbours in the east. Regardless of the global economic situation, it is clear that Eastern Europe is growing and will play an important role in the development of the entire continent. It is quite likely that the Eastern European countries will gradually catch up with the West in terms of living standards and GDP, at least the ones within the EU that benefit from relatively large subsides and unlimited access to Western European markets. This means good business opportunities, almost regardless of the industry or field of activity. Even so, the deeply rooted corrupt and inefficient ways may well take at least one generation to wipe out (in many countries, people are still relatively poor and the temptation to take illegal short cuts is very high). Hence, anyone aspiring to do business in the region will need to be aware of the local cultural peculiarities and risks. Personal contacts and diligent analysis are always needed in order to make a successful business. Unfortunately, statistics cannot always be trusted and everything needs to be verified and double-checked. Owning a controlling majority in the target business is usually a must and organizing strict corporate governance procedures is advisable. Finally, if something seems too good to be true, it probably is.

Finally, let me mention a striking example of the conquest of consumer markets in Eastern Europe. In 2005–7, my team and I were heavily involved in working for the management team of a large Nordic producer of consumer goods. The producer is a leader in its niche and is known for producing high priced and high quality products for premium consumers.

Our client had been active in Russia and some other Eastern European countries within the EU, but they didn't do any business in large countries like Ukraine, Romania and Kazahkstan. The task of our team was to analyse the markets and create a strategy for how the clients' products could reach the leading position they had in other markets, where the client had been active for a longer time.

After months of gathering and analysing official (and unofficial) customs and statistics data, interviewing hundreds of consumers and industry experts and meeting tens of wholesalers and resellers in each country, we were able to present some surprising results for our client: it turned out that in most of the markets analysed, this client's products were being widely sold. Our client had no idea about this, and they had never shipped anything to these markets. Instead, their products were bought through bigger wholesalers in Russia, and transported through customs with incorrect (low-tariff) customs labels (and probably sometimes without any customs declaration whatsoever) before being sold on to the retailers. In some of the markets, the products were sold in high-end consumer shops and, in one market, the brand even had stronger price and brand position than in the markets where our client was actively controlling their marketing efforts. In the end, our recommendation was to gradually establish own imports and good contacts with the high-end retailers, while trying to avoid hurting the already strong market positions that had been established through the uncontrolled grey imports!

Indeed, the past few years have been a historic time for Europe, and we should take the opportunity to benefit from this continued development, both economically and culturally. At least, for me, what started in those gloomy Latvian halls some 10 years ago, has led me to many experiences I would not have dreamed of having otherwise. I hope the coming years will bring more of these adventures and opportunities as European integration continues.

Questions

1 What developments of the European business environment does the CEO of Excedea note?
2 What does EU enlargement imply for business consultancy?
3 What FDI flows does the CEO of Excedea observe, and why?
4 What will be the future of FDI in Europe?
5 What are the opportunities and challenges when focusing on increasingly Eastern markets?

Note

1 For further information, see http://www.excedea.com; see also Suder's *Doing Business in Europe* video series on the SAGE Website and YouTube for illustrations of this case.

The Expansion into Europe of Multi-Latinas: A New Breed of Competitors

By Albert Schram, PhD, Maastricht University School of Business and Economics and Ionara da Costa, PhD, UNU-MERIT, Maastricht

Although Indian and Chinese companies are better known for expanding into Europe and buying up assets, a new breed of multinationals (MNCs) has appeared: the multi-latinas (MLs), or multinational companies owned by Latin Americans. The Boston Consulting Group (2009) identified 100 MLs with yearly revenues over USD500 million. Among those, 34 are Brazilian, 28 are Mexican and 21 are Chilean. The largest seven of those make up more than half the revenue.

The underlying reasons for the emergence of MLs are the solid economic growth in many Latin American economies, and the expansion of the middle class. During the last two decades, Latin America has been growing at less than double digit rates, but despite several crises most economies have shown 4–5 per cent average growth during prolonged periods. Five countries – Brazil, Mexico, Chile, Peru and Colombia – now have investment grade ratings, which make the cost of capital for national as well as foreign investors substantially lower.

What propelled MLs to venture into other markets was, first, that after the liberalization of the 1990s they found themselves in a new competitive environment with their own backyard under threat, and, second, the saturation of national markets despite strong growth, as Latin American markets are rather small. In the current economic crisis, MLs have been more exposed to drops in revenues than other MNCs, but their strong financial position will probably allow them to bounce back quickly.

Compared to other MNCs in rapidly developing economies, state ownership in MLs is minimal, and most MLs started out, and remain, as family-owned companies to some degree. By contrast, the capital of Chinese MNCs, for example, is 69 per cent state-owned. Furthermore, MLs have a strong regional focus, and dominate in their home Latin American markets. MLs represent a wide range of industries, whereas Indian MNCs, for example, are concentrated in relatively few industries, with a focus on manufacturing, pharmaceuticals and IT. Through dealing with macro-economic instability and a complex regulatory and political environment in Latin America, MLs have bred focus, flexibility and resilience.

MLs have a number of distinguishing characteristics, which allows them to potentially expand rapidly into Europe:

1   Large family ownership and strong visionary leadership.
2   Operational discipline and innovative technologies.
3   Business model innovation.
4   Low indebtedness and good financials.
5   Cultural and linguistic affinity with Europe, and previous contacts with Europe.

Out of the 70 MLs we have identified based on different sources, 26 have established units in Europe, of a total of 87 subsidiaries in the region. Four cases of expansion into Europe by MLs are illustrative: CEMEX (cement, Mexico), Pollo Campero (fast food, Guatemala), Viña Concho y Toro (wine, Chile) and Sabó (car parts, Brazil).

The cement industry is highly concentrated and CEMEX is one of the three largest cement producers in the world, along with France's Lafarge and the Swiss-based Holcim. CEMEX is one of the most remarkable corporate success stories emerging from Latin America, and in fact from emerging economies in general. It is a top cement company in major markets across the world, including the USA, Spain, Egypt and the Philippines. With 16 subsidiaries, including an innovation centre in Switzerland, Cemex has the strongest presence in Europe amongst the 26 MLs we have identified that have productive presence in the region. Its growth strategy has been executed by acquisition, frequently targeting underperforming corporations with a potential to be restructured and streamlined 'the CEMEX way'. In its home market, it has a market share of 90 per cent. The company has put great effort into e-enabling all its operations, achieving high efficiency in production, business-to-business trade and logistics. All companies acquired by CEMEX are to be called CEMEX, and adopt the 'CEMEX way'. Another company-specific advantage is in marketing. CEMEX realized that for a large share of its market, cement was not a bulk commodity, but rather a consumer good sold by the bag. While other companies are selling cement, CEMEX is selling a middle-class 'dream' of owning a house, and building solutions to families, with appropriate financing.

A milestone in CEMEX's internationalization was the expansion into Spain in 1992, 500 years after Spain's colonization of Latin America began. CEMEX took over the two biggest Spanish cement companies, Valenciana and Sanson, for €1.5 billion, making this the largest takeover in the cement industry up to then. Although there were many operational risks, this was offset by a number of benefits:

1   CEMEX could deploy cement output from Spain and export it from Europe to the USA, in order to bypass punitive US import duties on Mexican cement.
2   It facilitated access to capital markets.
3   It allowed debt consolidation, saving about €80 million in interest payments a year.
4   Compañía Valanciana de Cementos became the umbrella-holding corporation for all future CEMEX international acquisition.

CEMEX also took over cement companies in the UK (RMC in 2005 for USD5.8 billion), Australia (Rinker in 2006 for the impressive USD13 billion) and many others in the USA, making developed country markets a source of one third of its cash flow, and making the company less dependent on volatile emerging markets. As *The Economist* noted: 'Queen Victoria, whose subjects built or financed much of Latin America's infant infrastructure, would not have been amused' (30 September 2004).

Pollo Campero (PC) is another case which shows the strong growth potential of multi-latinas. It has more than 7000 employees and more than 260 franchised restaurants in Central America, Mexico, the USA, Europe (Madrid) and Asia (Shanghai and Jakarta), with average sales of USD1.8 million per restaurant. The chain has grown from operating in three countries in 1994, to 11 countries in 2007. First, PC followed its customers along the traditional immigration route to US cities. Customers were attracted to superior flavouring and country-rooted branding. In fact, the flights from Guatemala to Los Angeles were called the PC flights, due to the dominant smell of fried chicken in the airplanes brought by Guatemalan families. PC was asked to use scent-proof packaging. In 2007, it made a deal to hire restaurant space from Walmart stores in the USA.

In its home market in Guatemala, PC started as a downstream retail component of an investment company's poultry-farming operations. In its branding in Guatemala, PC has given a lot of attention to corporate social responsibility and has provided humanitarian assistance in the wake of natural disasters. Expanding into the US market allowed it to find new markets with similar consumer characteristics, reduced currency risks and exposure to economic volatility.

Expansion into Europe went through Spain. The only comparable restaurant chain in Spain is Kentucky Fried Chicken. In 2000, it established a strategic alliance with an experienced Spanish fast-food company, Tele Pizza. PC integrated Tele Pizza corners into its restaurants, and Tele Pizza was obliged to reciprocate in all its Spanish locations. The groups can be considered more complementary than competitive, and PC products could be home-delivered by the Tele Pizza's scooter fleet. Earlier competitors, KFC and Pizza Hut, had also used the formula of combined restaurants. PC's objective was to operate about 50 outlets in Spain as soon as possible. The success of PC in Spain has attracted a lot of attention, and requests for franchises all over Europe.

Viña Concha y Toro shows the power of a market diversification strategy. It owns the third most famous wine brand in the world, after Gallo (California) and Hardy's (Australia). Its export strategy has focused on market diversification. It was driven to expand internationally due to the low per capita consumption in its home market, Chile. One of the company's main achievements in the past few years has been its growth in the European market. Increasing revenues in Europe have been originating largely from sales growth of about 15 per cent in Scandinavian countries and Eastern Europe and about 6 per cent in the UK. Viña Concha y Toro's strength in foreign markets is the result of decades of work dedicated to building strong sales relationships with distributors. It has opened its European distribution office in the UK. It has taken advantage of a shift in the world wine market to new world wines, in particular in those markets where wines from traditional wine-producing markets could be contested. Viña Concha y Toro has developed a number of wine brands such as Casillero del Diablo, which are easily recognizable even for inexperienced consumers.

Sabó is an example of a truly multi-national company. It is probably not as well known as the previous companies discussed, or as Brazilian MNCs, like Petrobras, Embraer and Vale. This may be due to the fact that Sabó produces auto parts, having car makers as their clients instead of final consumers. Yet, this Brazilian company is one of the most internationalized companies in the country, and occupies the 37th place in the *América Economía*'s ranking of the 60 largest MLs. In addition to its home country, Sabó is present in eight countries, including Argentina, the USA, Germany and Hungary. With five units in Europe, Sabó is among the MLs with a strong presence in the region. It has plants in Germany, Austria and Hungary, the latter being the home country of its founder, José Sabó; and technical commercial offices in Italy and the UK. Sabó began its internationalization from Europe, as it followed General Motors as a supplier for its operations in Europe, Opel. In 1993, Sabó had already acquired the German-based Kako, taking over three plants in Germany and one in Austria. Sabó's success in expanding abroad can be related to three factors: first is its focus on a niche market (sealing and conduction for the automotive industry); second is its aggressive strategy for international expansion, which is considered as a way to survive the increased competition in both its home and international market; and third is its smooth process of succession, a major problem for many family-owned companies.

Questions

1 What are the main characteristics of each industry, in terms of ownership and capital expenditure?
2 What kind of market entry mode is preferred by each of the four companies? How is this related to the characteristics of products, home markets and competitive environments?
3 How sensitive are the sales of these companies to economic downturns or upturns in Europe? When can one expect acquisitions of further expansion? In the long run, how sensitive are sales to aging population effects?
4 What have been the key opportunities for each of these four companies to enter the European market?
5 What are the key skills for managers of these companies in Europe?
6 Constitute or download a list of multi-latinas for analysis. In the future, given demographic and socioeconomic developments in Europe, what kind of MLs would you expect to expand into Europe? Why?

Bibliography

Boston Consulting Group (2009) *The 2009 BCG Multilatinas. A Fresh Look at Latin America and How a New Breed of Competitors are Reshaping the Business Landscape.* Available at: http://www.bcg.com/documents/file27236.pdf

Da Costa, I. (2009) *Database of MLs in Europe* (UNU-MERIT). *América Economía,* April, p. 24. Available at: http://www.americaeconomia.com/revista/ediciondigital.aspx?edition=1081

Inter-American Development Bank (2009) *From Multilatinas to Global Latinas: The New Latin American Multinationals – A Compilation of Case Studies.* Available at: http://www.iadb.org/intal/intalcdi/PE/2009/03415.pdf

All rights and permissions have been obtained by the authors of this case study.

The European Market for Schunk: An Audit of Europeanization

By Professor Gabriele Suder, SKEMA Business School and Matthias Poguntke, GGS

Introduction

The German engineering company Schunk GmbH & Co. KG (Schunk) has been operating internationally ever since the early 1980s.[1] However, it took them over 35 years before they first crossed their home market's borders. Today, Schunk exports to 50 nations, owns 22 sales offices abroad and produces or carries out engineering assignments on three continents. Most of its investments primarily target markets and locations within the European Union.

In the context of the global economic crisis, the hyper-internationalization of activity in the sector and the increasingly wide integration of the European market, Heinz-Dieter Schunk, the founder's son and CEO of the Schunk holding, had to decide upon the development of the firm's international strategy; he is the company's Senior General Manager and manages the company together with his daughter, Kristina Schunk, and his son, Henrik Schunk. He thought back to the company's cross-border evolution, and asked his team to help him audit and evaluate the benefits and challenges of the EU market grouping effects on the firm.

Founded in 1945, Schunk currently employs around 1700 people, and in 2008 accounted for generated sales topping €200 million. The company manufactures products for industrial handling and automation, and prides itself on being the leading expert in automation due to its award-winning leadership in technological engineering. As a larger medium-sized engineering company in both size and scope, it could rightly be considered as one of the typical backbone industries of the German economy.

This case study focuses on corporate Europeanization (as defined by Suder, 2007) strategy and analysis.

Schunk's Europeanization

Intra-European activities

Schunk had greatly evolved from the garage in which its founder, the late Friedrich Schunk, had turned his passion into a profession. He started his business in Lauffen, the city on the river Neckar in Swabia, south-west Germany, where the headquarters are still located. In 1964, Heinz-Dieter, his son, joined the company, which at that point had eight employees. Heinz-Dieter's vision brought the firm its particular drive for technological leadership and – after a period of internal growth and consolidation – committed the company to a strategy aiming for international leadership across borders.

Background: European integration and business

For Heinz-Dieter and his team, a comprehensive chronological audit helped to analyse the importance of the European market. In 1951, six years after the creation of Schunk, the Paris Treaty set up the European Coal and Steel Community that, together with the other main treaties of the European Economic Community and Union, was the foundation for the European Union.

Ever since that time, the continent has grown closer together in what is called European integration or Europeanization. This has enabled businesses to grow inside a European Union where geopolitical, administrative and political borders have increasingly been removed. Having lived through the years of Euro-optimism and Euro-pessimism that shaped the EU market, Heinz-Dieter was aware that the ongoing EU integration was not restricted only to political significance. This Europeanization was evolving to facilitate the exchange of goods, services, capital and labour within Europe and its market. It came to cover more than 490 million citizens, consumers and partners. Heinz-Dieter saw that the commercial transactions of European companies were increasingly conducted inside the EU, because of a market characterized by a particularly low level of (political and economical) risk and uncertainty.

The EU evolved into the most advanced form of economic integration in the world, reducing transaction costs and increasing efficiencies. Companies like Schunk started to work across borders in Europe, raising performance and profitability. European diversity held huge potential for value creation through the transfer and exchange of knowledge, human capital and cross-cultural competencies – for those companies capable of handling it.

The 2004 and 2007 enlargements of the EU potentially translate into an enlargement of opportunities for competitive companies and for Member States' economies. Exporting companies were observed to be over 16 per cent more productive than local companies. Simultaneously, new Member State economies were found to benefit from Europeanization in the 10 years after accession to the EU. Schunk made strategic moves into Eastern and Central Europe, but was not yet present in countries such as Romania and Bulgaria, other than through traditional export and distribution channels.

What's more, costs of international commercial procedures decreased by more than 50 per cent as a result of European harmonization. These costs generally vary from 2 per cent to 15 per cent of merchandise value. In one note, Heinz-Dieter read that according to the EU, harmonization saves intra-European corporations approximately €300 billion per year.

Heinz-Dieter also realized that Framework Program 7 (published by the Commission and approved by the Parliament and then by the European Council) was conceived to attract R&D activity and foreign investments into Europe. It thus helped to foster growth and streamline European firms so that they could compete successfully, obtaining stimuli for innovation and research.

In 2008, most investments into the EU came from the USA, Switzerland and Turkey (all in special partnerships with the EU), and increasingly from Asia and South America. Schunk had opened entities in all of these countries. Schunk's management anticipated that, yes, these countries would bring competition, but they would also represent a great pool of partnerships, employment modifications, infrastructures and knowledge.

But, clearly, apart from increased competition, certain complex and specific rules for EU members limited the efficiency and fluidity of the European market potential. For example, intellectual property rights still could not be obtained for the whole of Europe without painful translation and cost. Schunk, for example, had to invest around €20,000 into turning an accepted German patent registration into a European patent. It was clear that companies needed to learn how to counterbalance the effects of such barriers.

Heinz-Dieter's team began its Europeanization audit with an overview of localization. As Table 1 shows, the chronological sequence was organized so as to shed light on the opportunities stemming from EU enlargement and Schunk's moves, and to note gaps and available opportunities. Columns one and two listed the countries of activity and (if given) their year of EU accession. Columns three and four gathered export and distribution start ranges. As with many enterprises, including Schunk, these dates were not given explicitly by year since the processes developed in a smooth transition and only gradually became institutionalized.

The fifth column highlights the moment in time when Schunk invested in locally staffed sales offices: the so-called 'Intecs'. Some of the mentioned locations are served from other countries' Intec. In this case, the location and year are listed. The sixth column evaluates whether the countries were EU members when Schunk entered the location, and the last column shows the latest specific Country Risk Index (CRI) from the Coface (2009) ratings.

A first analysis

As far as Heinz-Dieter remembers, the analysis seemed to indicate that, for simple export activity and distribution, EU membership had not been taken into account too much in the past. However, this membership was obviously considered very important for risk-bearing foreign direct investments (FDI): 13 out of 15 countries included in the list were EU members at the date of FDI placement. Furthermore, Switzerland was seen as closely related to Germany and the EU as a member of the European Free Trade Area (EFTA) and the European Economic Area (EEA). Only Turkey could be considered as somewhat EU distanced, despite its customs union with the EU which, to a certain extent, facilitates business.

The team then decided to develop certain trend lines in order to further clarify Schunk's Europeanization background (Figures 2 to 4).

Case Study Table 1   *Schunk's Europeanization timetable*

Country	EU since	Export	Distribution	FDI Intec	FDIEU	CRI
Australia	1995	early 80s	late 80s	2000	Y	A1
Belgium	Founder	early 80s	early 80s	1989	Y	A1
Croatia	–	late 90s	late 90s	–		A4
Czech Rep.	2004	ear ly 90s	late 90s	2005	Y	A2
Denmark	1973	early 80s	late 80s	2003	Y	A1
Estonia	2004	early 90s	late 90s	–		A2
Finland	1993	early 80s	late 80s	–		A1
France	Founder	early 80s	early 80s	1994	Y	A1
Great Britain	1973	mid 80s	late 80s	I998	Y	AI
Greece	1981	mid 80s	late 80s	–		A2
Hungary	2004	early 90s	late 90s	2005	Y	A3
Iceland	–	late 80s	late 90s	–		A1
Ireland	1973	mid 80s	late 80s	UK 1998	Y	A1
Italy	Founder	early 80s	early 80s	I998	Y	A2
Latvia	2004	early 90s	late 90s	–		A3
Liechtenstein	–	early 80s	early 80s	Swiss 1989	N	A1
Luxembourg	Founder	early 80s	early 80s	Belgium 1989	Y	A1
Netherlands	Founder	early 80s	early 80s	2001	Y	A1
Norway	–	mid 80s	late 80s	–		A1
Poland	2004	early 90s *	late 90s	2004	Y	A3
Portugal	1986	mid 80s	late 80s	Spain 2002		A2
Romania	2007	late 90s	early 2000s	–		A4
Russia	–	early 90s	early 2000s	–		B
Slovakia	2004	early 90s	late 90s	2006	Y	A3
Slovenia	2004	early 90s	late 90s	–		A1
Spain	1986	mid 80s	late 80s	2002	Y	A1
Sweden	1995	mid 80s	late 80s	1996	Y	A1
Switzerland	–	early 80s	early 80s	1989	N	A1
Turkey	–	early 90s	late 90s	2007	N	B

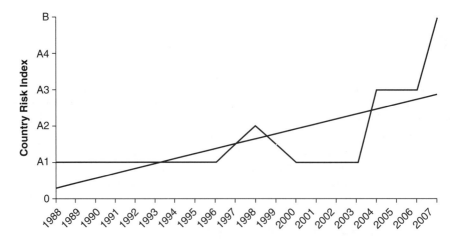

Case Study Figure 2   *Trend of country risk indices and Schunk's FDI over time*

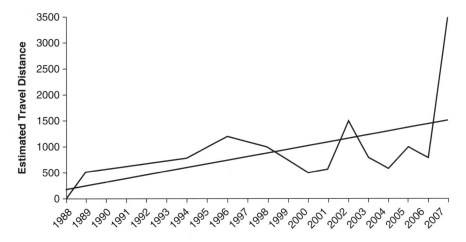

Case Study Figure 3 *Trend of estimated travel distance and Schunk's FDI over time*

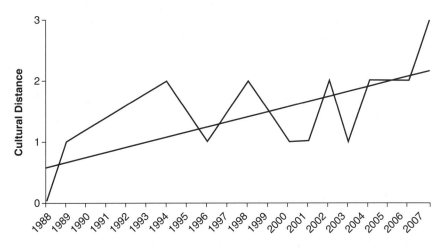

Case Study Figure 4 *Trend of cultural distance and Schunk's FDI over time*

It was concluded that, seen from this angle, Schunk had incrementally shifted its risk-, culture- and distance-related comfort level. This indeed reminded the auditors somewhat of the management theory of the Uppsala school of internationalization. Under Heinz-Dieter's guidance, the company gradually grew more self-confident while learning to manage international affairs. But were there additional internal and external dimensions of Europeanization to be taken into account beside those factors of risk, cultural distance and proximity?

Because organizations that also act outside the EU, or manage multilateral country relations, have to consider more constraints than firms that act exclusively within the community, the team decided to determine five specific 'challenge levels' (Figure 5). In this, the 13 EU countries with Schunk's FDIs were determined as locations of '1st

	Level 1	Level 2	Level 3	Level 4	Level 5
Relation directions	bilateral	multilateral	bilateral	multilateral	bilateral
Internal EU context	x	x	x	x	x
External EU context			x	x	x
External European context					x

Case Study Figure 5   *The four stages of the Intra-Europeanization Challenge*

level' challenges. Here, Schunk enjoys bilateral relations between the country of activity and Germany in an internal EU context.

Ireland, Luxembourg and Portugal represent the second level because they are EU members but are not served directly from Germany – for example, Ireland is served through the UK. These examples represent Schunk's handling of multilateral country relations in an internal EU context.

Switzerland represents a third-level challenge as now Schunk has also left the EU and manages bilateral relations from internal and external EU perspectives. Lichtenstein represents the fourth level because it is not an EU Member State, and is served through Switzerland. Here, Schunk handles multilateral relations between non-EU members and Germany in an internal and external EU environment. Turkey combines a high CRI and certain levels of cultural and geographical distance. Due to Turkey's double location as both a European and an Asian country, doing business there is a transition from Europeanization to internationalization. The team determined this environment as representing the fifth challenge level. Schunk's non-European facilities are linked to Europe from the outside. The company maintains export and distribution relations to Argentina, Australia, Brazil, Canada, China, India, Indonesia, Iran, Israel, Malaysia, Mexico, Singapore, South Africa, South Korea, Taiwan, Thailand, Ukraine, the USA and Venezuela. Production facilities are located in the USA and China.

Is a vast European home base an asset?

Interestingly, at this stage the auditors realized that each step of European integration could be determined as a carrier of risks and opportunities. To gain a deeper understanding of the effects of this for Schunk, related strengths, weaknesses, opportunities and threats (SWOT) required evaluation. Therefore, Heinz-Dieter and the audit team determined a scenario of an entirely Europeanized industrial automation business as a basis for analysis. The team characterized this environment as follows:

The Europeanized scenario

Automation companies face harmonized legislative and vocational settings throughout the continent. Competition and buyer potential are high, and this largely mature market is homogenized. Resources flow freely steered by demands and opportunities. The war for talent accelerates because these talents have grown in a borderless Europe and are geographically flexible. Work happens where it's done best in terms of price and quality. EU Member States and their EU institutions shape a democratic, transnational decision-making process that reduces red tape, harmonizes major industrial, competition and trade law (amongst the many other spheres overseen by the EU) and speaks to the world with one voice. Market imperfections are smoothed out but not entirely removed. The European market has therefore turned into a vast home base for its companies that hold opportunities and challenges for them. The team identified the following issues and classified them as a small-scale SWOT analysis.

Europeanization opportunities

Opportunity: Europe has become Schunk's vast home market, a wider, less risky and closer base for trade

Supportive Strengths: The enterprise is experienced in diversified markets, has a strong technology portfolio, a valuable brand and is the world market leader in industrial handling. It is related to a valuable 'Made in Germany' image.

Obstructive Weaknesses: Schunk recruits its workforce very locally: 92 per cent of the German-based workforce is born in Germany. The remaining 8 per cent largely consists of people with an immigration background. The European Intecs are 99 per cent staffed locally. German expatriates lead some of them. Consequently, the scope of different cultural horizons is relatively limited within the German headquarters. This could potentially lead to an atmosphere of limited cultural openness. Furthermore, Schunk, at least in Germany, has a somewhat Swabian image. Some of the attributes related to this are personal directness, stringent task orientation and a focus on being down to earth. Not all cultural backgrounds favour this kind of attitude. At the same time, its major customers do not always see Schunk as innovative. Investigations have shown that, although the company presents a huge amount of highly innovative products each year, this does not seem to be the reason why its main customers choose the company. Instead, they seem to focus their appreciation on the robustness and reliability of Schunk's components and systems.

Opportunity: Europeanization offers cooperation potential

Supportive Strengths: Due to its existing technological portfolio, Schunk is a very attractive partner for other firms. The workforce is prepared to utilize the opportunities resulting from this. Existing networks to firms and universities demonstrate Schunk's general networking abilities.

Obstructive Weaknesses: So far, Schunk has not favoured joint ventures or strategic alliances as a mode of cooperation. The company strives rather for high vertical integration.

Any data exchange is seen as potentially critical. Schunk's preference for finding internal solutions also affects the software side of operations. Many of the internal software systems are specialized and therefore somewhat complicate cross-border data exchange.

Opportunity: Harmonized patent, liability and economic legislation

Supportive Strengths: Schunk has a strong patent department and a strong consulting base for such issues. The products are machine subparts. These generally relate to simpler liability obligation regulations. The high vertical integration, to some extent, internalizes risks.

Obstructive Weaknesses: A lot of the patent and liability legislative consulting come from the outside.

Opportunity: Exchange of goods and services without borders

Supportive Strengths: Schunk's export department is strong and has many years of experience in cross-border distribution and international on-time delivery.

Obstructive Weaknesses: Schunk's sourcing is mainly steered by its German headquarters. Although the international facilities obtain their sourcing in a decentralized fashion, most transactions (e.g. steel prices) are harmonized with Germany. The important 'Made in Germany' approach limits production and sourcing flexibility to some extent. Generally, Schunk has limited experience in international production cooperation with external partners.

Opportunity: Quickly changing opportunities favour the agile!

Supportive Strengths: Schunk's workforce and its technology portfolio support agility. The company's owners are quick decision makers. They favour a mixture of analysis and intuition for decision-making, and have proved to have managerial foresight. Because Schunk is owner-operated and relatively small, decisions can be made more quickly.

Obstructive Weaknesses: Owner operation may potentially block decisions: in case of internal discrepancies, decisions might lead the company in the wrong direction because the owners are free to decide against internal consultancy. The favoured intuition base also risks leading to dead-ends because the contemporary markets are very complex and often hard to fully understand intuitively. This can result in high agility but low adaptability because it is not clear what to adapt to. Survival in the modern business world remains exclusive to the most adaptable and not to the fastest or strongest.

Opportunity: European capital market integration; capital mobility

Supportive Strengths: Schunk demonstrates a proven record of being a reliable business partner. Both Schunk's basic financial situation and the market potential can result in a promising future. Schunk has an excellent credit record and so far has been able to sustain its success.

Obstructive Weaknesses: Schunk does not favour dependence on external funds. Only a few house banks have access to Schunk. In the long run, this could potentially lead to other banks becoming uninterested in Schunk, thus making it harder to raise money when it is needed.

Europeanization threats

Threats: Competition grows increasingly stiff

Supportive Strengths: Schunk has vast experience in international business. The company claims to be the competence leader in its sector. Although the data about market share are difficult to identify, and often leave room for interpretation, Schunk is certainly seen as a very strong player in the industrial automation market. Furthermore, Schunk is very responsive to new demands. Due to relatively systematic market monitoring, Schunk knows what to develop. The level of product quality is very high.

Obstructive Weaknesses: As already mentioned above, Schunk is only seen as innovative by its customers in a limited way. Instead, it has a robust and reliable image. The strong focus on 'Made in Germany', to some extent, limits the international sourcing potential.

Threats: Borderless markets vs borderless bureaucracy

Supportive Strengths: Schunk is very experienced in managing multilateral international relations. The enterprise already maintains a good network of university cooperation partnerships that has worked well for many EU-funded projects.

Obstructive Weaknesses: Schunk, so far, mainly relies on its membership in the German Engineering Association (VDMA) for lobbying on the European level. Generally, Schunk is a somewhat self-centered enterprise. Whatever can be solved in-house is solved in-house. This basic pragmatic business attitude can potentially result in an atmosphere of impatience and impulsive action.

Threats: The centralization tendencies of the EU make business harder to do with EU externals

Supportive Strengths: Schunk is very experienced in managing multilateral international relations. Its global network is well developed. The globally located organization provides the potential to circumvent European bureaucracy to a certain degree.

Obstructive Weaknesses: The 'Made in Germany' approach makes it harder to exploit non-German value chain potentials. The company is perceived as a larger version of an SME rather than as a multi-national enterprise.

Threats: Demography accelerates war for talents: how to attract the best?

Supportive Strengths: The cooperative company culture helps to attract potential employees. Schunk's family ownership business gives an image of sustainability. This attracts people who seek security and prefer uncertainty avoidance to risk taking. As with other smaller corporations, the career potential is high for people who perform above average: they can potentially take responsibility faster and climb the career ladder quickly. Schunk offers job profiles which are interesting, engaging and provide development potential.

Obstructive Weaknesses: Schunk's monetary compensation model is only competitive in a limited way when compared to other companies in the region. This certainly applies to the headquarters, located in the middle of the German engineering centre around Stuttgart. However, within this ideal business environment, Schunk's headquarters are relatively isolated in terms of location with less than optimal connections to the Autobahn (motorway) and mass transit. This makes the daily commute more difficult for employees. Schunk has low visibility to industry outsiders and cannot easily attract potential employees from other industries.

Threats: European market imperfections smooth out; 'Made in Germany' then becomes less important

Supportive Strengths: Schunk is a quality market leader in its business. The firm is internationally present and potentially is able to exploit international imperfections through its production in the USA and China.

Obstructive Weaknesses: Although Schunk is internationally active, it still has relatively little experience in exploiting international market imperfections. Due to the 'Made in Germany' approach, international cost advantages have only been exploited in a limited way so far. The brand is built on 'Made in Germany'.

Critical success factors in the European context

Heinz–Dieter's future Europeanization strategy needs to rely upon further audit of the company's critical success factors (CSFs). His team has started to pinpoint the distinct firm and industry CSFs that are embedded in the Europeanized context. On the firm level, factors have been named that are vital for reaching the self-imposed aims of the mission statement. On the industry level, the business basics of the industrial automation environment within Europe have been considered.

Firm level critical success factors in the Europeanized context

Schunk's (2009) mission statement 'Better for you is better for us' highlights the company's customer focus. Schunk (2009) also cites reliability, perfection, pioneer spirit, will to perform, customer linkage and responsibility. These attributes were merged with a collection of related conditions, tasks and demands. Table 2 shows the results.

These conditions have helped the team to envision tasksrelevant to Schunk's business. The term 'critical' in CSF is ambiguous in that it has both a positive and a

Case Study Table 2   *General subgrouped conditions, tasks and demands related to firm level success*

Attributes	Related Conditions, Tasks and Demands
Better for You is Better to Us	> employee skills and motivation (understand customers and cultures, solve problems, be reliable, recognize demands, generate demands) > organization (be present, take customer view, foster customer view, scrutinize customer value, innovation no end in itself, offer information) > knowledge (know customer needs, know the industry, know the branch)
Reliable	> technology and tools (QM, PM, reachability, mature products, incremental innovation) > employee skills and motivation (keep promises, service, sales team has to know what they could promise) > time-factor (timelines, delivery reliability) > emergency plan (claim management, priorising, risk evaluation, risk minimization, risk consciousness, avoid surprises)
Perfect	> technologies and tools (QM, process management, innovation, new products, production ability, testing ability, PLM, ERP) > employee skills and motivation (human capital, employee training, employee skills, war for talent) > organization (perfection not as end in itself, strategy)
Pioneer Spirit	> employee skills and motivations (recognizing new application fields, implementation of latest tools, war for talents) > knowledge (technology knowledge, material knowledge, collect new ideas, patent monitoring) > organization (BDM, will to invest, foster ideas, sales foster PS, sales compensation supports PS, PS beside products (e.g. worktime models)) > innovation (radical innovation, innovation management, advanced engineering and production, recognize new ideas)
Willing to Perform	> employee skills and motivation (training, qualification, competitive monetary compensation, performance must pay off, job enrichment) > organization (recognize and foster talents, foster flexibility and ideas, team approach, measure performance not work hours, 'we' feel)
Customer Linked	> organization (be present, mutual trust, make information available) > employee skills and motivation (understand customers, understand and appreciate cultures, multilingual) > technologies and tools (reachability, web-page, modern IT, CRM, partserver) > customer motivation (customer events, knowing process owners, quick reaction, be present at fairs)
Responsibly	> employee skills and motivation (responsibility must pay off for employees, employee training) > organization (seeking solutions not failures, foster and enable responsibility, structures, delegation, bottom up approach, decentralization)
Economical	> organization (sales drive, calculate prudent, focus on core competencies) > knowledge (reducing risks, cost optimization, make or buy, cost monitoring)

negative meaning. The positive sense is vital and the negative, dangerous. If interpreted positively, then Schunk's firm level CSFs could be identified as:

FL CSF 1: 'Attract and maintain a motivated, qualified and strong employee base in Europe.'

FL CSF 2: 'Deploy state-of-the-art technologies in all European organizational domains.'

FL CSF 3: 'Focus all organizational senses and cognitions on European customers.'

FL CSF 4: 'Utilize the organization to excel in understanding and serving European customers.'

FL CSF 5: 'Monitor and steer the link between customer needs and economic success.'

Industry level critical success factors in the Europeanized context

Schunk is an active part of the European industrial automation business. Most of Schunk's turnover is generated within Germany and the European Union. Generally, about 35 per cent of turnover comes from international operations. This is a comparatively low level for a firm located in the world's second largest export market, Germany. However, this percentage is not altogether correct. Many of the modules that are sold to German customers are included in systems that are then sold to customers abroad. Therefore, the real export quota is significantly higher than that apparent from the actual turnover.

EU law and regulation have influenced the whole of Schunk's industry sector in the past few decades. Most recently, the revised Machinery Directive 2006/42/EC, implemented by the end of 2009 by all concerned parties, now regulates the documentation that has to be furnished and held for machinery within the EU. Schunk's products are almost exclusively so-called 'partly completed machines' that only operate if integrated into a system. Although these are subject to limited documentation, it still requires a significant effort to fulfil the level of conformity demanded.

An analysis of industry level CSFs applies to all companies in this industry. The team determined six industry-specific attributes. Based on these attributes, indicators and success factors that enable firms to compete in Europe were identified (Tables 3 and 4). In the next step, the team combined subgroups that then helped to finally formulate the IL CSFs.

The industry level CSFs were identified as follows:

IL CSF 1: 'Monitor, understand and actively learn from European competition and markets.'

IL CSF 2: 'Offer and promote products and services with a demanded price performance ratio.'

IL CSF 3: 'Monitor, understand and form written/unwritten rules for the European industry.'

IL CSF 4: 'Constantly design and question the company strategy to maintain flexibility.'

Case Study Table 3 *Attributes and factors of the automation industry in Europe and worldwide*

Attribute	Success Factors
Competitive	> global competition (knowing the competition, market knowledge, branch knowledge) > product related (innovation, prize, portfolio, solutions, process excellence, cross selling abilities) > company related (level of awareness, fair presence, clear strategy) > human ressource related (ability to attract talents)
Regulated	> norms and guidline (knowing norms update norms) > networking (be active in norm regulation organs, attend industry organizations) > strategy (offer adapted portfolios, economy of scale)
Technologized	> capabilities (R&D, knowing tools and technologies, recognize ideas) > networking (university cooperations, supplier networks, industry cooperations) > sales (technology plus service) > organization (innovation management)
War for Talents	> Job offer (competitive salaries, work live balance, job enrichment) > organization (social engagement, intercultural abilities of the company) > activities (talent screening, recognize talents, foster talents, recruiting events, offer practical semesters)
Glocalized	> capabilities (intercultural abilities) > knowledge (knowing countries, knowing regions, market knowledge) > organization (internationalization, global and local presence, adjusted process chain, clear strategy) > human ressources (flexible employee base, employee base that values other cultures)
Reliability demanding	> performance (perform reliability, show reliability, high support level) > organization (foster reliability, clear strategy, process excellence, flexibility) > human resources (willing employee base, flexibility)

IL CSF 5: 'Maintain the level of technological capabilities that fits to your strategy.'

IL CSF 6: 'Recognize and utilize ideas and business opportunities for the organization.'

IL CSF 7: 'Form and promote vocational settings and tasks that attract European talents.'

IL CSF 8: 'Create and foster an international and intercultural organizational mindset.'

IL CSF 9: 'Know and be aware of all global, European and local aspects of the business.'

IL CSF 10: 'Create and expand a financial setting that builds independence and strength.'

Case Study Table 4   *Attributes and indicators of the automation industry in Europe and worldwide*

Attribute	Indicators
Competitive	> global competition (many companies, economies of scale, high level of internationalization, continent specific market leader) > product related (commoditization, prize wars, dumping) > human ressource related (war for talents)
Regulated	> norms and guidlines (many norms, many industry guidelines, many unwritten standards, economies of scale enforce standards) > law and legislation (strategic industry, continent specific rules)
Technologized	> technology (many patents in this sector, high R&D quota) > sales (technology based sales, product focus)
War for Talents	> recruiting activities (recruiting events, job fairs, headhunter calls, mass of job offers) > internationalization (brain drain, European Blue Card) > gouvernmental (efforts to grow amount of engineering student)
Glocalized	> global (global competition, global production global companies rule the markets, international war for talents, global R&D) > local (local networks, local market leaders)
Reliability Demanding	> costs (very expensive downtime costs in automation systems, high level of investment) > commitment (automation sytems are a long-term commitment for both parties, strategic investments for buyers, 24/7 service) > danger (product malfunction dangerous for body and goods)

The way ahead ...

Schunk's economic success had proven that the firm possesses sound capabilities in a multicultural environment. Heinz-Dieter Schunk's team identified clear evidence that the long-term internationalization experience had provided the necessary learning and confidence to act on each European market.

The progress of European integration facilitated Schunk's internationalization as well as its sustainability-driven business. The understanding of this particular European context (which is harmonized and diverse at the same time) has enabled his firm to exploit market imperfections while enjoying Europeanized conditions in terms of logistics, common commercial policies, an extent of IP protection, innovation stimuli and euro-zone effects.

Nonetheless, Schunk has also increasingly been exposed to competition which enjoys similar advantages of scope and scale in Europe. Thus, essential questions to consider are: How to avoid giving ground to those competitors? Should more ground be covered in Europe? Should they develop and display a more culturally open atmosphere inside the company? Use knowledge transfer and exchange mechanisms that reinforce the internal cohesion of the German and non-German workforce and units? If the stringent focus on 'Made in Germany' is a key strength, does it at the same time also bear potential risks because it limits Schunk's sourcing and sociocultural possibilities? So far, Schunk mainly relies on its membership in the German Engineering Association (VDMA) for lobbying on the European level. Would it be possible for Schunk to engage in EU lobbying and institutional relations independently? Would this transform Europeanization from being just an asset into being a winning strategy?

The Europeanization audit gave Heinz–Dieter Schunk a sound overview of past accomplishments (see Figures 6 and 7), and showed a solid incremental Europeanization. At the same time, the audit now provided the potential to serve as a road map into further Europeanization, providing deeper involvement and greater awareness of the

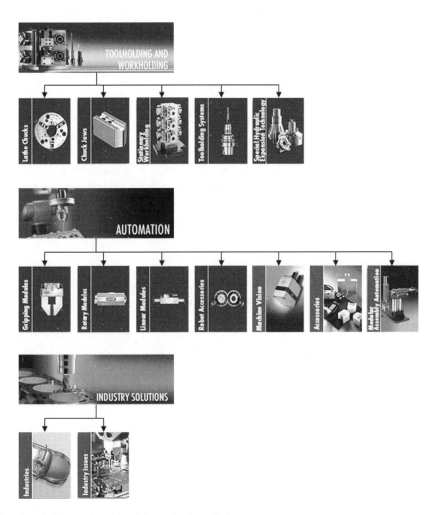

Case Study Figure 6   *Schunk's product portfolio*

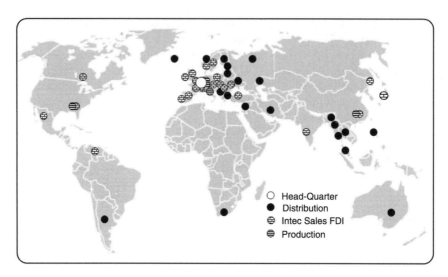

Case Study Figure 7   *Overview of Schunk facilities*

Source background picture: http://www.yellowtools.us/cp21/cms/YT_pictures/weltkarte.gif

pros and cons of European integration. The critical success factors gave insight into where to concentrate the resources, which would have to be evaluated in the context of Schunk's overall internationalization. Heinz-Dieter has now started to consider Lithuania and Estonia, but also the EU's special partner Russia, as locations worth looking into.

Distribution:

Argentina, Australia, Brazil, China, Croatia, Estonia, Finland, Germany, Greece, Iceland, Indonesia, Iran, Israel, Latvia, Malaysia, Norway, Romania, Russia, Singapore, Slovenia, South Africa, Taiwan, Thailand, Ukraine

Sales Office Intec (FDI):

Austria, Belgium/Luxembourg, Canada, China, Czech Republic, Denmark, France, Great Britain/Ireland, Hungary, India, Italy, Japan, Mexico/Venezuela, Netherlands, Poland, Portugal, Slovakia, South Korea, Spain, Sweden, Switzerland/Liechtenstein, Turkey, USA

Production:

Lauffen/Neckar (Germany), Hausen (Germany), Mengen (Germany), Morrisville (USA), Hangzhou (PRC), Milano Region (Italy)

Engineering:

Lauffen/Neckar (Germany), Hausen (Germany), Mengen (Germany), Morrisville (USA), Milano Region (Italy)

Questions

1 What impact has European integration had on Schunk's internationalization/localization decisions?

2 What advice would you give to Heinz-Dieter for future Europeanization (choose one country and one mode of entry) and why?

3 Make suggestions of other aspects of 'Doing Business in Europe' that Heinz-Dieter's team should have audited to assure the efficient use of the Single Market potential.

4 What organizational functions would mostly benefit from a more 'European'-scaled company?

5 Address alternative entry modes for Schunk in further detail. What is the best entry mode to adopt when your company has only very little knowledge of the country of choice for market entry?

6 Which EU institution would you recommend as the primary EU lobbying target for Schunk? Underpin your argument with an explanation that refers to the institution's organization and tasks and Schunk's concordance with any of the European Union and/or this institution's objectives.

Note

1 This case study was first published at European Case Clearing House (ECCH), Cranfield, 2010, ref. 310-063-1 and TN ref. 310-063-8; all rights reserved.

Bibliography

Coface (2009) *Country Risk Ratings.* Available at: http://www.coface-usa.com/CofacePortal/US_en_EN/pages/home/wwd/inform/Country_risk/Country percent20Risk per cent per cent20Ratings.

Daniel, D.R. (1961) Managment information crisis. *Harvard Business Review*, vol. 39, no. 5, pp. 111–21.

Johanson, J. and Wiedersheim-Paul, F. (1975) The internationalization of the firm: four Swedish cases. *Journal of Management Studies*, vol. 12, no. 1, pp. 305–22.

Luostarinen, R. and Welch, L.S. (1988) Internationalization: evolution of a concept. *Journal of General Management*, vol. 14, no. 2, pp. 34–46.

Oviatt, B.M. and McDougall P.P. (1994) Toward a theory of international new ventures. *Journal of International Business Studies*, vol. 25, no. 1, pp. 45–64.

Schunk, H.D. (2009) *Company Philosophy.* Available at: http://www.schunk. com/schunk/schunk_websites/worldwide/philosophy.html?submenu=202&submenu2=0&country=USA&lngCode=EN&lngCode2=EN (accessed 28 January 2009).

Suder, G. (2007) *Doing Business in Europe*, 1st edn. London: Sage.

European Chief Executives in the Merger Maze: Coping with Multiple Realities

By Dr Jacqueline Fendt, ESCP Europe

In a global economy characterized by liberalization and consolidation, many leaders today are busy reinventing their organizations, preparing or digesting a merger, attacking new markets or outsourcing tasks and downsizing their workforce. But many such experiences, especially mergers, still fail to deliver on their promise and often destroy substantial human and financial corporate value. The reasons – more often than not – lie in the social, psychological and cultural challenges of the post-merger process. These are particularly challenging in European companies, given their extreme plurality in language, culture and – last but not least – the diverse European visions of capitalism that are so different from the Anglo-Saxon model. European leaders in a globalizing world, and especially in the increasingly frequent transatlantic mergers, have to marry the European notion of capitalism, the Social or *Rhine* capitalism, based on corporatism and stakeholder consensus, with the exigencies of the more shareholder-based Anglo-Saxon capitalism.

A seven-year empirical research project on German and Swiss CEOs in global post-merger situations uncovered some powerful challenges these executives faced in their complex integration endeavours. Forty mergers in such varied industries as banking, airline, automotive, IT, engineering, life sciences, hotel management and food manufacturing were studied and the actors themselves, CEOs and top executives, spoke up and candidly shared how they went about solving problems and how they struggled between art and science in their thought processes. The research identified three generic types of leadership patterns – the *cartel*, the *aesthetic* and the *videogame* executive – and proposed a taxonomy of leadership behaviour that seems particularly propitious to post-merger performance, dubbed the *holistic* executive.

The cartel executive: 'life is power'

Cartel executives have a strong desire for control and power maximization. They are solitary, no-nonsense, facts-and-figures executives who do not mingle much, except in their restrained circles. Such leaders grew up in protected markets, trade organizations and barriers, and have a low tolerance for ambiguity. Their leadership is instrumental, utilitarian and focused on the conservation of power and unconditional control. Their secretive, power-based lobby has been highly successful in a stable world where this leadership style had served well for decades. In the management team, they usually form a coalition with the Chief Financial Officer. Such leaders are hard workers, bold decision makers and have an unflinching determination, a well-oiled network among the highest political and economic leaders and a long-term strategic perspective.

The aesthetic executive: 'life is beauty'

This type of leader is all about image. Their day's work begins with a thorough reading of the press that largely determines actions and priorities. They have multiple personal media appearances, often as carefully staged as those of a pop star. Their rhetoric is smooth, their metaphors well-oiled and their PR consultant is never far away. This style posits a dualism with the leader on one side and the followers on the other, which mystifies leadership and jeopardizes true collaboration. Such leaders believe that they can use the media for their own purposes but often end up being used by the media. Also, their successful public appearances bring them to mistake their perceptions for realities and thus the curtain over the stark truth often remains closed until it's too late. Still, the *aesthetic* executive has distinct strengths, namely a high awareness for effective, systematically planned communication with various stakeholders, a process view of change, intuition and loads of charisma.

The videogame executive: 'life is a game'

Videogame executives are acutely lucid, very well informed, anti-authoritarian and unsparing with classic leaders, who they consider mediocre, cynical and mendacious. To them, change is not a programme but simply a fact of life. They aptly use visual, symbolic communications first hand and by all available electronic means, and aptly raise their mission at hand to a level of worthwhile human adventure rather than an astute business deal. They have a playful but effective capacity to enthuse and want to have fun above all. They believe that doing a good job and being a good citizen does not have to come at the price of cynicism and sacrifice of family life and bonding with friends. It goes without saying that they tell the truth, even when it's ugly: they see themselves and their followers as 'in it together'. Video-gamers don't think in hierarchies and terms of 'moving to the top' but rather prefer multiple experiences. They believe in diversity, do not mind losing face before colleagues and easily volunteer unfinished bits and pieces of solutions in management meetings. In their logic, to make mistakes is essential and helps them to progress. Video-gamers are explorers, not exploiters: they hop from project to project and get bored rather quickly as soon as the task gets repetitive. They stick it out as long as the game lasts.

The holistic executive: 'life is multiple realities'

Leaders who performed best in complex, constantly shifting environments were those who combined the strengths of the three foregoing leadership styles. These *holistic* executives have a long-term vision and a powerful network, are highly determined and have the tenacity to stick it out as the cartel leaders did. They work equally closely with all management team members, including the HR manager. Like the aesthetic leaders, holistic executives are process-conscious, know the value of planning and communication with diverse stakeholders and use their charisma to the full to gather rank and file around a strong, shared higher-echelon goal. Like video-gamers, they are technology savvy, creative and view mistakes as opportunities for growth and innovation, and inspire colleagues through tough times with their candour, vulnerability and empathy. Above all, holistic leaders are pathological and passionate learners: they have a high tolerance for ambiguity, refuse to cede to complexity with binary 'either–or' decoys and instead support diverse alternatives. Incorporating plural viewpoints brings enjoyment to the merger process, which becomes a social and factual discovery trip. Choice is presented as a configuration of value rather than a selection from mutually exclusive alternatives and permits to innovate with hitherto untested third positions.

A people focus

Merger integration is, above all, a social and thereby leadership challenge. In leadership theory, different sets of behaviour are said to be particularly apt at coping with different company life stages, for example transitional situations require analytical leadership, start-up companies thrive on creative behaviour, adaptive situations need conceptual leadership, growth companies need a production focus and consolidation situations require a behavioural style. The problem is that a post-merger situation is simultaneously consolidative, starting, adaptive, growing and transitional. In this maze of juxtaposed entrepreneurial situations, the CEO would have to concurrently be analytic, conceptual, behavioural, production-focused and creative! The holistic executive comes closest to this as he or she manages the critical post-merger challenges, namely to:

- tap to the full the immense learning potential of two companies combining resources: this necessitates a learning vision and new management and learning processes and structures;
- move the organization from hierarchies to networks, that is to bring more accountability and power to the workplace. In poorly managed mergers, the contrary happens;
- keep the best talents on board and attract new ones from the market. Many companies plan to acquire human assets, which are then drained by poor integration. Talent turnover, which is normally at about 20 per cent, can rise to 75 per cent in post-merger phases;
- shape a new culture. The way change and uncertainty are managed, how the CEO treats people, the clarity, integrity and coherence of management action and the solutions found for the inevitable losers in a merger process, will determine staff commitment and the future culture of the merged company (see Table 5).

HR managers are ideally placed to second the CEO in these issues (see Box 1): they show a richer insight into how to manage the human factor in mergers than CEOs,

Case Study Table 5　*Taxonomy of European leadership behaviour in mergers*

Characteristic, dimension	Cartel	Aesthetic	Videogame	Holistic
Value system	Life is power and control	Life is beauty	Life is a game	Life is multiple realities
Ethics	Within the law	Code of conduct	Add value	Add value, respect
Social embeddedness	Solitary	Elitist	Unselective	Diverse, selective
Purpose of learning	To obtain something	To be someone	To become someone	
Knowledge	Is a possession, a means to an end	Is a product to be acquired	Is constructed	
Leadership	Directive	Analytic	Conceptual	Integrated
CEO's personal merger involvement	Until closing of deal	Until communication and integration plan	Until boredom	Permanent
Organizational perspective	Systemic organization	Systemic self-organization	Systemic networking	Co-active self-organization
Communication	By head of comms	By CEO		
Communication means	Formal verbal statements	Multiple personal appearances	By images, symbolic acts, systems	Mixture of verbal and image, systems
Main entrepreneurial	Degree of control	Degree of media support	Degree of excitement	Integrated focus
Time dimension	Decades	Next quarter	The time of a game	Long- and short-term
Subconscious learning mode	Instinct	Intuition (automated expertise)	Intuition (holistic hunch)	Both types of intuition
Human diversity	Little diversity	Diversity		
Medium diversity	Single, medium (verbal)	Reduced media (verbal, some images)	Multimedia	
Degree of planning	High		Low	High to permit improvization

(Continued)

Case Study Table 5   (Continued)

	Long-term dominance	Short-term results	Adventure	Integrated
Vision	Long-term dominance	Short-term results	Adventure	Integrated
Determination	High, permanent	Medium	High, until boredom	High
Internet literacy	Low		High	
Rhetoric	Poor	Excellent, universal	Excellent but addresses only the 'young'	Excellent, diverse
Attitude towards mistakes	No mistakes		Mistake-making as a resource	
Networking	Stable, long-term, confined to few peers	Reduced network	Intense, multiple partners, alternating, temporary	Both long-term and alternating networking
Perception of uncertainty	Is an inhibitor and must be reduced	Is related to some temporary factor and must be managed	Is a fact of life and must be integrated in the game tactics	Is a fact of life
Relationship with external stakeholders	Lobby	Communication, negotiation	Invited to join the game or ignored	Communication, negotiation
Notion of complexity	Reduce	Communicate, explain	Discover, enjoy, drop when bored	Discover, communicate, explain
Task dimension	Exploitation and exploration (sequential)		Exploration	Exploration and exploitation (simultaneously)
Films	The Godfather trilogy, Wall Street	Sideways, American Beauty, Kageshuma	Martix, Erin Brockovich	All types
Videogames	None	Chess, flight stimulator	All types	All types

Source: Table synthesized from Schuler et al (2005), pp. 214–216

as they are the turnstile between top management and the organization. Yet, except with holistic leaders, HR is still often involved late, sometimes only when human problems escalate. Holistic executives recognize the value of an early HR involvement and attribute a key role to the HR manager.

Box 1   Critical HR tasks in mergers

Before the merger:

- Contribute to defining the merger objectives;
- Bring an HR and a knowledge view to the selection of a potential merging partner;
- Assess the human and skills value of the potential partner (HR due diligence);
- Advise the CEO on human and cultural merger issues;
- Plan the integration process as a learning process.

During the integration phase:

- Assist the CEO in the structure and design of the new company from a knowledge perspective;
- Assist the CEO in acculturation leadership;
- Select the integration manager, design and manage the teams;
- Retain key managers and talent, recruit new talent, promote diversity;
- Manage the change process, negotiate with and motivate stakeholders;
- Examine extant HR policies and practices, select and implement the new policies and practices.

During stabilization:

- Be a knowledge and learning ambassador to the CEO and the organization;
- Solidify culture, leadership and staffing;
- Assess strategies, structure and processes from a knowledge perspective;
- Assess and adapt HR policies and practice;
- Monitor stakeholder concerns;
- Manage learning.

(*Source*: Adapted from Schuler et al., 2005)

Questions

1   What European specificities must be taken into account in merger management?
2   What makes leadership so challenging in mergers? What leadership behaviour would you adopt to make your merger successful?
3   Why is it that after four decades of international merger experience, many leaders still fail to achieve their strategic objectives and most mergers result in the destruction of substantial financial, strategic and human value?

4   What are the key human resources issues that must be addressed for successful merger integration:

(a) in the pre-merger phase?
(b) immediately after the merger?
(c) in the later integration/stabilization phase?

Bibliography

Fendt, J. (2005) *The CEO in Post-Merger Situations: An Emerging Theory on the Management of Multiple Realities*. Delft: Eburon.

Schuler, R.S., Jackson, S.E. and Fendt, J. (2005) Managing human resources in cross-border alliances, in H. Scullion and M. Linehan (eds), *International Human Resource Management: A Critical Text*. Basingstoke: Palgrave Macmillan. pp. 202–235.

Suder, G. (2007) *Doing Business in Europe*, 1st edn. London: Sage.

All permissions and rights obtained by the author of the case study; first publication of this case study in Suder (2007).

The Europeanization of Marimekko: International Growth and Single Market Effects

By Professor Gabriele Suder, SKEMA Business School and Aalto University of Economics

At the end of October 2007, it was announced that the former president and CEO of Sampo Bank Plc, Mika Ihamuotila, was to become President and CEO as well as principal shareholder of Marimekko Corporation with a 13 per cent ownership investment of his own; 10 per cent of the shares were acquired from the company's leader at that time, Kirsti Paakkanen, and 3 per cent from Finnish Varma Mutual Employment Pension Insurance Company.[1] In the week of his arrival, Marimekko's shares surged 12 per cent in Helsinki, after solid 3Q figures and the announcement of this being a change of generation and expertise in the company's leadership. This new era came in the form of a former highly successful banker driven by the desire for change and a family-rooted passion for the sector, ready for a full set of new challenges in his life. Marimekko was a leading Finnish textiles and clothing design company, and was 57 years old at that time, with great international growth potential.

Mika Ihamuotila observed Marimekko's success in Japan, the emerging success in the USA, and the market share in Nordic countries that had grown steadily in the past few years, but also the market share in the rest of Europe that had suffered tremendously in the mid 2000s and was – despite sound growth figures arriving in the year 2007 – not yet that stable.

Introduction

As part of the Finnish textile industry, Marimekko is an integral part of a large market grouping of more than 500 million consumers and more than 20 million companies: the Single Market of the European Union.

The group designs, manufactures and markets premium clothing, interior decoration textiles, bags and other accessories under the Marimekko brand. Its designs are distinctly known across Finland and abroad. The European Union states: 'textiles and clothing are among the most traded goods in the global economy. After China, the EU is the world's second largest exporter of textile products.' A 2005 surge in imports from the Far East had caused significant damage to this sector in Europe, and the international economic outlook had weakened notably during the second half of

2008, when economic growth slowed down globally into the 2010s. In Finland, growth slowed down quickly towards the end of that year of 2008. At the beginning of 2009, the economic outlook for the Finnish textile and clothing industry further weakened significantly when the number of orders diminished and profitability dropped. In addition, international competition, counterfeit products and illegal imports were weakening the sector.

Deregulation and liberalization of the EU market had led to a business environment that is uniquely integrated but also particularly challenging. It is conceived to enhance competition and, through this, the competitiveness of European companies worldwide. In this context, Marimekko's management decided to give its Europeanization[2] of cross-border activity a boost, in addition to its interests in the USA and Japan.

This case study sheds light on the strategy of incremental Europeanization of Marimekko; on its challenges and on the benefits stemming from this Europeanization. It also illustrates the importance for European business of adapting to the changing globalized business environment, using advanced politico-economic market group effects to enlarge its home base.

Marimekko: a Finnish design

Marimekko is, first and foremost, a distinctly Finnish company. 'Finnishness' is an important factor in the brand due to its local roots and the origin of its designs; also, most of its employees are Finnish. In 2008, the Marimekko Group employed 414 people, 398 of whom worked in Finland; and amongst the total of 370 employees in 2009, 353 worked in Finland. Also, all three fully company-owned factories are located in Finland. Marimekko's own plants produced slightly less than half of all the products sold by the company and its focus on local knowledge is underpinned by primarily Finnish manufacture.

However, Marimekko also has *subcontractors* abroad that manufacture some minor proportion of its products, and, in the late 2000s, outsourcing from main sites to Finnish and foreign suppliers grew noticeably in all product lines. Marimekko's foreign subcontractors are mostly from the EU area and its international sales are mainly from that area (despite important stakes in Japan), of which Finland has been a Member State since 1995.

Typically for this industry sector, *exporting* is the cornerstone of Marimekko's market entry strategy abroad. In 2008, altogether 27 per cent of the firm's net sales came from foreign operations and exports. Intra-EU operations accounted for 17.4 per cent of total operations (see Table 6).

Overall, Marimekko products were sold in over 40 countries, and – amongst those – in 22 out of the 27 EU Member States at that time. In this period, Marimekko declared its main target to be an increase of international sales by 20 per cent annually.

By the end of 2008, there were around 30 *concept stores* abroad operated by retailers, which Marimekko has considered as the best channel to grow internationally.

Case Study Table 6   *Net sales by market area (in € million)*

	Market Area	Market Area	Market Area
	Finland	Nordic	Rest of Europe
1999	19.6	2.4	2.5
2000	23.638	2.954	4.247
2001	28.959	3.129	6.509
2002	35.937	3.481	5.807
2003	43.297	4.160	5.568
2004	50.244	5.136	5.183
2005	54.180	6.074	2.674
2006	53.826	7.373	3.655
2007	56.826	8.581	4.725
2008	59.175	9.423	4.700

Marimekko products have been manufactured under *license* in Finland, Sweden, The Netherlands, the USA and Denmark.

By 2009, Marimekko had 23 *stores* of its own in Finland, one in Stockholm (Sweden) and one in Frankfurt (Germany). At the end of March 2009, the company added a subsidiary to its cross-border investments: in the UK, Marimekko UK Ltd was created to administer the operations of the Marimekko store in London. The store was acquired from Skandium Ltd on 1 April 2009.

Despite the global economic crisis starting at the end of 2008, Marimekko's net sales increased by 5 per cent to €81.1 million in 2008 (from €77.3 million in 2007). In Finland, its net sales grew by 4.1 per cent to €59.2 million (from €56.8 million in 2007). Most of the international growth came from the neighbouring Nordic countries and in the market area referred to as 'other countries', where Japan is the most important country for exports. The breakdown of the net sales by product line, including all market areas, demonstrates that 36.9 per cent of sales come from clothing, while interior decoration accounts for 46.5 per cent and bags for 16.6 per cent.

Marimekko's industry sector in Europe

Marimekko is part of the textile and clothing industry. According to the European Commission, the definition of this industry comprises the treatment of raw materials, the production of knitted and woven fabrics, finishing activities such as bleaching and printing, and transformation of fabrics into usable products (see http://ec. europa.eu/enterprise/textile/development.htm).

The industry had undergone significant strain: in the late 2000s, the European textile markets were suffused with textile products from the Far East, in particular from China, Vietnam, Bangladesh and Sri Lanka. Imports from those latter four countries accounted for almost half the imports of textiles into Europe in

2009 (Eurostat, January 2009). They represented strong competition to Euro-Mediterranean textile activities (linked to the European Union since 1995 through a partnership and free trade agreement) and helped European textile firms that were hoping to hold onto competitiveness through cheap manufacture and outsourcing in Morocco, Tunisia, Turkey and Egypt, as a circumvention of high labour costs in Europe. European manufacturers there benefited from geographical proximity and higher quality standards.

This scenario was soon to change. The WTO Agreement on Textiles and Clothing, which eliminated quantitative restrictions on imports into the European textiles market, was signed in 2005. This agreement stirred much concern amongst those producers who held privileged access to the EU market comprising, at that time, 25 Member States. The resulting global liberalization of textile and clothing exports was followed by the end of the textile import monitoring system between the EU and China which created its own challenges for the European textile and clothing industry (see http://www.ec.europa.eu/trade/issues/sectoral/industry/textile/pr091007_en.htm).

Because at the same time, ATC (Agreement on Textiles and Clothing)/Multifiber agreements with, for instance, the Mediterranean countries, were phased out, China was able to increase its exports to the EU massively at the beginning of 2005. Consequently, the EU imposed quotas that were immediately used up by importers (wholesalers and retailers) who hoped to get their orders in as soon as possible, and as cheaply as possible, using up those quotas instantly. This led to the deadlock of about 75 million items of imported Chinese garments in European ports in summer 2005.

The following September 2005 textile deal ('Memorandum of Understanding') between EU Trade Commissioner Peter Mandelson and the Chinese Commerce Minister Bo Xilai resulted finally in the release of those textiles and the further opening of the EU market under a monitoring system, in 2008, allowing for action to be taken in case of a new surge in imports that would cause serious harm to EU industry. The Chinese scenario had a major impact on the organizational structure and operations within Europe.

At the same time, Marimekko's management decided to further increase its cross-border activity and to strengthen its design.

Marimekko and EU integration

Marimekko had begun its cross-border activities more than half a century ago. In the 2000s, however, Marimekko was still in the early stages of internationalization, if measured by market share and market entry strategy.

Milestones in Marimekko history

The company had started exporting as early as 1956, and the first company-owned retail outlet was opened in 1960 in Stockholm, Sweden (Stengg, 2001). This was a natural choice for expansion due to the small psychic distance between the countries as well as the high demand of Marimekko products in Sweden. Even today, Sweden is amongst the five biggest exporting countries for Marimekko in Europe, having gained its pole position since the mid 2000s when consumption of Marimekko's Grünstein products fell dramatically (Karesvuori, 2004). The Nordic countries, separately listed in the Annual Reports due to their importance, have always been easily accessible for Marimekko for cultural, logistical and common market advantages, and, thus, a strong brand awareness. In 2009, a new concept store was opened in Copenhagen, Denmark and Marimekko's own shop in Stockholm was refurbished. The openings support Marimekko's long-term internationalization strategy and strengthen the company's presence in the Nordic capitals.

Some other milestones in Marimekko history are of great interest in this context. In 1974, Marimekko was listed on the Helsinki Stock Exchange, quite an unusual move in an industry dominated by privately owned SMEs. In 1979, the (known-to-be passionate) leader of Marimekko, Armi Ratia, passed away. The impact on the firm was great, and is thought to be one of the main reasons for the decline in sales at the beginning of the 1980s. In 1985, Marimekko was sold to Amer Group Ltd and its shares were removed from the stock exchange. Marimekko's business strategy was renewed and, amongst other activities, outsourcing of production began. The advantageous cost-cuts, however, raised issues in regard to the quality of the garments. Sales began to further decline, and the brand image suffered further. In 1991, the company Workidea, owned by Kirsti Paakkanen, bought Marimekko, and Paakkanen took over as the new head of Marimekko.

The company went public again in 1999, and, as a turning point, results got back to their status quo ante in the Finnish market with a new design team supplemented by several, young talents as well as top names in the industry. In 2000, Marimekko acquired a Finnish firm, Grünstein Product, which manufactured leather and fur products, outdoor clothing and other branded products, and had a strong foothold, in particular, in Germany. This move opened up significant export channels to countries such as France, Russia and the USA at that time.

The company's position in international markets in the 2000s strengthened substantially through numerous Marimekko concept stores that were set up by retailers, based on the strong design and quality concepts of Marimekko. Most of the international expansion was led through concept stores, licensing sales and cooperations. Exports were handled directly and through local agents. The concept stores exposed Marimekko's colourful print design as a differentiating factor. Several Marimekko exhibitions organized around the world also helped increase exports and drove the recognition of the Marimekko brand. A sales target of 20 per cent growth in international sales annually was then set. The major countries for export for Marimekko were Sweden, Denmark, Norway and Germany, and – outside of Europe – Japan and the USA.

Indeed, Marimekko's international sales increased significantly from €9.4 million in 2000 to €21.9 million in 2008. Sales in the Nordic neighbour countries have experienced a steady increase of between 15 and 20 per cent annually since

1999. However, sales stemming from the rest of Europe (which had increased by more than 50 per cent from 2000 to 2001 with the acquisition of Grünstein Product Oy) fell dramatically from 2002 onwards when Grünstein was hit by increasing competition on the continental European market and a fire ravaged its facilities in 2003. Grünstein was finally sold in 2004, and the European market picked up at a moderate pace through shop openings and efficient marketing efforts in Germany, Belgium, Spain, Portugal and other countries. These efforts were also rewarded by the 2007 licensing cooperation agreement with Sweden's H&M (Hennes & Mauritz AB) and the Design Management Europe Award for outstanding management of creative assets.

European integration effects

In 1961, Finland became an associate member of the European Free Trade Association (EFTA) and, in 1986, a full member. EFTA members entertained free trade arrangements amongst themselves and bilateral trade agreements with the EEC (the predecessor of what is now called the European Union), thus expanding the access of Finnish firms to the European market significantly.

Membership of its home country in a free trade union significantly eased Finish companies', and Marimekko's, internationalization opportunities, mainly into the rest of Europe, including its Nordic neighbours, through the benefits of free trade areas, such as the lifting of import restrictions amongst EFTA members, and the European Economic Area (EEA). For those EFTA countries joining the EEA (excluding notably Switzerland), members began to incorporate two-thirds of the EU legislation. This was paving the way for Finland, among other countries, to join the EU for a more harmonized playing field.

Finland joined the EU, with its (partially) supranational powers, in 1995 (together with Austria and Sweden). Cross-border operations and further growth were now facilitated significantly because of market group effects that came from the EU's advanced European integration: in particular, for shift and share advantages, for the harmonization of economic policies, the abandoning of much red tape and transaction costs in intra-EU trade, and the reduction of economic, financial and political risk. The harmonization of the political, economic and regulatory is part of this environment. Customs, tariffs or any other type of restrictions no longer hindered Marimekko's export activities to other Member States and were harmonized across the entire market. A common customs tariff of all EU members towards imports from non-EU countries added an advantage in terms of supplies from abroad and international competition (Stengg, 2001). Finland now had direct and full influence and impact on/from trade policy instruments such as taxation and tariff instruments, anti-dumping duties against injurious imports, local content requirements and rules of origin for all actors in the market, funding opportunities for cross-border R&D and innovation initiatives, standards and IP protection, and similar regulations common to organizations in the Single Market.

The voice of united European voices in international negotiations added negotiation power to the Finnish industry and to a sector under strain across the common market.

For instance, Marimekko was part of the EUROCOTON member companies that had filed an anti-dumping complaint in 1996, against a certain type of cotton bed linen. The complaint led to anti-dumping fines mounting up to 20 per cent of anti-dumping duty on, amongst others, Indian exports in 1997. The case was then taken to the WTO in 1999 by India, and taken to the WTO panel in 2000, where European representatives support its industry with a common voice, and was asked to bring its measures into closer conformity with WTO rules. The WTO backing of the EU in 2000 was later nuanced and revised.

In 1999, the euro-zone came into effect, based on the Treaty on the European Union (Maastricht Treaty) signed in 1992. The euro later proved efficient when handling global economic crises for the stronger EU economies including Finland. More immediately, the common currency helped reduce economic, financial and transaction costs further between the members of the EMU. It was first adopted by 12 Member States, and then grew to 16 euro members by 2010, with an increasing cohesion to the euro-zone by CEE countries.

With one of the two foreign sales subsidiaries of Marimekko located in the euro-zone, benefits of this alone were considerable. But the EU also provided challenges. The economic union and the opening up of the market increased competition and trade creation, especially after the 2004 enlargement which added 10 new Member States, with another two countries joining the EU for full membership in 2007, and pre-accession negotiations and agreement well under way for more countries to join, in particular Croatia and Macedonia, and later, Iceland.

The widening of the European market was prepared by the Treaty of Nice signed in 2001, and resulted in an enlarged EU Single Market of more than 500 million citizens (and potential customers) through the biggest accession of all, in 2004 (coinciding with Grünstein's loss of competitiveness in Germany).

The process of trade liberalization, according to the WTO Agreement on Textiles and Clothing, had been completed in 2005 (Stengg, 2001) with implications, in particular, for competition on the EU market which, all at once, had become openly accessible to low-cost competition that had been previously diverted: 'The significant labour cost differential between many third world countries and Europe put prices under constant pressure.' In this time period, Marimekko invested in new printing and digital screen-making equipment, in a new 'Design, meet the user!' design competition for new talent and innovation, and in international growth through brand and design.

For the EU to remain competitive, firms had to focus on higher productivity or excel in other competitive strengths such as innovation, quality, creativity, design and fashion in this wide market. The textile and clothing industry also became increasingly active in the field of institutional relations, including those in Brussels and Strasbourg that govern the biggest part of regulations implemented in the European marketplace.

Marimekko's interests in common EU market regulations

Marimekko has multiple interests that are influenced by the European market and its regulation. They are based on the company's values (that are defined on the company website, http://www.marimekko.com/eng) and include issues such as:

EU internal trade: as Marimekko's international operations are mainly based on exports, a well-functioning EU trade environment is vital for the company's success. It is important that EU internal trade functions according to common policies, and, as a result, that cross-border European trade is as easy and cost efficient as possible.

International trade agreements on textiles and clothes: the general development of the textile sector is of interest not only to Marimekko but to all actors in the textile industry. International trade agreements on textiles and clothes represent an increasingly important development in this sector in Europe. Both the multilateral and bilateral free trade agreements negotiated by the EU are interesting for Marimekko. According to the European textile and clothing industry, these negotiations should be governed by the principles of reciprocity and symmetry, and the outcome 'should be visibly and undeniably free trade between the EU and the trading partner concerned' (European Commission, 2008).

Intellectual property rights (IPR): Marimekko's core competence and competitive advantage are largely derived from its designs. Therefore, fighting counterfeiting is of greatest importance to Marimekko. Violations of its IPR were handled, for example, in the case of unauthorized use of the poppy pattern (Unikko design) by Dolce & Gabbana in 2008. It appears quasi impossible for the company alone to deal with the worldwide IPR issues, stemming from over 3000 patterns and designs. In addition, the EU lobbies in the World Intellectual Property Organization (WIPO) (Euratex, 2006). Finland can – within the strong negotiation position of 27 countries together – have a greater impact in voicing concerns.

Environment: environmental responsibility and ecology are very important concerns for this company (Lehtinen, 2009). Environmental regulation is part of the EU-governed legislation that supersedes national law on many occasions (80 per cent of Member States' laws are of EU origin) including, amongst others, the EU regulation concerning the use of chemicals such as those used in design manufacturing. Marimekko implemented the REACH regulation (Regulation 1907/2006) which entered into force in 2007. Although Marimekko is a downstream user and is therefore not obliged to register, it voluntarily pre-registered all substances used at the Herttoniemi fabric printing factory. Also, Marimekko, as an importer of certain goods including chemicals, is required to inform the Chemicals Agency and downstream users if a product imported by it contains a specified amount of a substance causing specific concern.

Water, waste water and transport are equally important for Marimekko's activities. The EU transport policy and the goal of the EU Commission to '… aim at fostering clean, safe and efficient travel throughout Europe, underpinning the internal market of goods and the right of citizens to travel freely throughout the EU' (see http://www.marimekko.com/ENG/marimekkocorporation/socialresponsibility/ environmentalresponsibility/frontpage.htm) coincide with the development of flexible human resource movement as well as the movement of goods within the Member States. The EU-wide initiatives allow companies to deliver goods anywhere in the EU in the most practical manner, instead of having to deal with red-tape considerations. The utilization of packaging is arranged in accordance with the Government Decision 962/97 and the EU packaging directive. As the website reads: 'The ecological aspects of product packaging are becoming increasingly important at Marimekko.'

Another example is the possible introduction of a uniform sizing standard for clothing in EU Member States as requested by European clothes manufacturers. The introduction of such a policy has been discussed and would not only make purchasing textiles more convenient for consumers but the manufacturing process would benefit from a simplification of production.

Marimekko's EU interest representation: shaping the market

Marimekko's interests are, directly and indirectly, represented at the EU institutions that shape the Single Market and its business environment. Multiple actors and interest groups can be appropriate for institutional relations. Some lobbying strategies require higher or lower resources, permanent or sporadic presence in Brussels and direct and/or indirect lobbying strategies. In any circumstance, it is essential for the company to play an active role in the institutional arena (in which its competitors and partners are active too), and to find the right partners to cooperate with. Some of the institutions and organizations in this context are as follows.

The European Commission (CEC)

The CEC stresses its need and desire for consultation with stakeholders of the EU, and provides an opportunity to impact legislation at its early stages. At this early stage, an 'issue' is being drafted as a 'proposal' initiating the decision-making process. It is thus a prime EU institution to lobby. As Marimekko's interests are varied, there are multiple policy areas, which affect its operations, and, thus, multiple Directorate Generals (DGs) that constitute the Commission.

Enterprise and industry governs, amongst other areas, the free movement of goods and the use of energy that are important for manufacturers like Marimekko. Another important area for Marimekko is *Internal Market and Services* as protecting industrial property and industrial designs are among its portfolio of policy sectors. *Trade* is in charge of the EU trade policy, which is important for all actors in the textile sector, taking into account, for example, the impact of the WTO trade agreements. Chemical use and ecological issues are among the key policies of the *Environment* directorates general and, as a result, decisions made there have an effect on Marimekko's operations. Heads of Units in these DGs can be contacted easily with information provided to the approximately 20,000 civil servants that are in charge of the various dossiers, and to about 9000 external experts.

The European Parliament

The Members of European Parliament (MEPs), directly elected in their constituencies every five years, are accessible without difficulty and play a central role in developing the business environment in the EU (see the European Commission's *Charlie McCreevy Portfolio* at http://ec.europa.eu/commission_barroso/mccreevy/portfolio_en.htm), in particular because they are close to citizens and companies, and because the European Parliament has gained significant power in the past decade, and through the Lisbon Treaty (the simplified European Constitution). This is thus another central institution for Marimekko to lobby. Finland counted 14 members in the Parliament in 2009, members of important committees and commissions preparing the adoption of legislation by, for the most part, co-decision with the Council. Participation in theme-oriented committees within the Parliament is crucial: the most appropriate committees (and their MEPs) for Marimekko are the Legal Affairs committee (responsible for intellectual property law), the Internal Market and Consumer Protection committee (responsible for identifying and removing potential obstacles to the functioning of the internal market), and the Industry, Research and Energy committee (responsible for the EU's industrial policy). All of these committees have Finnish representation.

Ministries on the national level

National ministries offer Marimekko an indirect way in to the Council of Ministers and, on a head-of-state level, to the European summit. Lobbying on the national level requires fewer resources but needs to be well defined. The most relevant ministry for Marimekko is the Finnish Ministry of Employment and Economy. Although lobbying nationally requires fewer resources, its outcome is debatable as it is possible that the national government does not deliver the desired end result because of last-minute bargaining (Suder, 2007). For certain decisions, such as the enlargement of the EU, the Council needs to have obtained the consent of the European Parliament to be able to adopt the legislation. For most other legislation and for the EU budget, a co-decision of both institutions is needed. The direct powers of ministers are hence limited, but their lobbying is of interest because it spans across national and supranational institutions.

The Federation of Finnish Textile and Clothing Industries (Finatex)

Marimekko is a member of this national interest group, which can be identified as a lobby, training and service organization. Finatex has about 200 members, which altogether employ almost 10,000 people. That is over 90 per cent of the total for the Finnish textile and clothing sector. The main mission of the federation is to 'enhance the business potential of members operating in the highly competitive Finnish and international markets by furthering their business and labour-market interests' (see the European Parliament's *Your MEPs* at http://www.europarl.europa.eu/members/public/geoSearch/search.do?country=FI&language=EN).

The European Apparel and Textile Organization (Euratex)

Euratex is the voice of the European textile and clothing industry supporting its members' interests in the context of the EU's institutional framework and the EU's international obligations. Finatex is one of its members. Euratex has the objective of creating 'an environment within the European Union which is conducive to the manufacture of textile and clothing products'. It is in close contact with the different decision-making institutions of the EU. In recent years, Euratex' major concern areas have included, for instance, the objective of a smooth transition to the quota-free era, promoting intellectual property legislation and supporting environmental protection (see the Finatex presentation at http://www.finatex.fi/html_en/presentation.htm).

The Confederation of Finnish Industries (EK)

All Finnish business sectors and companies of all sizes are represented by EK. Finatex and Marimekko are members of this confederation. EK supports 'a better and more competitive operating environment for the business community in Finland' on an EU level because it is the EU which increasingly regulates the rules concerning Finnish companies (see the Euratex mission at http://www.euratex. org/content/mission.html).

Expert groups

Amongst the great number of interest groups and lobbying experts at the EU, some are officially (CEC) registered expert groups. For Marimekko, groups that advise the Commission in preparing policy initiatives and legislations in its field are those related to free trade agreements, intellectual property rights (no groups focusing solely on IPR in the textile sector can be found), and the textile and clothing industry in general. Some other such groups are:

> *Expert Group on Trade Facilitation*: 'to provide a forum for discussion between the Commission and Member State experts on issues relating to Trade Facilitation, notably in relation to the WTO' (see the Euratex mission at http://www.euratex.org/content/mission.html).

Expert Group on Tariffs: 'to provide a forum for discussion between the Commission and Member State experts on issues relating to Tariff Negotiations, notably in relation to the WTO' (see the EK's *About Us* at http://www.ek.fi/www/en/about_us/index.php).

Expert Group on Best Practices on Strengthening the IPR Enforcement of EU Industry and SMEs: 'to provide an opportunity to review existing IPR enforcement support measures to identify best practices and to make policy recommendations in this field' (see the EK's *About Us* at http://www.ek.fi/www/en/about_us/index.php).

Contact Committee for Copyright in the Information Society: 'to establish close cooperation between the institutions of the Member States and the Commission on issues relating to copyright in the information society; to monitor the development of policies in the area of copyright in the information society; to facilitate the exchange on information, experiences and good practices in the area of copyright in the information society' (see the European Commission's *Register of Expert* Groups at http://ec.europa.eu/transparency/regexpert/detail.cfm?ref=1025&l=all).

Advisory Committee for Coordination in the Internal Market Field: to advise the CEC in regard to the Internal Market.

Expert groups which focus on a narrower section of the textile industry include:

Accords Textiles Pays Tiers: discusses technical/practical aspects of the textiles licensing system (SIGL): the management of licences for imports of textiles, clothing, footwear and steel to the EU; information on quota levels for imports of clothing, footwear and steel products applied in the EC (see the European Commission's *Register of Expert* Groups at http://ec.europa.eu/transparency/regexpert/detail.cfm?ref=1025&l=all).

In some instances, partnering up with other textile and clothing companies (that support the same issues as Marimekko at a given moment in time) becomes important in gaining 'voice' and power. Partner(s), depending on the issue in question, are clothing-related (for instance, Ivana Helsinki and Nanso) or design-related topics (such as Artek and Iittala), or focused on interior decoration textiles (for example, Finlayson and Luhta Home), to mention only the Finnish stakeholders. In regard to IPR issues, cross-industry cooperation proves effective: Marimekko joins forces with companies from other industries combating or supporting the same issues, no matter their home base or sector.

Marimekko and EU enlargement

The textile and clothing industry plays an important role in the manufacturing sector of many of the new Member States of the EU countries, in particular in accession countries of the (biggest) 2004 and 2007 enlargements of the Single Market. For example, the share of textiles and clothing in the overall manufacturing production in the Baltic States was over 11 per cent, followed by Romania and Slovenia with approximately 10 per cent. The share of textiles and clothing manufacturing in the EU-15 (the 15 Member States that had already grouped between 1957 and 1995) for comparison was 4.2 per cent on average at the time. Also, manufacturing employment in textiles and clothing denoted a large share, with 24 per cent in Lithuania, 15 per cent in Slovakia, 14 per cent in Estonia and 13 per cent in Poland. The EU average was approximately 7.6 per cent. The new EU member countries were able to offer existing Member States not only skilled and cheaper labour, but an opportunity to outsource their production to achieve lower costs in proximity, and a vast new market. Many EU countries did so, exporting EU fabric to low-wage Eastern European countries, which then took care of the transformation into finished pieces of clothing for re-import into the western part of the EU. Since the EU enlargement in 2004, mass production within the EU has been altogether repositioned. Initially, the majority of textile and clothing manufacturing was shifted to Central and Eastern Europe, and then from there to Bulgaria and Romania. Some production has also been shifted towards the Mediterranean area, historically linked to the EU and enjoying special partnership agreements (see the European Commission's *Register of Expert Groups* at http://ec.europa.eu/transparency/regexpert/detail.cfm?ref=1025&l=all).

Even though production prices in Asia would have been cheaper, these countries offered the advantage of being close to the European market, furnishing reliable products because of EU regulations, and with privileged import conditions. Turkey's accession to the EU would also significantly affect the textile and clothing industry within the EU. At the end of the 2000s, Turkey (in a customs union with the EU) was indeed ranking second among the EU's biggest suppliers of clothing right after China. Turkey also has approximately 2.5 million workers employed in its textile and clothing sector.

For Marimekko, the opportunities associated with the enlargement of the EU not only provide the company with wider market opportunities but also facilitate the development of operations and prolong the life cycles of the company's products (see the European Commission's *Enlargement* at http://ec.europa.eu/enterprise/textile/enlarg.htm). EU membership increases the purchasing power of the new joining countries (normally within less than 10 years), and consequently also increases demand for goods and services. Additionally, the removal of trade barriers with more countries makes it easier to enter markets previously dominated by domestic producers. Further, Marimekko could consider saving on its production costs by moving some of its manufacturing to new EU countries.

Along with an intention to adopt the euro, new member countries must accept the *Acquis Communautaire*, abiding thus to all EU regulations. For companies such as Marimekko, the risks and costs of doing business with these countries is reduced as their legal systems strengthen, corruption and fraud is reduced, and the market economy functions. The adoption of those tools eliminates fluctuation risks and exchange costs. Specifically, the 2004 enlargement welcomed, amongst others, the country of Lithuania as a new member. After gaining independence, Lithuania's clothing and textile sector had experienced tremendous growth and turned into one of the country's main employer industries. The industry attracted a considerable amount of foreign capital (see the European Commission's *Textiles and Clothing in the Euro-Mediterranean Region* at http://ec.europa.eu/enterprise/textile/euromed.htm). Lithuania's close proximity to Finland makes this location particularly attractive for Marimekko. Mika Ihamuotila, CEO of Marimekko, recently stated that the company has decided to concentrate on developing its internationalization in locations where there is the most natural demand for the company's unique products and designs. The Nordic countries and Japan are a good example; the Baltic countries may lead to a step forward. Certainly the greatest challenge, stemming from EU enlargement, for the textile and clothing industry is the increased competition from opening markets. The WTO Agreement on Textiles and Clothing eliminated quantitative restrictions on imports, which leads to competitive strain in the EU, and affects the new Member States more than the older EU countries. Those new EU countries, which rely heavily on textile production, experience increased pressure to modernize and restructure the sector, in the face of mass production being relocated to developing countries. Additionally, they incur extra costs in regard to respecting the *Acquis Communautaire* and its regulations in the fields of environmental protection and health and safety. The new member countries do, nonetheless, benefit from their close proximity to Western Europe, a very mature market, which results in higher speeds of delivery for products, compared to China, for example, which transports its clothing products to Western Europe by sea.

Impacts of Europeanization

The Europeanization of Business Operations deals with advanced forms of organizations that reflect the diversity of markets and cultures, the diversity within companies, as well as the scope of their operations (Suder, 2007; Tekniikka & Talous, 2008). Mika Ihamuotila, Marimekko's new CEO and president, announced that 'the Marimekko concept stores – both the company's own shops and those owned by retailers – continue to play a key role in the internationalization of Marimekko. This strategy allows us to present the Marimekko brand in depth and to expand our loyal customer base. Our geographic focus will be on areas where the Marimekko brand is already recognized. The goal is to have a sufficient number of stores in each region, so that each shop can benefit from the economies of scale in marketing and other areas.' Marimekko's leadership could not help but wonder what further benefits it could yield from additional market integration. How Europeanized should Marimekko become, and what options are available in terms of benefiting more from market group effects and integration in Europe? Would a company with strongly emphasized Finnish origins be able to leverage more advantage from this large and deeply integrated market, so as to gain further competitive advantage?

In its early stages of true cross-border Europeanization, Marimekko had long been influenced by EU integration. When Finland joined the EU in 1995, Marimekko's export activity did become easier due to the harmonization of the political and economic environment. However, the firm lost out on serving major markets at that very time in the context of its Grünstein challenges. With the biggest EU enlargement in 2004, competition did certainly increase but, also, access to skilled workers, suppliers and talented designers increased across Europe.

The possible Europeanization of consumer preferences, needs and purchasing power raised questions as to marketing strategies in and across Europe, and affected growth strategies, with new locations, new licensing agreements, new European awards and events, and new stores; European integration will continue to fundamentally affect Marimekko and European industry overall. The company is prepared to seize the opportunity.

Questions[3]

1 How did market integration shape Marimekko's business environment?
2 Is European integration a benefit for Marimekko or rather a challenge? Why?
3 Compare Marimekko's net sales development (Table 6), company evolution and the chronology of market integration in the European Union, and report your findings.
4 Does Marimekko's expansion strategy follow the Uppsala model? Do you find its international strategy consistent with its ambitions? Could outsourcing be a benefit?
5 For Marimekko, was the euro a benefit or a challenge during the economic crisis and following it?

Notes

1 I would like to thank Marimekko for the information and validation, and to SKEMA Business School and to Aalto University for the support provided. This case study is intended as a basis for class discussion rather than as an illustration of either effective or ineffective handling of management situations. © 2010 Gabriele Suder. All rights reserved. First published by the European Case Clearing House (ECCH), Cranfield, 2010, reference no. 310-102-1.

See also G. Suder's *Doing Business in Europe* video series on the SAGE companion website http://www.sagepub.co.uk/suder2e and YouTube for illustrations of this case.

The author would also like to thank Tiina Alahuhta-Kasko, Manager at Marimekko, her student team at HSE/Aalto (H. Leino, M. Lindroth, J. Karimaa, S. Norovuori, P. Oinonen, M. Paavola, N. Salmelainen, H. Salo), T. Wierenga at SKEMA, and Marimekko for permission to use the image of its pattern. This pattern, *Kaivo*, a classic design of Maija Isola, the most well-known designer at Marimekko, is credited. © Marimekko Corporation. All rights reserved.

2 Europeanization is defined in two interlinked ways: (1) as that of European integration of economies and the development of common policies and regulatory harmonization of EU Member States; and (2) as that of an advanced level of

organizational response to Single Market benefits, i.e. an organization and/or business activity and strategy that reflects the diversity of the European market as much as its shareholder nationality, partners and suppliers, market expansion, human resources and/or management (Suder, 2007).

3 Questions and Teaching Notes (TN) adapted and partly quoted from Suder/ Lesser, ECCH TN, ref. no 310-102-8.

Bibliography

Euratex (2006) *Going Down the Free Trade Agreement Route: The position of the European Textile and Clothing Industries.* Available at: http://www.euratex.org/download/ publications/papers/euratex_position_on_future_ftas-nov-2006_final.pdf

European Commission (2008) *Copyright and Neighbouring Rights.* Available at: http:// ec.europa.eu/internal_market/copyright/index_en.htm

Karesvuori, A. (2004) *Marimekko 1998–2002: A Case Study.* Helsinki School of Economics. Available at: https://cie.hkkk.fi/26E00400/materiaali/Marimekko.pdf

Lehtinen, H. (2009) *Hiljaista sodankäyntiä.* Available at: http://www.fashionfinland. com/fi/ilmiot/artikkeli/hiljaista_sodankayntia

Stengg, W. (2001) The textile and clothing industry in the EU – a survey. *Enterprise Papers*, No. 2. Available at: http://ec.europa.eu/enterprise/library/enterprise-papers/pdf/enterprise_paper_02_2001.pdf

Suder, G. (2007) *Doing Business in Europe*, 1st edn. London: Sage.

Tekniikka & Talous (2008) *Marimekosta rakennetaan nuorempienkin brändi.* Available at: http://www.tekniikkatalous.fi/viihde/article56371.ece

Managing Change at Unilever

By Dr Joanna Scott-Kennel, University of Waikato/ Aalto University of Economics

Introduction

It is hard to imagine a world without Lux and Dove soap, Sunsilk shampoo, Impulse and Axe deodorants, Pond's Cream, Omo and Surf washing powders, Cif cleaners, Rama and Flora margarine, Iglo frozen foods, Lipton tea, and Ben & Jerry's and Wall's ice cream. It is almost as hard to imagine they are produced by one company. Yet this is the reality. These brands, which are familiar parts of the daily lives of tens of millions of people worldwide, are made and sold by Unilever. (Jones, 2005: 1)

Unilever is one of the largest food and customer care product companies in the world. This case documents major changes to strategy and structure in response to European economic integration. It focuses on the dilemma of one of Unilever's line managers, who, along with his peers, is given responsibility for implementing the new strategy in practice.

Unilever's history

In the 1890s, William Hesketh Lever, founder of Lever Bros, wrote down his ideas for Sunlight Soap – his revolutionary new product that helped popularise cleanliness and hygiene in Victorian England. It was 'to make cleanliness commonplace; to lessen work for women; to foster health and contribute to personal attractiveness, that life may be more enjoyable and rewarding for the people who use our products'. (http://www.unilever.com)

Unilever was created by the merger in 1929 of Lever Brothers (British) and Margarine Uni (Dutch) and is jointly owned and managed by two parent companies: Unilever Ltd with its head office in London and Unilever NV with its head office in Rotterdam.

By the 1950s, Unilever was one of the world's most international businesses. In Europe, Unilever employed over 200,000 people and held huge market shares in its two original products: edible fats (two-thirds of the market share for margarine in Germany, The Netherlands and the UK) and soap and detergents (one-third of the

Western European market). Its products included ice cream and frozen foods, tea, soup, personal care products and chemicals. It owned a large trawling fleet, fish retail shops, restaurants, a road transport fleet, advertising and market research agencies, paper and packaging factories, and was one of Europe's largest oil milling operations.

In addition to its operations in Europe, Unilever had a large business in the USA, which, by the end of the World War II, accounted for one-fifth of total sales. During the war, Unilever had diversified from its long-established soap and detergent business in the USA by acquiring T.J. Lipton, the largest tea company in the USA, and the toothpaste company Pepsodent. Unilever also had substantial business interests (largely in soap and detergents) in Latin America, Africa and Asia, and owned the United Africa Company, the largest trading company in West Africa.

Regional integration

European integration opened up the possibility of a more international approach to the production and distribution of branded products across the continent. There was evidence that US firms were already reaping the benefits of treating Europe as a single market. Unilever, however, had a culture of decision-making, marketing and production organized at the local (national) level. This was hardly surprising for a business which was selling consumer products where tastes, habits and legislation were likely to be especially divergent between countries, and which had grown through merger and acquisition rather than organically. Acquired companies typically had their own strong corporate identities and brands. Not even the operating companies that made and sold Unilever products used the name Unilever (Jones and Miskell, 2005).

As European integration progressed in the early 1950s, the challenge for management became how to secure economies of scale without losing local market knowledge. It was clear that Unilever needed a new business model. However, formation of Europe-wide product group divisions in the 1970s, far from being a direct response to European integration, was highly contentious and the difficulties Unilever encountered took well over a decade to resolve (Jones and Miskell, 2005).

One area of contention was the newly devised position of 'World Coordinator'. First assigned to the promising business areas of personal care (toothpaste, shampoo, conditioner, perfume, make-up, skincare and shaving products) and food (including tea, soup, ice cream and other frozen and processed foods), and by 1962 to key business areas (edible fats and detergents) and, finally, to more disparate operations (paper, packaging and print), the role of the World Coordinators was to ensure that new brands were developed with an international market in mind. However, their function was to advise rather than to direct – and that advice was often ignored.

Despite further attempts at structural change (European Coordinators in the late 1960s, and European Product Divisions in the 1970s), national managers continued to resist central direction and leadership. Nationally based operating companies retained considerable autonomy in both production and marketing decisions. This had major implications for complexity and costs within the business. In the late

1970s, for example, Unilever estimated that while Procter & Gamble (P&G) supported 186 detergent brands worldwide, it was selling a total of 665. Some brands (such as *Sunsilk* shampoo and *Pepsodent* toothpaste) were sold in multiple markets but continued to be formulated, manufactured and marketed differently in different countries in Europe and elsewhere.

Time for change

Vitality is at the heart of everything we do. It's in our brands, our people and our values. (http://www.unilever.com)

Unilever's strategic approach had been a highly effective way of building a truly multinational business but was now out of step with the increasingly globalized competitive landscape. Here, battles were being fought and won with global scale and know-how coupled with top-down, strategically driven allocation of resources. By the late 1990s, Unilever had evolved into a highly complex matrix structure organized and managed at global, regional (such as Europe) and country level for each of the main product divisions: Home and Personal Care; Retail Foods and Icecream; and Food Solutions (business-to-business foods division). Each division and each country had its own separate management, marketing, human resources and administrative functions.

In the 1980s and 1990s, volume growth averaged a mere 2.5 per cent and Unilever began to lose advantage relative to competitors. In order to remedy this situation, a five-year 'Path to Growth' strategy was launched in 1999 with the goal of achieving sustained growth. The new strategy delivered brand focus, improved global buying, drove up margins and improved capital efficiency, but, unfortunately, failed to transform Unilever's growth performance. This was despite a cut in the number of brands from 1600 to 900 by 2001, the sale of DiverseyLever, Elizabeth Arden and Unipath in the same year, and further sales in 2002 of 87 businesses without acceptable growth or margin potential.

In 2004, the 'Vitality' mission was launched and the new Unilever brand rolled out, including a new logo representing the diversity of Unilever, its products and people. By early 2005, however, approximately 14 per cent of Unilever's businesses were still performing badly. It was clear that a new business model combining effective organizational structure with a strategy for growth was needed at Unilever – 'one that combined a more active, aggressive, top-down approach to managing and building our portfolio', said Patrick Cescau (Unilever, 2007a), Unilever Group Chief Executive.

Unilever today

150 million times a day, someone somewhere chooses a Unilever product. From feeding your family to keeping your home clean and fresh, our brands are part of everyday life. (http://www.unilever.com)

In February 2005, Unilever announced a series of significant changes to streamline its management and leadership, encourage vitality in the company and deliver faster decisions and execution. Antony Burgmans was appointed non-executive chairman of both Unilever N.V. and Unilever PLC while Patrick Cescau took on the new role of group chief executive, responsible for all operations.

The 'One Unilever' strategy entailed a major organizational change programme designed with the vision of creating a seamless company operation where duplication was eliminated and innovation shared. Richard Rivers, Head of Strategy, explains how the new strategy was set in motion.

> First, we focus on attractive businesses ... that are growing faster than average ... that are favoured by demographic and consumer trends and especially Vitality. Second, we like businesses ... where we can combine global leadership with strong local positions [and] will benefit from our brands and our technology. Several of our personal care categories tick all these boxes – Deodorants, Skin, Hair [and] Foods categories also fit the bill. Like Savoury, Ice Cream and Tea, where, again, big global brands, marketing and technology can make the difference (even if we haven't yet fully realised the opportunity). (Unilever, 2007b)

Through 2005 and 2006, Unilever conducted a comprehensive review of category strategies and applied a disciplined 'strategy into action' approach so that every unit had portfolio priorities and investment status (priority or non-priority), by brand and by category. The 30 per cent of the business which received priority investment grew strongly, and Unilever started to grow market share as a result.

In July 2008, with the release of the company's latest performance figures, Patrick Cescau reported:

> our performance in the first half year has been good in what has been a challenging environment. We have delivered 7 per cent underlying sales growth and an underlying improvement in profitability while maintaining competitiveness. The changes already implemented in the business have made us nimbler and better able to respond to the market conditions. We are doing so against our clear priorities of maintaining competitiveness, improving margins and investing selectively to gain market share. (31 July 2008, http://www.unilever.com)

The challenge of change

> Unilever employs 223,000 people in 100 countries, has over 20 nationalities in its top 100 leaders and thinks of itself as a truly multi-local multinational. (http://www.unilever.com)

By reducing the layers within the top management structure, Unilever gains greater simplicity, clarity of leadership and accountability. The new company structure is led by the Board, chaired by Michael Treschow, and operational authority is delegated to the Group Chief Executive, Patrick Cescau. He also chairs the Unilever Executive (UEX), consisting of three regional presidents (Europe, Americas, Asia/AMET), two category presidents (Foods, and Home and Personal Care), the Chief Financial Officer, the Chief Human Resources Officer and the General Counsel and Joint Secretary. Figure 8 illustrates Unilever's new streamlined structure.

In terms of implementation of the strategy, the Foods, Home and Personal Care categories are responsible for innovation and developing Unilever's 400 brands. Their single-minded role is to drive to true global advantage – and to leverage best practice across the world. The regions are responsible for activating the brands, regionally and locally, deepening customer relationships, profit and loss and business growth. They are totally focused on deploying investment and executing in line with the strategy (Unilever, 2007a).

While rationalization and restructuring of activities worldwide achieved the desired company structure, the challenge of managing the changes through people remained. In the words of Patrick Cescau, Unilever CEO: 'the new business model is not just the growth strategy. The other half of it is the organization, the people, the capabilities and ways of working, the mindset that can deliver the growth strategy.' Formerly distinct country and business groups are now merged and support functions integrated by region, rather than by country. This, however, has meant a reduction in manager and employee numbers, and more challenges for those who remain.

Putting it all into practice

Although the 'One Unilever' strategy was heralded as a major leap forward in terms of achieving levels of efficiency comparable to global competitors, putting it into practice was less than straightforward. The Western European regional headquarters were now based in Rotterdam but Unilever had diverse and still relatively autonomous operations all over Europe. Key to efficiency was reducing duplication between operations based in different countries, whilst following

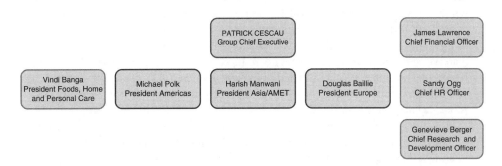

Case Study Figure 8   *Unilever's organizational structure*

Source: Unilever, 2008

global strategic objectives. In the Human Resources area, for example, the strategy envisaged Unilever would:

> *maintain an effective Leadership Supply system for our most leveraged roles and teams, complemented with a fully aligning talent strategy. Align, energize and inspire our people. Help them grow. (Unilever, 2008)*

Translating such global aspirations into day-to-day country-specific operations required reorganization at the regional level. Implementation would require major changes for many of Unilever's subsidiaries.

The challenges facing those working at Unilever Finland, just one of several in the Nordic region, were illustrative of the wider issues associated with balancing country- and regional-specific organizational change. The main issues seemed to arise at the line manager level, in particular. Many high-potential employees had been promoted from specialist brand marketing positions to the new and more demanding line manager roles. The new positions required management of other brands as well as employees down the line, some of whom were based in neighbouring countries. Frederik, who had recently been promoted to line manager, explains:

> *We were really thrown in the deep end after the 'One' strategy started to take effect. I not only had to manage another two brands, but also two new brand 'assistants' in Sweden and Denmark. How was I supposed to get the best out of them, when I was still learning my own new job?*

Before the new strategy, Frederik had been the Nordic area brand manager for Magnum ice cream. He was in charge of tailoring brands and promotion for Nordic markets originating from the European regional product and brand development team in Italy (the 'brand developers'). In order to ensure consistency in brand image and careful timing of promotional activities, he worked closely with customer marketing teams in the Nordic countries. These teams were responsible for reaching customers through successful launch of the brand at the store level. The customer marketing team would then liaise with Unilever's Key Account Managers, each of whom managed one large customer, to ensure the products were stocked.

Frederik had been pleased with the effectiveness of the previous summer's TV advertising campaign which had been well supported by in-store posters and promotional material and had managed to keep sales high despite cooler weather than average. Kesko, one of Unilever's clients based in Finland, owned the K-market, K-Supermarket and K-City-Market chains and had made generous allowances for Magnum SKUs (stock-keeping units) on the shelves that year which had helped keep turnover high.

However, as winter approached, Frederik wondered if the sea change at Unilever signalled stormy weather ahead for the newly appointed line managers – himself included. It seemed to Frederik that his workload had tripled almost overnight, and he felt ill-equipped to deal with all the new demands his job was making on him. First of all, Solero and Carte d'Or ice cream had been added to his portfolio – and not just in Finland but the whole Nordic region. While he was the first to admit he loved the ice-cream business, getting his head around dealing with new customer marketing managers, different customer segments, different pricing and promotion strategies and different marketing channels for all three brands in all four countries was certainly going to be a challenge!

And that wasn't all. He was now expected to take on the role of both manager and leader! His brand assistants in Sweden and Denmark would look to him for advice and guidance on how the products should be marketed there. In line with broader directives from Unilever global and the European headquarters, the VP of Marketing of Unilever Nordic had already briefed his group on the importance of being able to motivate and inspire others. Although Frederik had attended the briefing, he still didn't have a clue how to get started – his assistants weren't even based in Finland! He also found his administrative role had grown along with his new staff responsibilities. He would now be responsible for PDPs (Performance Development Planning – annual performance review and development discussion processes) and play an important role in the promotion of more junior staff.

Unilever Finland's HR Director, Ilkka Korpelainen, soon realized that Frederik was not alone in feeling disillusioned. He knew that something had to be done – and fast. He also knew that 2008 was not going to be an easy year. Patrick Cescau, Group Chief Executive, had announced his retirement after 35 years of service with the expectations that Unilever's growth would rise beyond the 3–5 per cent target range.

Four years ago we set out to transform Unilever and to get the business back on track ... I leave with a real sense of pride in what has been achieved, but also great confidence in the company's ability to pursue the opportunities that lie ahead. (Unilever, 2007a)

Ilkka wondered to himself how they would not only pursue these opportunities, but also meet the challenges ahead.

Questions

1 Why and how did Unilever change its management strategy in Europe? Compare and contrast Unilever's former multinational approach to strategy with the new 'One Unilever' strategy.
2 What challenges and opportunities does Frederik face (related to Europeanization)?
3 Being as creative as you can, design a change management strategy that addresses these challenges. Your strategy should offer practical solutions to help Unilever's managers, like Frederik, put the strategy into practice.
4 What alternative options would you recommend, in line with the objective of 'how to secure economies of scale without losing local market knowledge'? What does one need to know about the different European locations and cultures to make sound decisions in this context?

Recommended reading

Bird, A. (2009) McKinsey conversations with global leaders: Paul Polman of Unilever. *McKinsey Quarterly,* October, pp. 1–10.

Crawford, B., Gordon, J.W. and Mulder, S.R. (2007) How consumer goods companies are coping with complexity. *McKinsey Quarterly,* Web exclusive, May, pp. 1–13.

Haden, P.D., Sibony, O. and Sneader, K.D. (2004) McKinsey on consumer goods: new strategies for consumer goods. *McKinsey Quarterly,* December, pp. 1–6.

Hass, S., McGurk, M. and Mihas, L. (2010) A new world for brand managers. *McKinsey Quarterly,* April, pp. 1–7.

Bibliography

Jones, G. (2005) *Renewing Unilever: Transformation and Tradition.* Oxford and New York: Oxford University Press.

Jones, G. and Miskell, P.M. (2005) European integration and corporate restructuring: the strategy of Unilever, c. 1957 to c. 1990. *Economic History Review,* vol. 58, no. 1, pp. 113–39.

Unilever (2007a) Interview with Patrick Cescau, Group Chief Executive, 13 March. *Speeches and Interviews.* Available at: http://www.unilever.com

Unilever (2007b) Interview with Richard Rivers, Head of Strategy at Unilever, 13 March. *Speeches and Interviews.* Available at: http://www.unilever.com

Unilever (2008) Interview with Ilkka Korpelainen, HR Director at Unilever Finland, 1 September. *Speeches and Interviews.* Available at: http://www.unilever.com

Altran: Launching a Corporate Representation Office in Brussels

By Professor Gabriele Suder, SKEMA Business School

Introduction

In 2001, an important decision was taken by the Belgian Executive Management of Altran, a major player in European innovation consulting: to entrust the analysis of an 'opportunity for Altran to position itself at *European Institution level*' to a business development manager.[1] This was the beginning of a project for the launch of the company's representation office in Brussels at the heart of European policy making. Altran is a group of more than 180 companies serving more than 500 partners worldwide, a group which engages in strategy, innovation, technology and engineering consultancy.

This 2001 decision to move into the heart of Europe was based on various factors. Among these was the physical position of Altran in Brussels, close to the European decision-making process. Also, the young Business Development Manager came forward with a convincing and ambitious proposal to create a representation office for the group. This manager was, at the time, in charge of Space and Defence at Altran's offices in Belgium and had graduated from business school, specializing in European Affairs.

His analysis of the opportunities indicated good conditions for Altran to start developing its contribution to European policies and projects following a professional and organized process that included the following:

- an increase in allocated resources for research;
- a focus on small- and medium-sized enterprises (SMEs) and innovation;
- Altran geographical coverage;
- an international crisis: a need to find new markets; reorientation to public sectors;
- a change in the European institutions in 2004 (new Commission, new Parliament);
- a refocus of the Lisbon agenda.

The high degree of diversification of the group's business domains and its geographical coverage were indicators for Altran's main opportunities in the project: with its various competencies of technical consultation in fields such as energy and environment, telecommunication and information, and transport, the group was leading the European market in its sector of technology and engineering consulting. Also,

Altran's geographical diversification into markets reached from the EU, throughout regions such as those of Eastern Europe and the Mediterranean, to North and Latin America, and into the Asia-Pacific region. A remarkable development of Altran's revenues on a year-on-year sales basis reinforced its operations: a great increase in its US market share of 75 per cent and its Latin American of 50 per cent at the turn of the millennium provided the corporation with sound international weight, while Altran was still to reach its full potential and advance into new markets such as Oceania and the African, Caribbean and Pacific (ACP) countries.

The Belgian branch of Altran analysed and examined the project's potential and their findings led to the decision to focus on short-term return on the investment, given the lack of experience in the field of EU corporate representation.

However, the success rate was to remain insignificant, and the group's internal and external challenges at this time forced it to reconsider its strategy, and to realize what potential was to be exploited through new objectives for the project.

Altran's target business area, coverage field or coverage clients were unlimited from the beginning. However, at the second stage, the group concentrated on a small pilot project with a limited number of companies so as to create a sound and solicited expertise. Altran focused on EU contribution and image investment for business development. Only then, it was recognized, would it be sensible to diversify its target business area and partners so that both short-term and long-term return on investment could be met for Altran itself, its future clients and partners (the term used by the firm for existing clients). This case will now give valuable insight into the complex and difficult path that leads to the launch of a successful corporate representation office in Brussels.

The project

With an analysis of the group's opportunities for a launch of a corporate representation office in Brussels, during 2001, the project was rapidly considered worthwhile, though not strategic for the whole group. In the short-term, the go-ahead was given for a focus on high-quality proposals to public institutions' calls for tender and proposals, and for the development of new expertise and know-how with rapid returns on investment. In the long-term, this was potentially to widen into the further development of services and new competencies at Altran, and a proposal to the clients to act as an interface for European programmes.

The main objectives were hence two-fold: first, to ascertain Altran's expertise in EU affairs management and, second, to then also serve its clientele.

In Phase 1 of the project, the European office was created and operated with six Altran pilot companies. From January 2002 to December 2003, this analysis and test phase analysed the potential for effective business in Brussels, aiming to prove the concept following a 'strategy in action 'approach, that is, to design the concept by starting to produce actions and results. The focus was mainly on business development and short-term return on investment. Altran companies were selected for their interest, their knowledge and their capacity to work on European projects, and an external partner was added, working in a cluster approach. The European office started to produce project proposals concerning services for the European institutions. After a year of activities, the success rate was rather low.

In Phase 2, the involvement of more Altran companies (more than 180) came to broaden the scope of action (Figure 9). A Phase 3 was to enter the collaboration with clients, and to develop new services by targeting the private sector.

Given the low success rate of the European office at the beginning, the Altran European office team analysed the concurrent key factors of future success, and with this the needs that were to be satisfied to obtain efficiency in its operations. These factors were noted to be the:

- commitment of the companies to provide key human resources during the entire proposal preparation;
- commitment of the Board = decision-making on strategy and action plan and convergence with group strategy;
- industrialization of the process starting with one key sector (pilot project then growth);
- thorough process/methodology with tools;
- anticipation and coordinated action between business and representation actions (building image to make business which develops image).

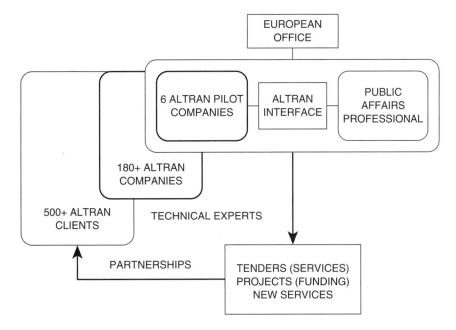

Case Study Figure 9   *ALTRAN client and partnership interface relations*

In addition, management recognized that the project's future was based not only on technical competencies, but also on networking skills and experience at the EU institutions. On the one hand, the high quality of human resources and the skills of its employees were necessary; on the other hand, an external partner selection process was to add the missing experience. Hence, the European office analysed 50 European public affairs companies, of which it interviewed 10. Of, these companies 7 were interviewed by the recruitment team to reinforce the focus on their compatibility with the Altran corporate culture, and, finally, with seven proposals having been received and presented, one company was selected to work with the European team.

In a similar fashion, the Altran Companies Selection Process, of those companies to be part of the six pilot companies in the project, followed the EU tendering approach. Six companies in six different key European markets were selected – France, the UK, Spain, Italy, Germany and Belgium – and shared investments per month.

The structure of this organization was developed as illustrated through the diagram in Figure 10:

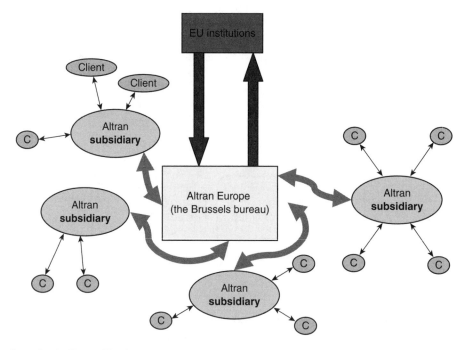

Case Study Figure 10   *Inter-organizational diagram*

'Strategy in action'

This two-step strategy has a strong readability for non-experienced individuals as it can be summarized through the diagram in Figure 11:

Case Study Figure 11   *Strategy in action*

The early two-steps strategy of the European office consisted in an analysis of poten-tiality of its operations, and the development of activities that would ensure return on investment so that the office could prove its worth. In analysing potentiality, the team highlighted the main areas of development that its office would offer to the group. Probably one of the most important features to be aware of was the potentiality of a strong and close relationship with EU institutions. What would such a relationship pos-sibly deliver to Altran? As part of the analysis, the team studied the methodology of the EU policy for funding, the main actors, and the way in which the EU discloses informa-tion on funding programmes with a call for tenders that only allows for a short applica-tion period for interested organizations. Anticipation and follow-up of annual calls were found to be essential in this field of activity, which requires a medium- to long-term approach. Moreover, the great diversity in the range of programmes likely to co-finance projects of Altran's entities involves specialization and selectivity (see Figure 12).

The internal structure of the Altran group is composed of an exceptionally wide range of companies. Each of them is specialized in one or more fields of activity that may find affinity with EU sectorial and horizontal policies. Also, Altran's geographic development evolves in areas that are part of the EU's strategic interests. This estab-lishes the 'portfolio' of Altran's competencies that can contribute to EU expertise and, vice versa, benefit from European partnerships, funding, services and market contracts, and the international political agenda. Nonetheless, reaching this type of relation necessitates the excellent knowledge of the two sides, of all players in the EU policy-making arena, and of Altran's structures, specializations, developments and engineers. It needs organization and planning.

The 'strategy into action' approach was meant to be a 'learning from failures' approach. The objective was to learn how to do by doing. This strategy had to directly link Altran's domains of competence with the direct implementation of returns. From January 2004 to January 2005, this second launch phase hence concentrated on con-ceptualization. During this phase, the European Office dedicated its activities to the reformulation of objectives and design of a new concept, and the structuring and creation of a modus operandi. The main focus was that of a definition of Altran's contribution to the EU, and image investment for its business development.

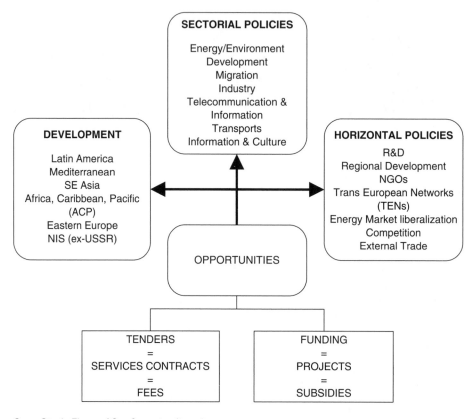

Case Study Figure 12   *Opportunity scheme*

Company specificities shape the methodology

Altran specializes in scientific consulting, and has acquired great experience in this domain, particularly in Europe. The group's internal organization is relatively fragmented, given the more than 180 entities that constitute the group. Altran is, hence, to some extent, comparable to a grouping of SMEs: each entity specializes in a precise field of activity(ies).

In 2002, Altran was hit by an accounting scandal. It was alleged that various members of the board of directors at the time were accomplices in manipulating and falsifying the company accounts. On 11 September 2002, the COB (the French market supervisory authority, now called AMF – Autorité des Marchés Financiers) filed a complaint against three of the group's directors on charges of dissemination of false information and manipulating quotations. By October 2002, Altran's shares had plummeted with a 45 per cent loss in value. Altran then allowed external auditors to check the company accounts.

On 30 January 2003, a legal inquiry was initiated against the directors and Altran joined in as civil plaintiff. These legal proceedings followed a case opened by the prosecutor in October 2002, the same date that a press article was published on the results of the first half of 2002 (on 8 October 2002, the results of the first half of 2002 were published with the comment 'audited figures under review'). Altran immediately asked its auditors, in concert with the COB, to perform a thorough audit of the 2001 accounts and the accounts for the first half of 2002. When the audit was completed and the results corrected, the auditors confirmed the authenticity of the 2001 accounts and those of the first half of 2002 published on 15 October 2002. The auditors informed the prosecutor that, to the best of their knowledge, no other item was likely to attract his attention. At the end of 2004, each of the three directors was subsequently cleared of any wrongdoing.

This crisis undeniably affected Altran's image and reputation. To make matters worse, the Altran scandal occurred in the shadow of the Enron and WorldCom accounting scandals, which shook the financial world. The case also highlighted two very concerning issues within the Altran structure. The first was a lack of accounting checks and regulations at the time. This is illustrated by the ease with which the employees involved in the scandal appeared to have falsified and manipulated the accounts. The second was poor corporate governance and a lack of communication with the business world and shareholders. This last problem no doubt created further damage to Altran: the corporation's secrecy in the case and about their affairs in general did nothing to fan the speculation and rumours during the scandal nor the negative publicity that Altran received from the media. Rumours circulated about the highest annual turnovers of employees in the industry. The direct impact of this was that Altran's financial results were very unconvincing in the 2002, 2003 and 2004 exercises.

Indirectly, the European office project suffered from the necessity of the group to dedicate its main financial and human efforts to redressing the company, minimizing and reducing damage done to the company by the scandal, and replacing its management. Since the EU lobbying project is a project with a long-term aim, with little possibility of significant immediate results, Altran's priorities lay elsewhere.

However, the new top management recognizes that, in Altran's aim to be the European market leader in innovation, European representation, European credibility and European influences are vital key factors. Logic dictates that only credible, ethical, trustworthy and valuable actors are permitted into the microcosm of successful public affairs managers at the EU. The name-and-shame principle of Brussels has a reputation!

The European office of Altran was, after the low rate of success in its early years, forced to set new objectives that would extend from the short- to the long-term on the timeline, and be complemented by an internal lobbying for the office's cause in the long run. In 2005, Altran underwent an important reorganization and analysis of its strategic orientations, following the appointment of Christophe Aulnette, former CEO of Microsoft France, as new CEO for the group. A new board was recruited and the management decided to change the governance of the organization. After three years of discussions, preparation and development of the project, Altran decided to officially launch its European office.

The European office now focused on a revised timeline:

- In the short-term: Altran is aiming at developing high-quality proposals and projects for public institutions, while benefiting from the expertise of an EU professional through a reinforced partnership with non-Altran competencies. Moreover, Altran experience and know-how can be considered as a 'push power' to create new projects and programmes.
- In the short-term/medium-term: Altran is aiming to influence the development and innovation of European technological trends. Thus, there exists a real will to become a partner of the EU in the field of scientific consulting.
- In the long-term: Altran is aiming to develop new services and competencies by choosing more specific partners inside the group, thus choosing more fields of competencies. Another aim is to propose an interface on European programmes to Altran clients, helping them improve their understanding of these sometime policies and their opportunities (see Figure 13).

The strategic relevance of 'fighting on all fronts' at the EU level can only be based on a corporate culture, and may otherwise well be classified as a waste of resources and energy. A company such as Altran, composed of more than 16,000 employees, can be well advised to create a small conglomerate of preferred partners for a set of European affairs. Only strong links between fewer companies allow the necessary level of collaboration that is required to implement an efficient bureau in Brussels.

The difference in the timelines lies in the fact that public institutions think in terms of months and years, when companies have shorter periods. This feature stems from the fact that companies and public institutions diverge in terms of objectives: the former needs to be profitable, the latter to represent the interests of citizens. This divergence has to be taken into account and developed to sort out a strategy consistent with collaboration with EU institutions.

This requires exactly the same 'mental gymnastics' as a business plan: you need to think about processes before applying them. The creation of a modus operandi is probably the best way to see all the issues that are about to rise, and to solve them

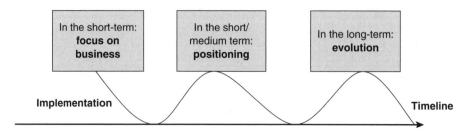

Case Study Figure 13   *Time management of the European Office*

with anticipation. The interpretation of objectives, methods and timelines can make or break relations between the corporate and public sectors in Europe.

Questions

1 Why did Altran set up a European representation?
2 What were the main challenges in this endeavour?
3 What alternative solutions could the group have used to increase its public affairs management in Europe?

Note

1 The author would like to thank Nicolas Rougy for his insights and support, as well as the students on the MIM European Business programme for their input into this case analysis. This case study was first published in Suder (2007).

Bibliography

Suder, G. (2007) *Doing Business in Europe*, 1st edn. London: Sage.

Haier: A Global Chinese Corporation Feels at Home in Germany

By Dr Bernd M. Linke, Friedrich Schiller University of Jena and Dr Andreas Klossek, Technical University of Freiberg

Introduction

When you go to Orly airport in Paris today, you will surely pass around the highway surrounding Paris and probably see some of the many advertisements that Haier, the largest producer of white goods (such as refrigerators, washing machines, dishwashers) in China, has placed there.[1] Today, Haier is present in European countries like France, the UK, Italy, Spain, The Netherlands and Germany, as well as in many other countries in Eastern Europe. Being a Chinese company with strong Chinese cultural roots, how did Haier manage to successfully enter the European market? Based on the example of Germany, this case will demonstrate how Haier entered the European market and how it managed to get along with a multiplicity of challenges and opportunities.

Stages in Haier's development

Today's Haier Group started out in 1984 as a small 'collective enterprise' (on the lines of a German cooperative) with 20 workers in the Eastern Chinese coastal city of Qingdao, a former German colony about 530 kilometres south-east of Beijing. In the year of its foundation, the fledgling company teetered on the brink of bankruptcy on account of mismanagement and inferior product quality. At this point, the city government appointed the deputy manager Zhang Ruimin, being 35 years old at the time. Today, Zhang still serves as a CEO and Chairman of the Board of Directors for the Haier Group. From the day of his appointment as CEO, Zhang decided to concentrate on Haier's core business, which was making refrigerators. His primary goal was to establish a strong brand within this product segment, synonymous with excellent product and service quality across Asian markets.

This decision characterized the first phase in the Haier Group development between 1984 and 1991, the so-called 'brand-building' stage (see Figure 14). A story which is still told about this period has come to epitomize what the company stands for: One day, Zhang Ruimin ordered 76 faulty refrigerators to be lined up in front

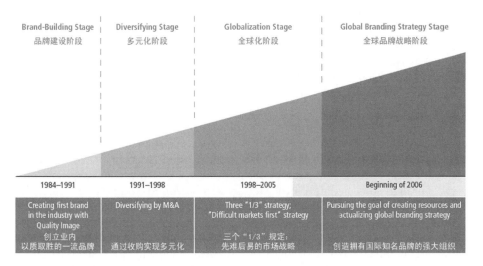

Brand-Building Stage 品牌建设阶段	Diversifying Stage 多元化阶段	Globalization Stage 全球化阶段	Global Branding Strategy Stage 全球品牌战略阶段
1984–1991	1991–1998	1998–2005	Beginning of 2006
Creating first brand in the industry with Quality Image 创立业内 以质取胜的一流品牌	Diversifying by M&A 通过收购实现多元化	Three "1/3" strategy; "Difficult markets first" strategy 三个 "1/3" 规定： 先难后易的市场战略	Pursuing the goal of creating resources and actualizing global branding strategy 创造拥有国际知名品牌的强大组织

Case Study Figure 14   *Haier's globalization strategy (adapted from Deloitte & Touche)[1]*

of the factory and had them smashed up with sledge-hammers in front of the assembled workforce. He also personally demolished a refrigerator, which is now in the Haier museum. This spectacle was designed to instil in the workforce a higher awareness of the need for quality and discipline. It also highlighted the strategy of the corporation, which was trying to gain a foothold in the market as a manufacturer of high-quality appliances. In order to achieve this, Zhang also aimed at achieving a permanent improvement in quality management through a joint venture with Liebherr, a German company in the refrigerator business. Liebherr was also the model for the current name of the corporation as 'Haier' is the Chinese way of writing the phonetic version of the German word 'Herr'.

After some years of rapid growth, the corporation, which in 1991 was renamed 'Qingdao Haier Group', finally embarked on a second development stage in which it deliberately diversified into other areas. An important stepping stone was the acquisition of the huge, though heavily indebted, state enterprise Qingdao Red Star Electric Appliance in 1993. With the acquisition of Qingdao Red Star's washing machine division Haier added a new, though complementary, product segment to its product portfolio of white goods. In the same year, Haier was listed on the Shanghai Stock Exchange and used the money raised in this way to finance a new production line in Qingdao. This 'diversifying stage' lasted until the late 1990s (see Figure 14) and included numerous forays into areas such as air conditioning equipment, TVs, PCs and mobile phones. On top of this, however, Haier added areas that were highly unrelated to Haier's core business, such as real estate and financial and tourist services – a pattern found in many other large Asian corporations, too.

During the next stage (1998–2005), the corporation became increasingly international as a result of many partnerships with foreign companies, resulting in the 'globalization stage'. This phase saw the advent of production joint ventures with partners elsewhere in Asia: when it came to making direct investments, Haier first went to close locations such as Indonesia and the Philippines (1996) or Malaysia (1998). The geographical and cultural proximity of these locations resulted in lower costs of foreignness, which are common when going abroad (see, for example, Zaheer, 1995). Moreover, these locations also offered significant advantages that stemmed from low labour costs. Later, and in line with Johanson and Vahlne's (1977) process model of gradual internationalization behaviour based on accumulated learning and experience, Haier formed sales joint ventures with partners in the USA and Japan. In 2001, Haier acquired the Italian company Meneghetti, including its design centres in Lyon and Amsterdam, which made Haier the first Chinese company in modern history to acquire a European company. Through this acquisition, Haier gained a sound foothold enabling its European expansion.

Today, Haier has eight globally dispersed R&D centres, over 40 production facilities spread all over the world and more than 58,000 point of sales spread across 160 countries. In concordance with this, Haier is currently pursuing its fourth development stage, i.e. the 'global branding strategy stage' (see Figure 14). By this means, Haier is specifically aiming at popularizing its brand worldwide through gaining market shares. At Haier, this strategy is called 'market first, profit second' in order to stress the basic idea of gaining a strong branding and market foothold first and high profits later. The strategy peaked in December 2009 when Haier 'reached the top spot in major appliances brands by market share for the first time' (Haier, 2009), according to Euromonitor International. In this vein, Haier is currently aiming at penetrating markets all over the world, with Europe and, most specifically, Germany being among the most important ones.

Haier Deutschland GmbH as a European role model

Today, Haier's European organizational structure includes the central sales office in Varese, Italy, and several sales branches in Germany, France, the UK and The Netherlands. In August 2006, the German sales branch was transformed into a self-contained and more flexible 'GmbH' (the German pendant of the British 'Limited'). The GmbH is the most common corporation form in Germany and, by this means, signals trustworthiness and a long-term focus, thus making it an 'employer of choice'. There were several good reasons for the decision to found an independent subsidiary in the shape of a GmbH: the expansion of business in Germany – particularly the amount of invoicing and the number of employees at the German location – made it necessary to transform the sales branch into a company with the legal status of a GmbH. The transformation also showed the significance of the German market for Haier, as the German CEO, Sun Shubao, remarked: 'We are fully aware of the strategic importance of the German market for our European business. This is the heart of Europe, and this is where we have to be successful – there was not the slightest doubt about that in our minds from the very beginning.' The appointment of the

German Kurt Weiss as general manager of the Sales and Marketing department of Haier Europe Trading in 2005 shows the importance of the German market for Haier's European business and brand-building strategy (Bell, 2008).

In the course of the transformation of the German branch, new structures were introduced. For example, in 2006, Haier introduced a team assembling system, referred to as the '1 + 1 + n system'. Each team had to consist of one external industry specialist (1), one specialist with a Chinese background (1) and, depending on situational requirements, of several local employees (n). External experts, whatever their nationality happened to be, had many years of sales experience in the industry and had already been involved in successful market entries of corporations they were previously with. This practice was based on a model from the American market, where the corporation's success was largely due to top US manager Michael Jamal, who has been working with Haier since 1994. The Chinese specialists were sent out from the central offices in Qingdao and held firm-specific knowledge and experience. Hence, the combination of external and internal specialists resulted in an amalgamation of different types of knowledge and experience, as well as in a dissemination of the newly created knowledge inside the company through the Chinese specialists once they returned to the headquarters or joined other locations around the world.

With regard to the appointment of top executives, this meant that, as a rule, the leadership of local sales companies consisted of local managers and staff sent out from China. In Germany, Haier Deutschland GmbH is currently headed by Sun Shubao, who studied German and has already worked successfully for Haier in other important foreign markets. A local deputy general manager supports Sun. On the second level, another Chinese executive is in charge of the finance department, while being supported by a German auditor who gained a great deal of experience at subsidiaries of numerous foreign companies, many of them Japanese corporations. These two '1 + 1'teams are supported by 'n' local employees, including a local team of product managers, sales assistants and field service staff. Altogether, there is currently a total of 22 employees (19 local, 3 from China) working at Haier Germany.

The sales strategy of the Haier Group in Germany

Current sales efforts of Haier are oriented towards making the brand known on a wide scale. For example, as a sponsor of the Olympic Games 2008, Haier contributed several exemplars of a recently introduced new washing machine that washes without powder as a 'green' product in order to facilitate the 'green Olympic Games in Beijing'. In highly competitive Germany, Haier is currently working on improving its image by trying to document the quality and good operating data of its products. Obtaining certificates and recommendations from product testing institutes and foundations are as crucial as the launch of marketing and distribution partnerships with companies such as Eismann, a German frozen food home-delivery service. At the same time, the corporation is enlarging its range of products. In addition to refrigerators, washing machines and dishwashers, Haier is hoping to turn flat-screen TVs, which are manufactured in Poland, into another source of income. This is an unusually wide range of products when compared with other German manufacturers of white goods.

In addition to this, maintenance and repair services currently constitute other important challenges. Like many of its competitors, Haier has decided not to provide these by itself, but to entrust them to an established and experienced service and maintenance company. In order to be able to minimize repair costs during the warranty period, Haier has identified a requirement for action in two areas: rigorous quality management to reduce the need for repairs and excellent marketing management to increase sales of products. Quality improvement and the development of higher quality products are mainly the two tasks of the Chinese plants, whereas 'popularizing their profiles in the markets' is the task of the local marketing departments. Success will materialize only if both sides – quality management and marketing of the plants in China and the subsidiary in Germany – jointly work together. To achieve this, the product managers of the various Chinese plants keep in touch regularly with their local German counterparts and visit Germany to evaluate the quality and features of their competitors' products, to acquire a feeling for what German customers like and to get to know the peculiarities of German consumer predilections.

Building a common corporate culture

There was hardly any communication problem between the German workforce and the Chinese management. This was largely due to the great deal of intercultural competence that the Chinese management prides itself in, as stemming from its intercultural knowledge and experience with other foreign subsidiaries within the Haier Group. Yet, if other global locations were involved in a decision-making process – for example, central offices in Qingdao or individual plants in China – differences in work rhythm and communication patterns became apparent. For this reason, Haier Germany also enlisted the help of external consultants in order to make corporate procedures and processes more transparent and easier to deal with. It also intended to standardize the hierarchy levels in the various locations. Furthermore, the corporation was promoting the creation of a common corporate culture. The central offices in Qingdao were not primarily concerned with enforcing all their own ideas and notions of value, which would resemble an ethnocentric strategy (Perlmutter, 1969), but rather with combining positive cultural habits from around the world – resembling more of a kind of geocentric strategy (1969), and probably more fitting with Haier's current developmental stage of the 'global branding strategy stage' (see Figure 14). Haier thus attempted to combine the advantages stemming from its global network of operations: American entrepreneurship, German thoroughness and Chinese cultural roots.

This geocentric thinking also becomes apparent when looking at Haier's mission statement, which emphasizes two main issues: committed environmentalism and interpersonal values. This approach is also symbolized by the 'Haier Brothers', i.e. an image of children from various ethnic backgrounds who are playing together. Contributing to this symbolic statement, the 'Haier University' was set up in Qingdao in order to ensure that these values will continue to play a central role in the corporation. Within the university, however, there is also a traditional Chinese garden which, despite Haier's international character, symbolizes its Chinese roots.

In China, Haier is perceived as a role model corporation, which has been successful in foreign markets for a long time and pays its employees far more than other Chinese companies. Thus, it is hardly surprising that, in recent years, Haier has been able to attract many talented young people from famous universities. As a result, with an average age of 30 (and of 38 within top management), employees at Haier are rather young – an orientation that might also fit well with habits in Europe, thus possibly contributing to recruiting young local talent.

In order to promote the previously described values in all various locations worldwide, there are frequent team meetings (both virtual and face-to-face) as well as educational opportunities for Chinese employees and for those with different nationalities. As in many other international corporations, the global integration of the corporate culture continues to be one of the most important challenges of the future. Through the aforementioned measures, Haier's German branch could act as a role model for this attempt.

Questions

1 How did Haier manage its entry into Europe?
2 What location-specific advantages did Germany provide Haier with?
3 How did Haier manage its human resources and overcome intercultural differences, and what are the implications that can be drawn for other foreign subsidiaries in Europe?

Note

1 This case study was written by Bernd Michael Linke (Friedrich Schiller University of Jena, Germany) and Andreas Klossek (Technical University of Freiberg, Germany) and was first published in the authors' study 'Chinese Companies in Germany: Chances and Challenges', which was sponsored by Bertelsmann Foundation and Deloitte (the study can be accessed at http://www.bertelsmannstiftung.de/cps/rde/xbcr/SID12ED87F35090242B/bst_engl/xcms_bst_dms_27517_27534_2.pdf). The authors would like to thank both for granting the permission to reproduce this case study. © Bertelsmann Foundation. The authors would also like to thank Gabriele Suder and an anonymous reviewer for their insightful suggestions and comments. All rights obtained by the authors of this case study.

Bibliography

Bell, S. (2008) *International Brand Management of Chinese Companies*. Heidelberg: Physica.

Haier (2009) Haier ranks #1 in global major appliances brands market share. Available at: http://www.haiereurope.com/en/contents/haier-ranks-1-in-global-major-appliances-brands-market-share (accessed 17 March 2010).

Johanson, J. and Vahlne, J.E. (1977) The internationalization process of the firm: a model of knowledge development and increasing foreign market commitments. *Journal of International Business Studies*, vol. 8, pp. 23–32.

Perlmutter, H.V. (1969) The tortuous evolution of the multinational enterprise. *Columbia Journal of World Business*, vol. 4, no. 1, pp. 9–18.

Zaheer, S. (1995) Overcoming the liability of foreignness. *Academy of Management Journal*, vol. 38, pp. 341–63.

Glossary

Absolute advantage
Goods that a nation can produce more efficiently than its competitor(s).

Acquisition
Where one company forcefully takes over another company.

Anti-dumping duties
Tariffs in the form of import duties that are established so as to counteract the injurious effects of selling a product (normally a commodity) at a price below cost of production or below domestic price in the export market.

APEC
Founded in 1989, this is the largest market grouping with privileged European Union (EU) relations. APEC members are Australia, Brunei, Malaysia, Singapore, Thailand, New Zealand, New Guinea, Indonesia, Philippines, Taiwan, Hong Kong, Japan, China, South Korea, Canada, USA, Mexico and Chile: 21 members of over 2.5 billion people and 47 per cent of world trade.

ASEAN
This Association of South East Asian Nations has 10 members, who aim to accelerate economic growth and social inclusion through their association of 600 million people.

Benchmarking
A marketing technique that relies on observation of competitors' management style to retain best practice.

Business angel
Mainly an individual investor providing capital (and often advice) for business ventures.

Cash flow management
This is about controlling money inflows and outflows so that the firm has enough resources for doing business at any given moment in time.

CEC
The Commission of the European Communities was first established on the basis of the EC Treatys and is one of the EU's main institutions. The CEC's major responsibilities are the initiation, formulation and coordination of Community policy.

Change management	A discipline of management that uses knowledge, tools and resources to provide a particular business with a strategy for a period of organizational change within a company.
Common external tariffs	Taxes levied on imports into member states are the same all over the market group. At the same time, these members do not exercise internal tariffs.
Common Law	The legal system in which judges refer to the judgment made in previous cases to create or redefine the law.
Common policies	A set of issue-related rules, decisions and measures adopted by the common institutions of independent member states of a market (or similar) group, that are implemented either by these common institutions or the member states or both.
Comparative advantage	In the case that one nation produces two goods more efficiently than another, both parties still benefit from an exchange and should specialize in the production of the good for which they have the greatest relative advantage.
Competitive advantage	A sustainable advantage that a company enjoys over the competition.
Competitiveness	The ability of a country or region to compete with other countries or regions.
Corporate culture	A set of norms, values and beliefs that are shared by the members of one company.
Customs union	Here, there are no barriers to trade among members and a common trade policy with respect to non-members.
Decentralization	Decision-making in organizations is dispersed to the managers who are closest to the action, often country managers.
'Deep' economic integration	A sharing of common policies and rules between countries and enhancing the authority of the organization.
Double taxation	Where a company or person has to pay twice the income tax for the same source of revenue to the different countries in which it is operating.

Dumping	Where the export price of a product is under-average compared to the corresponding product, the 'like product', on foreign markets, under specific conditions.
Economic Union	The integration of economic policies and the free movement of goods, services and factors of production.
Economies of scale	Companies reduce their production costs by increasing their quantities to supply a bigger market.
EEA	The European Economic Area, with its 30 members, allows certain EFTA members to participate in the EU Single Market. Switzerland is the only EFTA member not to have joined the EEA.
EFTA	The European Free Trade Area was established in Stockholm in July 1959. Its members entertain bilateral free trade agreements with the EU, and many are part of the EEA (Lichtenstein, Norway and Iceland until membership of the EU, but not Switzerland, see above).
European institutions (main)	The European Commission The European Parliament The Councils of Ministers or Council of the European Union The European Council The European Court of Justice
European Union	Primarily but not exclusively an economic union covering the majority of the European continent; the world's most advanced form of economic integration in terms of 'deep' integration. Member States remain independent and sovereign, but pool sovereignty in certain areas of common interest (see also Common policies).
Europeanization	European integration of economies and the development of common policies of EU Member States. Advanced forms of organization that reflect a diversity of markets and cultures; diversity within companies as well as in the scope of their operations.

Euro-zone

Also called the Euro-area or Euroland; EU Member States that have adopted the single currency to replace their own national currencies.

External economies of scale

Free mobility of factors of production translate into lower production costs.

Federalism

A school of thought that argues that member states of an international organization should form a unity but remain independent in terms of internal affairs.

FDI – horizontal

Where equity funds are invested across borders in the same branch of activity. Typically, this is motivated by cost and market-access considerations.

FDI – vertical

Where equity funds are invested across borders with product stages in different locations, providing inputs (backward) or outputs (forward) for the domestic production process. Typically, this is motivated by the fragmentation of production and relative factor costs.

First mover

An attempt to gain advantage by preceding competitors when making a strategic move in the market and 'occupying' it.

Foreign direct investment (FDI)

Where firms invest outside their home country and control their foreign assets.

Four freedoms

In the EU, the frontier-free area guarantees the freedom of movement for people, goods, services and capital.

Franchising

A special form of licensing, where the use of trade marks or assets of a company is granted to an independent firm that pays a fee.

Free trade area

An area where barriers to trade among member countries of a market group are removed – examples are NAFTA in North America and EFTA in Europe.

Functionalism

A theory which suggests that states cooperate in specific areas and functions, creating cohesion through the mechanisms established thereby.

Globalization

A compression of time and space that increases the frequency and duration of linkages between any given actors in the international environment.

Harmonization	Where national laws are brought into line with one another to achieve free movement of labour, goods, services, capital or similar initiatives of countries collaborating with each other and engaging in economic (or similar) forms of integration, rules and standards, that are commonly decided and that are coordinated and monitored in similar fashion across all Member States.
Indirect exporting	Exporting via a partner in the manufacturer's home country.
Infant industry	An industry, mainly a new and developing sector, that is considered insufficiently mature to compete on equal terms with international rivals.
Insourcing	Delegating tasks to services inside a company, in opposition to outsourcing, often in the quest for control of quality or knowledge.
Internal economies of scale	Greater production translates into lower production costs, characteristic of the objectives of a common market.
Internal tariffs	Tariffs applied between members of a market group for cross-border trade amongst them.
Joint venture	Where a company joins a partner – two or more partners share a project that is limited in time, purpose and quantity, often done to mitigate risk.
Licensing	A licensor makes an asset available to licensee(s) in exchange for compensation.
Lisbon Strategy/Europe 2020	The EU's common goal and strategy to increase European competitiveness and growth, stimulating a knowledge-based economy, innovation, employment and social cohesion.
Lobbying	The term is generally used interchangeably with public affairs management or interest intermediation. The main function of this activity is to make one's voice heard and known, and to therewith influence a given public administration.

Local content requirements   Some defined fraction of a good needed to be defined as 'produced locally'.

Maastricht criteria   Criteria which allow a member state to define its ability to adopt the euro (price stability, budget deficit, debt, interest rates, exchange rate stability).

MERCOSUR   The Southern American Common Market, comprising Argentina, Brazil, Paraguay, Uruguay and Venezuela. The grouping was formed to encourage integration among members via the free movement of goods and services. The main objective is to ensure the economic and political stability of the region.

Multinational firm (MNE)   A corporation that has its headquarters in one country but also operates in others.

NAFTA   The North American Free Trade Agreement – the world's largest free trade zone in terms of surface area. It is the main trading partner of the EU and comprises the USA, Canada and Mexico. The main aim of NAFTA is to eliminate impediments to trade of goods and services, to facilitate their movement across member states and to stimulate commerce and internal investments.

Offshoring   Operations moved across borders are controlled by the owner company, which monitors the company involved in the activity in the country.

Oligopolies   Few firms dominate a market, in contrast to the monopolistic market in which one firm dominates; both markets show a high degree of concentration of supply structures, in opposition to the low-concentration structure of a competitive market.

Outsourcing   External acquisition and purchase of services and products that were previously produced in-house, that is, subcontracting to an external company a part of the service in the business.

Patent   An exclusive right granted for an *invention*, that is, a product or process that provides a new way of doing something, and offers a new technical, useful solution to a problem.

Political integration	Political cooperation between member states and consequential full or partial harmonization of issues or initiatives.
Political union	The final, most accomplished stage of integration of independent states collaborating through political and other (economic, social) integration.
Private sector company	A company that cannot offer its shares to the public and restricts the right to transfer them.
Privatization	Where the government sells public goods and services to private investors.
Product life-cycle	A product goes through different phases from introduction through maturity to standardization, allowing company and country to switch from product to product at different moments in time in different locations, hence shaping international trade patterns.
Public sector company	A company owned by the public, or a company that is owned by stockholders who are members of the general public and which is traded publicly. Ownership is open to anyone who has the money and inclination to buy shares in the company; the government often owns a minority of shares.
Qualified majority voting (QMV)	Decision-making at the EU is, in most cases, based on the Council of the European Union's QMV, with each Member State casting votes in proportion to the size of its population.
Schengen area	An area in which most EU countries and some EFTA countries have abolished major checks on people travelling between them (except when required to maintain public order or national security), named after a town in Luxembourg where the agreement was signed. It includes a common visa policy and effective controls at external borders.
Single Market	An integrated marketplace – a market that marries competitiveness with certain social ideals (welfare, human rights, equality and many others). This market offers opportunities to those corporations that recognize the pros and cons of convergence, and that make the

most out of the diversity of cultures, languages, business practices and management styles.

Small and medium-sized companies (SMEs)

Enterprises which employ fewer than 250 persons and which have an annual turnover not exceeding €50 million and/or an annual balance sheet total not exceeding €43 million.

Strategic alliances

Collaborative ventures between international firms.

Subsidiarity

Decisions must be taken as closely as possible to the main concerned stakeholder. EU decisions are thus only feasible when more effective than national, regional or local level decisions.

Subsidies

Monetary assistance granted typically by a government to a person, organization or business in support of activities.

Trade mark

A distinctive sign which serves to identify goods or services as those produced or provided by a certain person or enterprise only.

Transnational company (TNC)

A firm that coordinates and controls operations across borders through an organizational design that allows for local responsiveness.

Unanimity

Unanimous agreement, that is, all countries have to agree. At the EU, this is used at the Council for major decisions.

Value added tax (VAT)

A general consumption tax on goods and services; in Europe, VAT on goods traded between one EU Member State and another is not collected at the internal frontier between tax jurisdictions. VAT rates between Member States differ; the EU sets a minimum rate only.

Venture capital

Financial capital that is furnished in support of early-stage, high-potential and high-growth start-up companies.

Voluntary export restraints

An exporting country may self-impose export limitations in response to threats of trade barriers from the target market.

Wider integration

Further enlargement of the EU, not only geographically but also in the number of states.

Index

Note: Page references in **bold** type relate to the glossary

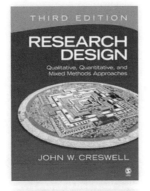
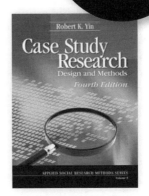

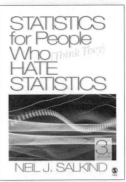

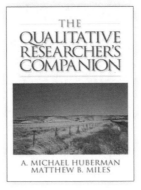

Research Methods
Books from SAGE

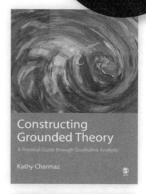

INTERPRETING QUALITATIVE DATA THIRD EDITION

DAVID SILVERMAN

Qualitative Research & Evaluation Methods

3 EDITION

Michael Quinn Patton

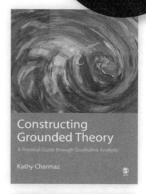

Constructing Grounded Theory
A Practical Guide through Qualitative Analysis

Kathy Charmaz

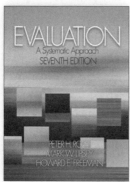

EVALUATION
A Systematic Approach
SEVENTH EDITION

PETER H. ROSSI
MARK W. LIPSEY
HOWARD E. FREEMAN

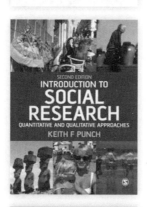

SECOND EDITION
INTRODUCTION TO
SOCIAL RESEARCH
QUANTITATIVE AND QUALITATIVE APPROACHES
KEITH F PUNCH

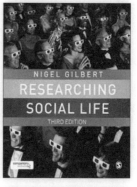

NIGEL GILBERT
RESEARCHING
SOCIAL LIFE
THIRD EDITION

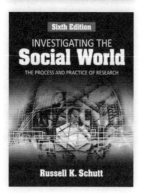

Sixth Edition
INVESTIGATING THE
Social World
THE PROCESS AND PRACTICE OF RESEARCH

Russell K. Schutt

AN INTRODUCTION TO
QUALITATIVE
RESEARCH
UWE FLICK
EDITION 4

DEVELOPING
EFFECTIVE
RESEARCH
PROPOSALS

Keith F Punch
SECOND EDITION

www.sagepub.co.uk

SAGE